Accounting Education for the 21st Century

The Global Challenges

Accounting Education for the 21st Century

The Global Challenges

Edited by

Jane O. Burns
Texas Tech University

and

Belverd E. Needles, Jr.
DePaul University

PERGAMON

in association with the
International Accounting Section
American Accounting Association
and the
International Association for Accounting Education and Research

U.K.   Elsevier Science Ltd., The Boulevard, Langford Lane, Kidlington,
            Oxford OX5 1GB, U.K.

U.S.A.   Elsevier Science Inc., 660 White Plains Road, Tarrytown, New
            York 10591-5153, U.S.A.

JAPAN   Elsevier Science Japan, Tsunashima Building Annex, 3-20-12
            Yushima, Bunkyo-ku, Tokyo 113, Japan

First edition 1994

Library of Congress Cataloging in Publication Data

British Library of Congress Cataloging in Publication Data

A catalogue record for this book is available from the British Library

ISBN 0-08-042405-8

Accounting Education for the 21st Century: *The Global Challenges*

Edited by

Jane O. Burns
Texas Tech University

and

Belverd E, Needles, Jr.
DePaul University

TABLE OF CONTENTS

Accounting Education in Developing Countries

Accounting Education in Developed Countries

Instructional Innovations in Accounting Education

Performance Evaluation in Accounting Education

Ethics and Professionalism in Accounting Education

International Accounting Standards

Further Issues in Accounting Education

Introduction

There is little disagreement that the world economy has entered an era of global interaction on a scale rarely experienced before. Financial markets in various parts of the world operate twenty-four hours a day as capital seeks involvement in this global economy. Countries that are still mostly agrarian are forming active stock markets. Trade agreements in the European Community and North America, the breakup of the former Soviet Union, the emergence of China as an economic power, and the commercial development of many countries in Southeast Asia and South America are just a few examples of the forces at work. After a long period of indifference, the importance of international accounting standards and international auditing standards to the free flow of capital throughout the world has resulted in heightened interest in the work of the International Accounting Standards Committee on international accounting standards and the International Federation of Accountants on international auditing standards. Within emerging countries, business enterprises must develop internal management controls that allow them to compete in a world market. Government units, consequently, must work with and regulate this growing market economy. The rapid, and sometimes startling, social, political, technological, and economic changes that are taking place in the world economy have led to increasing recognition of the key role that accounting and accountants in all countries play in the process of economic development. This recognition, in turn, emphasizes the need for quality accounting education.

The purpose of this publication, "Accounting Education for the Twenty-First Century: The Global Challenges," is to provide an up-to-date view of the state of accounting education throughout the world and to focus on the global challenges facing accounting education as we approach the Twenty-First Century. It consists of sixty-five papers that have been carefully edited and organized for the reader into the following nine parts:

Part I: Global Views of the Needs and Future of Accounting Education
Part II: Accounting Education in China and Russia
Part III: Accounting Education in Developing Countries
Part IV: Accounting Education in Developed Countries
Part V: Instructional Innovations in Accounting Education
Part VI: Performance Evaluation in Accounting Education
Part VII: Ethics and Professionalism in Accounting Education
Part VIII: International Accounting Standards
Part IX: Further Issues in Accounting Education

This book contains the refereed and plenary papers presented at the Seventh International Conference on Accounting Education, which was held October 8-10, 1992 at the Marriott Crystal Gateway Hotel in Arlington, Virginia, USA. At this conference, 440 accounting educators and professionals from forty-eight countries came together to share their views on how accounting education in their countries and/or regions of the world are, or should be, addressing the changes taking place in the last decade of the Twentieth Century.

Papers submitted for the program were reviewed by the Seventh International Conference on Accounting Education Task Force, a committee of the International Accounting Section (IAS) of the American Accounting Association. Committee members, appointed by 1991-92 IAS President Juan Rivera, were:

- Jane O. Burns, Chair
  Texas Tech University
- Abdel A. Agami
  Old Dominion University
- Shirley Dennis-Escoffier
  University of Miami (Florida)
- Michael A. Diamond
  University of Southern California
- Thomas G. Evans
  University of Central Florida
- Gary K. Meek
  Oklahoma State University
- Walter F. O'Connor
  Fordham University
- Lee H. Radebaugh
  Brigham Young University
- James A. Schweikart
  University of Richmond

Authors submitted their papers to the chair of the Task Force. The chair assigned the papers to the committee members, based on their knowledge about the paper topics. Each committee member selected knowledgeable individuals to participate in the review process. All papers were subject to a blind review and were evaluated by two or more reviewers. Each committee member summarized the reviews for each paper for which he or she was responsible and forwarded a recommendation to the committee chair. Papers were accepted, based on these recommendations, by the committee chair.

The Arlington, Virginia USA (1992) conference represented by this publication was sanctioned by the International Association for Accounting Education and Research (IAAER) and hosted by the American Accounting Association (AAA). It honored a tradition of similar conferences that began thirty years ago in Urbana, Illinois, USA (1962), and that continued through conferences held in London (1967), Sydney (1972), Berlin (1977), Monterey (1982), and Kyoto (1987).

IAAER was the idea of Professor Seigo Nakajima and came into being in advance of the Kyoto conference. Professor Nakajima and his colleagues sought support for the Kyoto Conference from the international academic community. He proposed a small association with a wide geographical spread. Early in 1984, through a mail process of nomination and election, Paul Garner, Dean Emeritus of the University of Alabama (USA), was elected the inaugural President. Professor Nakajima then convened a meeting in Toronto, August 1984, at which Professor Garner was installed as President. At that meeting, a constitution was approved and John Brennan, University of Saskatchewan (Canada), was elected as the first Secretary/Treasurer. Four vice-presidents representing different geographical regions of the world were subsequently elected, again by a mail ballot conducted by Professor Brennan. The vice-presidents were Professors Edward Stamp (Europe), Vernon Zimmerman (North America), Murray Wells (Australia and the Pacific), and Seigo Nakajima (Asia).

The main function of the IAAER in 1984 was to sponsor the Sixth International Conference on Accounting Education. The presence of an international sponsoring body enabled the Conference Organizing Committee to obtain financial support for the Conference from the Japanese Science Council. The Conference was an outstanding success and afterwards the Organizing Committee was left with a surplus of $10,000 US.

It would have been entirely proper for the Organizing Committee to have donated the $10,000 to the Japan Accounting Association, which ac-

cepted the responsibility for the Conference. However, to the great credit of Kyojiro Someya, Seigo Nakajima, and the Japan Accounting Association, the funds were donated to the IAAER in order to provide seed funding for the Seventh International Conference. At that time, Professor Garner conducted an informal mail survey of the IAAER members and resolved to continue the Association with the following objectives:

1. The International Conference would be held every five years in conjunction with the World Congress of Accountants.

2. A central information source on conferences, seminars, and exchange opportunities for academic accountants would be provided.

3. The infrastructure for cooperation and the exchange of information between national academic accounting bodies would be provided.

4. Research and publications in international accounting would be sponsored.

5. The IAAER would act as the international representative and contact point for academic accountants, as required by such bodies as the United Nations, the International Federation of Accountants (IFAC), and other international agencies.

6. The IAAER would liaise closely with the IFAC on all matters relating to accounting education and research.

Following acceptance of the objectives listed above in Autumn 1988, Murray Wells was elected President and the Executive Committee was reconstituted. The new Committee consisted of Sidney Gray (V-P Europe), Belverd E. Needles, Jr. (V-P North America), Kyojiro Someya (V-P Asia), and Don Trow (V-P Pacific). Norlin Rueschhoff was elected Secretary/Treasurer and later became Editor of the newsletter *"Cosmos Accountancy Chronicle."*

The new Executive Committee arranged with Gerhard Mueller, President of the American Accounting Association, for the AAA to take responsibility for the Seventh International Conference. The AAA, in turn, appointed a Planning Committee with Belverd E. Needles, Jr. as its Chairman. More recently, the IAAER also resolved that the same format be followed in the future and asked the French Accounting Association to accept responsibility for the organization of the Conference in 1997 when the World Congress will be held in Paris.

The editors wish to acknowledge the planning committee of the Seventh International Conference on Accounting Education which consisted of:

- Belverd E. Needles, Jr., Chair
  DePaul University
- Tom A. Gavin
  University of Tennessee at Chattanooga
- Sidney J. Gray
  Warwick Business School
- Morley W. Lemon
  University of Waterloo
- William Markell
  University of Delaware
- Seigo Nakajima
  Ferris Jogakuin Women's College
- Walter F. O'Connor
  Fordham University
- Norlin G. Rueschhoff
  University of Notre Dame
- Murray C. Wells
  University of Sydney

- Jane O. Burns, Chair, Paper Selection Committee
  Texas Tech University
- Juan M. Rivera, Chair, International Accounting Section
  University of Notre Dame
- André Zund, AAA Board Liaison
  An Der Hochschule St. Gallen

Their help and encouragement is very much appreciated. We also want to thank Murray C. Wells for his assistance in providing information for the above history of the IAAER and JoNoel Lowe for her editorial services in preparing this manuscript for publication. We also want to thank staff members of the American Accounting Association, Beverly Harrelson, Assistant Publications Coordinator; Sara Laurie, Proofreader; and Laurie Rayburn, Publications Coordinator, for their fine work in editing, proofing, and producing this large and complex work. Finally, we appreciate the support of Paul Gerhardt, Executive Director of the American Accounting Association.

Global Views of the Needs and Future of Accounting Education

The Changing Face of the Profession — Green Ink Fortified by Vintage Wine

Peter D. Agars

INTRODUCTION

I am very honoured to address this distinguished Conference of accounting educators — a conference of people who mould the future of the profession.

The International Conference on Accounting Education and the International Federation of Accountants (IFAC) go back a long way — your conference has been held immediately prior to World Congresses of Accountants for 30 years. We have also had links between IFAC's Education Committee and educators through the work of some very dedicated people. But I believe that this has not been enough and that we need to look at a number of other avenues that we can use to collaborate in achieving our complementary goals.

A THEME : "GREEN INK FORTIFIED BY VINTAGE WINE"

In choosing a theme for this address I looked for something that builds upon the strong foundations of the profession (the green ink) and also reflects the progress and maturing of our international profession (the vintage wine). Your President, Professor Murray Wells, will also attest that as a South Australian, I have a natural interest in vintage wines.

The foundation of our profession's development — *the green ink phase* — provided a strong focus on roles that were the exclusive preserve of the accountant and only the accountant — for example, auditing. From this arose a set of values, ethics, and standards of technical services of which we are justifiably proud. We should never undervalue these strengths.

However, the world we serve and seek to influence has been changing rapidly, and some of our values and attitudes have not kept pace and are in need of change. For example:

- In many countries the public practice area was regarded as *the* profession. Traditional notions of independence could conceive of only a self-employed professional being truly independent — hence only the self-employed public practitioners could be thought of as professional accountants.

- The traditional audit dominance of the profession tended to shape the core of accounting education. Many saw audit as *the* heart of the profession, which every undergraduate should study.

- This tended to emphasise the profession's historical roles — such as analysing and attesting to past results rather than building on this analysis to help enterprises produce better future results.

- There was a strong focus on methods and techniques — the green ink pens — rather than on a broader education in concepts and processes.

- The tools of the profession were largely manual and transactional rather than electronic and analytical.

- Accounting for the young graduate was often more akin to the sweatshop of apprentices than the rigorous challenge of young professionals and their integration into the wider business enterprise environment.

If this traditional role of accounting is the *green ink*, what is the *vintage wine phase* of our development? It is a reflection of many changes that have already taken place and some yet to come.

- It reflects the maturing of our profession with

  - A recognition of professionalism across the broader spectrum of accounting — not only in public practice but also in commerce, industry, government, and education.

  - A recognition of the extensive common ground in technical concepts across all of these areas.

  - A profession that is truly global in its outlook and services.

- It reflects the mellowing of the traditional view of a profession that required a dominant technical preparation. Abilities to analyse and evaluate, to exercise judgment, to understand a broad range of economic, social, and ethical concepts and values and to communicate ef-

Peter D. Agars is Deputy President, The International Federation of Accountants.

fectively with a wide range of people have become equal in importance to the solid foundation of technical excellence.

- It reflects the long-term view that the vintage winemaker must subscribe to. It nurtures a strong commitment to the future needs of the profession, and the society it serves rather than a short-term response to the immediate pressures of the day. It recognises that the education programs of today must be designed to meet the needs of the accountant of the year 2000 — not the needs of yesterday or today.

- It also reflects a commitment to quality — the kind of quality we expect from the results of vintage planning, a quality that is driven by client or enterprise needs rather than by the whims of a profession.

THE RELEVANCE TO IFAC

How can IFAC contribute to this maturation and customer satisfaction process? The first part of the answer to this question is to give a brief overview of IFAC. The second part is IFAC's strategic plan, which I will come to shortly.

IFAC was formed in 1977 by the world's major national accountancy bodies. It was established as the peak international body for the profession with the overriding objective of developing and enhancing a coordinated worldwide profession with harmonised standards.

IFAC promulgates, through the work of its Council and various committees, a range of standards and other pronouncements on audit, education, ethics, financial and management accounting, public sector, and other professional matters. It also promotes the objects of the profession through a network of other international organisations, professions, regulators, and so on. In round terms, it represents some 110 national professional bodies covering one million accountants in 80 countries.

IFAC also supports the work of the International Accounting Standards Committee and the harmonisation of accounting standards, but IFAC does not control the program of IASC. However, both organisations share the same national accountancy bodies as constituents.

IFAC encourages and recognises four regional organisations (FEE, IAA, CAPA, and ECSAFA), which perform vital roles in the national and regional development of the profession.

During the first 15 years of IFAC's existence, it has achieved the majority of its initial objectives

— principally to build a robust and respected international framework for the profession, with a strong representation from all major regions of the world, and to develop and promulgate a set of core professional standards and pronouncements. IFAC is now poised to lead the second phase of development of the international profession — hence the release of the publication *Towards the 21st Century - Strategic Directions for the Accountancy Profession.*

STRATEGIC DIRECTIONS

The mission of IFAC has been restated as follows:

> The International Federation of Accountants (IFAC) is the worldwide organisation for the accountancy profession. The mission of IFAC is the development and enhancement of the profession to enable it to provide services of consistently high quality in the public interest.

To achieve this, IFAC Council has adopted five objectives, namely:

- Enhance the standards and development of the profession by issuing technical and professional guidance and by promoting the adoption of IFAC and IASC pronouncements.

- Foster a strong and cohesive profession by providing leadership of emerging issues, coordinating with regional organisations and member bodies, and assisting them to achieve strategic objectives.

- Assist with the formation and development of national and regional organisations which serve the interests of accountants in public practice, commerce, industry, public sector, and education.

- Promote the profession's role, responsibilities, and achievements in advancing the interests of member bodies and in serving the public interest.

- Liaise with international organisations to influence the development of efficient capital markets and international trade in services.

Each objective is supported by a set of strategic directions and by a number of ongoing activities.

It would take more time than I have available to address these in detail. I would like to discuss just three major issues that are inherent in these objectives and will be strong influences on accounting education.

BROADENING THE BASE OF THE PROFESSION

The first of these areas is the broadening of the base of the profession. Whereas many professional accountancy bodies were established to serve the needs of the public practice arena of the profession, these now have a majority of members in commerce, industry, government, and education.

Figure 1 shows that in a sample of national professional bodies, public practitioners are generally below 50 percent of members. Indeed, less than 50 percent of the accountants represented by member bodies of IFAC are in public practice.

This is one of the key features of the changing face of the profession, and it has a dramatic impact on the education requirements of accountants. All accountants must have a strong core of education in accounting, economics, information technology, business law, social sciences, and quantitative methods to enable them to adapt to the changing business environment.

However, some areas such as auditing and taxation, which were once regarded as core subjects, are now more appropriately dealt with as specialist options at the fourth year or postgraduate level. Other specialist areas could include treasury, information technology, and management account-

ing. I am sure that we could have a long debate over what are the appropriate accounting specializations. Too often these are thought of in terms of where accountants practice their profession (e.g., the public sector) rather than in terms of the specialist body of technical knowledge required for a particular branch of accounting.

The concept that I am advocating here is not revolutionary. It has been put forward by many educators and is generally consistent with the 1986 report of the American Accounting Association Committee on the Future Structure, Content and Scope of Accounting Education (the Bedford Committee).

INFORMATION TECHNOLOGY

The second major issue is information technology. The complexity of corporate and governmental management; global competition; real-time commercial dealings with suppliers, financiers, and customers; and a demanding regulatory environment produce a dependence on information technology that was virtually nonexistent 20 years ago.

Information technology is having a profound impact on the role, knowledge, and skill needs of the accountant and the rapid pace of development will not abate. There is no area impacted more by this than accountancy education.

FIGURE 1
Members in Public Practice

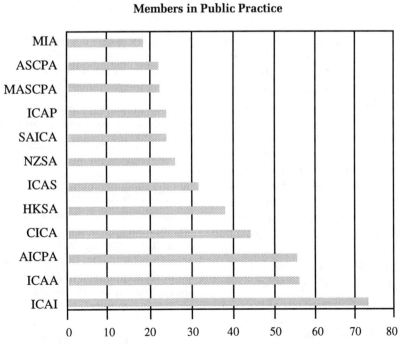

Percent of Members

The traditional response by many professional accountancy bodies and by IFAC has been to contemplate information technology mainly as a tool for use by accountants. Their focus has typically been on how to build information technology skills training into the undergraduate program and continuing education offerings.

Certainly information technology is presenting accountants with an array of new sophisticated tools for accounting functions but this line of thinking is rather limited.

Information technology is transforming the way organisations are structured, managed, and do business. Organisations of any substantial size need an information manager who can not only advise on the application of information technology to financial processing and reporting tasks but who can also

- Advise on the use of information technology to integrate financial and nonfinancial operating information.

- Use information technology for business analysis and business planning tasks.

- Advise on strategic investment in technology for internal and external purposes, such as linking with supplier and customer systems.

Functions of this nature are a logical extension of the professional accountant's role, both as the internal information manager and as the external adviser on these areas to clients. In an environment in which businesses are moving to open systems where they are not dependent on a single hardware brand, they often need independent external advice on the most cost-effective investment. Businesses should be able to turn to their professional accountant to evaluate the advice of the hardware and software vendors.

To enable it to evaluate the present and future impact of information technology on the accountant and the profession generally, IFAC Council commissioned a task force study, resourced by the Australian profession but advised by a panel of professionals from 11 countries. The task force has recently completed a report of exceptional quality and insight.

The report urges the profession to adopt a new vision for the role of the accountancy profession in relation to information technology.

The task force believes that

the accountant must become a skilled manager of the change process, must be able to determine the need for and form of strategic investment in information technology, and must be able to manage the associated risks. This contrasts heavily with

the image of the accountant as being backward looking, risk averse and slow to move.

The report suggests that business forces and information technology interact to provide a central technology application theme of connectivity. Technical connectivity will catalyse other forms of connectivity such as between

- Financial and nonfinancial information.

- Accounting and nonaccounting managers/departments.

- Clients and public accountants.

- Public practices and government/private institutions.

- Accounting systems with manufacturing systems incorporating robotics and process control.

The report discusses the impact of information technology on the various specialist functions and users. Among its 26 action recommendations are a number that impact on accountancy education. These relate to

- Expanding the definition of accountancy to encompass business information management and control.

- Defining, implementing, and monitoring the minimum levels of information technology competency required by accountants in various fields of practice.

- Creating specialist information technology programs and designations.

- Ensuring that accounting educators are able to maintain a knowledge of the "state of the art" of accounting business application by information technology.

- IFAC's taking a proactive role in research, information exchange, and other areas.

- IFAC's Education Committee working closely with member bodies, accounting educators, and other relevant parties.

The task force also concluded that the continuing professional education delivered by the professional accountancy bodies, as it relates to information technology, has at best been ad hoc and at worst nonexistent. In general, it has concentrated on skills acquisition in generic tools such as spreadsheets, not on broader management issues and specialist user requirements.

DEVELOPING NATIONS

The third major issue I would like to discuss is developing nations.

IFAC is often urged to do more to help advance the profession in developing nations, and this is an imperative under the strategic plan produced by IFAC.

In some countries, it is a matter of trying to assist in the founding of an accountancy profession as no structure or pool of professional skills currently exists. In some other countries still ravaged by civil unrest, it is almost impossible to ascertain whether any semblance of a profession even exists.

For these reasons, IFAC works mainly through regional organisations that understand local cultures and practices and have highly developed networks.

The solution to the problems of the profession in a developing nation and the way the solution is delivered may need to be quite different to what traditionally occurs in other countries.

To illustrate this point, developing nations often face serious problems in the management of their not-for-profit public institutions such as municipal corporations, hospitals, research centres, and universities. Many of these suffer from financial crisis, mismanagement, and a general lack of accounting and financial management skills. The proper functioning of these is fundamental to economic growth, but the free-market development of a local accountancy profession is likely to accord these institutions a low priority for the allocation of scarce accounting skills.

A plan for the development of a local accountancy profession may need to accord special attention to the education of accounting students in the specific requirements of not-for-profit public institutions as part of the prequalification education program. Otherwise the profession may not play a vital role in improving the economic performance of this crucial sector of a developing nation's economy.

IFAC has already produced technical and professional guidance that is of particular assistance to developing nations, and it has sponsored and funded some specific projects. However, a great deal more needs to be done, and the resource needs are so great that they exceed what might be considered realistic expectations of the profession from developed nations. For this reason alone, response by the profession must be delivered in partnership with international finance and aid organisations.

The profession's response to the needs of developing nations must be within a clearly defined structure of objectives, activities, and roles. Figure 2 is one option of framework needed. No doubt there are others.

CONCLUSION

IFAC Council has devoted considerable time during the past two years to formulating a vision for the accountancy profession to guide it into the 21st century.

IFAC recognises the value of the collective expertise of the national professional bodies and accounting educators in helping to achieve this vision. I am confident that through consultation and joint enterprise, core parameters will emerge for the education of accountants of the future. Together we can shape these parameters, formulate future concepts, and challenge our profession's tradition thinking.

The historical areas of the profession have already broadened to encompass new ideas and embrace new markets. The green ink has been fortified by the vintage wine in *practice*. It is our joint responsibility to ensure that the *education* of the profession is also fortified. Like all good winemakers, we must continue to improve the blend to produce even better results and to increase our share in the marketplace.

I look forward to the opportunity to meet with your association in the near future to discuss these issues that are of paramount importance to us all.

FIGURE 2
A Framework for Accounting Development in Emerging Nations

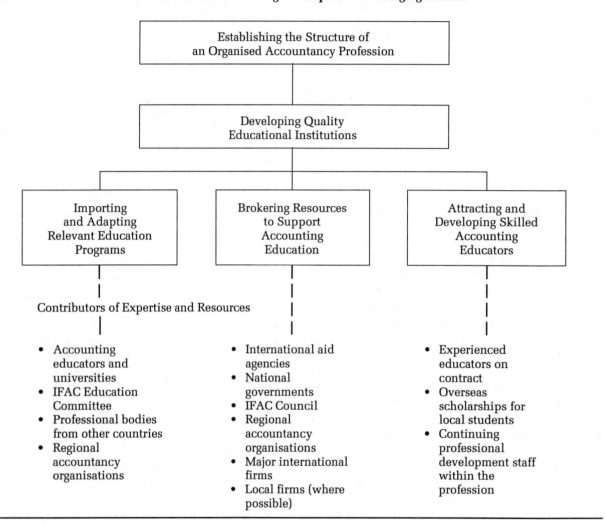

Global Challenges for Accounting Education

Gerhard G. Mueller

It is a singular professional honor for me to address this seventh International Conference on Accounting Education. I have attended all earlier venues of this quinquennial gathering except the inaugural meeting at the University of Illinois in 1962. This is the first time that the Conference has returned to the United States in the intervening thirty years.

At the second ICAE in London (1967), I presented a paper on curriculum aspects of international accounting. It was my proposition then (as it is now) that a separate international accounting course ought to be taught until full curriculum infusion of international accounting topics occurs. But I also stated, "In time a separate course on the subject will wither away at most institutions." Of course, the projected time frame was too optimistic, but the proposition itself still stands.

It is also worth recalling, ever so briefly, that in the spring of 1966 the Committee on International Accounting of the American Accounting Association based its recommendations for curriculum attention to international accounting matters on the following "practical reasons":

1. Expansion of international business and investment activities along with the related demands for international financial reporting, auditing, and accounting and auditing standards;

2. Emergence of international corporations (companies) owned and controlled in more than a single country;

3. Efforts toward economic regionalization and the consequent need for accounting developments transcending national boundaries;

4. Advancement of accounting thought on a multinational scale to foster better insight into conceptual matters and to avoid unnecessary duplication of research efforts.

These "reasons" are as valid today as they were 26 years ago—only more so! Has the international accounting field progressed much during the past quarter century? In a volume sense, there has been important progress. Twenty-five years ago we were largely talking about international accounting—and today we are doing it. Technical, managerial, pro-

fessional and regulatory attention to international accounting are certainly pervasive in today's environment. At the same time, some dark clouds are casting long shadows over the entire enterprise of higher education as well as the field of accounting in general. If the ship as a whole is threatened, we must do more than simply rearrange deck chairs. The challenges of the 1990s critically surpass those of the 1960s. I have every confidence that we can meet the challenges now facing us, but it will take new thinking, new commitment and new leadership. New wine in old bottles is not enough!

THE NEW HIGHER EDUCATION ENVIRONMENT

Hardly a day goes by without some major media attention to higher education. In the United States, books are published about *Profscam* and *Professors Who Seldom Teach*. Politicians from California to the United Kingdom are using budget reductions as enforcement techniques toward greater system efficiency and effectiveness. Most of Eastern Europe and the former Soviet Union suffer from an education gap since political polemics were the foundation of their erstwhile educational framework. In Mexico a massive student protest prevented the imposition of modest enrollment fees at the National University. In many developing countries the traditional university is condemned as elitist, colonialist, and largely irrelevant. For present purposes, three factors stand out among the many worldwide criticisms of higher education.

Higher Education is Now Big Business

In Japan new universities are springing up continually. Cambridge and Oxford in the United Kingdom now have management programs, and oil revenues in OPEC countries have become a major funding variable for indigenous universities. Since I know the situation best in the United States, I will use it as an example. Latest available statistics from the *Chronicle of Higher Education* (Au-

Gerhard G. Mueller is Hughes M. Blake Professor of International Business Management at the University of Washington.

gust 26, 1992) indicate that there are 3,559 operating colleges and universities in the United States These institutions serve a total student enrollment of 13,710,150. Faculty members total 379,373. Of the present U.S. total population, 20.3 percent hold bachelors, graduate, or professional degrees. Annual expenditures of public institutions add to $85.8 billion and those of private institutions come to $48.9 billion. Thus, in the United States alone we spend 1 and 1/3 trillion dollars each year on higher education. This is big business indeed!

Growing Globalization of the Environment

It is unnecessary to enumerate the pervasive globalization characterizing our present environment at an enclave like ICAE. Virtually all recent international accounting textbooks, handbooks, and research studies identify and analyze the dimensions of this globalization so that reiteration here would be redundant.

Widespread bureaucratization of higher education. It is my considered judgment that higher education is falling prey to more and more bureaucratic inroads. The big business dimensions already identified naturally spawn complex bureaucracies. As social institutions, colleges and universities are coerced into serving as role models for wide ranging social programs—comparative worth compensation schemes, equal opportunity and environmental protection pursuits, special recognition of animal rights, accommodations of alternative lifestyles and broad implementation of "political correctness." Aside from role modeling of social programs, faculty collective bargaining units influence curricula, faculty workloads, and often general employment conditions. Is university governance still the unequivocal domain of faculty or are various cadres of bureaucrats directly or indirectly managing most of what we do? Is the present management model of higher education truly in the public interest?

Today's Accounting Education Environment

The venerable tradition of accounting education is beyond question. It is a heterogeneous tradition in that there are strong feelings supporting university-level education for the profession, countered by equally strong feelings that institutes of practicing accountants should provide the requisite education. In my conference address five years ago at Kyoto I outlined different conceptual frameworks of our discipline and the corresponding educational approaches.

The majority of countries around the globe allocate to universities the task of accounting education. In my own country, the United States, this is a tradition of long standing. All U.S. professional accounting societies and institutes have long standing interests in accounting education and maintain generally well-funded education divisions and committees. This is especially the case for the American Accounting Association (AAA).

During the 1970s a wave of criticism broke over accounting education in the United States, which eventually led to a major survey among the AAA membership concerning the state of the art of accounting education in the United States. Professors Gary Previts and Joseph J. Schultz, Jr. were directly associated with this survey, whose results were published in 1989 as Accounting Education Monograph No. 10, *Reorienting Accounting Education: Reports on the Environment, Professoriate, and Curriculum of Accounting.* The general picture painted by this report was dark. Little curriculum innovation was reported, teaching methods employed were perceived to be stale and tradition bound, and professors found greater rewards and satisfactions in research.

These results only confirmed the 1985 special report of the American Accounting Association on the future, structure, content and scope of accounting education. The report is entitled "Future Accounting Education: Preparing for the Expanding Profession" (i.e., The Bedford Committee Report). Then, in 1989, in an unusual demonstration of interfirm unity, the (then) Big Eight professional accounting service firms published their white paper, *Capabilities for Success in the Accounting Profession.* The clear message of this practitioners' report was also concern over the quality and direction of accounting education. The white paper made it clear that "our focus is not on specific course content or the number of hours in the curriculum, but on the capabilities needed by the profession that should be developed through the educational process."

Against this background, the Accounting Education Change Commission (AECC) was established in 1989. During the course of this conference you will hear more about the AECC's purpose, direction of work, grants program, and public pronouncements. The AECC exists because of what I labeled the "malaise" in accounting education today (*Chronicle of Higher Education*, May 10, 1989).

Impotence of Accounting Research

Regrettably, we are faced with a similar problem in accounting research. If left uncorrected, a serious stalemate may well result. In essence, the crisis in accounting research is "market failure." In the last 20 or so years, accounting research has had no significant impact on the practice of accounting or accounting regulation. Accounting research is said to lack innovation. There has been no progress on fundamental issues in accounting and there appears to be no discernible demand for academic accountants or for accounting research by accounting firms, by industrial firms, or by regulators.

To address this issue, New York University hosted a panel discussion on the subject in November 1990 among recognized accounting researchers, practitioners, standard setters, and regulators. Since many of you have probably not seen the communique from this panel meeting, it is reproduced below (*1989-1990 Activities Report*, the Vincent C. Ross Institute of Accounting Research, New York University, pp. 5-7).

A STATEMENT OF THE STATE OF ACADEMIC ACCOUNTING

The Problem

There is a widespread sense among accounting researchers and practitioners that academic accounting, particularly on the research level, currently faces a serious crisis. Following are some symptoms of this crisis:

1. Unlike many other professional disciplines (e.g., finance, medicine, architecture), accounting research does not lead practice and/or policymaking. Indeed, it is difficult to recall one accounting research innovation in the last 20 or so years that has had a significant impact on the practice of accounting (having been adopted by CPA firms or by industry), or that meaningfully affected accounting regulation. Audit sampling and human information processing in auditing research are exceptions that prove the rule. In fact, much accounting research (e.g., economic consequences of regulation) tends to significantly lag real-life developments.

2. Most academic research areas are characterized by cycles of significant innovations—i.e., new ideas and concepts that periodically revolutionize the field, such as rational expectations in economics and options models in finance. Such innovations in accounting research are practically nonexistent. Indeed, information content studies in financial accounting and agency theory in managerial accounting have been imported from other disciplines. There

do not appear to be any built-in regenerative forces in accounting research.

3. Despite considerable research effort, it does not seem that we are any closer now than we were 20-30 years ago to addressing the fundamental issues in accounting, such as the optimal choice of accounting standards and the optimal structure of accounting institutions. This lack of progress is clearly manifested in accounting textbooks which are virtually no different today than those that were in use decades ago. Not surprisingly, the same is true for accounting instruction. There thus appears to be a general lack of progress in addressing fundamental accounting issues and in the instruction of accounting.

4. There appears to be no discernible demand for academic accountants or for accounting research by accounting firms (except in auditing), by industrial firms or by regulators. A strong demand for academicians exists in most other professional disciplines, such as finance, computer science and the biotechnology industry. During the late 1970s and early 1980s, both the FASB and the SEC initiated a few research projects (e.g., the FASB's financial instruments project). There appears to be a general lack of appreciation by our constituencies of accounting research. These constituencies are, of course, partly to blame for the lack of interest. But some of the fault also lies with us.

5. On the education front, in the last decade, the MBA student majoring in accounting has become an endangered species. Accounting is essentially a mere service area in graduate business schools, facing potentially diminished clout, budget support and supply of Ph.D. candidates. While the low salaries paid by accounting firms to MBAs is clearly an important factor in the disappearance of accounting majors in MBA programs, the lack of significant research and teaching innovations have also contributed to this troubling phenomenon. In some schools, deans are already questioning the justification of paying high compensation for accounting faculty who merely provide service courses. Indeed, the way accounting is currently taught does not provide "high-powered" (and high salaried) accounting researchers an advantage over broadly trained practitioners.

Thus, we seem to be witnessing a "market failure" phenomenon in academic accounting, particularly in research. Despite the serious weakening of demand for our product (by accounting and industrial firms, regulators, students), there are no self-correcting forces to provide inducements to change the nature and course of our research and teaching. What are some reasons for this "market failure"?

The Reasons

There does not seem to be a single, dominating reason for the "market failure." Rather, a combination of reasons apparently led to the present unsatisfactory state of affairs. Following are some of our conjectures:

1. Accounting researchers apparently suffer from insecurity about their field of study, leading them to perturb fairly secure research paradigms (mostly those that have been accepted by economists) within an ever-narrowing circle of accounting academics isolated from the practice world. There is very little reward in the current academic system for experimentation and innovation that has potential for impacting practice.

2. Perhaps reinforcing this sense of insecurity is the relative weakness of entry-level Ph.D.s in accounting and institutional knowledge. Such weakness in understanding one's own field can be maintained with impunity in accounting since, under existing incentives, thorough accounting knowledge is not needed for publishable research, and hence, promotion and tenure. The persistent use of old research paradigms and researchers' increasing ignorance of accounting institutional knowledge exacerbate the difficulties of communicating with our natural constituencies: accounting firms, corporations, government, etc.

3. Research funding and remuneration (mostly by accounting firms) is generally unrelated to the results and relevance of research. Again, an exception—KPMG's Research Opportunities in Auditing—proves the rule. This concerted funding with a clear objective contributed significantly to auditing research. In other accounting areas, however, research funds are disbursed independently of results. A much different situation exists in the sciences.

4. Increasingly, areas of research and curriculum have been surrendered to other disciplines. (Consider, for example, security analysis, the valuation of financial instruments and other themes in corporate finance.) In curriculum development, the domain of accounting seems to have been defined narrowly. We have not had much intellectual entrepreneurship in the field of accounting. Issues like mergers and acquisitions, leveraged buyouts and corporate governance could just as well have been approached as issues in accounting/tax rather than in finance.

5. Reinforcing the above is a tendency for senior accounting academics to judge and reward the performance of juniors also on the basis of a narrow definition of what constitutes academic accounting. This tends to discourage researchers from innovating in ways that would make our products more desirable and more in demand.

6. The regulation of financial accounting may be one of the reasons for the lack of interest of accounting practitioners in research. Much of the demand for financial accounting services presently stems from regulatory processes, i.e., the SEC, the FASB, the AICPA and others. Contrast this with the finance industry which is much more responsive to market forces. There, the initiative comes from entrepreneurs who are alerted to market opportunities, whereas within the accounting industry, demands for new products are generated primarily as a result of the regulatory process.

Information technology challenge. Another serious impediment to our educational efforts coming from the current environment is the paradigm shift toward information technology (IT). Sounding the alarm most eloquently on this topic is Robert K. Elliott, Assistant to the Chairman of KPMG Peat Marwick (U.S). Bob Elliott is a past AAA Vice President and a current AECC Commissioner. He contends that the present educational approach to accounting is based on concepts and methodologies spawned by the industrial and post-industrial eras. But these tools are flawed in our age of IT and the results produced by today's accounting are at best only marginally relevant and quite possibly seriously misleading ("The Third Wave Breaks on the Shores of Accounting," *Accounting Horizons*, June 1992, pp. 61-85).

Legislative intervention. Since many in today's accounting environment believe that accounting education is not what it ought to be, there has been a concerted effort in several countries to remedy the perceived shortcomings by legislative intervention. Again, we have a good example of this type of activity in the United States. When the leadership of the American Institute of CPAs (AICPA) became convinced that the best remedy for the perceived accounting education shortfalls would be a 25 percent increase in the time devoted to higher education for entry to the profession (i.e., the 150 semester credit hours/five years of required college/university proposition) they opted for regulatory action. Since many accounting academics were unsure whether simple expansion of required study time would overcome the perceived shortfalls, the AICPA apparently concluded that the academics alone would be unable to correct their ways in timely fashion. Thus, a major effort was launched to get local state legislatures to mandate five years of higher education as a prerequisite to professional licensure. Heavy political lobbying was unleashed to where, at the time of this writing, 25 of the 53 individual U.S. jurisdictions now mandate five years of higher education as a CPA prerequisite. My own state of Washington, as well as our largest state, namely California, has not yet adopted the five-year sanction. The entire approach continues to be controversial since it will make professional education more costly, restrict entry into the profession, and increase the cost of professional services. But the key point is that accounting educators were judged unable to put their own house in order and therefore, regulatory corrective action decided upon.

The schism between academe and practice. To conclude this brief litany of environmental signals to our accounting education enterprise, let us recognize that a host of knowledgeable observers finds a lack of interaction, understanding and cooperation between accounting academics and practicing accounting professionals. Observation tells us that medicine, law and engineering, for instance, have regular and substantive interactions between educators and practitioners. Why not in accounting? This answer is elusive, particularly since our sub-field of auditing boasts good cross-fertilization between town and gown.

Today's accounting education environment is not as benign as it was at the time of the 1967 London Conference. In the three decades since then, we have all attempted to make our field more respectable academically. While this effort has succeeded by and large, we may have overshot the mark. Also, we have tended to take our students for granted. Accounting graduates have been in high demand worldwide, and thus we may have relaxed a little too much on the quality control of our teaching activities. When electronic computers first became commercially viable, we had qualms about accepting their applications as part of our field. Now IT is posing a similar challenge. Do we really care whether our research has measurable consequences in practice? Will we change our work product only in response to government mandates? These are some of the issues that will preoccupy us at this conference over the next few days.

Some Development Ideas for Accounting Education

If the accounting education malaise is anywhere close to the consensus opinions of knowledgeable observers (partially referenced above), it is time to answer the clarion call for change. Mind you, I am not downhearted or otherwise negative about the state of the art in accounting education. Quite the contrary! But, I am thoroughly convinced that we must bring about a number of major changes in our endeavors or we will all have cause to worry about decline and loss of relevance.

Moving toward the change mandate, the AECC has formally accepted the challenge by moving productively forward with demonstration projects and the publication of Position Statements and Issues Statements. As mentioned already, these will be discussed later during the conference.

To illustrate the type of developmental efforts that might prove useful in turning around the effectiveness of accounting education, I would like to put forward a half a dozen developmental ideas likely to make a difference if acted upon.

Integral view of education. The schism existing in the present accounting environment between academics and practitioners of the discipline has been alluded to. Similarly, there is considerable debate about the compatibility of research and teaching. My predecessor AAA President, Professor William Beaver of Stanford University, developed as the program theme for his AAA administration the integral nature of accounting teaching, research and practice. This theme is now a part of the AAA Mission Statement (attached), which defines "accounting education" as including teaching, research and practice as interdependent elements of the educational process. We have spent much fruitless time and effort to differentiate between research and teaching in terms of faculty performance measurements and priorities for faculty workloads. Similarly, there has been too much name calling, albeit politely, between the modeling/analytical and the applied/professional camps of accounting research. The segmentations involved have brought primarily grief. It is time to pull the field back together and avoid the narrow focus of artificial specialization.

Unbounded intellectualization. It is instructive to reread the expert assessment of the relevance and productivity of accounting research offered by the knowledgeable panel convened at NYU and quoted earlier in this paper. These experts agree that we have intellectualized the field of accounting to the point of serious separation from practice and real-world applicability of research results. Many of our young Ph.D. accounting researchers have no practical professional experience and therefore operate almost totally in a world of abstraction.

Let me draw an analogy to political science. The intellectualization of that particular field has produced a plethora of model building, theory construction, abstraction and analysis. Yet none of this mighty intellectual arsenal even faintly suggested— much less predicted—the convulsive end of Marxism in Eastern Europe and the disintegration of the former Soviet Union. Intellectualization for its own sake is an empty set. A turn in the road we take seems called for.

Learning versus teaching. Developmental ideas about learning come in many different stripes. They are sometimes referred to as output or assessment measures, often related to student characteristics and generally subject to an expectations gap. The AAA has recognized the significance of this topic through the creation and support of its two-year-old Pedagogy and Curricula Section.

The traditional view of teaching is that the teacher "knows best"—what is to be taught, how it is to be taught, and when it is to be taught. It was believed that motivated and dedicated students would gain all needed educational prerequisites from this process. Specifically in accounting in the United States we assumed that this process was automatic. Accounting Ph.D. programs offer virtually no courses or seminars in pedagogy, have only limited teaching experience requirements through mostly "swim or sink" teaching assistant appointments, and our Ph.D. students are told quite consistently that research represents intellectual output whereas classroom work is a necessity that "goes with the territory."

The AECC is embarked on several initiatives to put teaching back into the accounting education mainstream. Yet we need to go one step further. We need to become genuinely concerned about the learning potential of our students and how well

we challenge, foster and eventually help to realize such potential. Put differently, effective teaching is a necessary but insufficient condition for effective learning. The earlier the new accounting professoriate accepts this proposition, the brighter the future of accounting education is likely to be.

Team scholarship. Following up on the idea that "learning" is the one and only real product of higher education, university leaders are increasingly opining that "team scholarship could help strengthen scholarly traditions" (Donald N. Langenberg, Chancellor, University of Maryland System, *Chronicle of Higher Education*, September 2, 1992, p. A64). In the Op Ed piece cited, Chancellor Langenberg points out that the university's basic "producer" is the faculty member and that the basic "production unit" is a group of faculty members. Groups of faculty are typically organized as departments around a recognized academic discipline or sub-discipline. Here are selected excerpts from the referenced point of view:

> Individual faculty members deliver parts of the product. But it is the department and the university of which it is a part that are held accountable for the delivery of the whole. Thus it is appropriate to focus on the productivity of the *faculty group*, not that of individual faculty members.
>
> The department would be rewarded financially on the basis of [periodic] evaluations and would itself decide how to distribute its collective reward among competing demands for individual salary increases, enhanced administrative services, new faculty appointments, and the like.
>
> [Team scholarship] has long been reality in academe—multidisciplinary research teams, team teaching, surgical teams in university hospitals.
>
> Collective accountability could generate all sorts of improvements. When everyone's next salary increase (including that of the department's Nobel laureate) depends on a good evaluation of the entire department, Physics 101 is unlikely to be taught by the new graduate student who can barely speak English.
>
> Indeed, team scholarship potentially could strengthen scholarly traditions. Giving departments greater responsibility for successfully delivering the university's product could help shield individual faculty members from inap-

propriate intrusion by politicians, administrators, or even colleagues and, at the same time, enhance the university's accountability to its clients.

However one might react to Chancellor Langenberg's ideas, the time is clearly at hand to rearrange the structure of universities to assess more critically the value added of our individual and collective faculty efforts and to design standards and measures of performance for each of the four types of scholarship defined by Ernest L. Boyer, President of the Carnegie Foundation for the Advancement of Teaching. Team scholarship might just be one way to deal with the strong winds of criticisms blowing across the landscape of accounting education.

The lure of total quality management (TQM). One of the most talked about management topics in the United States currently is TQM. Entire organizations have been restructured in its name, many have lost their jobs because of it, and TQM consulting activities are booming widely. Naturally, the idea has come to university campuses as well. Some faculty have become TQM specialists, a fair number of business schools teach TQM courses, and a few university administrative units are employing TQM in their work processes. At my own university, the Treasurer's Office functions completely on a TQM mode and several TQM courses are offered in the business school. Other courses have been infused with TQM ideas and our executive programs now extend to TQM coverage. What, if anything, has TQM to do with accounting education?

First of all, TQM (or CIQ—Continuous Improvement of Quality) focuses largely on process rather than subject matter. The latter has been the mainstay of accounting education for a long time. As this subject matter incessantly grows and becomes more complex, so does the frustration over limited resources available for accounting education. Maybe process improvements would enhance our educational product even though subject matter, scope and complexity seem to have put the discipline beyond reach of the typical four-year undergraduate degree program.

This thought leads to a second point. With the growth in many countries of greatly detailed financial accounting standard setting and an abundance of financial reporting regulations, the intermediate and advanced financial accounting courses have become albatross-like in their attempts to cover, one by one, all applicable rules, standards and regulations. Some intermediate accounting textbooks will soon have to be purchased by weight (in kilograms!) rather than in terms of subject matter coverage. Maybe a TQM approach would prove useful in finding a way through the intermediate and advanced financial accounting maze. This might be done by sorting out coverage of basic ideas and propositions and relying on judicious critical analysis of selected cases and topics rather than grinding through most of the rules, standards and regulations in existence.

Also TQM, in relation to the accounting curriculum, might just provide more efficient and effective results than simply growing linearly with the detailed growth of subject matter as is implied by the 150-semester credit-hour proposition now advocated and lobbied strongly by our American Institute of CPAs.

Finally, apart from its process-oriented dimensions, TQM is predominantly an output framework. In contrast, accounting education is traditionally characterized by input dimensions—test scores of students admitted to the study of accounting, academic degree levels of faculty teaching accounting, and professional experience and awareness levels of instructors in programs seeking special discipline accreditation. Maybe the TQM idea could help us in accounting education to deal with information overload and ambiguity—both of which seem ever present today. Memorizing and regurgitating more and more rules, standards and regulations is not the answer. Sensitivity to underlying basics, critical analysis of new facts and events, plus continuous streams of learning seem like more plausible solutions.

The globalization factor. Earlier in this paper I alluded to the growing globalization of our planet's environment. Accounting is no exception. The very existence of this conference is testimony to the global dimensions of accounting education.

We are still unsure, though, how to best deal with the globalization factor in accounting education. Should there be separate courses on international accounting or should there be infusion of international dimensions in some, most, or all of the courses we teach? How might we cover sensitivity to international or comparative issues in Ph.D. programs? Are international student exchanges or cross-border professional internships a good solution to provide our students with exposure to international ideas? And how do we pay for all these admittedly rather costly internationalization factors?

Again, many viable alternatives present themselves and by now many globalization experiments

are underway. The curriculum portion of this issue was the topic of my paper at the 1967 London
Conference. Among the things we have learned
since that time is the fact that international alone
is not going to stand up any better than domestic
alone. Stephen D. Harlan, the Partner in Charge of
international activities at KPMG Peat Marwick in
the United States, probably is quite realistic with
his theme, "Think Global—Act Local" ("Striving
for the Future: Developing a Global Mindset," *Euro
Sphere*, May/June 1992, p. 2). Obviously, we all
want to be nationals at home—Swiss in Switzerland, Australian in Australia, Swedish in Sweden,
and Nigerian in Nigeria. But, over and above that,
we must think globally to be relevant in today's
environment and to produce students who can be
competitive on a global scale. This conference will
obviously help all of us to do just that. Therefore,
it is well to briefly set the stage now for the themes
of this conference.

Topical Themes for the Conference

Comments offered so far have strengthened the
proposition that the global state of health of accounting education is not the best it has ever been
and that today's accounting education environment
is confronting all of us, whatever passport we carry,
with some substantive challenges. Without malice
of forethought, I have sketched six developmental
ideas that might be useful in meeting our present
challenges. In order to set the stage for all of the
conference sessions and panel discussions compos-
ing the conference program, I would like to comment briefly on the menu of conference topical
themes developed by our Planning Committee. The
list of conference themes identifies our present
professional crossroads and is daunting in and of
itself. I challenge all conference participants to
surface these topical themes and address their effects, consequences, and approaches to possible
solutions throughout the conference whenever appropriate.

*Accounting education needs in developing
countries.* The current thrust of this challenge is
that exporting accounting education approaches
and methodologies from the industrialized countries is of little help and may even be counterproductive. The World Bank is pursuing an interesting pilot program in Indonesia. In 1991, the U.N.
Centre on Transnational Corporations published
Accountancy Development in Africa. Also the U.N.
is taking various lead roles in addressing accounting educational needs in Eastern Europe and the

CIS. The International Accounting Standards Committee (IASC) has launched an active project on
the needs of developing countries. After years of
neglect this issue is finally getting the attention it
deserves.

*Accounting education issues in changing
economies.* Here we are concerned with accounting education responding to changing economic
environments. This issue already received attention earlier in my paper. Cases in point include the
"Relevance Lost" argument made by leading management accountants in the United States Their
point is that traditional cost accounting concepts
do not serve well in post-industrial eras. In Japan,
we have the phenomenon of dozens of American
colleges and universities operating local academic
degree programs. The Erasmus program in Europe
permits university students much greater freedom
to undertake courses at institutions other than their
respective home universities. The OECD has published a research report entitled, *Alternatives to
Universities*. Changing economies are fostering
changes all around us.

Ethics and values in accounting education.
The practicing profession around the world is increasingly confronted with the question of whether
it should be asked to serve as a police agency vis-
à-vis unscrupulous and possibly even fraudulent
business managements and their transactions. But,
before we review the ethics of others, there is the
question of ethics for practicing as well as academic
accountants. How well can one teach ethics in the
classroom? Are the Professionalism and Ethics
seminars and publications series of the AAA worthwhile? Where were the outside auditors when major financial swindles rocked Japan, the United
Kingdom, and the United States? How about academics not serving as expert witnesses in court
cases involving firms from whom they have received research and other grants? Or, still closer to
home, selling complimentary textbooks made available to instructors for examination purposes? Many
issues spring from this line of thought.

*The influence of national cmmissions, com-
mittees, and inquiries on accounting education.*
Major national inquiries into accounting education
are currently happening in the United States, New
Zealand, and Japan. Important committee level attention to accounting education is taking place in
Canada, Brazil, Mexico, several EC countries, the
Nordic countries, several mid-eastern countries,
and in a number of places in Africa. Apparently,
there is almost no national environment void of

some questioning regarding accounting education. What will the influence of these inquiries be? Can the academic accountants put their own houses in order or will it take outside political or professional sanctions? Which part of the accounting education process is the most vulnerable? The national commissions now in existence, or about to be created, bear very close watching. If they cannot somehow bring about a good measure of much needed change, accounting education as we now know it will clearly be in jeopardy.

Accreditation/common standards of excellence. Strong ministries of education characterize the Code Law Countries, whereas common law tradition puts lesser emphasis on central control. In Code Law Countries, standards of excellence for accounting and other education are simply prescribed and enforced. Common Law Countries have a greater tolerance for privately financed and organized universities which, in turn, produces wide quality differences across the full spectrum of colleges and universities. With respect to Code Law Countries, is standard setting by education ministries enough or does accounting education need the additional safeguard of private/professional program accreditation? In Common Law environments, with their pronounced variability in interinstitutional quality of accounting education, how does one get to common standards and their enforcement? Is the separate accreditation of accounting education programs by the American Assembly of Collegiate Schools of Business (AACSB) an effective tool that should be copied elsewhere? Substantive research on this question is long overdue.

The influence of computers and information systems on accounting education. Access to personal computers and a reasonable array of accounting-related software is still a major difficulty in most developing countries. Yet availability alone does not mean effective use—as is well illustrated in many industrialized countries. There appears to be agreement that a formal course covering computerized accounting information systems should be a part of any forward-looking accounting curriculum. The Certified General Accountants Association of Canada has pioneered strongly computer-based curricula throughout its non-university accounting education program. From several perspectives, substantial progress in this area is at hand. Nevertheless, the age of information technology (IT) is still waiting to be invited into the home of accounting education. To reiterate, this particular

point is made in Robert Elliott's, "The Third Wave Breaks on the Shores of Accounting," cited earlier in this paper. The IT challenge is not unlike the one emanating from changing economies and ethical values—either accounting education embraces them quickly or it must risk growing irrelevance.

Education needs of practicing professionals in developed and developing countries. This is a topic thoroughly addressed by the Education Committee of the International Federation of Accountants (IFAC). In fact, the international education guidelines issued by the IFAC Committee go a long way toward identifying and dealing with the needs referenced here. Key is the issue of life-long learning. No formal university and/or professional pre-entry level educational package will satisfy the continuing educational needs of practicing professionals. This puts the entire profession (i.e., academic and practicing) into the educational enterprise subject to joint responsibility. Obviously, practicing professionals must engage in effective and efficient continuing professional education (CPE) from whatever provider source. Licensing authorities may in fact require certain quantities of CPE. At the same time, colleges and universities have a responsibility to provide post-degree learning opportunities commensurate with the needs of the practicing profession. By and large, most of these relationships are still at the incubator stage and require serious attention.

Instructional innovations and materials in accounting education. A large part of the reason for the existence of national commissions assessing accounting education seems to be the lack of innovations surrounding what we do in the classroom. Many AAA committees have made this point since the mid 1950s. The Price Waterhouse Foundation study group on introductory accounting said so in 1971. Professor Zeff wrote editorials about it and now the AECC has picked up the challenge. Developments in countries outside the United States are quite parallel even though somewhat less intense. How fair to students is it in 1992 to base entire textbooks on the double entry bookkeeping paradigm? Why should intermediate textbooks incorporate accounting rules, standards, and regulations literally detail by detail? There is indeed a challenge of innovation in accounting education.

The influence of regulatory bodies on accounting education. In the beginning, one might say, professional accounting bodies determined the contents of accounting education. In most English-speaking countries, professional (i.e., qualifying) bodies still screen university courses as to which are acceptable as appropriate "accounting education." In the United States the American Institute of CPAs has made curriculum proposals for almost one hundred years, has pronounced what the "common body of knowledge" is and has now taken the stand that no one without at least five years of collegiate, formal education may become a member of the AICPA after the year 2000. Throughout Europe, but especially in Switzerland, Holland, and the Scandinavian countries, accounting education curricula reflect heavily the typical content of professional examinations. Clearly, accounting education is not independent of the regulatory bodies existing in each accounting environment. Five years ago at Kyoto I argued that accounting exists now as an independent discipline and should be so recognized at the university. But this proposition is difficult to maintain in the face of the growing influence of regulatory bodies on accounting education. Somehow a workable combination of the seemingly divergent interests between accounting regulators and accounting educators has elluded us.

Evaluation of performance in accounting education. As stated earlier in this paper, learning is the one and only product of institutions of higher learning. Can we realistically evaluate the quantity and quality of learning? Are grades assigned by instructors a reasonable evaluation index? Is performance on a professional examination? How about salaries obtained by graduates upon entering the profession? Why not peer evaluations of professors by their colleagues in other university departments? Is demand for accounting courses to be considered in evaluating accounting education programs? Evaluation of our product causes us great difficulties as educators. About the only thing we seem agreed on is that evaluations should be academically based. Maybe the intellectual quality of students attracted to accounting education is the best we can do. But then, entry-level measures can hardly be said to be measuring performance. I think the point is made that this topic is worthy of your attention at this conference.

Using international data sources in the classroom. One strong champion of this idea is the International Accounting Section of AAA. Its various clearing houses cover case availabilities, syllabi exchanges, electronically driven databases, and other sources of educational materials. Utilizing educational sources originating in a variety of countries and environments seems strongly in keeping

with today's global challenges. My personal view is that classroom utilization of international data sources ought to be encouraged at every turn. Moreover, I feel that truly international accounting education conferences like the one we are now attending or the annual meetings of the European Accounting Association (e.g., Madrid, 1992), or the Asian Pacific Conference on International Accounting Issues (New Zealand, 1992), provide an incredibly good opportunity to exchange information about sources of data and their use in various classroom settings among colleagues from the world over. Useful information about international accounting conferences and meetings is provided in the newsletter of one of our co-sponsoring organizations, namely the International Association for Accounting Education and Research. The newsletter in question is entitled *Cosmos Accountancy Chronicle.*

Comparison of accounting education systems. Comparative studies often yield positive results. Comparative law has established itself as a sub field as has comparative development in humans, public policy, and urban planning. Environmental management is currently receiving much comparative attention. Even though comparative studies in accounting education are likely to be informative, and seem certain to lead to better exchanges of educational materials and various accounting related databases, we should not set expectations too high. Accounting education systems are certainly culture bound. Effective and efficient delivery in one system may be only of marginal use in other systems. There are significant accounting education tradeoffs between non-university professional systems and graduate and undergraduate systems at the collegiate level. In Germany and Japan, the accounting education systems deliver highly abstract theoretical materials, whereas more applied pragmatic materials come to the fore in the English-speaking countries. In some systems, accounting education stands on its own, whereas in other systems it is built into economics or even broader social science perspectives. Thus, comparative systems study must be undertaken with great care, unlike variables must be identified and the generalizability of results is typically limited.

Problems of faculty recruitment and retention. Faculty development in accounting is clearly one of the more difficult challenges internationally. Earlier in this paper we defined "education" as an interactive combination of teaching, research, and professional service. Is the heavy emphasis on research in U.S. Ph.D. programs an appropriate background for *all* accounting faculty? European universities do not have the concept of the North American graduate school. Serious university research then happens at university institutes and research centers. Is this the right place to develop accounting faculty? In many Asian countries, in part due to very low levels of university salaries, accounting educators either have a professional practice background or combine active professional practice with active university teaching. Such joint venture faculty characteristics are also found all over South America and characterize the situation in the Netherlands. Maybe the portfolio effect of different accounting faculty backgrounds is a strength rather than a weakness. But we must also recognize, particularly in the developing countries, that accounting faculty salaries are often so parsimonious as to make it not feasible for even highly motivated individuals to accept full-time faculty appointments. Despite these challenges, we must remind ourselves that over the last quarter of a century accounting has clearly achieved university discipline status and that some migration of accounting faculty into professional practice and its reverse seem to be encouraging.

Other related international accounting education topics. This paper probably has raised more issues than any one conference can deal with. Therefore, rather than adding to the menu of focal topics, I would like to reiterate four core ideas touched upon earlier. First, accounting education should be seen as a broad, integrative endeavor that comprises research and service as well as teaching. Second, our many high-powered research skills and methods should be applied to education issues along with discipline issues. Third, all of us should invest more attention in some change ideas like team scholarship, focus on learning, TQM processes and the IT paradigm shift. Last, as today's accounting educators, we have no monopoly on preparing tomorrows entrants to the profession. Liberal arts graduates find attractive career opportunities in professional accounting service firms. Thus the educational package we deliver must stay relevant—and international! Thank you for your attention.

The Mission of the American Accounting Association Is to Improve Accounting Education

The Mission Requires	Therefore, The American Accounting Association
A Broad View of Accounting	Regards accounting as the intellectual discipline concerned with the measurement, communication, and use of decision-oriented information.
An Integral View of Education	Accepts education as including both the enhancement and transfer of knowledge and skills for obtaining knowledge. Teaching, research, and practice are interdependent elements of the educational process.
Teaching, Research, and Practice Interface	Promotes reciprocal interactions among teaching, research and practice that reinforce their complementary nature.
Broad Institutional Support	Maintains, and enhances synergies among, a wide range of components critical to its mission. These include committees, commissions, special-interest sections, regions, meetings, continuing education, and publications, which, in the aggregate, support teaching, research, and services to academia and practice.
Public Responsibility	Fosters awareness and acceptance of the responsibilities that follow from the effects of accounting and accounting education on important economic, social, and political policies and decisions.
Cooperation with Others	Considers its complements with other organizations, institutions, and persons in formulating strategies, setting objectives, and allocating resources.
Global Perspective	Comprehends the global nature of accounting and accounting education and interacts with other organizations, institutions, and persons around the world that share its mission.
Continual Improvement	Periodically assesses the quality of accounting education and refines its strategies, objectives, and activities to assure continual improvement.

Approved by
AAA Executive Committee and Council
April 1991

The Skills and Competencies of Accountants

Murray C. Wells

There is little doubt that migration is going to be one of the major issues in international affairs in the 1990s. The movement of people on a scale not previously contemplated is already evident, both as refugees and as authorised and unauthorised migrants. Many of those refugees and migrants have skills and professional qualifications and the recognition and use of those skills is not only a human rights issue but is also a matter of economic necessity. It makes no sense at all for receiving countries to spend scarce educational resources retraining people who are already trained in a recognised field such as accounting. Similarly, it is unrealistic and unreasonable to expect newly arrived refugees or migrants to expend time and money to acquire skills they already possess. In neither case am I suggesting that there are no local conditions, legal requirements or elements of local professional practice that will require special training. But, thanks to the inherent advantages of double-entry bookkeeping, basic accounting practices are the same throughout the world and people trained in one country usually have little difficulty in adapting to practices in another country.

Despite the universality of accounting practices, most countries allow their professions to erect barriers to entry. Newly arrived accountants must submit proof of their qualifications which, if accepted, will allow them to enter the profession. In most cases, however, the qualifications required reflect the educational system of the receiving country. Little or no allowance is made for the different educational or experimental arrangements that are common elsewhere. Accountants who have obtained their qualifications through a process that is different from the prevailing system in their new home are frequently disadvantaged and may even be prohibited from practising their profession in their adopted country.

Recognition of this problem has led UNESCO (Convention of the Recognition of Studies, Degrees and Diplomas) and a number of other international and national bodies (for example, the 1968 Federal German Vocational Training Act and more recent developments in the United Kingdom, United States, Australia and New Zealand—for information and examples of assessment and test instruments, the International Centre for Research on Assessment, Institute of Education, University of London, UK) to propose the development of competency-based standards which might be used to assess the skills and competencies of migrants as well as to inform local educational institutions. Many professions have accepted that challenge and, within the accounting field, I am familiar with the work already undertaken by the Charted Association of Certified Accountants and the Charted Association of Management Accountants in Britain; the Australian Society of CPAs and the Institute of Chartered Accountants in Australia; and the New Zealand Society of Accountants. There may be others, and I apologise if I have not recognised national bodies of accountants which are active in developing competency-based standards. The important point is that those professions have recognised the need for a defensible mechanism by which they can assess the skills and competencies both of migrants and new domestic graduates. Present methods of accreditation, which usually involve a review of inputs in the form of curricula, textbooks and physical facilities, cannot evaluate the quality of the teaching, the abilities of the students or the extent to which practical experience has enhanced the skills of the graduates.

We should not be surprised that the development of statements of professional competencies have not, generally, been well received by universities. Senior university administrators see threats to university autonomy and the prospect of increasing demands being placed on them by those professional bodies which develop competency-based standards. The universities fear that those professions will have objective criteria by which to judge the output of universities instead of the input criteria now commonly used (qualifications of faculty, student/staff ratios, number of students in a class, computers per students, and so on). This will, possibly, lead to the professional faculties placing irresistible demands on university administrators for larger slices of the financial pie. Arts and sciences faculties which do not have the support of professional associations will find it hard to compete in that environment.

Murray C. Wells is a faculty member at the University of Sydney, Australia and is outgoing President of IAAER.

Another complaint of university administrators is that competency standards might dominate professional training to the exclusion of the accepted university values. That is, graduates are expected to have not only the specific skills demanded of them by the profession they wish to enter, but they are also expected to be literate and numerate, be able to think independently and to express themselves clearly. I find those arguments less than convincing. Indeed, we might argue that all of those "higher" attributes are expected by professional groups and the lack of them is currently a cause for complaint by employers, generally. But more importantly, I am not aware of any suggestion that the competencies that might be demanded by a professional group should be interpreted as the maximum expected of a graduate. On the contrary, competency-based standards are more likely to be the minimum demanded, leaving room for each university or college to put its own stamp on its graduates. No one denies that professions are based on the possession of a body of specialised theoretical knowledge. But possession of that knowledge does not guarantee that the individual can or will act professionally:

> Competency assessment is not about measuring performance, but rather about making judgments based on evidence which can then be assessed as being sufficient to infer that an individual is competent. (Clive Chappell, *Competency Update* NOOSR, Australia, August/September 1992)

Whether the individual does, in fact, use the skills and competencies he or she possesses is also outside the assessment process and a matter for the employer or client to judge.

DEVELOPING COMPETENCY-BASED STANDARDS

The usual method of deriving competency-based standards for accountants is to undertake a series of detailed studies of the things that accountants do as well as to ask members of the profession and academics what changes might be expected over the next five or ten years. Delphi studies are commonly used and there have been criticisms of them. I have no doubt that the methods used could be improved and refined. But that is not a good reason for delaying the development of standards. Rather it suggests that we have much to learn about the methods and the outcomes. We will learn by experience and the standards will improve. Alternatively, if no attempt is made, the accounting profession will be open to charges that it has no objective method for assessing the compe-

tence of graduates, that it denies people of diverse backgrounds the opportunity to practice their profession and denies migrants and refugees the opportunity to use their training and experience in their new homeland. More importantly, without competency-based standards, professional accounting bodies run the risk of even greater legislative interference than is currently the case if they cannot demonstrate that they have defensible mechanisms for evaluating the skills and competencies of people wishing to enter the profession, And, in my view, the methods currently used around the world are not defensible!

THE ROLE OF EDUCATORS

Members of the IAAER might ask what this has to do with an international association devoted to accounting education and research. I have raised the matter here because I believe it is indicative of the role which the IAAER can play, in association with bodies such as IFAC and the UN Center for Transnational Corporations, in promoting accounting education around the world and in facilitating technological and educational transfer. It would not be in the best interests of educators to allow the professional bodies or legislators alone to determine the competencies of accountants—education clearly plays a key role in developing the "theoretical body of knowledge" which underlies professional practices. Educators and researchers are best placed to develop that body of knowledge and devise ways for disseminating it to those who want to join the profession. Similarly, if there is to be a defensible mechanism for evaluating the skills and competencies of migrants and others who have trained or practised under an educational and initiation system which is different from the one they are seeking to enter, then educators have a key role to play in developing those mechanisms.

One of the roles of the IAAER is to facilitate the sharing of experiences in developing evaluation criteria and testing processes. A conference such as this provides an opportunity for those experiences to be shared and lessons learnt. It is no coincidence that one of the topics for the panel sessions later in this conference is the international transferability (reciprocity) of accounting qualifications. Nor should we be surprised that the topic has been canvassed within the recent Uruguay round of GATT negotiations as part of a movement to establish an international framework for the trade in services. I have no doubt that we will all hear much more about that topic and the development of appropriate assessment methods in the future. Similarly, I have no doubt that the IAAER together with its counterpart, IFAC, will become increasingly involved in the movement to facilitate the international transfer and assessment of accounting education and training.

The IAAER also provides a forum in which the leaders of national academic accounting bodies can assemble to discuss matters of current interest or concern. I have raised one such issue here to illustrate why the IAAER became, in effect, a federation of national academic accounting bodies. There is no other mechanism for the interchange of the information and experiences that reside within those bodies and for the resolution of disputes that will inevitably arise through the rising tide of migration and the demand for skill recognition.

I have been greatly privileged to have had the opportunity to participate in the emergence of IAAER as a significant contributor to the develop-

ment of accounting education and research throughout the world. We, as accountants interested in teaching and research, are at the threshold of international developments which will have a powerful effect on world trade and the movement of people. I invite you all, as individual members of the IAAER, to participate in and contribute to the internationalization of accounting and in particular to the development of credible mechanisms that will facilitate the transfer of accounting knowledge and skills. I am also delighted that my colleagues and I on the outgoing Executive Committee are able to pass on these great responsibilities to the outstanding team of people you have elected to the incoming Executive Committee. There is important work to be done, and Sid Gray and his team are well qualified to do it. Please give them your support and lend your weight and expertise to the further development of accounting as the international language of business

Accounting Education in China and Russia

The conference program included six papers that provide an inside view into the evolving accounting profession in China and Russia and the need for revitalizing accounting education.

The role of accounting in China and Russia is undergoing significant change. In the past, the focus was on maintaining financial reports for national planning and centralized control over the economy. There were no shareholders and no perceived need for independent auditors. Instead, educational programs emphasized detailed record-keeping functions. Today, the national governments realize that an accounting system capable of measuring financial performance by accounting professionals is necessary to enable their transition to a market economy and to attract foreign investments. Accounting education is in transition too, preparing accountants who can facilitate the transfer from state ownership to privitization and who can perform a vital role as their countries move toward global economies.

Accounting Education in China

Barry J. Cooper, Tang Yun Wei, and Lynne Chow

In the late 1960s and early 1970s, when extreme leftist thinking dominated China, accounting was required to be simple and easily understood by anyone. Accounting education suffered greatly in that period, and most accounting departments of institutions of higher learning were closed down. Soon after the start of the modernisation campaign, government officials and business managers found that qualified accountants were badly needed in order to help achieve their economic aims. Accounting regained its former position, and accounting education began a period of rapid development. Tertiary, vocational and adult education are the main components of the accounting education structure.

HIGHER EDUCATION IN ACCOUNTING, FINANCE AND ECONOMICS

Accounting is an integral part of the programmes in finance and economics at the universities. Since the 1980–1985 Development Programme for National Education in Public Finance was formulated in 1980, the number of students in finance and economics courses has increased sharply.

The rapid expansion of the accounting and auditing specialities is a direct response to the increase in demand for accountants. Since China's economy has been changing from a highly centralised economy to a planned commodity economy, economic activities have become increasingly complicated. Accountants are now required to be more and more involved in decision-making and financial control of the enterprises and other institutions.

Overspecialisation in Finance, Economics and Accounting

In contrast to many Western universities, finance, economics and accounting programmes in Chinese universities are highly specialised, often industry oriented. It was found by the State Education Commission that the total number of different kinds of specialities in economics and finance increased from 37 in 1982 to roughly 80 in 1986. The major factor behind this increase is the proliferation of finely divided specialities in the same subdisciplines.

Several factors account for this situation. First, it was influenced by the needs of the centralised and physical planning system which has shaped the Chinese economy and government since the 1950s. In this system, most of the cadres in the government organisations and enterprises are obliged to carry out faithfully the policies and directives issued. There is little opportunity or need for them to think independently and with initiative or a sense of responsibility. Very specialised and very vocationally oriented economics and finance education seemed appropriate for preparing cadres to execute these limited functions.

Second, in the initial period of the People's Republic, China decided to follow the model of higher education institutions and curricula developed in the Soviet Union. In this model of tertiary education, the university system consists of a large number of highly specialised institutes offering finely divided training programs to facilitate rapid expansion of higher-level manpower, according to the specialised occupational requirements of the planned economy.

Third, many universities and colleges are administered and financially sponsored by line ministries. These sponsoring ministries want to secure the economic and finance graduates for the enterprises under their auspices, and this induces them to strengthen and expand their existing hold over the specialised institutes under their jurisdiction. This is another reason for the tendency toward further specialisation of the department and curriculum structure of the universities in economics and finance.

The situation of overspecialisation has been a major defect of the education system, and is now being questioned in tertiary education. Emphasis is now starting to be placed on general principles rather than on narrowly specialised programmes.

Development of Textbooks

Many accounting textbooks are outdated and have been developed along industry lines. They

Barry J. Cooper is Associate Professor at Royal Melbourne Institute of Technology, Australia, Tang Yun Wei is Vice President at Shanghai University of Finance and Economics, China, and Lynne Chow is Principal Lecturer at Hong Kong Polytechnic, Hong Kong.

are largely a host of rules and methods from uniform accounting regulations stipulated by the government for different economic sectors, together with some explanations. Alternative approaches justifiable from an accounting viewpoint are not explored and analysed sufficiently.

The development of high-quality teaching materials is by no means easy. The best method of improving the teaching material and teaching approach is to establish a highly qualified teaching force. The interruption of accounting education, caused by the Cultural Revolution in the late 1960s and early 1970s, created a big gap in the provision of teachers. Most teachers are either relatively old or very young, having graduated in the early 1980s. A strong tendency towards "inbreeding" also exists in most Chinese universities. Young faculty members are usually graduates from the same university. This increases the insular character of each university and hinders the development of a unified academic world on a national scale. In recent years, another factor compounding the scarcity of a teaching force is that many promising young faculty members have gone abroad to further their study and have chosen not to return. Upgrading teaching standards and teaching materials is an imperative task for accounting education.

Teaching Methods

Most undergraduate courses consist of one-way delivery of lectures and test paper examinations at the end of each semester. Teachers confine themselves to elaborating on details of textbooks, and students are used to taking notes and memorising what is said in the textbooks. Few courses are found to include much two-way communication between teacher and students such as discussions in small group tutorials or presentations by students in the classroom. The case study approach is not popular in class teaching.

Broadening the Common Body of Knowledge

An important step has been taken by the State Education Commission to reverse the situation of overspecialisation, and to establish a curriculum of specialities of finance and economics suitable to the Chinese environment. A Curriculum Development Seminar on Chinese Economics and Finance Education was held in 1987. More than a dozen foreign professors from famous universities in the United States, the United Kingdom, Japan, West Germany, Australia, Canada, and more than 20 Chinese professors from different universities were invited to participate in the seminar.

The foreign experts provided advice on economics, finance and accounting subjects in the universities, and personally observed the education process in economics and finance. They submitted a report which made valuable recommendations. The proposed minimum core programme for the Bachelor Degree for all economics, finance and management specialities is shown in Table 1.

Six additional management-related core courses are management accounting, organisational behaviour, marketing, production management, corporate finance, and business policy and strategy. The purpose of these core courses is to give students fundamental knowledge in economic theory and methods. This can provide an adequate foundation for understanding the more specialised courses, and establishing the ability to deal with the new economic and management problems the students will encounter in their future jobs. The programme also serves the purpose of overcoming the present problem of specialised courses which are too narrow and too vocationally oriented.

Development of Key Accounting Departments

While a large number of new accounting departments have been established in tertiary institutions, their standard varies significantly. Some of them are quite satisfactory in terms of teaching staff, research ability and library collection, while some are not quite as good. Procedures have been taken to evaluate the standard of these newly established departments by the State Education Commission and other supervisory organisations.

At the same time, the State Education Commission selects, through a rigorous evaluation procedure, key departments in universities all over China, with the aim of further developing these departments to achieve an internationally recognised standard, and setting examples for other departments in these specialities.

More specifically, the key departments are each required to reach the following standards:

• Expertise to develop doctoral, master's and bachelor's studies up to international standards.

• Ability to accept and direct foreign visiting scholars and to undertake high-level research projects.

• Ability to participate in solving theoretical as well as practical problems emerging in economic reform, and to provide a contribution to significant decision making in the nation.

• Ability to join various international academic exchange activities, to present research results

TABLE 1
Proposed Minimum Core Programme for the Bachelor Degree of Economics, Finance and Management Specialities

Subjects	Number of Credits
Basic Course	
Political Economy	8
Micro/Macroeconomics	6
Mathematics	9
Statistics	4
Accounting	3
Computer Applications	3
Applied Courses *(Students must choose 3 out of 4)*	
Public Finance	3
Money and Banking	3
Comparative Economic Development	3
International Trade and Finance	3
Total Minimum Score (including the 3 applied courses)	42
Other Courses (including additional courses in economics, finance and management)	78
Total for the Bachelor's Degree	120

of international standards, and the ability to explore new research areas and contribute to the development of the speciality.

Two accounting departments, one in the Shanghai University of Finance and Economics (under the auspices of the Ministry of Finance) and the other in Xiamen University (under the auspices of the State Education Commission), were accredited as key accounting departments. They were required to work out a detailed plan to achieve the objectives listed above. The plan was then examined by a group of well-known professors and accountants. Their success in implementing the plan will be evaluated periodically as unsatisfactory performance could lead to loss of status as a key department.

Accounting Education Reform

Most large accounting departments are established in the universities and institutes under the jurisdiction of the Ministry of Finance. In order to update and upgrade accounting education, the Ministry of Finance encourages the universities and institutes under its jurisdiction to undertake comprehensive accounting education reform.

This includes identifying the objectives and guidelines for accounting education, revising accounting curricula, rewriting suitable accounting textbooks, improving teaching methods, improving the methods of examination and grading, changing from a term system to a credit system, emphasising ethics in education, etc.

Based on the quality of accounting education reform in some universities, the Ministry of Finance selected two accounting departments, one in the Shanghai University of Finance and Economics and the other in the Zhongnan University of Finance and Economics, as experimental departments. A brief introduction to the current situation of these departments will give a general idea of the development of accounting education in universities in China.

At Shanghai University of Finance and Economics (SUFE), the main objective is to equip regular full-time students with broad and comprehensive knowledge, to enhance their ability to adapt to the needs of the four modernisations, and to develop their potential for high-level responsibility in China's enterprises. SUFE has adopted the credit accumulation system where a total of 2,739 class hours are required. The students must earn 163 credits, of which 123 are for compulsory courses, 28 for elective courses, and 12 are for the social survey, year-end thesis and graduate thesis.

At the Zhongnan University of Finance and Economics, the total class hours are about 2,890. Students are required to earn 150 credits during four years, of which 101 are for compulsory courses, 37 for elective courses, and the remainder for social survey, year-end thesis and graduate thesis.

As already indicated, SUFE has started the five specialised core courses of Elementary Accounting, Finance Accounting, Cost Accounting, Management Accounting and Auditing, which represents a significant change from the old accounting curriculum structure which was based on the line industries. These new core courses were not simply based on Western accounting textbooks, but were developed through a major effort to combine the theory and China's reality. Several distinctive features can be observed.

The core courses are offered in order of increasing difficulty. Together with some specialised and elective courses, they form a relatively complete disciplinary system. As the State Education Commission has recommended that 10 core courses be integrated into the curricula of all specialities of finance, economics and accounting, some adjustments are likely to be required soon.

So far SUFE has offered 36 elective courses, and other courses in accounting and economics related to specific national economic departments. In addition, SUFE arranges for the sophomores and juniors to go to factories or CPA firms for practical experience, or to conduct social surveys in accordance with the policy of combining theory with practice. It improves the quality of teaching and makes possible social investigation through the utilisation of "the second classroom."

The drastic change of textbook materials from uniform accounting regulation-oriented to more theory-oriented books has put the teachers under pressure to devise new instructional strategies. Also, classroom lectures are now less teacher oriented, and students are encouraged to participate in class. This change in emphasis has achieved some success and is considered another factor contributing to better educational quality.

Great efforts have also been made to improve the quality of the teaching staff. At SUFE, more than a dozen accounting faculty members have been sent abroad to further their study. They have been exposed to other education systems and new subjects that are not well developed in China. On return, they combine what they have learned abroad with the Chinese socioeconomic system, and are making a valuable contribution to accounting education. At the same time, the department has been engaging in active international academic exchanges, and has been undertaking joint research projects with scholars from other countries. A number of well-known outstanding academics who have been invited to the department to give lectures have brought in updated knowledge of accounting theory and practice.

Another measure taken by the department is to encourage faculty members to carry out research and participate in various conferences to present their research results.

Through these initiatives, the quality of the teaching staff in the department has been notably strengthened and a vigorous academic ethos gradually established. Those who proposed the reforms realise that in order to reach an internationally recognised standard, there is still a long way to go.

SECONDARY VOCATIONAL EDUCATION AND ADULT EDUCATION

The undergraduate programme is important in training professional accountants. However, China's modernisation programme needs millions of accounting staff, not all of whom can possibly be trained through the tertiary education system.

It is also unjustifiable from the economic viewpoint, because the qualification requirements of staff differ. Some of them are expected to assume the responsibility of high-ranking management, while many of them are required to do only semi-senior or junior work.

The State Education Commission has therefore determined that China must strive for a greater development of vocational technical education, with the emphasis on secondary vocational technical education. To this end, the State has decided to train, during the period of the Seventh Five-Year Plan, nearly 10 million graduates from the full-time

TABLE 2
SUFE Category of Courses

Category	Courses	Credits	%	Hours	%
Political theory	14	28	18.5	465	17.0
General basic courses	6	39	25.9	821	30.0
Finance and economics	4	13	8.6	225	8.2
Specialised courses	10	43	28.5	734	26.8
Elective course (min)	16	28	18.5	494	18.0
Social survey & thesis	—	12	—	—	—
Total	40	163	100.0	2,739	100.0

secondary schools. The number of vocational technical schools of finance and economics, especially the vocational training schools of accounting, increased sharply in the late 1980s. These schools can be classified into three categories.

- The specialised secondary schools directly under the finance bureau of the provinces, autonomous regions and municipalities. These schools primarily produce semi-senior staff for the provinces, autonomous regions and municipalities, who become the main body of staff for public finance and taxation. The students enrolled are graduates of senior middle schools and it takes three years for them to go through the programme.
- The specialised secondary schools directly under the finance departments of the prefectures, cities and districts. The major task of these schools is to train semi-senior staff for the departments of public finance and taxation. The students enrolled are graduates of junior middle schools, and the period of schooling is four years.

The specialised schools of public finance. The major task of these schools is to train relatively senior staff of the departments of public finance and taxation and other related departments. The students enrolled are graduates of senior middle schools and the schooling period is three years.

In these secondary schools, a higher specialised education programme has been developed in the fields of finance, economics, accounting, management, etc., similar to diploma courses in some other countries. The Shanghai Li Xin Accounting Institute is one of the schools offering exclusively such higher specialised accounting programmes. The students admitted are graduates of senior middle school, and it takes students three years to complete the programme.

Adult education is another important component of the system of education in finance and economics. Great emphasis has been placed on adult education by the State Education Commission and the Ministry of Finance. Many of the current management and accounting staff graduated during the Cultural Revolution, and the training they received is generally insufficient, so they, and others who wish to improve themselves, need further training.

Adult education takes many different forms. Many universities are now providing adult school programmes for adults who already have a job. These programmes range from those leading to a bachelor's degree to other short-term, specially designed programmes. All applicants must hold a job relating to the specialities they study.

Other forms of adult education include radio broadcasting and television colleges, correspondence colleges, factory-run colleges for staff and workers, rural colleges for country people, management cadres colleges, etc. The most popular programmes offered in this way are accounting, auditing, finance, economics and law. It has been projected that during the period of the Seventh Five-Year Plan, the country will need altogether 167,500 teachers for the adult education programme in finance and economics alone.

Some universities have also conducted short-term programmes jointly with foreign partners. For example, the Shanghai University of Finance and Economics has conducted training programmes in accounting for joint ventures and in auditing, jointly with the international accounting firms of Coopers & Lybrand and Touche Ross & Company. The training centre of SUFE and the Economic Development Institute of the World Bank have jointly run various short-term programmes on project management. The university has also conducted independently a controllers research programme and an audit teachers programme.

Adult education has been developed at a very fast pace. It has produced a large number of graduates who have filled the shortage in the fields of finance and economics. At the same time, it has also exposed some problems in education quality. Some of the programmes are not well organised and some lack qualified teachers.

Aware of this fact, the State Education Commission decided in 1990 to stabilise the level of educational programmes, and place the emphasis on quality rather than on quantity. Surveys and investigations have been made to evaluate various programmes, and a guideline is being produced to ensure a healthy development of adult education.

CONCLUSION

Accounting education is closely related to the demand for accountants, which in turn depends on the level of economic development. After disastrous setbacks during the Cultural Revolution, the accounting profession and accounting education has since gained a high level of momentum.

Accounting training in tertiary and secondary professional schools, as well as in adult education, was characterised by expansion on a large scale during the 1980s. However, the State Education Commission and other supervisory organisations are now becoming more concerned with the quality of education. A nationwide survey was recently conducted on university education in the fields of finance, economics and accounting, which highlighted weaknesses including narrowness of the subject matter taught, overspecialisation, outdated textbooks and unsatisfactory teaching methods.

Several critical measures have since been taken to improve the situation, such as the establishment of common core courses, launching of accounting reform, and the key accounting department accreditation scheme. Some of these measures have shown favourable results.

Secondary professional schools are managed by different industries and regions. They produce large numbers of accounting staff who are expected to be employed in the less advanced positions. This is an important part of the educational structure. Adult education takes many forms in meeting different requirements. It has been developed at a rapid pace and probably too fast to ensure consistent quality. However, stabilising the programme and improving the quality is the current policy of the State Education Commission.

BIBLIOGRAPHY

Amoy University, Fujian, China. 1987. *Accounting for Joint Ventures with Chinese and Foreign Investment* (in Chinese).

Fudan University, Shanghai, PRC. 1987. *Proceedings of the Curriculum Development Seminar on Chinese Economics and Finance Education*. Fudan University Press.

Shanghai University of Finance and Economics. 1988. *Financial Accounting*. Vols 1 & 2 (in Chinese).

————, and the University of Texas at Dallas. 1987. *Accounting and Auditing in the People's Republic of China: A Review of Its Practices, Systems, Education and Development*.

Tang Y. W., L. Chow, and B. J. Cooper. 1991. *Accounting and Finance in China — A Review of Current Practice*. Hong Kong.

A Western Accountancy Programme for the People's Republic of China

Barry J. Cooper and Anthea L. Rose

PROJECT FRAMEWORK

This paper reviews an accountancy training project which has been conducted in China since 1989, under the auspices of the UK Chartered Association of Certified Accountants (ACCA).

The establishment of a programme of Western-style accountancy training in a country such as China poses a number of problems; it requires a range of resources and skills and the co-operation of a number of different organisations, each of which will have its own particular reasons for being involved. This paper discusses those problems and resources and argues that the project provides a model for effective co-operation between the accountancy profession, the education system and employers, and between East and West.

The key to the success of the project has been an appreciation by all those involved that no system—be it of professional organisation, standards or education and training—can simply be lifted from one context and imposed on another. Education and training programmes must both derive from best international practice and be geared to the context and needs of the countries concerned. The accountancy training project needed also to be flexible and capable of responding to changing—and often unanticipated—needs.

As the project has progressed, it became clear that it could not be restricted to providing Chinese accountants with a Western-style professional education. Participants needed to see how to *apply* that education in practice; the managers and others to whom they would be reporting and who would be using the information which they provided needed to be made aware of the concepts and methods the newly trained accountants would be using.

This paper looks at

- the background to the project;
- the participants in it;
- its development; and
- the move to Open Learning.

The paper then indicates how the ACCA and the educationalists involved evaluate the success of their work so far and, finally, gives some interim thoughts as to key issues raised.

BACKGROUND

Accounting plays an important role in business management and economic development. This simple statement had not been fully recognised in China until the recent economic reform programme. In recent years, accounting in China has acted as a controlling link between state enterprises and their respective ministries. The function of accounting has been to monitor and check the achievement of planned tasks fixed by state authorities.

In fact, the accountancy profession virtually ceased to exist in China after the 1949 Revolution. In the later 1960s and early 1970s, accounting was required to be simple and easily understood by anyone without effort. Accountancy education suffered greatly in that period and most accountancy departments of institutions of higher learning were closed down. The profession only began to be re-established in the early 1980s. Soon after the start of the modernisation campaign, government officials and business managers recognised that accountants with a different sort of expertise would have key roles in helping them to achieve their economic aims. Accounting then regained its former position.

One of the key features of China's economic reform has been the introduction of foreign capital and technology. To attract foreign investment, the government has allowed foreign investors to form joint ventures with Chinese enterprises or to establish wholly owned subsidiaries and branches in China. By the end of 1988, more than 12,000

Barry J. Cooper is an Associate Professor at The Royal Melbourne Institute of Technology and Anthea L. Rose is a Deputy Secretary at The Chartered Association of Certified Accountants in the United Kingdom.

enterprises with foreign capital investment had been approved, including 250 wholly foreign-owned enterprises. The role of joint venture enterprises as one of the means by which China will co-operate with foreign companies to forward the development of its economy has created a particular need for Chinese knowledge of, and expertise in, Western accounting practices.

Accountants in China need now to be aware of the impact on business of interest rates, inflation, growth, uncertainty, financial structure and the cost of capital. As the state is no longer determining all the operational conditions of all economic organisations, accountants working outside the state sector have a new responsibility—to ensure that enterprises themselves generate adequate working capital, improve their efficiency and earn a positive return on funds. These accountants need to acquire the techniques of effective internal financial management and to recognise that management of cash, debtors, creditors and stocks is fundamental to the profitability and survival of the enterprise.

The joint venture programme is not, however, the only area in which the Chinese authorities are seeking to develop the accountancy profession. The country's internal economic development requires more and better information and greater clarity as to what that information means, and people who can use it. An idea of the scale of the action which is required can be gained from one simple statistic. The most recent figures show that, as at 31 December 1988, there were approximately 7,000,000 staff engaged in accounting activities in China. A figure recently quoted by the Chinese Institute of Certified Public Accountants, however, estimates the number to be now nearer 9,000,000. Either way, there are millions of accountants in China—although the majority of them are at bookkeeper level with very few qualified professionally in the Western sense. It seems that government enterprises will now be looking for improved financial management systems designed to encourage efficiency and effectiveness and attention has to be paid to the accountancy requirements of that (substantial amount of) economic activity which will remain under government control.

THE PARTICIPANTS

On the Western side the project has primarily involved two organisations—the United Kingdom's Chartered Association of Certified Accountants (ACCA) and the Department of Accountancy of Hong Kong Polytechnic—working with a Chinese Counterpart organisation, the China Association for International Exchange of Personnel (CAIEP). As the project grows, other training organisations and educational institutions in Australia and Europe are becoming involved.

The ACCA is the largest international body offering professional accountancy education. It has conducted examinations outside the United Kingdom since the 1930s. It has substantial experience in assisting the development of the accountancy profession in many countries, including the development of examination, administration and ethical structures, and advice on the development of accountancy training programmes. It is directly involved in the provision of auditing and accountancy training in over 100 countries and has considerable experience in design and delivery of training. In particular, it has been instrumental in developing accountancy in the Far East region—notably in Hong Kong, Singapore and Malaysia. It has developed an innovative Open Learning programme covering the whole of its syllabus—the only such programme in the world relating to professional accountancy training.

While the ACCA was thousands of miles from China, the Hong Kong Polytechnic's Accountancy Department was (relatively, anyway) on the spot. It had the advantage of having taught the ACCA's syllabus, members of staff who had themselves qualified as ACCAs, a number of Mandarin speakers and an interest in developing knowledge of accountancy in China.

The importance which the Chinese side placed on developing an accountancy and financial management training programme is indicated by the nature of the organisations which have been involved in the project and the fact that the Chinese partner, CAIEP, has designated it as one of its key programmes to upgrade financial skills in China. CAIEP is the sister organisation to the State Bureau of Foreign Experts; both report to the State Council, which in turn reports directly to the Prime Minister. CAIEP is a nationwide non-profit, non-governmental organisation, engaged in international exchanges of professionals. It is directly supported by the Chinese government and has close business relationships with various commissions, ministries, provincial governments, municipalities and local factories and enterprises. CAIEP co-ordinates the ACCA–CAIEP training programme with representatives from the Ministry of Finance, the Chinese Institute of Certified Public Accountants (CICPA), the Audit Administration, the Ministry of Foreign Economic Relations and Trade

(MOFERT), the State Tax Administration and the State Education Commission.

THE DEVELOPMENT OF THE PROJECT

At the outset, the participants envisaged the project as having three major components:

- providing a selected group of Chinese accountants with an intensive accountancy education programme;

- finding placements for them to give them practical accountancy experience and enable them to qualify as ACCAs; and

- developing links with a small number of business/economics universities so that they could take on the teaching of the ACCA programme within China.

The first goal was to establish the ACCA Professional Qualification Programme (PQP) and, with it, a group of men and women in China who would gain internationally recognised accountancy training and who would provide a core of qualified accountants familiar with Western accountancy concepts and practices. They would be well placed to represent China's interests in joint venture enterprises and also in China's own multinational enterprises. They would also provide skills to assist China's economic development and the financial control of new initiatives in the various areas of enterprise reform.

The PQP was delivered initially through a programme of courses in Hong Kong. Over a period of 18 months, the first group of students from China undertook three six-week periods of intensive training in Hong Kong. There have been two intakes of participants, with a third scheduled for January 1992. Based on an initial selection of around 40 of the applicants on each occasion, an evaluation course is conducted in Beijing each year, and approximately 25 people are selected to join the programme.

The PQP does not, however, stand on its own. As the full ACCA qualification is a professional rather than an academic course, it not only requires passing examinations but also practical experience. In any case, it was understood from the outset that students would not only learn the practical aspects of accounting but also familiarise themselves with how the capitalist system operates. Recognising the need for practical experience to supplement the training, a programme is being put in place to provide work experience in Western companies. Work placements have already begun in Hong Kong and are now being implemented in the United Kingdom.

The third element of the project has been the development of links with selected universities to serve as a support base for the programme. This was viewed as a particularly important element in it—as the aim was not to create dependency but to transfer skills as quickly as possible. So the idea was to train initially a group of teachers from these institutions who could then themselves continue the programme. The development of these links is progressing in Beijing and Shanghai and will be extended shortly to Guangzhou and Xiamen.

This part of the programme has served to enhance academic links between the Accountancy Department at the Hong Kong Polytechnic and Chinese institutions, in terms of research, course development and staff exchange. Particularly strong contacts have been established with the Shanghai University of Finance and Economics and the University of International Business and Economics in Beijing. Ultimately, the Polytechnic's own students will benefit from the knowledge and insight acquired by staff through their interaction with Chinese programme participants and Chinese academic institutions. Eventually the profession, academia and China itself all gain from this co-operative effort.

THE MOVE TO OPEN LEARNING

Major concerns have been overcoming shortages of teachers and of learning materials—and the wide dispersal of students. The Open Learning (OL) approach can address these concerns, and the training programme is moving to be based on it.

Adoption of the OL mode allows tutorial support from outside China, supplemented by intensive revision courses in Beijing. This method is more cost effective than the previous system of taught courses and allows the programme to be expanded at a reasonable cost, an important aspect as currently the ACCA is funding the project itself.

OL replaces the teacher in the conventional classroom context by thoroughly researched and expertly prepared workbooks and audio tapes. OL workbooks are exactly what the name indicates: books to be worked in. Their attractive design, lavish use of space to work in and careful use of words encourage learners to get to the heart of the skill they are tackling, by working their way actively, and interactively, through the text. Study sections are short; objectives and the teaching are clear; there are many practical work-based examples and activities.

Most conventional study manuals and correspondence courses ask students to read, memorise and reproduce what they find in the text, which is a passive form of learning. OL requires them to undertake activities where they review what they read, consider how they can use it and satisfy themselves that they have understood it. They learn by thinking about the topic and by doing. OL is active learning.

With the workbooks standing in place of the teacher, the role of the tutor becomes that of helping the students with problems or areas of difficulty and providing a focus for discussion of matters of interest. This enables better use of available teaching resources. Teachers and tutors have less preparation, less formal lecturing and use of well-researched, expert and fully piloted packages; this enables them to concentrate on the business of guiding, supporting and counselling students.

OL also takes as one of its key objectives the equipping of learners to apply what they have learned in their work. This approach represents the best and most up-to-date practice in the field of professional education and training; learning is directly related to the requirements of the work environment. Use is made of business-related settings and problems, and examples are like those which accountants meet in the course of their work. The examples are practical and relevant so that learners can develop the skills and abilities which will help them to work as professional accountants.

OL is particularly suitable for use in China, where the accountancy profession needs to undergo rapid development, because:

- it can be introduced very quickly and can thus help to develop relevant capability for current and future needs in the shortest practicable time;

- it can provide a vehicle for speedily providing, and widely disseminating, a vocabulary of Western accounting terms and for introducing the most modern approach to accountancy practice;

- particular care has been taken to ensure that the language level is appropriate for learners for whom English is not the first language;

- it is proving to be rather more effective than traditional teaching and learning methods—which have meant high dropout rates and low pass rates in the rigorous professional accountancy examinations;

- its modular format enables elements which are regarded as particularly suitable to be selected from it; and

- it enables optimum use of available teaching resources.

The ACCA programme is the largest ever single OL project in any subject area, providing over 2,700 hours of learning. It is leading the field in terms of innovative accountancy education development and was developed with a budget in excess of US$5 million over a three-year period.

The ACCA intends that, after an initial five-year period, CAIEP will arrange for the workbooks to be printed locally under licence. The ACCA considers, however, that it is important that, in the initial stages of the programme, the workbooks should be used as published in the United Kingdom. This is to ensure that the learners in China are working with material which is as clear and well-presented as possible. Once the Chinese side has built up familiarity with the programme, it will be better placed to produce the material (or elements from it) locally. In due course, it may be appropriate to translate certain modules of the material for specific teaching and learning applications. The ACCA has begun the process of translation (with adaptation to the local environment) in a number of other countries, and so is acquiring experience of what is involved in this process.

EVALUATION OF THE PROJECT: SOME PROBLEMS ...

The project has not been without its problems. A number of issues have had to be, or are being, addressed. These include

- the difficulties in creating an awareness and proper understanding amongst Chinese employers of what the ACCA qualification really means and in convincing them of the commitment required of both trainees and their sponsoring enterprises (for example, two of the three initial trainees who were seconded to work placements in Hong Kong (with one of the major professional accountancy firms) were recalled to China after only 18 months; employers seem to be quite ready to withdraw trainees from the examinations at only a few days' notice on account of pressures of work);

- language difficulties which have arisen with some candidates and occasional language misunderstandings between the project team and CAIEP. It is often the case that the same words can have different meaning in Chinese and Western accounting contexts. The inclusion of a Mandarin speaker in the project team has helped to minimise such misunderstandings;

- inexperience of Western commercial values among the Chinese students and in CAIEP itself. Conversely, the project team has needed to develop an appreciation of how China does business;

- the fact that much of what the students have learned on the ACCA programme is not necessarily immediately applicable or usable, and employers, with limited background of the relevant disciplines and concepts, have not always understood how to make best use of the knowledge;

- the pressure on the students to pass what are undoubtedly difficult ACCA examinations in order to justify continued support from their employers, particularly when there are no local teachers qualified to provide tutorial support and the students themselves are widely dispersed geographically; and

- the fact that a major motivation factor for the students is the opportunity to obtain an internationally recognised qualification and overseas work experience. The opportunities to find suitable work placements are, however, restricted, particularly since most of the Chinese employers are generally reluctant to release their employees for a substantial period. This has created difficulties, as three-year placements are normally necessary to meet professional experience requirements.

Some of these problems are of the practical kind which would beset any large-scale project which seeks to bridge very different cultures. Some, however, reflect the difficulties of this particular educational initiative.

The project's decision to allow students to begin their studies midway through the professional examinations underestimated their difficulties of studying in a foreign language, learning the very different culture of taking Western examinations and knowing what examiners expect, and dealing with terms which were unfamiliar. The policy has now been changed to have students sit the introductory examinations.

As has been mentioned, there have also to be arrangements to introduce non-accountant managers to the principles and practices being applied by the newly trained accountants. The programme is now expanding to include general finance management training, short "one-off" training courses (covering topics in auditing, software developments, international business, et al.) and exchange study visits.

...AND THE BENEFITS

All sides feel they have benefited from the cooperation. The Chinese side has gained valuable exposure to the Western way of doing things and,

with the OL programme, access to one of the most advanced systems of accountancy education in the world. The ACCA, which is one of the few professional accountancy bodies with a truly international perspective, is establishing both a presence for itself in China and an educational and commercial bridgehead between Hong Kong and China. The project management team is gaining valuable contacts and experience in dealing with the complex cultural, business and professional environment in China. The Polytechnic has acquired new teaching and research opportunities and has participated in a valuable tri-partite academic link between itself, the Shanghai University of Finance and Economics and the University of Glasgow. The academic link programme covers staff development, course development and technology transfer. Apart from the benefit of a regular series of visits between the institutions, a major research project has already been completed, resulting in the publication by Longman of *Accounting in China*.

The project has also highlighted a familiar issue—that of achieving the right balance between academic education and professional training and ensuring that the two do not become divorced. In many Western countries, including the UK, there is a distinction between academic education and professional training; this is not, however, an absolute divide but a matter of emphasis and there is, in fact, a very close relationship between the two with considerable overlap between the substantive intellectual foundation of academic training and professional qualifications.

Over a long period, this has been manifest in a number of ways. Academic accountants sit on committees, particularly the education committees, of professional bodies and frequently give lectures and undertake research projects for them. The profession influences education provision by setting examinations and accrediting educational courses as fulfilling parts of its examination requirements. Many accountancy academics regard a professional qualification as an asset to their teaching and research, especially when these have a practical focus, and accountants often move between professional and academic positions.

So while the academic integrity of longer—degree and other—courses is safeguarded, the material does not ossify but is flexible and adapts rapidly to changing requirements. Equally, the practice of accounting is rooted in a solid foundation and changes are based on sound principles. It would be all too easy to lose sight of this in the development of accountancy education and training in China. It will be important to ensure that, as the programme progresses, the training of the new practitioners goes hand in hand with the development of university accountancy education. Hence, the project's concern to include university teachers in the training programme. The involvement of a major professional body (which itself has strong links with the world of academic accountancy) and an academic accountancy department should ensure that China avoids the danger of a division between practical and academic spheres.

CONCLUSION

The project is dependent on co-operation between the professional accountancy body, an organisation in China and a group of educational institutions. The accountancy training being provided fills an educational and professional need, and the work experience placements not only provide worthwhile practical experience but are also helping to bridge the cultural gap between China and the West. In many respects, this project follows the general principles established by the Co-operative Education Movement over many years.

Above all, although many economies are moving towards free markets, all are doing so differently and those involved in training have to be aware of their individual characteristics so that support can be tailored to make a meaningful contribution. Training must not impose others' preconceptions but must be sensitive to the needs of those being trained to be able to go back to their own milieu and to function effectively there.

The project has provided valuable lessons of the awareness and sensitivity which is necessary, the problems to avoid and the successes to be sought.

Accounting Practices and Education in Russia and Other Republics of the C.I.S.

Adolf J. H. Enthoven and Jaroslav V. Sokolov

INTRODUCTION

The purpose of this presentation on accounting in Russia and other CIS republics is to sketch (1) economic and political changes, (2) the historical developments in accounting, (3) the structure of financial and managerial accounting and auditing, and (4) the educational process of accounting and the requirements needed to enhance accounting education and research.

Accounting in the former Soviet Union [now CIS—Commonwealth of Independent States—comprising 11 of the former 15 republics of the USSR] has not been a well-recognized discipline since the 1920s. Under the centrally planned economic structure of the USSR, accounting essentially consisted of record keeping and statistical recording. The new economic direction toward more market-oriented economies has resulted in drastic changes and heavy demands on practicing accountants and accounting educators. Intense international assistance is needed by our practicing and academic accounting colleagues in the former Soviet Union and East European countries (especially from agencies such as the World Bank, International Monetary Fund, European Bank for Reconstruction and Development, United Nations, and bilateral agencies). However, underlying all these changes is the requirement to reorient the accounting educational system.

If better and more effective accounting practices and standards are to be executed, we believe educational institutions must play a major role. Intense efforts have been initiated and are being carried out; however, these are neither comprehensive nor well coordinated as yet.

THE SOCIOECONOMIC AND POLITICAL STRUCTURE AND CHANGES

The Union of Soviet Socialist Republics (USSR), as it was known, was the largest country in the world, with a territory of 22,402 square kilometers, crossing 11 time zones. It has common borders with 12 nations and is washed by two oceans and 12 seas; 75 percent of its territory lies in Asia and 25 percent in Europe. The population is just over 290 million people, of whom slightly less than 50 percent are Russians.

In 1990, the Soviet economy entered into a painful transition process. In order to understand how a superpower with a tremendous output of many basic products can encounter enormous economic disproportions, one must take a closer look at the centralized economic mechanism that prevailed in that country for almost 60 years—from the early 1930s to the late 1980s.

The major features of the Soviet centrally planned economy were designed in the early 1930s and were based on a dogmatic interpretation of Marxian socialist theory. The main principles included the following:

- The state owns and controls most of the nation's property.

- The plan is the main element of the economic mechanism; the plan is law.

- Plans are worked out within central economic agencies and are vertically imposed and controlled.

- Procurement and distribution of products are centrally planned and organized.

- Practically all prices are fixed centrally, and, basically, so are wages.

- Accounting, reporting, auditing, and statistics are plan oriented.

- The bank (actually, one) is a controlling rather than a credit institution.

- All foreign transactions are monopolized by the state through a few institutions.

- The whole economy is based on obedient execution of orders coming out of "the center" which "always knows best."

The trend toward independence of different republics started in 1988, when national fronts were created in the Baltic republics. The movement toward economic and political sovereignty accelerated enormously in 1990, when most of the republics, including Russia, passed legislation according to which republican laws take precedence

Adolf J.H. Enthoven is a Professor at the University of Texas at Dallas, and Jaroslav V. Sokolov is a Professor at the Institute of Commerce and Economics, St. Petersburg, Russia.

over Soviet laws. Combined with increasing economic decentralization in the USSR, these developments are creating a new business environment, in which management of cultural/regional differences is becoming more important.

The socioeconomic and political developments in the Soviet Union show that reform is a long-term cyclical process and also requires vast judicial changes. It is a process that has brought radical changes to the Soviet political system. The "traditional" Soviet Union has been disintegrating, and the centralized economic mechanism is being transformed as the privatization of the economy takes place.

A HISTORICAL SKETCH OF ACCOUNTING AND AUDITING IN THE FORMER SOVIET UNION

Since the inception of this enormous state in Eastern Europe and Asia in A.D. 862, the evolution of its accounting system has reflected the many changes in its administrative and economic functions. Based on three historic turning points, the development of accounting in Russia can be divided into three periods: (1) 862-1700, development of a simple Russian accounting system; (2) 1700-1917, introduction and development of the European double-entry accounting system; and (3) 1917-present, adaptation of the established European double-entry accounting system to the requirements of a new socioeconomic order.

The third period (since 1917) has been characterized by radical social and economic changes. For the purposes of accounting history, this period began on July 27, 1918, when the Soviet of People's Commissars of Russia adopted and Lenin signed the decree on commercial books. This document was only partially related to accounting. Radical changes in the organization of accounting began to take place in the fall of 1918.

The ideas of cost accounting and profit were rejected. "Extraordinary accounting" replaced commercial accounting. Its basic ideas were adopted officially in the *Basic Regulations on State Bookkeeping and Reporting* (1920). These regulations were consistent with ideas proclaimed by party and state leaders.

Lenin stated four requirements for socialist accounting:

1. *Openness.* There is no place for commercial secrets; all registers must be accessible to everyone.

2. *Mass character.* All of the adult population of the country must participate in the process of accounting.

3. *Responsibility.* Not only values and the process of their creation and circulation must be under control but also the activities of executives responsible for them.

4. *Simplicity.* Accounting must be clear to every literate man.

Of these four requirements, only the third survived.

After the New Economic Policy (NEP) was initiated in 1921, the traditional accounting methods, practice, and principles gradually were reintroduced. While the NEP was in effect, joint stock companies and joint ventures with foreign firms were established, and foreigners were given the right to take concessions in Soviet territory. The use of commercial credit and notes became widespread.

The NEP had begun to be eliminated by 1930, a process that had a serious negative effect on further development of accounting in the Soviet union. First, almost all accountants were labeled as "bourgeois," and those who were accused of bringing harm to the national economy were physically eliminated. Second, the economic life of the country was simplified radically. Joint ventures and joint stock companies were stigmatized, as was commercial credit. Trusts were forced out, and management of factories passed to the commissariats (ministries). Factories remained formally responsible for their own accounting, with more and more official propaganda being devoted to the subject but, in reality, the more this self-accounting was advertised, the less it was implemented in practice.

Under the new conditions, the so-called "self-accounted factory" could not become bankrupt. Both profitability and nonprofitability were of symbolic character, and the main criterion for every factory became the plan. When a factory fulfilled its plan, losses were not taken into account; but, if the plan was not fulfilled, even giant profits could not help the management escape punishment (including capital punishment). Thus, fulfillment of plans became the most important objective of accounting. This approach fully corresponded to the principles of the "administrative command system" and led to the unique concept of socialist accounting, which retained the basic principles of the double-entry system but introduced many original features.

Every aspect of accounting was proclaimed an integral part of national economic accounting. This national economic accounting itself comprised three kinds of accounting—bookkeeping, statistical accounting, and operational accounting—but their unity was mostly for show. Accounting was carried out in factories, and the information was taken from the system of accounts. Financial statements of factories were summarized first by central branch administrative boards and then by ministries. Thus, all the information required to be reported to the upper levels of the hierarchy was provided by accounting, which summarized but did not consolidate balance sheets. Statistical accounting included all forms required by the state offices of statistics. Operational accounting, which provided financial statistics on operations, was carried out by the factory for its own rather than external use.

Centralized management of accounting had as its goal the unification of every sphere of accounting activity. The chart of accounts was unified first of all through the branches of the national economy and in the last 30 years (since 1961) has been unified for the whole economy.

The term "management accounting" is foreign to the Russian accounting tradition, evoking inadequate associations in the minds of Soviet administrators and accountants. In the Soviet Union cost accounting and prime-cost calculation never have been treated as an independent branch of accounting but only as an integral part of unitary accounting. Cost accounting is nothing more than an analytical expansion of the Main Production account. The idea of two parallel accounting branches—financial and management—seems extravagant. However, cost accounting in the Soviet Union has a long history. It came into being in the Middle Ages in monasteries that used it to calculate the results of their economic activities.

FINANCIAL ACCOUNTING, AUDITING, AND MANAGEMENT ACCOUNTING

Financial Accounting

The western reader should take into account that the Soviet Union was a state with a socialist structure. The accounting objectives and functions have been different from those of the West because of distinct socioeconomic conditions and objectives. These differences may remain for the time being while the transformation process takes place. In setting principles or norms, for example, western countries have been motivated by profit making, while in the Soviet Union the focus has been more on physical production to serve public requirements.

The Soviets have been applying a single accounting system with three subsystems:

- Statistical record keeping for aggregate economic data, including volume of production, cost of production, productivity, productive capacity, and resources;

- Operational-technical record keeping, which physically monitors the movement of materials and products within a plan; and

- Financial record keeping dealing with assets, liabilities, revenues, and expenses in financial terms.

Comparability is achieved by using the standard chart of accounts, by which various pieces of accounting information are accumulated and systematized. The present chart of accounts for business activities was approved originally in March 1985 by the USSR Ministry of Finance, and by the USSR Goscomstat, the State Committee for Statistics (the statistical office). The chart contains over 70 so-called synthetic accounts (that is, aggregated, combined, or first level) and subaccounts (second level) that are used in bookkeeping depending on the requirements of control and reporting. This chart was revised in October 1990 and again in October 1991. It was adopted in Russia in December 1991.

Balance sheets and income statements are drawn up, based on the chart of accounts. The objective of these financial reports is to provide information about the financial position and performance for a given period. The financial reports must fully reflect the results of all economic operations, as well as the availability of cash, fixed assets, and inventory.

What is needed most of all is the development of a sound theoretical base for Soviet accounting, a conceptual framework that should contain fundamental concepts and assumptions capable of guiding the setting of standards for financial reporting and managerial decision making. The incorporation of international standards into such a framework would be warranted; however, domestic standards have to be seen in the context of the socioeconomic structure and environment—a careful process of induction and deduction. Such an evaluative process demands theorists and practitioners well versed in accounting concepts and methods. Therefore, the standard-setting process in the Soviet territories may take some time yet.

Until 1930, the main objective of the accounting system in the USSR was to calculate profit and income. After 1930, this objective changed to fulfilling plans and safeguarding valuables (material and monetary assets) to prevent theft. Enterprises belonged to one of the ministries, a situation implying that all profits were paid to those ministries and, hence, that the enterprises could not manage their own financing. Authorities said that their system of pricing, not the good operations of the enterprises, earned profit. A universal chart of accounts was created and had to be used in all kinds of enterprises. The principle of valuation was acquisition (historical) cost. The government fixed prices, and inflation did not formally exist.

Differences between Soviet and Western accounting have been the result of both historical traditions and the distinct Soviet economic system. In the USSR, to serve the national planning system, the accounting system has been subject to strict centralized control.

Since the economic reform of A. Kosygin went into effect in 1964, the previously dominant goal of controlling plan fulfillment has been steadily losing significance, to the point that it has almost disappeared. That goal has been replaced by two new principal goals: (1) control for safeguarding material and monetary values and (2) control of business transactions.

The first goal arises from the legal functions and the second from the economic functions of accounting. The same accounting elements—documentation, inventory taking, chart of accounts, double entry, balance sheet, calculation, valuation, and reporting—are used whether measuring the legal or the economic functions.

The *balance sheet* is the basic reporting form that predetermines the chart of accounts and at the same time has as its basis the accounts of the general ledger. Accounts comprise synthetic (main) and analytic (supporting) accounts. During the entire Soviet period, the balance sheet has been defined as the instrument that shows the assets of an enterprise, along with the funding sources for those assets, at a definite moment in time. That is, the balance sheet is a statistical conception of groups of assets correlated and in balance with their respective liabilities.

Financial reports are the source of most statistical information in Russia and other republics. The state regulates the composition and the structure of these reports. The Ministry of Finance, in coordination with the statistical offices (SCS), carries out methodological supervision of reporting; determines its volume, structure, and forms; and also prepares instructions for filing. The procedure for report preparation and submission is set out in the "Regulation on Accounting Statements and Balance Sheets." SCS agencies have the right to cancel departmental reporting that is not in accordance with acting statutory regulations.

The balance sheet is the central and most important reporting form because it contains a full and detailed description of both assets of the enterprise and sources of their creation. The form has two columns, one for the beginning and the other for the end of the period, so readers can draw conclusions about changes in assets for the accounting period. All other reporting forms only clarify the balance sheet or provide more details and analysis.

Auditing

Auditing has a different meaning in the Soviet Union than in the West. Until recently there were no auditors, in the western meaning of that term (although traditionally local auditing societies were contemplated in 1894 and 1909 in Russia). Because there are no shareholders in the Soviet Union (as yet), and because nearly every creditor is a state enterprise, only designated state agencies are entitled to audit accounting statements.

The absence of auditing until a few years ago is another peculiarity of Soviet accounting practice. The concept of auditing was contrary to the traditional ideas about control. According to Lenin's views, accounting and control were not private affairs but matters of national concern.

COST AND MANAGEMENT ACCOUNTING

Internal operational management systems are a conglomerate of very different methods independent of each other. Therefore, it is difficult to speak yet about "management accounting," although cost accounting and cost analysis are practiced extensively, mostly by administrators. What is called management accounting in the West does not exist in the Soviet Union (now CIS) as either a comprehensive concept or a clear discipline and practice. The training of specialists in the administrative aspects of accounting falls into three subject-matter areas:

- Operational accounting,
- Cost accounting and cost calculation,
- Analysis of economic (business) activities.

Operational accounting is very specialized, according to its application. It exists in various forms—such as technical operational accounting, manufacturing operational accounting, and selling operational accounting—according to the industry or activity and therefore often merges with the planning and control of operations of a technical and administrative nature.

By means of operational accounting, management achieves control over: (1) execution of contracts, (2) the meeting of plan goals, (3) "dispatcherization," (4) internal reporting, (5) special purpose reporting, and (6) projections.

Cost accounting and *cost calculation* form the second component of Soviet (CIS) "managerial" accounting. Costs are expenditures of material, labor, and financial resources for the production of goods or services. This formula was transformed, however, by Marx's theory that both costs and prices in the end are determined by labor expenditures.

Analysis of business activities is the third component of managerial accounting. It is more an extension of operational accounting, as referred to previously, than it is financial analysis.

ACCOUNTING EDUCATION, RESEARCH AND DEVELOPMENT

Existing Structure

Accounting education in the republics is conducted at universities, colleges, and vocational schools, in specialized courses, and directly at the workplaces. In the former Soviet Union 150 schools have accounting faculties, and anyone with ten years of secondary education can enroll after passing entrance exams. The prestige of accounting has been extremely low.

Accountants with higher education are required at a minimum to know:

1. Theory and methods of research to solve various accounting, controlling, planning, and financing problems;

2. Methodology for planning and forecasting major indicators of an enterprise's performance, accounting techniques, and preparation of reports;

3. Economic and technological processes and the organizational structure of enterprises in different branches of the economy, as well as mathematical models and their applications;

4. Modern means of data processing, including electronic data processing;

5. The basics of law and of labor and environmental protection.

Higher education provides not only professional skills but also career opportunities. A university graduate can be appointed chief accountant or deputy to the chief accountant, accounting analyst, revisor (auditor), expert in law-enforcing agencies, or professor of accounting at vocational training schools or courses. Those gifted in research can continue with postgraduate studies and later work in universities or research institutes.

Reforms in Accounting Education

Accounting education and training in the republics of the former Soviet Union are currently subject to considerable evaluation and restructuring. The following organizational structure is envisioned for the training of accountants:

- Practical training and study of accounting techniques (under experienced supervision at a firm) for young employees;

- A network of courses (studies held both at employer organizations and in class sessions);

- Technical school training (professional schools can provide a sizable number of accountants);

- Academic institutes with strict admission requirements both for entry and during the process of study.

One way to enhance accounting education efficiently might be to prepare an *accounting manpower inventory* and *accounting development plan* that would set forth the future needs of the various areas of accounting and auditing. Because of the great shortage of educators and trainers, the development of *accounting training centers* and the types of updating to be undertaken could be based on the manpower needs of various sectors of the economy. In this regard, too, the areas requiring greater concentration and more text materials may have to be spelled out. For example, considerably more training might be needed in electronic data processing (EDP) systems and procedures, management accounting, computer auditing, and related areas. Internally, a *manpower inventory* could serve as a framework for resource programming and capital investment and help shape educational directions under the socioeconomic five-year plans. Such a comprehensive accounting development program should fit existing and projected needs in (1) manpower development, including foreign scholarships; (2) expatriate manpower needs; (3) teaching aids and materials; (4) building requirements; (5) short-course programs, for instance, travel cost; (6) research and translation funding; and (7) miscellaneous elements.

Good interaction between the educational institutions and the various CIS associations of accountants would be beneficial, and international accounting firms might be helpful in conducting certain courses and supplying course materials. Specialties to be covered in accounting also might be appraised and set forth. Methods to be used for continuing accounting education also need to be addressed specifically.

The contemplated redirection of accounting and auditing clearly will pose a considerable strain on the educational and training process and institutions. Because accounting has not in the past been adequately recognized as a desirable field of learning and practice because of its dogmatic methods and statistical orientation, a new emphasis may have to be put on educational aspects of accounting. The existing training institutes may have to be reoriented, and new directions for education and training, including teacher training, may have to be offered. This whole reorientation process needs careful appraisal in the context of CIS socioeconomic objectives, taking into account such factors as

- The existing setup and teaching materials,
- The desired direction of various fields of accounting,
- Text materials to be translated and developed,
- Updating and reorienting existing and new faculty,
- Funding needs to execute the new direction,
- Desired foreign technical assistance,
- Physical requirements, including teaching aids.

As for some specific educational/training activities to be pursued, the following are suggested:

1. Elaborate new conceptual frameworks and basic curricula for new guidelines in accounting education need to be implemented, because former narrow specialization for training accountants by sectors of economy is losing its importance.

2. The conceptual framework for the new curricula should include training in distinct areas such as financial accounting, managerial accounting, and auditing (as opposed to existing accounting specialization by accounting branches of the economy).

3. The role and scope of training of accountants in legal issues and mechanisms of the market economy should be increased dramatically, and accountants should acquire a deeper understanding of international economic activities and their accounting implications.

4. Accounting training/education needs to be enhanced for three main categories: students, practitioners, and trainers. Further differentiation is needed in training accountants and bookkeepers for specific functions and levels of responsibility.

5. Case studies, a powerful educational tool, should be used and applied in teaching.

6. Leading western and international accounting texts and cases should be translated from English, French, German, and other western languages for Soviet educational and practice purposes. Domestic authors should be stimulated as well to prepare textbooks.

Research

The further development of accounting education and training in the various areas should go hand in hand with research covering the areas and topics of accounting to be developed. The amount of research in accounting and auditing has been relatively limited (except for the work of certain scholars), partially because of the lack of funding but also because accounting has not been considered a discipline of high standing. Undoubtedly this attitude is and will be changing, and accounting research, both *applied* and *theoretical*, will have to be brought up-to-date. (Applied research deals, for example, with the development of accounting and auditing standards, a conceptual accounting framework, transfer pricing, and accounting for price changes, whereas the more *theoretical*, basic accounting research should delve into the normative and conceptual aspects of accounting.)

Organizational and research aspects in the former Soviet Union also need to be researched. The objective would be to study current problems and promote the development of accounting and auditing, integrating theory and practice. In the past, methodology was based on both dialectical and historical materialism. A fundamental task now is to establish a framework of accounting and auditing theory and methodology adapted to the new economic order and circumstances. Presumably, the various associations of accountants could also play a vital role in the development and distribution of research materials and bulletins devised for this purpose.

Among the tasks of the CIS accounting associations would be motivating research, summarizing past experiences to serve the economy, investigating new requirements and problems, carrying out international exchanges, and fostering friendly relations with foreign organizations. Because accounting traditionally was not recognized as a separate discipline in the Soviet Union but was taught in conjunction with economics and finance, the development of a specific accounting concentration with distinct areas of knowledge may be necessary. Furthermore, the trend toward a market economy requires a distinct reorientation, including accounting for capital market institutions (stock exchange), costing for pricing, performance measurement, and so forth. Such an orientation also will be needed for effectively appraising the financial activities of prevailing state enterprises and outlining better courses of action to follow (in the form of cost-benefit/effectiveness appraisals).

Accounting education reform has a long way to go. More emphasis might be placed, for example, on class discussion about case studies than on lectures and more on encouraging students' enthusiasm than on passive acquisition of information. Educators also would put greater emphasis on developing the ability to analyze and solve practical and theoretical problems and cases independently.

Advanced programs of accounting education for postgraduates would be perfected. Both quantity and quality of the program would be stressed to meet the urgent requirements for high-level accounting specialists.

A new set of textbooks is to be developed and published according to the needs of the new accounting education program. Educational reform in accounting has far-reaching effects not only on education but on research and practice as well. Ongoing educational reform is expected to extend to professional schools and other training programs in the coming years. The influence of educational reform on accounting education cannot be ignored. Appropriate attention needs to be given to educating and training a large number of various types and levels of accountants and auditors. The current big demand for accountants is reflected in the sizable salaries accountants are able to command today.

CONCLUSION

It may be apparent to the reader that due to the transformation stage the former Soviet Union is passing through, the need for extensive international technical assistance will be substantial in order to assist the CIS in sound economic growth and development. The resources of the former USSR are vast and its people are endowed with great intellectual skills which undoubtedly would make these republics again major players in the international arena.

As educators, we have a special mission to assist our colleagues in the CIS—and other countries—in their transformation process. There are many aspects and areas where we can be helpful when requested by the CIS republics. However such efforts should be well coordinated and well thought through because many current haphazard activities would not be leading to the optimum form of educational and practice development. One of the first steps we suggest is the development of a *comprehensive accounting inventory and development program* covering the many facets of accounting education and practices in the context of the future socioeconomic development patterns of the CIS. Such an "accounting educational development program" hopefully can be undertaken or sponsored by such highly regarded international organizations as the World Bank, the International Monetary Fund, European Bank for Reconstruction and Development and the United Nations.

Such a comprehensive feasibility study—taking into account all areas of accounting (micro and macro) —may constitute the basis for specific technical and financial assistance projects on a unilateral or bilateral basis.

Accounting Education in Russia
(Existing Approaches and Changes)

Valery V. Kovalev and Jaroslav V. Sokolov

Accounting education has a long and strong tradition in Russia. Currently, we have the following system for the training of accountants:

- Accounting institutes (more than 100) with strict admission requirements for entry and monitoring during the process of study;

- Technical school training;

- A network of courses (studies held both at employer organizations and in class sessions);

- Practical training and study of accounting techniques for young employees (under experienced supervision at a firm).

The main peculiarity of our accounting education is the lack of "professional certification," as Westerners know the term. Russia has more than two million accountants, accounting technicians, and bookkeepers, but the term "accountant" has a different connotation. To be qualified as an accountant means to have a diploma after graduating from an institute of higher education (five to six years) or a technical school (three to six years), specializing in accounting. Traditionally, the accounting profession was not very popular and was underpaid. Therefore, many women fulfilled accounting functions. About 80 percent of the students involved in accounting programmes are female. However, as a consequence of the currently changing role of accounting, and because it has greater significance and offers more rewards, more men are now attracted to these positions.

It's possible to say that an original methodology towards accounting training exists in Russia. Actually, there are four approaches which could be separated in accordance with two main characteristics: (a) education objectives and (b) education methodology.

The first characteristic means the choice made by a trainer (1) to teach students the technical accounting procedures only or (2) to teach them to understand the essence of these procedures. The second characteristic means the choice of a dominant methodology used in the education process. Generally speaking, there are two of them: reflection and dogma (see Exhibit 1).

The first approach is the most widespread in the system of higher education, but simultaneously it is the most unsuccessful and has no future. The main idea of this approach consists of a methodology of training students to fill in ledgers and books in a proper manner manually or in computerized form. This extremely technical work is accompanied by teaching some scholastic theories (politology, political economy, economics, etc.), trying to indicate the link between accounting and its political and economical environment. The training process itself is aligned with practice as much as possible. It means that a set of blank forms (invoices, vouchers, bills, etc.) is given to the students and they are taught to work with them like a bookkeeper of an ordinary enterprise. The sequence of items for understanding is the following: basic document — transaction — account — financial statements.

The main advantage of this approach is the following: a student works with real documents and becomes familiar with the sequence of basic accounting procedures. This approach has some disadvantages: (1) the fulfillment of technical procedures is quite incompatible with the goals of political and economical understanding; (2) the predominance of technical procedures in accounting education complicates the clarification of both the logic of economic transactions and their reflection in the accounting system; (3) there is no single set of technical procedures used in all enterprises, so methods learned by students are quite subjective and could be useless in many instances.

The second approach consists of some methodological procedures used for training bookkeepers (not accountants). The period of training is less, so no "high theories" are used. Its scope is quite unequivocal — pure technical orientation. It's a curious matter but this approach has turned out to be more effective for training bookkeepers than the first one, because the students' heads are not ob-

Valery V. Kovalev and Jaroslav V. Sokolov are faculty members at St. Petersburg Institute of Commerce & Economics, Russian Federal Republic.

EXHIBIT 1

Methodology / Objectives	Reflection	Dogma
Technical procedures	1 Based on some scholastic backgrounds; dominates in universities	2 No accounting theory; dominates in technical schools and short-term courses
Understanding of accounting procedures	3 Based on comprehensive accounting theory; exists in some universities	4 Based on behavioral aspects of accounting; it is experimental in its nature, but could be applied in schools and universities

scured by useless "high theory essays" (for their level of professional qualification).

The third approach is taking place at some universities offering postgraduate programmes. The accounting philosophy is the basis of this form of accounting education. The students have to understand some basic concepts and postulates of accounting: double-entry system, the framework of accounting, the essence of basic balance equations, and so on. The sequence of items for understanding is the following: balance sheet — account— basic document. The basic documents are seldom used in classes; all explanations are given with the use of "T-account" formats. The main advantage of this approach is the distinct clarification of the logic of the accounting cycle. In this way the students can understand the essence of their future work much better. Among the main disadvantages are the following: (1) a certain lack of practical experience, so it's quite difficult for a graduate to work at an enterprise with real documents; (2) a scholastic approach dominates in understanding and solving some real accounting problems — a person begins to discuss some meaningless categories (for example, has a basic document been a part of the method of accounting or not?) instead of making practical decisions in accounting.

The fourth approach is getting underway. It raises a paradoxical goal: to teach a person the logic of accounting procedure not through understanding a reflective analysis but through the mechanism of conditioned reflexes. This approach could be called the "behavioral approach." It has been developed in the spirit of the old Russian physiological school of Professors Pavlov and Bekhterev. Some basic logical accounting proce-

dures are given to students in a way that in being practitioners in the future, they will be able to fulfill these activities subconsciously as a reaction to some stimulus. The students must operate with these procedures quite automatically, but sometimes there will be a break-even point and some of them (not all!) will clearly understand the essence of these procedures.

This is theory, but what has been done in practice? An important element of improving accounting in Russia during the period of transition to a market economy is the development of curricula for students, practitioners and academics in Western accounting. This work was begun in 1989 when a workshop on the subject of accounting for joint ventures operations was organized in Moscow by the U.N. and the Ministry of Finance of the U.S.S.R. Several training programmes were developed jointly by Russian and Western specialists.

Our institute is involved in the realization of these programmes. We carried out two weeks' programmes together with trainers from the accounting firms of Coopers & Lybrand and KPMG. Some of the participants of these programmes are working now in the branches of these firms in Russia.

During the fall of this year, a programme for "training the trainers" will be organized in four educational centres in St. Petersburg, Moscow, Kiev, Tashkent. Educators from the northern part of Russia, including the Baltic Republics, will be gathered in St. Petersburg Institute of Commerce & Economics for a 19-week session. The programme is sponsored by the British Council. After the completion of the programme, 10 to 15 participants will be selected to go to the United Kingdom for a four-week period for additional studies.

The remarkable park of changes in accounting education in Russia is the publication of the most popular Western accounting textbooks. These books were selected by us together with our American colleagues. Among them there are the books written by Professors Belverd Needles, Robert Anthony, Gerhard Mueller, Eldon Hendriksen, Glenn Welsch and others. Many prominent Western specialists do help us in this work. Among them are Professors Adolf Enthoven and Belverd Needles from the United States, Professors Sidney Gray and Clive Emmanuel from Scotland, Anthony Rouse from ACCA, Lorraine Ruffing from the UNCTC, David Barton from Houghton Mifflin, Louis de Winter of Irwin, and many others. We are fully sure that jointly we shall overcome the problems encountered in the process of development and change of accounting education in Russia. I think the time of intentions to do something for the improvement of accounting education in Russia has passed. The time has come for action. So the well-known slogan could be applied to the current situation: it's not for us to reason why, it's just for us to do and die!

Recent Developments in Accounting Education in Russia

Lorraine T. Ruffing

INTRODUCTION

I would like to thank the International Association for Accounting Education and Research and the American Accounting Association for giving the United Nations the opportunity to make a presentation on recent developments in the former Soviet Union. For those of you who aren't familiar with the work of the United Nations in the field of international accounting, some background is necessary in order to put the Soviet initiative into perspective. The United Nations has been concerned with the quality of corporate accounting and reporting since 1973 when a Group of Eminent Persons noted that there was a serious lack of both financial and nonfinancial information on transnational corporations. This and other deliberations led the Economic and Social Council to establish an expert group — the Intergovernmental Working Group of Experts on International Standards of Accounting and Reporting (ISAR) in 1982, although the Group had existed in one form or another since 1975.

ISAR has three main objectives: first, to serve as an international body for the consideration of international accounting and reporting issues; second, to make a positive contribution to national and regional standard-setting; third, to take into account the interests of developing countries in the field of information disclosure. In this regard, ISAR is the only international accounting forum where developing countries and countries in transition participate in decision-making on a regular basis. It is particularly committed to the task of promoting the harmonization of national accounting standards in order to improve the transparency and comparability of financial and nonfinancial information.

ISAR or the Group undertakes a number of concrete activities in the field of research and technical cooperation which have become more and more relevant to accounting education. It is concerned with accounting education because it has realized that the implementation of internationally accepted accounting principles depends on accountants who are not only adequately educated but also have a global perspective.

For example, the Group will devote its entire annual session this March to the topic of accounting education. Recently, a number of academic accountants met at the United Nations to advise on the topics to be discussed in March. In their opinion, the present narrow approach to accounting education has not equipped accountants to cope with an increasingly complex financial world—and as I will discuss shortly—it has not prepared them to meet the challenges in countries in transition either. Core accounting courses need to teach broad principles rather than national practices which change constantly. Accountants must become analysts rather than narrow specialists.

Therefore, ISAR will be looking into the 21st century to see what challenges accountants will face and how they should be trained. ISAR hopes to contribute to the discussion and to help accountants meet their responsibilities in the global marketplace. By facilitating accounting development and helping accountants meet future challenges, it hopes to promote harmonization. As long as accounting education focuses on national practices, it could even be an obstacle to harmonization. On the other hand, adequately trained accountants might be able to more easily understand and apply internationally accepted accounting principles.

The group of academic accountants invited to the United Nations also designed a questionnaire to collect information on the status of accounting education today and its future direction. It has been mailed to all member Governments as well as to some professors of accounting and presidents of accounting associations. I would like to ask some of you at the Conference to fill it out since on-the-spot interviewing will help me in interpreting mailed-in responses.

ACCOUNTING REFORM IN THE NEW INDEPENDENT STATES

Now I will focus on the technical cooperation activities in the former Soviet Union. As I men-

Lorraine T. Ruffing is Chief of the Accounting Section of the U.N. Transnational Corporation and Management Division.

tioned earlier, one of the objectives of ISAR is to help countries in the process of standard setting. In 1989—long before various Western countries decided that the former Soviet Union was serious about reform—the Ministry of Finance approached the former Centre of Transnational Corporations (CTC)—for help in three areas: accounting, free enterprise zones and joint ventures. It was thought that such assistance would increase the flow of foreign direct investment, which was one of the mandates of the former CTC.

The Ministry was feeling pressure from many sides including from the Western partners of joint ventures—they wanted better information about their investments. They were extremely reluctant to risk sizable amounts of capital—indeed the average amount of foreign capital per joint venture never exceeded $1 million. Luckily, the Soviet Government realized that a crucial step in its transition to a market economy was the development of an accounting system capable of measuring financial performance at the enterprise level. It also realized that the adaptation of international accounting standards according to their needs might be more useful than adopting the national standards of another country, which would facilitate investment with partners from only that one country. In other words, it saw that the use of international standards could more quickly integrate them into the global economy. It had gained these insights from its participation in ISAR. This approach differs from that of some Eastern European countries which have sought advice on a bilateral basis or have engaged one of the Big Six to draft accounting legislation. This approach does not allow for much "due process" within the country. On the other hand, involving international organizations does allow the Government to take advantage at relatively low cost of the work which has been done in various multilateral settings; it can also avoid favouring one national system or firm over another; and lastly, it can receive advice that is both objective and sensitive to its particular needs since the international organization should have no special interest beyond harmonization.

The pressure, after the breakup of the former USSR, has become even more acute than ever since the various new independent states would like to undertake a rapid privatization of the state enterprises. The State Governments, the public, and potential investors need to be assured that the public resources of these state enterprises are being safeguarded and transferred in an equitable manner. This requires good accounting and auditing sys-

tems as well as the development of professionals who not only know their job but also know their professional responsibilities.

To make a long story short—the result of the request by the Ministry of Finance was the creation of an international Task Force on accounting reform and the design of an accounting education programme. The United Nations has adopted an integrated approach to accounting reform, accounting education and the strengthening of the profession. As we shall see, each of these elements depends on the other — there can be no accounting reform without retraining and the support of the profession. There can be no profession without reform and education. And education depends on the efforts of the profession. Therefore, each of these efforts has to be thought through and coordinated. Some of these efforts have already yielded tangible results. For example, the main accounting document for all productive enterprises in the NIS—the chart of accounts—has been revised by the Task Force according to internationally accepted accounting principles and recently has been adopted by Russia, Belarus and Moldova. It is now possible for investors, creditors, government officials and the public to use the chart of accounts to draw up financial statements which will indicate the enterprises' financial position and performance.

Accounting reform will continue in the Russian Federation under the International Advisory Board on Accounting and Auditing—the successor to the Task Force. It met in Moscow on 20 July and agreed on its programme of work, which includes drafting an accounting law, an auditing law and further improvements to the chart of accounts. The Board's decision to keep the best in the accounting system—the fact that each enterprise uses the same chart of accounts—is a tremendous advantage if one wants transparency and comparability in accounting information. However, modifications are necessary so that the accounting system produces financial statements which contain the information needed for investment decisions.

The Board has been organized by the United Nations Transnational Corporation and Management Division successor to the CTC, the Russian Parliament and the Ministry of Finance. It includes Russian experts and experts from international organizations such as the European Commission, the IASC, IFAC, OECD, the UN and the World Bank. Among the Russian experts are nongovernmental ones such as the President of the Association of Accountants— a concrete example of the government sharing power with the private sector. The Board has three committees: one on accounting, one on auditing and one on education. The work by Russian and foreign experts will be funded by the EC. The World Bank has also undertaken an additional effort to reform accounting for financial institutions. It is working closely with the Central Bank of Russia and is keeping the Board informed of its progress.

With the breakup of the former Soviet Union and the reluctance of the New Independent States to take direction from Moscow, there is a very real chance for accounting systems and requirements to begin to diverge with all the same drawbacks as in the rest of the world. Therefore, the United Nations, the Organization for Economic Cooperation and Development and the Ukrainian Ministry of Finance invited accounting experts, both government and private sector, both international and NIS to attend the International Conference on Accounting Reform in the NIS, 14-15 July in Kiev. The Conference gathered Vice Ministers of Finance, heads of accounting departments and leading academics from eight different states to discuss the future of harmonization in the NIS. They agreed to create the Coordinating Council on Accounting Methodology so that they could exchange information and promote the harmonization and modernization of their accounting systems. In the founding resolution, the eight states pledged that national accounting standards will be based on the recommendations of the Council.

THE ACCOUNTING PROFESSION IN THE NEW INDEPENDENT STATES

Accounting reform will be very difficult to implement without the active support of accountants, auditors and bookkeepers throughout the FSU. They will be called upon to take up new roles and functions. Formerly, their main duty was to supply information to central planners about the fulfillment of production targets. Now they must advise either management or the stockholders. Professional organizations can help in this process.

The first step was already taken in December 1989 when the Association of Accountants, CIS was formed. The first president is Prof. Anatoly Sheremet, Chairman of the Department of Accounting at Moscow State University. It has more than 300,000 collective (firms) and individual members. The individual states are also establishing their own associations but they maintain close ties with the parent association, and there are plans to convene a congress of an International Association of Accountants and Auditors in the NIS in December 1992. The members of these associations are accountants or are experts in related disciplines. The parent association has established refresher courses, it is advising members, it is developing ethical norms and it is gathering information on the establishment of the profession. In this context, ISAR produced a report on the Organization of the Accounting Profession and the Role and Qualifications of Auditors, which contains useful information and is available in Russian.

The former Centre and former DRT-Inaudit also organized a seminar to acquaint Russian auditors or "controllers" with the audit process and to discuss issues surrounding the organization of the profession. Russian auditors are very concerned about what will happen if they certify accounts and later they are proved to be incorrect. They also are puzzled about the nature of "independence" and what it means not only in relation to their clients but also in relation to government authorities.

Within the Association (CIS), there is the Institute of Professional Accountants whose members are considered auditors if they have successfully completed the certification process and obtained a license. There are approximately 130 Institute members at the present time. The Ministry of Finance has delegated the granting of auditors' licenses to the Association (CIS). The training of auditors is confined to experienced, well-qualified individuals who undertake a nine-week study programme offered by the Centre on Accounting and Auditing at the Academy of National Economy, or by Moscow State University, or by the Russian Economic Academy (Plekhanov Institute). Approximately 30 percent of those who complete the course go on to seek the auditing license, which is obtained by passing written and oral exams given by the Association of Accountants (CIS). At the current rate of certification, only 200 auditors a year will be produced. This in contrast to the potential demand which is in the thousands. The actual demand will of course depend on the requirements of the new auditing law. As mentioned above, the new Board will be reviewing such a law in the near future. If all privatized enterprises, small and large, must be audited, this would require, according to some recent estimates, 1.2 million auditors—clearly an impossible target for any association or educational programme.

ACCOUNTING EDUCATION IN THE NIS

Accounting reform cannot succeed unless the three million bookkeepers and accountants in the NIS are retrained. First, I would like to give you a thumbnail sketch of accounting education in the

NIS and then go into some of the new programmes which have been designed to meet the need for retraining.

The present educational system provides five years of secondary schooling to all students. At age 15 years, students are divided into three streams: technical school (two years), technikum (three to four years) or secondary school (two years). Only the latter enter institutions of higher learning such as an academy, institute or university and will earn a diploma in five years. In a further three years of post-graduate study, they can become candidates of science and after three additional years, doctors of philosophy.

Annually, approximately 60,000 bookkeepers are trained in technical schools (two years), 40,000 bookkeepers in technikums (three to four years) and 7,000 accountants in institutes or academies. There are about 171 higher education institutes which offer accounting courses. Currently, the total teaching staff in 41 institutes which specialize in accounting and finance numbers 342 professors; 150 doctors of science; and 1,800 candidates of science. The total number of accounting trainers in technikums and technical schools is about 6,000. The curricula, texts and courses for accounting diplomas have traditionally been set by a methodological council composed of university accounting professors which met at the Moscow Finance Academy and was supported by the Ministry of Finance. The council had the responsibility to set curricula, to designate courses as obligatory or nonobligatory depending the type of diploma and to ensure consistency in accounting education across the various institutes.

The United Nations, together with some members of the Association of Accountants, CIS, designed three different curricula to retrain accounting professors, students and practitioners. During 1990 to 1991 over 400 upper-level university students were retrained by international accounting firms on a pro bono basis using the UN curriculum. The international instructors were assisted by Soviet accounting professors. The students, who were fluent in English, were able to rapidly assimilate new concepts and terminologies in the two- to three-week period. Therefore, it was never true that "There probably are not 300 Soviets out of 300 million who know how to read a profit and loss statement" (J. Hertzfeld, "Joint Ventures: Saving the Soviets from Perestroika," *Harvard Business Review*, Jan-Feb. 1991). One constant criticism by Soviet accountants of foreign courses and workshops is that they are too elementary. The curriculum for

university students has subsequently been revised and is currently being tested at Moscow State University this September and October.

A detailed programme has also been designed for 120 top accounting professors or for "training the trainers." Briefly, the programme consists of an intensive pilot course which has already been given followed by a 10- to 12-week course in financial and management accounting in four centres of excellence in Russia, the Ukraine and Uzbekistan. After this a select number of participants will go abroad for a semester's study to deepen a particular aspect of their knowledge. This programme is very expensive and was clearly beyond UN resources. However, the U.K. Know How Fund was interested in building on UN efforts and is funding the programme and the British Council is administering it. The Association of Accountants, CIS and UN are serving in an advisory capacity. The goal is to build academic links between Russian, Ukrainian and Uzbek institutions and U.K. educational institutions so that they can develop curricula and retrain the faculty both in the designated "centres of excellence" and in the institutes affiliated with them. It is hoped that these 120 professors will form a cadre of Soviet trainers and reformers who will be key players in the transition to the market economy. Thus, the programme has the potential to exert a considerable multiplier effect.

The programme for practitioners is being studied by the European Commission and might be executed by the Chartered Association of Certified Accountants, which is known for its long-distance techniques and materials. The World Bank is also considering programmes for practitioners. There is also a draft programme written by a special Soviet commission to reform education on four levels on a long-term basis.

An integral part of any education programme is the translation of the appropriate textbooks. Six textbooks were chosen by the Association (CIS) and the United Nations for translation and publication by Finance and Statistics Publishing House in Moscow. The editor of the series is Prof. J. Sokolov, St. Petersburg Institute of Economics and Commerce, who is one of the Conference's speakers. One title by Prof. Mueller et al. is already available. More than 20 Russian translators have worked on the *Principles of Accounting* by Belverd Needles et al. and it is expected to be completed this fall. There is a great need for truly international textbooks which emphasize international practices rather than national ones. There has been an attempt to eliminate national practices from the translated texts. Translating accounting terms precisely is a major stumbling block and it won't be resolved until there exists an accounting dictionary or glossary in Russian. International organizations such as the EC and World Bank should incorporate the translation and development of appropriate textbooks into their programmes.

Regarding other training programmes, it is almost impossible to keep up with other national and international efforts. In March ISAR reviewed many of these programmes and the report of the Secretary General on this subject is available to you (E/C.10/AC.3/1992/7). Recently, both the European Commission and the World Bank have undertaken several fact-finding missions to determine what should be done in accounting education and commercial education. Final proposals for programmes are being formulated at this moment and the press coverage of them is highly inaccurate.

RESPONSIBILITIES OF ACADEMIC ACCOUNTANTS INVOLVED IN PROGRAMMES TO ASSIST COUNTRIES IN TRANSITION

In order to bring my comments to a close—I would like to discuss some guidelines for the design of accounting education programmes in the countries in transition. I think that academic accountants have a responsibility to ensure that these programmes meet local needs rather than national interests. I strongly urge either this Conference or the Association to make a statement on the duties of those accountants and professional associations involved in assisting accountancy development in countries in transition. If these technical assistance programmes are overly nationalist, we risk opening—in the words of one editor—"a Pandora's box" and setting back harmonizaton and modernization for at least a decade.

In my opinion, the designers of really useful programmes of accountancy development must have good knowledge of international accounting, the local accounting environment and recent developments in the local country or state. Particularly, a knowledge of what is happening in accountancy reform is crucial to the relevance of the initial curriculum. It is also important to have a good grasp of the problems which are likely to occur as countries in transition try to implement internationally accepted accounting principles and practices. For example, how can they make the transition to accrual accounting when 90 percent of the accounts receivable aren't receivable?

It is also desirable to have some knowledge of the local language. Accounting was never a presti-gious field in centrally planned economies. Therefore, accountants were not allowed to travel widely and are usually not great linguists. Given the absence of a glossary or dictionary, the interpreters have a very difficult time. Therefore, it is best if there is a Russian speaker among those designing and delivering the programme.

It goes without saying that the use of internationally accepted accounting principles and practices will be influenced by the local accounting environment. The positive features of the previous system should be preserved. In a recent letter, one deputy finance minister said, "We want to use our domestic experiences to the maximum and to preserve accounting and reporting methods which are compatible with international accounting standards." Indeed, this is the only feasible course given the large number of bookkeepers and accountants in the NIS. I have encountered frustration and anger in Soviet accountants when they are confronted by Western experts who purport to show them the way to the market economy while knowing little or nothing about the existing system and what bridges must be built between the two.

One should distinguish between bookkeeping which is the recording of transactions and accounting which is concerned with disclosure and measurement issues. It is perfectly possible to keep the current uniform bookkeeping system intact through the chart of accounts while at the same time making modifications in it so that it produces useful information for drawing up of the financial statements. This will considerably reduce the costs of retraining bookkeeping staff while a new generation of accountants is being educated. The chart is accompanied by detailed instructions for its use. These instructions are necessary because they reduce the number of independent interpretations which must be made by bookkeepers. Some Eastern European countries no longer require the chart of accounts but have not produced any detailed instructions for fulfilling the new accounting requirements which are based on the 4th and 7th EC directives. Thus, they have cut the bookkeepers adrift. The common format of the chart of accounts also makes it possible to provide various government officials such as statisticians, economists and tax collectors with the information they need. It would be a pity to give up such an important tool and only later have to design new tools to collect information for each of these users.

The chart of accounts will also make certain accounting procedures easier such as the consolidation of various individual accounts. It will also provide strong assurance that detailed accounts underlay the financial accounts and make the audit trail much easier to follow, thereby allowing the auditors to concentrate on how the enterprise is being managed.

As you can see I'm not an advocate of "shock therapy." The NIS do not need a revolution to produce useful accounting information. Shock therapy risks killing the patient (which the economists are in the process of doing) and destroying the building blocks from which an adequate accounting system can be produced. Therefore, I'm a bit critical when Western professors refuse to learn anything about the chart of accounts; refuse to incorporate it into their courses; insist that accountants in the NIS forget about it and jump immediately to Western-style balance sheets and income statements. Such an approach is nationalist and in the end will slow down the transition.

I mentioned earlier that we must make a distinction between bookkeeping and accounting. It is important that Western professors learn the bookkeeping system before they attempt to teach Western-style accounting. In the reform effort it is important to provide rules for both bookkeeping and accounting. Perhaps it is best to let the Ministries of Finance together with the accounting profession continue to set the detailed rules of bookkeeping while the Parliaments legislate the basic accounting and auditing laws. These laws should form the framework for accounting and auditing and should change relatively seldom whereas the chart of accounts and detailed instructions should be changed as needed. Gradually, an institution must be created that can formulate and implement national accounting standards which cannot be accommodated in the basic legislation or the instructions to the chart of accounts.

It is very important for those involved in accountancy development to have a comprehensive picture of what is required in the areas of reform, education and the strengthening of the profession. I hope that my remarks have brought this picture into better focus. I believe that many participants in this Conference are facing the challenges which I have described and I would again urge this Association to provide them with guidance so that they can better meet the challenge of this century.

Reform of Economic Systems and University Accounting Education in China

Yu Xu-ying

HISTORICAL REVIEW

Since the founding of our Republic, the economic system was copied basically from the former Soviet stiff patterns of the early 50s until the reform in China.

General Characteristics

1. Unitary ownership

   All enterprises were owned by the state, and merely viewed as the "appendages" of government organizations at various levels.

   (1) Working capital and fixed funds utilized by the enterprises were appropriated by state budget according to production quotas and used without remuneration.

   (2) Profits were remitted to the state, while losses were made up by an appropriation from the state. The state assumed responsibility for profits and losses as a whole.

2. Centralized management

   (1) The state took the enterprises as the object of its direct management.

   (2) Decisions about what products to produce, quantities to produce, and selling prices of products were made by the state at various levels.

   (3) Economic dealings between enterprises were wholly linked up through mandatory plans of the state.

3. Being isolated from the international community

   This situation made it difficult for the people to know what had happened in the outside world.

4. Consequences of the old system

   (1) Lack of vitality in businesses.

   (2) Lack of motivation to workers.

   (3) Slow economic growth.

The Impact of the Original Economic System on Accounting Practice

1. The accounting system implemented was also characterized by high degree of centralization.

2. Adopting a single, highly standardized uniform accounting system mainly for centralized economic planning and controlling, managers of enterprises were basically not the users of accounting information.

3. The unification and simplification of accounting work decreased the level of sophistication and expertise required of accounting personnel and transformed the accountancy profession into a career of no significance.

The Impact of the Original Economic System on Accounting Education

1. The low-level quality requirements of accounting personnel had a negative impact on accounting education.

2. The main requirement for university students majoring in accounting was to learn unified official accounting regulations embodied in related accounting textbooks without making sufficient theoretical analysis.

3. The main peculiarity of accounting university education in that period was to lay emphasis on training narrow technical specialists lacking of adaptive and creative abilities.

SOME MAJOR BREAKTHROUGHS MADE IN ECONOMIC REFORM (1980–1991)

The unsuccessful results of practicing China's original stiff economic system for the past 30 years convinced people that China must reform the original economic system on the basis of restructuring it as a whole, rather than amending or fine-tuning it.

The economic reform began in 1979 with the introduction of a family-contract responsibility system in rural areas. The overall reform of the urban economic system (the center of national economic system) started in 1984.

A Basic Recognition

Affirming China's economy as a socialist commodity economy is the prerequisite for China's eco-

Yu Xu-ying is a faculty member at Xiamen University, P.R. China.

nomic reform. The new economic system has to adapt itself to the basic requirements of socialist commodity economy. Accordingly, the replacement of original highly centralized economic system with a commodity-based economic system, and implanting a mechanism that combines both planned economy and market regulation would be considered as the goal of current economic reform.

Major Breakthroughs made in the Economic Reform Concentrating Mainly on the Following Three "Shifts"

1. Ownership shifted from unitary to diversified

    As the reform deepens, various forms of ownership such as collective, individual and private, and foreign-funded, have been developed simultaneously. The general trend shows that the percentage of state ownership tends to decrease, while the percentage of nonstate ownership tends to increase. The fact that the ownership of social resources becomes diversified would be beneficial to vitalizing the whole national economy.

2. Management shifted from centralized to decentralized

EXHIBIT 1
Changes of the Percentages of National Gross Industrial Output Value Produced in Enterprises with Different Ownership Forms

Ownership Form	Percentage	
	1980	1990
State-owned	76.0	54.54
Collective	23.5	35.76
Individual and private	0.5	5.34
Foreign-funded	0	4.36
Total	100.0	100.0

Source: No. 2, 1992, *Economic Science* (Bimonthly)

EXHIBIT 2
The National Gross Industrial Output Value Newly Added in 1990 Produced in Enterprises with Different Ownership Forms

Ownership Form	Percentage
State-owned enterprises	27
Township and village enterprises	40
Foreign-funded enterprises and joint ventures	33
Total	100

Source: No. 4, *Tech-economics Management Research* (Bimonthly)

EXHIBIT 3
The National Retail Sales Done in 1989 in Enterprises with Different Ownership Forms

Ownership Form	Percentage
State-owned	39.10
Collective	32.20
Individual and private	28.25
Joint ventures	0.45
Total	100.00

Source: No. 7, 1992, *China Economic Structure Reform* (Monthly)

The scope for mandatory state plans reduced, while the scope for market regulation enlarged in the process of reform, due to:

(1) State-owned enterprises acquiring greater dependence on production and marketing;

(2) Diversification of the ownership of enterprises;

(3) Development of non-national economy.

3. International relationship shifted from being detached to opening to the outside world

    (1) Lessons from history

    "History has taught us that a very important cause of China's long-time stagnation and backwardness was that China closed off. China cannot detach itself from the world for development" (Deng Xiaoping). Modernization and internationalization are closely related in contemporary world. Recognition and understanding of the new characteristics of contemporary world led China to actively carry out her policy of opening up to the outside world at the beginning of the last decade.

    (2) Three main forms were adopted to promote cooperation and exchange with foreign countries and regions (Hong Kong, Macao, and Taiwan) in order to attract foreign capi-

EXHIBIT 4
Changes of the Percentage of Goods Subject to Different Pricing Models

Goods Category	Percentage	
	1980	1991
State-set	92	25
Market-priced	8	75
Total	100	100

Source: June 1992, *China Today* (Monthly)

EXHIBIT 5
Utilization of Foreign Capital (in Billion US¥)

Year	Foreign Loans		Foreign Direct Investments	
	Project	Amount	Project	Amount
1985	72	2.688	3,073	1.959
1986	53	5.014	1,498	2.244
1987	56	5.805	2,233	2.647
1988	118	6.487	5,945	3.739
1989	130	6.286	5,779	3.773
1990	98	6.534	7,273	3.755
1991	108	6.888	12,978	4.666
Total	635	39.702	33,779	2.783

Source: No. 9, 1992 *Quantitative and Technical Economics* (Monthly)

tal, absorb advanced achievements of civilization and science and technology.

A. Attract foreign investments used to establish Sino-foreign joint ventures, cooperative ventures, or solely foreign-funded enterprises as well as foreign loans for the construction of highway, port, oil fields, power station, etc.

B. Establish transnational corporations abroad

It is an effective approach to develop an externally oriented economy for China.

C. Establish Special Economic Zones

It is a successful aspect of China's opening to the outside world. SEZs play an important role as windows and bases in China's economic and technological cooperation and trade with other countries and regions.

There are five special economic zones at present, namely Shenzhen, Zhuhai, Shantou, Xiamen, and Hainan. The first four were set up in 1980 and the last in 1988. The industrial output of the first four increased 17.7 times over the decade to 1990. Together the five

EXHIBIT 6
Overseas Direct Investments (Billion US¥)

Year	Project	Amount
1982	43	0.037
1991	1,008	1.400

Source: Issue 3, 1992, *International Business Administration* (Bimonthly)

SEZs produce one-ninth of the country's exports and have one-fourth of the total foreign investment. Such has been the measure of their success and justification of the SEZ experiment.

The Impact of the above Three "Shifts" on Accounting Practice

The primitive and uniform accounting system originally stipulated and implemented can no longer adapt to the new economic environment and must be broken through and further enriched and developed, mainly due to:

1. Managers of enterprises have been given greater decision-making powers in production and marketing. They become the main users of accounting information. As the economic interest and relationship are becoming more and more diversified and complicated, creditors, investors and other interested parties become the users of accounting information as well. Accounting has to seek to satisfy the needs of these users.

2. There have been lots of Sino-foreign joint enterprises, foreign-funded enterprises, and enterprises run by compatriots from Hong Kong, Macao, and Taiwan located in the Special Economic Zones and other vast opened areas. These enterprises would want to operate their business in the light of relevant international conventions (including international accounting conventions).

3. International economic intercourse and multinational operations demand accounting to serve as business language in communication.

4. The new situation provides accounting with a much more important and vital role to play.

The Impact of the above Three "Shifts" on Accounting Education

1. The new condition and environment raise new demands for a large number of broadly educated accounting experts qualified to undertake the modernized accounting work to meet the needs of China's modernized economic construction.

2. Such kind of "new-type" accounting experts cannot be expected to bring up from the old accounting education system which has been closely linked with the original economic system.

3. We are confronted with the arduous task of building up a new accounting education system which can comprehensively reflect the results of the developments and achievements of contemporary accounting science in the world and the relevant international conventions.

SOME PRELIMINARY EXPERIENCES GAINED IN ACCOUNTING EDUCATION REFORM AT XIAMEN UNIVERSITY

The Orientation of Accounting Innovation and Modernization in China

1. The main accounting subjects that stemmed from the original uniform accounting systems developed on "departmental" basis, and materialized as Industrial Accounting, Agricultural Accounting, Commercial Accounting, Bank Accounting, Capital Construction Accounting, etc. These subjects confined the learner's knowledge to a narrow pragmatic field and hindered both the development of accounting theory and the training of accounting personnel with up-to-date knowledge and ability to serve China's modernization. A new system of accounting subjects superseding this old one has become inevitable.

2. China's economy is socialist commodity economy. It is in this respect that China's economy has much in common with the economies of economically advanced Western countries. We should be broadsighted, emancipate our minds from the traditional restraints, and regard the abundant achievements of Western accounting originating from commodity economy as the common cultural wealth of human societies that is applicable to all countries.

   In order to keep pace with the contemporary developing trends in accounting fields, we should face the whole world to determine the orientation of our accounting innovation and modernization. It means that the way to get our original accounting innovated and modernized lies in introducing, digesting, and assimilating the scientific achievements of Western accounting and making them serve our needs.

3. Modern accounting in Western countries is developing in a multidisciplinary direction with broad theoretical foundations, and further subdivided into several "subjects," such as Accounting Theory, Financial Accounting, Management Accounting (including Cost Accounting), International Accounting, Government Accounting, Macroaccounting, Auditing, etc. The multidisciplinary character of modern accounting subjects facilitates bringing up broadly educated "new-type" accounting personnel with sound theoretical foundation and strong creative ability that will enable them to fit broader role.

The Effective Measures Adopted to Widely Draw on the New Developments and Achievements of Western Accounting

China had isolated itself from the international community for the past 30 years since the founding of our Republic. This situation made it very difficult to draw on the new developments and achievements of Western accounting, and get them integrated into our new accounting education. The main measures adopted to overcome these difficulties are to

1. Actively develop suitable forms of scholarly communication and intercourse between Xiamen University and a dozen of notable universities in the West starting from early in the last decade. These academic relationships make it relatively easy for the scholars concerned to learn and understand the latest developments and achievements in their areas of specialties.

2. Actively invite a good many professors in Western universities to give a series of lectures on new emerging areas of Western accounting to Chinese teachers and students. These notable professors did not simply help the participants to acquire related new knowledge in their specialties, but also put emphasis on conceptual and theoretical foundation of accounting and research methodology as well. Their enthusiastic support and help are of great significance.

3. Implement a program of joint training at home and abroad of promising young teachers and students (mainly doctoral students). They are given the opportunity to spend at least one year at a related Western university to pursue further studies so as to broaden their academic insight, enrich their professional knowledge, and improve on the quality of their academic training.

General Description of What Our University Has Done in Accounting Education Reform

Accounting education in our university includes two broad stages: undergraduate and graduate; the latter is further subdivided into two levels: master's level and doctoral level.

1. Undergraduate Program

   (1) A guiding principle for developing a better accounting curriculum.

       Expanding the view of accounting from a narrow discipline to a broad multidisciplinary perspective was the basis of developing a better accounting curriculum in the Accounting Department of Xiamen University. This new recognition of the true nature of accounting should make it possible for university students majoring in accounting to achieve a sound grounding in general and business education. The student will also take more thought-enlightening and less-structured optional subjects which will broaden their horizons of knowledge and develop their analytical ability.

   (2) Main modern accounting subjects were already integrated into our new accounting education.

       The basic four-year program of accounting specialty at Xiamen University is composed of three main segments (some political theory courses omitted). (See Exhibit 7.)

       The contents of this program have been enriched and expanded by the introduction of the main subjects of Western accounting into the curriculum. This was an important step to provide students with new expertise and update their professional knowledge.

       This curriculum is a combination of two approaches: a series of new courses were added without interfering with the content of some existing courses (such as Indus-

---

EXHIBIT 7
Curriculum for Accounting Major (Undergraduate)

General Basic Course
Political Economics
Foreign Language
Advanced Mathematics
Computer Languages
Chinese
Economic History
Chinese History

Basic Courses in Finance Economics
Statistics
Planning Management of the National Economy
Public Finance and Credit
Enterprise Management
Financial Management of Industrial Enterprises
Economic Laws

Specialized Courses

Required
Principles of Accounting
Industrial Accounting
Capital Construction Accounting
Economic Activity Analysis of Industrial Enterprises
Western Financial Accounting
Sino-Foreign Joint Venture Accounting
Auditing
The Application of Computers in Accounting

Optional

Offered by Accounting Department
International Accounting
Western Auditing
Issues in Accounting Theories
Issues in Management Accounting
Value Engineering Analysis

Offered by Other Departments
Contemporary Western Economics
International Trade
International Finance
Marketing
Elementary Operations Research
Mathematical Statistics
Logic
Psychology
Organizational Behavior
Human Resource Management
An Introduction to New Emerging Sciences

trial Accounting, Capital Construction Accounting, etc.). So it is a curriculum in transition. Our attempt and efforts to reform accounting education have achieved preliminary success and have laid a solid foundation for further in-depth and greater development.

2. Graduate Program—Master's Level

    The accounting master's program was initiated in 1978 at Xiamen University. It is one of the first established training bases for accounting master's students in China.

    (1) The main purposes of the master's program

    The three-year master's program is designed to prepare students as "new-type" accounting educators and accountants equipped with modern accounting science to meet the needs of educational and economic reform.

    (2) The structure of the master's program

    The structure of the master's program consists of two years of course work (including educational practice) and one year for social investigation and graduate thesis.

    The Accounting Department of Xiamen University offers six specialized areas for master's students. They are Accounting Theory, Financial Accounting, Management Accounting, International Accounting, Auditing, and Financial and Cost Management.

3. Graduate Program—Doctoral Level

    The accounting doctoral program was initiated in 1982 at Xiamen University. It is one of the first established training bases for accounting doctoral students in China.

    (1) The main purposes of the doctoral program

    The object of the doctoral program is to train selected individuals to become capable of undertaking creative research work in the main areas of modern accounting. The doctoral program is also considered as an important means for developing younger academic pioneers in their specialties.

    (2) The structure of the doctoral program

    The structure of the doctoral program consists of two years of course work and research practice, one year of study in a foreign university if joint training at home and abroad is feasible, and one year for social investigation and dissertation.

The Accounting Department of Xiamen University offers two specialized areas, Accounting Theory and Management Accounting, for doctoral students.

The common required courses designed for doctoral students in the college of Economics of Xiamen University are

> Research on Classical Economic Theories
> Research on Modern Economic Theories
> First Foreign Language
> Second Foreign Language

The advanced studies in specialized areas are primarily in the form of seminars directed by the supervisors.

In the seminars offered to doctoral students, historical, global, and comparative perspectives are emphasized. This is an effective way to develop students' critical and analytical faculty that is vital to their long-run academic career.

Doctoral students are also assigned as the supervisor's research assistants, and conduct certain research work under the guidance of their supervisors. This would provide the students with opportunities to learn the scientific research methodology, to develop their actual research capacity, and to make some practical contributions.

Dissertation is a key step in the training of doctoral students. China's regulation of academic degrees requires a dissertation to integrate theory with practice, apply advanced professional theories and methods to study and analyze issues of theoretical and practical significance, and obtain some creative results. The quality of the dissertation reflects the breadth and depth of the students' theoretical mastery as well as their ability in applying theoretical knowledge to study, analyze, and solve complicated practical problems.

Joint training at home and abroad is an important form of training doctoral students encouraged by the State Commission of Education and warmly praised by doctoral students themselves. The doctoral students attend at least a one-year study in foreign universities after completing their basic course work at home. The essence of this form of training is to make it possible for doctoral students to learn more effectively the contemporary new developments in their specialties and to quicken their academic maturity as well.

EXHIBIT 8
Curriculum for Accounting Master Candidate

Common Required Courses	**Specialized Courses***
Research on Basic Economic Theories	Advanced Financial Accounting
Foreign Language	Advanced Management Accounting
Operations Research Principles and Application	Specific Issues in:
Accounting Information System	Accounting Theories
	International Accounting
	Auditing
	Financial and Cost Management

Other Optional Courses from Disciplines Outside the Accounting Department
Research on Contemporary Economic Theories
Advanced Mathematical Statistics
Specific Issues in:
    Public Finance
    Financial Management
    etc.

* These courses are required only for the graduates specializing in corresponding area and are optional for other graduates.

FUTURE OUTLOOK

Ten-odd years have elapsed since China embarked on the policy of reform and opening to the outside world. China's great achievements gained during this period have attracted worldwide attention. It is justifiable for all of us to be proud of these achievements. But now China has come to a crucial period for further development. The contemporary world situation urges our country to grasp the current favorable opportunity to stride forward on this successful path more rapidly. Unfortunately, there are some things, especially some types of rigid idea which hampers China from advancing with giant strides. Under these circumstances, Deng Xiaoping, the chief architect of China's reform and open policy, made some important comments on accelerating China's reform and opening wider to the outside world, especially on issues concerning attributes of Socialism or Capitalism in reform and opening, and the relationship between Socialism and market economy, during his tour of South China last January. Deng's sagacious comments soon became a powerful weapon to surmount ideological and theoretical obstacles existing continuously in some people's minds, and have far-reaching significance to accelerate China's reform and opening.

Under the enlightenment of Deng's comments, a new theory concerning socialist market economy emerged and has been developed rapidly. The theory of socialist market economy is an important breakthrough on the basis of current theory of socialist commodity economy. According to the theory of socialist market economy, China has to run to socialist market economy, establish a complete socialist market system, and let the market mechanism play the dominant role in the allocation and utilization of social resources. This new theory also requires that China's domestic market system should be closely linked to the big sea of the whole world market system. This is the necessary condition for China to keep pace with the general trends of global developments and to speed up her process of modernization. Inspired by Deng's above comments and equipped with socialist market economy theory, China enters a new stage of marketization of her economy and opening ever wider to the outside world.

Accounting is the language of business. Accompanied by the development of China's socialist market economy, the trend of internationalization of accounting practice and education in China will be also enhanced. It can be seen that China's new accounting model, based on socialist market economy, is becoming more and more compatible with the accounting models of many Western countries. As to accounting education, the guiding principles concerning education reform, stipulated by the State Commission of Education, emphasize three aspects (e.g., facing the world, facing the future, and facing modernization). These principles materialize in accounting education. We will lay emphasis on training new "externally oriented type" or "internationalized type" accounting experts to meet the needs of developing China's market-oriented, externally oriented economy.

Accounting Education in Developing Countries

The conference program included eleven papers that focus on accounting education in one or more countries which are frequently referred to as developing countries. These papers provide background information about both the accounting profession and accounting education in several countries. An important common theme in these papers is that accounting is playing an increasingly important role in economic development and socio-economic evolution. The demand for qualified accountants and accounting faculty exceeds the supply. The growing need for a more advanced accounting education system is crippled by the shortage not only of accounting faculty but by relevant accounting instructional materials. Because of the lack of published materials developed within their countries, most educators turn to western textbooks which often do not meet the specialized needs of their students.

Developments in Indonesian Accountancy

Katjep K. Abdoelkadir and Hadori Yunus

INTRODUCTION AND OUTLINE

We are greatly honoured and pleased to address you about accounting developments in Indonesia, as we think our Indonesian structure and process may have considerable impact on other countries trying to get to the "take off" stage in accountancy—both from a practice and educational point of view.

In Part I of this paper, we will cover the historical development of accounting in the Republic of Indonesia. The second part, will deal with our important Accountancy Development Project, while in the third part, we will touch upon the educational aspects which play such an important role in our enhancement of public and private sector accounting and auditing.

Since this paper is limited by its size, we will not be able to cover all our elements in detail, but we will be pleased to answer fuller questions at this conference or in subsequent correspondence to you. One of the most valuable benefits of a conference such as this comes through the sharing of ideas and experiences—not only amongst ourselves as educators, but also, on a broader level, among the countries which we represent.

Indonesia is currently in the middle of an evolution of our accounting systems—in the public and private sector—with a major reform program currently in progress with the assistance of the World Bank. A number of important policy and organizational changes have been introduced, on which we will touch later.

A BRIEF HISTORY OF ACCOUNTANCY IN INDONESIA

The history of accountancy in Indonesia can be divided into three periods: the period before World War II, the war years, and the period after Indonesia obtained independence. This part will cover important developments in each of these periods.

Before World War II

Accountancy in Indonesia can be traced back to 1642, the year in which the Dutch Governor General of the Nederlands East Indies (a colony which included most of present-day Indonesia) issued a regulation concerning the administration of cash receipts, receivables and the budget for garrisons and ship-dockages in Batavia (now Jakarta) and Surabaya.[1] Part of the regulation dealt with the use of the Journal. The Journal is a book in which all transactions are recorded before they are transferred to the Journal. The purpose of the Journal is to make sure that the debit and the credit entries are equal. The regulation issued by the Dutch Governor General also explained the use of a ledger and the method for correcting errors in the ledger.

The first internal accountants in Indonesia were Englishmen. According to Stibbe and Stoomberg,[2] "Messrs. Nijst and Verbiest said in their book about accountancy, that the first accountants in the Nederlands Indie (Indonesia) were Englishmen. They are not public accountants, but accountants that worked for a big English firm. . . ." The first Dutch internal accountant was sent to Indonesia in 1896.

In 1907 the first government accountant, van Schagen, was sent to Indonesia from the Nederlands to open the State Audit Agency. The formal opening of the Agency occurred in 1915. In 1918 Frese & Hogeweg opened the first public accounting office in Indonesia.

Bookkeeping was first taught to Indonesians in high schools and special schools, such as the Handelschool or the Middelbare Handelschool (schools specializing in trade). Enrollment in these

---

[1]A.S Sapi'ie, *sejarah Perkembanngan Akuntansi Indonesia*, Unpublished Master Thesis, University of Indonesia, 1980.

[2]Ibid.

Katjep K. Abdoelkadir is the Executive Secretary, Indonesian Coordinating Agency for Accounting Development (CAAD), Vice Chairman, Indonesian Institute of Accountants (IAI) and a lecturer at the University of Indonesia.
Hadori Yunus is the Managing Partner of Dr. Hadori & Rekan, an Indonesian public accounting firm, and a lecturer at Gadjah Mada University.

schools was usually limited to Indonesians with special status, such as the children of the head of a district or the children of a wealthy businessman.

Private tutoring in bookkeeping was given by Dutchmen who worked for the Tax Office, the Audit Office, or the Treasury. This tutoring was given after office hours—in Dutch, using Dutch accounting textbooks. Each tutor had his own exam and certificate.

On March 20, 1925, in Semarang the "Bond van Vereniging voor Handel Onderwijs" (Trade Teachers Association) was established to regulate the training of bookkeepers outside school. Bookkeeping courses were classified as Bond A and Bond B, which were roughly equivalent to basic and intermediate accounting, respectively. The Bond conducted a uniform examination and issued its own certificate.

During World War II

During the early years of World War II, while the Dutch still held Indonesia, almost all of the important jobs in the Ministry of Finance were held by the Dutch inhabitants. In March 1942 the Japanese captured Indonesia, and the Dutch inhabitants who did not flee to Australia were put in concentration camps. The Japanese occupation of Indonesia opened a large number of vacancies in the Ministry of Finance. To fill these vacancies, the Japanese trained Indonesians. Four different courses were offered:

1. Course A: For the post of Assistant-Inspector for the Ministry of Finance, the applicant had to be a lawyer and had to undergo six months of training.

2. Course B: Initially divided into Course B-1 for Tax Controllers and Course B-2 for Tax Officers, the courses were later merged into a single course. Applicants had to be high school graduates, and their training lasted one year.

3. Course C: For a position as an Assistant Accountant, an applicant had to be a high school graduate and undergo three years of training. Completion of the course of Assistant Accountant was equivalent to obtaining a Bachelor of Arts Degree.

4. Course D: For a position as a bookkeeper, applicants had to graduate from Middelbare Handelschool and complete an additional year of training. Satisfactory completion of Course D was equivalent to completion of Bond B.

About 150 applicants were accepted for the four courses. Initially the Japanese allowed Dutch experts to teach the courses. However, when Japan began to lose important battles to the Allied Forces, the Dutch experts were no longer allowed to teach. The teaching was briefly continued by a few Indonesian experts.

Due to financial problems and other difficulties, the courses were discontinued in 1943. The participants were appointed to positions in the Ministry of Finance. Those who had been following Course C or Course D were required to prepare themselves for an examination which was given in 1944 and was equivalent to Bond B.

Some of the participants of these training courses later became well known for their expertise in taxation and accountancy. Among them were the late Prof. Sindian Jayadiningrat and Prof. Rachmat Sumitro, who wrote many books on taxation. The trainees also included Prof. S. Hadibroto and Prof. Soemardjo Tjitrosidojo, who are still recognized as experts in accountancy.

After Indonesian Independence

Indonesia declared its independence on August 17, 1945, just three days after Japan had indicated a readiness to surrender to the Allied Forces. After the close of the war, the Dutch attempted to regain control over Indonesia. However, they could not overcome the resistance of supporters of the new national government. Eventually, the territory of the former colony was divided. A portion was placed under Dutch administration, and the remainder was ceded to the Republic of Indonesia.

In 1948, while control over much of the Indonesian territory was still in dispute, the MBA (Moderne Bedrijft Administratie) was introduced. The courses combined the curricula of cost accounting and advanced accounting.

There were still a number of Dutch accountants who worked for the Ministry of Finance after Indonesia obtained independence. To replace the Dutch accountants with Indonesians, the government sent students to England, to Holland, and to the United States to study taxation, accounting, and other fields of study. The government of Indonesia continues to send students overseas for graduate work even today.

Use of the title of accountant came under regulation in Indonesia with the passage of Law No. 34/1954. According to the law, the title of accountant may be used only by those who have earned a bachelor's degree in accounting (formerly a master's degree until 1987) from a state university or from another accredited institution, or by those who have earned a bachelor's degree from an unaccred-ited institution and have also passed an examination administered by an "Expert Committee," appointed by the Ministry of Education and Culture. The law required new accountants to register with the Financial and Development Supervisory Board upon graduation from an accredited institution or passage of an "Expert Committee" examination.

In 1953 Universitas Indonesia in Jakarta became the first Indonesian institution to offer a program of study leading to a master's degree in accounting. The university's program, which followed the Dutch system of education for accountants, required a student to earn a master's degree in economics and then spend two years of concentrated study in the field of accountancy. The first four students to become qualified accountants through the completion of the university's program graduated in 1957. Shortly after their graduation, Universitas Indonesia introduced a new program of study for prospective accountants. The program was called the "guided study system" and was modeled after a plan used in the United States. Under the guided study system, a student could earn both his baccalaureate and master's degree in accounting in five years.

Meanwhile, in 1957 the Minister of Finance established a school for training accountants to work for the Ministry. Originally called the Sekolah Tinggi Ilmu Keuangan Negara (STIKN), the school became the Institut Ilmu Keuangan (IIK), and later the Sekolah Tinggi Akuntansi Negara (STAN).

State universities outside of Jakarta began to establish departments of accounting in early. 1960's: Universitas Padjadjaran in Bandung (1961); Universitas Sumatera Utara in Medan (1962); Universitas Airlangga in Surabaya (1962); Universitas Gadjah Mada in Yogyakarta (1964); Universitas Brawijaya in Malang (1977); and Universitas Andalas in Padang (1978). Private universities also began to offer courses in accounting: Universitas Parahiyangan in Bandung (1965); and Universitas Trisakti (1969), Universitas Tarumanegara (1972), and Universitas Atmajaya (1973) in Jakarta.

Some of the universities modeled their programs on the Dutch system of education, while others chose to follow the American plan of study. This dualism in methods of education for accountants persisted until 1977.

In 1977 the Ministry of Education and Culture organized the Board of Consortium of Economic Sciences (BCES). The BCES issued a ruling which directed universities to follow a uniform curriculum in preparing students for a master's degree in accounting.

The vast majority of new accountants in Indonesia are educated at the state universities. Although one of the private universities (Universitas Parahiyangan) introduced a program in accounting as early as 1965, only 12 graduates of private universities had been awarded a master's degree in accounting by the beginning of 1978. It is not known how many of the 12 graduates passed the Expert Committee examination and thereby became entitled to call themselves accountants. In contrast with the private institutions, the state universities had granted a total of 1,763 master's degrees in accounting by the start of 1978.

The Ministry of Education and Culture classifies every department (fakultas) of every private university after evaluating the facilities for teaching, the teaching staff, and the curriculum. There are three possible classifications. The highest classification is "Disamakan" (Equated), which signifies that the Ministry considers the overall quality of the fakultas to be on a par with that of a fakultas in the same field at a state university. No state examination is given to a student who earns a degree from a fakultas that has been classified as "Disamakan." The degree is considered to be equivalent to a degree from a state university.

The second classification is "Diakui" (Recognized), while the lowest is "Terdaftar" (Registered). Students who receive degrees from fakultas that have been classified as "Diakui" or "Terdaftar" must pass a state examination in order to demonstrate competence equal to that of a student who has earned a degree at a state university. The Ministry of Education and Culture appoints a committee to supervise the administration of examinations by fakultas classified as "Diakui." An appointed committee takes charge entirely in the administration of examinations to students who receive degrees from a fakultas that is merely "Terdaftar."

Representatives of two agencies of the Ministry of Education and Culture, the Directorate General of Higher Education and the Board of Consortium of Economic Sciences, have outlined a program for improving accounting education in Indonesia.[3] The program is divided into short-term and long-term objectives.

A. Short-term objectives:

1. To improve the facilities of existing institutions by
    a. providing sufficient quantities of up-to-date textbooks
    b. translating foreign textbooks used by the accounting departments into Indonesian
    c. providing electronic equipment for the accounting laboratories
    d. increasing the number of classrooms

2. To improve the teaching staff by
    a. arranging upgrading programs for teaching staff
    b. arranging staff development seminars
    c. providing opportunities for staff members to continue their education abroad
    d. providing greater financial incentives for staff to develop accounting education
    e. offering courses in accounting to staff members whose expertise lies in a field other than accounting

3. To consider the establishment of a department of accounting at any state university that can satisfy the following criteria:
    a. the employment of at least four accountants as full-time instructors, or the employment of at least two accountants as full-time instructors and four accountants as part-time instructors
    b. the inclusion of at least one senior teacher among the full-time instructors

4. To encourage an exchange of ideas with educators in the field of accounting abroad by inviting foreign professors to serve as guest lecturers, to assist in developing a curriculum, to improve teaching methods, etc.

B. Long-term objectives:

These long-term objectives have been incorporated into a ten-year accounting development program which is being financed by the World Bank. The program is intended to accomplish the following:

1. To study the needs of accountants through an institutional approach. The objectives of an institutional study would be
    a. to determine the supply of and the demand for accountants
    b. to determine the capacity to produce competent, good quality accountants through the universities in Indonesia
    c. to determine the classification of accountants in Indonesia
    d. to direct the allocation of accountants and assistant accountants to various sectors of the Indonesian economy.

2. To establish four accountancy development centers within the university's faculties of economics and the Ministry of Finance Sekolah Tinggi Akuntan Negara (STAN). These centers will
    a. provide training to broaden the capabilities of accountancy teachers and practicing accountants
    b. develop courses and teaching materials with greater relevance to the needs of the Indonesian economy
    c. carry out practice-oriented research projects in order to improve current methods of accounting in Indonesia.

The early development of Indonesian Accountants' Association (IAI) was very slow due to its small membership and its lack of recognition from business, government, and the academic community. Not until its third congress in December 1973 did the IAI take any significant actions. At its third congress the IAI adopted and undertook to publish the following:

1. Generally Accepted Accounting Principles (GAAP)

2. Generally Accepted Auditing Standards (GAAS) and

3. Code of Professional Ethics

The norms embodied in the Principles and Standards and the Code of Ethics were taken primarily from statements of accounting norms in the United States. Some were also taken from "A Statement of Australian Accounting Principles," and "Wet op de Jaarekening van Ondernemingen" from the Netherlands.

In July 1974 the IAI established the Yayasan Pengembangan Ilmu Akuntansi Indonesia (Indone-

---

[3]M. Salaki, *profesi Akuntan di Indonesia Kini dan Dimasa Mendatang*, Unpublished Master Thesis, University of Indonesia, 1979.

sian Accountancy Development Foundation) for the purpose of directing the growth and development of the accounting profession with regard to the needs of private business and the needs of the community at large.

IAI started to participate in the international forum by sending representatives to the first meeting of accountants from ASEAN countries in Manila and also to the Eighth Congress of the Asia and Pacific Accountants in Hong Kong in 1976.

At the end of 1976 the President of Indonesia in his Decision No. 52/1976 established the first stock exchange in the country. With the establishment of the stock exchange, the need for public accountants was greatly increased. Public accountants are required to audit and to give unclassified opinions on the financial condition of corporations that elect to "go public" (to trade their securities on the stock exchange).

On March 27, 1979, the President issued Instruction No. 6/1979, which further increased the importance of public accountants. In the instruction, which is known as the March 27 parcel, the government tried to increase its tax revenues by offering incentives to corporations. However, to be entitled to these incentives, corporations had to have their financial statements audited by public accountants. To implement the President's instruction, the Ministry of Finance issued Decree No. 108/1979. On May 1, 1978, a body known as Seksi Akuntan Publik (the Public Accountants' Section) was established within the IAI. To become a member of Seksi Akuntan Publik an accountant must pay an initial fee of Rp 50,000 (about $25), and monthly dues of Rp 10,000 (about $5). Some of the large public accounting firms pay these fees for their accountants. At present the section has about 300 members.

In 1967 the Minister of Finance authorized the public accounting firm of Arthur Young to establish a joint partnership with an Indonesian accountant, Santoso Harsokusumo. The ruling for this partnership stated that:

1. The name of the partnership should show both names: Arthur Young and Santoso Harsokusumo.

2. The partnership must show a list of five foreign corporations that will become its clients.

3. The partnership cannot audit state corporations.

4. The partnership cannot request favorable facilities which are available for other types of foreign investments.

5. Foreign accountants working in Indonesia should abide by Law No. 34/1954.

6. The partnership should assist in training Indonesian accountants.

7. The partnership should assist in developing the Indonesian accounting profession.

8. The partnership should abide by all Indonesian government regulations.

The following year Sycip, Gorres and Velayo from the Philippines formed a partnership with Utomo.

In 1971 a new Minister of Finance was sworn in. The new Minister revoked the ruling stipulating the conditions of the joint partnership. In place of the ruling he issued Decree No. 76/1971, dated February 8, 1971. The decree added a reciprocal clause and a three-year time limit to the original terms of the partnership. The reciprocal clause stated that Indonesian accountants must be given permission to work in the United States in the case of the partnership between Arthur Young and Santoso, and in the Philippines in the case of the partnership between Sycip, Gorres and Velayo and Utomo. The two foreign accounting firms could not accept the new terms, and the joint partnerships were liquidated.

Foreign accounting firms are able to operate in Indonesia today as correspondents. Although the relationship is technically a correspondence, in practice the firms operate in much the same as they did under the original joint partnership agreement. In addition to Santoso and Utomo, the following Indonesian firms have established a correspondence relationship with a foreign accounting firm:

1. Go Tie Siem with Thurquand & Young since 1971, and with Klijnveld, Kraijenhof & Co. since 1974.

2. Tan Eng Oen with Price Waterhouse since 1971.

3. Sujono Sudomo with Peat, Marwick, & Mitchell between 1971-1977.

4. Sudiendro with Peat, Marwick, & Mitchell since 1977.

5. Suparman with Coopers & Lybrand between 1971-1979.

6. DLP Siregar with Coopers & Lybrand since 1979.

7. Hendra Darmawan with Touche Ross International since 1975.

In 1976 the Minister of Finance revoked Decree No. 76/1971 and replaced it with Decree No.

1681/1976. The new decree relaxed the restrictive terms affecting foreign firms. However, foreign accounting firms have displayed little interest in changing their legal status. They apparently are satisfied with the correspondence relationship.

THE INDONESIAN ACCOUNTANCY DEVELOPMENT PROJECT

The Republic of Indonesia (Indonesia) recognized clearly, about 20 years ago, that, in order to develop effectively economically and financially, good accountancy systems and procedures were a sine qua non. Such an effective framework required, of course, sound education, training and research, and, of course, effective institutional frameworks to develop such activities. We didn't have a viable professional institute nor were our educational institutions geared for the future requirements.

At independence in 1945, there was no significant stock of professionally qualified accountants and auditors. The Indonesian Institute of Accountants was not formed until 1957. [It presently has about 4,300 members of whom some 900 are licensed to practice publicly.]

The Government of Indonesia sought the assistance of the International Bank for Reconstruction and Development (IBRD or World Bank) in developing its overall accounting framework, e.g., education. Extensive feasibility studies were carried out in the 1970s and 1980s resulting in various assistance programs. The principal one is the one now in process, i.e., a $165 million accounting development project covering a five-year period. We hope to continue this project with the assistance of the World Bank, resulting in another five-year project. As you may have noticed, we're speaking about sizable funds of money and comprehensive projects. By the way, these are for accounting development alone, while of course many other development projects are under way with international organizations, especially the World Bank, IMF and Asian Development Bank. Let us return to the 1988 "Accountancy Development Project" still in progress, and as you can see it has many components.

The objectives of the project are to (a) assist the government to improve accounting practices in both the public and private sectors; and (b) support the government's program to improve the quality of accounting education and prepare for future demand for accountancy manpower. The project finances specialist services, training, equipment,

books, development of instructional materials and operating costs. Specifically, support is given to (i) implementing the first phase of a modernized government accounting system; (ii) improving government auditing services; (iii) raising the quality of accounting staff; (iv) increasing the scope and efficiency of the capital market; (v) strengthening the role of the professional association of accountants and introducing a series of accounting standards; (vi) improving the quality and management of accounting education in the secondary, tertiary and informal subsectors; and (vii) expanding accountancy training capacity in higher education and nonformal education.

Significant long-term benefits are expected from this project in the form of improved public stewardship, more effective control over national revenue and expenditure, improved auditing, capital market expansion and a strengthened accountancy profession. Underlying the execution of this project was a series of fundamental weaknesses encountered in our accounting structure; let us enumerate some of those as they may well "ring a bell" with many of you:

1. Archaic accounting practices.

Archaic accounting practices limited the effectiveness and efficiency of accounting and auditing activities throughout the public and private sectors in Indonesia. This situation reflected the deficiencies of inherited accounting conventions. More fundamentally, it resulted from the scarcity of professional and technical staff who are adequately trained in modern methods of accountancy.

2. Deficiencies in government accounting.

The most conspicuous problem occurred in the public sector. Deficiencies in government accounting hampered public administration in two key respects: they compromise public stewardship by limiting the government's ability to ensure that public funds are used for their intended purposes and they obstruct budget planning by not providing accurate and timely information on public resource availability and cost of program options. Improvements in government accounting practices and parallel efforts in staff training in Indonesia were needed to close the serious gaps in timeliness and accuracy of existing government accounts. One indication of the problem was the long delay—about two years—between the time that central government expenditures were made and the time those expenditures were reported to Parliament. Another was the existence of major and irreconcilable differences between different data series on the same transactions, resulting from fragmented accounting systems and from the absence of a uniform chart of accounts.

3.   Shortcomings of the government budget process.

Further deficiencies in government accountancy arose from shortcomings of the budget process, including excessively short-term and fragmented budget allocations, incomplete coverage of public enterprise transactions, and blurring of distinctions between capital and revenue items. Improvements in the timeliness, completeness, and accuracy of government accounts would contribute both to better planning of public expenditures and to improved implementation of investments and routine government activities.

4.   Scarcity of competent government accountants and auditors.

The scarcity of competent government accountants and auditors also limited the scope for improving tax audits as a means of increasing revenues through better compliance with corporate and personal income and other taxes. Significant improvements in compliance with corporate income taxes and other taxes require the introduction of consistent accounting standards and the enforcement of statutory audits. This in turn implied an expanded role for the professional association of accountants in development of accounting standards, certification of accountancy skills, and provision of auditing services.

5.   Private sector shortage of accountants with up-to-date skills.

The private sector was also hampered by a shortage of professional and technical staff with up-to-date skills in accountancy. Management accounting as a tool of managerial efficiency was virtually nonexistent. Financial disclosure requirements for private firms were very limited.

6.   Improved and uniform reporting methods needed.

Development of improved and uniform reporting on enterprise performance is a prerequisite to the further expansion of the nascent market for private securities. The government aim was to increase the share of private savings in total domestic savings. The goal of expanded private sector savings was more likely to be met if the stock market could be made to assume a more active role in capital mobilization. As a prerequisite for improved investor confidence in the private securities market, appropriate standards for reporting the financial performance of enterprises needed to be de-

veloped and put into practice. More generally a study of the existing market's operation was to be carried out with a view to identifying appropriate changes to invigorate the market as a source of investment capital.

The above-mentioned issues were related to accountancy development in five broadly-defined areas: (a) government accounting and auditing, (b) private-sector accounting, (c) capital market, (d) accountancy manpower supply and demand, and (e) accountancy education.

It would carry us too far to elaborate on each of those issues but let us touch on some of those of relevance to you, I think:

1.   Private sector accounting and auditing.

The private sector comprises Indonesian public and private companies (including about 300 public accounting firms), cooperatives, partnerships and sole traders. The quality of accounting in the private sector varies widely, tending to be better in those companies which have foreign investors or are listed on the local stock exchange (which imposes certain reporting standards); but in general the development of accounting had fallen behind that of other skills required in industry and commerce. Accounting systems frequently did not provide adequate financial control, and few accountants and managers were trained to produce or use accounting information as a management tool.

To some extent this situation can be attributed to a general absence in Indonesian law of regulations of the type which in other countries frequently enforce the maintenance of basic standards of accounting. The Indonesian Companies' Act and Commercial Code are anachronisms dating back to colonial times and are silent on accounting matters; there were no statutory reporting requirements for companies; and there are no audit requirements (apart from listed companies).

A second factor which in other countries frequently contributes to the maintenance of accounting standards is the presence of a strong professional body of accountants. In Indonesia, the professional body—the Indonesian Institute of Accountants (IAI)—is relatively young and has not yet developed the stature to command wide respect among businessmen and other potential users of accounting and auditing services.

2.   Accountancy education and training programs.

Prior to Independence in 1945 and to the nationalization of Dutch enterprises in 1957, most accounting practices in government and in the private sector followed Dutch accounting conventions. Because most senior positions involving accounting were held by expatriate staff, in-country accountancy training was initially limited to bookkeeping courses offered in trade and commerce institutions. These lower-level training programs have evolved into two main categories of accountancy instruction: the accountancy courses offered in the Ministry of Education and Culture's (MOEC) general secondary schools (SMAs) and secondary commercial schools (SMEAs) and the nonformal courses in accountancy administered by various government and private agencies, often through short-term, in-service training.

In order to help meet the growing demand for qualified accountants in government service, new legislation was enacted in 1961 to require that all qualified applicants for professional certification as accountants must complete at least three years of government service before certification would be granted. However, this legislation has been retracted.

This measure, however, proved insufficient to meet government needs, and in 1975 the Ministry of Education and Culture (MOEC) approved the establishment by the MOF of its own accountancy training institute, the State School of Government Accounting (STAN). The STAN pre-service accountancy courses are offered at two levels: a three-year adjunct accountant course (called the Diploma III level), and a five-year accountant course (called the Diploma IV level), which also requires a thesis and working experience as a adjunct accountant. Diploma IV graduates are eligible for certification by MOF as Registered Accountants. STAN trains about 400 graduates per year in its pre-service Diploma III and Diploma IV programs of accountancy. In addition, STAN offers an extensive program of in-service training for government accountants and auditors—usually in the form of several weeks' training courses on specific topics of accounting or auditing practice.

There are currently a total of 85 universities, institutes, and academies which offer post-secondary courses of accountancy, but there are important differences among these programs in terms of their size and quality. The vast majority of Registered Accountants in Indonesia are graduates of STAN and the eight state universities with accredited accountancy programs.

A general problem with accountancy training programs of all kinds is the shortage of qualified teaching staff and teaching materials for the new

methods of accountancy which are now widely adopted in the private sector and which are about to be introduced in the public sector.

This problem resulted from the dualism which has characterized accountancy training programs for most of the past 35 years. Following the nationalization of Dutch companies in 1957, private sector companies progressively replaced the former, inherited accounting practices with more modern accounting practices—particularly, of North American origin. At the same time, government accounting has continued to follow the earlier Dutch practices. There had thus been a need for accountancy training at all levels to provide instruction in both the old and new systems of accounting. As the government has progressively become committed to modernization of government accountancy and as the private sector's adoption of new accounting practices has become widespread, however, the need for maintaining a dual system of accounting education no longer exists. Recognizing this fact, the MOEC moved early in the 1980s to prepare new curricula for accountancy education at all levels. These curricula are now complete and in operation, but their effectiveness is impaired by teachers' unfamiliarity with the new techniques and with the lack of suitable Indonesian language textbooks, teachers' manuals, and other teaching materials. The Accounting Development Project is aimed at overcoming these shortages.

3. Accounting manpower supply and demand.

It may be apparent to you that we were in dire need of an adequate inventory of accountants and an effective educational planning framework to serve our future socioeconomic needs in Indonesia. Therefore, a thorough accounting manpower study had to be prepared, and this study is now in its final stages. Let us briefly touch upon the scope and contents of this study as it will play such an important part in developing accounting education and training in our economy in the years ahead.

The objectives of the study were

- to provide information to assist in the determination of new, additional and modified training curricula as well as to determine qualification levels, specialization requirements and validation criteria that may be required.

- to determine future allocations of accounting manpower; training of accounting personnel in the various areas (specializations) and branches of accounting; additional retraining (updating) requirements; and continuing professional education demands all likely to arise from the present and future stock of accounting manpower in both the public and private sector. As such, the study will help formulate the respective training programs required to satisfy the future needs of the Indonesian Economy.

- to provide information for the economic management of manpower currently allocated, and to be allocated through 1999, to accounting, financial management, auditing, and associated economic activities, particularly to determine new, additional, and modified training curricula and delivery systems, with qualification levels, specialization requirements, and validation criteria which may be required.

The focused activities of the study are to

a. Make an inventory of the stock of accounting manpower in the government and private sector by employment classifications in Indonesia identified by the principal locations of their professional/commercial training as at the end of our recent five-year plan, REPELITA IV (March 31, 1989);

b. Estimate the stocks of accounting manpower by employment classifications as at the end of each REPELITAS I, II and III: also identified by the principal locations of professional/commercial training. The needs for accountants should be set forth by Central Government, regions, provinces and districts to the extent possible;

c. Forecast the stocks of accounting manpower by employment classification, levels of qualification, and by sectors of the economy which are likely to be required by the mid-points and ends of new REPELITAs V and VI, taking into account (to the extent feasible) the demands of these economic development programs; and

d. Forecast the impact on existing professional commercial training centers in Indonesia of the results in (3) above. As such this forecast should include the areas of specializations, levels of accounting, and respective bodies of knowledge required.

This comprehensive study should help us in shaping our future practice and educational direction. We feel that such a manpower survey is important for a developing economy like Indonesia in allocating our financial and manpower resources in an effective and efficient way, and linking our accountancy with our future socioeconomic requirements. It is important, however, that the agency or firm, undertaking such a study is clear about the objectives, scope and content of such a survey. Specific terms of reference (TOR) are to be spelled out with such an institution based on competitive bidding. Such TOR's are to cover all elements and procedures to be covered.

4. Governmental accountancy and auditing reform.

Previously we indicated the need for a good governmental accounting system and their reforms taking place in Indonesia. Let me elaborate on a few points.

An array of accounting and auditing activities is carried out in the public sector to enable the government to comply with constitutional and legal requirements governing collection and use of public funds. All government departments and agencies maintain accounts of their receipt and use of funds, accounts which are routinely audited by their internal audit staff under the supervision of each department's or agency's Inspector General. External audits of government departments' and agencies' accounts are carried out by the Supreme Audit Board (BPK), which reports directly to Parliament. A parallel audit agency for the executive branch of government, the Financial and Development Supervisory Board (BPKP), functions as the government's internal auditor.

Central control of government expenditures is vested in the Ministry of Finance's Directorate General for Budgetary Affairs. This Directorate General is responsible for ensuring that cumulative expenditures of government departments and agencies under each budget category are consistent with budget allocations in the annual budget law.

The MOF's State Financial Accounting Center is responsible for maintaining consolidated accounts of all central government expenditures and revenues and for reporting them to Parliament in the form of the Annual Budget Realization Report.

In addition to central government ministries and agencies, public sector accounting functions are carried out by other levels of government and by public enterprises. There are four levels of government below the central government: (a) provinces (27 in number), (b) regencies and municipalities (294), (c) subdistricts (3,500), and (d) villages (58,000). All have their own budgets; most can levy taxes and charges; and most have their own secretariats, including accounting staff. There is a complex flow of budgetary transfers within this government hierarchy—typically, from top to bottom. And there is an equally complex flow of accounting and auditing information in the reverse direction, principally for the purpose of documenting and justifying budget authorization and payments. At least 400,000 civil servants are employed in regional government administration at various levels. It is logical to presume that about half this number is engaged in accounting functions of some description.

There are also over 200 public enterprises at the national level, and a much larger number of small enterprises managed by regional governments. Together, they constitute an important part of the productive sector, accounting for about 25 percent of national fixed capital formation and a roughly similar share of national value added.

The governmental financial administration system is complex, and government accounting practices had failed to keep pace with the increased size and complexity of the government's financial transactions since independence. They had fallen behind the private sector, where more modern accounting practices were being adopted. Moreover, government accounting practices had not developed beyond their historical role of measuring compliance with mandated budget allocations. In particular, they had not evolved to reflect the newer functions of accounting as an instrument of performance efficiency and effectiveness, widely adopted elsewhere both in public administration and in the private sector.

Our Accountancy Development Project also focused on this area, and major efforts have been carried out since the start of our project to improve the system, with the assistance of a great number of outside consultants. Our governmental training institute (STAN) is heavily involved in training and updating personnel for the public sector (as conveyed under our section on education). The government operates its own school for Government Accounting Education and Training (STAN) which has programs at both the technician and the fully qualified registered accountant level. Staff development will provide for graduate level study overseas at both the master's and Ph.D. levels.

Let us briefly touch upon the agency, of which I am Executive Secretary, and my Agency is playing an important role in coordinating all these activities.
5. The Coordinating Agency for Accounting Development.

Tim Koordinasi Pengembangan Akuntansi [Coordinating Agency for Accounting Development or TKPA/CAAD] was formed in 1985 by a joint de-

cree of the Ministry of Finance and the Ministry of Education and Culture. The agency is responsible to both ministries through its steering committee which includes senior officials from both ministries. The Coordinating Agency for Accounting Development is a unique agency created specifically to coordinate and stimulate accounting development.

TKPA has a broad and sweeping mandate with respect to fostering improvement of accounting standards, practices, and education in both the private and the public sectors. TKPA itself is primarily concerned with acting as a think tank and change agent as well as providing a coordination and information role.

From 1985 to 1988 the activities of TKPA were financed by the government of Indonesia and were almost exclusively concerned with planning the Accountancy Development Project. During the period 1988-1994 the financing of TKPA is through the Accountancy Development Project [ADP] funded by the World Bank and the government of Indonesia. Within that project, specific program areas relating to education and culture are managed through the Ministry of Education and Culture. Governmental and private sector programs are managed through the Ministry of Finance. TKPA is responsible for stimulating planning evaluation and monitoring the entire range of development activities in accounting within Indonesia.

In our opinion, any country that seeks to improve its whole accountancy structure and process should be sure that all components are well coordinated. Moreover, underlying all this is the need for a clear and comprehensive feasibility study, which may take between one to two years to set forth specifically—by all elements to be covered—the nature, required changes, impact and costs/benefits of such program activities. International and regional development agencies (such as the World Bank, ADB and UN) will be pleased to assist in such feasibility studies.

As we hopefully made clear, our Accountancy Development Project is an ambitious, long-term project to implement a defined program of improvements in the accounting and auditing infrastructure of the country. It is divided into components dealing with education and components dealing with practice. It also provides the funding for the ongoing activities of TKPA/CAAD.

The present planning and funding horizon is to December 31, 1994. The funding of the five-year project is U.S. $165 million financed jointly by the government of Indonesia and the World Bank. We do hope to have a second project, a continuation of many components, also jointly financed between our government and the World Bank. We feel we still have a sizable road ahead of us to improve our accountancy and auditing systems at all levels and areas in a viable way, and to link it with our rapidly growing economic development requirements.

INDONESIA'S EDUCATIONAL STRUCTURE AT THE ACADEMIC LEVEL

The national education policy is set by the Ministry of Education and Culture, and accounting education must follow the national policy. To remedy deficiencies in education, it has been decided to standardize the education system with the main goal of increasing educational productivity.

Uniformity of accounting education was decided in 1975, and at the higher education level was followed in 1979 by the new degree and nondegree programmes, with associated changes in the curricula and syllabi. The main objective of uniformity in accounting education is to ensure that accountants produced are of the same standard throughout the country. However, the changes in the higher education level have not yet been followed by adjustment at the elementary and secondary levels nor in nonformal education.

Changes in secondary and nonformal education must be brought into line with the principal educational policies at the higher education or professional levels. The administrative officials are aware that this has not yet occurred, because changes to education programmes at certain levels could not be achieved as quickly as the policy makers had intended. The general and accounting educational structures are shown in Figure 1.

According to the Decree of the Ministry of Education and Culture in 1979 and 1982, and higher education system has been divided into degree and nondegree programmes. The accounting education programme at the Faculties of Economics of state and private universities must be a degree programme. The accounting programme at state institutes or private organizations must be a nondegree programme. The cumulative credit hours and length of study can be seen in Table 1.

At present, only Gadjah Mada university has an S2 programme in accountancy with an emphasis on management accounting. This programme began in 1984 to 1985.

There are more than 48 state or public universities, polytechnics and teacher training institutes providing higher education, and more than 200 other universities, institutes and academies operated by government departments and private organizations. The rough estimate of the total student body in higher education all over the country is approximately 1,000,000 students.

The numbers of universities, institutes and academies which offer accounting programmes are:

1. State universities and institutes: 14
2. Private universities and institutes: 25
3. Polytechnics: 6
4. Academies of accountancy: 40

Total 85

In 1988, three new departments of accountancy were opened at state universities, and three other polytechnic commerce schools have been built in other cities. Based on Act No.34/1954, state universities and institutes can educate accountants, and private universities and institutes which have been approved by the Directorate General of Higher Education can educate accountants through preprofessional and professional examinations offered by the Board of Consortium of Economic Sciences.

The Indonesian government and the accounting profession are currently under great pressure

TABLE 1
Credit Hours and Length of Study
Degree and Nondegree Programme

No.	Degree	Nondegree Credit Hours	Cumulative Study	Length of (Year)
1	–	D I	40-50	1-2
2	–	D II	80-90	2-3
3	–	D III	110-120	3-5
4	S1	D IV	144-160	4-7
5	S2 (Master)	Sp I	180-194	6-9
6	S3 (Ph.D.)	Sp II	228-233	8-11

Notes: D = Diploma Sp = Specialist S = Stratum

FIGURE 1
General and Accounting Education Structure in Indonesia

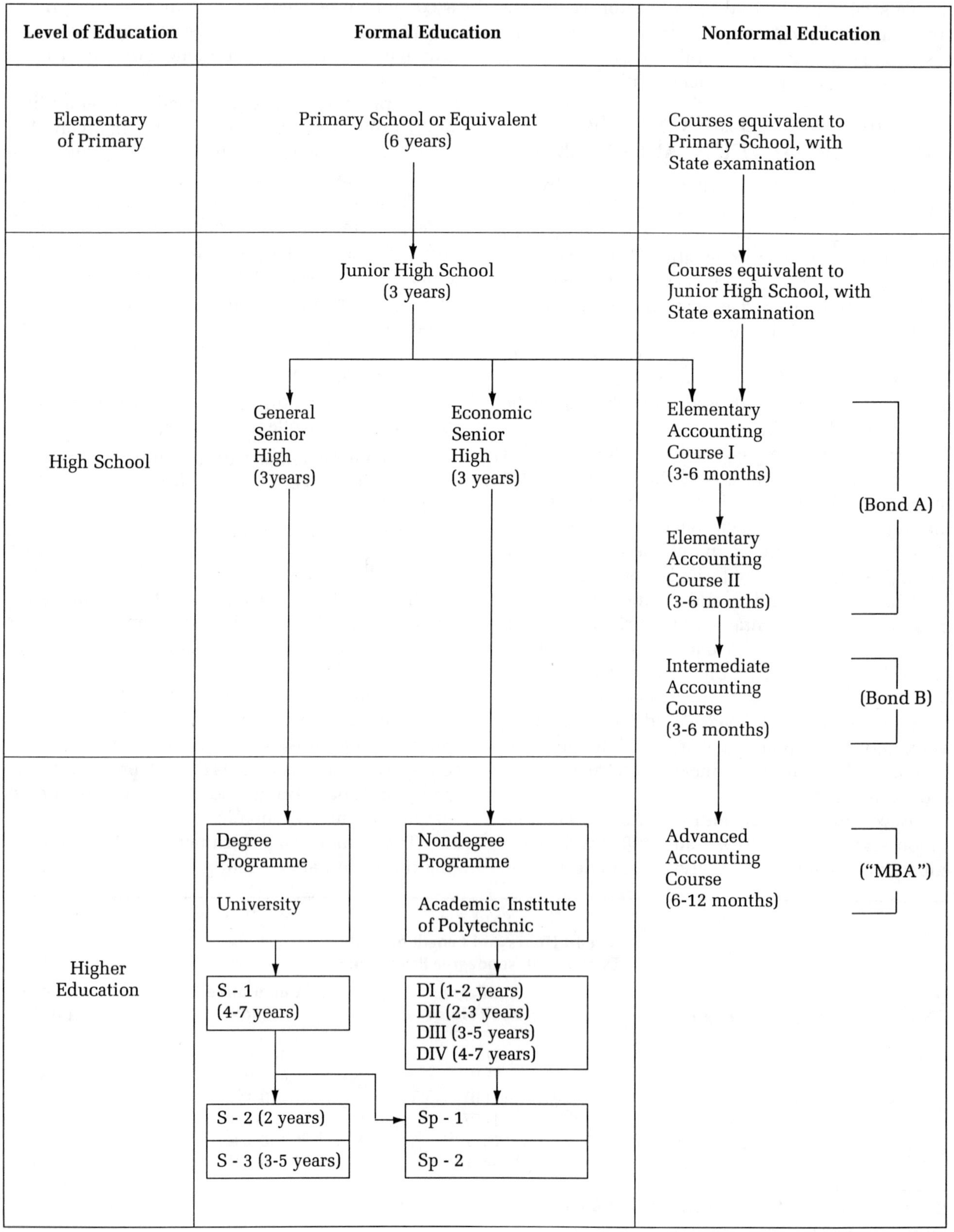

to meet the demands which challenge them. They have suffered from a shortage of qualified accounting personnel, despite the considerable increase in numbers as a result of accounting education at the higher education level. However, quantity of accountants is not the only problem. Many of them qualified years ago and developments in the discipline have been rapid. Improving the standards, technical skills, and overall professional competence of the existing stock of accountants seems a difficult task. It is a challenge to the individuals as well as to the profession and to the government.

There has been a policy of economic liberalization since 1966. The oil boom in the 1970s and the decline in oil revenues in 1982 to 1983 led to a marked weakening of the foreign exchange reserves, triggering a comprehensive adjustment effort. New financial reforms were undertaken by the Indonesian government beginning in June 1983, with the abolition of interest rate controls and ceilings by the Central Bank, a change in the Central Bank's funding role, and the introduction of new money market instruments. These measures were introduced together with a large devaluation, tax reform, and streamlining of public sector investment and subsidy programmes. The government has enforced the recent economic policy by deregulation of major economic sectors, which are now much more liberal and open to market forces.

Changes include new banking and financial institution systems and revised capital market requirements and regulations. All of these changes have forced the accounting profession to play a bigger role in economic development.

To create professional accountants who are able to fulfill the needs of development, a strong, systematic and professional approach to their education and training is required. Such a system must be developed at all levels: the basic elementary, the high school, higher education, and continuing professional education. The development of accounting education and professional education must be implemented on a long-range planning basis, regardless of the economic conditions. To achieve optimum results, these must be based on sound short-term and long-term planning.

The strategy of accounting development in Indonesia has been set up following the establishment of CAAD in 1985. The main objectives are twofold: firstly, to develop accounting education at various levels; secondly, to develop professional accounting in both governmental and private sectors. Measures to be taken by CAAD as part of the development plan

are: to improve accounting standards and practices, to organize the application of accounting standards and practices in stages, and to develop a uniform and unified accounting education system.

The construction of the strategy considered the existing conditions in accounting education and in the profession, the need to integrate the accounting profession with education, and anticipated developments in the socioeconomic environment. The main points of the strategy for accounting development are mentioned below.

1. There is an integrated plan to develop accounting education and the accounting profession, in order to maximize the use of the limited expertise available, and to promote efficiency in using facilities and infrastructures.

2. Planning for education is twofold:

   a. Short range planning:

      (1) To improve educational programmes in an integrated system at various levels of education, including stages of education, curricula and syllabi, as well as textbooks, computers, and other references.

      (2) To promote and upgrade the quality of teachers, lecturers and other educators at all levels through workshops, internship programmes and scholarships, either domestic or abroad.

      (3) To increase educational facilities, including libraries, books, computers and other services.

   b. Long-range planning:

      (1) To stabilize the orientation of accounting education through scientific research.

      (2) To develop postgraduate programmes (master's and Ph.D. degrees) in accounting.

      (3) To promote cooperation and coordination with and between universities and educational institutions, nationally and internationally.

      (4) To promote research in accounting for development.

3. At the professional level, there are two aspects:

   a. Short-range planning:

      (1) To promote and reorganize the professional institutes in order to perform their duties better than before.

(2) To make improvements in some specific areas where early action is required. These areas include the governmental accounting systems, internship and training systems for government accounting trainers, the accounting and reporting requirements of the capital market, accounting principles, auditing standards, code of ethics, and continuing professional education.

(3) To review the existing laws and regulations relating to the profession and work cooperatively with the government for their modernization.

b. Long-range planning:

(1) To promote cooperation, coordination and integration between professional institutes in accounting and other closely related professional fields.

(2) To promote cooperation and coordination between the Indonesian accounting profession and their regional and international counterparts.

(3) To promote the role of the IAI in the community by increasing empirical research

into accounting practice, publications, improving relations with government agencies and legislative bodies, as well as by continuously improving the level of competence of its members.

(4) The crucial role of government is acknowledged. The government has included accounting development in the National Economic Development Plan. The establishment of CAAD was a governmental initiative. Government will continue to play a decisive role in both the educational and the professional levels.

CONCLUSION

In this brief outline I hopefully conveyed the need to undertake a systematic and comprehensive approach towards the accountancy development in a rapidly developing economy. It requires the coordination with many sectors and departments in the government and with private industry and the accounting profession. A coordinating agency, as we have in Indonesia, to link all these elements is essential. We believe we have been successful in Indonesia, but we still have a long way to go.

Accounting Education in the Perspective of Economic Development in India: In Retrospect and Prospect

OBJECTIVES OF ACCOUNTING EDUCATION IN THE PERSPECTIVE OF ECONOMIC DEVELOPMENT

The modern economic activities are characterised by complicated organisational systems the management of which calls for a large amount of quantitative information. The uncertainties that are found in the operations of modern enterprises require advance planning which is becoming more and more sophisticated. The type of information required and the nature of uses to which accounting and other quantitative information are being put these days have become so varied that specialised training is required.

In the developing countries such as India, there is a constant endeavour in promoting large-scale development of industries and infrastructure required for such industries. For this purpose it is necessary to mobilise all the available resources and put them to the optimum use. There is thus the need to absorb the latest innovations in science and technology for faster growth. Though the accounting profession has been rendering a useful service to the community in the above-mentioned spheres of activity in India, there is scope for further improvement. These can be achieved by the adoption of more sophisticated management techniques which are the outcomes of a good education system.

The objectives of accounting education should therefore be (1) development of human resources in this particular area in keeping with societal needs (2) help in solving business problems at the micro and macro levels. Many developing countries the educational system is geared towards financial reporting. Accounting education, he argues, should take into account socioeconomic objectives and provide the necessary tools for economic development.

INTERNATIONAL ACCOUNTING INFLUENCES AND CHANGES

Some important changes have taken place in the international socioeconomic field in recent years. These have bearing on accounting and hence on accounting education in a country. The important changes are:[1] (1) Third World economic development, (2) regionalisation and internationalisation, (3) growth of multinational enterprises, (4) involvement of the public (government) sector in accounting operations, (5) social responsibility awareness and (6) international communication. Now nations throughout the world are moving closer together regionally and internationally. These regional and international activities require better economic-financial data identification, collection, measurement, processing and reporting. The growth of multinational enterprises has also changed international accounting demands. The public sector has been playing a significant role in many developing economies in the world.[2] There has therefore been a growing attempt towards closer supervision, regulation, and control by governments of financial measurement and disclosure.[3]

It is true that in keeping with the above international influences, accounting modifications and improvements are taking place in many countries to cater to the changing socioeconomic conditions and demands. But the responses very often come late to the challenges posed.

ACCOUNTING EDUCATION IN INDIA

In the above perspective, we now briefly discuss accounting education in India. We first give a

---

[1]Adolf J. H. Enthoven, Accounting Education — its Importance and Requirements — An Economic Development Focus, Fifth International Conference on Accounting Education, 1982, pp. 4–11.

[2]India has developed a gigantic public sector whose contribution in the country's economic development is phenomenal.

[3]B. Banerjee and D. K. Chakraborty, "Regulation of Accounting in India — An Overview," *Research Bulletin*, ICWAI, January and July , 1988, pp. 56–65.

Bhabatosh Banerjee is at the University of Calcutta.

brief account of the same during the preindependence period. We then describe the developments during the postindependence (1947) period both in respect to professional education and academic education. This is followed by a discussion on perspectives for further development.

ACCOUNTING EDUCATION IN THE PRE-INDEPENDENCE PERIOD—A BRIEF ACCOUNT

India was under British Rule for about 200 years. So its education system was greatly influenced by the British system. But until the Companies Act of 1913, the audit of the company accounts by qualified accountants was not made compulsory. At that time there were a few qualified accountants in the country. These accountants got their required training and certificate for practice from the Chartered Institutes in the United Kingdom and Canada. Within a few years, the Government of Bombay instituted a scheme of awarding Government Diploma in Accountancy (G.D.A.) on passing the prescribed qualifying examination and on completion of articleship of three years under an approved accountant in practice. This scheme was approved by the Government of India in 1919. But the number of persons enrolled as G.D.A. from 1919 to 1932 does not indicate popularity of the diploma course.[4] In 1932 the Indian Accountancy Board was constituted and the Auditors Certificate Rules were promulgated. These rules prescribed a two-tier examination system known as Registered Public Accountants (RPA) Examination. The G.D.A. Examination was stopped in 1934. The Accountancy Board kept functioning in an advisory capacity to the Governor General in Council. The accountancy profession made some headway under the Accountancy Board. During the period 1933 to 1947, 10,739 professional accountants were enrolled.[5]

Over the years, need for an autonomous association to administer and regulate the profession of accounting was felt. After World War II, the Accountancy Board accepted the stand for autonomisation of the profession and pressed for necessary action by the Government.

DEVELOPMENTS OF ACCOUNTING EDUCATION: THE ROLE OF PROFESSIONAL INSTITUTES

It was only after independence that the Commerce Ministry, Government of India, appointed an Expert Committee to examine the scheme. Ulti-

mately, in 1949, the Institute of Chartered Accountants of India (ICAI) was formed, pursuant to the provisions of the Chartered Accountants Act of 1949 as an autonomous body of the first accounting profession in India. In 1959 the Institute of Cost and Works Accountants of India (ICWAI) was formed by an Act of Parliament.

In order to assess the effectiveness of the two professional institutes, let us examine separately for each Institute the trend in the enrollment of students as one of the measures of its popularity over a period of about three decades, and growth in membership as a criterion for providing qualified accountants to serve the growing demand from different sectors of the economy.

The Role of the Institute of Chartered Accountants of India (ICAI)

The Chartered Accountancy Examination conducted by ICAI is now divided into three parts: Entrance or Foundation, Intermediate and Final. In 1949, it was divided into only two parts — First Examination and Final Examination. Initially, the entry qualification to the C.A. course was graduation. Over the years, the entry qualification has been changed to 10+2 standard[6] with a provision for a Foundation Course under the proposed scheme. Presently, admission to the Entrance Examination is restricted to a graduate or one undergoing the graduation course. Commerce graduates securing not less than 50 percent marks and other graduates securing not less than 55 percent marks may take up the Intermediate Course directly. Coaching has been made compulsory since 1956. The first Preliminary Examination was held in November 1956. The qualifying marks in each of the two Intermediate and Final Examinations have been prescribed at 50 percent. The Institute requires articleship for a period of three years as a precondition to successful entry into the profession.

Let us now look at the response from the students since 1949 for professional courses. Table 1 shows that while the number of students entering the profession has grown considerably over the

---

[4]G. P. Kapadia, *History of the Accountancy Profession in India*, ICAI, 1973, p. 316.

[5]Kapadia, pp. 456-7.

[6]At present, the basic structure of education in India is generally 10+2+3, that is, 10 years of schooling, 2 years for higher secondary education in schools and colleges and 3 years for graduation in colleges.

TABLE 1
Students Enrolled for C.A. Courses

Year	Students Enrolled Annually	Average Annual Increase	
		Number	Rate (%)
1949–50	257	—	—
1964–65	2,822	171	11.76
1969–70	2,915	19	0.66
1974–75	3,464	110	3.51
1979–80	10,133	1,334	21.75
1983–84	8,660	(-) 368	(-) 3.84
1987–88	12,753	1,023	10.06
1988–89	13,990	1,237	9.70
1989–90	13,305	(-) 685	(-) 4.90
1990–91	12,791	(-) 514	(-) 3.86
Compound Annual Growth Rate	—	—	10.7

Source: Annual Reports of the ICAI.

years the growth rate has not at all been consistent. The entry to the profession is partly dependent on number of students graduating in various disciplines. Among the various disciplines commerce graduates are predominant. A random sample of members' qualifications shows that about 85 percent of the members have a commerce background. The fast growth in the number of students can be attributed to the growth in commerce as a discipline at the graduation level during this period.

Regarding growth in membership, Table 2 summarises the position since 1950 at five-year intervals (with the exception of first two years). A membership of 1,685 in 1949–50 has at the end of 1990–91 increased by 35 times to 58,998. The annual compound growth rate has been 9.1 percent. From the above trend, it appears that the profession will be having many more members at the turn of the present century. For example, taking a little lower annual compound growth rate, say 7 percent, the membership of the Institute is expected to reach 1,11,200 by 2000 A.D.

The growth in the profession does not depend on input alone — the availability of gainful opportunities to the output is another vital factor that

TABLE 2
Members of ICAI

As on (1 April)	No. of Chartered Accountants	Average Annual Increase	
		Number	(%)
1950	1,685	—	—
1951	1,948	263	15.6
1956	3,379	286	11.7
1961	4,942	313	7.9
1966	7,332	478	8.2
1971	11,227	779	8.9
1976	16,763	1,107	8.4
1981	25,438	1,735	8.7
1986	40,278	2,968	9.6
1988	49,324	4,523	10.7
1989	53,134	3,810	7.7
1990	56,573	3,439	6.5
1991	58,998	2,425	4.3
Compound Annual Growth Rate	—	—	9.1

Source: Annual Reports of ICAI.
Note: Chartered Accountants include both the categories — those who are in service and those who are in practise.

contributes to growth. As far as the gainful opportunities for the output are concerned, there are two avenues — statutory practice avenues as auditor and employment opportunities as accountant. Based on the joint stock companies at work in the last three decades, the number of companies per chartered accountant is shown in Table 3.

About 67 percent, on an average, of the chartered accountants are in practice while the remaining 33 percent are in service or otherwise. It has been observed that in the past an annual growth rate of about 3.8 percent in the economy and that of 6 to 7 percent in the industrial sector have been adequate to absorb without any difficulty an annual compound growth of about 9 percent in the number of chartered accountants.[7] The government has been envisaging a much higher growth rate now which may seem to be adequate for absorbing the projected growth in the membership.

The Role of the Institute of Cost and Works Accountants of India (ICWAI)

In India, a company limited by guarantee, and known as Institute of Cost and Works Accountants, was set up in 1944 with the objects of promoting, regulating and developing the profession of cost and management accountancy. Under the Cost and Works Accountants Act, 1959, the Institute of Cost and Works Accountants of India (ICWAI) came into being on 28 May, 1959.

The cost accountancy examination is now divided into three parts: Preliminary, Intermediate and Final. Initially, it was divided into two parts only — Intermediate and Final. The entry qualification is now graduation but with a 10+2, one can take it with a preliminary examination. Like ICAI examinations, the qualifying marks have been fixed

at 50 percent. Coaching, postal or oral, has also been made compulsory. Although no prequalification articleship is necessary, one is to have an experience of at least three years in the industry for admission into Institute's membership.

The students' response for the course as measured by the enrollments of students may be shown in Table 4. From the students' point of view, the cost accountancy course has some distinct advantages over the other professional course, viz., taking the course while in employment, pursuing other courses simultaneously, no bar on upper age limit, no compulsory training. In spite of these, the response from the students does not appear to be convincing. One reason might be very low success rate among the students. For example, the percentage of students completing costing examination (Final) to the number registered over the period, 1968–72 to 1984–86, was only 2.76.[8] The low success rate is also corroborated by the number of members of the Institute. Table 5 shows the profile for members of the Institute since 1944. The compound rate of growth has been 13.6 percent. Taking a little lower compound rate of growth, say 10 percent growth factor, the number of members expected at 2000 A.D. may be estimated at 23,300. This number may be considered to be inadequate in view of the rate of growth of joint stock companies in the country. In India, maintenance of cost records [sec. 209 (1) (d)] and audit thereof [sec. 233-

---

[7]K. Gupta, "The Profession in 2001 A.D. — A Quantitative Profile," *The Chartered Accountant*, March 1982: 595.

[8]D. C. Bajaj and K. M. Pranamurthy, *Cost and Management Accountancy in Free India — Retrospect and Prospect*, 30th National Convention of ICWAI, 1988, P.C. 4.3.

TABLE 3
Avenues of Practice by Chartered Accountants

Year	No. of Companies	No. of C. A. in Practice	Companies per C. A. in Practice
1961	26,149	3,380	7.7
1971	30,322	7,421	4.1
1981	62,714	16,636	3.8
1986	1,22,159	28,772	4.2
1988	1,56,500	33,540	4.6
1989	1,77,730	39,002	4.6
1990	1,98,553	41,456	4.8
1991	2,20,721	43,426	5.1

Source: Company News and Notes, Government of India, and Annual Reports of ICAI.

TABLE 4
Students Enrolled for ICWAI Examinations

Year	No. of Students Enrolled	Annual Growth	
		No.	%
1968–69	7,068	—	—
1973–74	13,783	1,343	14.3
1978–79	22,278	1,699	10.1
1983–84	37,856	3,116	11.1
1984–85	25,062	(-)12,794	(-) 34
1985–86	18,744	(-) 6,318	(-) 25
1986–87	18,344	(-) 300	(-) 2
1987–88	21,065	2,721	15
1988–89	20,458	(-) 607	(-) 2.9
1989–90	22,333	1,875	9.2
1990–91	25,686	3,353	15.0
Compound Annual Growth Rate	—	—	6.0

Source: Annual Reports of ICWAI.

TABLE 5
Membership Profile of ICWAI

Year	Total Members	Average Annual Growth	
		No.	%
1944	25	—	—
1960	433	26	20.9
1970	2,272	184	18.4
1980	4,804	253	7.8
1985	6,018	242	4.6
1986	6,405	387	6.4
1987	6,853	448	7.0
1988	7,438	585	8.5
1989	8,035	597	8.0
1990	8,643	608	7.6
1991	9,869	1,226	14.2
Compound Annual Growth Rate	—	—	13.6

Source: Annual Report of ICWAI. About 12% represents those holding certificate of practise.

B] has been made compulsory for selected industries/companies. Up to 31 March 1991, 37 industries have been brought under the purview of maintenance of necessary cost records. There were 5,367 companies for which a cost audit was ordered for the 10 years from 1977 to 1987. The demand for cost auditor is therefore likely to increase in the coming years.[9]

ACCOUNTING EDUCATION AT THE COLLEGE AND UNIVERSITY LEVELS

In India, accounting education at the college and university levels is offered generally as part of the graduate (B. Com.) and the postgraduate (M. Com.) programme in Commerce. Prior to indepen-dence, the British system dominated the commerce education in the country. Professional education, as stated earlier, played a more important role in the field of accounting education. Accounting was nowhere recognised as a separate discipline. A few premier Indian universities, viz., Bombay, Madras and Calcutta Universities, used to impart commerce education to serve the vocational needs of trade and industry. This attempt was, however, sporadic in nature. In some cases, commerce courses were more or less ancillary to the economics courses. In most academic institutions, the number of full-time

[9]B. C. Ghosh, W. C. Yoong, and B. Banerjee, Mandatory Audit of Cost Accountancy — An Indian Experiment, Pan Pacific Conference VI, Sydney, 1989.

teachers was far less than the part-time or guest lecturers who were mainly professional accountants. This naturally stood in the way of proper development of commerce education in the country.

The position, however, changed after independence particularly since 1960s. In early 1970s the universities began recognising the lacunae in the commerce curriculum in the light of new demands on accounting education that emerged and started the process of restructuring their courses. Accountancy was included as a core subject at all levels — higher secondary, undergraduate and postgraduate courses. There is, however, a great deal of diversity among the course structure and course content from university to university.

There are a number of problems (structural and environmental) of the present college and university education systems. The important ones are outlined below.

1. Excluding a few universities in Northern and Western India, India does not have a separate discipline of accounting education as distinct from commerce education as is prevalent in most of the developed countries.

2. The more brilliant and ambitious of the student community generally pursue careers in engineering or medicine and, as a result, business studies, in general, attract only the second best.

3. Accounting courses are heavily problem-oriented stressing more on computational skills and procedural aspects and less on conceptional aspects or on decision situations. There is little coordination at different levels of education — secondary, higher secondary, undergraduate and post-graduate levels.

4. College and university libraries are not well equipped with adequate number of text and reference books.

5. Teaching methodology is not scientific in that it depends predominantly on lecturing and problem solving, the latter taking away even as much as 80 percent of the class time.

6. There is no scope for providing practical training in accounting areas at the graduate or postgraduate level due to low rapport with industry and business.

Keeping in view some of the above problems, the University Grants Commission (UGC) is now giving more attention to improvement of the state of commerce education in the country. More financial assistance, recurring and nonrecurring, is being given to colleges and universities. With a view to improving the teaching methodology it has, of late, formed six nodal academic staff colleges (one each in Andhra Pradesh, Assam, Delhi, Pondicherry, Rajasthan and West Bengal) to impart periodical training to commerce teachers. For reducing diversity in course structure and contents among different universities, it organised a seminar in Delhi in April 1989 to suggest a model course structure both for B. Com. and M. Com. together with some P. G. Diploma courses. Perhaps more such seminars may be useful in arriving at a greater consensus on this crucial issue.

RESEARCH IN ACCOUNTING

Research is considered as the key to developments in any education system. It may be of a basic and applied nature. Although there is wide scope for research in accounting in Indian universities, efforts made at different quarters so far do not show an encouraging picture. According to a survey made by Indian Council of Social Science Research (ICSSR) in 1976, completed research projects and doctoral theses awarded by Indian universities in accounting and allied areas were only 25 in number.[10] The position, however, changed significantly in late 70s and early 80s. Table 6 shows the relative position of research in accounting vis-à-vis that in commerce and management from 1975–76 to 1985–86. Until 1990 out of 326 dissertations in commerce and management only 57 relate to accounting (including auditing and finance). There are some problems in this area too. Some of them are as follows.

First, teachers are given very little incentive in terms of lesser work load and infrastructural support. Shortage of faculty, inadequate space, and nonavailability of adequate funds generally stand in the way. Second, publications of these are few and far between. Third, there is a lack of proper coordination between industry and academic institutions, the result being that there is very little effort for application of the theory/knowledge into practice. Industry response for supplying data and for funding research projects is not worth mentioning.

PERSPECTIVES FOR FURTHER DEVELOPMENTS

In regard to the nature and type of present accounting education and its problems, as outlined

---

[10]S. K. R. Bhandari, *A Survey of Research in Accounting Theory*, (ICSSR, 1976), pp. 22–24.

TABLE 6
State of Research in Accounting vis-à-vis Researches in Commerce and Management during 1975–76 to 1985–86

Year (1)	Ph.D.s Awarded in Management (2)	Ph.D.s Awarded in Commerce (3)	Total Ph.D.s Awarded Cols. (2) + (3) (4)	Ph.D.s Awarded in Accountancy (5)	Percentage of Accounting Ph.D.s to total Ph.D.s (6)
1975–76	10	15	25	5	20.0
1976–77	23	27	50	12	24.0
1977–78	42	29	71	13	18.3
1978–79	42	32	74	13	17.6
1979–80	37	20	57	11	19.3
1980–81	43	34	77	11	14.3
1981–82	59	37	96	15	15.6
1982–83	54	29	83	14	17.0
1983–84	65	35	100	19	19.0
1984–85	64	28	92	18	19.6
1985–86	77	30	107	20	19.0

Source: ICSSR Dissertation Abstracts, 1975–76 to 1986–87.
Results Computed.

in the previous paragraphs, a few suggestions may be made for its improvement. Some *structural changes* are required to be made. At the postgraduate level, separate accounting departments should be formed under the College of Business Studies to impart accounting education. Present postgraduate courses in most universities allow interested students to take professional courses simultaneously or after completing the study. At the university level, we should no longer serve as feeder organisations to professional institutes. In designing future courses, more attention should be given to the conceptual *foundation* of the accounting subjects. The postgraduate courses should be meant for those only who want to either enter the teaching profession or subsequently to pursue research for doctoral degree. In order to ensure effective teaching, the present practice of having more than 100 students per section in some universities should be discontinued and the *number* should be restricted to 50. New universities may be set up to cope with the increasing number of students.

A better coordination among curricula framing bodies at different levels is desirable. The curricula up to graduate level should be designed in such a way that it partly meets the requirements of the professional institutes and partly the requirements of higher education in that those who will come out successful at the graduation level may either pursue higher education or may shift for professional qualification. At the postgraduate level, the curricula should put more emphasis on theoretical and research aspects.

Another important aspect relates to teaching *methodology*. In teaching, *what* and *how* questions are important. Therefore, a deliberate *plan* of how to perform the teaching functions could contribute to *teaching effectiveness*. There should, therefore, be proper course planning for accounting education right from the higher secondary level. The audiovisual systems should be introduced. Group discussions, debates, quizes, seminars, workshops and continuing education should also be part and parcel of the education programme.

Accounting education should be consistent with national and international developments and environments. As accounting training will find itself increasingly part of the total socioeconomic scene, it also needs to respond to dynamic changes and to be future oriented. Research of a basic and applied nature in accounting will have to be viewed as the key to future developments and improvements. Continuing education should also become a major part of accounting education. To frame the structure and curriculum of accounting education accordingly, a few suggestions may be made as follows.

There is widespread lack of attention to *international accounting issues* in the present accounting curriculum in India. Greater emphasis on *accounting standards* should also be given in the course structure so as to make accounting measurements more precise, more credible and more comparable. Certain other areas of accounting like *human resource accounting* (HRA) and *social accounting* (SA) should also be incorporated. Other areas that require proper attention are *management accounting and financial management*. In a developing country resources are scarce and they are required to be allocated to the priority sector(s) for balanced development of the economy. Introduction of proper management accounting techniques in government activities would result in a much better management of the economy. During the last few years there has been considerable change in the policy of the government with regard to installation and *use of computers* in government and semigovernment organisations. But we do not have an adequate number of trained accountants to handle the situation. This should also be taken care of.

There is total lack of emphasis being given to the agricultural sector which provides food to the 70 percent of the country's population. Thus, the areas of *farm accounting, farm management,* and *farm costing* can no longer be left out of the accounting courses in India. Another area to be developed is *accounting and management problems of the unorganised sector* in the economy. This sector is represented by small and cottage units and self-employed professionals. Another important area that requires careful consideration is the *public sector accounting*. In India, the public sector employs about 67 percent of the workers and 79 percent of the paid-up capital employed in the organised sector. The existing accounting education and training method given by the professional institutes and universities suit the requirements of the private sector better than those of the public sector. A change in outlook with consequential changes in syllabi and training methods is also a necessity of the day.

The Impact of Accounting Education on Economic Development in the Caribbean

Robertine A. Chaderton

INTRODUCTION

Background

Although the West Indies Federation collapsed in 1962, various professional groups and other bodies have continued to collaborate on economic and other matters, proceeding slowly if not erratically along the road to regional unity. The Caribbean Community (CARICOM) was formed by the Treaty of Chagaramus in 1973 as a movement towards unity and to minimise the disadvantages that "smallness" imposes on development. At present it operates as a loose trading agreement between the islands. There are 13 members and three observers. Appendix 1 discloses some demographic and economic indicators of the countries. This paper deals with the CARICOM member countries in general and Barbados, Jamaica and Trinidad and Tobago in particular as those are the campus locations of the University of the West Indies (UWI).

The Institute of Chartered Accountants of Caribbean (ICAC) was incorporated in October 1988 as a limited company registered under the Companies Act of Jamaica. The regional institutes are its members. The founding members were the Institute of Chartered Accountants of the Bahamas, Barbados, Belize, Guyana, Jamaica, St. Lucia, Trinidad and Tobago. There is a board made up of one director from each territory from whom are chosen a president, vice president, secretary and treasurer. The initial project is to launch the regional professional accountancy qualification. Curriculum development and the writing of textbooks for taxation and law are the current preoccupation of select members. The aim is to produce the first examinations in 1993. Financial and other assistance has been received from the Chartered Association of Certified Accountants (CACA), the International Federation of Accountants (IFAC) and the Certified General Accountants Association of Canada (CGA).

The size and growth of the membership are seen in Table 1. The professional bodies of Jamaica, Barbados and Trinidad and Tobago are described in the remainder of this section. There are some similarities as well as differences.

Jamaica

The Institute of Chartered Accountants of Jamaica (ICAJ) was formed in 1965. Full membership to ICAJ is restricted to Jamaican citizens who pass the Institute's examination or other recognized examinations and obtain the required practical experience. The founder members of the institute were mainly members of the recognised British professional bodies — Institute of Chartered Accountants in England and Wales (ICAEW), Institute of Chartered Accountants of Scotland (ICAS), and the Chartered Association of Certified Accountants (CACA).[1] Non-Jamaicans who were ordinarily resident prior to the Institute's incorporation and who were members of certain recognised bodies were admitted to full membership. In order to unify the profession, in the early years of ICAJ, the council agreed to allow members of the Association of International Accountants, British Association of Accountants and Auditors, and the Society of Commercial Accountants to become members, if they had ten years of experience and had passed examinations in auditing, Jamaican taxation and financial reporting as set by the University of the West Indies (UWI).

There are two categories of membership of ICAJ — the associate member (CA) and the fellow (FCA). Five years of approved practical experience are required for admittance as an associate. This experience may be obtained in commerce, industry, pub-

---

[1]CACA was formerly known as the ACCA and is still referred to as such in the Caribbean; whenever this acronym is used in this paper, it means the Chartered Association of Certified Accountants.

Robertine A. Chaderton is a Lecturer in Accounting at the University of the West Indies and a member of the Institute of Chartered Accountants of Barbados.

The author acknowledges the constructive comments of colleagues at the University of Manchester. She would also like to thank the Association of Commonwealth Universities and The British Council for their support in funding her doctoral research.

TABLE 1
Professional Accountants in the Caribbean

(a) Professional Accountancy Bodies in the Caribbean

Country	Professional Body	Date of Incorporation
Antigua	Institute of Chartered Accountants of Antigua and Barbuda	
Bahamas	The Bahamas Institute of Chartered Accountants (BICA)	1971
Barbados	Institute of Chartered Accountants of Barbados (ICAB)	1974
Belize		
Grenada		
Guyana		
Jamaica	The Institute of Chartered Accountants of Jamaica (ICAJ)	1965
St. Lucia		
St. Vincent		
St. Kitts-Nevis	St. Kitts-Nevis Association of Chartered Accountants	1991
Trinidad & Tobago	The Institute of Chartered Accountants of Trinidad & Tobago (ICATT)	1970

(b) ICAC Membership

	Members of Territorial Institutes	
	December 31	
Country	1989	1991
Bahamas	202	227
Barbados	176	176
Belize	29	28
Guyana	30	40
Jamaica	450	443
St. Lucia	44	38
Trinidad & Tobago	426	413
	1,357	1,365

lic practice, the government service or a combination. A practising certificate is granted after two and a half years in a practising office. Fellowship is automatic after ten years of associate membership or five years in practice. The growth of its membership is seen in Table 2.

There are no examinations set by ICAJ, but in 1984 a joint examination scheme was established where the Institute's students are registered with and sit the exams of ACCA. At March 31, 1991, there were 1,366 (1989: 1,149) students registered with ICAJ.

The pass rate of these examinations is very low; over the period 1982–1990 only 127 persons completed level III. Preparation for the examinations is either by correspondence courses with institutions in the United Kingdom or attendance at evening classes locally. Graduates of the UWI with the B.Sc Accounting obtain exemptions on a subject-by-subject basis and may get up to eight exemptions.

In 1975 the UWI introduced an M.Sc (Accounting) at Mona in Jamaica to assist with training of professional accountants. ICAJ agreed that graduates of the M.Sc programme would be admitted to membership after a period of 30 months of approved practical experience in a firm of chartered accountants, or industry, commerce or government. The M.Sc programme covers the same subjects as the ACCA — taxation, executorship, accounting theory, auditing, as well as project evaluation and financial management, quantitative business analysis and computer applications among other subjects; the focus, however, is Caribbean (Jamaican where the legal and taxation provisions are specific). This meant that within 15 to 18 months, a graduate could be eligible to begin the work experience unlike a nongraduate who had to take at least five years. It was an innovation which ICAJ found difficult; it was not ready to hand over the approval mechanism from the United Kingdom ACCA body to UWI (Mendes 1992).

In October 1987 the ICAJ decided to withdraw recognition of the M.Sc (Accounting) and holders of the M.Sc (Accounting). After 1987/88, M.Sc

TABLE 2
Institute of Chartered Accountants of Jamaica (ICAJ)

(a) Membership Growth

	1977	1991
Fellows		
Public practice		160
Other		103
Associates		
Public practice		17
Other		116
Affiliates		
Public practice		6
Other		26
Members — overseas		18
Members — retired		5
	280	451

Source: ICAJ Newsletter, several issues

(b) ACCA/ICAJ 1990 Examination Results

	June		December		Total		
Level	Entered	Passed	Entered	Passed	Entered	Passed	%
I	296	34	257	17	553	51	9
II	405	22	428	26	833	48	6
III	40	9	52	8	92	17	18
Total	741	65	737	51	1,478	116	8

Source: Institute of Chartered Accountants of Jamaica 1991 Annual Report

Accounting graduates are required to pass or be exempted from the ICAJ qualifying examination. The designated areas for the ICAJ qualifying examination are financial management, advanced financial accounting, auditing and investigation, tax and tax management, and company law. Pending the introduction of this qualifying examination, the ICAJ has decided to use Level 3 of ACCA as its qualifying examination. Some of the holders of the M.Sc (Accounting) degree avoid the ACCA route by registering with an American state (usually Colorado), which accepts non–USA residents as students and they write the CPA examination.

Barbados

Unlike Jamaica, the Barbados Institute of Chartered Accountants (ICAB) comprises persons who have obtained a professional qualification from any of the recognised overseas bodies 1-9 listed in Appendix 3 and five years of approved accountancy experience. The Council of ICAB issues practising certificates to some of its members who satisfy certain prerequisites. ICAB was incorporated in 1971 and its membership has grown as seen in Table 3.

ICAB is also unique in the region in that the 1982 Companies Act gave it the right to determine who can be appointed as an auditor.[2] It also gave the international accounting standards (IAS) legal backing since the responsibility for setting standards applicable to financial statements has been placed on ICAB. ICAB has adopted certain IAS.

ICAB's joint examination scheme with ACCA started in 1981. Preparation for the ACCA is like correspondence courses with institutions in the United Kingdom and the use of the Open Learning Material recently introduced by the ACCA. The exam results were as poor as those of Jamaica (Table 2). The local chapter of the CGA through a private organisation offers courses that take the form of 12-week self-study sessions with tutorials. Many persons have switched to the CGA although the fees are higher, since there is the contact with tutors and higher completion rate. The local chapter of the CMA formerly offered preparation by the same method; now that a degree is a prerequisite for registration in the CMA program, a new arrangement

---

[2]The Barbados Companies Act 1982-54, sec 153 (2), (3).

TABLE 3
Institute of Chartered Accountants of Barbados (ICAB)

(a) Membership Profile

	82/04/30	89/04/30	91/04/30
UK Designation			
ACCA		87	91
ICAEW		20	27
ICMA		4	2
ICAS		2	1
		113	122
Canadian Designation			
CA		18	24
CGA		17	32
CMA		10	68
		45	68
American Designation			
CPA		2	5
	90	160	195

Source: ICAB Annual Report: Several years.

(b) ICAB/ACCA Examination Results, Selected Years

	1985	1986	1987
No. of registered students — all levels	293	275	255
No. completing level III	4	5	3

Source: Records of ICAB, various years

through UWI is being introduced. The B.Sc Accounting and B.Sc Management Studies graduates of UWI, Cave Hill Campus in Barbados also receive up to 8 exemptions from ACCA and can receive up to 10 exemptions from CGA and CMA if the right combination of courses are taken in the degree programme.

In 1983 ICAB commissioned a study to ascertain a process of certification which would have been acceptable for the island. It considered all levels of expertise — accounts clerk, corporate accountant, financial director and public practitioner (Chaderton 1990). However, it was never implemented and ICAB fully intends to participate in the regional method of certification.

Trinidad

The Institute of Chartered Accountants of Trinidad and Tobago (ICATT) was formed in 1970. Members and or graduates of the accountancy bodies 1-9, 11 in Appendix 3 are eligible for admission to ICATT after a period of approved work experience. The membership comprises mainly of persons qualified with the ACCA. Unlike the other countries surveyed, many of its members are employed in government and state enterprises.

ICATT administers professional examinations for a student body of over 1,000 in Trinidad and Tobago. The majority of them write the ACCA. There was an arrangement similar to that in Barbados for the Society of Management Accountants of Ontario's (CMA) examinations. There are several privately run institutions on the island which prepare students for the British professional accounting exams Association of Accounting Technicians, Chartered Institute of Management Accountants and Institute of Chartered Secretaries Association (AAT, CIMA and ICSA) as well as for the ACCA.

The ACCA examination results in Trinidad have been as poor as in the other two countries surveyed (Table 4). In an attempt to stem the change to Canadian examinations, a summer school was held to prepare for the December 1991 examinations and the results were improved.

Many of the persons in Trinidad who have the ACCA qualification attended full-time courses in

TABLE 4
Institute of Chartered Accountants of Trinidad & Tobago (ICATT)

(a) Membership profile

	1988	**1991**
UK Designation		
ACCA	302	308
ICAEW	33	28
CIMA	12	6
ICAI	3	
ICAS	2	2
AIAA		3
ACIS	9	1
	361	348
Canadian Designation		
CA	14	13
CGA	2	3
CMA	14	17
	30	33
American Designation		
CPA	4	4
Other		
M.Sc (Accounting) UWI	15	20
	410	405
Members resident overseas		19
Retired members not resident in Trinidad & Tobago	24	14
		33
	434	438

Sources: ICAN Vol 14 No 4 December, 1988. ICATT List of Members 1991.

(b) ICATT/ACCA Examination Results December 1988

Level	Sat	Absent	Passed	Referred	Failed
I	289	176	204		389
II	217	154	143		295
III	41	0	7	1	33

the United Kingdom sponsored by the government of Trinidad and Tobago.[3]

The St. Augustine campus of UWI in Trinidad introduced the M.Sc Accounting programme in 1975. It was not identical to the Jamaica programme in content but was similar in that it had a Caribbean focus (Trinidad taxation was taught). ICATT agreed that the graduates of the M.Sc Accounting programme would be admitted to membership after "thirty (30) months adequate and appropriate accountancy experience." That acceptance was withdrawn in 1991 on the grounds that "it does not provide adequate professional training of a suitable standard required for a professional accountant."[4] If holders of the M.Sc Accounting degree after 1984 wish to become members of ICATT, they would have to approach one of the overseas professional bodies listed in Appendix 3 for certification. Fortunately, the 1929 Companies Act, which is in operation in Trinidad and Tobago, does not require accountants practising in the country to be members of ICATT as is required by the

[3]During the period 1963–1985, 50 scholarships were given annually for persons to travel to the United Kingdom to study for the ACCA examinations. It was estimated in 1984 that it cost TT $180,000 per person for persons in public office and TT $74,500 for persons not in public office over four years; this is the average period for completing the ACCA in the United Kingdom (Address by Minister in the Ministry of Finance and Planning at the formal opening of "Accountants Week" 1985 at Trinidad Hilton, March 1985)

[4]ICAN Institute of Chartered Accountants of Trinidad and Tobago Newsletter, December 1991.

Public Accountancy Act of Jamaica or the 1982 Barbados Companies Act.

REGIONAL ATTITUDES

Very little has been written on accounting in the Caribbean; one of the reasons is that the people are very typically third world in the respect that they do not like to respond to questionnaires. To obtain empirical data for my doctoral dissertation, it was necessary to use interviews as part of the field work. The Caribbean has an oral tradition. "Memories were and are the lifeline of Caribbean culture."[5] Sixty-five persons from the business community on four Caribbean islands (Antigua, Barbados, Jamaica, Trinidad and Tobago) were interviewed to ascertain their attitude towards the accounting profession. The transcripts of the conversations were verified by 45 percent of the interviewees. They included accountants in public practice, in government, in industry and commerce, bankers and employees of other financial institutions, as well as top civil servants/government employees. The response to two questions which are pertinent to this paper will be summarised.

Q: *What is the contribution of the accounting profession/accountants to the economic development of your country?*

Of 35 answers, the recurring response was that accountants do not contribute very much to the economy of the country. It was considered that

> ... economists deal with macro policies; accountants monitor the systems, keep the books and control expenditure ... (Civil Servant/Government employee) and

> ... their impact is minimal in the micro and small business sector ... (Banker)

The responses of two other bankers are worthy of mention:

> ... In that they are responsible for the preparation of the customers' financial statements, they make a contribution, but most statements are usually late ...

> When a business folds up some blame is placed on the accounting firms. In our commitment letter there is a precondition of up to date financial statements, so we depend on the accountants.

The phrase "accountants are not proactive" occurred in 10 percent of the answers. The accountants themselves had this to say:

> The professional firms are mainly involved in auditing and I think that they see it as their duty to issue the annual management letter; this suggests solutions and can influence decision making,

therefore they have an impact on the economy. (Accountant in industry)

> Generally accountants make peripheral contributions to economic development. I believe they see their role as attempting to be good bookkeepers and good corporate/regulatory agency reporters. Their role as advisors and strong influencers in the management of resources in under-rated. That is why I like the broad based approach to management accounting training. I believe it can contribute more to economic development. . . (Accountant in industry)

> The contribution an accountant can make depends on his/her education and how others outside the profession view it. In their circle, the profession is a business entity and is an employer (Accountant in public practice)

The above are but a sample of the responses received, but they provide an indication of a common perception of accountants and their role in economic development of the region. As the last response noted, the education influences the contribution. Tables 1, 2 and 3 show that the accountants in the Caribbean follow by and large the training of industrialised countries on either side of the Atlantic. They perceive their role to be the same as that of their counterparts in those countries. Table 4 shows the examination structure of the ACCA as it currently stands. As will be shown in the next paragraph, they operate in a different environment. ACCA professional accountants should be adequately qualified to be more than "bookkeepers or corporate reporters."

Caribbean Business Environment

There is a scarcity of human resources in the Caribbean and the region cannot afford to have accountants who are so specialised. Accountants are one group of professionals for whom a work permit on most Caribbean islands is easy to obtain. The capital market environment in which auditors in Canada, the United Kingdom and United States serve is minuscule in the region.[6] Most commercial enterprises are private entities; and the company law which regulates the activities of accountants is outdated (Appendix 2).

---

[5]"Old Folks' Tales" by Camilla Reed, *South May 1991*, 74.

[6]The Jamaica Stock Exchange has 44 companies listed; there were 13,892 transactions in 1989 valued at US $89,818; the Barbados Stock Exchange has 14 companies listed and the market capitalisation in 1990 was US $301.34 m; the Trinidad & Tobago Stock Exchange has 30 companies listed in 1990, there were 4,716 transactions valued at US $5,536,797 in that year.

The effect of using the United Kingdom Companies Acts of 1862, 1908 and 1929 seriously affects the legal support for the actions of accountants. The Acts do not demand financial disclosure which is necessary for developing commercial entities in which there could be confidence. Shareholders, employees and the general public have been denied the protection which subsequent Companies Acts in the United Kingdom have provided. Government is involved in many commercial ventures and except for Trinidad, very few accountants are employed in the government service.

On interviewee suggested, "There needs to be less auditing and more business advice; management needs advice on productivity and efficiency."

Q: *What are your views on the Caribbeanisation of the accounting professional exams?*

Of the 15 answers received to this question, 90 percent of the interviewees were in favour of some form of Caribbean accreditation, but there was the overriding preoccupation with the global acceptance of the certification and the desire for portability. The Caribbean has always used emigration as an escape route when the economic climate became unsatisfactory or difficult. Emigration explains the slow growth in the membership (Tables 2, 3, 4). Persons holding Canadian accounting qualifications have found access to Canada and the United States easy within the past 5 to 10 years.

A sample of answers which expressed some of the concerns are as follows:

I would hope that the Caribbean exams will include information on offshore business . . .(Accountant in practice)

Although the accounting profession has many standards which should be followed so that financial statements are in accordance with GAAP, the Caribbean still has some issues that are unique to the area. Local accounting exams particularly at the lower levels will have the advantage of making the student more aware of these issues and allow him/her to be more responsive to them, when they arise . . . Accountant in public practice)

I am not sure that we need to Caribbeanise the profession other than to set papers in Law and Tax. People should be allowed to have two designations; they should have an outside designation and then have a regional qualification which had tested them in Caribbean Tax and Law . . . I am against re-inventing the wheel (Accountant in Commerce)

Every support should be given to ICAC. I think that the accounting professional exams should be linked to the university . . . (Accountant in public practice)

Each of these comments requires further elaborations. There are a number of business topics which are particularly important to the Caribbean and which are not examined on any of the overseas professional qualifications. These include offshore business, hotel accounting (tourism is one of the largest foreign exchange earners in Jamaica, Barbados and the Bahamas), accounting for agricultural entities (most Caribbean economies are dependent on the export of primary products such as sugar cane, bananas and citrus fruit) (Hope 1986).

The sociopolitical history of the region has influenced the Caribbean countries and their business environment. The accountant operating in this environment therefore ought to be aware of this and its implications. It is generally possible to give more informed advice when one understands how the economies are structured in relation to the world stage and the problems of "smallness" (Ramsaram 1989). All the CARICOM countries have from time to time had to negotiate with the IMF and World Bank, and accountants are used occasionally. Unless one has been exposed to literature on these organisations, decisions may not be taken in the best interest of the region. None of the ACCA courses provide techniques for dealing with developing economies although the majority of ACCA members reside and work in the third world (Chaderton 1991).

The need to have two designations is economically unsound and financially impossible in some countries where foreign exchange is scarce. A comparison of the Membership Handbook of the ACCA and of ICAJ reveals that a growing number of persons have let their ACCA membership lapse. This is mostly due to inability to pay the subscriptions. The ACCA's annual membership fee is £80 (at the conversion rate of J $30 = £1 in January 1991 this is J $2,400 or US $300) and the membership fee for ICAJ is J $1,550 (US $195). The unwillingness to accept that the Caribbean business environment is special and capable of supporting a recognised professional qualification is a matter of deep regret, and which needs to be changed as matter of urgency.

There appears to be a limited desire for the professional qualification to be linked with the UWI; this is not unreasonable and has a precedent. The UWI has been in existence for 40 years and has been recognised as an institution which produces quality. The medical and legal professions in the region have been Caribbeanised through the university. However, the problem with the M.Sc Accounting programme in both Jamaica and Trinidad as discussed earlier gives cause for concern.

CONCLUSIONS AND RECOMMENDATIONS

The directorate of ICAC has a challenging opportunity to be a part of a change mechanism that can influence the course of the economic development of the Caribbean region in the future change. A Caribbean examination for the accounting profession must ensure that the next generation of accountants understand the Caribbean environment and the institutions which exist there while at the same time be able to communicate with their counterparts overseas.

Problems

The immediate exercise which ICAC is undertaking has inherent problems as there has been no harmonization of company law and taxation within the region. The preparers of the texts are, however, dealing with the topics generally and then compiling separate sections on the legislation of the larger member countries of CARICOM. It is the duty of the respective Institutes to lobby government to update the company law.

The size of the student population is clearly a negative aspect of a regional accreditation process; however, as mentioned above, accountants are still being recruited from overseas; therefore there is currently a shortage, not an over supply. When ICAC takes a look at the entire profession, it may be advisable to develop an accreditation process where individuals can move from the technician stage right through to the public accountant or financial controller/finance director.

There is a growing literature on the differences between the objective of a professional qualification and a university degree. The university provides the theoretical framework behind accounting, the discipline. The professional qualification comes after the work experience has been obtained. The responses received when a survey was carried out in Jamaica and Trinidad to ascertain the attitude of the business community to the M.Sc Accounting programme revealed a level of ignorance as to exactly what was covered in the degree programme (Mendes 1992). The fact that the hierarchy of the Institutes in the Caribbean qualified by the apprenticeship method and are not holders of a university degree is a problem that can be dealt with only by the passage of time.

Conclusions

In assessing the positions that accountants filled in the Caribbean, it is noticed that they aspire to top management positions in private and public sector enterprises; therefore their training and examinations ought to equip them to fill these positions (Williams 1989). It seems ironical that there are so few management accountants in the region when most qualified accountants outside the firms of chartered accountants occupy positions of management. This is perhaps one of the reasons why they are perceived as making very little contribution to the economic development of the countries.

In the United Kingdom and Canada, there are separate bodies for the training of management accountants (CIMA and CMA) and for accountants who work in the public sector there is the Chartered Institute of Public Financial Analysts (CIPFA); in the Caribbean no such separation exists nor is there any necessity. The certification should allow the professionals to move freely from one sector to the other.

The results of the ACCA examinations have been pathetic and frustrating. That a profession in a developing country can effectively be built up by persons studying through correspondence courses is a myth. Part-time study is both a lengthy and expensive process. The high literacy rate of the region as shown in Appendix 1 would tend to indicate that there is deeper underlying reason why individuals take so long to complete the ACCA. This evidence is supported by the results of CGA and CMA programmes which offer tutorial assistance as well as mandatory submission of assignments before an individual is allowed to write the examination. There is an imposed discipline.

If the accounting profession is to take its place alongside the older professions of medicine and law, it is necessary for a higher calibre of person to be qualified. A university degree produces an individual with a broader base of knowledge than does a professional qualification. Most of the accounting professional bodies in North America require a degree as entry into the profession and with a university already established in the region, it seems the appropriate way to develop. The work experience would be provided by practitioners. Without the exposure to a university education, accountants may continue to be marginalised in the society.

Recommendations

It is therefore recommended that using the expertise of the ACCA and the other international accounting bodies, there should be curriculum development of a programme to better prepare professionals to meet the needs of the region. It is strongly recommended that courses on project evaluation and project management be included. Management accounting at the highest level would expose the accountant to behavourial aspects of accounting measurement, strategic planning, organization design and control (Williams 1989). These are areas of extreme weakness in the Caribbean business environment.

Computer skills are necessary for the effective functioning of accountants. The Caribbean is not like some other third world countries; many enterprises have computers owing to the geographical access and exposure to the United States

Employers need to be given more information on the academic content of local training programmes so that hiring practices can be more streamlined and job descriptions more realistic. Economic development of the region can only be enhanced if there is a partnership between the private sector and the public sector with feedback to the educators.

In order to ensure that Caribbean-accredited accountants can function in the international arena, there can be comparative sections in subjects such as taxation and law. However, that should not be a priority. The creation of an awareness of the problems of the region and how accountants can help to solve them would reap long-term benefits.

APPENDIX 1
Demographic and Economic Indicators of CARICOM Members

Country	Area (square miles)	Population '000 (Mid-1989)[1]	Per capita GNP 1989 US $1	Life Expectancy 1989[1]	Literacy %[1]
Antigua & Barbuda	108	78	2,030[2]	74	88
Bahamas	5,380	249	11,320	68	93
Barbados	166	256	6,350	75	98
Belize	8,866	184	1,780	68	n/a
Dominica	290	82	1,160[2]	75	80
Grenada	120	94	1,900	69	98
Guyana	83,000	796	340	64	86
Jamaica	4,411	2,400	1,260	73	82
Montserrat	40	12	2,583[2]	n/a	76
St. Kitts-Nevis	104	41	1,520[2]	69	88
St. Lucia	238	148	1,810	71	80
St. Vincent & the Grenadines	150	113	840[2]	70	80
Trinidad & Tobago	1,980	1,300	3,230	71	97
CARICOM Observer States					
Dominican Republic	18,712	7,000	790	67	68
Haiti	10,714	6,400	360	55	23
Suriname	63,036	437	3,010	67	80

Sources: [1] World Development Report, 1991.
[2] World Development Report, 1991 (figures at 1985).

APPENDIX 2
Caribbean Countries and Companies Legislation

Country	UK Act on Which Based	Status
Antigua, Bahamas, Dominica, Montserrat	1862 or earlier	
Belize, Grenada	1908	
Guyana	1908	amended 1961
St. Lucia	1908	amended 1948
Trinidad and Tobago	1929	new legislation in process
Jamaica	1948	amended 1967
Barbados	1982	operative with amendments from January 1985

Source: Based on the Report of the Working Party on the Harmonization of Company Law in the Caribbean Community, CARICOM Secretariat, Georgetown, Guyana, 1979 (Updated).

APPENDIX 3

1   Chartered Association of Certified Accountants (ACCA)
2   Institute of Chartered Accountants in England and Wales (ICAEW)
3   Institute of Chartered Accountants of Scotland (ICAS)
4   Institute of Chartered Accountants in Ireland (ICAI)
5   One of the Provincial Institutes/Ordre of the Chartered Accountants in Canada (CA)
6   The Institute of Certified Public Accountants of the United States of America (CPA)
7   The Institute of Cost and Management Accountants in England (CIMA)
8   The Society of Management Accountants in Ontario (CMA)
9   The Institute of Certified General Accountants of Canada (CGA)
10   The University of the West Indies (Mona Campus, Jamaica) M.Sc programme before 1984
11   The University of the West Indies (St. Augustine Campus, Trinidad) M.Sc programme before 1984

APPENDIX 4
The Current Examination Structure of the ACCA Certification

Level 1	Paper
1.1	Accounting
1.2	Cost and Management Accounting I
1.3	Economics
1.4	Law
1.5	Business Mathematics and IT

Level 2	
2.1	Auditing
2.2	Company Law
2.3	Taxation
2.4	Cost and Management Accounting II
2.5A or	Executorship & Trust Law & Accounts
2.5B	Effective Management
2.6	Decision Making Techniques
2.7	Management Information Systems
2.8	Regulatory Framework of Accounting
2.9	Advanced Accounting Practice

Level 3	
3.1	Advanced Financial Accounting
3.2	Financial Management
3.3	Advanced Taxation
3.4	Auditing & Investigation

REFERENCES

Chaderton, R. A. 1991. The Education of Professional Accountants in Barbados. *Comparative International Accounting Educational Standards*. Center for International Education and Research in Accounting, Department of Accountancy, University of Illinois: 237–243.

———. 1991. The Association as an Exporter of Accounting Technology. *The Certified Accountant* (July): 8,9.

———, and P. J. Taylor. (forthcoming) The Accounting Systems of the Carribbean: Their Evolution and Role in Economic Growth and Development. *Research in Third World Accounting* (Vol. 2).

Demas, W. G. 1990. *Towards West Indian Survival.* Occasional Paper No. 1. The West Indian Commission.

Hope, K. 1986. *Economic Development in the Caribbean.* Praeger Publishers.

Mendes, M. 1992. *Innovation in Professional Accountancy Education at the University of the West Indies (Jamaica): 1968-88.* Unpublished M.A. (Ed) thesis, UWI Library.

Ramlogan, V. 1985. The Education of Accountants in Trinidad and Tobago. *ICAN: Journal of the Institute of Chartered Accountants of Trinidad and Tobago* Vol. 11, No. 3.

Ramsaram, R. 1989. *The Commonwealth Caribbean in the World Economy.* Warick University Caribbean Studies. Macmillan.

Williams, R. 1989. The Role of the University of the West Indies in Accounting Training in the Caribbean. *Caribbean Finance and Management* (Summer): 8–13.

Accounting, Development, and the IFAC Guidelines

G. D. Donleavy

It would seem self-evident that the overriding need of the poorest economies is to advance to the global mean of wealth and income. This relativist view of poverty, however, leads readily to "marketist" complacency that holds "the poor are always with us;" therefore systematic alleviating action is a statistical impossibility. Poverty, however, has an absolute reality more important than its relative one. Eight hundred million people on earth (3/4 of them in Asia) are estimated to lack the basic essentials of living in terms of food, shelter and freedom from disease.

If poor people were just like the rich except for their assets, then returns on investment should be much larger in LDCs than in developed countries as labour costs would be so much smaller. Similarly, if we confine assets to human resources, then educated people in LDCs should earn far more than their counterparts in developed countries (Stiglitz 1989). Several recent studies (Lucas 1988, Stiglitz 1987, Romer 1986) argue that a major difference between the first and third worlds is sourced in the nontransferability of lessons arising from "learning by doing" (Arrow 1962), which obliges LDCs to specialize in technology or products with low learning potentials. Stiglitz (1987) hypothesized that the ability to learn may itself be learned and that such abilities may be localized. He adduces the Silicon Valley phenomenon as exemplifying learning externalities, where the intellectual ferment in the area facilitates productive innovation. Hoff (1988) shows that since economic development involves entrepreneurs taking risks which do not always come off, entrepreneurial success or failure conveys lessons for other entrepreneurs. Such lessons are not readily transmitted in LDCs, and the result is too few entrants into new industries. It would seem, then, that a major development need is to avoid the mistakes of others *before* applying the Mexican proverb;—hacemos el camino caminando—we can make the path by walking it (Edwards 1989 127).

The function of education especially relevant to LDCs is "conscientization" according to the influential work of Paulo Freire (1972). This neologism denotes the enlargement of an individual's cognitive map by imparting a critical awareness of the nature and causes of the individual's underlying condition. Insofar as that condition can be epitomized as poverty, Freire characterizes it as cross-culturally universal in its most important aspects: no savings, child and female hard labor, informal and usurious moneylending networks, overcrowding and domestic violence, provincial world view alienated from that of the nearest urban culture, sensitivity to local status distinctions, second-hand clothing at best, inability to defer gratification, and, the feature most amenable to cure by conscientization, that by fatalism.

Although studies such as Mohan and Sabst (1988) of Colombia show that extra educational supply reduces rather than increases economic inequality, the view still persists that education intensifies the distinction between manual and mental labor and that creates an intelligentsia alienated equally from its personal roots and from its foreign richer counterparts (Rossides 1984). When some of those counterparts visit an LDC as expatriate experts, they bring their own conditioning to the problems of LDCs so that many endeavours remain fruitless because their ideas cannot take root in new cultural soil. Advising Africa, for example, has become a major industry with at least 80,000 expatriates at work south of the Sahara at a cost of more than US$ 4 billion a year. The volume of magazines, books, periodicals and papers concerning development continues to increase, while there are so many conferences on development that attendance has almost become an industry in itself. (Edwards 1989 116). The ex-president of Zimbabwe, Canaan Banana (1987), is quoted thus on the subject of "armchair intellectuals":

> Time and again, now and in the future, they face the bleak disjuncture and mismatch between lengthy and laborious theories, decked out in figures and ornate expressions, and the ugly, undecorated and sordid reality of rural poverty.

G. D. Donleavy is Academic Director, the Business School, at Hong Kong University.

If people can analyze, design, implement and evaluate their work in a critical fashion, they stand a good chance of achieving their objectives. However, a system of education and training that relies on experts will never be able to do this, because the attitude of the expert prevents people from thinking for themselves (Edwards 1989 119). The challenge to educators is to transfer experience, know-how and technology to LDC students without facilitating an intellectual cargo cult or becoming an academic policeperson for neocolonialism.

ACCOUNTING EDUCATION

In July 1991, the International Federation of Accountants Education Committee issued a codification (IEG 9) of its six education guidelines issued between IEG 1 in February 1982 and IEG 6 in November 1989. All the IEG statements on prequalifying education are now in IEG 9. Its key prescriptions are set out below.

- Entrants to candidature for the professional examinations should be educated to the equivalent of university matriculands (SAT equivalent in the US, A level GCE in the Commonwealth) (IEG 9 para 13).

- Professional education courses should provide historical, ethical and theoretical perspectives on accountancy (IEG 9 15a).

- Such courses should also teach interpretation, conceptual integration, proposal formulation and adequate communication skills (IEG 9 15b).

- All courses should address the core subjects of accounting (financial and management), information technology, auditing, tax and business finance and the supportive subjects of economics, law, maths with statistics, behavioral sciences and management (IEG 9 19) but these may be weighted in ways appropriate to local circumstances (IEG 9 18). The courses need to last three years' full time or its equivalent (IEG 9 22).

- Courses should end with a test of professional competence; and public confidence is said to depend on "the adequacy of the professional exams" (IEG 9 33). The design of the exams should require students to demonstrate the skills deemed (in IEG 9 15b) to be desirable (IEG 9 40).

- There needs to be a period of approved practical experience (IEG 9 50) and that would preferably last no less than three years (IEG 9 54).

- The accountancy qualification itself should be regarded as of equivalent standard to a university degree (IEG 9 60).

None of IEG 9's supportive outline syllabi in behavioral sciences (IEG 9A 53-60) or management (IEG 9A 61-68) mention cross-cultural studies, although the academic literature on international accounting is deeply imbedded in them. (e.g. Mueller 1968, Amenkhienan 1982). This omission corroborates the view voiced by such writers as Briston (1978), and Boussard (1980) that the Anglo-American accounting priorities are globally dominant at the expense of other priorities, especially LDC priorities. The critique of such dominance is now well known. But, as the IEGs have ignored it, it may be worth encapsulating the critique's main points here.

- Anglo-American accounting centers on the assumed information needs of equity stockholders in reasonably efficient markets, but non-American markets are not very efficient and non-Anglo-American financial cultures are not equity dominated (Mudogo 1986, Mueller 1968).

- The English Chartered Association of Certified Accountants has offered ready-made training and examination packages to nascent accounting bodies around the world, which has spread English accounting priorities to places where they may represent barriers to development (Briston and Kedslie 1991, Osiegbu 1990, Mudogo 1986).

- The US domination of the economies of the Americas has led to the inappropriate copying of AICPA forms of organisation and accounting practice throughout that continent (Davila 1991).

- The principal lending agencies from the World Bank down lend chiefly on a project financing basis and expect to see Anglo-American–style proposals, reports and accounts in respect to such financing (Seidler 1969, Hopkins 1986).

- LDCs need more emphasis on governmental and macro accounting, on management accounting, on fiscal policy creation (Prawiro 1991) and on courses that "conscientize" students (Freire 1972).

- LDCs are chronically short both of professional accountants and of accounting technicians but failure rates at Anglo-American–style local professional exams are very wastefully high (Gbenedio 1977, Rivero 1990).

It is relevant to the decision about the kind of accounting that should be taught in LDCs to review the issues involved in continuing discussions of accounting's prime justification. Unsurprisingly perhaps, the IEGs amplify, but do not depart from, the US AICPA recommendations by Roy and MacNeill (1967) two decades earlier. So, law gets

4 lines, economics 10, in the syllabus specifications, following the post Trueblood orthodoxy well captured in the following catechism from the Bedford Report (AAA 1986);

> Economics is the root discipline of accounting. Research in the economics of information emphasizes the importance of cost benefit trade-offs in deciding on the complexity of formal information systems. For example, the widely used accounting model is only one source. Accounting students should be well grounded in cost benefit thinking and should recognize that an accounting system is not necessarily always the optimum way to gather information.

The doyen of academic accountants in the developmment accounting field, Enthoven (1973 112/3) defines accounting thus;

> The development of economic facts—based on real world phenomena—involving measurements and their further appraisal and supply—in the form of costs and benefits—to enable evaluations and decisions about activities and the allocation of resources.

It is submitted that these definitions express a hope rather than an experience. The rise of decision usefulness as the rationale for accounting is traced by Watts and Zimmerman (1979) to the perception that the 1929 Crash was caused partly by inadequate corporate disclosure, although there was little supporting evidence for such a view. Stewardship somehow got associated with excessive secrecy. If the New Deal Securities Act was the start of decision usefulness, its ascendancy was marked by the Trueblood Report (1973), which said financial statements should "serve primarily those users who have limited authority, ability or resources to obtain information and who rely on financial statements as their principal sources of information about an enterprise's activity (p19)." In other words, accounts are for those without inside information. However, the Trueblood Report had a wider view of usefulness than many of those who have since cited it, for it declares that one objective of financial statements is to report on the "activities of the enterprise affecting society which can be determined or measured and which are important to the role of the enterprise in its social environment" (p55). The acknowledgment by the decision usefulness school of the importance of such imponderables as probabilities, the expected present values of alternative outcomes' cost-benefits, and environmental impact data imply that "hard" accounting data are less relevant to important decisions than the phantom quanta that eco-

nomics itself has been questing ever since John Stuart Mill first opened the Pandora's box of marginal utility. These important decision quanta include subjective assessments of benefits, probabilities and political frictions. Hopkins (1986 173) aptly quotes Churchman (1968) on the choice between alternative valuation methods thus;

> About all that the decision maker can do is pick on one aspect of the situation and push that as hard as possible, arguing against his enemies that they are failing to sense the true situation.

A previous secretary general of the United Nations, U Thant, went further than Churchman and held it is decisions which create resources, not resources which limit decisions (Said 1991 507). The point here is that it could be counterproductive to raise LDC students' hopes of the decision usefulness of accounting when much of the most important data cannot be captured by any accounting system yet created.

In contrast with the idealistically normative views of the decision usefulness school, Boussard (1980, 138) declaims "accounting protects and legitimises the owner's rights"; an assertion, however misconceived, that many LDC focused writers echo and for them "owners" mean neocolonial foreign developed country institutions. For Oliga and Samuels (1986) by way of example, the aim of acccounting in LDCs should not be to highlight efficiency but to highlight exploitation.

Enthoven (1973) argued what is now an orthodoxy to which great lip service is paid: that since accounting systems operate within a socioeconomic framework, they need to to be in tune with it. It is easy to exemplify the nonfulfillment of that need. Indonesia has some 4,000 accountants in a population of some 170 million, but lecturers are so poorly paid that most have second jobs which means that good teaching practice is a rarity; infrastructures are inadequate and hardly any textbooks in Bahasa are available (Foo 1988). Even India teaches behavioral science up to graduate level without automatically or necessarily including cross-cultural paradigms (Sishtla 1990).

Agami and Alkafaji (1981 145) define an accounting educational system as "students, faculty, curriculum and resources [library, computers, facilities, financial resources, innovations and technology] that are ideally combined harmoniously and efficiently to meet the educational needs of a given society." Panama quite well exemplifies the opposite of such an ideal. Accounting degrees yield only five percent of their students to professional certification, partly because two-thirds of the students are part-time evening mode and partly because the degree requires a dissertation to be completed (Rivero 1990). Nigeria has a system of practical training and courses in Recognized Training Centers, but there are too few teachers and inadequate facilities (Osiegbu 1987). As a final example from the *embarras de pauvresse*, centralization of curriculum control and textbook printing for its very conventional Chartered and Cost and Management professional accounting courses has not produced satisfactory results in Bangladesh, not even a more efficient allocation of accounting resources (Ghosh 1990).

Arthur (1988) has shown how socially suboptimal institutions may persist when path-dependent processes are important. An example of this is the retention round the world of the qwerty keyboard long after the reasons for inventing such a deliberately inefficient process have not merely disppeared but actually reversed with the replacement of manual typewriters by word processing technology. More generally, when there are increasing returns from adopting a particular innovation, the path chosen by the initial adopters may lock in the system for an overlong time. This, it is submitted, models the Anglo-American paradigm's hold on the world quite well.

In a wide ranging review of his personal experience of accounting education in Pacific LDCs, Hopkins (1986) pointed out the importance of the conflict in allocating scarce educational resources between the attraction of overseas recognition of an Anglo-style exam-based qualification and indigenized curricula useful and relevant to local problems. He reported how the Manila Report of accounting academics in 1984 had recommended that development plans should be country specific. However, do different sociopolitical conditions always justify the differences presently found? For example, the total practising qualifying period for professional certification is five years in such countries as Zimbabwe, six years in Chile and five to seven years in Kuwait (Needles 1990).

Within one country, educational investment decisions are an extreme example of defined costs today, indefinably vague benefits the day after tomorrow. The costs are distributed across all taxpayers while the direct benefits focus on the graduate employed. Across national frontiers, cooperation is limited by the different *social* rates of discount different countries apply to educational investment. Differences between private and social

rates of return to education significantly impact ministerial decisions on educational resource allocation. As an extreme example of a society's attempt to recover its educational investment outlays, Indonesia's Diploma III accounting students face government bonding for 15 years as the price of their education. However, in other respects, Indonesia has mismanaged its accounting education. The World Bank's Accounting Development Project in Indonesia failed because it was part of a wider technical education development project whose managers did not see accounting as a particularly important component of the package (Briston et al 1990). US experts arrived to find equipment and facilities money already spent. The associated Accounting Development Center effort was not a success, since many of those involved had no idea of its mission, how it should be managed or what it should achieve. It seems that project administrators and managers need thorough briefing, if not extensive training, before educational development projects are implemented.

Investment in accounting education, of even more general business education, in the Americas south of the USA is little better than in the rest of the Third World. There are only three doctoral schools in management studies throughout Latin America in Mexico, Rio and Sao Paolo. Virtually all business education is strongly influenced by, or directly linked to, the USA. Davila (1991 29) characterizes the effects thus:

> The values and assumptions of North American thinking have come to dominate, without adequate testing or refinement, much of management education in the region. Extreme pragmatism, anti-intellectualism, conformism through lack of criticism, acceptance of managerial ideologies and the idea that management theories are value free, and deep seated ethnocentrism might all said to be features of this insidious form of intellectual dependence.

Business schools should, he believes, become active agents of change in regional management education by indigenizing its content.

In the USA itself, the Anderson (AICPA 1986) and Bedford (AAA 1986) reports concluded that the large increase in employer requirements for technically skilled entrants necessitated the addition of a fifth year to accounting programs. The fifth year is seenas enhancing communication skills, enhancing awareness of ethical aspects *and* raising the status of accountancy to that of law and medicine both of which *require* graduate education. The Philippines is to introduce a professional year at the end of its accounting degrees though employers there have been found to believe that an undergraduate specialization in accounting is one of the worst preparations for a successful accounting career (Roque 1986). Status raising of accountants is perhaps not quite so urgent in fulfilling the basic needs of LDCs.

BANDAIDS FOR LDC ACCOUNTING EDUCATION

Graves and Berry (1989) were impressed with the late GDR's chart of accounts approach and its permitting of supernormal profits only if workers achieved a favorable efficiency variance against the standard incorporated into the unit pricing system. Since all wage levels were fixed by the State, such variances were the only way for workers to increase earnings by way of participating in value added within the GDR's pre-market system. Value added reports have now almost a long history of advocacy since the UK's Corporate Report (1975) and were explicitly argued by AlHashim (1982) to be more useful to LDC governments than conventional income statements. Their presentation, interpretation and limitation should perhaps play the role in LDC financial accounting education that the P & L (UK) or Income Statement (US) does in Anglo-American accounting education.

Ability to engage in corruption has been argued (Harendra 1989) to result from a combination of quasi monopoly of power or authority by one party and need by the other to control material political risk, to solve indivisibility problems or merely to reap the benefits of network externalities. The Treadway Report (1987) in the USA advocated the compulsory inclusion of ethics into undergraduate accounting degrees, partly because, surmise Chua and Matthews (1991), recent trends have been away from professional values towards trading ones. Professional powers and privileges have an ethics price tag beyond what is acceptable in ordinary trading relationships. Insofar as the accountant sings the song written by her/his client when it is out of tune with the wider expectations of society, the business of accountancy slides from being a profession to being a mere trade. Doctors do not do the surgery required by the patient nor lawyers frame the law desired by their clients, but accounting treatments in the "decision" framework are vulnerable to just such refraction. For example, India has not yet fully codified its accounting, so inventory and depreciation numbers can be ambiguous, confusing and open to abuse, unaffected

by the presence of the largest international accounting firms (Khambata and Khambata 1989).

Ethics as a core element throughout the accountancy education process can scarcely be overemphasized. Not only does it reduce the dangers of corruption by sensitizing students to its nature and manifestations, but also it is quite central to the accountants' claim for professional status. A professional paid by a client but acting as an agent for society is not just a skilled employee. It is submitted that this message can not be too deeply embedded in accountancy education, least of all in corruption vulnerable LDCs. It is not so much a resurrection of professional "noblesse obige" as a reconfirmation that Accounting has *two* intellectual parents—a mother in Law as well as father in Economics. It is evident that the stewardship aspect of accountancy is relevant here. It is submitted that the conflict in academic accounting between decision usefulness and stewardship as *the* primary rationale is a quite false conflict. Accounting as a human system, per Ijiri (1983), means human complexity. Telling ourselves or our students that accounting is fundamentally about decision usefulness not stewardship is about as sensible as saying nutrition is fundamentally about drinking not eating.

Williams et al. (1988) report that most empirical research evidence about educational output is about attempts to change those outputs while the significance of the outputs is taken for granted. Outputs are said to include (p 158) "those embedded in Dewey's conception of education as a civilizing influence in human society and the ideals commonly inscribed in Latin on university insignia." In this connection, a useful tool for thinking about education for development is the civilization screen which I have developed from the well-known BCG screen with its dogs and cash cows. The horizontal axis scales economic development with any measure appropriate for the occasion (but GDP per head in default of any other). The vertical axis scales civilization and is usable to capture any aspect of that concept not intrinsic to economic development; for example, artistic work in foreign national art museums, rate of violent crime per thousand persons per year, citation counts of the use of the word *civilization* adjacent to the word (say) *Chinese* in all the humanities periodicals surrveyed by a CD database such as those of University Microfilms International at Ann Arbor, Michigan. In the top right quadrant, equivalent to BCG stars would be countries both developed and

those of University Microfilms International at Ann Arbor, Michigan. In the top right quadrant, equivalent to BCG stars would be countries both developed and civilized such as France. At the lower left would be those which are neither, such as Sudan, the equivalent of BGC dogs. At lower right are regions highly economically developed but lacking something on the relevant dimension of civilization such as Belfast or the Bronx. The upper left would be countries with developed cultures that were not yet economically advanced, such as China, India and much of Arabia. It is these "question mark" countries that are are particularly sensitive to the westernization price tag of development. They look at Iran as an example of excessive development insuficiently balanced by core values of indigenous civilization. The 45 degree line on the civilization screen represents a balance between economic growth and cultural development, with France as the exemplar of economic advance without adoption of Anglo values or structures. It is submitted that since France, Germany and Japan all provide radically different accounting frameworks to the Anglo one and all three are both rich and free from undue cultural colonization, they need to be studied on a comparative basis by accounting students in LDCs. It is urgently necessary to move away from accounting courses

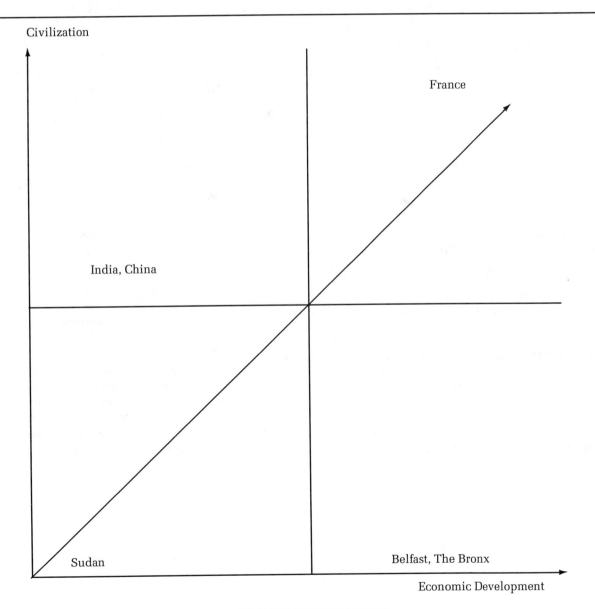

THE CIVILIZATION SCREEN

the differences between her/his own culture and that of Anglo-America.

Some Islamic writers such as Alam (1991) have stressed the tensions between Islam and western financial frameworks in the areas of interest (prohibited under Shari'ah), speculation (prohibited), and Zakah as a kind of redistributive tax (mandatory). Partly to mediate fundamentalist pressures, Indonesian education includes compulsory courses on the national secular ideology of pancasila (Hadibroto 1991 74). Agami and Alkafaji (1987) report that many Arab universities offer courses suited closely to the local milieu. King Abdul Aziz University in Saudi Arabia, for example, offers courses in Islamic accounting systems, agricultural accounting, oil and gas accounting, cooperative accounting, national accounting and Zakat accounting. China's Shanghai University of Finance and Economics has a course called Financial Accounting in Western Countries, which rather neatly contains the Anglo-American paradigm within controllable pedagogic bounds (Lou and Zhang 1991 216). It is recommended that other LDCs take from such examples and segregate traditional Anglo-American accounting explicitly in their syllabi, while also introducing practitioner-led courses on accounting as it is actually done in the home country concerned.

Communication skills are important areas lacking in accounting graduate entry-level employees in the USA (Grange and Peck 1991) and in LDCs (Lim et al. 1991 for Malaysia, Tipgos 1991 for southeast Asia generally). In Asia, the familiarity and the dangers of the experience of lecturing to a passive student audience as the main teaching method are widely recognized, even in China now (Lin and Deng 1991). Research is needed on the relationship between new graduate communication skills and their exposure to interactive teaching methods. In the meantime, courses explicitly addressing this area would seem to be needed on a mandatory basis in most cultures. A semester of Business English will not cut it. Priestley (1989) reports her pioneering venture in London, channelling

textbooks and academic literature from British academics to African universities. An organized distribution channel for second-hand textbooks seems to be a project within the reach of the World Conference of Accounting Educations. Its desirability is obvious.

The Association of Accounting Technicians (AAT 1989) has some 2,000 members and 10,000 students round the world. Some countries such as Swaziland already recognize the AAT exams as qualifying their citizens for the designation "registered accountant." It intends to develop a worldwide second tier with harmonized applicable professional standards, partly by promoting international recognition and partly by other means such as encouraging local AATs such as the Zimbabwe AAT or starting local branches of its own UK–based organization (as approved by Briston and Yunus [1991] for Indonesia). In the context of harmonizing accounting standards, Hove (1986) of Harare has argued that LDCs do not need to partcipate in the process while it is being attempted in the same way that accounting technology was transferred without any consideration of the needs of LDCs. A similar caution is appropriate for the AAT's ambitions and for accounting educators involved in furthering them.

CONCLUSION

Knowledge is only useful if the listener needs the knowledge, understands it, wants to use it, can use it, and is not prevented by circumstances from using it (Klonda 1986, 5).

The above quotation is recommended for memorizing by all involved in the LDC accounting education process. It can scarcely be doubted that the IEG 9 stipulations would have been rather different had the IFAC panel heeded the wise words therein. Byron once asked: Is it civilization when a cannibal uses a knife and fork? This Conference might like to ask whether it is education when an LDC student learns the accounting procedures for applications and allotment of equity capital.

REFERENCES

AAA American Acounting Association. 1986. *Further Accounting Education: preparing for the Expanding Profession*, AAA Committee on the Future Structure, Scope and Content of Accounting Education [the Bedford Report] Sarasota: AAA.

AAT Association of Accounting Technicians. 1989. Overseas Policy Statement by Council. London (9 March).

AICPA American Institute of Certified Public Accountants. 1986. *Restructuring Professional Standards to Achieve Professional Excellence in A Changing Environment*. Report of the Special Committee on Standards of Professional Conduct for CPAs [the Anderson Report] New York: AICPA.

Agami, A. M., and Y. A. Alkafaji. 1981. Accounting Education in Selected Middle Eaatern Countries. *International Journal of Accounting* Vol. 23, No. 1 (Fall): 145-168.

AlHashim, A. I. 1982. International Dimensions of Accounting and Implications for Developing Nations. *Management International Review* Vol. 22.

Alam, K. F. 1991. Shari'ah, Financial Dealings and Accounting Practices. 552-562 SEAUTA Conference, Jakarta.

Amenkhienan, F. E. 1982. *Accounting in Developing Countries A Framework for Standard Setting*. Ann Arbor: UMI Research.

Arrow, K. J. 1962. The Economic Implications of Learning by Doing. *Review of Economic Studies* Vol. 29 (June): 155-173.

Arthur, B. 1988. Self Reinforcing Mechanisms in Economics. *The Economy as an Evolving Complex System*, ed. P. W. Anderson and K. J. Arrow. Reading, MA: Addison Wesley.

Banana, Canaan, quoted in M. de Graaf. 1987. *The Importance of People*. Bulawayo: Hlekweni Friends Rural Service Centre.

Boussard, D. 1980. Accounting As An Artifact. *International Journal of Accounting* Vol. 16, No. 2 (Spring): 125-147.

Briston, R. J. 1978. The Evolution of Accounting in Developing Countries. *International Journal of Accounting* Vol. 14 (Fall): 105-120.

————, S. L. Foo, and H. Yunus. 1990. Accounting Education and Workforce Requirements in Indonesia. *Comporative International Accounting Education Standards*. Center for International Education Research in Accounting, University of Illinois.

————, and M. J. M. Kedslie. 1991. The Internationalisation of Professional Accounting: The Role of the Chartered Association of Certified Accountants. South East Asia University Accounting Teachers Conference, [hereafter SEAUTA] Jakarta: 518-527.

————, and H. Yunus. 1991. The Role and Training of Accounting Technicians: IFAC's IEG No 7 and Its Relevance for South East Asia. SEAUTA Conference, Jakarta: 528-538.

Chua, F. C. K., and M. R. Matthews. 1991. Professional Ethics, Public Confidence and Accounting Education. SEAUTA Conference, Jakarta: 366-381.

Churchman, C. W. 1968. The Systems Approach. Delta Books: viii.

Corporate Report (The). 1975. *Accounting Standards Steering Committee*. London Institute of Chartererd Accountants in England and Wales (August).

Davila, C. 1991. The Evolution of Management Education and Development in Latin America. *Journals of Management Development* Vol. 10, No. 6: 22-31.

Edwards, M. 1989. The Irrelevance of Development Studies. *Third World Quarterly* Vol. 11, No. 1: 116-1135.

Enthoven, A. J. H. 1973. *Accountancy and Economic Development*. North Holland: Amsterdam.

Foo, S. L. 1988. Accounting Education Systems in Southeast Asia; The Indonesian & Singaporean Experiences. *International Journal of Accounting* Vol. 23, No. 2 (Spring): 125-136.

Gbenedio, P. O. 1977. The Challenge to the Accounting Profession in A Developing Country: The Nigerian Case, PhD Thesis. University of Cincinnatti (August).

Ghosh, S. N. 1990. A Comparative International Study of the Education of Professional Accountant: A Case Study of Bangladesh. *Comparative International Accounting Education Standards*. Center for International Education Research in Accounting: University of Illinois: 97-108.

Grange, E. V., and R. L. Peck. 1991. Trends in Accounting Education in the United States. Proceedings of the Third Annual Conference of Accounting Academics. Hong Kong (March): 458-465.

Graves, O. F., and M. Berry. 1989. Accounting's Role in Successful Economic Development — Some Normative Evidence from the GDR. *International Journal of Accounting* Vol. 24, No. 2 (Spring): 189-220.

Gray, S. J. 1988. Towards a Theory of Cultural Influence on the Development of Accounting Systems Internationally. *Abacus* Vol. 24, No. 1: 1-15.

Hadibroto, H. S. 1991. Accounting Curriculum Development In A Developing Country: The Indonesian Experience. SEAUTA Confernece, Jakarta: 74-81.

Harendra, K. D. 1989. The Genesis of Economic Corruption; A Microtheoretic Interpretation. *World Development* Vol. 17, No. 4 (April): 503-511.

Hoff, K. 1988. Essays in the Theory of Trade & Taxation under Incomplete Risk Markets, PhD thesis. Princeton University.

Hopkins, R. W. 1986. Accounting Education and Development — Some Personal Reflections and Perspectives. Proceedings of the New Frontiers in Accounting Education in South East Asian Universities (herafter New Frontiers) Singapore: 121-177.

———. 1991. Accounting Education, Professionalism and Socio Economic Development. SEAUTA Conference, Jakarta: 323-330.

Hove, M. R. 1986. Accounting Practices in Developing Countries: Colonialism's Legacy of Inappropriate Technologies. *International Journal of Accounting* Vol. 22, No. 1 (Fall): 81-100.

IEG 9, International Education Guidelines. 1991. *Guideline on Prequalification Education, Tests of Professional Competence and Practical Experience of Professional Accountants.* New York: International Federation of Accountants (July).

IEG 9a. Appendix to IEG 9.

Ijiri, Y. 1983. On the Accountability Based Conceptual Framework of Accounting. *Journal of Accounting and Public Policy* Vol. 2.

Khambata, F., and D. Khambata. 1989. Emerging Capital Markets: A Case Study of Equity Market in India. *Journal of Developing Areas* Vol. 23, No. 3 (April): 425-439.

Klonda, A. 1986. *Primary Health Care: Who Cares?* Lilongwe; Private Hospitals Association of Malawi.

Lim, C. C., S. S. Deri, Boh M., and F. Samad. 1991. The University Accounting Education. The Malaysia Scene. SEAUTA Conference, Jakarta: 67-73.

Lin, Z., and S. Deng. 1991. Educating Accountants in China: Experiences and Prospects. *Balance: The Afro Asian Journal of Accounting* (Winter).

Lou, E. Y., and W. Zhang. 1991. Innovation in Accounting Education in China: A Review and Critique. SEAUTA Conference, Jakarta: 212-220.

Lucas, R. E. Jr. 1988. On the Mechanics of Economic Development. *Journal of Monetary Economics* Vol. 22 (July): 3-42.

Mohan, R., and R. Salst. 1988. Educational Expansion & Inequality of Pay: Colombia 1973-8. *Oxford Bulletin of Economics & Statistics* Vol. 50, No. 2 (May): 175-182.

Mudogo, E. 1986. In Search of Requisite Accounting Information in a Predominantly Subsisence Economy: The Papua New Ginea Case. New Frontiers Conference, Singapore: 863-882.

Mueller, G. G. 1968. Accounting Principles Generally Accepted in the US versus Those Generally Accepted Elsewhere. *International Journal of Accounting* (Spring) in ed. S. J. Gray. *International Accounting and Transnational Decisions.* Butterworths.

Needles, Belverd E. Jr. 1990. Standard for International Accounting Education: A Consideration of Issues. *Comparative International Education Standards.* Center for International Educational Research in Accounting, University of Illinois: 1-31.

Oliga, J. C., and J. M. Samuels 1986. Towards Accounting Development in Third World Countries. New Frontiers, Singapore: 883-903.

Osiegbu, P. I. 1987. The State of Accounting in Nigeria. *International Journal of Accounting* Vol. 22, No. 2 (Spring): 57-68.

Prawiro, R. 1991. Accounting Development for Economic Development. Opening speech at the 1-8 SEUTA Conference, Jakarta.

Prentice, C. A. 1986. Admission Tests for Accounting Schools in Indonesia. New Frontiers in Accounting Education in South East Asian Universities. Singapore: 772-780.

Priestley, C. 1989. University Book Famine Initiative: The International Campus Book Link, *African Affairs* Vol. 88 (October): 353, 583-584.

Rivero, J. M. 1990. The Accounting Profession and Accounting Education in Panama: A Survey. *Comparative International Accounting Education Standards* qv Briston et al 1990.

Romer, P. 1986. Increasing Returns and Long Run Growth. *Journal of Political Economy*, Vol. 94 (October): 1002-1038.

Roque, F. D. Jr. 1986. The University and Economic Development through Accounting Education. New Frontiers Conference, Singapore: 272-281.

Rossides, D. W. 1984. What is the Purpose of Education? *Change* (April): 14-46.

Roy, R. H., and J. H. Macneill. 1967. *Horizon for A Profession.* New York; AICPA.

Said, A. M. 1991. Social Responsibility and Accountability. SEAUTA Conference, Jakarta: 495-509.

Seidler, L. 1969. Nationalism and The International Transfer of Accounting Skills. *International Journal of Accounting* (Fall).

Sishtla, V. S. 1990. Economics Development under Five-Year Plans and Accounting Education in India. *Comparative International Accounting Education Standards*, qv at Briston: 213-236.

Stiglitz, J. E. 1987. Learning to Learn: Localized Learning and Technical Progress. *Educational Policy and Technical Performance*. P. Dasgupta and P. Stoneneman eds. Centre for Economic Policy Research, Cambridge University Press.

———. 1989. Markets, Market Failures and Development. *American Economic Review* Vol. 79, No. 1 (May): 197-203.

Tipgos, M. A. 1991. Regional Accreditation: A Strategy for Allocating More Resources In Southeast Asian Countries. SEAUTA Conference, Jakarta: 316-322.

Treadway, J. 1987. Report of the National Commission on Fraudulent Financial Trading.

Trueblood Report [short title]. 1973. Study Group on the Objectives of Financial Statements. New York: AICPA.

Watts, R. L., and J. L. Zimmerman. 1979. The Demand and Supply of Accounting Theories: The Market for Excuses. *The Accounting Review* Vol 54 (April): 297.

Williams, J. R. J., M. G. Tiller, H. C. Heving III, and J. H. Scheiner. 1988. *A Framework for the Development of Accounting Education Research*, Accounting Education Series #9. Sarasota: AAA.

Future Problems and Challenges of Accounting Education in Small States

Charles A. Francalanza

INTRODUCTION

The purpose of this Seventh International Conference on Accounting Education is to explore and study the challenges that accounting education will face in the 21st century. The brochure announcing this conference listed several topics relating to accounting education and from the areas presented, it can be seen that the organisers wanted to be as encompassing as possible. They have, however, again failed to make any specific reference to an area of international accounting, which is rather unique in nature and which, if trends at the time of writing in the Soviet Bloc, Eastern Europe, and other parts of the world continue, is growing in importance. This area is concerned with the problems and challenges of accounting, and consequently accounting education, in small countries. It may be argued that such questions are adequately addressed in the growing literature on accounting in developing countries. This need not be so because the characteristics of the accounting environment in India and Pakistan are totally different from those outlined later in relation to such countries as Luxembourg and Malta.

This apparent lack of interest in the problems of small states is not limited to accounting. In other disciplines, however, there seems to be a growing awareness of such particular questions. The Commonwealth Secretariat, for example, as a result of the decolonisation process of the British empire that has taken place since World War II, has shown special interest in the economic problems of small countries and has organised or sponsored different conferences on this subject.[1] On a European level, six micro European states met in Andorra in 1987 to discuss the socioeconomic relations of micro states with the much bigger members of the European Community.[2] Also, much of the economic analysis taking place in the Caribbean and South Pacific, two regions with a large number of small states, discusses the problems facing small countries.

What is actually meant by the term "small country"? The classical criteria of smallness are population, area, and the size of the economy as measured by GDP. According to the 1989 World Development Report of the World Bank.[3] 130 countries/territories have populations of less than ten million. Sixty-one of these, or 33 percent of all counties, have a population of less than one million. These micro states have a population of about 0.3 of 1 percent of the total world population and they occupy an area of about three percent of the total world living area. Their average per capita income, excluding three oil-producing countries, is only around 88 percent of that of the world average income. Forty-five countries have a surface area of less than 5,000 square miles; most of them are islands.

In theoretical economic terms, a small country is one that is small enough that the quantity of goods and services it produces is too small to affect their prices. In other words, the small country, from a micro point of view is a "price taker." At the macroeconomic level, smallness may be defined as such that the country's expansion or contraction will not influence the overall economic activity in the rest of the world. There are some exceptions to this as, for example, a few small oil-producing countries.

The purpose of this article may by now be evident. It aims to deal with accounting in small states and, more specifically, with the problems facing accounting education in such small states now and

---

[1] In 1972, a conference in Barbados addressed the question related to the development policy in small countries. In 1981, the Commonwealth Secretariat sponsored a conference organised by Alister McIntyre, Deputy Secretary-General of UNCTAD, on the problems and policies in small countries. In 1983, the Commonwealth Study Group discussing the world financial and trading system addressed the particular disadvantages of 20 ministates with populations of less than half a million.

[2] 'Les Micro Etats et la Grand Europe', Andorra, 7-13 September, 1987. The participating states were Andorra, Liechtenstein, Luxembourg, Malta, Monaco, and San Marino.

[3] World Bank, *World Development Report 1989*, the World Bank, Oxford University Press, 1989.

Charles A. Francalanza is a senior lecturer at the University of Malta.

in the future. Small countries vary a lot with regard to climatic conditions, physical and human resources, welfare levels, and political, social, and cultural characteristics, and future developments in accounting education can consequently be different in each small state. There are, however, certain features and problems that, due to their size, are common to most, if not all, small states. These form the basis of this essay. For reasons of familiarity, examples of these common traits are drawn from the conditions and developments in Malta, a micro Mediterranean island state of little more than a third of a million inhabitants with a land area of less than 200 square miles.

The article is divided into four sections. In the first, the characteristcs of the accounting environment and accounting education in small states is outlined. The second section describes the effects that such characteristics can have on present-day accounting education in such states. The third section looks at examples of factors that may have an effect and that therefore have to be considered when planning future accounting education in small states; the fourth section contains some general recommendations for developing what is essentially small-state–friendly accounting education.

THE GENERAL ACCOUNTING AND ACCOUNTING EDUCATION CHARACTERISTICS OF SMALL STATES

In this section only the characteristics related to size will be outlined. This is being done to avoid, as far as possible, any confusion with other types of countries, like developing countries, whose characteristics overlap those of some small countries. Because of this constraint, the distinguishing features are reduced to a few in number but, as will be shown in the following section, their effect on accounting education is still extensive. The characteristics are divided into two groups. The first group deals with the accounting environment in general. As pointed out earlier, knowledge of such a background is essential since it has a profound effect on accounting practice and accounting education. The second group of features will illustrate the actual accounting education situation in small states:

General Accounting Environment

1. *Nature of Business Units*

   Due to the constraints of the domestic market, the great majority of local concerns are very small in size.[4] In such entities, where the owners frequently keep for themselves the day-to-day running of the business, although there still is a place for the normal financial and management accounting techniques and procedures, there is little scope for the specialisation of personnel and resources found in larger concerns. The accounting function in all its aspects falls under the responsibility of one person who is also very often entrusted with duties of general management and company secretaryship.

   The few relatively large concerns that exist are in most cases subsidiaries of large foreign multinational companies. They are set up as simple production units with the functions of financing and marketing performed at the foreign head office. Any financial reporting carried out, although conforming with local laws, is aimed primarily at meeting head office control and consolidation requirements.

2. *The Proximity of Participants*

   Due to the relatively few numbers involved, company directors, bank managers, and others in the forefront of business activity are very often on a first-name relationship. In such an environment, there is a tendency towards informal, frequently unrecorded, means of communication, and an adequate amount of information about local business affairs is always available in the social "grapevine." As a result, external financial reporting is afforded a lesser dimension than in larger countries.

3. *Lack of Accounting Regulation*

   It is true that local commercial and company laws exist but, typically, these rely on foreign influence, primarily that of the former coloniser.[5] Court cases dealing with, for example, aspects of accounting measurement are few and far between. Indigenous accounting standards are rarely issued[6] and for such regulations, the pronouncements of either the Inter-

---

[4]According to the Census of Industrial Production, in 1984 Maltese manufacturing units numbered 1,473 and contributed nearly 30 percent of the gross domestic product at factor cost. Of these, 1,157 (79 percent) employed less than ten workers. Only 24 (2 percent) employed more than two hundred workers.

[5]In Malta the first and only piece of legislation concerning the form and duties of business units is the Commercial Partnership Ordinance (CPO) of 1962. Since Malta is a former British colony this law relied heavily on the British Companies Act of 1948. However, whereas the British Act has since been amended six times, the Maltese CPO has remained unchanged.

[6]For example, in Malta the Accountancy Profession Act was passed in 1979 (amended in 1986). Inter alia, this Act set up the Accountancy Board and provided for the establishment of maltese accounting standards. Up till the time of writing this paper, no accounting standards have as yet been issued.

national Accounting Standards Committee or of the former coloniser are relied upon.

4. *Small Size of the Accounting Profession*

The accounting profession in small states counts to only a few hundred[7] with a consequent insufficiency of funds and facilities. The members with the inclination and the time to take an active part in the affairs of such organisations are disencouragingly few, with the same names cropping up year after year in the different committees. In such a setting, it is very difficult to start and sustain certain initiatives like an accounting journal and, as a result, public debate on matters relating to accounting, both practical and theoretical, cannot be cultivated.

Accounting Education Environment

1. *Nature of Accounting Education*

Undergraduate accounting education is provided to the relatively small number of students either on a full-time basis at the local university or polytechnic or on a part-time basis, by the local professional institution. Foreign accounting qualifications are also studied for either when no local accounting teaching institution exists or when a place in the local institution is not obtained. Tuition for such foreign qualifications is obtained either through full-time study at a foreign institution or through correspondence courses sent for from the country of the foreign examination.

A fast-growing development today is that of continuing education. With the ever-increasing pace of the process of change in accounting theory and practice, knowledge acquired during the school years is more rapidly becoming obsolete. Accountants are therefore continually seeking to learn new techniques and procedures through participation in various types of courses and seminars.

2. *Teaching Staff*

In the local accounting teaching institutions, there is usually only one or two specialists in each particular branch of accounting. The committing of members of staff to the speciialisation in and teaching of specific topics, like the budgeting process, is an unaffordable luxury. In many areas related to accounting, such as taxation amd computing, the services of practitioners in these areas on a part-time basis are obtained.

3. *Accounting Teaching Material*

Accounting textbooks and other teaching material originating in small countries are practically unheard of. The local student market is simply not big enough to render such initiatives viable with

the numbers of students diminishing in the higher stages of accounting programmes. Because of this, the teaching material used in class is either imported, usually from the former coloniser, or, in the case of local subjects such as law and taxation, is in the form of lecturer's notes, which vary according to the particular lecturer.

THE EFFECT OF THE ABOVE CONDITIONS ON ACCOUNTING EDUCATION

The general effect of the above environmental characteristics on accounting education is to limit it in a number of ways. The following are some examples.

The fact that accounting teaching institutions are small as regards staff, space, facilities, and numbers of students means that accounting programmes offering a wide range of optional subjects are impossible or uneconomical to provide. Accountancy students, therefore, have to follow the same courses with little or no opportunity for specialisation.

The fact that accounting departments are small in size also means that each member of the academic staff, from the senior down to the most junior, has unavoidably to be entrusted with a relatively heavy share of administrative duties. This may impinge on the time set aside for such academic matters as the preparation of lectures, setting and correction of examination papers, and programme development and coordination.

Moreover, the above situation affects the few research projects undertaken. As a result of the limited library facilities and the consequent reliance on foreign sources for particular reference material, research projects take an abnormally long time to be finished. In addition, due to the lack of specialists in the same area of accounting, discussions and the seeking of advice on research work being undertaken on local topics are very difficult or simply impossible.

The part-time members of staff, when they are found in the limited local situation, are constrained by their own personal time-tables. Very often they are on campus only at the time of their classroom sessions. Because of this, communication between them and the full-time members is limited, affecting the cohesion of the accounting department.

---

[7]The number of maltese qualified accountants is presently about 400 although lately it has been increasing at the rate of about 30 every year.

In many respects, the foreign textbooks and other teaching materials used are alien to local conditions. The foreign names, amounts and quantities, currencies, and laws and situations used and quoted tend to make students treat the study and solution of the case studies and problems found therein as simply classroom exercises with little relevance to local real-life situations. An additional problem is that, when the teaching material comes from some country other than the former coloniser, even the accounting terminology used may be unfamiliar.[8] These problems of unfamiliar teaching materials are more pronounced in financial accounting and reporting where the reference to the requirements imposed by foreign laws is normally not compatible with the local legal requirements. The laws and regulations in the country of origin of the accounting textbooks, usually the former colonial power, are, as a rule, changed and expanded much more frequently than in the small countries using them. Obviously the textbooks are updated accordingly, and a situation then arises as to where to find examples and problems for discussion conforming with current local legal requirements. Students in small states have to use the older editions of foreign accounting textbooks that may seem to be out of print.

In summary, it can be stated that, as a result of the conditions outlined above, change in accounting education is very slow, and when it does take place, it is carried out to follow foreign developments, not as a result of some study of changes in local accounting conditions. The attitude towards accounting education is still that of stressing accounting methods as the focal point of the educational process with considerable importance being attached to the ability of students to apply those methods to more complex problems as in the case of sophisticated consolidation puzzles. There is still the rigid adherance by teachers to double-entry bookkeeping as a basis for the teaching of financial accounting while in cost and management accounting, emphasis is usually placed on the learning of technical procedures. The fundamental concepts underlying financial and management accounting are not dwelt on too much. Accounting theory is introduced only in the later stages of the programme, usually with no standard plan and very often ending up being an explanation of the requirements of foreign accounting standards, which, in their majority, bear little or no relevance to current local conditions.

FACTORS AFFECTING FUTURE ACCOUNTING EDUCATION IN SMALL STATES

Most of today's independent countries gained their independence in the post-World War II period. As with newborn children, the first few years were quite probably characterised by insecurity, dependence, and teething troubles of varying lengths and degrees of intensity. Once this period has passed, however, each country begins to take on its own individual identity and slowly embarks on the social, political, and economic routes that it deems best for its future existence and development. The former influence begins gradually to wane and is replaced by the ones encountered in the new paths that the country has decided to follow.

The small independent countries in the world today have reached different stages of this process of change. Most probably, many are starting to take a closer look at the structures and institutions which they inherited on the day of their independence and studying whether and, if in the affirmative, how they should best be changed. Naturally, accounting also falls under this scrutiny. As stated many times by different authors, accounting does not take place in a vacuum, and if its environment changes, then the accounting function has to make a corresponding change if it is to maintain or, better still, increase its relevance as the most important micro and macro information-providing mechanism.

The same applies to accounting education. In spite of the limitations constraining them, those in charge of such education are in duty bound to study and assess the different perspectives and changes in them taking place and adjust their output accordingly. Only in this way can their end-product, that is, the future accountants, be prepared to properly serve their employing entities in the future. The following sections briefly deal with four aspects that will surely influence future accounting education in small states.

1. *The Objective Function of Accounting*

As already pointed out in a previous section of this article, due to the various constraints brought about by small size, change takes place very slowly in small states. Most probably, the

---

[8]In Malta, accustomed as we are to British terminology, we have this problem with American accounting terms. Ordinary terms like "common stock" and "accounts receivable" make students uneasy while others like "in substance defeasance" simply bewilder them.

perception today of the nature and objective of accounting is not very different from that prevailing at
the time of the former coloniser. The attest function
of accounting still predominates and a career in auditing with a public accounting firm is still the aspi-
ration of many student accountants. Obviously, all
this has an important bearing on the accounting education being provided. The real objective function
of accounting within the ambit of the local environment is, however, now increasingly being understood. Emphasis has to be put on the word "real"
because it is now being recognised that, given certain aspects in the general accounting environment
like the proximity of the accounting information users, the aim of accounting in small states is not the
attest function, but the provision of relevant information for making economic decisions by the various user groups has been emphasised in larger countries in the last few decades. Also, given the situation prevailing in many small states in which the
absence of a stock exchange, banks, and government
agencies, not the outside shareholders, are the primary users of accounting information, management
accounting information and all that it entails as regards valuation and the qualitative characteristics of
the information provided, is more relevant than that
being currently provided in annual financial reports.

2. *The Role of the Accountant*

A brief review of the work of the accountant in
small states points to the growing importance of
familiarity with aspects of business other than the
traditional accounting ones. First of all, due to the
increasing demands of commercial and economic
expansion and the influence of the large international accounting firms, the variety of services currently offered by the local public accounting firms is
much wider than that provided previously. Secondly,
due to the small size of the average business unit,
the industrial accountant in small states cannot be
limited to specific activities. In other words, whereas
in large concerns the accountant is part of a team of
management specialists, in small firms, where the
size of such a team is very much reduced, although
accounting in all its aspects would still be the
accountant's prime responsibility, that role can easily be turned into that of a general management cum
financial factotum. The impact of the computer on
the accountant as the prime provider of information
should also not be forgotten. Its increasing availability even to small firms and the growing awareness of
its immense capabilities in the handling of information are creating a new business environment requiring differently equipped professionals.

3. *Prevailing National Conditions and Future As-
pirations*

The current local commercial and business
conditions and the way these will be affected by
the new directions that the country may be presently embarking upon will obviously have an important bearing on the knowledge that accountants
should have and on the services they will be required to provide in future.[9] Such changes can even
mean the demise of long-standing industries and
the coming to the fore of new ones with a consequent change in the services provided by, and
therefore knowledge required of, accountants and
it is inconceivable how the impact of such matters
can be ignored in the preparation of local future
accountants.

4. *International Harmonisation of Accounting
Education*

Two features that are common to most small
states besides their size and that are a direct result
of this characteristic are their openness to international events and their reliance on foreign sources
for investment funds. Small states go to great
lengths to attract international capital to their
shores offering very tempting investment packages
to achieve this important goal. The presence of an
efficient accounting profession would be an invaluable additional attraction, and it is therefore in the
best interest of small states to have an internationally recognised local accounting qualification. The
attainment of such a status for accounting credentials would be greatly assisted through compliance
with the international efforts being made to achieve
harmonisation in accounting education both on a
global and regional level.[10]

GENERAL RECOMMENDATIONS ON FUTURE ACCOUNTING EDUCATION

The implications of the conditions and expectations outlined in the previous sections are obvi-

[9]For example, local conditions will surely change in Malta
as a result of initiatives undertaken in the last few years,
namely, the application for EEC membership, the opening of a local stock exchange, the establishment of the
island as an offshore business centre, and the commencement of oil exploration.

[10]Examples of such international efforts at accounting education harmonisation are the seven International Accounting Education Guidelines issued by the International Federation of Accountants since 1982, and the 8th Directive
of the European Economic Community (adopted in March
1984 and intended primarily for member states), which
deals with the qualifications of auditors.

ously far reaching for accounting education in small states. They will involve adjustments in what is to be taught to future accountancy students, the material to be used, as well as the emphasis to be placed on the various aspects of the accounting curriculum.

Specific recommendations on such matters are difficult to propose since these would have to take into consideration the conditions and characteristics of the individual country. These should therefore be left to the accounting leaders in each particular state. Certain general suggestions could, however, be briefly proposed here since they follow naturally from the conditions and problems outlined in the previous sections.

Thus, the present importance given to laws, rules, and accounting standards, very often not really relevant to the local situation since these are those found in the imported foreign textbooks, should be drastically redimensioned. Rules and regulations change with changing circumstances, and knowledge narrowly based on them quickly becomes obsolete with the result that time devoted to continuing accounting education is "wastefully" spent in familiarisation with the new rules and standards instead of new proposals on theory and state-of-the-art processes and data systems. The fundamental part of the future accounting programme should instead be made up of conceptual thinking on and analysis of the present accounting measurement, valuation, and disclosure criteria and their alternatives. Only in this way would future accountants be equipped to evaluate and choose from alternatives when the need for decisions in such matters arises. As regards the foreign and international accounting standards that have to be used in the absence of local ones, these should not be imposed on students simply because they have been issued. They should be sifted and consideration given only to those bearing relevance to the local context as balanced by pressures for international accounting harmonisation.

The conditions prevailing in small states point to the fact that the emphasis placed on the different subject areas of the accounting curriculum need not necessarily be the same as in large countries. The relative importance of financial accounting and reporting on the one hand and general management and management accounting on the other may have to be readjusted. Many factors, national and international, accountancy related or otherwise, have to be considered to arrive at the right balance. Certain suggestions could, however, be of general relevance. Thus, due to the importance of the general

management area to the average accountant in small states, certain areas such as operational research, organisation theory, and the behavioural sciences, and such practical subjects as the law and procedure relating to meetings are very pertinent and, where lacking, adequate space should be afforded to these areas in the accounting curriculum. The same can be said of the economic and commercial impacts of the aforementioned new directions and initiatives taken at a national level. Also, in spite of limitations, provision should be made in the syllabus, even on an optional basis, for areas dealing with the requirements and complexities of the new service industries such as insurance and tourism, which may be coming to the fore as a result of the new economic directions being undertaken by the country concerned.

The computer and modern electronic data processing should be treated as the revolution in information systems that they truly are. Even in small states they are generating a new background against which accounting has to be taught. Their impact should therefore permeate through the whole accounting programme and not be treated as a single subject inserted in the earlier stages of the course.

Needless to say, for students to obtain the greatest benefit from such changes, it should be ensured that there is maximum coordination and cohesion among the different subject areas of the accounting curriculum. Students should not perceive the accounting programme as a series of related but unconnected disciplines. They should clearly understand the purpose of learning a topic and the reasons for its particular position within the accounting curriculum. The material covered during their studies would then make more sense and they would be better equipped and thus more confident to face the challenges met in their future careers.

An important corollary to the above suggested changes is that the teaching material would have to be given a local orientation. It has to be accepted that in those subjects where the theories involved have universal relevance, the content would still have to be provided by the foreign textbook, today increasingly embellished by such supporting material as workbooks, software and videos. Such theories should, however, be given a local flavour through the development of notes, problems and case studies for discussion. As regards the 'local' subjects, every effort should be spent to develop local material of a more permanent and diffused nature than the traditional lecturer's notes frequently used at present. It was earlier stated that, given the size of the local market, attempts at developing local teaching material are definitely uneconomical. The present situation is, however, untenable on different grounds, and mechanisms suitable to local conditions should be set up whereby native experts in the different fields are given adequate opportunity and compensation to develop such material and to keep it current with changes in local conditions.

CONCLUSION

As indicated by the title, the purpose of this paper is to draw attention to the challenges facing future accounting education in small states. The advancement of accounting education in such states could be rendered an easy process if all that is done is to simply follow the developments in the large leading countries. On the other hand, it can become a very onerous task if the local environment is also taken into consideration. Although some general suggestions on these lines were made in the last section, the underlying characteristic of small states which pervaded the whole of this paper has been the restricting effect of size on all aspects of accounting and accounting education. Due to this constraint, it is doubtful whether small states have the resources to individually tackle such an important issue. It would therefore seem opportune to end this paper with appeals firstly for help from the large advanced countries and international bodies in all matters dealing with accounting education and secondly for the setting up of international mechanisms where the problems and challenges in accounting and accounting education common to small states can be addressed on a formal and, if possible, continuing basis.

Action and Results Oriented Research and Consultancy Approach to Third World Accounting Education and Professional Development

J. B. Ato Ghartey

Professions adapt to transformations in human values that give rise to them. As such, with the advent of the new Europe and the demise of the Cold War, the accountancy profession in the Third World needs to begin the arduous task of self-study and reevaluation. The self-study is needed to propel the profession through the evolution necessary to meet the needs of society in the New World Order and the next century.

In the process of self study and re-evaluation, the concern for global improvement and harmonization of accounting practices finds itself at the forefront. Considering the volume of trade and socioeconomic activities between the North and the South, and international concerns to improve and harmonize the quality of accounting practice, it would be prudent in the study process to reassess some of the perennial problems of accounting education and development.

In the past generation, literature and consultancy reports on the deficiencies and proposed remedies of Third World accounting education and development proliferated. What was found to be in critical supply was effective on-sight, hands-on action to provide a conceptual framework and operational guidelines for accountability, and establishing the institutional framework for improving the quality of accounting education and development in the Third World.

As part of institutional building for global management development and consolidation, the United Nations, The World Bank, and the African Development Bank, for example, set up a capacity building fund for Africa in 1991. To ensure that accountancy education and professional development receives its due share of this fund and other sources of funds, and apply the funds in a cost-effective manner, this paper uses Africa as a case study of Third World regions to

1. Recommend the review, update and consolidation of studies on Third World accounting education and development needs;

2. Establish the foundations for a progression from apparently sterile, normative and prescriptive research/consultancy and technical assistance to collaborative, action and results-oriented research/consultancy and technical assistance;

3. Provide further thrust to the concept of establishing regional centers of accounting education and development in the Third World; and

4. Present and sell the principle to national governments, management of the recently established African Capacity Building Fund, international and bilateral organizations, and the general public that development of accounting education and practice deserve as much priority and support in management capacity building and economic development programs as do other leading professional disciplines.

The paper draws on a generation of extensive international experience in accounting education, research, and practice. It is the result of many international assignments and hands-on experience as a student, professor, professional practitioner, and consultant in several African and Western countries.

The 1988 *Annual Report of the International Monetary Fund* (IMF) identified 134 developing countries distributed in five geographical world regions as follows (p. 217): Africa 48, Western Hemisphere 33, Asia 28, Middle East 16, and Europe 9. In line with international development priorities and focus in the 1980s, the discussions in this paper focus on Africa. However, because of the environmental and other similarities of Africa with other parts of the Third World, the recommendations and proposals would provide a model that would be potentially generalizable and adaptable to other Third World regions.

J.B. Ato Ghartey is Professor of Accounting at the University of Massachusetts. He is currently on leave of absense as technical adviser for The Institute of Chartered Accountants (Ghana).

JUSTIFICATION FOR ACTION AND RESULTS-ORIENTED RESEARCH AND CONSULTANCY APPROACH

Within the past generation, literature and consultancy reports on Third World accounting deficiencies and proposed remedies have burgeoned. The United Nations, the World Bank, International Federation of Accountants (IFAC), United States Agency for International Development, and publications of several other international, regional, and national organizations and institutions, and seminars, symposia and conferences of professional and academic accountants have endlessly responded to the anxieties of the problems and deficiencies of Third World accounting and their repercussions on international relations and commerce. The most recent and comprehensive of these studies for Africa is *Accountancy Development in Africa Challenges of the 1990s*, published in 1991, and prepared by the United Nations, the World Bank, and the International Labour Organization (the Joint Study).

The problems and deficiencies constitute an endless list. With slight modifications the list could be adapted to different regions or countries in the Third World. The list includes a dearth of qualified accounting personnel, lack of meaning and direction of accountability, untimely and unreliable information systems, unnecessary bureaucracy, inadequate or nonexistent professional, education and training institutions, inadequate or nonexistent institutional linkages, obsolete governmental accounting systems, and failure or inability to employ or retain qualified and competent accounting and management personnel.

There is almost universal acknowledgement and consensus on what the major accounting deficiencies and problems in the Third World are. What is in doubt is how to get effective action to mitigate the problems and shortcomings. The two most recent international deliberations on Third World accounting are the Asia and Pacific Conference on Accounting Education and Development (APCAED)[1] held in Manilla, Philippines, in November 1984, and the African Accounting Conference held in Abidjan, West Africa in December 1988.

Both the Manilla and Abidjan conferences concurred with Third World accounting concerns and anxieties that have been expressed within the past generation, and the need to improve the quality of accounting education and practice in the Third World. Both conferences identified the major con-

straints to the development of accounting education in their environments as the dearth of appropriate education/training institutions, and human and other resources needed to sustain and manage Third World economies. Publication of IFAC Education Guideline No. 7 in 1987 was a response to the Proceedings of the 1984 Manilla Conference.[2] This publication provides guidelines on education requirements for accounting technicians.

To date the emphasis of assistance and guidance on Third World accounting development has been on production of a proliferation of documents on diagnoses and prescriptions for the accounting problems and deficiencies. The manpower and other resources needed to implement the prescriptions continue to be either inadequate or in critical supply.

Theoretical and applied research that do not require immediate action have their time and place in the search and advancement of knowledge. However, effective accountability which would help spur efficient allocation and utilization of resources, and improve the quality of Third World accounting requires more than endless replication and reproduction of sterile reports and literature. It takes time, money, and productive resources to produce consultancy reports and literature. Therefore, accounting diagnoses and prescriptions that are intended to be acted on but that remain not acted on or implemented constitute a waste of and a drain on resources.

What is needed now for Third World accounting development is action and results-oriented research and consultancy that would enable the profession to reap the benefits of a generation's investments in accounting diagnoses and prescriptions. Action and results-oriented research and consultancy in the form of provision of on-sight, hands-on personnel and other resources are required urgently. These resources are needed to provide the leadership, guidance, and on-the-spot assistance to implement research and consultancy proposals, and improve the quality of professional accounting education and development in Third World environments.

Traditional Third World accounting research and consultancy have normally taken the form of

[1]*Proceedings of Asia and Pacific Conference on Accounting Education for Development*. IFAC, Asia Development Bank, World Bank, 1984.

[2]International Federation of Accountants, *Guideline on Education Requirements for Accounting Technicians*, (IEG 7) IFAC, 1987.

brief or intermittent stints by experts to Third World environments, and subsequent publication of research findings or submission of consultancy reports. Almost invariably these publications and reports have piled up and remained unacted on. Among the reasons for the inaction are lack of appropriate personnel and other resources, and inadequate inertia or follow up on the reports or proposals.

What action and results-oriented research and consultancy would seek to do would be to inject **commitment, willingness, perseverance**, and **partnership** (CWPP) into Third World accounting research and consultancy.

Commitment. Long-term commitment to live, work, and relate to colleagues in the Third World environment provides an opportunity to understand and appreciate the environmental and professional subtleties of other cultures. It also provides the researcher/consultant time and the opportunity to discuss, test, and obtain preliminary feedback on proposals and recommendations before the research results are published or the consultancy reports are submitted and/or implemented.

Willingness and Perseverance. To minimize the dangers of contributing to the list of sterile publications and reports, the researcher/consultant must have the willingness and perseverance to live in the Third World environment for a protracted period to foster and guide the research publication or consultancy report to its logical policy audience or destination for appropriate action.

Partnership. Partnership of the researcher/consultant with the implementing organization, institution or client in the form of active participation, cooperation, and collaboration is required if the desired proposals or recommendations of the research or consultancy project are to be attained. Finally, partnership through the action and result-oriented research/consultancy approach would provide an effective contribution to the critical manpower problems, brighten the prospects of getting recommendations and proposals acted on, and provide the chance for the researcher/consultant and local counterparts to share each others' knowledge, learn from each others' experience, and benefit from each other's abilities.

ASSESSMENT OF CURRENT EDUCATION AND TRAINING NEEDS

Action research and consultancy require top intellectual talent and qualifications. Only six of the 51 countries in Africa achieved or became independent before 1960. It would be an understatement to suggest that socioeconomic and political developments in Africa within the past generation make it almost mandatory to review and update, assess the current status and needs of accounting education and development, and propose a potent approach to mitigate accounting problems and deficiencies in the Third World.

Since the 1960s African countries established or expanded their secondary and higher education programs and curricula to suit their national human resource needs. Most countries have established schools for law, medicine, engineering and other professional disciplines. Students in these professional disciplines stay in school and enjoy the benefit of full-time tuition and guidance before writing their final entry-level professional examinations. These examinations are normally administered wholly or in part by the educational institutions that teach the students.

A few countries have succeeded in establishing local professional bodies. Currently, professional accounting bodies in 16 African countries are members of the International federation of Accountants (IFAC).[3] Accounting institutions, on the other hand, that are set up specifically for the education/training of terminally qualified professional accountants are a rare phenomenon in Africa. The 1991 Joint Study, for example, was unable to provide definite answers on countries that provide full-time tuition for the education and training of terminally qualified professional accountants. If such institutions do exist, that would be a very recent phenomenon.

At the professional level, accounting students usually work and study part-time through the non-formal education process to prepare for their examinations. As might be expected, failure and dropout rates have been extremely high. Thus, while professional accounting students face the normal educational constraints in Africa — such as inadequate classroom facilities and lack of textbooks and other instructional elements — they are also subjected to additional constraints such as the lack of appropriate educational institutions in their home countries. As might be expected, failure and drop-out rates have been extremely high. The high failure rate has been a matter of grave concern to

[3]The 16 countries are Botswana, Egypt, Ghana, Kenya Lesotho, Liberia, Libya, Malawi, Morocco, Nigeria, South Africa, Swaziland, Tanzania, Tunisia, Zambia, and Zimbabwe.

some national governments and international donor agencies.

Almost all the universities in Africa are government owned and rely almost exclusively on the governments for their financial support. Realizing the importance of accounting to the development of Africa, governments would normally be expected to devote as much time, effort and resources to accounting as to other professions. However, a 1988 World Bank Policy Study on Education in Sub-Saharan Africa, and the 1988 World Development Report cautioned that the most devastating damage to African higher education is the rapid erosion in the 1980s of the progress made since the 1960s by African governments to build an indigenous African capacity to produce tertiary education teachers, research scholars, and high-ranking analytical and professional personnel.

As financial crisis of the governments deepened, education and research budgets were typically subject to early and severe cuts. Stagnation or decline in higher education and research output, and in the capacity to produce quality education, graduates, and researchers jeopardized Africa's long-run ability to take advantage of worldwide advancement in technology and human development. The World Bank Study recommended that over the long run, Africa can survive and prosper only by fully developing its major resources, people, especially those with skills acquired in tertiary education.

Accountancy education at the professional and tertiary levels were not given as much attention by African governments as to other professional disciplines. With the current financial constraints most African countries are currently facing, it is unlikely that individual African countries can devote substantial amounts to make up the shortfalls in resource allocations to the development of the accountancy profession. In view of this, it is reassuring to note the encouragement and assistance international organizations and other institutions have been providing to the continent.

The World Bank has provided various types of assistance for training and education in financial management in several countries. Various departments and offices of the United Nations and its specialized agencies, the Commonwealth Secretariat, the United States Agency for International Development (USAID), the Canadian International Development Agency (CIDA), the Australian Development Assistance Bureau (ADAB), the German Foundation for International Development, the British Overseas Development Agency, the French Ministry of Cooperation, and the Swedish, Danish, Finnish and other Aid Agencies have similarly provided support for the training and education of African accounting personnel. The assistance provided includes provision of resident experts to manage projects and train counterparts, provision of on-the-job training either locally or overseas, organizing or sponsoring conferences, seminars and workshops, provision of scholarships to Africans to study abroad, and provision of lecturers to teach at African educational institutions.

As a general principle, however, bilateral and multilateral agencies do not make resources available on a countrywide basis for accounting training and education. Currently, only the World Bank considers making resources available for this purpose. Most other multilateral and bilateral sources of technical assistance are mainly interested in improving financial management of local institutions utilizing their project funds. The major reason for this disinclination to develop and/or reform the total financial management education of the host country is that donor/lender concern is normally limited to the technical level, not the policy level.

To date international efforts to improve accountability requirements or the quality of accounting education and development in recipient countries in the Third World have generally been piecemeal, uncoordinated, peripheral in nature, and not well articulated. Such programs and technical assistance creates a duplication of effort and do not get to the heart of the matter.

THE CASE FOR ESTABLISHING REGIONAL CENTERS FOR ACCOUNTING EDUCATION AND DEVELOPMENT

A sample of 50 African universities in the 1988 World Bank Study indicated that 12 of the universities had enrollments under 1,000 students. Only 13 had enrollments over 5,000 and several of these institutions had universities dispersed over more than one campus. This proliferation of small universities precludes exploitation of economies of scale in higher education. It also deprives the institutions of the academic advantages of mass concentration of critically needed highly specialized faculty, staff and physical resources. It is appropriate to guard against such duplication and dissipation of funds when providing for facilities for full-time terminal education/training for professional accountancy and development.

Ultimately, Africa will continue to develop only to the extent that it can take advantage of the worldwide explosion of knowledge and generate knowledge pertinent to African problems. These functions require top intellectual talents and qualifications: the people with professional qualifications and/or master's and doctoral degrees whose careers are in research and development, teaching and training of middle level and high level manpower, and providing the technical leadership and complement to socioeconomic development.

In the 1980s especially, most African countries faced economic and financial crisis. This made planning difficult and stalled the process of localization of accounting and other manpower needs in the continent. There are several multiplier effects. Many faculty members and other highly qualified and experienced personnel unable to cope with inadequate salaries and deteriorating living conditions left their home countries for greener pastures. Nigeria, Uganda, Ghana, Sudan, Zambia, Sierra Leone, and several other countries have lost most of their best talents to international organizations and overseas institutions. Aware of the conditions in their home countries, newly qualified Africans overseas (sometimes educated at their government's expense) are unwilling to return to their home countries. For the qualified people who remain in their home countries, there is a constant need to supplement one's salary with a second job or other business interests. This leads to weakened discipline, lower employee morale and loyalty, neglect of duty, and increases in the incentives and temptations for corruption and inadequate accountability.

Given the continent's limited resources, its inability to provide the needed educational and research facilities or attract and retain suitably qualified faculty and staff, the current diseconomies of scale in the universities, and the unavoidable costly sums required to ensure high-quality research, graduate and professional development programs, it is recommended that the most effective way of accelerating the development of accounting education and practice for the benefit of African and other Third World regions would be to reactivate and implement the concept of Regional Centers of Accounting Education and Development. The concept of creating regional centers of accounting education and development has immense benefits and substantive professional and international support. In fact, such centers have already been established in the Third World for certain professional disci-

plines. Also, regional accountancy bodies have been formed. These include the Arab Society of Accountants, African Accounting Council, Association of Accountancy Bodies of West Africa, federation international des experts compatables Francophones, and Eastern, Central and Southern Africa Federation of Accountants (ECSAFA). However, establishment of regional accountancy educational centers still remains a far cry.

Examples of established regional centers of education and development in Africa for selected designated professional disciplines are the African Regional Center for Engineering Design and Manufacturing (ARCEDEM), the Regional Institute for Population Studies (RIPS), and the African Institute for Economic Development and Planning (IDEP). ARCEDEM, RIPS, and IDEP are sponsored by the United Nations Economic Commission for Africa (ECA), and their directors report to the head of ECA. All three institutions operate under a cooperative arrangement between a number of African countries and the United Nations. RIPS is located in Accra, ARCEDEM in Ibadan, Nigeria, and IDEP in Dakar Senegal.

ARCEDEM promotes cooperation among African countries in the field of engineering design and manufacturing, and promotes its activities by establishing national centers of engineering design and manufacturing as well as a network of such centers in African countries. RIPS carries out research on demographic problems with special reference to the economic and social development programs of the countries it covers. RIPS also provides in-service training to a number of trainees drawn from member countries. IDEP provides specialized postgraduate training to government officials in African member states in economic development, planning and related fields. It also undertakes research and advisory/consultancy services in African countries on socioeconomic problems.

The creation of centers of accounting education and development in African and other regions of the Third World on similar lines as ARCEDEM, RIPS, and IDEP would help mitigate problems associated with national resource inadequacies and far-flung international resources, by being able to maximize the benefits of available resources through cooperation and coordination at regional levels. Nigeria, for example, has a population of over 10 times that of most other countries in Africa. Bigger countries such as Nigeria with a huge market potential for professional accountants, and reasonably well-established infrastructure for accounting education and professional development could have one center to themselves. Similarly, regions with well-developed and cohesive regional organizations such as the ECSAFA could have one center to themselves. On the other hand, such countries as Gambia, Togo, Niger, Chad, Liberia, and Burkina Faso with relatively smaller population and rudimentary infrastructure for accountancy education and development could pool resources to form regional centers with countries with better established infrastructure. For example, English-speaking countries such as Gambia, Liberia and Sierra Leone could join Ghana. And French-speaking countries such as Togo, Guinea, Burkina Faso, Niger and Chad could join Senegal.

In the Final Report of the Conference of Ministers of Education and Those Responsible for Economic Planning in African States organized by UNESCO in 1982, the ministers reaffirmed the need for international cooperation as a means of remedying the present shortcomings of African higher education, especially in the highly specialized fields. Furthermore, both the 1984 Manila Asian and Pacific Accounting Conference and the 1988 Abidjan African Accounting Conferences reiterated the need for and advantages of regional cooperation in accounting education and development.

The regional accounting centers would be staffed by teaching, technical, and management personnel possessing internationally acceptable minimum qualifications and professional standards, and contain sufficient research and instructional resources. The centers would also need diplomatic status in order to insulate their operations from national political and socioeconomic constraints and developments. The type of diplomatic status envisaged would be equivalent to that granted to similar regional institutions that have already been established.

AIMS AN OBJECTIVES OF THE THIRD WORLD REGIONAL ACCOUNTING CENTERS

The following might be considered as a tentative set of aims and objectives for the regional accounting centers in the Third World:

1. Serve as a central resource pool in formulating, coordinating, monitoring and evaluating accounting education and training policy for the designated Third World region,

2. Locate, channel and coordinate research and development funds and resources to be utilized for the benefit of accounting development in the region,

3. Provide postgraduate education (ultimately at the master's and doctoral levels), research and executive development opportunities for accounting professionals and educators within the region,

4. Conduct research in accounting and related fields with emphasis on the region,

5. Develop, adapt and harmonize accounting standards, practices and instructional materials to suit the various environments in the region,

6. Develop accreditation standards for curricula and education/training institutions, and provide an independent examination or accreditation system to measure, certify, and sustain accounting educational standards in the region,

7. Provide continuing professional education for accountants,

8. Liaise with accounting practitioners, educators and established institutions in various countries to develop accounting standards, practice and education,

9. Assist countries to loosen their apron strings with their colonial legacies and masters, and adopt an open and objective approach for global insights and directions to accounting education and professional development,

10. Assist countries already possessing accountancy bodies with professional training and development,

11. Encourage and assist countries without legally established professional bodies to establish such institutions,

12. Develop cooperation and interchange of ideas between accountants and professional bodies in the region, and the international accounting community at large,

13. Assist with other appropriate measures with respect to promoting effective accounting standards and sustained development within different countries and the designated region.

The creation of centers for accounting education and development in Africa and other parts of the Third World, based on the above aims and objectives, would help to mitigate problems associated with both national resource inadequacies and far-flung international efforts and resources. It would also provide a clearly defined direction and focus for accountancy development in the Third World at the regional and international levels.

SUMMARY AND CONCLUSION

The concept of regional cooperation to develop professional fields or disciplines is not alien to the Third World region. Regional centers of education and development in certain professional disciplines have been operational for almost one generation. It is now time for the accounting profession to wake up from the apparent lethargy and present a case for creation and funding of such centers for the development of the profession in the Third World.

In 1991, the United Nations, The World Bank, and the African Development Bank set up a joint capacity building fund for Africa. One of the objectives of the fund is to consolidate and strengthen the infrastructure for management manpower development in the continent. The two major objectives of this paper are

1. To present and sell the idea to the accounting profession, the national governments in the Third World, the management of the African Capacity Building Fund, other international organizations, and bilateral and multilateral organizations, that development of accounting education and practice deserves as much priority and governmental and international support, and international regional centers of excellence, as do other leading professional disciplines.

2. To establish the foundations for a progression from apparently sterile, normative, and prescriptive research/consultancy and technical assistance.

Presenting a persuasive argument for the funding and establishment of the centers requires updated and substantive documentary evidence that would best be gathered by field research. Policy makers need to be convinced that the project proposals are beneficial and feasible. This process involves lobbying and collaborative action. Effective collaborative action requires physical presence in the Third World environment for a protracted period.

There is an urgent need to divert Third World accounting development focus from sterile reports and studies that are rarely acted upon, to develop efforts for a concerted plan of purposeful effective action. This paper uses Africa as a case study of Third World regions to propose a pioneering study

and experiment on action and results-oriented research and consultancy, and provide a further thrust to the concept of establishing regional centers of accounting education and development.

If regional Centers for Accounting Education and Development are established in Africa, it would be the first set of regional/international centers provided exclusively for accounting education and development in the continent. As a major regional or national body recognized by individual African governments, other countries and governments and the international community and organizations, the Center would have the reputation and major role to

1. Serve as a model for the establishment of similar centers in other Third World Regions.

2. Serve as a clearinghouse for international accounting bodies and other institutions and organizations on issues concerning African accounting.

3. Have access to regional and international skills, technical support and resources to achieve its objectives.

4. Recruit and retain high-quality faculty and staff and provide them with internationally acceptable and competitive remuneration and benefits.

5. Minimize national governmental interference from accounting education and development. At present the survival of most accounting education programs depends on the direction of individual government policies and priorities.

6. Insulate the centers and their staff from national political detractions and domestic extracurricula executive responsibilities.

7. Collaborate with governments, donors and lenders to ensure adequate provision of resources for accounting education and development.

8. Minimize the proliferation and duplication of national efforts, donor and technical assistance, and funds.

9. Increase the ability to monitor progress of various sources of funds invested in accounting education and development.

10. Increase the retention rate of qualified African accountants in the continent. A lot of the Africans who are sponsored to study abroad for overseas qualifications do not return home on completion of their studies. Providing the education and training to the students in Africa would minimize this aspect of brain drain.

11. Promote harmonization of accounting education, practices and standards in the continent and the world at large.

The Third World must intensify efforts not only to create and promote its own capacity to develop its indigenous intellectual and professional resources but also to provide and sustain the professional environments in which such highly specialized talent can be productive. The longer term improvement in the quality of accounting education and practice would be realized and sustained through the establishment of programs and centers of excellence for postgraduate education, research, and continuing and executive development programs. By establishing such specialized, high-quality programs and institutions, Third World governments would provide their students and others with an attractive alternative to the more costly foreign study (with the extreme high risk of not getting the student to return home), create incentives for professionals and university researchers to pursue their work in their geographic regions and address the serious problem of brain drain.

Profound changes are required in professional accounting education and development in the Third World. As useful as consultancies and theoretical research may be, fundamental change cannot be expected to result from these alone. Instead, such change will come about only by putting a greater thrust to transforming into action what has been contemplated.

Educational institutions, public officers, the accounting profession, and the general public in Africa and other parts of the developing world need to pay more attention to the concept of accountability so that all individuals may understand and appreciate better their own responsibilities and need to be accountable to their communities. Such awareness and educational process to enhance the level of international confidence in Third World accountability and financial reporting need adequate resources and well-staffed education/training and research institutions, as well as competent and devoted professional guidance and leadership. The desired accountability guidance and leadership would be most effectively provided by the regional centers in Africa and other regions of the Third World.

A Comparison of Accounting Education Systems in Australia, the United States of America, and the People's Republic of China

Yi-fen (Grace) Hu and John A. Marts

INTRODUCTION

This paper is a brief description of accounting education in China today and a limited comparison to accounting education in Australia and in the United States. The principal author has taught in the Chinese university system since 1981 and was a visiting professor at an Australian University for one year and at a U.S. university for two years. It is from this exposure that this paper is written.

INSTITUTIONS

In 1987, using the latest figures available, approximately seven percent of the PRC's institutions of higher education was dedicated to the teaching of finance and economics which includes the offering of degrees in the field of accounting. Another six to seven percent offer accounting concentrations within a given discipline such as Shanghai Marine Transportation College, Southwestern University of Agriculture, and the Shanghai College of Foreign Language. The principal institutions offering concentrations or degrees in accounting are universities of finance and economics. Although this seems like a small number of institutions offering the accounting discipline, the number has increased dramatically since the open policy began in 1979. In 1979 there were only 22 finance and economic institutions in the country. Today there are 74 (Appendix A).

Other than regular universities and colleges, as those in the United States and Australia, the PRC has several correspondence and evening colleges, adult self-study programs, and secondary vocational and technical schools which offer accounting majors as well as TV universities.

University Affiliation—Higher Authority

The university system in the PRC is operated almost in its entirety by the government. However, each university is affiliated with a specific higher authority within the government. For example, some universities are affiliated directly with the State Education Committee, some with a particular industry ministry such as the chemical ministry, some with the People's Bank of China, and others with provinces and cities (Appendix B). Usually, universities affiliated with the State Committee are comprehensive institutions and are of higher prestige. Prestigious universities from all affiliations are known as key universities, with approximately ten percent of all universities fitting into this category.

Although having universities affiliated with so many different higher authorities lends itself to duplication of programs, the PRC believes that this system has its advantages. Among the advantages are a closer relationship with industry, a better chance at obtaining graduates into specific fields, and if the Ministry attaches importance to accounting education, a better funding arrangement can be made. Institutions that are ministry related will teach from that ministry's perspective as well as being able to provide real-world contacts for the students in that particular field. The institutions also have easy access for student internship programs which all students must go through before graduation. From the ministry's viewpoint, they may enjoy priority in obtaining graduates from the universities and colleges under its leadership. This is important because the supply of graduates is usually less than the demand.

The prestige and status of a university in the PRC is determined similar to the determination in the United States or Australia. Status is based on the accomplishments of the institution and its faculty and the diversity of its programs.

CURRICULUM

Most accounting undergraduate programs in the United States and Australia dedicate approximately

Yi-fen (Grace) Hu is an Associate Professor, Southwestern University of Finance and Economics, PRC and is a visiting Associate Professor at the University of North Carolina–Wilmington, and John A. Marts is a Professor at the University of North Carolina–Wilmington.

25 percent of the course work to accounting. The balance is divided between business administration courses (25 percent to 35 percent) and liberal arts, math, and science (40 percent to 50 percent). The average student can finish degree requirements in these countries in four years. The total number of semester hours varies from 120 to 130 for a four-year program.

At Shanghai University of Finance and Economics, the typical curriculum for an accounting major is 164 semester credit hours of which 146 are required and 18 are electives. Accounting-related courses make up 33 percent of the required course work (Appendix C). The curriculum provides for 35 hours of other business course work and the balance is from a basic core of languages and math, and political and ideological courses. The student is required to take four years to finish the bachelor's degree.

In addition to the class work, the undergraduate must write a thesis before receiving a bachelor's degree. Students may choose a topic from a suggested list prepared by the Accounting Department or they may choose their own topic after discussion and approval by the department. Instructors are assigned as advisers to each degree candidate to assist the student with the paper. The thesis for an undergraduate is mainly a review of the literature; however, innovative ideas and original research are encouraged. The length of the thesis is about 5,000 Chinese characters. The student must defend the thesis before a committee of faculty that teach in the area of the thesis.

At universities that offer the master's degree in accounting, the required time length is three years. Approximately 30 semester hours are required plus a 20,000 Chinese character thesis in order to receive a master's degree (Appendix D). Master's students will spend some time after completing the course work traveling around gathering data for the thesis. Some universities invite faculty from other universities to participate in the defense of the thesis, although this is not a requirement.

Doctoral programs in the PRC are two and a half to three years long which includes a dissertation and a second foreign language. Doctoral students will also spend time after completing the course work traveling around the country gathering data for the dissertation. The length of the dissertation is about 50,000 characters. The defense of the dissertation is similar to that of the master's thesis but the defense committee must include faculty from other universities.

STUDENTS

Majors

In the United States and Australia students select which university or college to attend and what their major will be. This is assuming they can meet the entrance requirements for the university and in some cases the major. Most programs in the United States do not require the declaration of a major until the student's junior year. At some institutions the student must apply for admission to the business school or accounting program during their sophomore year. The requirements usually include an above-average GPA for all courses taken and a high GPA in the principles of accounting courses.

In the PRC students select 20 universities and the majors they would like to pursue before sitting for the National Uniform Entrance Exam. The 20 universities are divided between key universities and nonkey universities and are listed in order of their preference. If the student meets the criteria of his or her first choice of schools and majors, then he or she is admitted to that program. If the student does not meet the entrance criteria for his or her first choice then he or she moves down the list to the next school, etc.

Caliber of Students

In the United States and Australia the caliber of students entering a university depends on the entrance requirements of the school. Some universities and colleges pride themselves on the quality of their program and hold very high entrance standards; therefore, all students have relatively similar academic abilities. However, it seems that the majority of institutions have entrance requirements that allow admittance of marginal students as well as the highly qualified. This is especially true in the state-supported university systems.

In the PRC, leveling is not a problem due to the selection procedures used in the admissions process. Most students admitted into the accounting programs have similar abilities.

Student Financial Support

In the United States and Australia, the student is responsible for obtaining the necessary financial support to attend school. This might come from scholarship, grants, loans, part-time jobs or parental support.

In the PRC, the government pays for the students to attend school for higher education. The students are provided with free room and tuition. The students have to pay for their own food as well as their books and supplies. If the student needs additional funds, which all students do, his or her family will provide whatever assistance it can. Scholarships are also available from the institution as are awards for outstanding social work or outstanding social surveys as well as for other activities. About one-third of the students receive scholarships or awards. Part-time jobs are not looked upon favorably in the PRC in that the student is supposed to be going to school full-time and, therefore, should not have time for a job.

Class Schedule

In the United States and Australia, students are allowed to arrange their schedules as they choose. In consultation with their advisers, they can choose the time of day and the semester in which they take their courses. Although they must meet prerequisites, they are given a lot of flexibility as to when and, for some classes, which instructor they will have. Even after they have registered for a class, they can drop it and add another or withdraw from the course altogether. In the PRC a student's class schedule, dates and times, are assigned by the university.

Teaching Methods

In the United States and Australia there are many different teaching styles and methods used in teaching small classes as well as large classes. Currently in the United States innovative teaching methods are being encouraged, as well as integrating more relevant information into the curriculum provided by various groups such as the Accounting Change Commission of the AAA. The methods most commonly used to date involve lecturing on the material and then going over the homework assignments in class. At some major universities, the basic accounting courses are taught in large sections for the lecture portion and then are broken down into smaller sections for tutorial purposes and homework analysis. These are usually taught by graduate teaching assistants. In Australia, at Melbourne University, the "lecture" is given to very large classes (300+ students). Students then attend tutorial sections, about 20 students, taught by the professors and lecturers in the department. Regardless of a professor's rank he or she holds tutorial sections. This is true even for the highest ranking professor even if he or she was not the one responsible for the lecture class. In addition, experienced

accountants from outside of the university are sometimes invited to act as tutors. During the tutorial, rolls are called, important materials of the course are explained and emphasized, questions are asked and answered, and some homework problems are dealt with. The grading of the homework problems in the United States as well as Australia varies from instructor to instructor. Some grade for accuracy, some grade for effort and others collect it just to see if the student attempted the work and no grade is given.

In the PRC usually all classes are relatively small and the lecture method is used to cover the desired material. The instructor may arrange some tutorial sessions when he or she feels that they are needed. Homework in the PRC is turned in regularly. If a text for a given course has end-of-chapter assignments, the instructor will assign problems from the text or problems prepared by the instructor. If the text does not have questions supplied, the instructor will prepare all of the homework questions. The student is required to work and turn in all assigned material. The homework is then graded for correctness as well as completeness. The instructor or the instructor's assistant will do the actual grading of this work and assign a grade. Students are required to do the homework on their own but occasionally the instructor sees the necessity and may arrange a class meeting to do homework.

If a student wants to ask an instructor for assistance outside of class in the PRC, he or she can make an appointment with the instructor since the instructor is not required to have set office hours. This differs from Melbourne University in Australia where professors do not have set office hours but students can go to their instructor's office at any time. If the student's professor is not available, any other professor in the department has the responsibility to help the student.

Examinations

In the PRC, usually two exams are administered each semester, a mid-term and a final. Comprehensive exams are prepared from questions developed by the instructor and approved by the group leader or the vice-chairman of teaching within the department. A relatively new item being developed at some universities to facilitate the preparation of exams is the preparation of a test bank for each course. Each instructor is requested to develop questions for the test bank. The bank is then given to the Department of Academic Affairs. The Department of Academic Affairs then prepares the exams from this test bank. In preparing the exam they follow certain criteria set out by the instructor, such as the percentages of objective and subjective questions and the chapters which the test covers.

The exams are graded by the instructor or the instructor's assistant. The final grades for a class are approved by the academic group head. Sometimes, in some universities, the administration suggests a rough percentage of A's that will be given for a course. If a given instructor's grades do not fall within this range he or she may be asked to review and adjust the grades accordingly, if necessary, or make a case for the variance.

In the United States there is much more diversity in administering and grading of exams. It is usually up to the individual instructor to develop his or her own exams. The instructor can decide to have two exams or as many as he or she wants during the semester. They can be comprehensive or noncomprehensive. They can be specifically designed by the instructor or they can come from a test bank provided by the textbook publisher. Some universities require a common exam at the principles level since there are so many TAs teaching at that level, but very few have common exams for upper-level courses. The grading of the exams is up to the instructor also, unless it is one of the common exams mentioned previously. Some professors use computer scan sheets for the grading of the objective format questions. Each instructor determines his or her student's grade based on his or her own criteria. Some give credit for class participation, outside projects and classroom reports besides averaging their test grades.

At Melbourne University the final accounting examinations are drafted by the course leader in concurrence with all of the professors teaching that particular course. The exam is administered at the same time to all of the students taking the course regardless of their regular class schedule. The students are assigned examination numbers for identification purposes so that when grading takes place the grader cannot identify whose paper is being graded. The point allotment for each question as well as credit for partial correct responses are decided before the exam is graded.

When the students have finished taking the exam, the papers are put into numerical order for ease of tracking. If there were ten questions on the exam, ten professors are assigned to grade one problem each. This might mean grading the same question on hundreds of papers.

After all of the professors are finished with the grading, they total the score for the whole paper. Staff members then input the individual question grades into the computer and check the output with the hand tallies to double check the process before the final grade is posted. Any paper that has a score close to the passing percentage is checked for errors in grading. Statistics are calculated on each question to determine content areas that need work or poor questions. The statistical results are provided in the form of graphs for each question. The analysis of examination performance is considered an important tool in improving teaching performance.

Internationalizing the Accounting Curriculum

The recent push in the West to internationalize the accounting curriculum is also taking place in the PRC. Most of the accounting programs in the PRC already include a Western accounting course in the curriculum. Some programs also require a course in Chinese-foreign joint ventures accounting. A few universities, such as the Central Institute of Finance and Banking, have established degree programs with foreign accounting as a specialty (Appendix E).

Internship Programs

The internship program is considered an important part in the PRC's accounting education process. The students normally have one or two internships in their junior and/or senior year. The accounting students serve their internships in factories, banks, CPA firms, or government offices. Instructors are in charge of the program and make the contacts and arrangements with the various organizations. They are also available to give students guidance and help during the internship period. After the internship period the students are required to write reports on their experiences. During the internship the host organization, if it has room, may provide a place for the student to stay, either in the organization's dormitory or at a nearby guest-house or hotel. If the host organization does not provide the accommodations, the university will do so if the university is too far away for commuting.

In the United States and Australia internship programs vary from university to university. Some are paid internship positions; some are not. Some require the student to work full-time for a semester; others only require part-time work. At a few institutions, the internship is a required part of the degree program. Without it a student can't graduate.

Job Placement

Most universities and colleges in the United States and Australia offer a job placement service to their graduating students. These services help to prepare resumes, hone up on their interviewing skills, and in most cases seek recruiters from various companies to come to campus to interview the students. From there it is up to the student to find his or her own job.

The State Education Committee is the higher authority on job assignment in the PRC and works with a yearly plan based on the supply and demand of college graduates. Organizations which have vacancies they wish to fill with accounting graduates pass these requests onto their higher authority. At each stage, the requests are consolidated and passed upward. The requests are then accumulated at the State Education Committee to be matched with the supply from the various universities.

The State Education Committee, through its matching process, then prepares a job placement plan indicating how many graduates from which universities are to be assigned to the various ministries, or provinces, or cities, etc. After careful consideration of items such as the student's home area, the student's grades and potential, and the specialties needed, the university will place the student. During this process the student may also express his or her desire for a particular job or location. Some universities have experimented with allowing their top students to pick from the list given to the university, thereby rewarding the best and brightest.

Faculty Development

Most universities and colleges in the United States and Australia have faculty development programs. Some are in the form of travel funds to attend educational conferences and some are in the form of paid sabbaticals. The PRC also has faculty development programs for its accounting faculty. In recent years faculty have been allowed paid sabbatical leaves to do research for papers and books or on-site research. Some universities may also send faculty to other universities to study. In addition, the various ministries have offered programs for faculty development. For example, in 1987 in cooperation with the World Bank, the State Education Committee sponsored a one-year training program at Xiamen University with Dr. V. R. Zimmerman and Dr. H. P. Holzer from the University of Illinois as keynote instructors. University accounting departments from all over the country were provided a quota for a certain number of professors to attend.

Accreditation

The PRC does not currently have an accreditation body similar to the AACSB in the United States; therefore, it is difficult for an outsider to know which universities are considered the best in a given field. The method most often used relies on the level of degree offerings at the various institutions. To gain approval to offer master's and doctorate's degrees, a university must make application to the State Education Committee. The committee evaluates the university based on resources and the status of the faculty. As of 1987 there were only 17 universities that could confer accounting master's degrees and only seven that could offer accounting Ph.D. programs. Ph.D.–granting institutions gain this status through the professors. Individual professors are granted permission to have Ph.D. students. That professor then guides the candidate through the program.

Currently, the only written ranking of accounting programs in the PRC was a 1988 report by the State Education Committee. This report ranked the Department of Accounting at Xiamen University and Shanghai University of Finance and Economics as being the leading programs.

On-the-Job Accounting Education

In the United States when a student graduates and enters the work force he or she finds his or her educational process has just begun. In that the demands for accounting information are ever changing, accountants, public or private, must continually educate themselves to keep abreast of the latest techniques. To help them with this education process, most employers provide continuing education programs for their employees. Some of these are in-house programs; some are in the form of continuing professional education programs offered by proprietary firms or accounting societies and associations.

In the PRC continuing education is provided through a three-tiered system.

The Three-Tiered Accounting Education System in Industry in the PRC

Accountants in industry must be well trained. Even though they possess a bachelor's degree in accounting, that alone does not guarantee success, as there is much beyond accounting theory to assimilate in the real world. In addition to having the basic competencies in accounting, a successful accountant in industry must have

1. a strong desire to contribute and accomplish;

2. an exploring mind and perseverance;

3. good communication and interpersonal skills; and

4. knowledge of production and economic activities in an enterprise environment.

Communication and interpersonal skills are extremely important because management in China is very much mass oriented. Mass participation is crucial to enterprise achievement. Similarly, "budgetary participation, managerial performance, and job satisfaction" have been important issues in American industry and accounting literature in recent years. Direct laborers, on-site engineers, inventory clerks, etc., are the ones who work on the front lines, and whose participation and knowledge are essential to achieve enterprise goals. The accountant must know how to communicate with these people.

Where the college leaves off the accountant's education, the industry picks up. China utilizes a three-tiered continuing education system for accounting personnel in some industries. In the chemical industry, for example, the three tiers are Ministry of Chemical Industry, Province or Local Bureau of Chemical Industry, and Enterprise.

Ministry of Chemical Industry

The Ministry sponsors training programs for senior and sometimes mid-level accounting personnel, including directors of accounting departments in major- or ministry-affiliated chemical enterprises. Experienced accountants from the chemical industry serve as principal lecturers, with training programs lasting three months to one year. The programs cover general accounting theory but place more emphasis on accounting issues facing the chemical industry or a particular industry specialty (e.g., chemical machinery, rubber, fertilizer). Occasionally the Ministry also sponsors training programs in universities to update accounting personnel from the chemical industry on specific topics. For example, in 1980, the Ministry sponsored a training program on accounting for Chinese- foreign joint venture enterprises in Xiamen University. An affiliate of the Chemical Ministry, the Beijing College of Chemical Industry, offers an associate degree in accounting to students from within the industry. The students are recommended for this program by the accounting supervisors from the various chemical companies.

Province (or Municipal) Bureau of Chemical Industry

The bureaus sponsor training programs for accounting personnel from major province-affiliated or city-affiliated chemical enterprises, sometimes through participating universities and colleges.

Enterprise

The enterprise often sponsors a half day of accounting study time on a weekly basis. In addition to covering new accounting regulations and/or government documents, participants discuss their accounting work, exchange ideas, and brainstorm problems confronted by the enterprise. Sometimes vocational study programs are organized along departmental lines for front-line cost accountants. The enterprise also holds several "enterprise management" programs to enhance the managerial skills of middle- and upper-level managers, at which departmental directors give presentations related to their particular areas.

APPENDIX A
Distribution of the 74 Chinese Universities
and Colleges of Finance and Economics

By Location		:	By Number of Students	
North China	17	:	<300	5
Northeast	11	:	300–500	7
East	18	:	501–1,000	25
Central South	15	:	1,001–1,500	13
Southwest	6	:	1,501–2,000	10
Northwest	7	:	2,001–3,000	8
	74	:	3,001–4,000	4
		:	4,001–5,000	2
		:		74

APPENDIX B
Examples of Higher Authority Structure for Higher Education in China
(Institutional Affiliation)

<u>**Higher Authority**</u>

1. State Commission of Education

Beijing University
Qinghua University
Xiamen University
Sichuan University

2. Ministries:
   Finance

Shanghai U. of Finance & Economics
Central Institute of Finance & Banking
Northeast U. of Finance & Economics

   Chemical Industry

Beijing College of Chemical Industry
East China College of Chemical Industry

   Agriculture

Southwest U. of Finance & Economics

   People's Bank of China

Southwest U. of Finance & Economics

3. Provinces and Municipalities:
   Shanghai

Shanghai U. of Science and Technology

   Chengdu

Chengdu University

APPENDIX C
Shanghai University of Finance and Economics Curriculum
(Department of Accountancy — Undergraduate Accounting Major)

		Credit/Hours
A.	Ideological Education Courses:	
	1. Situation and Policy	4/131
	2. Basics of Law	2/30
	3. Philosophic Theory of Life	2/19
	4. Ideological Training of University Students	2/34
	5. Professional Ethics	1/17
B.	Political Theory Courses	
	1. Political Economics	8/151
	2. History of China's Revolution	3/51
	3. Philosophy	4/70
C.	General Basic Courses (Fundamental courses)	
	1. Chinese	3/45
	2. Calculus	8/136
	3. Linear Algebra	2/38
	4. Basics of Computer Application	4/76
	5. Foreign Language	20/350
	6. Physical Education	10/172
D.	Specialty-Related Courses	
	1. Business Writing	3/42
	2. Industrial Enterprises Administration	3/57
	3. Statistics	4/76
	4. Finance	3/57
	5. Money and Banking	3/51
	6. Western Economics	4/68
	7. International Trade	2/38
	8. International Finance	2/38
	9. Introduction to Business Law	2/38

(*Continued on next page*)

APPENDIX C (Continued)

E.   Specialty Courses:
       1.   Accounting in English   6/113
       2.   Basic Accounting   5/95
       3.   Financial Accounting   10/178
       4.   Cost Accounting   8/132
       5.   Managerial Accounting   3/57
       6.   Auditing   3/54
       7.   Computerization of Accounting   4/76
       8.   Chinese–Foreign Joint Ventures Enterprises Accounting   2/36
       9.   Western Accounting   5/95
       10. Accounting Theory   2/36

Total Required Courses (89%)   146/2658
Total Options Courses (11%)   (Prescribed 6%, 11/197)
                                     (Random 5%, 7/137)   18/334

Total   Accounting Major   164/2992

        Auditing Major (course offering: more emphasis on principles,   165/2993
              financial auditing, economic benefit auditing,
              sampling auditing)

        Accounting pedagogical Major   129/2331

APPENDIX D
Xiamen University
Graduate Curriculum for Accounting Degrees

Master's Degree	**Credits**	**Semester**
A. Special topics on accounting fundamental theory research (domestic)	4	1
B. Special topics on accounting fundamental theory research (foreign)	4	1
C. Research on Financial Management Topics	3	1
D. Advanced Cost Accounting	3	1
E. Special Topics on Western Accounting	3	1
F. Management Accounting	4	1
G. Capital	4	1
H. Foreign Language	5	2
I. Thesis		2

Ph.D. Degree

	Credits
A. Basic courses:	
1. First foreign language (intensive foreign language training for one semester at foreign language institute)	3
2. Second foreign language (reading knowledge)	3
3. Materialist Dialectics Methodology (philosophy notes by Lenin)	3
B. Specialty basic (fundamental) courses:	
1. Research on "Capital" (Volume 3)	3
2. Research on Economic Accounting and Economic Performance	3
C. Specialty Courses:	
1. Research in Socialistic Accounting Theory & Method	4
2. Research on Western Financial Accounting Theory and Methods	4
D. Dissertation	1 – 1.5 years

APPENDIX E
Central Institute of Finance and Banking
Foreign Accounting Speciality

Undergraduate	Semester	Credit/Hours
1. Ethics	1	3/42
2. Political Economics	2	10/169
3. History of Chinese Revolution	1	4/68
4. Principles of Marxism	1	4/68
5. English	6	24/768
6. Maths	2	8/138
7. Writing	1	3/51
8. Probability and Statistics	1	4/68
9. Linear Algebra	1	3/51
10. Program Design Language		
11. Computer Application	1	2/34
12. Physical Education	4	4/130
13. Principles of Accounting	1	3/51
14. Industrial Accounting	1	5/85
15. Foreign Trade Accounting	1	4/68
16. International Trade	1	3/51
17. Import and Export	1	3/42
18. Western Financial Accounting	1	6/124
19. Accounting for Chinese–Foreign Joint Venture Enterprise	1	4/68
20. Western Financial Management	1	4/68
21. Management Accounting	1	4/68
22. Western Auditing	1	3/51
23. Introduction to Law	1	2/34
24. Internship and Report		4/4 weeks
25. Thesis		10/15 weeks

Restricted Optional Courses

	Semester	Credit/Hours
1. Western Economics	1	3/51
2. Principles of Social Economic Statistics	1	3/51
3. Business Law (Economic Law)	1	3/56
4. Introduction to Insurance	1	2/34
5. International Taxes	1	2/28
6. Industrial Enterprise Management	1	3/51
7. Finance and Credit	1	4/68
8. International Accounting	1	2/34
9. Typing	1	2/34
10. International Credit	1	3/51

Aligning Accounting Education and Training to the Skills Needs in Developing Nations: The Case of SADCC

Shabani Ndzinge

INTRODUCTION

Accounting education and training should be geared towards satisfying the accounting skills needs as dictated by the economic environment. Once the nature of accounting skills needed is known, accounting education and training programmes should, in their design, be aimed at improving and guiding accounting practice and, of course, education and training. There is a need for alignment of accounting education and training with practice. This is particularly so in developing countries where, due to the severely limited resources, there is a need to shorten the time span it takes to produce accountants. It is also crucial that the production of accountants in developing countries be speeded up to fill the gaps that currently exist in most of these countries. This also demands the alignment of accounting education and training with practice.

A call is made for the design of accounting systems which cater to the financial information needs of economic planners in developing countries and for such systems to be in line, overall, with the socioeconomic environments in these countries. This poses a challenge to both academic and practising accountants to not only design the needed accounting systems, but also to reorientate their education and training programmes. This would in turn demand the local production of more educational and training materials to reduce dependence on less suitable overseas ones.

In this paper the shortcomings of existing accounting education and training programmes are discussed. In particular, these do not adequately address themselves to the accounting skills needs of the Southern African Development Conference (SADCC) countries. The paper seeks to explain the current state of affairs and make a case for reform as well as for regional cooperation.

THE CURRENT STATE OF AFFAIRS

Just as is generally the case throughout the British Commonwealth and in certain other parts of the world today, to become a practising accountant in all of the SADCC countries except Angola and Mozambique, one has to sit professional accounting examinations of one institute or another, even after the successful completion of a relevant first degree. To qualify as an accountant through the Chartered Association of Certified Accountants (ACCA) route now common in this region (see later sections), the holder of a relevant first degree would normally need an absolute minimum of two years of full-time study and three years practical experience in the United Kingdom. The road to a full professional qualification such as certified or chartered accountant is, therefore, a fairly long and difficult one.

In Angola and Mozambique there is no emphasis on professional accounting training in the manner in which this is undertaken in the other SADCC countries. However, some fully qualified expatriate accountants are employed in certain industries in these countries (Rowe et al. 1986, 41). Accounting education exists only at the secondary school level in both these countries. As a result of this, the discussion that follows relates only to the first seven English-speaking members of the SADCC.[1]

It has already been pointed out in the previous section that accounting education and training should be geared towards the provision of skills that are needed in the particular economy. It is essential that the types of accounting skills needed in an economy should be known before accounting education and training programmes can be designed to produce those skills. This would normally require a thorough assessment of the accounting skills needs of the particular economy. As economies generally change with time, the continuous monitoring of economic changes and the implication thereof on accounting education and training is necessary. Accounting programmes

---

[1]The author has not been able to collect data on accounting education and training in Namibia.

Shabani Ndzinge is at the University of Botswana.

should, therefore, be reviewed as and when necessary as dictated by economic changes. It is important, therefore, that accounting academics together with their practising counterparts should engage in research activities all the time in order that review of accounting programmes does not significantly lag behind. At times it may even be necessary to carry out research in collaboration with those in allied fields such as economics and statistics. Accounting programmes that do not address themselves to the needs of an economy are an obvious waste of human and material resources.

Existing University Programmes

Just as is the case with accounting practice, Anglo-American influence on accounting education in English-speaking SADCC has been considerable. The first degree programmes are very similar to those of the United States in particular. Most, if not all, of these undergraduate programmes could, with a few modifications, pass for American and British accounting programmes (Markell 1985, 105). The course content of these programmes follows mainly the topics in textbooks, most of which are American.[2] There are almost no books or other teaching materials which have been produced locally. Furthermore, accounting is taught as if it is as universal as arithmetic. This is so despite the demonstrated need for accounting to be a product of its environment (see, for example, Perera 1989; Mirghani 1982; Samuels and Oliga 1982; Briston 1978; Needles 1976).

The economic environments of the United States and the United Kingdom are certainly not similar to those of the developing countries of the SADCC as is evidenced by the different degrees of economic sophistication and the composition of the respective economies. It is worth noting that Anglo-American accounting has even been criticised by scholars such as Briston (1978, 107) for failing to address the accounting information needs of the very countries it was designed to serve. What hope, if any, is there that accounting education programmes modeled after those of the developed Western countries can contribute to the development of accounting skills needed in the developing nations of the SADCC. Even though accounting programmes of the universities of this region have been positively evaluated by scholars such as Markell (1985), American accounting programmes with their bias towards enterprise accounting were used as the standard against which these programmes (SADCC universities'

programmes) were evaluated. No consideration was given to the vast difference in economic composition and sophistication between the developing countries of the SADCC region and the developed Western countries such as the United States of America.

The accounting programmes of the universities of Botswana, Copperbelt in Zambia, Dar-es-Salaam in Tanzania, Lesotho, Malawi, Swaziland and Zimbabwe are too academic in nature for graduates of these programmes to be of immediate value to accounting practice. There is very little attempt to align these to the local environment, except in courses such as company law and taxation. In most cases instructors use material and examination questions in American and British textbooks without any modification except, perhaps, occasional substitution of such immaterial things as names. To make things worse, further reading for students means more American and British books in the university libraries.

The nature of accounting programmes in this region, together with the use of American and British text and reference books, which in some cases cover phenomena that are of marginal importance to developing countries, makes accounting seem like a highly theoretical subject. It also makes it difficult for accounting graduates to develop themselves conceptually to become leaders in the development of accounting theory and practice in their countries.

There are several factors which have contributed to this state of affairs. These include (1) the fact that university accounting programmes were introduced in these countries long after the introduction of Western accounting practice; (2) the recruitment of expatriate academics; (3) the education of local academics in the West; (4) lack of understanding of the potential role accounting could play in economic development and (5) the acute shortage of financial resources needed for research and publication, among others.

On attaining political independence each SADCC country embarked on economic planning to achieve accelerated economic growth and development. In some of these countries, such as Tanzania and Zimbabwe, where significant economic activity took place under colonial rule, Anglo-American accounting systems were already in existence at the time of attaining political independence. In others Anglo-

---

[2]The author is familiar with accounting textbooks prescribed at the Universities of Botswana, Dar-es-Salaam, Lesotho, and Swaziland.

American accounting systems took root a few years after independence as their economies began to experience significant economic growth and development. There were no time and no indigenous accounting expertise to ensure the evolution of accounting in the same way that this has happened in developed countries. Foreign companies which invested in these countries and the international accounting firms which set up branch offices to service them brought along Western trained professional accountants and Anglo-American accounting systems. When academic accounting programmes were finally designed for the local universities, these were naturally based on the prevailing accounting practices as much as on the existing programmes of Western universities. There was never any assessment of the nature of accounting skills needed in the economies of these countries.

Accounting programmes in the universities of SADCC countries were designed largely by expatriate academics recruited from such countries as the United Kingdom, the United States of America, and other countries of the British Commonwealth where self-rule and the resultant manpower development had already spanned many years. It was much easier for such people to draw from their experiences elsewhere and to align the programmes to the existing accounting practices than to depart from what then appeared to be the norm in many developing countries of the British Commonwealth. It is doubtful if most of these academics appreciated the need for accounting to be suited to the particular environment within which it operates.

Local academic staff members are products of the very same Western system which produced their expatriate counterparts. There is a general lack of awareness of the potential contribution that accounting could make in the economic growth and development process (Perera 1989; Mirghani 1982; Needles 1976). As a result, there has been no attempt to assess each SADCC country's financial information needs and therefrom, the nature of accounting education and training except in Tanzania and Zambia (Enthoven 1977, 135). Even in those two SADCC countries where this was attempted, there has not been a significant shift from the Anglo-American accounting system. Either the assessments were not carried out properly or the now deeply rooted Western accounting systems made it difficult to effect radical changes.

Academic programmes in the SADCC universities fail to emphasize the role accounting could play in economic development. This state of affairs is a direct reflection of the nature of accounting and economics education at these universities. Academic programmes in these fields tend to be highly specialised and lack the necessary linkage that ought to exist between them. At the university of Botswana, for instance, there exists the so-called "single major" (which means specialised) programmes into which some of the most able students in the Faculty of Social Sciences are channelled. These single major programmes tend to play down the relationship between accounting and economics in particular. There is very little economics content in the accounting curricula and vice versa.

There is a first degree programme in accounting and economics catering for the weaker students who do not show the potential for the single major economics programme at the end of the second year of the four-year bachelor of arts degree programme. Even this first degree programme in accounting and economics is merely a combination of courses picked from the single major accounting and economics programmes. Any student of this programme who gains any knowledge of the linkages between accounting and economics does so in spite of the programme rather than because of it. In 1987 the programme was nearly discontinued at the request of the Accounting Department[3] with the support of some members of the Economics Department, on the ground that it did not serve any useful purpose. The state of affairs at the University of Botswana is representative of the situation at other universities in the SADCC region. Given this educational background, it is not surprising that there should be a lack of awareness amongst accountants and economists alike, of the potential role accounting could play in economic development.

Another factor related to the lack of awareness of the role accounting could play in economic growth and development is the severely limited research undertaken by academics in developing countries. There is also very little by way of regional conferences and workshops. This does not only prevent the sharing of ideas but also means that the curricula of accounting programmes are almost never influenced by what is or what ought to be going on in accounting practice. At times the contents of courses remain unchanged for many years despite the frequent changes in both the na-

---

[3]The author is a member of staff of this department.

tional and international economic and accounting environments. There are a number of reasons for this apparent inactivity of accounting academics. Financial resources needed for research are in very short supply. With the universities funded mostly by state governments which are besieged with numerous financial problems, research activities, which are often thought to be of little importance, receive a very low priority ranking for funding. There are hardly any close links between accounting academics and the accounting firms as well as the private sector at large, thus denying the former access to funds that could otherwise flow from the latter.

The shortage of funds together with the usually heavy teaching load makes it very difficult for academics to undertake research activities. To worsen things, it is not easy to publish articles from the developing world. Again, the shortage of financial resources has meant that there are hardly any journals in the region in which researchers could publish. Publishing in international journals is not easy because of the tight competition for space in the journals and perhaps the lack of appeal of issues that bear relevance to developing countries only. In any case an article published in an international accounting journal is as good as lost to the developing countries of the SADCC where university libraries subscribe to only a few such journals.

As a result of all these factors, and maybe a few others, university accounting programmes in the SADCC region remain largely Western oriented. They are, therefore, geared towards servicing the very accounting systems (Anglo-American) which fail to offer substantially useful financial information to the developing countries of this region. There is a need to redesign these programmes to suit the local socio-economic environments. A starting point ought to be the assessment of accounting skills needed in each individual economy of the SADCC countries. Given the similarity of the economics of these countries, there should exist common accounting skills needs in a number of areas. University accounting programmes could then be designed based on the appropriate accounting skills needs for each economy. Unless the necessary changes are effected, universities in this region will continue to produce accounting graduates who are not the best suited for the developing economies of the SADCC countries.

The Demand for and Supply of Professional Accounting Skills

The demand for accounting skills in the SADCC region has been established to be quite high. This has been revealed by several studies aimed at assessing the manpower needs of countries in this region (for example, Rowe et al. 1986; World Bank 1986). Even though all these studies based their assessment of the demand for accounting skills on Western notions, their estimates, taken together with the numbers of expatriate accountants in employment, serve to indicate the enormous task ahead of training locals to meet the perceived demand. Most of these studies paid little attention to the demand of accounting skills in the public sector. The actual demand is likely to be much higher than was estimated in most of these studies, perhaps with less emphasis on high-level qualifications.

In most of the SADCC countries, the ratio of fully qualified expatriate accountants in employment to that of local accountants is very high. There is an obvious need and desire to train locals in order to reduce the number of expatriate accountants in employment. It is natural government policy to train locals with a view to reducing dependence on expatriates throughout the sectors of an economy. Not only does the replacement of expatriates create employment opportunities for locals, but it also reduces the usually high costs of employing large numbers of expatriates. As Markell (1985, 100) noted, the recruitment of expatriates results in the employers incurring subsidy and relocation costs which could be avoided if suitable qualified locals were available. Naturally, expatriates need to remit part of their earnings to their home countries, and by so doing dip into the already meager foreign reserves of their host countries.

Existing Training Schemes

Professional examination schemes were launched fairly recently in most of the SADCC countries. The Institute of Chartered Accountants of Zimbabwe has the longest standing examination scheme. Prior to the launching of these examination schemes, nationals of the English-speaking SADCC countries who wished to qualify as professional accountants had either to study full-time or by correspondence for mostly British qualifications such as ACCA and ICMA. Very few qualified in this manner. For instance, only six nationals in Botswana (Stokes 1987), six Swzi nationals (SIA 1989), about 15 Malawians (Rowe et al. 1986, 11) qualified as professional accountants by 1987, 1989 and 1986, respectively. The solution to professional accounting training problems was rightly seen to lie in mounting local training and examination schemes. The outcome of this realization is the existing examination schemes of the various accounting bodies in this region. As it turns out, little has changed despite the launching of these examination schemes.

The Botswana Institute of Accountants (BIA), the Public Accountants' Examinations Council of Malawi (PAEC), the Swaziland Institute of Accountants (SIA) and the Zambia Institute of Certified Accountants (ZICA) all have examination arrangements with the ACCA. Registered students of these bodies sit all ACCA examinations with law and taxation papers substituted by local variant ones in the case of the SIA (SIA 1989, 14, 15).

The Lesotho Institute of Accountants (LIA), the National Board of Accountants and Auditors of Tanzania (NBAA) and the Institute of Chartered Accountants of Zimbabwe (ICAZ) all have their own examination schemes. The examinations of these bodies are structured in the very style of Western professional examinations except there is an attempt to incorporate as much as possible of accounting issues peculiar to their countries. This is particularly true in the case of NBAA where agriculture and cooperative accounting issues feature in its syllabus (NBAA 1984, 16). Neither accounting body in this region has moved away from Anglo-American accounting, whose emphasis is on private sector financial accounting and auditing.

As in the case of academics, there seems to be a general lack of awareness and concern of the role accounting could play in the economic growth and development of the countries of the region.

Relevance of Existing Examinations Schemes

Existing professional examination schemes do not result in any significant improvement of the situation that existed prior to their launching. Students still have to sit most, and in some cases, all of the ACCA papers. This means that the failure rate will continue to be unnecessarily high. There is no doubt that many such students will not succeed simply because of examination questions which relate to an economically developed country — the United Kingdom. This will continue to deny the countries involved of the skills of those who qualify to be accountants in these countries but cannot be because they did not pass ACCA examinations. Furthermore, it is doubtful whether there will be adequate tuition at the existing or proposed training arms of these accounting bodies.[4] With most of the economies of the SADCC countries registering positive economic growth (SADCC 1988, 4–11), these training and examination schemes are not likely to cope with the increase in

demand for accounting skills and would, therefore, not be able to reduce the already large number of expatriate accountants in these countries. Instead, the increase in demand for accounting skills may result in the increase of expatriate accountants recruited to fill the gaps. The existing situation would deteriorate further to the detriment of the SADCC countries.

Just as is the case with university accounting education, professional training and examination schemes were designed or adopted, as the case may be, without any due consideration of the financial information needs of the national economic planners and those of the public sector. This is presumably due to the lack of awareness of the potential role accounting could play in economic development, as well as to the desire amongst professional accountants to ensure the perpetuation of their privileged status and to safeguard the flow to them of high financial rewards accruing from the Western style of accounting bodies. Radical reform of the examination and training structures to make them more responsive to the needs of national economic planners, for example, would appear to jeopardise this privileged position of professional accountants. As a result, they cannot be expected to willingly effect such a reform process. As Briston (1978, 120) rightly concludes:

> [Anglo-American accounting] is widening the chasm between accountants and economists and making it more unlikely that a satisfactory information system for national economic planning and control will ever be attainable. Even if it is, it will be achieved, sadly, in spite of the accountancy profession rather than with its encouragement and guidance.

There is, however, an urgent need for reform. If the necessary steps are not taken to reform accounting education, training and practice, the potential that accounting offers the economic development process will never be fully exploited with the likelihood that suboptimal and erroneous national economic decision will continue to be made.

THE REFORM OF ACCOUNTING EDUCATION AND TRAINING

A case for reform of accounting education, training and practice has been made throughout the preceding sections of this paper. There is no doubt that Anglo-American accounting does not

---

[4]The SIA does not intend creating a training body. This was revealed in an interview with Robert Reed, then Technical Director of the Institute in May 1989.

adequately serve the economic objectives of developing countries such as those in the SADCC region. It has even been suggested that this system of accounting could possibly be harmful to these countries (Briston 1978, 110; Samuels and Oligia 1982, 87). It is, therefore, crucial that an assessment of the financial information needs of each SADCC country in the enterprise, public and national accounting sectors is carried out in order that appropriate accounting education, training and practice systems can be designed.

It is quite clear that reforms in accounting practice, education and training would not be achievable without pressure exerted upon the profession by external forces. It may be easy for academics to understand and accept the need for reform, but this may not necessarily be the case with professional accountants who are immensely rewarded by the existing accounting systems. It would not be easy for academics alone to persuade the professional accountants to effect radical reforms to accounting practice and training.

The Need for Government Intervention

There is, therefore, a need for SADCC governments to intervene if progress in this direction is to be achieved. Reforms which would further the course of economic growth and development should interest any SADCC government. This is particularly so given the fact that rates of economic growth forecasted in national development plans of these countries have been largely unattainable yet economic growth and development are the main focus of government economic planning. The Zimbabwe Government, for instance, based its first five-year national development plan (1986–1990) on the assumption that the annual rate of economic growth shall be 5.1 percent (First Five-Year National Development Plan) but this remained low with a growth rate of less than 1 percent in 1987 (SADCC 1988, 10).

Government intervention is justifiable given that in some of the SADCC countries a large percentage of the budgets of the statutory accounting bodies is borne by government. The governments of SADCC countries all assisted and continue to assist their national accounting bodies financially and in other ways to the extent that these bodies would not achieve much without all this assistance. It is only fair that these accounting bodies should contribute meaningfully to the process of national economic growth and development rather than for them to expend public funds and remain

appendages of United Kingdom accounting bodies.

All SADCC universities have well over fifty percent of their budgets met by government. They should strive to produce manpower that is suited to the socioeconomic environments of their countries rather than for them to remain in ivory towers. Given the millions that the individual SADCC governments spend each year subsidising universities and other institutions of higher education, they (governments) should make a deliberate effort to ensure that academic programmes of these institutions serve as useful a purpose as is possible.

Government intervention in accounting matters is nothing new. In the United Kingdom and United States of America where there is a strong desire for minimal government intervention in accounting matters, the profession in those countries has occasionally had to live with some form of government involvement in what are considered professional matters. The establishment of the Securities and Exchange Commission by the United States Government, for instance, is a good example of government intervention in an otherwise self-regulating profession. The appointment of the Sandilands Committee by the United Kingdom Government to deal with issues relating to inflation accounting serves as yet another example of government intervention. There is, therefore, much in favour of government intervention where the accounting profession is not seen to act in a manner consistent with the national socioeconomic goals. Such a move is even more justifiable in the case of the SADCC countries where national governments are now spending considerable sums of money to develop the accounting profession.

A CASE FOR REGIONAL COOPERATION IN ACCOUNTING EDUCATION AND TRAINING

The problems discussed above—the lack of understanding of the role accounting could play in economic growth and development, the acute shortage of financial and technical resources resulting in lack of research and publications and the production of more suitable text material, and the sitting of professional examinations intended for developed countries among others — are common to all the SADCC countries with a few exceptions. Even though it is ideal for accounting practices and education and training to conform to the particular needs of a country (Perera 1989; Hove 1986; Mirghani 1982; Samuels and Oliga 1982; Briston

1978; Needles 1976), regional cooperation in accounting education and training is recommended in this case because neither country is likely to overcome the foregoing problems on its own. Furthermore, the legal and economic conditions in the SADCC countries are quite similar.

Given the widespread shortage of financial resources, a lot more can be achieved if educational institutions pooled resources in areas such as research and publication. Professional accounting bodies could do the same. It would be easier for accounting academics, for example, to launch a regional accounting journal as opposed to each university attempting to run its own journal or relying exclusively on foreign journals. There are considerable benefits to be reaped from a jointly owned and run accounting journal. The pooling of financial resources would facilitate the regular release of journal issues; a wider readership would be achievable; the sharing of ideas across national boundaries would be enhanced; research on regional issues would be stimulated; and overall cooperation on academic matters would be easier to achieve.

A major task facing accounting faculties in this region is the design of programmes that are relevant to the accounting needs of developing countries. This involves a considerable amount of research for which funding is in short supply. The pooling of resources could alleviate the funding problem. The production of textbooks and other teaching material, such as cases, specifically for developing economies is central to the successful design of appropriate accounting programmes. This can best be achieved through co-authorship of textbooks. For purposes of securing funds for research and the production of textbooks and other teaching material as well as for regional cooperation in accounting education, it is advisable that co-authors should come from different countries of the region in as far as this is feasible.

There are opportunities for regional cooperation in professional accounting training as well. No one accounting body in this region has adequate resources to develop suitable study material for those who wish to become professional accountants. Most of the accounting bodies are not even in a position to hold continuing education seminars for their members. This is another area where accounting bodies could pool their meagre resources to develop their members further.

The shortage of both technical and financial resources necessitates regional cooperation in accounting education and training if this region is ever to produce the accounting manpower that is suitable for its economies. The similarities of the economies of this region should make it desirable and appropriate for regional cooperation in accounting education and training to be effected.

CONCLUSION

It is quite clear that universities and other educational institutions as well as professional accounting bodies in the English-speaking SADCC have adopted Anglo-American accounting education and training programmes and examination schemes with little or no modification to suit the local environment. Since Anglo-American accounting education and training are geared mainly towards satisfying the skills needs of the private sector, which dominates the economies of the developed Western countries, it can hardly be the best suited for the public sector–dominated economies of the developing countries of the SADCC region. There is a need to reform accounting education and training in these countries. What is needed are accountants who can assist the economic development process of these developing nations in a much more significant way.

The amount of reforms needed in accounting education and training in these countries is such that it would not be easy for each country to go it alone given the constraints imposed by severely limited resources. The similarity of the needs of these countries makes it possible for them to pool their meagre resources together to achieve what they probably could not achieve individually.

REFERENCES

Briston, R. J. 1978. The Evolution of Accounting in Developing Countries. *The International Journal of Accounting Education and Research* (Fall): 105–120.

Enthoven, A. J. H. 1977. *Accountancy Systems in Third World Economies*. North-Holland Publishing Company.

Hove, M. R. 1986. Accounting Practices in Developing Countries: Colonialism's Legacy of Inappropriate Technologies. *The International Journal of Accounting Education and Research* (Fall): 81–100.

Markell, W. 1985. Development of Accounting Education and the Accounting Profession in Third World Countries: Botswana. *The International Journal of Accounting Education and Research* (Fall): 99–105.

Mirghani, M. A. 1982. A Framework for a Linkage between Microaccounting and Macroaccounting for Purposes of Development Planning in Developing Countries. *The International Journal of Accounting Education and Research* (Fall): 57–68.

National Board of Accountants and Auditors. 1984. *National Accountancy Examinations Scheme — Examination Regulations and Syllabus* (Reprinted).

Needles, B. E. 1976. Implementing a Framework for the International Transfer of Accounting Technology. *The International Journal of Accounting Education and Research* (Fall): 45–62.

Perera, M. H. B. 1989. Accounting in Developing Countries: A Case for Localised Uniformity. *British Accounting Review*: 141–157.

Rowe, D. N., L. J. Motshubi, K. M. Mundea, J. Sampio, and A. M. Hegarty. 1986. *Study of Accountancy Training in the SADCC Region*, (November).

SADCC. 1988. Annual Progress Report July 1987 – August 1988. SADCC.

Samuels, J. M., and J. C. Oliga. 1982. Accounting Standards in Developing Countries. *The International Journal of Accounting Education and Research* (Fall): 69–88.

Stokes, K. C. 1987. *Proposals for the Development of the Accountancy Profession in the Republic of Botswana*. (December).

Swaziland Institute of Accountants. 1989. Membership Register.

World Bank. 1986. *Botswana, Lesotho, and Swaziland (BLS), Study of Public Administration Management: Issues and Training Needs*, Volumes I, II, III, and IV.

Enhancing Accounting Education in Developing Countries: The Case of Iran

Adel M. Novin and Ali Saghafi

Accounting plays a significant role in the economic development of any country. Effective accounting systems that result in the generating and reporting of sufficient relevant, reliable, and timely financial information may assist both governmental authorities and businessmen in developing countries by:

(1) facilitating the optimal allocation of available economic resources in order to improve the standard of living;

(2) preventing theft, misdirected efforts, waste, and other economic losses;

(3) measuring the performance and effectiveness of responsible units and investment projects;

(4) ensuring accountability for government expenditures and tax revenues;

(5) creating accountability for foreign investment, and, subsequently, attracting foreign investors; and

(6) improving accountability for foreign aid.

Enhancing the development of accounting profession in developing countries has received considerable attention in recent years. In this regard, Professor Mueller states [1988]:

> [A]s academic/professional accountants in the First and Second Worlds, we have to bring ourselves to recognize a substantive responsibility toward accounting development in the Third World. This is not a scientific argument. Some will consider it a matter of morality and ethics. Others see it as a matter of equity and fairness among the humans populating the planet. Still others would use economic arguments such as adequate standards of living for all. Interdependence—the global village idea—may motivate yet another group of accountants. Without express recognition of a clear responsibility we are likely to remain at the status quo.

Professor Enthoven [1983] makes the point even more forcefully by calling for the establishment of a U.S. accounting assistance coordinating body, involving professional and educational institutions.

OBJECTIVE OF THE STUDY

The absence of sound accounting education in developing countries, and, consequently, the shortage of qualified accountants, is one of the major obstacles preventing the development of accounting profession in these countries [Holzer and Chandler, 1981]. Thus, the enhancement of accounting education should remain at the forefront of the thrust behind the development of accounting profession in developing countries. However, many problems stand in the way of enhancing accounting education in developing countries like Iran. These problems require careful study (i.e., country by country) for the purpose of developing long-term solutions. Exploration of accounting education problems particular to Iran, along with remedial strategies to solve such problems, is the subject of this paper. More specifically, this study addresses the following questions:

1. What factors are obstructing the development of accounting education in Iran?

2. What is the degree of effectiveness of various remedial strategies for the enhancement of accounting education in Iran?

In order to describe the findings of the study in a proper context, the article begins with general background information on the status of accounting in Iran, followed by a description of the research methodology, results, conclusions and recommendations.

Adel M. Novin is a member of the faculty of Kent State University. Ali Saghafi is a faculty member of Tehran University, Iran.

GENERAL BACKGROUND

Currently, there are approximately twenty universities and colleges offering programs in accounting in Iran. Four of these universities offer graduate programs in accounting at the master's level, and three grant doctoral degrees in accounting. Admissions into the accounting programs at universities and colleges are based on national entrance examinations. Western accounting has dominated both accounting education and practice in Iran. Accordingly, Iran has not been able to construct a system of accounting to meet its own information needs. The Iranian economy, culture, social values, and the level of education and sophistication of average businessmen are dissimilar to those found in the West. Furthermore, Iranian capital and financial markets are less complex than their western counterparts. Yet traditionally, accounting education and practice in Iran have been based on the accounting education and practice in the United States and the United Kingdom, in part because it has become very difficult to isolate the bias of accounting educators and practitioners who have studied and practiced accounting under the United States and British systems from the accounting reconstruction process in Iran. At the present time, the accounting education program in Iran is based on the accounting curriculum in the United States, and there are no Iranian professional accounting examinations leading to certification, accounting and auditing standards are lacking, and the professional activities of accountants are minimal.

RESEARCH METHOD AND RESULTS

A survey of practicing accountants and educators in Iran was conducted to compile the necessary information for this study. The survey questionnaire was developed in Farsi based upon Novin and Baker's survey instrument [1990]. Thirty-five (35) practicing Iranian accountants who had a considerable familiarity with the accounting education and practice of Iran participated in the study. Sixty nine percent of the respondents possessed undergraduate degrees in accounting, 26 percent held master's degrees, and five percent doctoral degrees. More than 60 percent of the respondents were 30 years of age or older, and most had significant work experience with a mean number of years of experience of nine. The responses received are reported and analyzed in two major categories described as factors obstructing accounting education development and remedial strategies.

FACTORS OBSTRUCTING THE DEVELOPMENT OF ACCOUNTING EDUCATION

An open-ended question was used to compile information on factors obstructing accounting development in Iran. Respondents were asked to identify up to six factors obstructing the development of accounting education and practice in Iran and to indicate whether each factor is significant or very significant. Table 1 presents the most frequently mentioned factors that are obstructing the development of accounting education in Iran. According to the result, lack of sufficient qualified instructors is the most serious obstacle preventing the development of accounting education in Iran.

TABLE 1

Related Educational Factors Obstructing Development of Accounting Education and Profession in Iran

	Very Significant	Significant	Total
1. Lack of sufficient qualified instructors	11	2	13
2. Significant difference between education and practice	6	3	9
3. Lack of and/or outdated accounting textbooks in local language	5	2	7
4. Lack of sufficient research studies concerned with accounting	5	1	6
5. Lack of practical training for students during college education	2	2	4

Other educational problems noted by some of the respondents are lack of close cooperation between practitioners and universities and lack of continuing education opportunities for practicing accountants.

REMEDIAL STRATEGIES

Novin and Baker [1990] have identified a series of remedial strategies for enhancing accounting education and the accounting profession in developing countries. By placing their list of remedial strategies in the questionnaire, we asked respondents to indicate the degree of effectiveness of each strategy for enhancing accounting education in Iran using the following scale:

0=Not Effective
1=Least Effective
2=Effective
3=Very Effective
4=Extremely effective

Table 2 presents the rating results. Column 2 in the table presents the mean of ratings. The closer the mean to 4, the higher is the effectiveness of the method. The relative effectiveness ranking of various means in column 3 is based on the Coefficient of Variation (CV), that is, the standard deviation of ratings for each item divided by its mean. Although all the strategies in the list were viewed by most respondents as having some degree of effectiveness, enhancing accounting curricula was perceived to be the most effective strategy for the enhancement of accounting education in Iran.

CONCLUSION AND RECOMMENDATIONS

This paper provides evidence on the underlying obstacles to the enhancement of accounting education in Iran, and determines the effectiveness of various remedial strategies to solve these problems. Information obtained from respondents suggests recommendations in four areas: (1) the training and upgrading of accounting faculty, (2) focus on relevant accounting education, (3) textbooks, and (4) closer cooperation between academe and accounting profession.

TABLE 2
The Degree of Effectiveness of Various Means For Enhancing Accounting Education in Iran

	Mean	CV	Rank
- Enhancing accounting curricula in universities and colleges	3.14	0.220	1
- Providing practical training to accounting students during their college education	3.26	0.228	2
- Training and upgrading domestic accounting professors	3.09	0.240	3
- Developing accounting textbooks in domestic language	3.14	0.246	4
- Educating government officials about the role and benefit of accounting for economic development	3.40	0.249	5
- Encouraging profession—university cooperations	3.24	0.264	6
- Enhancing usage of computers for processing accounting data	3.00	0.268	7
- Enhancing publication and distribution of accounting journals	2.77	0.309	8
- Requiring and providing continuing education for accountants after graduation from college	2.74	0.323	9
- Initiating and encouraging students' Accounting Association activities	2.41	0.410	10

First, as noted by the study, the shortage of qualified instructors is the major obstacle preventing the development of accounting education in Iran. Several notable attempts have been made to solve this problem including offering of doctoral programs in accounting at three universities. However, due to the lack of faculty for teaching and supervising of doctoral students, the plan has not succeeded.[1] These universities have failed to fully utilize Iranian accounting professors living abroad for the instruction of doctoral courses and supervision of doctoral dissertations.[2] By adapting *formal* and *more effective* co-operative programs to involve Iranian educators at foreign universities in the instruction and supervision of doctoral students in Iran, much better results can be achieved. It is also critical that the doctoral students in the program be taught how to adapt the knowledge gained from abroad to the needs of their own country. They must come to realize that accounting and auditing practices in developed countries may not be completely relevant for Iran, so that adjustments will be necessary when it comes to the application of their knowledge.

Second, at the present time, the accounting education in Iran is based on the accounting curriculum in the United States, resulting in at least three major problems. First, the main emphasis of accounting education in Iran, as in the United States, is on financial accounting. However, based upon the economic and political structure of Iran, more emphasis needs to be placed on governmental, tax, cost, and managerial accounting. Second, a large portion of the subjects taught in accounting courses (in particular in financial accounting) are not applicable to Iran's needs, simply because Iran's business and economic environment is not as sophisticated as western countries. Thus, the content of accounting courses must be revised to accommodate Iran's business and economic environment. The fact that accounting students are taught the accounting of developed countries, not of developing countries, has complicated the development of accounting profession in Iran. Third, certain critical subjects such as accounting information systems and microcomputers are missing from the undergraduate accounting program in Iran. As a result, due to the lack of experience and relevant

---

[1]Currently there are only three qualified accounting professors with Ph.D.s in Iran.

[2]There are at least 25 Iranian accounting educators with Ph.D.s in the United States and Canada.

knowledge of the analysis, design, and implementation of accounting systems and computers, the accounting graduates are ill-prepared to bring about improvements in existing accounting systems and procedures in Iran. Consequently, Iranian accounting students, who will be the practitioners of the future, will not be prepared to remedy the deficiencies of existing accounting systems; thus these deficiencies are not likely to be corrected in the near future. Attempts should be made to incorporate an adequate number of courses covering topics in accounting information systems and application of microcomputers in accounting within the curriculum. Relevant accounting education, and consequently, relevant accounting practices, will generate a significantly higher demand and respect for accounting services.

Third, the content of accounting textbooks must be responsive to the business and economic environment of Iran and should focus on the financial information needs and level of sophistication of average decision makers within government and private sectors. Translating foreign accounting textbooks, and accounting and auditing standards without adapting them to local needs and environment is not a useful practice. As Briston states [1978]:

> Each country has its own political, social, economic, and cultural characteristics, and it is highly probable that the goals and thus the information needs of the managers of the economy will differ from one country to another. As a consequence, each country should be encouraged not to standardize the structure and specifications of its information system, but to create a system appropriate to its own needs.

Accounting educators, with the cooperation of accounting firms and government, should undertake an adequate number of research studies in order to answer such basic and vital questions as "Who are the present and potential users of accounting information in Iran?," "What are the characteristics and the level of sophistication of average Iranian decision makers?" "What are the accounting information needs of Iranian decision makers at both micro and macro levels?," "Do Iranian decision makers understand the content of financial statements and reports prepared based on western accounting systems?," "What type of accounting curricula, and consequently, accounting textbooks are needed for Iran's particular needs?," "What materials should be used for teaching?," and "What accounting and auditing standards should be covered in accounting textbooks given Iran's social, cultural and economic conditions?"

Finally, a closer cooperation between the accounting profession and universities should be encouraged. Such cooperation could be in the form of:

(1) having government and private accounting practitioners serve as members of Accounting Advisory Committees to colleges and universities, and

(2) inviting accounting practitioners to visit university classrooms and/or participate in student functions for question and answer periods.

The major product of such cooperation might well be the development of a dynamic accounting program that is geared to the business and economic environment of Iran. Increased cooperation could also result in the establishment of internship programs that would enable students to gain firsthand knowledge concerning the existing accounting systems and associated problems for class discussions. In addition, practitioners might provide the necessary resources to the faculty for conducting relevant research studies for the enhancement of accounting education and practice in Iran.

The results of this study provide an up-to-date list of accounting problems particular to Iran along with information on various remedial strategies for solving such problems. The findings of the study provide a guide for the government officials, accounting administrators, or accounting faculty members who face the challenge of enhancing accounting education in Iran.

REFERENCES

Briston, R. J. 1978. The Evolution of Accounting in Developing Countries. *International Journal of Accounting* (Fall): 105-120.

Enthoven, A. J. H. 1983. U.S. Accounting and the Third World. *Journal of Accountancy* (June): 110-112, 115, 116, 118.

Holzer, H. P., and J. S. Chandler. 1981. A System Approach to Accounting in Developing Countries. *Management International Review:* 23-32.

Mueller, G. G. 1988. Accounting Education and Scholarship in Developing Countries: What Are Our Responsibilities? Working paper, University of Washington.

Novin, A., and J. Baker. 1990. Enhancing Accounting Education and the Accounting Profession in Developing Countries. *Foreign Trade Journal* (October-December).

Accounting Education Development in Papua, New Guinea

Fabian Pok

INTRODUCTION

This paper examines the development of accounting education in Papua New Guinea (PNG). Accounting education development is examined from these perspectives. First, the historical perspective of the development of accountancy, including accounting education, before and after PNG became independent is discussed. Major accountancy development took place after independence. Second, government policies on accounting education are examined, and finally, the present state of university-level accounting education, and their shortcomings are addressed.

HISTORICAL PERSPECTIVES OF ACCOUNTANCY DEVELOPMENT

Europeans settled on the Island in the early 19th century. For the convenience of the colonists, the Island was divided into three sections. The western half was claimed by the Dutch (now Irian Jaya, a province of Indonesia). The eastern half was further divided. The northern half of the main Island and islands such as Bougainville, New Britain and New Ireland were claimed by Germany (known as German New Guinea). Britain ruled the southern part of the Island as a protectorate (known as British Papua). In 1888 Papua became a colony of Britain. It was placed under the authority of Australia in 1902, and became a colony of Australia in 1906 (Amarish 1979a; Hardman 1983).

During World War I, Australian soldiers invaded German New Guinea and the Island was under the control of the Australian Army. The military encouraged the German companies to continue developing plantations and other trading activities, but they were not allowed to repatriate their profits to Germany. The German planters thought that Germany would soon win the war; thus they would retain their plantations and continue trading. However, when Germany was defeated, the Australian Administration inherited the plantations in New Guinea from the Germans at very little cost. New Guinea became a mandated territory of the League of Nations (Goodman et al. 1985).

It is impossible to pinpoint when accountancy started in PNG. Evidence suggests, however, that with the advent of the colonial era, some form of accounting and auditing existed to provide financial information for owners and shareholders of both German and British companies based in PNG. At the same time, the earliest accountants to work in PNG were British and Germans brought in from the United Kingdom and Germany. After World War II, most accountants employed in PNG were from Britain, Australia and New Zealand (Juchau 1978).

As modern plantations and other industries expanded with capital investments from multinational corporations and Australian businessmen, there was a need for professional services including accounting. The first professional accounting firm to open a branch in Port Moresby was Coopers & Lybrand in 1959. Other professional accounting firms followed, opening offices in PNG to provide accounting and other services to the expanding business activities (Hardman 1983).

During the period of Australian rule, the Australian Government policy did not favour the participation of local PNG people in the public services, not only in accountancy areas, but in all aspects of public service administration. The TPNG era was administered exclusively by expatriate officers. The local employees were performing clerical tasks, for example, filing, records administration and making tea. There were few opportunities given for education, training and promotion of local employees. Baldwin (1978, 12) states:

> The Papua New Guinea public service was without significant local participation, it was, in fact, an extension of the Australian Public Service, dominated by Australian values and methods. The development of an Australian-type administrative system, staffed almost entirely by Australians, was based on the assumption that the Territory of Papua New Guinea would one day be integrated into Australia as the country's seventh state. To prevent the emergence of an educated anticolonial elite that might jeopardize the process, Australia pursued a policy of "uniform development" of the local population. In education, all segments of the local population were to advance at the same rate, and almost all effort was devoted to primary education.

Fabian Pok is a Postgraduate Student at the University of New England in Armidale, Australia.

The paucity of trained local applicants precluded serious efforts to localize public service or private business until "uniform development" should have proceeded much further. Consequently, those Papua New Guineans who entered the monetarized economy before the 1960s remained mainly as plantation labourers, domestic servants and low level government employees.

The Australian Government policy on "uniform development" in PNG had major implications for the local work force. The higher education institutions which were to produce the work force required by the country were nonexistent. The first major input into the development of higher educational institutions came from the recommendations of the Foot Report (1960). The Foot Committee was established by the United Nations Trusteeship Council to examine the Australian Government's efforts to develop higher education in PNG. The Report was critical of Australia's efforts and proposed that "every New Guinean capable of going to university and other higher educational institutions should be encouraged and assisted to do so." This report had immediate results. The Australian Government reacted to the Foot Report (1960) by appointing the Currie Commission of Higher Education (Currie Commission 1964). The Currie Report (1964) led to the establishment of the country's first university (University of Papua New Guinea [UPNG]) in 1966, and the Institute of Technology in 1968, which became a university (University of Technology [UNITECH]) in 1973.

The first intake into liberal arts and science courses started in 1966 and the first Papua New Guineans graduated from UPNG in 1970. The Institute of Technology has offered a Certificate and a Diploma in accountancy since 1968. However, the accounting graduates (degree level) from universities entered the job market just before independence. In UPNG, accountancy studies essentially began as a by-product of the economics program. UPNG wanted to develop courses in the sciences and the social sciences, including economics, law and the humanities. There was no plan to introduce business studies bacause UNITECH was producing diploma and certificate graduates in accounting. The Economics Department at UPNG decided that a satisfactory program in economics required some input from the discipline of accounting; therefore, one accounting lecturer was recruited to teach basic accounting to economics students. However, once the accounting discipline existed on campus, there were pressures from the

private sector to develop accounting programs for employees working in Port Moresby. As a consequence, a part-time Diploma in Commerce program was introduced initially in 1968, though only for students already in employment (Onedo 1981).

AFTER INDEPENDENCE

The economic development plan adopted at independence in 1975 gave priority to ensuring an equitable distribituion of benefits to forge national unity. Priority was given to rural development and equal distribution of income to each province. Higher education and manpower training was given low priority; Michael Somare, the founding Prime Minister (1973, 3) outlined his Government's policy thus:

> There is a new government in Papua New Guinea . . . We are moving away from past policies that emphasise economic goals and moving towards a more well-rounded program with the basic aim of improving the lives of Papua New Guinea people — not just increasing the gross national product.

He also saw higher education as creating elites within an emerging country like PNG.

> There are three different kinds of elites that can develop in our society that we need to be careful of. Firstly, there are expatriate businessmen who do not provide a fair deal for Papua New Guineans. Second, there are our own Papua New Guinean businessmen and employees of business who may forget their people back in the village and try to live too much like the European examples they have seen. And thirdly, there are well-educated people with prospects for good jobs and quick promotions in the public services.

Mr. Somare's Government policies had adverse effects on university education and accounting personnel development. Even though the Government saw higher education as fulfilling the work force needs, it was targeted at the wrong professions. We therefore examine the Government policy on higher education, including accountancy.

PNG GOVERNMENT POLICIES

The Government's education policy was to satisfy, in as economically efficient and educationally effective a manner as possible, the personnel demand being created by the economy for both localization and growth. The work force needs the Government saw were graduates in humanity studies to fill jobs in the public services vacated by expatriates after independence. The Government did not seriously address the work force needs in specialist areas such as accounting until the 1980s.

In 1980, Professor Wells of Sydney University was commissioned to review accounting education in PNG universities and its contribution to the work force needs. Wells (1980) was critical of the fact that the supply of accounting graduates was not adequately meeting the demand of both the public and private sectors. Based on that report, the Government set up a committee within the National Planning Office in 1981 to survey the supply and demand of university graduates. Table 1 shows the average output by UPNG between 1976 and 1981, as compared with the average graduate output required in the same years.

The survey shows an overproduction of graduates in arts, law and, to a certain extent, economics. There is underproduction in science (combined fields) and Accounting. Based on these findings, there was pressure from the public and private sectors to improve and increase the output of accounting graduates from the Universities. The Government began to realize that the emphasis on the work force requirement had targeted the wrong group. Therefore, there was a need to review and improve accounting education in PNG.

In 1982, the Government set up a committee known as the Policy and Planning Group for Accounting and Financial Management Education and Training (PPG). The terms of reference set by the Government for the PPG to examine and report back on were

1. to examine and describe the present state of education and training in the accounting and financial management fields;

2. to collect and analyze employers' reports on the performance of graduates and their expectation of graduates;

3. to collect and analyze data on the views of graduates relating to the adequacy of the training they received in institutions for the job they have been expected to perform;

4. to report on the quantity and quality of accountants required by level of training and to develop an appropriate career structure in the accountancy and financial management areas;

5. to set up specialist working groups as required to examine specific problems:

    (a) work force requirements;

    (b) accreditation of courses; and

    (c) standards and ethics.

6. to seek the cooperation and involvement of the education institutions and the employing organizations in both the public and private sectors; and

7. to report to the National Planning Committee with appropriate recommendations.

The PPG investigated the problems besetting accounting and financial management education and training and noted some deficiencies relating to accounting education. The PPG Report (1986, 5) states:

1. PNG is desperately short of experienced and trained accounting and financial management personnel at both the professional and sub-professional levels. This is having serious effects on both public service and the private sector.

2. At the professional level, both the Government and private sectors are overly dependent upon the services of expatriate accountants and financial managers. It appears this will be the case for many years.

3. Educational institutions are presently unable to supply an adequate number of accounting personnel at either the professional or the subprofessional level.

TABLE 1
Imbalances in Graduate Supply and Demand, 1976–1981

	Average Annual Graduate Output (1976–1981)		Excess Supply of Output
	Required	Produced	
Bachelor of Arts	50	57	7
Bachelor of Economics	21	24	3
Bachelor of Science	28	18	−10
LL.B	13	26	13
Bachelor of Accounting/Commerce	71	10	−61

Source: National Planning Office, August 1982.

4. Training resources in the universities and in both the public and private sectors are inadequate to meet their urgent needs in accounting and financial management.

5. Accounting/Commerce and related courses at various educational institutions differ in content and scope. This makes accreditation difficult.

6. The University of Technology, UPNG, and other appropriate institutions should liaise with each other to construct a curriculum more closely designed for users' needs and to provide a more appropriate foundation for professional examinations. In structuring the courses, coverage should also be given to the public sector as well as the private sector.

7. The general quality of current graduates produced by the universities is not what the employers desire.

8. The accounting graduates noted that the current university-level accounting programs need an overhaul.

The PPG concluded that the Government should use its authority to rectify the above deficiencies. They noted that these problems could be minimized in the foreseeable future.

In 1986, the National Planning Office conducted another survey to establish the output of university graduates between 1984 and 1992. This survey was to enable the Government to develop a Higher Education Plan 1986–1990 (Table 2). One of the most striking features is the high proportion of business-oriented graduates required by the work force. Accounting graduates are in high demand — 17 percent of all graduates, while another 13 percent of graduates are required with commerce or business studies degrees. A total of 30 percent of all graduates between the years 1984 and 1992 must have degrees in accounting, commerce or business studies.

The Second National Manpower Assessment Report set the work force needs, which were incorporated into the "Higher Education Plan, A Strategy for Rationalization 1986–1990." The plan (1986, 7) states:

> Priorities in higher education are reflected by the Second National Manpower Assessment Report (NMA2). They are broadly as follows: financial management (accountancy), management (general), professional scientific and technical areas. Universities will need to increase their output quite substantially to meet the demand of the economy.

TABLE 2
Required Output of University by Discipline
1984–1992

Discipline	Output Required	Percent
Arts	679	10
Economics	393	6
Science	424	6
MBBS	193	3
DBS	21	1
Agriculture	288	4
Law	161	2
Education	870	12
Commerce	334	5
Architecture/Physical Planning	108	2
Business Studies	593	8
Accountancy	1,219	17
Computer Studies	399	5
Surveying	112	2
Cartography	128	2
Applied Chemistry	86	1
Food Technology	27	1
Forestry	22	1
Building Economics	69	1
Civil Engineering	50	1
Electrical Engineering	45	1
Mining Engineering	254	4
Mechanical Engineering	288	5
Communications	20	1
Library Studies	190	3
TOTAL	6,969	100

Source: National Planning Office, May 1986.

> The greatest need is for more graduates in the business-type subjects such as accounting, commerce and business studies.

This led to the creation of the Department of Commerce in the UPNG in 1990.

Before 1990, commerce was a section within the Economics Department. The academic staff positions increased from 5 to 10 members and the Accounting Department was allocated funds from the University budget. The increase in positions will increase the intake of accounting students and, it is hoped, will improve accounting education in PNG. However, four of these positions have not been filled, including the Professor of Accounting, despite advertisements placed in both developed and developing countries.

The Government recently realized the acute shortage of specialist manpower in the scientific and accounting fields. The efforts of successive Governments to improve accounting education are so far encouraging; however, there are many deficiencies in accounting education, especially at the university level. There is need for more funds from both Government and international and regional agencies interested in improving accounting education in developing countries such as PNG.

UNIVERSITY-LEVEL ACCOUNTING EDUCATION

Interest in higher education in general and business education in particular is a relatively recent phenomenon in PNG. The Institute of Technology (now the University of Technology) located in Lae was the first institution of higher education to offer a business curriculum in PNG. The Institute began the program (beginning in the 1968 academic year) by offering a certificate and a diploma. The first graduates with accounting degrees did not enter the employment market until after 1973, when the Institute had gained university status. UPNG in Port Moresby had its first intake of students in 1966. It offered courses in humanities, economics, science, law, medicine and agriculture (Linge 1980). One or two accounting courses were introduced to economics students. The first diploma for part-time students in employment was offered in 1968. The degree program was introduced in 1971 and accounting graduates entered the labour market in 1974.

Selected aspects of the two universities in PNG offering degree programs in accounting are summarised in Table 3. Some of the institutions offering some business programs including accounting are shown in Table 4.

ACCOUNTING GRADUATES

Table 5 shows the number of diploma and degree-level accounting graduates from the two universities in PNG over the last 20 years (1970 to 1990).

There is a steady increase in diploma-level graduates. The degree-level graduates are also increasing, but very slowly. The difference in diploma graduates from UNITECH between 1970 and 1982, and 1983 to 1990 resulted from the Department offering a three-year degree program in 1970. Most students entered the three-year program rather than the two-year degree program. In 1981 UNITECH adopted a two-tier accounting education program. All students do two-year programs and those eligible continue for another two years of degree studies. The diploma graduates from 1983 to 1990 show a steady increase. In UPNG either students do a four-year degree program or a two-year diploma program. The diploma graduates can enroll for the degree program. With the creation of the new Department of Commerce at UPNG, the number of accounting graduates should increase, but it is not likely to meet the forecasted accounting personnel requirements (see Table 2). There may be a need to increase the capacity of existing institutions to produce degree-level accountants, or create new institutions to cater for accounting personnel requirements.

ACCOUNTING ACADEMICS

Table 6 presents a profile of full-time accounting academics by educational qualifications, rank and nationality. The table indicates that of the 13

TABLE 3
Selected Aspects of PNG Universities Offering Accounting Programmes

Aspects	UPNG	UNITECH
Date of Establishment	1966	1968
Date of Establishment of Accounting Programmes:		
Certificate	—	1968
Diploma	1968	1968
Degree	1971	1970
Post Graduate[a]	1986	—
Student Body	Both Male and Female	Both Male and Female
Medium of Instruction	English	English
Funding	Government	Government
Location	Port Moresby	Lae

[a] The postgraduate program refers to the Honours Degree offered at UPNG in 1986. However, in both institutions master's and Ph.D. degrees can be completed by thesis if there are supervisors and research facilities available.

TABLE 4
The Current Accounting Programmes in PNG Institutions

Institutions	Certification	Year Commenced	Location
Port Moresby Business College	Certificate, Diploma	1985	Port Moresby
College of External Studies	Certificate	1983	Port Moresby
Divine Word Institute	Certificate, Diploma	1985	Madang
Pacific Adventist College	Certificate, Diploma	1986	Port Moresby
Administrative College[a]	Certificate, Diploma	1974	Port Moresby
Technical Colleges	Certificate, Diploma	1980s	Various centres
UPNG	Diploma, Degree Honours	1968, 1971, 1986	Port Moresby
UNITECH	Diploma, Degree	1968, 1970	Lae

Source: Policy and Planning Group Report, 1986.

[a] The Administrative College is the only institution that offers both a cerfiticate and a diploma in Government Accounting and Financial Management.

full-time accounting academics at the two universities in PNG, none hold doctorate degrees, 11 hold master's degrees, one holds a bachelor's degree and the other a diploma in information systems. The Professor of the Accounting and Business Studies Department at UNITECH holds a master's degree. UPNG has advertised for a full professor, but the position has not yet been filled. Even UPNG has another four positions, which are vacant. The associate professor of UPNG holds a master's degree. The rest of the accounting academics are lecturers.

There is an acute shortage of qualified accountants at all levels of employment including university teaching. The shortage in the university-level

TABLE 5
The Summary of Diploma and Degree Awards in Accountancy Over the Last 20 Years (1970-1990)

Year	UPNG		UNITECH		Total	
	Diploma	Degree	Diploma	Degree	Diploma	Degree
1970	4	—	2	—	6	—
1971	11	—	2	—	13	—
1972	7	—	8	—	15	—
1973	31	—	5	15	36	15
1974	24	10	4	11	28	21
1975	21	5	2	34	23	39
1976	20	7	1	34	21	34
1977	15	8	9	37	24	45
1978	24	12	1	41	25	53
1979	11	27	1	30	12	57
1980	14	17	2	37	16	54
1981	12	30	1	46	13	76
1982	6	25	—	51	6	56
1983	6	23	40	17	46	40
1984	21	32	44	6	64	38
1985	18	28	38	44	56	72
1986	25	24	21	50	46	74
1987	7	18	70	26	77	44
1988	22	11	55	19	77	30
1989	38	9	49	13	87	22
1990	40	15	84	12	124	27

Sources: UPNG and UNITECH Students Records, 1970–1990.

TABLE 6
Characteristics of Full-time
Accounting Academics (1991)

	Institution		
	UPNG	UNITECH	Total
Academic Qualifications			
Doctorate	—	—	—
Master's	4	7	11
Bachelor's	1	—	1
Diploma	1	—	1
Rank			
Professor	—	1	1
Associate/Professor	1	—	1
Senior Lecturer	1	2	3
Lecturer	4	4	8
Nationality			
PNG	1	1	2
Non-PNG	5	6	11

Source: Adapted from UPNG and UNITECH Course
Handbooks, 1991.

teaching profession is seen from the composition of accounting academics by nationality. Only two accounting academics or less than 15 percent of all accounting academics in the two universities are Papua New Guineans. The majority of the accounting academics are from other developing countries, educated in developed countries.

The diversity in background of academics affects the teaching methods, textbooks and case studies used. The techniques and books used are geared towards the faculty from which the academics come or where they obtained their degrees. This is a serious shortcoming of accounting education in developing countries like PNG where training is geared to the wrong environment. Graduating students find themselves in the PNG environment which is quite different from the education they have received.

One factor which creates difficulty is that regulations restrict external consulting. This prevents academics from relating the PNG environment to the classroom for the benefit of the students. The two universities have formed consultancy companies, but the arrangements are between the universities and outside organizations. The university assigns the project to academic staff. If there is no accounting work available, the accounting academics are not utilized (Renagi 1980). In addition, due to the shortage of qualified academics, the high student/staff ratios and low funds, academics are unable to do empirical research and write textbooks relating to the PNG environment (PPG 1982). The shortage of accounting academics has implications for course development, student development, research and textbook publications (Gibbs 1990).

COURSE PROGRAMMES

The general makeup of the undergraduate accounting degree program of the two universities in PNG is shown in Table 7. A graduate of accounting must complete requirements in three areas: Liberal Arts, Economics/Statistics and Accounting.

The mix of courses in the two universities does not appear to be evenly distributed. This results from the fact that there is little consultation regarding course development between the two universities. The two universities originally set out in a competitive mode and this tension continues to exist (Onedo 1981). There may be a need for a committee made up of academics and accountants in practice to monitor course development to bring the two universities in line with the needs of PNG. Table 8 shows the variation in the undergraduate program. The Honours in Accountancy offered by UPNG is shown in Table 9. Other graduate pro-

TABLE 7
The General Makeup of the Undergraduate Accounting Degree (1991)

Requirements	UPNG		UNITECH	
	Credit Hours	%	Credit Hours	%
Liberal Arts	21	24	15	13
Economics/Statistics	15	17	30	25
Accounting: Compulsory	52	59	59	49
Elective	—	—	16	13
Total	88	100	120	100

Sources: UPNG and UNITECH Course Handbooks, 1991.

TABLE 8
The General Make-up of the Undergraduate Accounting Degree (1991)

	UPNG		UNITECH	
Title of Course	Credit Hours	Compulsory or Elective	Credit Hours	Compulsory or Elective
Introductory Accounting I	3	C	6	C
Introductory Accounting II	6	C	6	C
Commercial Law	3	C	4	C
Cost and Management I	6	C	6	C
Taxation	3	C	4	C
Data Processing	3	C	9	C
Company Law	3	C	4	C
Cost and Management II	6	C	6	C
Corporate Finance	6	C	6	C
Auditing	3	C	4	C
Intermediate Accounting I	3	C	—	—
Intermediate Accounting II	3	C	—	—
Advanced Accounting	3	C	6	C
Financial Accounting for Business Structures in PNG	—	—	4	E
Business Organization in PNG	—	—	4	E
Projects in Accounting	—	—	4	E
Government Accounting	—	—	4	E

Source: UPNG and UNITECH Courses Handbook, 1990.

grams such as master's and doctorate degrees can be offered by thesis alone.

The courses have no element of research which can help students to think critically and enhance their development. There are some courses relating to PNG but they are electives offered by UNITECH. Courses such as farm accounting, small business management, economic development accounting and government accounting greatly needed in PNG are not taught at universities. There may be a need to review these course programs in light of the requirements of PNG. There has to be a balance between international and national needs.

TABLE 9
Honours Programme in Accounting Offered by UPNG (1991)

Title of Course	Credit Hours	Compulsory or Elective
Accounting Theory	4	C
Business Policy	4	C
Auditing and Investigations	4	C
Development Accounting	4	E
Financial Theory and Policy	4	C
Advanced Management Accounting	4	C
Quantitative Analysis	4	E

Source: UPNG Course Handbook, 1991.

The course programs in the two universities have changed to a two-tier system. All students admitted to the degree programs must complete the diploma programs. Those who are eligible proceed to the degree programs. Those who cannot proceed make their way into the work force as bookkeepers or accounting technicians. Other students study part-time only for their diploma as required by their employers. Students completing the diploma at UPNG will be eligible to sit the accounting technician examination. The program will be upgraded to full British professional qualification status when UPNG adopts the professional program as part of its degree program.

The two institutions have secured funds from the International Development Program (IDP) to set up accounting programs at certificate and diploma levels on a external studies basis. The course programs are written at the Department of Accounting and Financial Management of the University of New England, Australia, and are reviewed by accounting academics in PNG to enable the program to be PNG orientated. This program will be available to individuals in employment in all parts of the country by 1992. It may alleviate the accounting personnel shortages in the middle management level. Students completing the certificate can elect to do the diploma and diploma graduates can enroll for degree programs (Eddie 1990).

METHODS OF INSTRUCTION

The most common method of instruction in the two universities is the lecture method. This method is commonly used for three reasons:

1. academics use the methods to which they are accustomed;

2. high student/staff ratio; and

3. lack of facilities.

The lecture method is used partly because the training most academic accountants have received is in an environment where the lecture method has been used. The lecture process is a one-way communication process and is not the most suitable method for students, especially in developing countries like PNG, where students are learning accounting terminologies for the first time. This learning process is passive and mechanical and tends to focus on description and techniques rather than allowing students to analyze the facts and develop their problem-solving skills (Abdeen and Yavas 1985). Such deficiencies in the intellectual growth of PNG students prevents graduates from thinking through the problem when presented with real-life situations. The analytical growth of PNG students could be achieved through case studies, practical sets, computer-augmented sessions and laboratory sessions. However, the high student/staff ratio does not allow small groups to discuss case materials, have laboratory sessions and use practical sets.

The lecture method is further encouraged by the nonavailability of teaching and research facilities including textbooks, case materials and other reading materials relating to the PNG environment. This is due in part to lack of academics and the current academics being preoccupied with teaching large classes and having no time for research. There is also a lack of funds to build more classrooms, purchase computers and publish books and case materials relating to PNG. All textbooks selected for use in accounting and auditing courses are authored in Western countries and are mostly obtained from America, Britain or Australia, and naturally they have not been written with PNG in mind. Continuous reliance on foreign materials may impede the development of a local accounting education applicable to PNG (Juchau 1981).

ACCOUNTING STUDENTS

Students from PNG are admitted to the accounting programs based on their results in the National High School examination. UPNG allows students to enter the science, arts or law streams. The Accounting Department falls under the Arts Faculty. All students in the first year of "Arts Foundation" take courses in humanities such as psychology, language, history, introductory math, etc. Those students desiring to enter the accounting stream must take introductory mathematics and economics and obtain grades at credit level or better before being admitted. Employers argue that English should be taken into consideration because graduates cannot communicate effectively in the workplace (Arreola and Torres 1988). During the next three years, students do accounting courses including economics, statistics and data processing. This program will change to meet the United Kingdom Accounting Technicians requirements when introduced. Students from the National High School will come straight into first-year accounting. In the first two years all students will do the diploma program and those eligible will continue on to the degree program.

At UNITECH, the Accounting and Business Studies Department offers three degree programs: (1) Accounting; (2) Management; and (3) Computer Studies. In the first year all students do similar units which introduce them to these three areas. Depending on where students' interests lie, they are streamed into that area. In the second year they complete the diploma while those eligible continue on to the degree program (White 1988).

Both universities have policies allowing mature-age students (nonschool leavers) in employment to enroll for diploma and degree programs. Some of the factors taken into consideration include fees, years of experience, matriculation courses completed, etc. Each year certain places are allocated to mature-age students. The two universities also take about 10 percent of all accounting students from neighboring South Pacific countries. A similar percentage of students is taken in other departments.

Most students come from a traditional village orientation where, in this setting, they speak their village language. Most have no background in commercial transactions and business procedures. General business knowledge is poor and they have similar views of the economy and the world (Wilson 1981). With these disadvantages, students need good coaching involving small group discussion and case studies to build up their analytical ability. However, this coaching cannot be provided because of the lack of qualified full-time accounting academics, funds and facilities. Most students are poor and are on government or private organization scholarships. They cannot afford to buy textbooks and the book allowance provided is inadequate; therefore, lecturers recommend cheap, out-of-date textbooks. Libraries do not have the necessary funds to buy textbooks and case studies, and even one or two textbooks bought by the library cannot adequately serve the needs of 30 to 40 students. The use of foreign examples in textbooks and case materials makes it difficult for the students to relate the information learned to their environment, making accounting a difficult profession to study.

Another factor that is deterring the progress of students is that accounting and bookkeeping programs are taught for the first time at the postsecondary levels, including the two universities. Accounting and basic bookkeeping are not taught in National High Schools and therefore students coming to universities have their first exposure to accounting only in the four years of study (Mudogo and Watson 1985; O'Neil 1990). O'Neill (p. 28) states:

> Accounting education is at most non-existent in schools at present. This is surprising in view of the chronic shortage of accounting skills at all levels in the country. The education authorities should be more receptive to the manpower needs of the country that they are at present . . . Moving to specific policies, I believe the first concrete step to be taken should be the introduction of accounting in National High Schools.

Given these handicaps, university's administrators and accounting academics in the two universities in PNG strive to produce the accounting personnel required at both the subprofessional and professional levels. Students' development is crucial to the type of accountants produced; however, due to shortages of academics, funds and facilities, this cannot be given full attention. The situation also determines the number of accounting students admitted to the program.

SUMMARY

Having examined the development of accounting and related accounting education in PNG, major developments have taken place since independence. However, accounting education in PNG is a recent phenomenon, including accounting programs taught in the two universities. Since 1980, the successive governments in PNG have developed a positive outlook towards improving accounting education and producing the personnel required. However, more needs to be done in terms of funding, but the present government does not have a plan regarding the funding of accounting education. In order to help PNG to progress there is a need to improve accounting education, including accounting programs at the university level, which in turn may minimize accounting profession problems in PNG. There is a great need for funding which should be provided by the PNG government and other international and regional organizations interested in accountancy and economic development in developing countries, including PNG.

REFERENCES

Abdeen, M. A., and U. Yavas. 1985. Current State of Accounting Education in Saudi Arabia. *The International Journal of Accounting* (Spring): 255–273.

Amarish, A. 1979a. The Plantation System. In A. Amarish et al. ed. *Development and Dependency: The Political Economy of Papua New Guinea*. Oxford University Press: 9–35.

Amarish, A. 1979b. The Transformation of Peripheral Capitalism, 1945–1987. In A. Amarish et al, ed. *Development and Dependency: The Political Economy of Papua New Guinea*. Oxford University Press: 36–48.

Arreola, M. M., and L. K. Torres. 1988. Employees Expectations of New Graduate Accountants: Some Findings. *Papua New Guinea Journal of Accounting* (December): 11–18.

Baldwin, B. G. 1978. *Papua New Guinea: Its Economic Situation and Prospects for Development*. International Bank for Reconstruction and Development.

Buckley, K., and K. Kugman. 1983. *The Australian Presence in the Pacific: Burns Philp 1914–1946*. George Allen and Unwin.

Currie Commission. 1964. *Report of the Commission on Higher Education in Papua New Guinea*. Government Publishing Unit.

Eddie, I. 1990. Externalisation of Accounting Programs at UPNG and UNITECH. *External Consultants' Report to the Executive Director of International Development Program*.

Foot Report. 1960. *Higher Education in Papua New Guinea*. League of Nations.

Gibbs, C. N. 1990. The Role of Education in Accountancy Development in Third World Countries: A Critical Appraisal. *Papua New Guinea Journal of Accounting* (September): 22–27.

Good, K. 1986. *Papua New Guinea: A False Economy.* Anti Slavery Society.

Goodman, R. et al. 1985. *The Economy of Papua New Guinea: An Independent Review.* The Australian National University.

Hardman, D. J. 1983. Public Financial Administration of Microstates: South Pacific Forum. *Public Administration and Development* 4(2): 141–154.

——. 1985. Accounting for Independence: South Pacific Forum. *Papua New Guinea Journal of Accounting* (June): 23–28.

——. 1987. Prefiguration in Colonial Accounting: The Territory of Papua New Guinea. *Accounting Forum* (September): 35–43.

Higher Education Plan: A Stategy for Rationalisation 1986–1990. 1986. Papua New Guinea Government Printer (May).

Juchau, R. 1978. Accounting Practice Problems in Fiji and Papua New Guinea. *The Australian Accountant* (May): 232–238

——. 1981. Accounting Education in the Developing Nations of the South Pacific. In H. J. A. Enthoven, ed. *Accounting Education in Economic Development Management.* North-Holland Publishing Company: 171–185.

Linge, C. 1980. Universities in Papua New Guinea and Their Role in the Pacific. *Pacific Perspective* (March): 46–48.

Mudogo, E. 1986. Accounting Education and Training in Papua New Guinea. *Papua New Guinea Journal of Accounting* (June): 8–11.

——, and E. Watson. 1985. *The Needs of Accounting Graduates and Their Employers.* Unpublished mimeo, University of Papua New Guinea (February).

National Planning Office of Papua New Guinea. 1982. *The First National Manpower Assessment Report* (August).

——. 1986. *The Second National Manpower Assessment Report* (May).

Onedo, O. 1981. *Accountancy and Business Studies Education at the University of Papua New Guinea.* A Submission to the Office of Higher Education.

——. 1984. Some Thoughts on Accounting Education in Papua New Guinea. *Papua New Guinea Journal of Accounting* (June): 12–16.

O'Neill, E. 1990. Accounting Education in Schools. *Papua New Guinea Journal of Accounting* (March): 25–28.

Policy and Planning Group on Accounting and Financial Management Education and Training. 1986. *Masterplan for Accounting Education and Training in PNG: A Critical Analysis,* A submission to the Papua New Guinea Government (December).

——. *Accounting Education and Training in Papua New Guinea.* A submission to the Papua New Guinea Government (December).

Renagi, L. 1980. Demand for Higher Education in Papua New Guinea. *Pacific Perspective* (March): 49–52.

Somare, M. 1973. New Goals for Papua New Guinea. *Pacific Perspective* (March): 49–52.

University of Papua New Guinea. 1991. *Students and Graduates Records.*

——. 1991. *Arts Faculty Handbook of Courses.* University Publishing Unit.

University of Technology. 1991. *Students and Graduates Records.*

——. 1991. *Department of Accounting and Business Studies Handbook of Courses.* University Publishing Unit.

Wells, M. C. 1980. *Accounting Education at the Two Universities in Papua New Guinea.* External Consultants Report to the Education Department (November).

White, M. 1988. Market Demand for Accountants in Papua New Guinea and UNITECH's Response. *Papua New Guinea Journal of Accounting* (June): 14–25.

Wilson, R. 1981. Papua New Guinea/Australia Commercial Training Programme: Work Experience for Undergraduates. *The Australian Accountant* (May): 284–286.

Needs of Accounting Education in Developing Countries: An African Case Study[1]

R. S. Olusegun Wallace and Maurice Pendlebury

INTRODUCTION

Few governments in Africa have systematic arrangements for the training and education of their accountants. Although advanced training for higher military officials has a long history, the recognition of the need for comparable programmes for accountants (and in many cases, other professionals) is a rare phenomenon. Acknowledgement of the need, principally from outside Africa, has not brought much action. The explanation of this failure is to be found partly in certain resistances, not unusual in any instance of education, and more importantly in several unresolved questions about the nature and purpose of accounting education.

Although this paper is about Africa, it should not be assumed that African countries are homogeneous in their accounting problems and cultural, legal, political and socioeconomic environments. They are, in many respects, more heterogeneous in their environments and sociocultural heritage than many of the industrialized countries. For example, in terms of economic well-being and standard of living, the oil- or mineral-rich countries of Africa are far superior to those possessing little or no oil/minerals at all (e.g., Nigeria and Ghana, or Botswana and Uganda). Given the heterogeneity in socioeconomic and political developments and cultural milieu, it would be misleading to analyze African countries as a single entity. In consequence, the emphasis of the paper is on those accounting education needs that apply to specific African countries and subregions. Essentially, we address pan-African problems.

The Nature of Accounting Education Needs

A study of the accounting education needs of a people is a study of how to upgrade the accounting infrastructure of their country. The issues to be analyzed are usually varied and include the funding, planning and structuring of accounting education, the creation of a market for the graduates of accounting education by, for example, promoting financial accountability and seeking to elevate the status of accounting profession and accountants in the relevant country. This paper's analysis of the needs of accounting education in developing countries is based on three a priori assumptions: (a) the accounting education systems presently available in these countries are inadequate, (b) specific actions are available which will correct them and (c) a choice has to be made between several possible actions. If extant systems are adequate, there is no requirement for further analysis. If extant accounting education systems are inadequate and solutions are not available, one no longer talks of "need analysis" but of the identification and evaluation of problems. If extant systems are inadequate and only one solution is possible, there is no choice to be made and analysis of needs is a question of determining when to rectify the inadequacy.

A study which provides insight into the accounting education needs profile of developing countries is important, not only because it satisfies the curiosity of international accounting scholars, but also because it seeks to provide essential information for developing countries seeking to upgrade their accounting infrastructure and for those countries intent on granting financial and technical aid for the improvement of accounting in developing countries. More specifically, the accounting education needs of developing countries may be analyzed for one or more of the following reasons: (a) for budgeting and planning purposes — to use as a basis for making funding requests, to set funding priorities and decision making about programme implementation; (b) for academic purposes — to facilitate our understanding of the problems of developing countries; (c) for policy pur-

[1]Although this paper deals with the African situation, many of the issues raised in it are generally applicable to other developing countries in Europe, Asia, Latin America and the Pacific.

R. S. Olusegun is Senior Lecturer and Maurice Pendlebury is Professor at the Cardiff Business School, University of Wales College of Cardiff.

The authors are grateful for the reading assistance of colleagues Roger Mansfield, Mike Peel and Neil Marriot at the Cardiff Business School.

poses — to make a case for a technical assistance programme and to create national and international community awareness and to direct attention to a problem in need of a solution or evaluation.

Whatever the reasons for analyzing accounting education needs, it can be argued that the role of a systematic analysis of a country's needs for accounting education is the reduction of uncertainty. The governments of developing countries, and those who desire to assist developing countries in their quests for economic growth, are uncertain about what (if any) programmes should be mounted to upgrade the accounting infrastructure of developing countries. Need analysis seeks to reduce this uncertainty.

The needs identified in this paper are those accounting education requirements of developing countries which, in our judgment, can be met.[2] A judgment about the inadequacy of accounting education is one about the expected or actual outcome of accounting education; an outcome which violates expectations.[3] The critical question is whose expectations are violated? For example, it might be perceived that there is an accounting education problem in a country if accountants trained under the current system in that country do not meet the expectations of the targeted users (e.g., stock market, public and private sector employers, national and international community) that depend on their services.

The remainder of the paper is in three sections. The next section summarizes the literature on the needs of accounting education in Africa and distinguishes between different types of accounting education needs. The third section identifies and discusses the needs of African countries for accounting education. The conclusion follows in the fourth section.

AN OVERVIEW OF THE LITERATURE

Little has been written specifically on the needs of accounting education in Africa. The existing literature on accounting education in developing countries has always started from the premise that accounting in these countries is in a poor state and is badly in need of improvement. There is no scarcity of studies which describe the inadequacies in the accounting education and practices of individual African countries. Many of these studies have been reviewed by Wallace (1990).

Table 1 provides a summary of the literature concerned with the upgrading of accounting education in developing countries.

However, two significant continental studies of African accounting were conducted between 1986 and 1990, one by the International Labour Office (Management Development Branch) which produced a discussion paper on the "Dynamics of Accounting Development in Africa," co-authored by Boland and Wallace (1987) and the other by the United Nations which reported the results of a major survey of accounting in the book *Accountancy Development in Africa: Challenge of the 1990s*. Much of the information contained in this paper is drawn from these two reports.

IDENTIFYING THE INADEQUACY OF ACCOUNTING EDUCATION IN DEVELOPING COUNTRIES

Need analyses can help to identify the discrepancies between external (as opposed to intrinsic) expectations of accounting education and its outcomes. Arising from this are the accounting profession's fear of supply failure and overreliance on the work of other countries.

Expectations Gap

An expectations gap would exist if there is a discrepancy between what people can or ought to receive from accounting education and what they are getting from it. Four types of expectations gap, which support judgments of need, are identified by Bradshaw (1972). The first is *normative need*, that is, a need to fill the gap perceived to exist between what an expert defines as an adequate level of accounting education performance and the actual performance of accounting education. Based on their experience and knowledge, it is believed that experts can provide guidance about what outcomes should be expected and about the levels of

---

[2]We are aware that other people may recognise different needs. Coming from two different cultural settings (one from a developing country, the other from a developed country), we sought to blend our two perspectives: one of us has been a keen observer of the needs of developing countries and the other has experienced and actually expressed some of these needs. Like those raised by many other authors, the issues we raise in this paper are normative but unlike them, our judgment on the inadequacy of the state of affairs of accounting in these countries seeks to avoid much of their ethnocentricism, because we emphasise those dissatisfactions experienced by the countries. What constitutes our interest in this paper is what the peoples of developing countries desire, intend, value and need for the upliftment of their accounting education.

[3]The exact role, purpose and utility of accountants in developed countries is also open to debate.

TABLE 1
Five Approaches Suggested in the Literature for Improving Accounting in Developing Countries

Approaches	Authors and Policy Prescriptions
1 The transfer of accounting knowledge from developed to developing countries by designated transfer agents such as transnational enterprises and accounting firms, special projects undertaken by the United Nations and its agencies, or other international or regional agencies (such as European Community) and universities from developed countries.	**Authors** Engleman (1962), Enthoven (1979 and 1981), Lowe (1967), Seiler (1966), Needles (1976) and Briston (1978). **Policy Prescriptions** Accounting systems of developed countries should be transplanted into developing countries in accordance with the needs of each country. But needs are determinable by evaluating the gap between what presently exists in a country and what is normatively believed to exist in that country.
2 To structure accounting in a developing country so as to provide information which can facilitate the economic evaluation of the activities of an enterprise by management, investors and government. The goal is to base the structuring "solely on general micro and macro economic principles rather than business practices, accounting conventions, tax or other narrowly conceived legislation" (Scott, 1970: 149). This model is described by Tipgos (1987) as Economic Evaluation Accounting (EEvA).	**Author** Scott (1970) **Policy Prescriptions** Accounting education and improvement programmes should meet the needs of the end users. To ensure that such needs are met, input to accounting structure should be improved — such inputs include education of accountants, legislative control and regulation of accounting and professionals.
3 The use of existing and potential accounting systems, techniques, procedures and data to enhance economic development within a country and among countries (AAA, 1977: 20). This model is described as Economic Development Accounting by Tipgos (1987).	**Author** AAA (1977) **Policy Prescriptions** The vehicle for undertaking the AAA proposal is an economic development educational programme which would incorporate "a conceptual socio-economic foundation of accounting education and training, a further specialization in various areas (branches) of accounting; a closer linkage between institutional, professional and educational programs; and a greater focus on forecasting techniques of both internal and external nature" (AAA, 1977: 22).
4 The development of a two-tier education system devoted to the production of accounting technicians and accountants.	**Authors** Tipgos (1987) and Briston and Wallace (1990). **Policy Prescriptions** Accounting workforce development should embrace technical and professional levels. Tipgos (1987) provides an illustration of a two-tier structure in Philippines while Briston and Wallace (1990) describe the three-tier and three-level structure in Tanzania.
5 The education and training of accountants as well as nonaccountants in the advantages and uses of accounting information. The training of the latter group of people would stimulate the demand for accountants.	**Authors** Wallace and Briston (1992) **Policy Prescriptions** That the development of a national accounting development programme should emanate from within a country and be concerned with the demand and supply sides of accounting education and the education of those responsible for ensuring the maintenance of the quality of accounting information.

Adapted from Wallace and Briston 1992.

service required to reach such outcomes. In many countries, there are systems by which accounting programmes, provided by institutions of higher education, are evaluated and accredited. Such accreditation systems provide normatively based expectations on accounting education courses. Normative expectations may be particularly useful in countries with little previous experience in accounting education. However, because of the dependence by many developing countries on many foreign experts, normative expectations can be unrelated to the environment for which they are set and can lead to the adoption of accounting programmes that may be too elitist for the target population. One good example is the apparently generous donation by the American Accounting Association of copies of dated editions of American accounting texts to countries in Africa. This donation was not only based on the belief that Africa needs American books based on an American environment, but there was also the assumption that they would help to solve problems. Unfortunately, the problems which those books seek to solve are American, not African. Rather than help accounting students to learn about their countries' accounting problems, they tend to Americanise them.

The second type of expectations gap is described by Bradshaw (1972) as *felt need*. This concerns the need which arises because the people of a country are dissatisfied with the outcomes of the systems operating in their own country. For example, the instructions provided by accounting educators may be considered inadequate by the end users (e.g., the accounting profession); this can lead to a felt need. The major accounting firms in the US have recently suggested that there is an urgent need for a reexamination of the accounting education in the US. The expression of a felt need depends on the insight that a country has into its own problems. If a need for a service is not felt by a country, it probably will not be provided. On the other hand, many of the felt needs for accounting education in some developing countries are unrealistic on cost/benefit grounds.

The third type of expectations gap relates to those indicated by the use of services. This gap, described by Bradshaw (1972) as *expressed need*, arises because the existing supply of accountants (in quantity and quality) is inadequate to the needs of society. Such a need can be expressed through a long lead time in the completion of annual audits because only a few auditors deal with the many requests for annual and *ad hoc* audits of companies, higher level of enrollment for accounting education courses or high level of remuneration packages for accountants. Another source of expressed need is the demand which may arise from a country's economic growth. It should be realised that evidence of demand for a service does not of itself suggest that the use of the service is appropriate or that the service itself is of a high quality.

The fourth expectation gap identified by Bradshaw (1972) is *comparative need*. This expectations gap is based on the performance of another country. If a country has fewer accountants per 1000 of its population than another country, or scores below the global average in one or more measures of accounting performance or the other, the country has a problem.

Expressed Need for Accounting Education

The needs for accounting education in a country extend beyond the education *of* accountants. They include the education of the citizens *in* accounting and education *for* accountants (postqualification training). There are usually three elements to the services offered by accountants: the supply of those services (which may be covered by the education of accountants to a minimum acceptable standard); the demand for the service (which may be covered by educating the population to change their attitudes towards accounting and accountability); the monitoring and supervision of the quality of the services produced (which may be covered by the provision of education for accountants and by the setting of accounting, auditing and ethical standards).

The need for accounting education and accounting services may be expressed when those in positions of power (such as politicians, government officers and journalists) understand the underlying principles of accounting and are in a position to demand the services they require. So the more educated the people are, the better placed they are to demand accounting and support any programme for the education of accountants. It is, therefore, essential in every African country (and indeed, in non-African ones) to establish and strengthen increasingly the attitude towards accounting and accountability as a way of thinking which would become more and more powerful as they become widely accepted. This accountability outlook cannot be established by force. It should depend on acceptance through proper understanding. The accounting profession in a country may, on its own or through the assistance of external parties, evolve a reasonable national accounting education programme; but such a programme can be accepted and implemented only when it is properly appreciated by persons capable of similar understanding.

Accounting Education Needs for Economic Growth

Many developing countries are relatively new nations, having attained their independence within the last 50 years. By definition, a new nation is one that must tackle and accomplish several urgent tasks simultaneously. The compelling goal is one of development (or modernization) with its many obvious (sometimes baffling and confusing) pathways. The more obvious ones are the maintenance of a country's political and (if possible) economic independence and freedom of action through improvement in the general education of its people, improvement of social and physical infrastructure, economic welfare and military and diplomatic activities.

Less obvious, more baffling and even more challenging are those pathways leading to the establishment of stable behavioural patterns within which the desired and needed economic development can take place. This is the province of accountancy and accountability, and in this province, it is urgent that a radical transformation should occur during the next decade, both in the provision of research and in the consequent output of systematic and constructive thinking.

Far more than the developed and established countries, the developing countries of Africa require the services of the most skilled, perceptive and sophisticated mechanisms of accounting and accountability that can be contrived. This is because they have less time in which to achieve comparable viability in their economic institutions and government. They have a greater need to avoid mistakes, being less able to afford them. Like the developed countries from which they have inherited dominant features of their accounting systems, they are confronted with the problem of keeping accounting practices and regulations abreast with the times. But their adolescent need for stability and national unity makes them face many additional problems of institution building and social development. Yet their equipment for this task is minimal. And though the need is perceived, too little provision has been made for constructive thought in this area, and too little instructive thinking has been made.

According to Lewis (1955), one of the problems inherent in the situation of developing countries is that they need better government than the developed countries, just because they are "back-ward," and can get worse government just because they are "backward." The relative wealth of a country is closely related to the quality of government. The richer a country is, in terms of gross national product per capita (GNPpc), the easier for it to buy the needed management. But rapid economic growth would lead to greater demands for more accountants and managers. However, many countries are more concerned with building up military arsenals than improving the accountability of their government and management. As a result, higher GNPpc is not enough if people are sick, the air is polluted and corruption is rife. Accountants in developing countries need training in the measurement and reporting of the quality of life of their people as well as in the measurement of national, corporate and individual income and wealth. In this respect, Seidler (1966) has noted that:

> ...the strength and extent of a nation's information system determines in large part the rate at which economic development will progress, and that accounting systems thus assume an important role in the development of emerging nations.

Felt Needs of Accounting Education

Massive and concerted work by accounting educators on the intangible infrastructure of economic growth and development in Africa has been urgently needed since independence. Intuitively, the more educated the accountants of a country are, the more likely they are to be able to perform better. Regrettably, however, evidence from some developing countries with better trained accountants suggests that training more accountants does not raise the standards of accounting—see Parry and Groves (1990) for evidence from Bangladesh, Rivera (1990) for Panama and Abayo and Roberts (1992) for Tanzania. In a field where many common problems challenge combined thinking and action, it remains true to say that most of the ongoing work proceeds in isolation and does not measure up to the need. And for the most part, Africa has yet to take the necessary steps away from the starting point, bequeathed by the colonial powers, on the road to integrated national accounting systems and to international harmonization in appropriate spheres.

In support of this suggestion, we present an impressionistic profile of the colonial accounting legacy and impact, raising questions and, thereby, indicating areas that demand thoughtful action based on systematic research.

THE COLONIAL ACCOUNTING LEGACY AND IMPACT

Almost all the countries in Africa are a creation of the imperial authority. Every African country is heterogeneous in culture and historical antecedents, having been formed through conquests, settlements following wars (usually outside Africa) between imperial powers and from a collection of previously autonomous polities. These differing historical antecedents and cultural diversity are reflected in the profiles of accounting to be found in Africa. Although other systems may be found, the accounting systems in Africa are largely based on those of the United Kingdom (anglophone), France (francophone) and Portugal (lusophone) (UN, 1991: 3).

The description of the state of accounting systems in these major groupings of African countries is based on the report of a survey on accounting in Africa conducted by the United Nations Centre on Transnational Corporations (UNCTC) (UN, 1991).

Anglophone Africa

Many anglophone countries in Africa need to review the regulatory frameworks of their accounting systems which are usually based on the United Kingdom Companies Act of (or before) 1948. They have not reviewed these acts despite the changes in the corporate and financial environments of their countries and in the international markets. Many of these countries, in line with the practice in the United Kingdom, have regulations (such as Accountants Acts and Income Tax Acts) which give recognition to and regulate the accountancy professions. Such acts also specify the keeping of accounting records and the filing of accounting returns by individuals and enterprises about their activities and their wealth and, as a result, give accounting and financial management high priority. The UN report suggested that those countries (such as Ethiopia, the Gambia, Mauritius and Uganda) which have no such acts should consider enacting them.

Francophone Africa

The UN report opined that 15 of the 17 francophone African countries are still closely tied to France and the *plan comptable* which was in place during the colonial era. The other two are in the process of enacting a law which would give pride of place to the *plan comptable*. The *plan comptable* imposes a uniform framework (plan or chart of accounts) for the recording of transactions

and presentation of financial statements. The framework also provides an operational linkage between (macro) national income accounting and (micro) accounting by enterprises. Because of the uniformity in operational definitions of accounting items, interfirm or intersectoral comparisons can be undertaken and enterprise accounts can be aggregated and analyzed at the sectoral and national levels. However, the *plan comptable* has proved too complex and the cost of complying with it may be a handicap for the development of small business.

A simplified accounting plan (for small business) exists, but many francophone African countries have not adopted it. These countries have also not modified the *plan comptable* which has been revised twice but has not been drafted to fit the needs of African countries. The UN report concludes that as a result, a great deal of reliance on tax law to determine what information should be disclosed exists and that this reliance undermines the development of accounting standards. The African Accounting Council has, however, developed a new accounting plan which seeks to incorporate many African contingencies but there are no takers of this new accounting plan as yet.

In francophone Africa, there is a distinction between persons who are both accountants and auditors (*experts comptable*) and those who can work only as auditors (*commissaires aux comptes*). Strictly speaking, *experts comptable* are appointed by management (as employees) to ensure that the books of accounts comply with the *plan comptable*. The *commissaire aux comptes* is chosen by the shareholders to certify that financial statements present a true and fair view of the operations and financial position of the reporting enterprise.

All francophone African countries have a National Accounting Council (*Conseil national de comptabilité*) which is responsible for the accounting regulation, especially the operational interpretation of the *plan comptable*. The Minister of Finance is usually the President of the Council whose members are drawn from professional associations, users of financial statements (such as employers, members of the chamber of commerce), the banking community, training and educational institutions and government nominees from the treasury, tax offices and the department responsible for national planning.

Lusophone Africa

These countries are those which had colonial experience under the Portuguese. The accounting systems in these countries are also based on a chart of accounts which sets out the requirements for company books of accounts, auditing and publication of financial statements. The accounting systems in these countries are in a confused state. This is because during the colonial period, the charts of accounts were produced and maintained by the Portuguese experts. On departure, the citizens of these African countries sought and got help from the Cubans and East Europeans who, rather than operate the erstwhile accounting systems, superimposed their own accounting systems.

There are no accounting bodies in lusophone Africa and, unlike anglophone Africa, an audit is not a meaningful part of an accountant's work.

On the basis of Table 2 and the conclusions of the UN report (1991: 29), African countries as a whole have the following problems in need of urgent solutions:

1. There are too few indigenous professionally qualified accountants especially if the number of indigenous accountants in each African country, relative to population, was compared with those in some developed countries—see Appendix 1 in Boland and Wallace (1987: 78) and Table 1 in Wallace (1990: 28).

2. Public sector accounting is weak and this might well be one of the reasons for the poor performance of many African countries in the management of their external debts and other fiscal problems. With the exception of Zimbabwe, no African country conducts systematic training, education and examination of its people in public sector accounting. Zimbabwe even has a professional accounting body for public sector accounting. Many African countries are taking steps to move away from their overreliance on central planning and socialist principles, in favour of a certain amount of capitalist market principles. This will mean the training of more accountants.

3. Accounting technicians are of poor quality; thus the few qualified accountants are not only performing tasks suitable for accountants of far greater experience than themselves but also undertaking tasks which might be sensibly undertaken by unqualified or partly qualified staff (this is in line with Parker's [1990] description of his early professional accounting experience in Nigeria in early 1958).

4. Low priority is given to accounting standards and their enforcement.

In summary, African countries have either inherited the accounting systems left behind by the colonial administration or imported accounting systems voluntarily from the countries from which they obtained their political independence or from their new political allies, as in the case of lusophone countries. As a result, African countries have not taken heed of Scott's (1970: 7) advice that

> developing countries should adopt formats for aspects of accounting that is, for education, legislation, professional associations, and accounting principles and techniques, which are neither those used by advanced nations when they were developing (because the environments of developing nations of the past are different from those of the present), nor necessarily those presently existing in advanced nations (which are adapted to a different kind of economic context). Instead, developing nations should adopt accounting which consists of [adaptations] of modern methods to the special conditions of today's developing nations.

The Needs of a Country for Comparing its Accounting Education

The usual distribution pattern of accounting profiles of countries appears in Figure 1, as an approximation of a normal curve (which could be skewed in either direction). A country may possess more efficient or adequate accounting education systems, while another may have less efficient and inadequate accounting education systems and have problems in need of solution. The usual problem is to seek to move the country's accounting education to the right of Figure 1.

When countries are compared, the usual situation is shown in Figure 2. One country's accounting education profile is at A, while another country's is at B. The problem is to move the country in A to the level of the country in B. Considerations of how to do this would lead to the vast subject area of the transfer of accounting education technology and accounting systems (Olsolie 1975: 206; Needles 1976; Wallace and Briston 1992). If country A can somehow obtain relevant transfer, then it can improve its accounting education system.

The term "relevant" is crucial. Consider a developing country with about 20 million people, two or three million of whom are in a position to become professionals of one sort or the other. On average, less than five percent of these people may seek to become accountants. But what shall they learn? Should the accountants in training learn how to account for exports from and imports into their country? How do the people in other countries ac-

TABLE 2
Supply of Fully Qualified Accountants in Africa

| Country | Existence of | | Fully Qualified Accountants | | |
	Accounting Body	Qualifying Examinations	Private Sector	Public Sector	Accounting Education
NORTH AFRICA					
Algeria	Yes*	Yes	47	..	9
Egypt	Yes	Yes	9,755(100)	100	45
Morocco	Yes*	No	128(?)	35	7
Tunisia	Yes*	Yes	104**	..	16**
WEST AFRICA					
Benin	Yes	No	71	75	2
Burkina Faso	No	No	3(10)	90	2
Cameroon	No	No	52	25	3
Chad	No	No	..	..	—
Côte d'Ivoire	No	No	25	..	..
Gambia	Yes*	No	4(5)	9	—
Ghana	Yes*	Yes	496	86	8+
Guinea	Yes*	No	5	..	2
Liberia	Yes	No	3(2)	..	7
Mali	Yes*	No	28(1)	6	—
Mauritania	Yes*	No	61	52	—
Niger	No	No	1(13)	109	5
Nigeria++	Yes*	Yes	3,225(40)	827	15+
Senegal	Yes*	No	38	..	..
Sierra Leone	Yes*	No	30(5)	17	8
Togo	No	No	402(495)	86	6
Zaire	No	No	15(?)	..	..
EAST AFRICA					
Burundi	No	No	—(5)	1	..
Ethiopia	No	No	11(3)	3	..
Kenya++	Yes*	Yes	1,370(150)	87	—
Madagascar	Yes*	No	30(2)	..	6
Mauritius	Yes	No	173	25	2
Rwanda	Yes	No	41	15	5
Uganda	No	No	31(3)	10	1
SOUTHERN AFRICA					
Angola	No	No	—(300)	..	..
Botswana	Yes*	No	74(25)	125	1
Lesotho	Yes*	No	6(43)	11	5
Malawi	Yes*	No	98(22)	39	—
Namibia	Yes*	No	57(8)	10	—
Swaziland	Yes*	No	—(45)	6	—(3)
Tanzania	Yes*	Yes	902(47)	..	—
Zambia	Yes*	No	120(330)	..	..
Zimbabwe++	Yes*	Yes	502(23)	..	1+
TOTAL (37)	26	8			

Key: * = Statutorily recognized
  ** = All foreign personnel
  + = Updated information obtained through direct contact, ( ) no of foreign accountants working in the country
  ++ = Stock exchange

Source: United Nations, 1991. *Accountancy Development in Africa: Challenge of the 1990s.*

FIGURE 1
Typical Distribution of National Accounting Education Profile

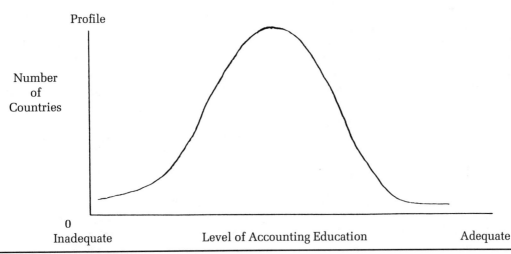

Profile

Number
of
Countries

0
Inadequate   Level of Accounting Education   Adequate

count for their domestic activities? Should the country train more public sector accountants rather than more private sector accountants, given the fact that there are more public sector activities in some countries than in others? Should accountants in African countries without capital market institutions study the accounting that is suitable for international capital and money and stock market activities?

The transfer of accounting knowledge may be undertaken by an accountant from one country going to work in another country, or by people from a developing country coming to study and work in a more industrialized one and returning to take up accounting jobs in their own country; or they may be transferred, as the USAID, and certain other bodies such as educational institutions from the US are trying to transfer them, through development and training programmes for accountants in developing countries. In every case, this involves the application of knowledge and practices evolved in one sociocultural environment in the circumstances of another.

With the exception of Needles (1976), Briston (1984) and Wallace and Briston (1992), there is vir-

FIGURE 2
Comparative Adequacy of Accounting Education

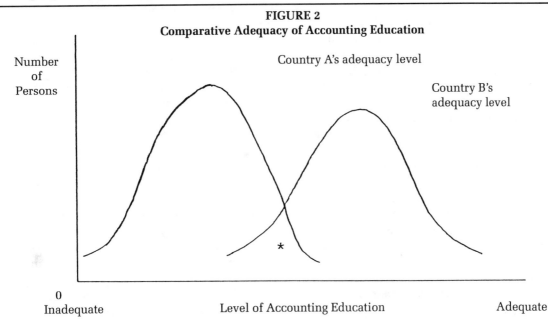

Number
of
Persons

Country A's adequacy level

Country B's
adequacy level

*

0
Inadequate   Level of Accounting Education   Adequate

*Some people in Country A have more than adequate accounting education than *some* people in Country B, but on the average, Country A's population is less kowledgeable or has less than adequate accounting education.

tually no discussion of this point in the literature. However, a developing country will seize upon what is available without examining the suitablity of this to its needs and tends to import a part or all of it through the help of funding and aid agencies. The rationale for this action is hard to explain and rarely discussed. Perhaps this lack of insight into what to learn explains why so many countries, after decades of laborious efforts to import both accounting education systems and accounting practices, discover that they are little more efficient at the end than at the beginning. According to Wesberry (1984: 150):

> The history of development assistance to improve accountability, as development agency officials are quick to point out, shows that five years after the assistance terminates there is rarely any existing evidence that it was ever provided in the recipient agency. Accountability systems disappear into the air like smoke once a development project ends.

Arising from the comparability need is the need for affiliation. Affiliation-oriented countries would tend to move toward international associations and the adoption of internationally recognised accounting practices and education standards. However, a strong need for affiliation may interfere with the drive towards the development of accounting education in a country.

Accounting Education Need for International Affiliation

Because there are common problems in accounting and because accounting must be established in every country, it is necessary, continually, to promote collaboration between all countries of the world and of Africa, both large and small, advanced and developing (in accounting terms). The motivation for affiliation plays a significant role in the adoption of foreign accounting practices and accounting education systems by African countries. In the pursuit of economic growth, African countries in need of foreign investments usually seek to convince foreign enterprises that they would permit them to adopt accounting systems of their home countries or those which are generally accepted internationally. Although international accounting standards (IASs) are prepared to serve as benchmarks against which all countries may compare their own accounting standards, IASs have been perceived by some African and other developing countries as applicable to their countries regardless of the stage of their economic development. Countries which adopt international

accounting practices and accounting education guidelines are probably doing so to take advantage of what such membership may bring. In addition, African enterprises that have borrowed funds from international capital markets are usually required to follow international accounting standards, the standards of the country from where the loan was granted or a modified version of these two standards. The essential feature about IASs and IFAC guidelines is that their pronouncements are available to members and nonmembers alike and so they provide each country the opportunity of carefully selecting aspects of those IASs and IFAC's auditing and education guidelines which fit their national priority needs and their environment. The ability to discriminate between the options offered in these standards and guidelines in the context of an African country's environment seems lacking. The accounting education programme which may meet this need for international affiliation is the education of the managers of the accounting profession and those responsible for setting national accounting standards and accounting education policies on how to determine whether an IASC's standard or IFAC's guideline is relevant to their country, and if not entirely relevant, how to adapt such a standard or guideline to suit their environment.

In one sense, the economic growth which developing countries are seeking is a process entailing the concurrent growth of superior technical, managerial and accounting skills. In principle, a people may acquire such skills spontaneously, by internal social processes, or they may acquire them by learning from others or by actually employing others to exercise these skills for them. In practice, a people normally does both, the resulting transformation being a complex interaction of internal and external influences (for an illustration of how Tanzania developed its accounting workforce, see Briston and Wallace 1990).

However, many countries in Africa are probably unable to develop, finance and sustain a national accounting profession or mechanism for the training of accountants.

We re-echo Enthoven's (1979) call for an international centre of accounting research in Africa. This centre can be constituted on lines similar to those of the United Nations Economic Commission for Africa (UNECA), and working closely with it, supplied with full-time staff specifically devoted to this task. The tasks awaiting such a centre include (1) the undertaking and promotion of systematic research into the many common accounting problems that confront most countries in Africa, not least of which is the establishment of viable accounting profession and accounting educational institutions; (2) acting as a technical agency for any future organisation that may be set up to promote harmonization of accounting practices, as between countries in matters where harmonization is desirable and practicable and assisting, generally, with the work of modification and restatement of IASC's standards that is underway in some countries; (3) serving as a coordinating centre and clearing house of information regarding how the accountancy reform activities in different countries are progressing and how particular problems have been solved in different national accounting systems, and also for providing facilities and assistance for projects for reform in particular countries.

CONCLUSION

We suggested in this paper that it is very important for developing countries to upgrade their accounting infrastructure. While there are many avenues along which such improvement can be attained, it has been recognized that there are various social, cultural and other obstacles which will act as barriers. Our concern in this paper has been primarily with what we referred to as "weak accountability levels."

One would naturally raise the question, "What is the solution?" We think the solution can be a two-pronged approach, one, to remove excessive controls and restrictions and to create a competitive market situation, and two, to reorientate the accountability philosophy of policymakers in developing countries.

The second approach of reorientating the accountability philosophy of policymakers can only be indirect and gradual. While competitive forces will no doubt compel many enterprises to take a close look at their efficiency situation, educational programmes might instil into management the elements of that frame of mind which seeks to build effective and efficient accounting systems.

A good many schools of accountancy in developed countries have been providing accounting education in their countries for people from developing countries and also taking courses to various developing countries. The purpose of these courses has been to concentrate on the education of accountants and accounting technicians. Pessimistic though it may sound, unless there is a perceptible change in the philosophy of the political leadership entrepreneurs and the top salaried managers in these countries, the efforts may not yield fruitful results. This is so, because one may find individuals who are imbued with knowledge of accounting techniques and theory acquired painstakingly but are unable to apply such knowledge effectively in a work environment. This is the situation that often prevails in a large number of enterprises in developing countries.

REFERENCES

Abayo, J. A., and C. Roberts. 1992. Does Training More Accountants Raise the Standards of Accounting in Third World Countries? Another Evidence from Tanzania. In R. S. O. Wallace, J. M. Samuels, and R. J. Briston, eds. *Research in Third World Accounting*, Vol. 2. JAI Press Ltd.

American Accounting Association (AAA). 1980. *Accounting Education and the Third World*. Report of the Committee on International Accounting Operations and Education 1976-1978. AAA.

Boland, R. G. A., and J. B. Wallace 1987. Dynamics of Accounting Development in Africa. A Discussion Paper. ILO.

Bradshaw, J. 1972. The Concept of Social Need. *New Society*, 30: 640–643.

Briston, R. J. 1978. The Evolution of Accounting in Developing Countries. *The International Journal of Accounting Education and Research* 14(2): 105–120

———. 1984. Accounting Standards and Host Country Control of Multinationals. *British Accounting Review* 16: 12–26.

———, and R. S. O. Wallace. 1990. Accounting Education and Corporate Financial Reporting in Tanzania. In R. S. O. Wallace, J. M. Samuels and R. J. Briston, eds. *Research in Third World Accounting*, Vol. 1. JAI Press Ltd.: 281–299.

Engleman, K. 1962. Accountancy Problems in Developing Countries. *Journal of Accountancy* (January): 53–56.

Enthoven, A. J. H. 1979. *Accounting Systems in the Third World Economies*. North-Holland, Elsevier.

———. 1981. *Accounting Education in Economic Development Management*. North Holland.

Lewis, W. A. 1955. The Economic Development of Africa. In C. W. Stillman, ed. *Africa and the Modern World*. Chicago University Press.

Lowe, H. D. 1967. Accounting Aid for Developing Countries. *The Accounting Review* (Vol. 42): 356–360.

Needles, B. E., Jr. 1976. Implementing a Framework for the International Transfer of Accounting Technology. *The International Journal of Accounting Education and Research.* 12 (1): 45–62.

Olsolie, C. C. 1975. *Legal Aspects of the International Transfer of Technology to Developing Countries.* Praeger.

Parker, R. H. 1990. Foreword. In R. S. O. Wallace, J. M. Samuels and R. J. Briston, eds. *Research in Third World Accounting,* Vol. 1. JAI Press Ltd.: xi–xii.

Parry, M. J., and R. E. Groves. 1990. Does Training More Accountants Raise the Standards of Accounting in Third World Countries? A Study of Bangladesh. In R. S. O. Wallace, J. M. Samuels and R. J. Briston, eds. *Research in Third World Accounting,* Vol. 1. JAI Press Ltd.: 117–140.

Rivera, J. M. 1990. The Accounting Profession and Accounting Education in Panama: A Survey. In B. E. Needles, Jr., and V. K. Zimmerman, eds. *Comparative International Accounting Educational Standards.* Center for International Education and Research in Accounting, University of Illinois.

Scott, G. M. 1970. *Accounting and Developing Nations.* University of Washington Graduate School of Business Administration.

Seiler, R. E. 1966. Accounting Information Systems and Under-developed Countries. *The Accounting Review* 25: 652–656.

Tipgos, M. A. 1987. A Comprehensive Model for Improving Accounting Education in Developing Countries. In *Advances in International Accounting,* Vol. 1, K. Most, ed. JAI Press.: 383–404.

United Nations. 1991. *Accountancy in Development in Africa: Challenge of the 1990s.*

Wallace, R. S. O. 1990. Accounting in Developing Countries: A Review of the Literature. In R. S. O. Wallace, J. M. Samuels and R. J. Briston, eds. *Research in Third World Accounting* Vol. 1. JAI Press Ltd.: 3–54.

———, and R. J. Briston. 1992. Improving the Accounting Infrastructure in Developing Countries. In R. S. O. Wallace, J. M. Samuels and R. J. Briston, eds. *Research in Third World Accounting,* Vol. 2. JAI Press Inc.

Wesberry, Jr., J. P. 1984. The Identification of Resources Available to Developing Countries for the Expansion of Accounting Education: Official Multilateral and Bilateral Assistance. In *Proceedings of the Asia and Pacific Conference on Accounting Education for Development,* held in Manila, Philippines (International Federation of Accountants, Asian Development Bank, and World Bank).

Accounting Education in Developed Countries

The conference program included seven papers that examine university accounting educational systems in developed countries. The common theme in most of these papers is that the current educational approach is inadequate for the demands that are being placed on accounting graduates. As accounting information requirements and technology change, accounting education must be responsive. New creative ideas for education must be developed and implemented. The papers contain ideas for change, examples or experiments of new approaches, and suggestions that may be useful for accounting education not only in developing countries but in all countries where accounting education is evolving.

An Accounting Education Program for the 21st Century: A Canadian Experiment

Z. Jun Lin and Al Hunter

INTRODUCTION

Accounting education is being challenged. Dramatic changes in technology and business environment are revolutionizing accounting practices. Accounting graduates often find that their school training fails to prepare them to cope with various practical situations rarely encountered in their classes. Criticisms of the current accounting education system have increased steadily and the pressure for change is mounting (Ingram and Charles 1980; Brown and Thomas 1982; Andrews and Norman 1984; and Sedki and George 1984). In North America, the United States accounting profession has taken the lead in providing stimulus to universities to overhaul and redesign their accounting programs. New programs are being tried to accommodate the changed professional demands for the next century. Especially during the past decade, practitioners and academics have joined to promote a revitalized accounting education (Bedford and Shenkir 1987; Sundem, Williams, and Chironna 1990).

In the mid-1980s, the Committee on the Future Structure, Content and Scope of Accounting Education (Bedford Committee) of the American Accounting Association (AAA) issued its initial recommendations to restructure university accounting education to meet the expanded demands of the profession (AAA 1986). The American Institute of Certified Public Accountants (AICPA) approved unanimously, in 1988, a proposed 150-semester-hour and five-year undergraduate accounting program beginning in 2000 (Bandy 1990). Recently, the Accounting Education Change Commission in the United States (AECC) outlined the objectives, knowledge requirements, curriculum structure, and guidelines for changes in accounting education for the 21st century (AECC 1990; Sundem et al. 1990; Engstrom and Wardlow 1991). In Canada, the accounting profession expressed similar concerns about accounting education (Hanna 1987). A guideline for accounting education reform has been recommended in "Education for the CA Designation: A Long Term Strategy," a study report by the Long-range Strategic Planning Committee of the Canadian Institute of Chartered Accountants (CICA) (CICA 1986).

There is a general recognition of the problems and the need for change in accounting education by the profession and academics. It is time for action. But a consensus has not yet been reached in the form of a definitive blueprint of a new accounting education program. It is argued that accounting education must direct students to become professional accountants with both broad knowledge and specific professional skills. Educators have a responsibility to plan and implement strategic changes in accounting education. Some pilot experiments in accounting curriculum changes, with varied versions, have been introduced in several educational institutions (Gibbins 1988; Pincus 1990).

One such experiment recently was implemented at a Canadian university. The Faculty of Management at The University of Lethbridge inaugurated a new undergraduate accounting program which incorporates a "liberal education" component and a fifth year professional diploma program. The University of Lethbridge's experiment demonstrates a unique and interesting pattern for reforming accounting education.

THE BACKGROUND OF THE UNIVERSITY

The University of Lethbridge, founded in the late 1960s, is one of the three public universities in the province of Alberta, Canada, located in the southern Alberta city of Lethbridge, about 220 kilometres southeast of Calgary and 130 kilometres north of the United States–Canada border. The Faculty of Management is a major part of the University. It offers a two-year management program to students who have first completed 20 preentry courses (i.e, they have spent two years in the Faculty of Arts and Sciences

Z. Jun Lin is an Assistant Professor and Al Hunter is an Associate Professor at The University of Lethbridge, Canada.

The authors are grateful to Dr. George Lermer, Dean of the Faculty of Management at University of Lethbridge, for his suggestions and comments on the earlier drafts of the paper.

studying philosophy, economics, political science, sociology, psychology, mathematics, statistics, history, language, and some introductory management and accounting courses). Two hundred and fifty third-year students are accepted into the management programs each year. Ten management degrees are available at the faculty. About one-third of the students choose the accounting major, or a double major with accounting. Upon completion of another 20 required courses (including 6 core management courses, 6 core accounting courses, and 4 courses in other management and nonmanagement areas) during the third and fourth year, students receive a degree of Bachelor of Management (accounting or a double major). Students can also opt for one of several two-degree programs, i.e, five-year programs lead to a Bachelor of Management and Education, a Bachelor of Management and Arts, and a Bachelor of Management and Science. A second degree in accounting is offered to students who have previously obtained a bachelor degree other than a management or commerce designation.

The Accounting Division within the Faculty of Management includes nine faculty members and some sessional instructors. The Accounting Education Resources Centre is an affiliated unit, which was founded in 1987 with financial support from the Accounting Education Foundation of the Institute of Chartered Accountants of Alberta. The Centre and the Faculty have been actively involved in the study and research in accounting education. To date, they have organized three biannual accounting case-writing competitions (nationwide and international), with a series of publications of the case books on financial accounting, intermediate accounting, and management accounting. One international workshop on computer applications in accounting was held in 1989. In May 1991, the Faculty and the Education Committee of the Canadian Academic Accounting Association (CAAA) jointly sponsored a conference on Curriculum Development in Accounting: Preparing for the Next Century, with 130 accounting educators and practitioners coming from Canada, the United States, Ireland, Britain, Germany, and some other countries.

THE GUIDELINES FOR CHANGES

The accounting division in the Faculty began the study of accounting education changes in late 1989. Reform of the accounting curriculum has been a major topic. Following a series of discussions, the faculty members reached consensus on the need for significant change in the accounting program to accommodate the new challenge from the profession. Reports and recommendations by the Bedford Committee AECC, and the CICA's Strategic Planning Committee were evaluated. Faculty members unanimously agreed that the undergraduate education should emphasize training students to become competent professional accountants through a broad-based education (e.g., "liberal education of accounting") to foster students' thinking, analytical and communication skills.

In particular, the accounting faculty members decided that the accounting education program should rest on three legs. The first, and the most important leg, is general education. General education is expected to motivate students to appreciate the existing heritage of structured and disciplined thought about private, economic, and social issues, which is at the root of all academic disciplines and applied social sciences. Hence, a "liberal education" approach should be adopted in the accounting program, with the goal of sensitizing students to accounting's social role and its response to social changes. A multidisciplinary knowledge base is needed to prepare accounting graduates to pursue their career under a dynamic social and business atmosphere.

"Liberal education," however, should not be proceded by completely isolating nonaccounting or nonbusiness from accounting courses. The faculty believed that other alternatives to having students complete a nonaccounting or nonbusiness undergraduate degree and then continuing accounting training would not be an effective pedagogical model for accounting education. Instead, nonaccounting or nonbusiness knowledge must be integrated with accounting knowledge training. Liberally teaching accounting is the key. Accounting courses should be the carrier of multidisciplinary knowledge and be taught contextual to the social, cultural, and economic environments of accounting.

Instruction is the second leg of university education, by which students can acquire specific knowledge of a discipline. The accounting faculty members agreed that instruction is a necessary and efficient means to convey some of the curriculum subjects because students can effectively accept the authority of the instructor and the textbook. But instructional education should not concentrate on technical and procedural accounting knowledge, at the expense of the underlying concepts and their social and economic implications. Although procedural knowledge is a necessary tool to perform accounting work, those technical materials may be inherently complex and often ambiguous and must be adapted in light of real-world situations. The approach of overstressing technical knowledge in traditional accounting education is problematic because it could not effectively accommodate the changing accounting practices with a dynamic business environment. Hence, the instruction component of university education should be aimed at directing students to acquire the rationale for accounting procedures and to develop a solid conceptual framework to understand and apply accounting procedures appropriately in the real world, instead of a mechanical repeating of specific technical procedures.

The third leg of accounting education is experience, which is a practical exercise of combining elements of instruction in the form of applying disciplinary knowledge to solve real-world problems and general education in the forms of understanding the complex interdependence between the profession and society and to interact with diverse groups of people (i.e., colleagues, supervisors, clients, and other people from within and outside the workplace). The accounting faculty members consented that separation of experience from education and instruction is generally a slow, expensive, and often painful route to wisdom. University education should encourage and assist students to

practise their knowledge and skills through the learning process. The development of problem-solving ability, interpersonal communication skills, and life-time learning is an effective means for students to cumulate experience, and should be another focus of change in accounting education.

Hence, the fundamental guideline of the accounting education reform at the University of Lethbridge is to design an undergraduate accounting program which will/can foster an effective integration of the educational, instructional and experiential modes of learning by carefully scheduling the three learning components into the new accounting program. Figure 1 displays a diagrammatical illustration of the knowledge components of the new accounting program.

THE DESIGN OF NEW PROGRAM

After several rounds of discussions and revisions in the past two years, the Faculty of Management approved a new accounting program in the Fall of 1990. The new program maintains some significant changes as outlined below.

1. Adopting an approach of "liberal education of accounting." "Liberal education" is a tradition at the University of Lethbridge, which has been

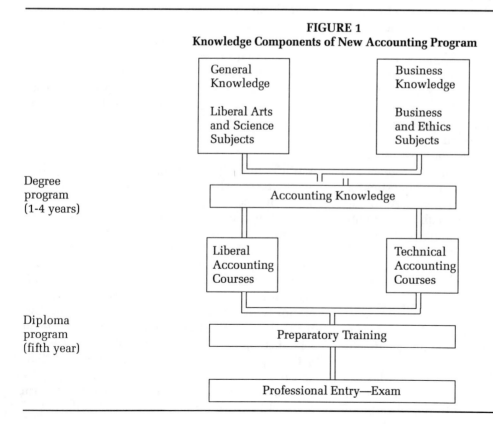

FIGURE 1
Knowledge Components of New Accounting Program

strengthened in the new accounting program. The new program shifts the focus of interest from the instructional to the general education. General knowledge courses have been considerably expanded even at the expense of the technical accounting courses. Knowledge on social sciences and humanities disciplines concerning human behaviour in a social, organizational and economic context, as well as optional courses from other arts and sciences, is enhanced in the new curriculum. Nonaccounting elements of business knowledge are also stressed. In particular, courses in finance, economics, and other related business areas such as Advanced Finance, Portfolio and Investments Management, Financial Institutes and Markets, Risk Management, Business Ethics, Management Policy and Strategy, and Advanced Economics are introduced as the selective for the accounting major in the new program. In addition, new accounting courses emphasizing the social and economic context of accounting, such as Behaviourial Accounting, Contemporary Accounting Research, History of Accounting, and International Accounting, are added in accounting curriculum, as an important component of "liberal accounting education." The purpose of such curriculum changes is to broaden students' vision, and to build a sound interdisciplinary knowledge base for accounting students. Tables 1 and 2 demonstrate a comparison of the curriculum changes under the old and new accounting program.

2. Reorganizing the instructional component of the program. The technical accounting courses have been redesigned, in light of the requirements of the profession. Some technical courses were restructured, others were cancelled. A significant part of the instruction-based technical accounting courses was shifted to a postdegree certification program called "diploma program" in the fifth year. The diploma program provides students an intensive preparatory training for professional entry examinations. Students must complete eight technical accounting courses, currently required by the professional organization, in two semesters. They will write, with the consent of the professional organizations in the province, the final examinations for the professional designations (i.e., CA or CMA) on completion of the diploma.

3. Strengthening the introductory accounting courses. The accounting faculty members all

---

TABLE 1
Faculty of Management
The University of Lethbridge, Canada

Old Curriculum of Accounting Program

I. Preentry requirements (The first two years)

Completion of 20 courses, including:

Introduction to Economics
Principles of Macroeconomics
Principles of Microeconomics
Introduction to Management
Introduction to Management Information Systems
Decision Analysis
Introductory Financial Accounting
Introductory Management Accounting
Mathematics
Introduction to Probability and Statistics
Quantitative Methods in Economics

9 nonmanagement courses (Arts and Sciences option)

II. Degree Requirements (The third and fourth years)

6 core courses in management:

    Management (Business) Law
    Marketing
    Organizational Behaviour
    Finance
    Personal Management and Labour Relations
    Policy and Environment

6 core courses in accounting:

    Intermediate Accounting I
    Intermediate Accounting II
    Accounting Topics
    Management Accounting II
    Accounting Theory
    Auditing Topics

4 management selective (including accounting)

4 nonmanagement selective

---

agreed that introductory accounting courses should provide a sound basis for further study in accounting and be a useful tool for nonaccounting students to obtain an understanding of accounting. Many efforts have been made to strengthen the teaching and learning of the two introductory courses of financial and management accounting under the new program. Not only have the computer-assisted learning laboratories been introduced, but also the supplementary material to the traditional textbooks are enriched by adding 1.5 hours per week "colour" section to the introductory courses. This "colour" section exposes students to literature and ideas underlying the conceptual issues affecting the accounting profession. Typical subjects covered are Information Economics, Theory of Principal-Agents, Property Rights, and History of Accounting Thought.

Discussions and analyses are stressed in class time, while technical exercises and problems are handled in the laboratory time.

4. Modifying pedagogical procedure to develop students' analytical ability. Under the new program, emphasis is placed on training students to become active thinkers instead of passive information recipients. Case studies are increasingly used in Intermediate Accounting, Ac-

---

TABLE 2
Faculty of Management
The University of Lethbridge, Canada

New Curriculum of Accounting Program (Effective July 1, 1991)

I. Preentry requirements (The first two years)

Completion of 20 courses similar to previous requirements, except for including Business Ethics as a required course, and adding laboratory and "colour" enrichment to the two introductory accounting courses.

II. Degree Requirements (Completion of 20 courses)

Third year

Semester 1:

Management (Business) Law
Marketing
Organization Behaviour
Finance II
Intermediate Accounting

Semester 2:

Behaviourial Accounting
Tax Policy
Personal Management and Labour Relations
Accounting Topics (cases)
(Nonmanagement option)

Fourth Year

Semester 1:

History of Accounting
or: International Accounting
Contemporary Accounting Research
(Management Option—Nonaccounting)
Corporate Financial Analysis
(Arts & Science option)

Semester 2:

Auditing I
Management Policy and Strategy
(management option)
(Nonmanagement option)
(Arts & Science option)

III. Diploma in Accounting (Completion of 8 courses)

Fifth Year

Semester 1:

Accounting Standards I
Auditing II
Personal Income Tax
Management Accounting II

Semester 2:

Accounting Standards II
Auditing III
Corporate Income Tax
Management Accounting III

counting Theory, Management Accounting, and Auditing courses to enhance students' problem-solving ability. The complexity of the cases is coordinated with the topics and the level of the courses. Interdisciplinary and unstructured cases (such as developing accounting standards for new accounting issues that have emerged in real world) are required at senior-level courses. Communication skills (verbal and written) and group performance are intentionally encouraged through various class assignments (such as case presentations, reading abstracts, class debates and discussions, literature reviews, data searching, and term papers), with a goal to help students to cumulate experience and ability of "learning how to learn."

5. Developing students' experience through field-training program. The experiential component of the learning is enhanced by students' participation in a co-operative education program. The co-op program, sponsored through the Canadian federal government's grants, integrates students' academic studies with relevant and productive work experience in industry, business, and government. Accounting is a major field of the co-op education program and students enrolled will work with an external employer during the summer time and extended term to obtain valuable work experience before their graduation. With the cooperation of the Alberta Institute of Chartered Accountants (AICA), the field-training time will count for the work experience required for the professional entrants.

IMPLEMENTATION AND PERSPECTIVE

The new accounting program was officially implemented on July 1, 1991. For a smooth implementation, both the old and new accounting programs are offered in a four-year transition period. Students already in the Faculty of Management, or who began an undergraduate program at the University of Lethbridge or other institution before January 1, 1991, could choose to follow the old rather than the new program. The option to select the old program will remain available until July 1, 1994. Students entering in the Summer term of 1994 or later must pursue the new program.

At present, the fifth year of certificate program, the diploma program, is not mandatory. Students in the new program may choose to graduate with a major in accounting after completing a 40-semes-ter-course program, without enrolling and completing fifth year courses. Those students seeking professional certification are strongly encouraged to continue in the fifth year study immediately on completion of their degree. Priority in registering for the diploma program will be given to accounting graduates. Courses listed in the fifth year program will not count for credits towards a degree after the transition period. Students completing the fifth year study will receive a Diploma Certificate in Accounting, in addition to the Bachelor of Management degree.

It is premature to assess the merit of the new accounting program at the University of Lethbridge. However, the new courses and teaching methods have evoked the student's interest in studying and expanded their knowledge and skills. Accounting education is no longer restricted to number-crunching techniques, but exploring a discipline built on multidisciplinary knowledge. It is hoped that the new accounting program will help accounting graduates to meet the new challenges to the profession in the 21st century.

The new accounting program at the University of Lethbridge is less than perfect at present. Some difficulties appeared from the current experiment. One major hurdle is related to the resources to operate the new program. The updated program raises the quality requirement for the faculty significantly. Since the University of Lethbridge is a relatively young university in Canada, it is hard to attract sufficient number of qualified faculty in the context of a general shortage of accounting Ph.D.s in the country. As well, it is difficult to find suitable textbooks or reading materials for some new courses, such as History of Accounting and Behaviourial Accounting. Although the Faculty of Management at the University of Lethbridge has made a strong commitment to self-development, external support from the profession and business community is helpful.

CONCLUSIONS

It is broadly recognized that accounting education must be revamped to meet the profession's needs in the next century. The Faculty of Management at the University of Lethbridge, Canada, has developed and experimented with a new accounting program in light of the changing demands from the profession. The new program is intended to integrate general education, instruction, and experience components of learning, by employing an approach of "liberal accounting education." Multidisciplinary knowledge and analytical skills are stressed in the curriculum and many technical accounting courses are shifted to a fifth year post-degree diploma program. Emphasis is placed on preparing students to become competent professionals with broad knowledge and proficient skills for a dynamic business environment. The experiment should generate some valuable lessons for the promotion of accounting education elsewhere.

REFERENCES

American Accounting Association. 1986. *Future Accounting Education: Preparing for the Expanding Profession.* A Special report by the Committee on Future Structure, Content, and Scope of Accounting Education.

Accounting Education Change Commission. 1990. Objectives of Education for Accountants: Position Statement Number 1. *The Accounting Review* (Fall): 307–312.

Addams, H. L. 1981. Should the Big 8 Teach Communication Skills? *Management Accounting* (May): 37–40.

Amernic, J. H., and H. B. Thomas. 1984. Accounting Students' Performance and Cognitive Complexity: Some Empirical Evidence. *The Accounting Review* (April): 300–313.

Andrews, J. D., and B. S. Norman. 1984. How Effectively Does the "New" Accountant Communicate: Perceptions by Practitioners and Academics. *The Journal of Business Communication* (Spring): 15–24.

Backman, R. J. 1989. The 150 Hour Requirement for Accounting Studies. *South Dakota Business Review* (December): 1, 6–7.

Bandy, D. 1990. Accounting Education at the Crossroads. *CPA Journal* (August): 12–13.

Bedford, N. M., and W. G. Shenkir. 1987. Reorienting Accounting Education. *Journal of Accountancy* (August): 84–91.

Birkett, W. 1987. Curriculum Issues in Accounting Education: Academic Viewpoints. *Australian Accountant* (August): 44–46.

Brown, J. F., and E. Thomas. 1982. Do Accountants Need More Education? *Management Accounting* (November): 26–29.

Canadian Institute of Chartered Accountants. 1986. Report of the Long-range Strategic Planning Committee, Education for the CA Designation: A Long Term Strategy.

Chambers, R. J. 1987. Accounting Education for the Twenty-First Century. *ABACUS* (September): 97–106.

Cherry, A. A., and M. J. R. Phillip. 1983. The Introductory Financial Accounting Course: Its Role in the Curriculum for Accounting Majors. *Journal of Accounting Education* (Spring): 71–82.

Dockweiter, R. C., and G. W. Carl. 1984. On the Use of Entry Requirements for Undergraduate Accounting Program. *The Accounting Review* (July): 496–504.

Engstrom, J. H., and P. S. Wardlow. 1991. Accounting Education Is Poised for Change: Will Government Accounting and Auditing Be Covered? *Government Finance Review* (February): 37–39.

Farley, A. A., and A. L. Ramsay. 1988. Student Performance in First Year Tertiary Accounting Courses and Its Relationship to Secondary Accounting Education. *Accounting and Finance* (May): 29–44.

Gibbins, M. 1987. Accounting Curriculum Development: An Alberta Example. *CA Magazine* (November): 60–65.

Hanna, J. 1987. The University's Role in Professional Accounting Education. *CA Magazine* (July): 50–54.

Huff, B. P. 1987. Educating Accountants for a New Era. *Massachsetts CPA Review* (Spring): 36–38.

Ingram, R. W., and R. F. Charles. 1980. Developing Communication Skills for the Accounting Profession (AAA).

Kelly, T. F. 1987. Educating Future Accountants. *CPA Journal* (August): 8–12.

Lentilhan, R. W., and T. K. Anthony. 1983. Professional Examination Preparation in AACSB Accredited and Member Schools. *Issues in Accounting Education*: 38–49.

Lourens, J. 1989. Accounting Education: Fighting the Wrong Battle. *Australian Accountants* (February): 21–26.

May, G. S., and C. AreValo. 1983. Integrating Effective Writing Skills in the Accounting Curriculum. *Journal of Accounting Education* (Spring): 119–126.

Pincus, K. V. 1990. Educating Accountants for the Twenty-First Century: Force for Change in Accounting Education. *Governmental Accountants Journal* (Summer): 59–61.

Porcano, T. M. 1984. An Empirical Analysis of Some Factors Affecting Student Performance. *Journal of Accounting Education* (Fall): 111–126.

Sedki, S. S., and J. P. George. 1984. The Accounting Practitioners/Accounting Educators Dialogue. *Journal of Accounting Education* (Spring): 163–166.

Sprouse. R. T. 1989. The Synergism of Accountancy and Accounting Education. *Accounting Horizons* (March): 102–110.

Sundem, G. L., D. Z. Williams, and J. F. Chironna. 1990. The Revolution in Accounting Education. *Management Accounting* (NAA), (December): 49–53.

Cross-Cultural Influences on Audit Quality: A Comparison of Pacific Rim, European, and North American Audits

James C. Lampe and Steve G. Sutton

The Securities and Exchange Commission reported that world financial market activity approximately tripled from a level of $1,700 billion in 1978 to over $5,000 billion in 1986 (SEC 1987). Not surprisingly, the Japanese share of trade increased during this time period while the United States share decreased from 52 to 43 percent. Paralleling the increased activity in international financial markets, multinational corporations (MNCs) also reflected the globalization of business during the 80s. Although losing in share to the Japanese, U.S.-based MNCs experienced much more growth than purely domestic counterparts. Many more U.S. companies who previously operated solely within North American confines have established trade contracts and joint ventures in other developed and developing countries.

This rapid growth in the the international financial market and MNC activity has also correspondingly increased international audit activity by U.S.-based CPA firms, by U.S.-based MNC internal audit departments, and by non-U.S. auditors.

One obvious indicator of rapidly increasing international activity by U.S. auditors is the merger activity of the large CPA firms. A commonly stated reason for this merger activity has been to better service the international community. Reports of the Institute of Internal Auditors also provide evidence that the decade of the 80s brought about increased education, training, and utilization of U.S.-based MNC internal auditors. (Vinton 1991). Similarly, the incidence of non-U.S. auditors performing fieldwork in the United States is also on the rise. For example, auditors from French, Japanese, and Italian manufacturing firms performed preacquisition audits on Firestone Rubber Company. This study is concerned with and reports results obtained from practicing international auditors on how cross-cultural factors influence audit quality. A general framework for recognizing cross-cultural influences is generated via clustering and nominal group techniques.

THE IMPORTANCE OF QUALITY

A second recognizable trend in recent business activity is increased emphasis on quality. While Japanese electronic products were considered inferior in the 1950s, emphasis on quality circles and other such programs have resulted in their now being recognized as the highest quality electronics producers with associated levels of demand and profitability. In order to compete, numerous U.S. and internationally based entities have begun some type of high-priority total quality management (TQM) program. Within the United States, increased interest in and competition for the Malcolm Baldrige National Quality Award is one clear indicator of the trend to focus on quality output for both products and services. Similar programs, such as the Canada Quality Awards, have been introduced in other countries.

Past Baldrige Quality Award winners have had varied descriptions of TQM such as "zero product defects," "six sigma," and "quality action approach." A common focus of all these varied programs, however, has been to better define, measure, and monitor both productivity and quality. This is difficult in production manufacturing and even more so when extended to services including the auditing function. Measuring and monitoring audit quality is difficult in domestic engagements and magnified when U.S.-based auditors perform audits in different countries. A common concern of audit customers is that the quality of the work performed and the degree of reliance afforded by the audit report are acceptable. The failure of an entity that has received unqualified audit reports from external auditors for several consecutive years raises questions about the quality of and value added by independent audits. When an internal

James C. Lampe is Arthur Andersen Professor of Accounting at Texas Tech University and Steve G. Sutton is an Associate Professor of Accounting at Arizona State University.

audit is performed for an area of a company and fails to detect significant control weaknesses that lead to a subsequent middle level management defalcation, audit quality and value are similarly questioned. The closure of the Bank of Credit and Commerce International (BCCI) has raised numerous questions regarding both internal and external international audit quality.

One of the clear problems of both domestic and international auditing is how to improve service quality by making the audit more effective and efficient. Greater effectiveness, at equal or lower cost, improves audit quality by providing higher levels of assurance to the readers of the audit report. Improved efficiency is attained when an equal or higher level of assurance is provided, other audit objectives are met, and lesser time or other resources are used in the audit process. Attempts to measure and improve audit quality must include consideration of both effectiveness and efficiency.

Several findings of prior service quality research are applicable to the study of international audit quality including (1) quantitative measures collected for audit process attributes improve the objectivity of audit evaluation (Sutton and Lampe 1991), (2) multiple quality measures, comprehensive of the entire process, are necessary to avoid manipulation of a single area to the detriment of overall quality (Adam, Hershauer, and Ruch 1986), (3) involvement and empowerment of the persons performing day-to-day tasks within the process are necessary to achieve an attitude for continual improvement (Shea 1986), and (4) continual monitoring of process productivity and quality via a set of benchmarks leads to multifold improvements in the monitored process (Lynch 1991).

All of the service quality research referred to in the previous paragraph has a central theme of identifying and measuring specific process factors as a means of improving service quality. Another research approach considered applicable to this study centers on the concept of developing knowledge clusters based on higher levels of abstraction as the field of international business develops and matures. A significant literature in the area of international management attributes has been developed on the basis of clustering methodology and some applications to international accounting and auditing have been recognized (Choi and Mueller 1978).

This type of research applied to the area of comparative management has attempted to establish clusters of countries based on similarities of relevant organizational variables. Ronen and Shenkar (1985) review eight empirical studies that use employee attitudinal data (primarily low and middle management level employees). A synthesis of these studies provides the basis for a cross-cultural clustering map for grouping like countries.

APPLICATION OF THE CLUSTERING APPROACH

In one example of a clustering methodology applied directly to international auditing, it was found that audit reports can be divided into five groupings of countries with similar practices (Hussein, Bavishi and Gangolly 1986). The current study combines a similar clustering technique with structured quality circle sessions in order to identify the attitudinal variables of both the auditor and auditee that impact the quality of the output from international audits. The previously referenced Ronen and Shenkar (1985) clustering map is presented in Figure 1 and serves as the basis for identification and discussion of variables potentially impacting the audit process as well.

The map in Figure 1 contains eight different clusters plus a group of four independent countries which represent most of the noncommunist world. The first, and most important, conclusion to be obtained from the mapping is that most countries can be clustered according to culture based on four attitudinal variables—work goals, values, needs, and job attitudes. The discriminant validity of these four variables is supported by the synthesis of the eight empirical studies. The resulting clusters consistently discriminate between the cultures represented by different countries. In addition to the grouping of countries within each cluster, Figure 1 illustrates per capita GNP as concentric distances from the center of the map. The most highly developed countries are closer to the center of the map and appropriately indicate more similar levels of development and attitudes even if not within the same cluster.

A better understanding of why certain countries cluster, as exhibited in the map, can be obtained from looking at other dimensions underlying the clusters. Ronen and Shenkar identify and discuss three other such interdependent dimensions in addition to the economic and technological development— geography, language, and religion. It can be generally observed that the countries with one of these elements in common often share all three. For example, the Latin American

FIGURE 1
Ronen and Shenkar's (1985) Country Clustering

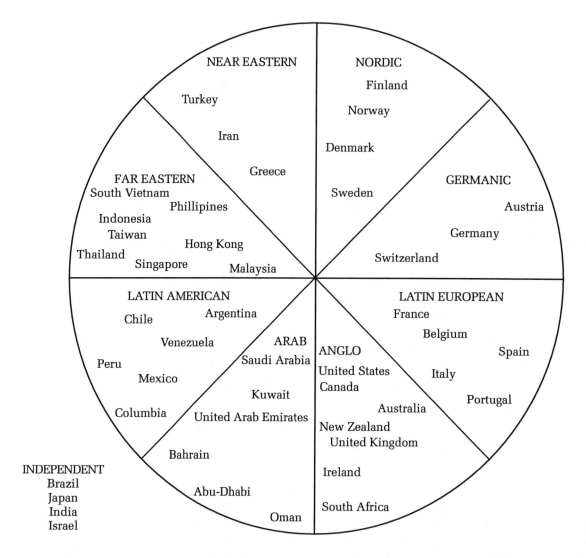

cluster is geographically contiguous with most residents of the member countries sharing the same language and religion. It can also be observed that people in Anglo countries speak English and people in Germanic countries speak German.

THE STRUCTURED QUALITY CIRCLE APPROACH

The primary premise behind quality circles is that the employees performing the day-to-day work are most familiar with the strengths and weaknesses of the process used to generate product or service output. When small groups of employees working on the same process are given the power to self-identify the problems they perceived to be most important to quality/productivity and subsequently analyze their causes, it is probable that problems not evident to higher levels of management will be identified and accompanied by innovative and efficient solutions (Shea 1986). Another advantage of quality circles is that the employee work force performing the tasks assume greater ownership of the problems and self-selected solutions in contrast to an agenda prepared by upper management and pushed down on lower levels.

A structured form of quality circles that has been used by the researchers with both internal and external auditors to identify the critical factors affecting auditors' ability to perform at the desired level of quality. A series of three eight-hour structured quality circle sessions have been conducted with groups of different teams of internal auditors from the United States who have had significant audit experience in the Pacific Rim, Europe, and Canada. These intensive data-gathering sessions have been based on a specialized form of nominal group techniques developed by Adam et. al. (1986). The four primary objectives of the sessions are to (1) define the audit process that is to be monitored, (2) identify the critical factors affecting audit quality and productivity, (3) generate a set of measures for monitoring each of these factors, and (4) to determine the relative importance of each of the critical factors to overall audit quality. The first two objectives have been performed and examined from two perspectives—first for domestic factors and then for additional international factors. (See Lampe and Sutton 1992b for more complete descriptions of this process methodology.)

IDENTIFYING U.S. AUDIT QUALITY FACTORS

The first phase of this study has been to identify a common set of factors that most auditors face in most audits that affect their ability to perform and complete the audit at the level of quality desired. All subjects participating in the study have had United States audit experience as their one common country of experience. For this reason, the United States is used as a benchmark from which to look at cross-cultural effects on audit performance. The objective is to use this benchmark set of audit quality factors and compare these to factors identified as critical when these auditors were auditing outside of their home base of operation—e.g., the United States This

particular study specifically compares three types of countries for cross-cultural effects: (1) countries identified via the Ronen and Shekar (1985) clustering as similar in language and level of economic development (i.e., other Anglo countries); (2) countries in other clusters that are considered relatively close in economic development and some cross-cultural factors but different in language and limited cultural factors (i.e., Latin European, Germanic, and Nordic countries), and (3) countries of quite diverse economic, language, and other cross-cultural dimensions (i.e., Far Eastern).

The subjects participating in this study represent six different teams of auditors selected to provide two sets of input for each of the three situations described above. Two participating audit teams have only U.S. audit experience, two audit teams have experience in countries of economic and other cross-cultural dimensions similar to the United States but different language, and two teams are experienced in countries from the Far Eastern cluster. This trichotomy provides a control from which to ensure that the domestic factors are not biased by the international audit experience of the other four teams.

The first output of the group processes is condensation of the audit process into three phases with 16 related quality factors. These factors were commonly agreed upon to comprehensively include the variations that impact an auditor's ability to efficiently perform and effectively complete a domestic audit. The three phases and 16 quality factors are summarized in Table 1.

To identify any potential bias from the internationally experienced audit groups, the consistency

---

TABLE 1
Domestic (U.S.) Audit Quality Factors

Planning Phase:
    Audit Staff Training &
        Experience Level
    Audit Manager Involvement &
        Support
    Auditee Cooperation & Availability
    Time Availability for Planning

Fieldwork Phase:
    Audit Staff Training &
        Experience Level
    Auditee Personnel Experience Level
    Auditee Cooperation & Availability
    Supervision & Review
    Significance (sensitivity) of Findings
    Time Constraints on Fieldwork

Reporting andReview Phase:
    Audit Manager Involvement & Support
    Auditee Cooperation & Availability
    Company Political Pressures
    Audit Staff Training & Experience Level
    Completeness & Clarity of Report 2
    Significance (sensitivity) of Findings

between the selection and rating of audit quality factors by the groups has been analyzed using Kendall's Coefficient of Concordance test. Since Kendall's concordance test uses rank data, the tests of consistency have been run separately for each of three stages in the audit process: (1) planning, (2) fieldwork, and (3) reporting and review. The results provide evidence of very high agreement between the groups for the planning (W = .51, p = .009) and fieldwork (W = .38, p = .019) phases of the audit, but week results for the reporting phase (W = .18, p = .535).

The strong agreement between groups with respect to common quality factors that influence the quality of processes within the planning and fieldwork stages of the audit provides a strong foundation for comparison with cross-cultural influences that may further affect audit quality. The single phase that has previously been identified to most affect total audit quality is fieldwork (Lampe and Sutton 1992a). Because there is strong agreement that relatively few factors (five planning phase and six fieldwork phase) provide a fairly comprehensive indication of quality over these processes in the audit, deviations in audit quality caused by performance in nondomestic countries is more likely to be measurable.

The lack of strong agreement (W = .18) and low significance level (p = .535) on what factors most influence quality for the reporting and review phase of domestic audits is considered a limitation for objectively measuring quality differences due to performing audits in international countries. It does not, however, weaken the foundation laid for the planning and fieldwork phases. Furthermore, the reporting differences between domestic U.S. and international reporting has been one of the areas with research support via other methodologies (Most 1989, Hussein et.al. 1986). Reporting is also one area that has been directly addressed by the International Federation of Accountants, International Auditing Practices Committee (IFAC 1983). This paper, therefore, continues with international comparison emphasis in the planning and fieldwork processes within the audit. In the following section, we discuss in more detail the rationale for the selection of the additional countries and how the countries were expected to compare with the United States factors.

CROSS-CULTURAL AFFECTS ON AUDIT QUALITY

As an alternative to the Ronen and Shenkar (1985) country cluster mapping, Lampe and Sutton (1992b) present an "impact cube" for evaluating the effect of cross-cultural deviations on the audit process. The impact cube uses the three dimensions to represent identified areas of cross-cultural influence: (1) English versus non-English speaking, (2) Eastern versus Western culture, and (3) developed versus developing economies. These three dimensions closely parallel with a combination of five dimensions used in Ronen and Shenkar (1985) for clustering countries:

Ronen and Shenkar	Lampe and Sutton
1. Language	1. English vs. non-English
2. Geography 3. Religion	3. Western vs. Eastern culture
4. Economic development 5. Technological development	3. Developed vs. Developing economy

The Lampe and Sutton (1992b) impact cube is shown in Figure 2 along with a mapping of a countries examined in this study: (1) Canada, (2) France, (3) Germany, (4) Netherlands, (5) Denmark, (6) Italy, (7) Indonesia, and (8) Singapore. The impact cube is designed such that the distance between the origin and the mapping point for a country in which the auditor will be auditing is reflective of the expected impact of cross-cultural variables on audit quality. Thus, the greater the distance, the more extreme the anticipated impact on audit quality.

As a means of confirming the expected similarities between countries of similar language and cultural basis, auditors having experience in Canada were used to evaluate cross-cultural effects on U.S. auditors. The impact cube would indicate that no cross-cultural effects should impact these auditors given the commonalities between the two countries on all three dimensions of the cube: in language (i.e., both English speaking, culture (i.e., both Western), and level of economic development (i.e., both developed countries).

The next set of countries entered into the study consisted of an array of European countries representing the Latin European, Germanic and Nordic clusters in the Ronen and Shenkar clustering model. These countries provide a test of the impact cube by varying the language dimension while minimizing differences in economic development and Western culture. The cultural differences cube would suggest that the non-language cross-cultural differences for each of the countries included in the three Ronen and Shenkar clusters (European, Germanic, Nordic) would be fairly small. The testing of this dimension is important in verifying the reasonableness of simplifying the clustering model into three dimensions for estimating impact on audit quality. The cube would predict that language has greater quality impact in Europe than for English-speaking countries, such as Canada or Australia, but less than when language is combined with other significant cultural differences.

The final country set includes Pacific Rim countries Indonesia and Singapore. Both countries represent extreme distance from the impact cube origin with large variations on all three dimensions. They also represent the Far Eastern cluster in the Ronen and Shenkar clustering model—a cluster that is considered one of the most diverse from the Anglo cluster. Given the high cross-cultural impact indicated by the cube, it is expected that U.S. auditors would have greater difficulties performing and completing an audit at desired levels of quality in countries falling at this point on the cube.

RESULTS ON CROSS-CULTURAL AUDIT QUALITY FACTORS

The structured group processes completed with the four audit teams having international audit experience provide an ability to identify additional factors or variables that affect audit quality in international settings. Furthermore, this methodology provides measures of different relative degrees of impact on audit quality when the same factor affects both domestic and international audits. First, a large set of audit quality factors affecting audit quality in international settings was generated. Subsequently, the key factors were identified by the individual audit team members for each of the identified countries with which they had experience in auditing. The results are summarized in Table 2 and separated according to the results for countries with relatively close cross-cultural settings and those with diverse cross-cultural settings.

From an overall perspective, it can be observed that the language barrier is perceived to have a significant impact in both dimensions summarized above. Interestingly, however, in the countries relatively close in economic development and Western culture orientation, the language barrier is considered less in impact than purely logistical travel-related factors. A contrary observation can be made for countries with lower levels of economic development and an Eastern culture orientation. In these countries, auditors rank the language barrier as the most important factor effecting audit quality. It is apparent that language problems are compounded by other cultural differences. While travel, on an absolute scale, is equally as important as in countries close to the United States on other bases, it is relatively less important than several other factors associated with economic and cross-cultural differences.

Effects in Similar Cross-Cultural Settings

To test the similarities between countries of a similar cross-cultural settings, U.S. auditors with experience in auditing Canadian-based auditees were asked to identify the key international factors having a significant effect on audit quality when performing these audits. All of the auditors with Canadian experience were in agreement that few, if any, of the international factors had been significant in performing the desired level of audit quality. Essentially, they felt that the only effects from auditing in Canada were the inconveniences resulting from having to clear customs on arrival and other travel-related factors similar to lengthy travel within the United States.

It is interesting, however, that the auditors noted they did not have experience in Quebec, but they perceived that this province would be signifi-

---

TABLE 2
Audit Quality Factors Arising From Cross-Cultural Effects

Relatively Close Cross-Cultural Settings	Diverse Cross-Cultural Settings
Time for Planning Before Fieldwork	Language Barrier
On-Site Timing Constraints	Level of Auditee Cooperation
Language Barrier	Audit Team Cohesiveness
Availability of Auditee	Cultural Practices
Broader Scope of Accounting Activities	Different Accounting Methods
Acceptance of U.S. Corporate Standards	Health Risks
	Distance for Review Meetings

NOTE: Factors are listed as ranked in order of audit quality impact

cantly different from auditing in the other provinces within Canada. In discussions these auditors had with other auditors and through experience in traveling through Quebec, the perception was that Quebec would assimilate more of the attributes of the European countries in the study—particularly France where it was perceived that other-than-language differences were greater than in the Germanic countries.

Effects in Relatively Close Cross-Cultural Settings

The European countries included in this study— (1) France, (2) Germany, (3) Netherlands, (4) Denmark and (5) Italy—provide representation from each of the Ronen and Shenkar (1985) country clusters that are considered relatively close cross-culturally to the United States (i.e., Latin European, Germanic and Nordic countries). These countries provide primary variation on the language dimension of the impact cube.

The additional factors affecting auditors' ability to achieve the level of quality desired are expectably a mix of travel-related constraints and cross-cultural effects based on language differences. Only three of the factors would be considered non-travel related: (1) language barrier, (2) broader scope of accounting activities and (3) acceptance of the United States corporation's standards. While the second and third items are certainly not reflective of the English versus non-English dichotomy of the impact cube, they encompass differences in the accounting "language" that would seem essentially consistent with the predicted impact. Another non-language result from the study is that there was notably more concern recognized by auditors with experience in Denmark and Italy as to the difficulties in auditee availability due to holidays, work hours, and auditee attitude. These difficulties have been grouped under "Availability of Auditee."

Effects in Diverse Cross-Cultural Settings

To test the diversity between countries of disparate cross-cultural settings, U.S. auditors with extensive experience in conducting audits in the Pacific Rim—primarily Indonesia and Singapore in this study—participated in the generation of cross-cultural factors affecting audit quality. These factors, summarized earlier in this section, indicate an array of variables that include all three dimensions of the impact cube: (1) language, (2) East/West culture, and (3) economic development. The fac-

tors range from the importance of the audit team maintaining high morale to differences in accounting and control practices to very basic health and self-welfare issues.

Beyond these basic factors, the auditors also noted an array of underlying auditor considerations contributing to deviations in the main factors. These considerations included the increased risk of auditor burn-out, expense limitations, the international political environment, equipment functionality, and local customs. It was also noted that the impact of many of the factors had an inverse relationship with the amount of international audit experience of the individual auditor. Re-phrased, auditors new to the international environment generally faced significantly more discomfort and concern in relation to more experienced auditors.

All auditors participating in this part of the study provide anecdotal support for the relative impact of each of the dimensions on the cross-cultural impact cube as displayed in Figure 2 and discussed throughout this paper. There was consistent agreement among the participants that developing nations were the most difficult to audit, Eastern culture countries were next, and countries with essentially only a language barrier had the least impact on audit quality with travel being the most important.

CONCLUSIONS AND IMPLICATIONS

As the globalization of the business environment continues to expand, both external and internal auditors in many countries are finding that audits are taking them to foreign lands more often. As these auditors experience new audit environments, they are discovering additional barriers that limit their ability to perform the level of audit quality desired. These new performance barriers can generally be classified as cross-cultural factors.

This study has examined the impact of key factors on U.S. auditors' performance in three different international regions: (1) North America, (2) Europe, and (3) the Pacific Rim. The results are consistent with theoretical frameworks proposed by Ronen and Shenkar (1985) based on studies of managerial attitudes and studies of auditors (Lampe and Sutton 1992b). The managerial cross-cultural mapping and the auditors cross-cultural impact cube are in agreement with empirical results provided in this study that (1) language barriers, (2) changes from Western to Eastern culture, and (3) auditing on site in economically developing coun-

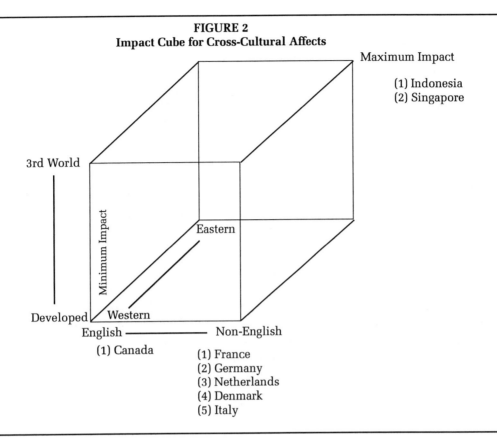

FIGURE 2
Impact Cube for Cross-Cultural Affects

Maximum Impact

(1) Indonesia
(2) Singapore

3rd World

Minimum Impact

Eastern

Developed / Western

English ——————— Non-English

(1) Canada

(1) France
(2) Germany
(3) Netherlands
(4) Denmark
(5) Italy

tries all provide significant impact on the quality of audit process performance. The study also identifies several specific factors within each of these dimension changes.

The results provided via this study imply that careful planning of the audit and preparation of the audit staff can mitigate many of the commonly encountered cross-cultural problems encountered. For European countries, pre-audit review of accounting procedures and scope used in the auditee country would allow the audit team to anticipate and become familiar with these cultural differences so that the language barrier can be minimized. For the Pacific Rim countries included in the study, it would appear that planning of the audit becomes even more critical. Compatibility of audit team members, technical support (including equipment needs), planning for family communication, and basic physical needs have all been identified as affecting audit quality in the Pacific Rim. Inclu-

sion of audit team members well-versed in the language of the auditee appears to be an invaluable aid to the completion of quality audits in all of the countries studied.

From a more general perspective, the study results imply that additional education and training (especially in the language and cultural history of an auditee) are required for international auditors. In the same way that there are industry audit specialists and EDP audit specialists, country or region audit specialists also appear to be highly desirable. Auditors performing audits in other countries will no longer be able to perform at desired levels of quality with training solely in U.S. accounting and auditing skills. Rather, there is increasing need for a much stronger background in nonaccounting subjects. Relatively greater emphases on liberal arts and economic education in addition to specific training in language and culture are needed.

REFERENCES

Adam, E. E., Jr., J. Hershauer, and W. Ruch. 1986. *Productivity and Quality Measurement as a Basis for Improvement.* University of Missouri-Columbia Business Research Center.

Choi, F. D. S., and G. G. Mueller. 1978. *An Introduction to Multinational Accounting.* Prentice Hall.

Hussein, M. E. A, V. B. Bavishi, and J. S. Gangolly. 1986. International Similarities and Differences in the Auditor's Report. *Auditing: A Journal of Practice & Theory* (Fall): 124–133.

International Federation of Accountants, International Auditing Practices Committee. 1983. *The Auditor's Report on Financial Statements* (IFAC, Audit Guideline No. 13).

Lampe, J. C., and S. G. Sutton. 1922a. An Application of Quality Circles to Measuring Bank Audit Quality. *Internal Auditing* (Spring): 24–38.

———, and ———. 1992b. International Auditing: Cross-Cultural Impacts on Audit Quality. *Advances in International Accounting* (Vol. 5).

Lynch, J. 1991. Monitoring Internal Audit Quality and Effectiveness. Presented at the Institute of Internal Auditors Research Foundation Symposium on Measuring Internal Audit Productivity, May.

Most, K. S. 1988. *International Auditing.* Canadian CGA Research Foundation.

Ronen, S., and O. Shenkar. 1985. Clustering Countries on Attitudinal Dimensions: A Review and Synthesis. *Academy of Management Review* (Vol. 10 No. 3): 435–454.

Securities and Exchange Commission. 1987. *Internationalization of the Securities Markets.* October.

Shea, G. P. 1986. Quality Circles: The Danger of Bottled Changes. *Sloan Management Review* (Spring): 7–18.

Sutton, S. G., and J. C. Lampe. 1991. A Framework for Evaluating Process Quality for Audit Engagements. *Accounting and Business Research* (Summer): 275–288.

Vinton, G. 1991. International Audit in Perspective: A U.S./U.K.Comparison. *Internal Auditing* (Spring): 3–9.

Customizing the Education Needs of Accounting Professionals: Two Australian Case Studies

Jillian C. Phillips, R. H. Keith Sloan, and John Dekkers

Accounting professionals in Australia, like those in other parts of the world, recognize that it is not practicable to become an expert in all areas of the profession. In response to this situation, the professional accounting bodies[1] now encourage specialization by their members and encourage universities to structure their business degree programs to permit students to take different paths through their studies, depending on the students' intended area of employment. A further response to the knowledge explosion in accounting has been that the profession is encouraging universities to purpose-design programs to meet specific needs and to fill perceived gaps in education for accounting professionals.

This paper presents case studies of two programs which commenced in 1991 and which reprecent innovations not only in their *raison d'etre* but also in their modes of instruction and other academic and administrative procedures. These two programs, the Master of Accounting Studies offered by The University of New England – Northern Rivers[2] and the Bachelor of Taxation offered by The University of New South Wales,[3] are both national programs which have been customized to meet the educational needs of accounting professionals and the profession itself. The similarities and differences between these programs are discussed, with an emphasis on the innovations that could become models for other purpose-designed programs in Australia or elsewhere. Some of the issues faced by the designers of these programs are also presented as a guide for others considering similar ventures.

BACKGROUND TO THE PROGRAMS

Because of Australia's small population, there are relatively few universities in the country, mostly set in or among large population centers, resulting in a large part of the population not be-

ing able to enroll in on-campus university programs. The accounting profession has therefore emphasized the need for universities to offer programs of study which will be accessible to students wherever they live, and a significant feature of both the programs that are discussed in this paper is their accessibility to a wide range of accounting professionals who are seeking upgrading.

The Master of Accounting Studies (MAS) was designed as a "conversion program," to provide an avenue whereby graduates from any (nonaccounting) discipline could undertake an intensive program of advanced study to meet the entrance requirements of the professional accounting bodies. While the emphasis in the program is on accounting subjects, studies in law, quantitative methods, economics and finance are also com-

---

[1]The major professional accounting bodies in Australia are the Australian Society of Certified Practising Accountants (ASCPA) and the Institute of Chartered Accountants in Australia (ICAA). The National Institute of Accountants (NIA) is also gaining recognition.

[2]Address: P.O. Box 157, Lismore NSW 2480, AUSTRALIA
Phone: +(61)(66) 20 3000.
FAX: +(61)(66) 22 1300.

[3]Address: P.O. Box 1, Kensington NSW 2033, AUSTRALIA
Phone: +(61)(2) 697 2272.
FAX: +(61)(2) 313 6634.

Jillian C. Phillips is currently ATAX Project Controller at The University of Central Queensland, and was formerly Acting Head, Centre for Accounting and Finance, University of New England – Northern Rivers during the development of the MAS program. R. H. Keith Sloan is a lecturer in Accounting and Finance at The University of New England – Northern Rivers, and was actively involved in the initial design and development of the MAS program. John Dekkers is the Director, Division of Distance and Continuing Education at The University of Central Queensland.

pulsory, and the professional bodies accredit the MAS using the same criteria as for undergraduate programs; that is, they specify a minimum core of knowledge and allocate to subject areas the approximate percentage of the total degree that each subject area should represent. The content of the program is therefore fairly rigidly prescribed and tends to emphasize the needs of public practice rather than commerce and industry. There are eight core areas of study and no electives in the MAS program. Students would most likely enroll in the MAS rather than a second undergraduate degree (majoring in accounting) for two reasons: the MAS is a postgraduate qualification and because of the intensive program of study it can be completed in fewer years than the equivalent undergraduate programs require. The opportunity to study at a distance is also an attractive feature of the program.

The Bachelor of Taxation (BTax) program is part of a range of purpose-designed programs (collectively referred to as ATAX) which represent an initiative of the Australian Taxation Office, Australia's equivalent of the IRS in the United States. The ATAX programs cover both undergraduate and postgraduate courses of study and have the stated purpose of increasing the competence and professional standards of taxation professionals in Australia, whether they be employed by the Australian Taxation Office or in the private sector. While tax legislation has become much more voluminous and complex in recent years, the coverage of taxation in undergraduate business programs was perceived to be diminishing,[4] and both the Australian Taxation Office and the public accounting firms felt the need to devote a considerable amount of their in-house training effort to bring newly employed graduates up to an acceptable level of technical skill and knowledge of taxation practice. This is not to imply that the Australian Taxation Office and the profession were advocating or supporting vocational training in place of education; rather, they saw value in a profession-related university education program, based on normal principles of academic independence and critical traditions, which is specifically tailored to meet their needs and the needs of their employees.

The Australian Taxation Office called for expressions of interest from Australian universities for development and delivery of a comprehensive taxation studies program, and, after an exhaustive selection process, The University of New South Wales was selected to fulfill these roles. The ATAX suite of programs currently comprises the Bachelor of Taxation,

Master of Taxation, and two Graduate Diplomas,[5] all of which are comprehensive programs in the traditional university sense. The BTax, the only one of the four ATAX programs offered in 1991, is the first undergraduate tax program to be offered by distance education in Australia.

The ATAX Director at The University of New South Wales, Professor Yuri Grbich, recently stated:

> The model of tax education reflected in the Bachelor of Taxation puts particular emphasis on professional competence. In implementing the model, we have related all our strategies back to the central question: How do we create a balanced academic program that will produce a competent and educated tax professional? The ideal product of a tax program is a multi-disciplinary, problem solving taxation graduate with a good grasp of the main elements of the existing tax system and the intellectual tools to respond effectively to a system which will continue to change during their careers.[6]

UNIQUE FEATURES OF THE PROGRAMS

Program Development

Each of these programs represents a departure from the norm for the institutions concerned. A particular feature of the ATAX programs, for example, was the collaborative and consultative nature of the processes that took place in the design, development and delivery of the programs between staff from The University of New South Wales, the Australian Taxation Office and the University of

---

[4]The BTax comprises seven semester subjects (courses) in taxation, compared with the one or two available in most undergraduate accounting programs.

[5]The Graduate Diploma in Advanced Taxation is broadly similar in its objectives and content to the past Master of Taxation (MTax) but is less onerous in its entry requirements, comprises fewer total subjects (courses), and does not require the same application of analytical skills as the MTax.

The Graduate Diploma in Taxation Studies is a form of "conversion course," like the MAS, which is designed to prepare students from other disciplines for work in taxation. It is intended to provide core training in taxation and basic component disciplines, approximating the BTax over a shorter time period. Unlike the MAS, it is not designed to prepare students for membership of the professional accounting bodies.

[6]Speech to the Technology in Education and Training Conference, Melbourne, September 17, 1991, at which the ATAX Program was presented with the Gold Award for Technology in Government.

Central Queensland,[7] whose roles will be discussed in more detail below.

Development of both the MAS and the ATAX programs involved considerable consultation with the professional bodies and the profession itself, with respect to curriculum design, instructional design and development of learning materials, delivery of the programs, and the student support system. The involvement of a wide range of experts in the development of the two programs has resulted in the incorporation of quality improvement and quality assurance procedures and measures into the programs.

Mode of Instruction

The intention of both programs was to be accessible to professionals already in employment, including those in geographically isolated places which do not permit on-campus attendance at a university. For both programs, the decision was made to initially offer the programs by distance education, which has the additional advantages of permitting students to study at their own pace (to some extent) and to apply their learning immediately in the workplace. However, given that Australian universities which offer programs at a distance are all dual-mode institutions,[8] it is conceivable that either program could be offered on-campus as well as at a distance.[9]

The decision to deliver the programs by distance education created some problems due to the Australian Government's decision in 1988 to designate a limited number of universities (currently eight) as Distance Education Centers (DECs), that is, those which are permitted to develop (as opposed to deliver) distance learning materials. In the case of The University of New England – Northern Rivers, it is part of the The University of New England network of universities, and The University of New England has been designated a DEC. However, The University of New South Wales does not have DEC status, and therefore the Australian Taxation Office and The University of New South Wales needed an additional partner. All eight DECs expressed interest in designing and developing the required materials, and ultimately the DEC at The University of Central Queensland was chosen to fulfill this role. The University of New South Wales is responsible for developing and delivering the course materials, while The University of Central Queensland provides the distance education expertise for both study materials development and course delivery.

In the delivery of each of these programs, extensive use is made of comprehensive stand-alone print materials, supported by nonprint materials such as audio- and videotapes, the use of communication and information-processing technologies, and face-to-face teaching where appropriate. Because both are national programs, the face-to-face component usually takes place close to where the students are located, as discussed below; that is, students are not required to travel long distances to meet residential or on-campus commitments. Currently, BTax students are required to meet some face-to-face commitments, while for MAS students the face-to-face component is optional (as are audioconferences and other learning opportunities created by the university).

Another similarity between the MAS and the BTax programs is that both have taken a relatively cautious approach regarding reliance on the emerging technologies. At present, delivery is based on sound experience, affordable systems and the pervasiveness of the carriers. Course developers have been mindful that they could exclude some potential students from their programs by relying on technology not widely available. However, the use of such technology at the learning centers is being further explored.

The Australian Taxation Office operations are decentralized, with around 20 regional offices spread among the seven States of Australia, and these offices form a nationwide network of learning centers for students in the ATAX programs. Currently, these centers are set up to provide audioconferencing, audio- and videotape playback facilities, and limited electronic communication, and it is intended in the future to provide facilities for videoconferencing and expert systems for interactive learning. The centers also provide the basis for student networking and mutual support groups, as well as for holding tutorials presented by local tutors.

---

[7]Address: Rockhampton MC Qld 4702, AUSTRALIA
Phone: +(61)(79) 30 9623.
FAX: +(61)(79) 30 9792.
[8]Dual-mode institutions are those that offer courses both on-campus and by distance education. In many cases, the same teaching staff are involved in preparing and delivering materials for both modes.
[9]It was originally anticipated that there would be a small intake of on-campus full-time MAS students at UNE-NR for 1992, mainly overseas students who wish to gain membership of the Australian professional accounting bodies in as short a time as possible. However, no full-time on-campus students are enrolled currently nor are expected in the foreseeable future.

By contrast, The University of New England – Northern Rivers currently has a limited number of Open Learning Centers, most of which are located within 500km (300 miles) of the university campus. To reach the students, "outreach" visits are conducted by teaching staff, often utilizing the premises and facilities (and sometimes the teaching staff) of other universities and colleges. It is intended in the near future to develop a wider network of study centers to which MAS students and others will have access.

In both programs, it is envisaged that the network of centers across Australia will be used for both student-initiated and university-initiated activities, including teletutorials, self-directed study groups, video viewing, tutorials presented by local tutors, audioconferences with staff and students at other locations, and various computer activities including on-line library searches, submission of assignments by electronic mail or facsimile, and computer-assisted learning. It is envisaged that, when fully established, the centers could also house a limited range of resources such as textbooks and videos. In the case of the Australian Taxation Office, the centers will also provide facilities for other user groups. For example, workshops and seminars may be presented for the community at large, or for taxation and accounting professionals; and the Australian Taxation Office itself could utilize the facilities for staff training and induction programs.

Academic Procedures and Issues

The development of course materials for distance students involves many fundamental issues and judgments—for example, what comprises quality instructional materials?—none of which will be discussed at length in this paper. Suffice it to say that in both the MAS and ATAX programs, the course developers have set out to use a cooperative, systematic approach to materials development and have set high standards with respect to perceived quality, covering both content and form. Development is necessarily a dynamic process, and it is acknowledged that regular revisions and periodic rewrites of print materials will be necessary, not only to deal with changes to content but also to incorporate new teaching/learning techniques and media.

While the MAS materials have been prepared mostly by academic staff from the host university, the ATAX materials have been written by, and in consultation with, specialists from major accounting and legal firms and from the Australian Taxation Office itself, as well as by academic staff from the host university. Both programs have also benefited from the input of respected academics from other universities, who are specialists in their field. The involvement of experts from other institutions and from the profession has insured that issues are debated during curriculum design (initially and ongoing), resulting in the courses having the correct focus for the current state of the profession.

Authors of course materials for the ATAX program, including academics of long standing, have the opportunity to attend a writers workshop, conducted at The University of New South Wales by University of Central Queensland distance education specialists. This workshop is intended to provide an overview of some distance education issues that impact on writers (with an emphasis on optimizing text for distance learning and identifying other media and learning strategies that optimize distance learning), as well as detailing specific procedural matters such as timelines, copy preparation, and the roles of various team members.

A materials development team for both the MAS and ATAX programs usually comprises the following:

- one or more authors, whose role it is to finalize the curriculum content; specify objectives; set questions and other activities to encourage interaction with text; write the material; document copyright material; proofread typeset material; and participate in evaluation

- a content validator, whose role it is to check content for accuracy, relevance and consistency; check readings and other resources for appropriateness; advise on student workload; and suggest improvements in these and other areas

- an instructional designer and/or a course development officer, whose role it is to ensure that content, process and outcome are consistent with learning theory; compose a style sheet of specific style features requested by the author or others; design materials from the copy provided by the author(s); advise on sequencing of content; assist in the selection of other instructional media; assist in the selection and development of student learning experiences; check quality and quantity of resource materials; edit original copy and proofread typeset copy; and coordinate the flow of materials

- editorial, graphic design, production and media specialists as required to support the materials development process.

Through experience, it has been found that all members of the team need to use their individual strengths to collectively achieve a quality product. However, what constitutes a quality product is not clear cut, and different perceptions of quality held by different team members can cause breakdowns in the materials production process. Conflicts that arise among team members are often based on time constraints; for example, authors who are academics often do not appreciate why they have to begin writing and submitting first drafts of materials for development testing some 15 months before teaching begins. Other authors are heard to cry "Whatever happened to academic freedom?" when a content validator or instructional designer dares to question the sequencing of content or the quality or quantity of the learning materials. Still others insist on assuming that distance students have the same learning needs as on-campus students, failing to take account of the relevant literature. The permanent and public nature of distance learning materials, together with the nature of distance students, places special demands on all members of the team, particularly while the definition of a "quality product" is unresolved! Whose ultimate responsibility is that product after all?

As well as designing and developing course materials, a number of academic staff are also involved in delivering the courses. For many staff, these courses provided their first experience in teaching at a distance. It is also true that in many cases the academic charged with presenting the course has not been involved in design and development of the course materials. This is another area for potential conflict; authors are often reluctant to impose their own views (particularly with respect to matters such as content and assessment items) on others, and those who have to actually teach from the materials often complain that they would "rather things be done differently"! The existence of learning materials does constrain flexibility in delivery, but this is not necessarily a weakness of distance education. These factors are not unique to the programs under discussion here, however, and are merely cited as factors to consider when distance education programs are being developed.

Teaching at a distance involves different strategies from on-campus teaching. Lectures, tutorials and seminars do not exist in the traditional sense and cannot be meaningfully replicated at a distance. These are often replaced by audio-conferencing and other forms of mediated communication, most of which are new to academics so far as interacting with students is concerned. Further, traditional forms of assessment such as class tests and examinations cannot be applied to distance students without modification.

Both The University of New England – Northern Rivers and The University of New South Wales have found that staff involved in distance education benefit from training in these areas, and manuals and workshops are currently being developed to assist academic staff to acquire skills in preparation of assignments for distance students, as well as in the use of audioconferencing, electronic mail and other media.

Several other issues which can be described as both academic and administrative are now considered. These revolve mainly around staffing for distance education programs. As the MAS and the ATAX programs were being developed by their respective universities, administrators were without precedent for determining matters such as how many "equivalent face-to-face hours" to allow authors, content validators and teachers of distance learners. This was further complicated by having some authors and other team members who were external to the universities, who naturally expected payment for their services. Some academics agreed to perform certain tasks if they were paid additional salary or allowed "amounts for academic pursuits" such as conference attendance or computer purchase; others indicated a preference for a reduced teaching load. However, determining the equivalence of these options, or even an arrangement acceptable to all parties, proved a difficult task. In most cases, the end result was based on individually negotiated contracts.

A related issue was the selection of staff to participate in the design, development and delivery of materials, but this is another issue which is not unique to distance education nor to the two programs being discussed here.

The structure of the programs, as opposed to their content, is another mixture of academic and administrative concern. Academics tend to think of structure in terms of "teaching weeks" and "hours per week," yet these concepts do not strictly apply in distance education which emphasizes the students' freedom to determine when and where they study. However, due to constraints such as examination dates, some formal structure is necessary, and this impinges upon content so far as quantity is concerned. Both universities found it useful to express learning time in terms of hours, and both divided the academic year so as to approximate teaching weeks.

Materials for the MAS, as for several other programs offered by The University of New England – Northern Rivers, are organized on a modular basis, where a module approximates four weeks' work. The purpose of modularization is twofold. Primarily, it permits students to choose their areas of study at a micro level; for example, students can select three modules in a related area and then treat those as forming a subject or course, even if no other student has put the combination together in quite the same way. While this selection is not permitted in the MAS because of the accreditation requirements of the professional bodies, it is popular in other programs. The second benefit of modularization is that compact modules of work are used as the materials for short courses, either as self-study programs or as employer-sponsored training programs, which any learner can undertake and later count towards a degree program. The modular form is indirectly a marketing tool for the programs at a later stage.

Another particularly popular innovation of the MAS was the offering of the program over three trimesters of study where each trimester provided the same workload as the traditional semester thus allowing students to complete the program much more quickly. (The trimester principle is not unlike the summer school principle which applies elsewhere, but which is relatively uncommon in Australia to date.)

One very positive outcome of the offering of these two programs of study has been the impact of distance teaching on face-to-face teaching. Academic staff involved in both authoring and presenting distance programs have reported that they have been forced to consider many aspects of their teaching in a new light rather than taking for granted that what they have "always done" necessarily represents the best way of doing it. For example, an instructor in International Finance, who had just authored his first set of distance learning materials, abandoned his traditional lecture-tutorial format for on-campus students in favor of the distance education mode which required students to individually consider the material to be learned prior to attendance at a workshop/seminar where the material was discussed by the group. The feedback from this group of students was exceptionally favorable.

Another positive outcome of the development of distance learning materials has been the use of these materials as resources for on-campus teach-ing. In some instances, they have become an important resource base. Given the way financial constraints are currently driving education, it may be that educators need to consider whether it is more appropriate to adopt selected distance teaching strategies for on-campus teaching rather than the traditional practice of adapting face-to-face teaching strategies for distance education.

This is not to say that there have been no negative consequences of the offering of these two programs of study. The mere fact that staff are involved in both on-campus and distance teaching creates conflict and pressure, to say nothing of the difficulties faced by those trying to work in trimesters in distance education and semesters for on-campus teaching. The question of what constitutes a full teaching load is asked as often as "But when can I go on vacation?"!

Administrative Procedures and Issues

The introduction of the MAS and the ATAX programs necessitated a number of changes to administrative practices and procedures at the universities involved, both within the teaching faculties and for administration generally. The long lead time required to produce quality distance learning materials and the involvement of a diverse range of professionals and organizations have already been discussed, and each of these has a major impact on administrative procedures. Another related factor is the wide range of university staff affected by any new program offering, particularly by a distance education program. Other specific differences will be considered briefly.

The MAS program is unusual in that it requires students to pay fees to the university offering the program,[10] a recent innovation in Australia. For example, the entire MAS program would cost a student approximately \$A7,000 to \$A9,000 in tuition fees, in addition to other costs incurred in any program of study. The charging of fees led to a number of administrative issues being considered at The

---

[10]The majority of students at Australian universities pay no tuition fees to the institution but are charged instead a Higher Education Contribution fee which is paid to the federal government. For a full-time student this amount is currently around \$A2,000 per year. Australian universities have only recently been permitted to charge students tuition fees, except for overseas students. However, many full-time students receive funding from the federal government, the amount being determined by a means test.

University of New England – Northern Rivers, ranging from the proportion of the fees to be taken by the central administration, through the allocation of fees to enhance library and other resources, to procedures for refunding fees to students who discontinue their studies. These are typical of the range of issues to be resolved when changes take place in program offerings.

A further aspect of the introduction of any new program is the impact on library resources. Libraries which service distance students, particularly at postgraduate level, generally need to offer extended loan periods as well as making other concessions with respect to photocopying of journal articles, lending of reference materials and so on. The time and cost involved in administering these additional activities should not be underestimated. Decisions also need to be made concerning packaging, responsibility for paying freight and other similar mundane matters.

A vital matter which would be best described as managerial rather than administrative concerns the management of the materials development process. Both The University of New England – Northern Rivers and The University of New South Wales found that authors in particular had unrealistic expectations about how late they could be in submitting their manuscripts for production. Because academics traditionally rely on their own resources (which can include choosing to "write" a lecture on the way to the lecture room), they can easily forget that all the other parts of the materials development team and process are relying on them. Late submission of manuscripts can lead to there being no time for pilot testing, adequate proofreading, and so on, all of which can be seen to affect the quality of the materials being distributed to students. Perhaps the most telling result of the authors' not meeting deadlines is that they often prepare too much material to constitute a reasonable student load, yet there is insufficient time to cull it. As well as potentially affecting student motivation and learning, this can also result in major cost overruns for the university providing the materials.

Other Issues and Considerations

The innovative nature of both of the programs described in this paper led to there being many practical issues to be resolved during the design and development phases as well as in delivery. Many of these issues relate to distance education per se, such as whether to offer various forms of face-to-face interaction to support the distance learning materials, and whether any such provision should be compulsory or optional, what form it should take, and when and where it should be offered.

Because of the inevitability that accounting and taxation professionals will use computers as a commonplace tool in their day-to-day work, computing has been incorporated into both the MAS and BTax programs. While BTax students undertake studies in computer information systems as a discrete topic, computing was integrated into all MAS topics where appropriate, with students being regularly required to prepare spreadsheets, use accounting software, and so on, as they proceed through the program. This led to the consideration of how to provide student access to computers.

BTax students have access to computers through their learning centers, but UNE-NR's Open Learning Centers do not yet house computers. Consideration was given by UNE-NR to various access options, including the university's buying the necessary hardware and software for loan to students, allowing access to the university's computers via a modem, and requiring students to attend computing lab sessions on-campus if they could get access no other way. For MAS students, it was resolved, at least for 1991, that they would simply be advised that access to a PC was an integral part of their studies and that if this posed any problems, they should contact the university. No potential students contacted the university in this regard, although it is impossible to determine how many were deterred from applying because of this stipulation. This is one of many issues which is being monitored during the early stages of the program's offering.

There are many other issues which deserve recognition, but which are beyond the scope of this paper. One issue which is of particular interest to academic staff involved in the development of materials for the two programs described above is recognition of that involvement for promotion purposes. Preparation of distance education materials is necessarily different from research in the traditional sense, but it is also different from teaching in the traditional sense, and should arguably be given some weighting when an academic is applying for promotion. UNE-NR's guidelines for promotion from lecturer to senior lecturer indicate that applicants should include "contributions to off-campus learning and other teaching methods" when describing their teaching experience, but there is no indication of how this information is treated.

CONCLUSION

In this paper, we have focused on selected issues surrounding innovative modes of instruction and on academic and administrative issues that have arisen to date out of the offering of two purpose-designed accounting programs in Australia. There are no doubt as many issues still remaining to be resolved as there have been issues discussed here.

Our intention has not been to itemize every detail of the two programs presented as case studies, nor to suggest that every aspect of them represents a model solution to a problem. Rather, the University of New South Wales' Bachelor of Taxation and the University of New England – Northern Rivers' Master of Accounting Studies have been presented as two examples of innovations in program development that were purpose-designed to meet the needs of accounting professionals in Australia.

Both programs were offered for the first time in 1991, and some formal summative evaluation has been undertaken, particularly involving evaluative feedback by students. To date, we can report that student feedback has been positive with respect to both programs,[11] that student dropout has been minimal, that the profession has given its endorsement and support to both programs, and that the ATAX Program was in September 1991 awarded the Gold Award for Technology in Government.

[11]MAS survey instruments provided the following general feedback:

Students are generally happy with access to teaching staff as required, teaching staff's timely response to answering machine messages, general administration of the subject, knowledge and supportiveness of teaching staff, reasonableness of suggested study time for the subject, layout of the materials, ease of reading the materials, relevance of content, appropriateness of recommended textbooks, usefulness of supplied readings, relevance of assessment items, appropriateness of feedback, value of audioconferences and workshops.

There were suggestions for improvement concerning timely delivery of materials, size of folders (not leaving sufficient space for additional pages of student work), timely return of graded assignments to students, size of groups for audioconferences, and some lack of structure in audioconferences and workshops.

The vast majority of students indicated that they would recommend the subject in its existing form to other students.

ATAX survey instruments provided the following general feedback:

Students are generally happy with most aspects of the learning materials and the course delivery (including assessment). Many thought the supplied readings for some subjects to be too voluminous, although all relevant. The majority found both audioconferences and face-to-face tutorials very useful, and many recommended that each of these be held weekly (although scheduling was recognised as a potential problem). One aspect of course delivery that needs attention, according to students surveyed, is assignment turnaround time.

An International Survey of Accounting Programs

Barbara Powell Reider and Donald N. Hester

The majority of four-year accounting programs in the United States devote the first two years of course work to general studies, and the last two years to intensive accounting and business classes. Students interested in becoming accounting majors may take only principles of accounting courses during their first two years of college. These students must wait until their junior year to finally see what a career in accounting involves. In the United Kingdom, accounting students blend their business and general course work over the same four-year period, and a more well-rounded education is emphasized (Grow 1987).

The focus of the United Kingdom baccalaureate accounting degree is a long-term career as an accountant, rather than the United States educational focus of immediate placement into the workforce.

American accounting educators have been criticized for not adequately preparing our students for their future career choices or even advising them of the wide variety of positions available. In some instances, our accounting programs focus heavily on preparation for the CPA exam and those few students who are recruited by the major public accounting firms.

Our study examines undergraduate accounting programs in the United States and eight other countries for similarities and differences in preparing students for an accounting career. Among the important issues we examine is the point at which an accounting student begins preparation for a career in a specialized field of accounting. If students plan to take the CPA/CA, CMA or CIA exams, they must be properly advised at the beginning of their studies to select courses which will help them pass these certifying exams.

How many faculty members are CPAs, CMAs or CIAs themselves? Knowledge of the three exams and the work that an accountant performs, in combination with learning from faculty members who are certified, should increase student interest in taking the certifying exams.

METHODOLOGY

We developed a survey which was sent to undergraduate accounting department chairpersons at 559 American and 78 foreign colleges and universities in 11 countries to address these issues.

The accounting programs surveyed were selected from a current directory (Hasselback 1991) listing institutions which grant accounting degrees.

The survey examined the number of students entering various accounting positions after graduation (auditing, management accounting, governmental accounting, financial accounting and tax); whether students and/or accounting faculty have the opportunity for internships in these five areas of accounting; the number of faculty members who are CPAs or CAs, CMAs or CIAs; and the accounting-related courses offered by colleges and universities.

RESULTS

Of the 559 surveys mailed to department chairpersons in the United States, 367 were returned. Fourteen of these questionnaires were unusable, so our results and analyses are based upon the 353 usable surveys (response rate equals 63 percent). Similar surveys were also sent to 78 accounting chairpersons at universities outside the United States Of the 33 responses received, one survey was unusable. Therefore, the foreign results are based upon the 32 usable surveys (response rate equals 41 percent) from eight nations. The country and number of usable responses are as follows:

Australia	7
Canada	12
England	4
Hong Kong	2
New Zealand	1
Scotland	4
Taiwan	1
Wales	1

No usable responses were received from Israel, Japan or France.

Number of Graduates

Table 1 illustrates the number of accounting students who graduate each year from colleges and universities in the United States and the eight foreign countries which responded to our study. These

Barbara Powell Reider is an Assistant Professor and Donald N. Hester is an Associate Professor at the University of Alaska Anchorage.

TABLE 1
The Annual Number of Accounting Graduates

The percentage of colleges and universities indicating the annual number of accounting graduates

Country	0–30	31–60	61–100	101–300	+300
United States	19%	25%	24%	27%	5%
Australia	—	—	17%	66%	17%
Canada	9%	18%	55%	18%	—
England	25%	50%	25%	—	—
Hong Kong	—	50%	—	50%	—
New Zealand	—	—	—	100%	—
Scotland	—	25%	50%	25%	—
Taiwan	—	—	100%	—	—
Wales	—	—	—	—	100%

Sample size:	United States	353
	Australia	7
	Canada	12
	England	4
	Hong Kong	2
	New Zealand	1
	Scotland	4
	Taiwan	1
	Wales	1

schools range from the small private colleges to major state universities.

Care must be taken when interpreting Table 1 because of the small sample size for each of the foreign nations. For example, it is highly unlikely that all accounting programs in Wales have more than 300 graduates per year.

ENTRY-LEVEL CAREER CHOICES

Where do accounting students begin their careers after graduation? Our survey asked the respondents to estimate the percentage of their institution's accounting graduates who entered careers in (1) auditing, (2) financial accounting, (3) governmental accounting, (4) management accounting and (5) tax. The results are presented in Table 2.

Respondents were given the following ranges for their answers: 0 to 20 percent, 21 to 40 percent, 41 to 60 percent, 61 to 80 percent, and 81 to 100 percent. To interpret Table 2, the figures across each of the five career areas are the percentage of total responses marked for that career. Therefore, the total across each row equals 100 percent.

The two accounting career fields which attract the highest percentage of graduates in the United States are auditing and management accounting.

Auditing attracts at least 21 percent of graduates at 76 percent of the universities and colleges, while management accounting attracts at least 21 percent of graduates from 52 percent of accounting programs.

Given the small number of responses for each country, direct comparison with American schools is difficult. However, the following results deserve attention:

- In Canada, 80 percent of schools reported that at least 41 percent of their graduates begin accounting careers as auditors.

- In England, 75 percent of schools reported that at least 41 percent of their graduates begin accounting careers as auditors.

- Of Canadian schools, 28 percent reported that many students (at least 61 percent of graduates) enter the field of financial accounting.

FREQUENCY OF SEPARATE TRACK OR DEGREE PROGRAMS

The next survey question examined whether accounting programs have developed separate tracks within their accounting degree, or whether separate degrees are offered for specialty majors within accounting. The five areas examined were (1) auditing, (2) financial accounting, (3) governmental accounting, (4) management accounting, and (5) tax.

Table 3 illustrates that for U.S. accounting programs, 10 percent offer a financial accounting track, 10 percent offer a distinct track for tax accounting, 5 percent of schools offer an auditing track, and 10 percent offer a management accounting track.

Even fewer American colleges and universities offer distinct degrees within the accounting department: 4 percent offer a tax degree, one percent offer a degree in management accounting and two percent offer a degree in financial accounting. When U.S. accounting programs are compared to foreign programs, other nations obviously place much more emphasis on specialized tracks and degrees.

Among American accounting programs which offer either a separate accounting specialty track or degree, we asked at what point (during the student's academic career) the choice was made to enter such a program. These results are presented in Table 4.

Within each of the five accounting specialties we examined, the years for election of a particular track or degree are presented. The sum across each row equals 100 percent. The results indicate that most track or degree programs begin in a student's junior year.

TABLE 2
The Percentage of Graduates Who Enter Five Career Fields

	0–20%	21–40%	41–60%	61–80%	81–100%	Total
Auditing						
United States	24%	43%	21%	8%	3%	100%
Australia	17	66	17	—	—	100
Canada	20	—	40	10	30	100
England	25	—	25	25	25	100
Hong Kong	—	—	50	50	—	100
New Zealand	—	100	—	—	—	100
Scotland	—	25	50	25	—	100
Taiwan	—	—	—	100	—	100
Wales	—	—	100	—	—	100
Financial Accounting						
United States	58%	38%	4%	8%	—	100%
Australia	50	50	—	—	—	100
Canada	43	29	—	14	14	100
England	100	—	—	—	—	100
Hong Kong	100	—	—	—	—	100
New Zealand	100	—	—	—	—	100
Scotland	50	50	—	—	—	100
Taiwan	100	—	—	—	—	100
Wales	—	100	—	—	—	100
Governmental Accounting						
United States	88%	10%	1%	1%	—	100%
Australia	50	50	—	—	—	100
Canada	67	33	—	—	—	100
England	100	—	—	—	—	100
Hong Kong	100	—	—	—	—	100
New Zealand	100	—	—	—	—	100
Scotland	100	—	—	—	—	100
Taiwan	100	—	—	—	—	100
Wales	100	—	—	—	—	100
Management Accounting						
United States	48%	44%	7%	1%	—	100%
Australia	83	17	—	—	—	100
Canada	45	55	—	—	—	100
England	33	33	34	—	—	100
Hong Kong	100	—	—	—	—	100
New Zealand	100	—	—	—	—	100
Scotland	50	50	—	—	—	100
Taiwan	100	—	—	—	—	100
Wales	—	100	—	—	—	100
Tax						
United States	70%	26%	3%	1%	—	100%
Australia	67	33	—	—	—	100
Canada	66	17	—	—	17	100
England	100	—	—	—	—	100
Hong Kong	50	50	—	—	—	100
New Zealand	100	—	—	—	—	100
Scotland	—	100	—	—	—	100
Taiwan	100	—	—	—	—	100
Wales	100	—	—	—	—	100

TABLE 3
Separate Track or Degree Programs

	Track	Degree
Auditing		
United States	5%	1%
Australia	40%	—
Canada	20%	10%
England	—	—
Hong Kong	50%	—
New Zealand	—	—
Scotland	50%	—
Taiwan	—	—
Wales	100%	—
Financial Accounting		
United States	10%	2%
Australia	80%	—
Canada	45%	—
England	25%	25%
Hong Kong	50%	—
New Zealand	—	—
Scotland	50%	—
Taiwan	—	—
Wales	100%	—
Governmental Accounting		
United States	2%	—
Australia	20%	—
Canada	—	—
England	—	—
Hong Kong	—	—
New Zealand	—	—
Scotland	—	—
Taiwan	—	—
Wales	—	—
Management Accounting		
United States	10%	1%
Australia	80%	—
Canada	60%	—
England	25%	25%
Hong Kong	50%	—
New Zealand	—	—
Scotland	50%	—
Taiwan	—	—
Wales	100%	—
Tax		
United States	10%	4%
Australia	—	—
Canada	11%	—
England	—	—
Hong Kong	50%	—
New Zealand	—	—
Scotland	50%	50%
Taiwan	—	—
Wales	100%	—

STUDENT AND FACULTY INTERNSHIPS

Our survey also inquired about the availability of either student or faculty internship programs. The survey results for this question are presented in Table 5.

The majority of U.S. accounting programs have internships available for students, but not for faculty members. Students may participate in an auditing internship at 82 percent of accounting programs, financial or management accounting internships at 80 percent of schools, and tax internships at 74 percent of programs.

Faculty at only 38 percent of responding U.S. accounting programs have an opportunity for an auditing internship. In management accounting, only 28 percent of institutions indicated that faculty members may participate as an intern. Lewis, Kagle, and Peters (1988) argue that more cost accounting internship programs are needed, and that the reward structure for faculty members should encourage accounting professors to gain experience in industry. Obviously, few accounting internship programs are currently available for accounting faculty.

When comparing the internship opportunities of American accounting students and faculty to their foreign counterparts, the United States clearly offers more programs. (Care must be made when interpreting results from a country with a single response to the survey, because a single positive response results in a 100 percent answer.)

PROFESSIONAL CERTIFICATION OF FACULTY MEMBERS

Students are more likely to learn about or be encouraged to take professional certification exams if their accounting professors show interest in such credentials. We asked survey respondents to indicate the percentage of their faculty members who were either CPAs/CAs, CMAs or CIAs or held other professional certification. The results from this question are presented in Table 6.

Twenty-nine percent of our sample's American colleges and universities indicated that between 61 and 80 percent of their faculty were CPAs. The percentage of U.S. schools with more than 80 percent of faculty who were CPAs was 49 percent. Therefore, 78 percent of respondents indicated that at least 61 percent of their faculty were CPAs. The other two certifications are not represented as frequently — in 78 percent of accounting programs, fewer than 21 percent of faculty are CMAs. In 97 percent of our sampled U.S. schools, fewer than

TABLE 4
U.S. Accounting Programs Grade Level for Entering Track or Degree Program

	Freshman	Sophomore	Junior	Senior	Total
Auditing	9%	9%	50%	32%	100%
Financial Accounting	15%	26%	55%	4%	100%
Governmental Accounting	10%	14%	55%	21%	100%
Management Accounting	9%	21%	64%	6%	100%
Tax	10%	11%	62%	16%	100%

TABLE 5
Percentage of Accounting Programs Which Offer Internships for Students and Faculty

	Students	Faculty		Students	Faculty
Auditing			**Management Accounting**		
United States	82%	38%	United States	80%	28%
Australia	50%	—	Australia	33%	—
Canada	67%	—	Canada	29%	—
England	25%	25%	England	25%	25%
Hong Kong	50%	50%	Hong Kong	—	—
New Zealand	—	—	New Zealand	—	—
Scotland	50%	25%	Scotland	25%	—
Taiwan	100%	100%	Taiwan	100%	—
Wales	100%	100%	Wales	100%	100%
Financial Accounting			**Tax**		
United States	80%	28%	United States	74%	31%
Australia	50%	—	Australia	50%	—
Canada	43%	—	Canada	38%	—
England	25%	—	England	—	—
Hong Kong	—	—	Hong Kong	—	50%
New Zealand	—	—	New Zealand	—	—
Scotland	50%	25%	Scotland	25%	—
Taiwan	100%	—	Taiwan	100%	—
Wales	100%	100%	Wales	100%	—
Governmental Accounting					
United States	61%	21%			
Australia	33%	—			
Canada	29%	—			
England	—	—			
Hong Kong	—	—			
New Zealand	—	—			
Scotland	25%	—			
Taiwan	100%	—			
Wales	—	—			

21 percent of accounting faculty members are CIAs. The results from foreign schools are also presented, but no interpretation is made due to the small sample size from each country.

COURSES OFFERED

The final survey question asked each respondent to indicate the accounting courses offered at his or her university. A list of 34 courses was included, and any courses that we had omitted could be added to our list. The results are presented in Table 7.

We were particularly interested in the number of financial accounting courses which were offered compared to the number of management and other accounting courses. Students may be influenced about their future career choices by the account-

TABLE 6
Faculty Certification

	0–20%	21–40%	41–60%	61–80%	81–100%	Total
CPA/CA						
United States	1%	4%	16%	29%	49%	100%
Australia	—	17%	17%	33%	33%	100%
Canada	18%	10%	27%	27%	18%	100%
England	—	—	100%	—	—	100%
Hong Kong	—	—	—	50%	50%	100%
New Zealand	—	—	—	—	100%	100%
Scotland	—	25%	75%	—	—	100%
Taiwan	—	—	—	100%	—	100%
Wales	—	—	—	100%	—	100%
CMA						
United States	78%	16%	4%	1%	1%	100%
Australia	100%	—	—	—	—	100%
Canada	67%	33%	—	—	—	100%
England	33%	—	67%	—	—	100%
Hong Kong	50%	50%	—	—	—	100%
New Zealand	100%	—	—	—	—	100%
Scotland	50%	50%	—	—	—	100%
Taiwan	100%	—	—	—	—	100%
Wales	100%	—	—	—	—	100%
CIA						
United States	97%	2%	1%	—	—	100%
Australia	100%	—	—	—	—	100%
Canada	100%	—	—	—	—	100%
England	100%	—	—	—	—	100%
Hong Kong	100%	—	—	—	—	100%
New Zealand	100%	—	—	—	—	100%
Scotland	50%	50%	—	—	—	100%
Taiwan	100%	—	—	—	—	100%
Wales	100%	—	—	—	—	100%
Other						
Australia	67%	—	33%	—	—	100%
Canada	60%	20%	—	20%	—	100%
England	100%	—	—	—	—	100%
Hong Kong	50%	50%	—	—	—	100%
New Zealand	100%	—	—	—	—	100%
Scotland	33%	67%	—	—	—	100%
Taiwan	100%	—	—	—	—	100%
Wales	100%	—	—	—	—	100%

ing courses offered (or not offered) at their university.

The majority of accounting programs in the United States offered Principles of Financial Accounting (90 percent), Intermediate Accounting I (97 percent), Intermediate Accounting II (96 percent), and Advanced Accounting I (95 percent). The management accounting courses most frequently offered were (1) Principles of Managerial Accounting (86 percent) and (2) Cost Accounting (93 percent).

Courses focusing on selected topics for the CPA exam include Auditing (95 percent), Income Tax for Individuals (93 percent), and Income Tax for Partnerships & Corporations (87 percent). A CPA Review course was offered at 24 percent of schools.

Courses which are most relevant for the CMA and the CIA exams do not fare as well. Intermediate Managerial Accounting is offered at only 16 percent of schools, Advanced Cost Accounting is offered by 54 percent of accounting programs, and only 15 per-

TABLE 7
Courses Offered

Accounting Programs Which Offer the Following Courses (% omitted)

	US	Aus	Can	Eng	HK	NZ	Scot	Tai	Wal
Accounting for Health Care Organizations	6	0	0	0	0	0	0	0	100
Accounting Theory	65	100	100	67	50	100	100	100	100
Accounting Information Systems	73	100	63	33	50	100	100	100	100
Advanced Accounting I	95	83	100	100	100	100	75	100	100
Advanced Accounting II	29	83	63	100	100	100	75	100	100
Advanced Cost Accounting	54	83	91	67	100	100	100	100	100
Auditing	95	100	100	33	50	100	100	100	100
Budgets & Controllership	15	67	9	33	50	0	50	0	100
Contemporary CPA Problems	15	50	9	33	50	0	0	0	0
Cost Accounting	93	100	81	33	100	100	100	100	100
CIA Review	1	0	9	0	0	0	0	0	0
CMA Review	3	0	9	0	0	0	0	0	0
CPA Review	24	0	0	0	0	0	0	0	0
EDP Auditing & Controls	23	67	36	0	50	0	50	100	100
Estate & Trust Tax Law	25	17	0	0	0	0	0	0	100
Governmental Accounting	58	17	9	0	50	100	25	100	0
Income Tax for Individuals	93	83	100	33	50	100	75	0	100
Income Tax for Partnerships & Corporations	87	100	72	33	50	100	75	100	100
Intermediate Accounting I	97	100	100	100	100	100	75	100	100
Intermediate Accounting II	96	100	91	100	100	100	75	100	100
Intermediate Accounting III	28	83	0	100	100	100	50	100	100
Intermediate Managerial Accounting	16	83	91	100	100	100	75	100	100
Internal Auditing	14	50	27	33	0	100	75	0	0
International Accounting	22	50	18	33	50	100	100	100	100
Management Consulting	3	17	9	0	0	0	0	0	0
Natural Resource Accounting	2	0	0	0	0	0	25	0	0
Not-for-Profit Organization Accounting	37	17	18	0	0	0	0	0	0
Oil & Gas Accounting	7	33	0	33	0	0	25	0	0
Principles of Financial Accounting	90	100	72	100	50	100	100	100	100
Principles of Managerial Accounting	87	100	72	100	100	100	100	100	100
Professional Ethics & Legal Responsibility	13	33	9	33	0	0	25	0	0
Regulatory Accounting	2	33	0	33	50	0	50	100	100
State & Local Taxes	6	0	0	0	50	100	25	0	100
Tax Planning & Research	30	67	18	33	0	0	25	0	100

cent of universities offer a course in Budgets & Controllership. A CMA Review was offered at 3 percent of colleges. Internal auditing is offered at only 14 percent of institutions, and a CIA review course is offered at only 1 percent of accounting programs.

Comparing the results of accounting courses offered in American programs to international programs illustrates that the United States lags in the offering of International Accounting, Internal Auditing, and Regulatory Accounting. Most U.S. programs offer only Advanced Accounting I while foreign schools also teach a second course in Advanced Accounting. Many foreign programs offer three semesters of Intermediate Accounting while their American counterparts generally offer the course over two semesters.

SUMMARY

We surveyed 559 major U.S. accounting programs and 78 foreign accounting programs to determine the status of the accounting education curriculum. If the majority of our accounting students eventually work in an accounting field other than financial accounting, our educational systems must prepare these students for their future careers. Our survey included the availability of a separate track or degree for specialized accounting majors, the availability of accounting internships both for students and faculty, the number of faculty members who hold professional certification, and the diversity of accounting courses offered.

The number of students who initially are hired as auditors and as management accountants is fairly close (Table 2). Perhaps American students plan their academic careers with short-range goals, such as finding a job immediately after graduation, rather than with more long-term plans. If history repeats itself, many of these present auditors will eventually find themselves employed as professionals in other accounting fields.

Very few U.S. schools offer special tracks or degrees for auditing, financial accounting, governmental accounting or tax (Table 3). The accounting curriculum nationally appears to be generic in its approach to meeting student needs.

Students in the United States are exposed to careers in various accounting fields with the accessibility of internships (Table 5). Respondents at 83 percent of accounting programs indicated that students have the opportunity for such internships in auditing. The lowest exposure to a particular career choice for American students is in governmental accounting where 61 percent of programs have internships. Students at many foreign universities are also able to participate in internship programs.

The accessibility of accounting internships for professors in the United States is low – 38 percent of schools offer auditing internships to faculty members, while only 21 percent of schools offer government accounting internships to their faculty. Faculty at foreign programs are also not offered many opportunities to participate in internship programs.

Professional certification (Table 6) is an important credential for accounting educators both here in the United States and abroad. The most popular certification remains to be the CPA or CA. In selected countries, the CMA is gaining popularity among academics.

We also examined the variety of courses offered by accounting programs in both the United States and the eight other nations. Most accounting programs offer similar courses:

- Principles of Financial Accounting
- Principles of Managerial Accounting
- Intermediate Accounting I
- Intermediate Accounting II
- Cost Accounting
- Income Tax for Individuals
- Income Tax for Partnerships & Corporations
- Advanced Accounting
- Auditing
- Advanced Cost Accounting

REFERENCES

Grow, B. L. 1987. The Land of the CPA. *Accountancy* (UK) 100 (July): 109–110.

Hasselback, J. R. 1990. *Accounting Faculty Directory.* Prentice Hall.

Lewis, R. J., A. R. Kagle, and R. M. Peters. 1988. Cost Accounting Internship Programs Needed. *Management Accounting* (March): 57–58.

Implications for Proposed Changes in Accounting Education: The New Zealand Experience

Kenton B. Walker and Lawrence A. McClelland

INTRODUCTION

There are repeated references to the shortcomings of accounting education in the United States (Bedford Committee Report, AAA, 1986; *Perspectives on Education: Capabilities for Success in the Accounting Profession*, 1989; Patten and Williams, 1990). With the formation of the Accounting Education Change Commission, several universities have embarked on a variety of programs to implement improvements in accounting education (Williams and Sundem, 1990). Few, if any, references to accounting education in foreign countries are made in the literature in the context of proposed changes to domestic programs. Overseas models of accounting education may provide insight to academics and the profession in the accounting education reform process.

The purpose of this paper is to describe an overseas accounting education model consistent with many of the changes called for in the United States, and the influences on foreign accounting education which may have led to the model selected. This paper assesses the influence of the accounting profession on education in New Zealand, describes the important features of the accounting degree program and the accounting honors program at the University of Otago, and concludes with a summary of the New Zealand accounting education experience for application in U.S. accounting programs.

INFLUENCES ON ACCOUNTING EDUCATION IN NEW ZEALAND

The New Zealand Society of Accountants (NZSA) exercises significant influence over accounting education in New Zealand. The Associate Chartered Accountant (ACA) certification is the most widely recognized professional credential in the country. Certificate holders must fulfill the education requirements of the NZSA, pass the NZSA's Final Qualifying Exam, and complete three years of practical accounting experience.

New Zealand does not have an independent accreditation body such as the AACSB in the United States. The formal standards for accounting education in the nation's seven universities, apart from the degree requirements of the individual institutions, are set by the NZSA. Rule 70(1) requires "completion of a degree, diploma, or postgraduate course ... recognized by the Education Committee" as a prerequisite for admission. In addition, candidates must successfully complete prescribed courses in professional studies (auditing and taxation), business law, economics, and communications.

Recognition (accreditation) of an accounting education program by the NZSA requires a formal review every two years by the chairman and two members of the NZSA Education Committee. The recognition process involves a visitation of the university to review curricula structure, course content, faculty qualifications, pass rates, and other matters that impact on the quality of the degree program. The stated purpose of the review is (1) to provide a mutually beneficial process that helps ensure the development and maintenance of high-quality accounting programs and (2) to facilitate a close liaison between accounting academics and professionals by providing a vehicle for regular contact, dialogue, and exchange of information with respect to accounting needs and developments. The recognition process is important for ensuring the competency of persons entering the

Kenton B. Walker is from the University of Wyoming and Lawrence A. McClelland is from the University of Otago in New Zealand.

profession because the Final Qualifying Examination "is not a retest of previous academic requirements" (New Zealand Society of Accountants, 1990).

The Final Qualifying Examination (FQE) is analogous to the Uniform CPA Examination in the United States. However, the structure of the exam is different from its U.S. counterpart, which examines technical competence in accounting theory, practice, auditing, and business law. The New Zealand exam places greater emphasis on a candidate's conceptual understanding of accounting issues and contains no multiple choice questions; each candidate must demonstrate good written communications skills. The FQE contains sections on the structure of the accounting profession (20 percent), technical pronouncements of the NZSA (35 percent), ethics and jurisprudence (25 percent), and current issues facing the profession (20 percent).

The FQE's section on the structure of the profession is broadly concerned with a candidate's knowledge of the role of accounting in society. Those sitting the exam are required to describe relationships between the NZSA and international accounting and auditing bodies, other New Zealand professional bodies such as the Institute of Internal Auditors and the Stock Exchange, and the accounting professions in the USA, Canada, the UK, and Australia. The technical pronouncements section examines a candidate's ability to explain the rationale for accounting standards and the practice and reporting problems each was designed to remedy. The candidate must demonstrate applications of accounting and auditing standards within the context of short case studies. The section on ethics and jurisprudence requires a candidate to discuss the contents of the Code of Ethics and rules of professional conduct, and to apply ethical pronouncements to hypothetical situations. In addition, a candidate must demonstrate knowledge of law and legal cases which affect professional liability. The current issues section requires a candidate to discuss important technical and professional issues facing the profession, and explain how the profession is responding to these issues with specific reference to leading professional publications in the USA, New Zealand, Canada, the UK, and Australia.

The recognition (accreditation) process and the structure and content of the FQE have a significant influence on the way accounting is taught in New Zealand. Accounting faculty are given wide latitude in developing and implementing curricula at New Zealand universities. Faculty responsibility in the process is magnified by the nature of the FQE examination, which addresses many of the issues that are receiving attention in the United States. The exam requires a conceptual understanding of accounting and business issues rather than mere technical competence, and a broader perspective of the role of accountants in society, including ethics and social responsibility. As a result, the accounting education programs in New Zealand emphasize the development of conceptual understanding, critical thinking, and communication skills, which in turn fosters the life-long learning process.

OVERVIEW OF THE ACCOUNTING PROGRAM AT THE UNIVERSITY OF OTAGO

The undergraduate accounting program at the University of Otago requires three years to complete a degree. Although students may earn a degree in accounting without completing all the course work required for admission to the NZSA, most students follow the course prescriptions required to gain admission to the professional society. Table 1 summarizes the accounting course offerings and degree requirements at the University of Otago, and the requirements for admission to the NZSA.

All accounting and other business courses consist of approximately 50 student contact hours, similar to a semester in the United States. Lectures are presented to groups of 150-300 students in the first and second years of the program, and in groups of 20-25 in the third year. An objective is to limit the size of second year lectures to groups of 40-50 students, but resource limitations currently prevent this. To provide close faculty contact with students during the first and second years, the class is broken into smaller tutorial groups of about 15-20 students. During weekly tutorial sessions, students interact with faculty and other students on topics of discussion, review and discuss homework problems, and present group assignments. About 50-60 percent of total student contact hours are devoted to large group lectures. Forty percent of total contact hours are devoted to the small group tutorial sessions in the first year and up to 50 percent in the second year.

Substantial emphasis is placed on developing students' written and oral communications skills

---

TABLE 1
University of Otago Accounting Course Offerings

Year	Course	Degree Required	ACA Required
1	Principles of Accounting	Yes	Yes
2	Cost Accounting	Yes	Yes
	Financial Accounting	Yes	Yes
3	Management Control Systems	Yes	Yes
	Seminar in Financial Accounting	Yes	Yes
	Plus One Elective:		
	Not-For-Profit		
	Financial Statement Analysis		
	Audit Theory		
3	**Professional Studies:**		
	Auditing	No	Yes
	Taxation	No	Yes
	Auditing Systems	No	Yes
	Estate and Tax Planning	No	Yes
	Research Methods in Accounting	Honors	No
4	International Accounting	Honors	No
	Accounting Theory	Honors	No
	Management Accounting	Honors	No

by incorporating significant writing and class presentation assignments in all accounting classes. Conceptual understanding of accounting issues and policies is emphasized early in the program, and especially in years two and three. Minimal time is devoted to technical accounting problems and memorization of reporting rules, part of the education process which is regarded by faculty and practicing professionals as the primary responsibility of employers. Small tutorial groups are also used to develop skills in using accounting software and electronic spreadsheets. In the first year accounting software practicum, students must design an accounting system (chart of accounts, report formats, etc.) as well as enter and process transactions.

The accounting degree program at Otago places early emphasis on a conceptual understanding of accounting, but at the expense of developing technical proficiency. First year accounting courses cover many topics found at an intermediate level in the United States. Coverage includes issues in revenue recognition, alternative valuation systems, and conceptual frameworks such as that of the Financial Accounting Standards Board. There are two

required courses in the second year, financial and management accounting. The management (cost) accounting course is similar in scope and content to its U.S. counterparts. The second year financial accounting course covers topics normally reserved for intermediate and advanced accounting in the American education model. A substantial portion of the course is concerned with consolidations, business combinations, equity reporting, and interpreting financial statements. The primary focus of the course is to develop a broader understanding of alternative business forms, capital formation and structure, and the strengths and weaknesses of publicly reported financial information.

The third year of the curriculum is significantly different from the U.S. model. Third year financial accounting seeks to develop an understanding of the functions and practice of financial reporting in the context of a complex economic, social, and political environment and the problems associated with providing and using financial information. The financial accounting course includes coverage of policy issues in the formulation and choice of accounting methods by firms and regulatory bodies, problems and alternative solutions to measurement and reporting issues, human resource reporting and social disclosure, conceptual framework issues, and the use and interpretation of information contained in reported financial statements. Reading material for the course consists primarily of journal articles taken from professional and academic journals.[1] Classes consist of no more that 25 students. Minimal time is devoted to lecture; students are responsible for class discussion, making presentations, and completing a number of substantial written assignments.

Management accounting in the third year emphasizes the interplay of the accounting system, human behavior, and organization dynamics in the context of management control system design and implementation. The course attempts to heighten student awareness of the human and social factors which affect accounting systems and to integrate accounting into the overall management framework. Materials for the course are equally divided between cases and readings from professional and academic journals. Topics covered include the contingency theory of control system and organization design, responsibility accounting, the influence of participation on motivation and control, control system design alternatives for different organization structures, new ideas and developments in management accounting, and the suitability of traditional management accounting techniques to the current business environment. Similar to third year financial accounting, class time is devoted primarily to student discussions, preparation and presentation of cases, and student reviews of topical issues covered in the readings. Substantial written assignments are required.

At each stage, the program attempts to address precisely the concerns of accounting education reformers in the United States: an emphasis on conceptual understanding of accounting issues and a de-emphasis of technical knowledge, greater focus on management decision making, improvements in oral and written communication skills, heightened awareness of the ethical and social issues facing the accounting profession, and the changing role accounting will play in a globalized economy. Accounting students at Otago benefit from reading a variety of view points to formulate informed opinions on conceptual and topical accounting issues. Accounting electives are constructed along similar lines as the required financial and management accounting courses but are focused on specific areas of interest.

THE ACCOUNTING HONORS PROGRAM AT THE UNIVERSITY OF OTAGO

The University of Otago offers a four year accounting honors degree for students of exceptional ability. The honors program offers students the opportunity to develop further their skills of analysis, criticism, and expression. The program seeks to enhance the ability of students to think critically in order to formulate and defend their view points, broaden their appreciation of the accounting profession, and build research skills. Each year, the top students in first year accounting are invited to apply for entry to the program. Approximately 15-25 students, roughly two percent—five percent of the first year accounting class—are accepted.

Second year honors students attend the same lectures as other accounting students. However, instead of attending small group tutorials, they attend special two-hour seminars each week, one each in financial and management accounting. These seminars are used to discuss assigned problems and selected supplementary readings from books and journals which are relevant to the topics being covered in the lectures. Students are required to prepare written summaries and critiques and make oral presentations. Their performance in the honors seminars accounts for 30 percent of the grade assigned to their second year course work.

Third year honors students are required to take the same courses as other accounting students. In addition, a course in research methods is required. The purpose of this course is to provide students with an understanding of the research process and methods. Topics covered include an introduction to logic for researchers (induction and deduction, falsification, theories, etc.), the philosophy of science and accounting theory, the scientific method (the nature and purpose of research, the research process), data collection and analysis (ANOVA, regression, correlation, nonparametric statistics, tests of significance, etc.), and elements of written expression. Lectures are presented by faculty from the accounting and philosophy departments.

---

[1]The reading list for the third year financial and management accounting courses includes articles from the *Journal of Accounting Research, Accounting Review, Journal of Accounting and Business Research, Management Accounting* (UK and USA), *Accounting Organizations and Society, Harvard Business Review, Accounting Horizons,* and other respected journals.

In their final year, honors students complete three additional courses in accounting, one seminar each in financial and management accounting plus one elective. The readings for these courses are typical of those found in many doctoral programs. In addition, students must complete an honors dissertation, an in-depth primary research investigation of approximately 10,000 words in length, supervised by a senior faculty member. Table 2 describes a number of representative papers completed during the past three years. Although the education process is substantially shorter, the quality of the completed research rivals that of some postgraduate work done in the United States. Some educators have questioned the worth of research skills to potential employers, but Otago's honors graduates are highly sought after by professional accounting firms and governmental units, particularly the national taxation authority and the auditor general's office.

SUMMARY AND CONCLUSIONS

Accounting education in New Zealand is instructive for improving accounting programs in the United States. The primary focus of the educational process in New Zealand is providing students with a conceptual understanding of accounting issues. However, their programs lag in other areas, namely the breadth of *business* education and a lack of general university study prior to undertaking accounting course work. The profession, through the NZSA, exerts a strong influence on the structure and content of accounting curricula taught in universities. Some accounting professionals and educators support a movement toward a four year accounting degree for admission to the NZSA following successful efforts to implement five year programs in the United States. But the NZSA does not emphasize the technical aspects of accounting in the examination process. Instead, it encourages critical thinking and expression of divergent view points, an understanding of the social and legal implications of professional activities, and the development of communication skills. The fundamental differences in the structure and scope of the qualification examination in the United States and New Zealand indicates that reforms in the Uniform CPA Examination may be necessary before substantive changes in U.S. accounting education programs can be effectively implemented.

Existing alternative models of accounting education, like the one used at the University of Otago, may serve to shorten the definition, evaluation, and implementation of improved accounting curricula in the United States and elsewhere. The success of the Otago honors program demonstrates that a broader conceptual understanding of accounting issues may be effectively taught in a reasonably short education process. The honors program increases job opportunities for graduates and encourages top students to pursue academic careers in accounting, which may serve to decrease the worldwide shortage of accounting faculty. But more importantly, Otago's education program demonstrates that the tripartite goals of critical thinking, self-expression, and life-long learning can be addressed in an expedient manner and in much less time than the five-year curricula that many American universities have adopted or plan to adopt.

---

[2] A five year curriculum and a broadening of a four year curriculum are, arguably, alternative solutions to the problems in the accounting education process identified by professionals and educators alike. The five year curriculum alternative addresses the shortcomings of accounting education by *extending* the education process. The AICPA initiative contemplates little change in the scope or content of *accounting* education. There primary concern is the broadening of knowledge and awareness outside of accounting and improving written and oral communication skills. The four year curricula alternative includes fundamental changes in the *accounting* education process. This alternative emphasizes a conceptual understanding of accounting issues, and the expanded role of accountants in contemporary society, and builds critical thinking and communication skills within an *accounting* context. The New Zealand experience suggests that these skills may be imparted within a three year degree program. Which alternative will serve as a better foundation for life-long learning remains to be seen.

TABLE 2

Representative Research Projects Completed by Accounting Honors Students

Project Title	Method/Descriptive	Statistical Technique	Pages
The Effect of a Qualified Audit Report on the Share Price Returns of the Firm	Abnormal returns analysis, effects of qualifications on investor decisions	Regression	136
Financial Information Presentation and Decision Accuracy	Effects of form and presentation on decision making, laboratory study	Nonparametrics	71
Inventory Planning and Control Systems: The Impact of Selected Contingency Factors	Contingency theory approach to inventory system design, questionaire survey	Descriptive, correlation analysis, factor analysis, regression	72
The Role of Economic Consequencies in the Choice of Accounting Methods: An Income Strategy Approach	Effects of political and debt contracting costs on income strategy choice	Probit, regression	50
Management Accounting System Design: The Influence of Organization Size, Perceived Environmental Uncertainty, and Personality	Relationship of factors with characteristics of MAS, questionaire data from CEOs and CFOs	Factor analysis, regression	65
Concentration and Pricing in the Audit Industry: Some New Zealand Evidence	Concentration of audit services and pricing effects, questionaire data from 259 companies	Regression	52
Intuitive Accounting Concepts and the Private Shareholder: A Measure of Financial Statement Usefulness	Effects of accounting experience on understanding of statements, questionaire	Descriptive, Chi-square	66
The Effects of Experience on the Perception of Auditor Independence	Interviews of practicing auditors	None	49
Standard Setting — The Extractive Industries in New Zealand	Factors influencing accounting policy choice in extractive industries in New Zealand, questionaire	Descriptive	85
Towards an Understanding of Audit Fees: An Empirical Investigation	Determinants of audit fees in listed and unlisted companies	Regression, ANCOVA	79
The Incremental Content of Cash Flow Information: New Zealand Evidence	Investigation of incremental information provided by cash flow reporting requirements, analysis of abnormal returns	Regression	57

REFERENCES

American Accounting Association, Committee on the Future Structure, Content, and Scope of Accounting Education (The Bedford Committee). 1986. Future Accounting Education: Preparing for the Expanding Profession. *Issues in Accounting Education* (Spring): 168-195.

Patten, R., and D. Williams. 1990. There's Trouble — Right Here in Our Accounting Programs: The Challenge to Accounting Educators. *Issues in Accounting Education* (Fall): 175-179.

Perspectives on Education: Capabilities for Success in the Accounting Profession. 1989. (New York: Arthur Anderson & Co., Arthur Young, Coopers & Lybrand, Deloitte Haskins & Sells, Ernst & Whinney, Peat Marwick Main & Co., Price Waterhouse, and Touche Ross).

Quality Assurance by Way of a Review Process with Respect to University Accounting Programmes: Preparing Candidates for Entry to the New Zealand Society of Accountants. 1990. (Wellington, New Zealand: New Zealand Society of Accountants).

Williams, D., and G. Sundem. 1990. Grants Awarded for Implementing Improvements in Accounting Education. *Issues in Accounting Education* (Fall): 313-329.

Australian Government Policy on Higher Education: Impact on Accounting Education

Joan D. Wells

INTRODUCTION

This paper describes recent Australian Commonwealth government policies and reforms in higher education (higher education in Australia is essentially postsecondary education, i.e. tertiary education) and their consequences for accounting education. The policy changes come during a period of cutbacks in the funding of higher education. These cutbacks are part of an overall attempt to control the total expenditure of the Commonwealth government which has been in budget surplus from 1987 to 1990 after more than 20 years of deficit spending. It became evident that without policy changes, further economies in education expenditure were not possible.

The three major areas of reform are as follows:

- A unified national system of higher education via amalgamations was initiated on the premise that cost efficiencies were capable of being achieved through economies of scale. Particular mention was made of the potential to reduce administration costs since larger institutions were noted to have lower administration cost per student than their smaller counterparts. (Dawkins 1987, 33)

- The higher education contribution scheme (HECS), where further funding is derived from charges set at approximately 20 percent of cost on all Australian students at universities and institutes. (The user pays principle.)

- The full fee paying scheme where overseas students are charged a fee based on the average cost to the university or institute.

Examining the changes instituted by the Commonwealth government—the amalgamations, the higher education charge scheme and the full fee paying scheme—it is difficult to describe these changes as reforms. It is much easier to see them as budgetary motivated changes made to design a system whereby further control over expenditure is possible —to reduce even further Commonwealth government expenditure on higher education.

Very real concerns have been expressed over the impact of these policy changes on the quality of tertiary education (Senate Standing Committee 1990, 1) and on the quality of accounting education specifically (Mathews Volume 1 1990, 64). The following is a brief description of current developments in higher education in Australia and the impact on the quality of accounting education.

CUTBACKS IN THE FUNDING OF HIGHER EDUCATION

The Commonwealth government assumed responsibility for the funding of higher education in 1974 taking over from the state governments. The Commonwealth government is the major supplier of funding for higher education in Australia. One of the first statements made in every Commonwealth budget on education over the period 1980–1990 has been that spending on education has increased in real terms (Commonwealth Budget Papers 1980–1991). No allowance is made for the fact that the student numbers have increased in every year. For the past three years no information about student numbers has been included in the budget papers! Information to complete this paper had to be obtained directly from the Department of Employment Education and Training (DEET).

Table 1 shows that real Commonwealth government funding decreased in six of the ten years. This table gives the total Commonwealth government operating, capital and research funding in millions of dollars which is deflated by the gross domestic product deflator (excluding farm produce) to give real funding each year.

Table 2 shows the extent of the drop in funding per equivalent full-time student (EFTSU) over the ten years. The total drop over the period is 24.78%. The average annual drop is 2.81% and over the period, spending dropped in eight of the ten years.

This decrease in real funding per student has occurred at a time of a stated government policy of increasing the retention rates and increasing the numbers of students in the tertiary education system.

Joan D. Wells is a member of the Department of Accounting, Faculty of Business, Swinburne University of Technology, Hawthorn, Victoria, Australia.

TABLE 1
Total Australian Commonwealth Government Funding for Higher Education throughout Australia
1980–81 to 1990–91

Year	Total Com Funding $,000,000	GDP NonFarm Deflator	Real Funding $,000,000
1980–81	1670.6	71.5	2336.5
1981–82	1859.8	79.7	2333.5
1982–83	2041.1	88.4	2308.9
1983–84	2115.2	94.5	2238.3
1984–85	2353.7	100.0	2353.7
1985–86	2546.0	107.1	2377.2
1986–87	2696.2	115.0	2344.5
1987–88	2885.2	123.4	2338.1
1988–89	2965.2	134.7	2201.3
1989–90	3394.1	142.8	2376.8
1990–91	3880.6	148.8	2607.9

Source: Commonwealth Budget Papers

AMALGAMATIONS

The Reform

The Honourable John Dawkins through the Green Paper (Dawkins 1987) and White Paper (Dawkins 1988) announced a major Commonwealth government "reform," a unified national system of higher education. The amalgamation process has been by far the greatest policy change that has been undertaken in higher education in Australia since the adoption of the Martin report in 1965.

Prior to the adoption and implementation of the present government policy, there was a distinc-

tion between education at a university and education at an institute of technology or a college of advanced education. The distinction was that the universities with their emphasis on research were more academically orientated, while the institutes and colleges with their emphasis on skill training were more practically orientated. This so-called binary system of higher education was adopted by the Commonwealth government on the recommendation of the Martin Committee Report on Higher Education commissioned by the Menzies Government and conducted from 1961 to 1965 (Davies 1989, 23). This distinction is becoming blurred

TABLE 2
Real Australian Commonwealth Government Funding Per Equivalent Full Time Student Unit (EFTSU)

1980–81 to 1990–91

Year	Total EFTSU '000	Funding Per EFTSU $	Per Annum (Decrease) Increase %
1980–81	252.3	9261	
1981–82	255.5	9133	(1.38)
1982–83	256.5	9002	(1.43)
1983–84	263.8	8485	(5.74)
1984–85	271.5	8669	2.17
1985–86	281.9	8433	(2.72)
1986–87	289.0	8112	(3.81)
1987–88	307.9*	7594	(6.39)
1988–89	322.9*	6817	(10.23)
1989–90	344.8*	6893	1.11
1990–91	374.4*	6966	1.06

Source: Commonwealth Budget Papers and * supplied directly by the Department of Employment, Education and Training

with the adoption by the present Commonwealth government of a policy of unified national system of higher education. Institutes and universities are being coerced into amalgamations with the threat of cutbacks in funding and/or the refusal of university status for those institutions which fail to cooperate. Australian tertiary education is in the throes of this amalgamation process with the objective of forming larger organizations which will be given university status.

Consequences

The process of amalgamation has by no means reached its conclusion. The cooperation of each state has differed as has the response of each institution. Amalgamations made in haste have ended in divorce in several instances; however, despite this, the number of institutions in Australia has been reduced from 54 to 34 (Baldwin 1990, 26–28), most of which now carry the title university. Whether the perceived economies of fewer large multicampus institutions actually eventuates remains to be seen. While some amalgamations are demonstrably beneficial, others are so contrived that the benefits are hard to imagine. Amalgamations of geographically remote campuses must lead to increased administrative costs. The upgrading of colleges of advanced education and institutes to university status is a shift away from low-cost institutions to relatively high-cost institutions.

THE HIGHER EDUCATION CONTRIBUTION SCHEME (HECS)

The Reform

This scheme was announced in the 1988/89 Commonwealth budget to take effect from 1 January 1989. It was established to help fund the planned expansion of Australia's higher education system. Under the scheme, students contribute about 20 percent of the average cost of a higher education place ($2250 in 1992). Each semester students choose either to pay up front or to defer payment. Up-front students pay 85 percent of their higher education contribution scheme liability for the semester direct to the institution. The Commonwealth pays the balance on their behalf. Deferring students accept a loan from the Commonwealth which pays their total liability for the semester to the institution. Students begin repaying these loans when their taxable income reaches a minimum level ($25,469 for 1990–91). The Australian Taxation Office collects this payment on behalf of the Commonwealth. The government announced that moneys

from HECS are to be paid into a trust fund account which is to be used to assist in funding the government's higher education equity and growth objectives. The HECS charge replaced the Higher Education Administration Charge of $250 per annum (approximately 4 percent of cost) which was introduced in 1987 and discontinued from 1989.

Consequences

The deterioration in the quality of teaching as a result of the overcrowding of physical facilities and the decreases in the staff student ratios (Penington 1988, 3), which has accelerated in the last three years, has taken place at a time when the students have been compelled to pay for their education. It would be reasonable to expect that when a user pays the principle would be adopted that Commonwealth government expenditure on a per full-time student basis would be maintained. Unfortunately, this is not the case. As well, the government is refusing to fund the unavoidable over enrollment of students throughout Australia in the 1991 year, while at the same time charging these over enrolled students their HECS.

FULL FEE-PAYING OVERSEAS STUDENTS

The Reform

The government announced guidelines in July 1985 which enable universities and colleges of advanced education to offer full fee courses for overseas students either in Australia or overseas. Institutions can offer new courses or extra places in existing courses to overseas students at full cost outside the current quotas. A typical charge for a business student is approximately $8,000 per annum in 1991. This goes directly to the institution and has been promoted by the government as a way for the tertiary sector to get additional funding.

Prior to the adoption of the present scheme, overseas students attending Australian educational institutions were required to contribute to the costs of their tuition through the Overseas Students Charge. Education of foreign students was seen almost exclusively as an element of the Australian foreign aid program. The charge grew from approximately 35 percent of the average cost in 1980 to 55 percent of the average cost in 1988. There was no new intake of subsidized students after 1 January 1990, as from that date all new overseas students were full fee paying. Overseas aid by subsidization of overseas students has been replaced by a system of scholarships.

Consequences

The introduction of the full fee-paying overseas students program as a means of boosting the export dollar at the same time as giving universities and other institutions the opportunity of generating additional funding has created more stresses on an already overburdened tertiary sector. Real questions can be raised over whether the fees charged actually cover the costs of educating these students and whether the funds generated by the fees charged get down to the faculty level.

The competition between Australian and overseas institutions to attract full fee-paying overseas students has led to the charges falling short of the cost and has led to overseas students being selected into some bachelor degree courses with matriculation scores below what is required of Australian students (Mathews 1990 Volume 1, 150–151).

IMPACT ON ACCOUNTING EDUCATION

Accounting in higher education has been fortunate in that its progress at a grass roots level has been examined in detail through the comprehensive Mathews' Report. The Commonwealth government commissioned a review of the accounting discipline in higher education which commenced in March 1989, concluded in June 1990 and covered courses conducted in 49 government-funded higher education institutions throughout Australia. It was chaired by Emeritus Professor Russell Mathews (1990 Volume 1-3).

The major findings of the review committee were the following:

* At both government and institutional levels there has been persistent neglect, underfunding and discrimination against accounting education throughout Australia.

* Student-staff ratios in accounting are far too high, academic salaries generally have fallen relative to average weekly earnings, whilst working conditions, teaching and staff accommodation and technical support are unsatisfactory.

* Major policy decisions on student growth and the introduction of full fee-paying students have been made for financial rather than educational reasons.

* Most of the funds from full fee-paying students have been used for purposes other than the enhancement of the quality of teaching programs.

Some of the major recommendations of the review committee were that

* The Commonwealth government should adopt a needs-based model for funding of accounting education, not the historical models of the past, and institutions should use the same model for funding accounting education internally.

* Funds from full fee-paying overseas students should be used to provide resources on a scale that is at least one-third higher than the level of funding per Australian student and full fee-paying overseas students should meet entrance requirements equivalent to those for Australian students.

* A target student-staff ratio of 16 to one should be adopted by institutions immediately. There should be no growth in commencing student places in accounting in the next triennium.

The cutbacks in real expenditure on higher education per equivalent full-time student by the Commonwealth government have led to a deterioration in the quality of tertiary education in Australia. The Mathews' Report highlights this deterioration in the accounting discipline (Mathews Volume 1, 64).

The Institute of Chartered Accountants and the Australian Society of Certified Practising Accountants in June 1991 issued a statement on guidelines for the accreditation of tertiary institutions by the professional accounting bodies (Johns and Cappaletto 1991). This statement follows closely the recommendations made by the Mathews' Report and reflects the concern of the professional bodies over the deterioration in the quality of accounting education. Few institutions, if any, under the present funding arrangements have a hope of meeting these accreditation guidelines.

To date the government has made no attempt to implement any of the recommendations of the Mathews' Report. The joint response by the Department of Employment Education and Training and the Higher Education Council to the Mathews' Report released in February 1993 rejected the major recommendations of this report.

CONCLUSION

All of the government policy changes covered in this paper have been executed through the vehicle of the Commonwealth budget and though announced as reforms, the main focus has been to reduce Commonwealth government expenditure on tertiary education.

The consequences of the current government policies on higher education in general and accounting education in particular have been to increase staff-student ratios and cause overcrowding of the physical facilities. There has without a doubt been a deterioration in the quality of higher education in Australia as a direct result of the cutbacks in real government funding per student. This deterioration has been magnified in its impact on accounting education because of the discrimination against accounting which has occurred historically through the relative weightings given the discipline in the allocation of funding both at a government and institutional level.

As a result of the current recession in Australia with an unemployment level currently around ten percent, a greater number of students are being retained in both secondary and tertiary education. This together with an increased demand for places from applicants with no immediate job prospects from the secondary schooling system has led to severe overenrollment in 1991. The Commonwealth government has refused to fund this Australian-wide overenrollment. Given these current developments in higher education, there can be no improvement in the quality of Australian tertiary education in the foreseeable future.

REFERENCES

Accounting in Higher Education — Report of the Review of the Accounting Discipline in Higher Education. 1990. (Emeritus Professor R. Mathews, Chairman) Volumes 1–3. Department of Employment Education and Training. AGPS, Canberra.

Ashenden, D., and S. Milligan. 1991. *Good Universities Guide to Australian Universities and Other Higher Education Institutions.* Manadarin, Australia.

Baldwin, P., Minister for Higher Education and Employment Services. 1990. *Assessment of the Relative Funding Position of Australia's Higher Education Institutions.* AGPS, Canberra.

Bureau of Industry Economics. 1989. *Exporting Australia's Tertiary Education Services.* Information Bulletin 16. AGPS, Canberra.

Davies, S. 1989. *The Martin Committee and the Binary Policy of Higher Education in Australia.* Ashwood House, Melbourne.

Dawkins, The Hon. J. S., Minister for Employment, Education & Training. *1990–1991 Programs, Department of Employment, Education & Training.* AGPS, Canberra.

———. 1989. *Higher Education Funding for the 1990–92 Triennium* (December). AGPS, Canberra.

———. 1989. *Supplementary Funding Decisions on Higher Education for the 1989–91 Triennium* (June). AGPS, Canberra.

———. 1988. *Higher Education a Policy Statement* (White Paper). AGPS, Canberra.

———. 1987. *Higher Education a Policy Discussion Paper* (Green Paper). AGPS, Canberra.

Hogbin, G.R., ed. 1988. *Withering Heights, the State of Higher Education in Australia.* Allen & Unwin.

Johns, A., and G. Cappelletto. 1991. *Guide-lines for Joint Administration of Accreditation of Tertiary Institutions, by the Professional Accounting Bodies.* A Proposal.

Mathews' Report. Refer to the *Accounting in Higher Education* reference.

National Board of Employment, Education and Training. 1989. *Report of the Task Force on Amalgamations in Higher Education.* AGPS, Canberra.

Penington, D. 1988. *"The Way ahead for Higher Education The University of Melbourne Response to the Green Paper." Tertiary Education for National Economic Objectives: Critiques and Alternatives.* Melbourne University Assembly.

Senate Standing Committee on Employment and Training. 1990. *Priorities for Reform in Higher Education.* AGPS, Canberra.

Strategies for Change in Accounting Education: The U.S. Experiment

Doyle Z. Williams

I am pleased to be invited to speak at this Seventh International Conference on Accounting Education and report to you on the reformation movement in accounting education in the United States.

To appreciate the background for current changes in accounting education in the United States, we need to review briefly the history of accounting education in the U.S. The first formal university accounting education programs were developed in the late 1800s and the early 1900s. As higher education expanded in the first half of the 20th century, accounting education programs grew steadily at both public and private universities.

Beginning in the 1960s, accounting enrollments, as in higher education as a whole, exploded. There was also an explosion of textbooks, although most were strikingly similar. Employment opportunities for accounting graduates grew along with enrollments until the mid-1980s when both began to level off.

Driven largely by the available textbooks, accounting curricula over the last 50 years have remained generally static. On most campuses, the curriculum has had a decidedly financial accounting orientation. While there are no national regulatory bodies prescribing accounting curricula, each of the 50 states, the District of Columbia, Guam, Puerto Rico, and the U.S. Virgin Islands have set education requirements for individuals to be licensed as certified public accountants. For the most part, the education requirements are similar and have remained unchanged until recently when almost one-half of the states have extended the standard four-year education requirement to five years. The movement toward a five-year requirement has provided an excellent opportunity for universities to reexamine their entire accounting curricula.

A Uniform CPA Examination is administered by all of the states for those seeking to be licensed as Certified Public Accountants. Like textbooks, the content of the examination has had a significant influence on accounting curricula over the years, especially at the undergraduate level.

During the late 1970s and the 1980s, the practice of accounting in both the public and private domains began to undergo significant change. Public expectations for auditors grew, business practice became much more complex, the international dimension of business expanded, technology advanced, the scope of practice broadened, and public practice became much more competitive.

FORMATION OF THE AECC

Accounting educators observed that practice was changing much more rapidly than accounting education. Out of this perceived need for change, I, as the incoming President of the American Accounting Association, appointed in 1984 a committee to examine the future of accounting education. The Committee, chaired by Norton Bedford, issued its report in 1986. The Committee called for fundamental changes in accounting curricula and how we teach accounting.

In the spring of 1989, the then largest eight (now six) accounting firms issued a paper endorsing the Bedford Committee report and called upon the educational community to begin the process of reforming accounting education. The firms pledged funding for this effort.

With funding assured for up to five years from the firms, in April 1989 the AAA Executive Committee agreed to establish a body to be a catalyst for change in accounting education. The name Accounting Education Change Commission (AECC) was selected. The Executive Committee empowered the President and President-Elect to name the 16 voting members of the Commission. The membership includes seven accounting professors, four public accountants, two industrial accountants, three nonaccountants, and two ex-officio members—the chief education officer of the American Accounting Association and the American Institute of Certified Public Accountants.

Doyle Z. Williams is the Chairman of the Accounting Education Change Commission.

The Commission meets four times annually, rotating meeting sites around the country. Meetings are open to the public.

WHAT IS THE AECC TRYING TO DO?

The Commission is not a regulatory or accrediting body. It must rely on persuasion to generate change in accounting education. The mission of the Commission is to be a leader in improving the academic preparation of accountants, so that entrants to the accounting profession possess the skills, knowledge, and attitudes required for success in accounting career paths. The AECC seeks to enhance the quality of accounting education consistent with the objectives of the AAA's Bedford Committee Report and the Sponsoring Firms' white paper, "Perspectives on Education: Capabilities for Success in the Accounting Profession." The AECC fosters continuing improvement in the education of accountants by working in collaboration with other stakeholder organizations.

In fulfilling its mission, the Commission seeks to serve as a forum to discuss issues; represent interests of stakeholders, including faculty, students, and employers; and be a catalyst for improvements in education of accountants through curriculum restructuring, promoting alternative education processes, encouraging the development of new and different educational materials, and speaking out on the appropriate allocation of faculty resources.

HOW IS THE AECC TRYING TO ACCOMPLISH THESE OBJECTIVES?

The Commission's primary focus is on reengineering the curriculum and improve how it is delivered. The Commission seeks also to address the infrastructure issues that can facilitate or impede curriculum innovation.

To convey its message, the Commission has an active speaking and publications program. During the first three years of the Commission's life, Commission members have appeared on over 200 programs and have authored over 30 published pieces. The Commission also publishes statements setting forth its views on topics related to its work. To date, two position statements and three issues statements have been published. The Commission has also awarded grants to selected schools to stimulate curriculum change.

Curriculum Changes

In 1990 the Commission issued as Position Statement No. 1 "Objectives of Education for Ac-

countants." The basic premise of this statement is that the objective should be to prepare students to *become* professional accountants, not *be* professional accountants at the time of entry to the profession.

The curriculum objectives of Position Statement No. 1 include teaching students to learn on their own—an attribute that will stand them in good stead throughout their lifetimes. In addition, students should be active participants in the learning process. They should be taught to identify and solve unstructured problems, learn by doing, work in groups, and learn how to use technology effectively, such as databases for researching issues.

Students' learning should focus on skills as well as knowledge. Especially important, students should develop good communication and interpersonal skills. In addition, their ethical and professional values should be enhanced. But of greatest importance, the curriculum should focus on the process of learning, not just teaching answers. Granted, this approach may lead to students not being able to readily recite specific professional standards, but the premise is that professional standards will change. If students can learn how to find answers, then they are well prepared for a lifetime career.

First Course in Accounting

A number of research studies have shown that one of the greatest influences on students deciding whether or not to major in accounting is the first course in accounting. In the United States, this course, usually covering an academic year, is taken by all business students. It typically includes introductory financial and managerial accounting, sometimes called principles of accounting.

Recognizing the importance of the first course in accounting in curriculum development, the Commission issued Position Statement No. 2 that follows up on the first statement on "Objectives of Education for Accountants." The statement points out the importance of the first course to both potential accounting majors and nonmajors. The statement notes that the first course shapes students' perceptions of the accounting profession, aptitudes and skills needed for successful careers in accounting, and career opportunities.

The major thrust of the statement is that the first course in accounting should be an *introduction to accounting* rather than *introductory accounting*. That is, the course should focus more on the role accounting serves in society and to organizations. It should have a greater user focus than the traditional first accounting course. It is expected that to accomplish its objectives, the course will be a rigorous educational experience.

The primary objective of the course is for students to understand accounting as an information development and communication function that supports economic decision making. Students completing the course should have a broad view of accounting's role in society, understand the basic features of accounting and reporting, understand fundamental accounting concepts in addition to the elements of financial statements, appreciate the role of accounting in taxation and other governmental measurements, understand that some accounting systems are more effective than others, possess enhanced analytical skills and the ability to confront unstructured problems, and appreciate the changing nature of the discipline due to economic and technological change.

Consistent with Position Statement No. 1, the statement on the first course in accounting, urges that teaching methods give priority to student interaction, such as cooperative learning or learning in groups. Again, it is most important that students learn to learn on their own.

In the United States, often the first course in accounting is taught by part-time faculty or graduate students. The Commission believes that the importance of the course calls for universities to place their most effective instructors in the first course. Those teaching this course should have a record of success in teaching, current knowledge of professional developmentsand should support points by citing relevant research, bring an integrative organizational approach, use real-world examples, and be enthusiastic and committed to teaching and the accounting profession.

In short, the first course in accounting is the window to the discipline and the profession for students. It should be broad based, convey the important role accounting serves, and help develop the skills of students. High priority should be given to assigning the most effective faculty to this course.

Grant Program

One of the primary strategies adopted at the outset by the Commission to stimulate curriculum change was to establish a grants program. In early 1990, five grants were awarded to four-year and graduate programs for the purpose of undertaking comprehensive curriculum change. These first round grants were made to Kansas State University, Brigham Young University, University of Massachusetts, University of North Texas, and Rutgers University. In 1991, five additional grants were made to four-year and graduate schools. This second round of grants was made to the University of Chicago, Arizona State University, University of Illinois and the University of Notre Dame (a joint grant), North Carolina A & T University, and the University of Virginia. These schools are in various stages of their projects. We look forward to them sharing the results of their efforts with the academic community at large over the next two to three years.

In the United States, many students attend a two-year college prior to going on to a four-year college or university. Most of these two-year colleges offer an introductory accounting course that is transferred or accepted by the four-year colleges and universities. Recognizing the important role of two-year colleges, in the spring of 1992 the Commission made grants to two two-year colleges to revise their beginning accounting courses. These schools are located in Iowa and Arizona. Work on these grants began this fall. Also, the Commission issued in August 1992 Issues Statement No. 3 on the importance of two-year colleges for accounting education.

Infrastructure Changes

The Commission recognizes there are several infrastructure issues that affect the ability to change accounting curricula. One of the most significant is the lack of faculty incentives for curriculum development and course design. It is widely recognized in the United States that research typically is weighted more heavily than teaching for tenure, promotion, and annual reward purposes. There is broad-based support in the Commission for the model of scholarship espoused by Ernest Boyer, President of the Carnegie Foundation for the Advancement of Teaching. This model states there are four dimensions to scholarship—discovery of knowledge, integration of knowledge, application of knowledge, and scholarship that supports teaching.

To call attention to the need for greater recognition of the scholarship of teaching, including curriculum development and course design, in the reward structure, the Commission published Issues Statement No. 1, urging priority for teaching in higher education. This statement calls for more emphasis on teaching and curriculum and course development. The statement points out that for these activities to occur, the reward system must provide sufficient incentives, which may require a shift in the allocation of faculty resources. This statement has enjoyed widespread support, including endorsement by several academic and professional bodies. As a follow-up, the Commission issued in August 1992 an exposure draft of a proposed Issues Statement on "Defining, Evaluating, and Rewarding Effective Teaching."

Another infrastructure issue is accreditation. In the United States, traditionally there has been one nationally recognized body for accreditation of business and accounting programs—the American Assembly of Collegiate Schools of Business. Over the years, accreditation standards have tended to be very subject-matter specific, leading universities to interpret the standards in terms of specific courses, often stifling curriculum innovation. The Commission played a key role in the redrafting of the accreditation standards to allow for greater innovation and experimentation. The new standards are missionbased, allowing a wide range of institutional objectives. They also focus on the quality of the educational experience provided to the student, rather than just input measures. Finally, they emphasize continuous quality improvement.

Another impediment to change in accounting education has been the regulatory requirements of the various states and the CPA Examination. The Commission believes that the regulatory requirements should permit flexibility and innovation and a variety of educational paths for entering the profession. It also believes that preparation for entry-level professional examinations should be separated from the academic curriculum. The Commission presented its views on this subject in Issues Statement No. 2.

Finally, if we are successful in changing the nature of accounting education, then we must be concerned about the reception the practicing community will give accounting graduates of such programs. If the Commission is successful in its efforts, future graduates will have a different set of skills than did those in the past. To help address the bridging of the new curriculum with practice, the Commission issued recently an exposure draft of a proposed Issues Statement on "Improving the Early Employment Experience of Accountants." In this statement, the Commission offers recommendations for employers, faculty, and students for bridging students' expectations gap between their studies and their first job.

Prospects for Success

The Commission began in the fall of 1992 the fourth year of its originally budgeted five-year life. Surveys have revealed a consensus for change in accounting education and support for the work of the Commission. Numerous accounting programs are undertaking major curriculum revision. Faculty workshops are springing up on how to teach accounting differently and more effectively. Although it is too early to see the end product, authors and publishers report significant changes are underway in many forthcoming textbooks. Change in accounting education is taking hold.

What will be the legacy of this experiment to change the core of accounting education? I believe the rigid, traditional accounting curriculum of the past 40 years will give way to a variety of curriculum approaches. The long-held view that one size fits all will vanish. Some common goals will emerge, such as greater emphasis on communication skills, interpersonal skills, and solving unstructured problems. There will be less emphasis on financial accounting and more attention to integrating all aspects of the discipline. The changes will be implemented in a variety of ways, as demonstrated by the work of those receiving Commission grants.

In the early 1970s, a major effort, funded by Price Waterhouse, was undertaken to change accounting education, particularly the introductory course. However, that effort did not take root. I have been asked why I am optimistic that this effort will succeed. I firmly believe this effort will succeed for several reasons:

1. Employers demand a different product. If accounting programs do not produce properly educated graduates to meet the changing practice environment, employers will look elsewhere for its talent.

2. There is a broad cross-section of stakeholders committed to improving accounting education.

3. The experiment involves comprehensive curriculum change, not just pieces of the curriculum.

4. The five-year requirement movement provides an excellent opportunity for reexamining the total curriculum.

5. There is greater awareness and acceptance among accounting educators of the need for change. Accounting educators are more accepting than in the recent past of the notion that education should be for more than preparation for the CPA Examination.

6. Emerging technology (e.g., custom textbook publishing) permits faculty to tailor teaching materials for local use.

7. There is renewed interest in the academy for recognizing faculty efforts in curriculum development and course design.

In short, I believe the timing is right for major change in accounting education in the United States. The future of the discipline depends upon it.

I understand there is an old Mexican proverb that says, "He who doesn't look ahead stays behind." That proverb describes the underlying philosophy behind the Accounting Education Change Commission.

Professor Warren Bennis at the University of Southern California says managers do things right while leaders do the right thing. I look forward to reporting to you at the Eighth International Conference on Accounting Education the outcome of this grand experiment to change accounting education in the United States, and whether or not the Accounting Education Change Commission has been a manager, a leader, both, or neither.

Instructional Innovations in Accounting Education

The conference program included sixteen papers that contain descriptions of innovative approaches used by the authors in the accounting curriculum. These innovative approaches were developed primarily in response to public criticism that traditional instructional methods are deficient, particularly in developing critical thinking and communication skills among students. In most instances, the experiment was designed for a specific course but is transferable to other courses. The authors describe the use of cases, databases, group learning projects, writing assignments, integrative computer programs, expert systems, and local or international internships and the integration of all courses into a business cycle approach. Some of the experiments include the use of unusual games, cases, or methods designed to motivate students.

Some Exploratory Applications of Suggestive Accelerative Learning and Teaching (SALT) in Accounting Education

Kwabena Anyane-Ntow

INTRODUCTION

The purpose of this paper is to suggest to accounting educators and professionals to explore the possible application of suggestive accelerative learning and teaching (SALT) in accounting education in order to achieve easy and efficient assimilation of ever-increasing knowledge base in accounting and allow sufficient amount of time for conceptual understanding and applications. Emphasis on teaching the body of knowledge required to be a professional accountant has been the traditional approach by most accounting programs. The present environment within which accounting practice takes place renders this approach to teaching ineffective. Thus, products of accounting programs are often inadequately prepared to handle the dynamics of real-world situations. The knowledge explosion, the proliferation of information-processing technology, and the exponential rate of growth in accounting rules and regulations, coupled with time limitations in accounting courses have made it impossible to learn the enormously growing amount of facts in accounting. This problem is compounded by the need to spend time on conceptual understanding of accounting and learning to exercise judgment. The result has been that graduates generally learn more about standards, rules and procedures without being able to effectively apply their knowledge in real-world settings. Thus, forcing ever-increasing knowledge into a constrained curriculum has squeezed out important items, yet graduates are able to learn only a relatively smaller percentage of the accounting knowledge base.

The Accounting Education Change Commission has proposed movement from a knowledge-based educational program to a process-oriented approach as a solution to this problem (AECC 1990). This is also intended to help prepare graduates to become professional accountants rather than to be professional accountants at the time of the entry to the profession (AECC 1990).

Achieving a balance between the knowledge-based approach and the process-oriented approach is essential for producing competent entry-level accounting professionals. Suggestive accelerative learning and teaching (SALT) may just be a technique that could provide accounting programs a viable alternative. Several research results have suggested that SALT can make learning easier and up to five or more times faster than conventional teaching methods (Schuster 1972, 1976; Lazanov 1975, 1981).

THE SALT SYSTEM

SALT is a peak performance technique based on a holistic and whole-brain functional approach to learning and teaching in any learning or educational environment. The purpose is to accelerate the rate at which information is acquired and amount of information that can be retained and retrieved. The system was developed in Bulgaria by Georgi Lazanov of the University of Sophia in 1956 and brought to the United States by Donald Schuster of Iowa State University.

It uses subtle suggestions through positive speaking, positive expectations and positive feedback to students. The psychophysiological brain principles involved are as follows: The human brain is divided into left and right hemispheres. Nobel Laureaets Roger Sperry and Robert Ornstein of the California Institute of Technology found that the two hemispheres are connected by a complex network of about 300 million nerve fibers called Callosum. They showed that each of the hemispheres has different functions. The left brain is associated with language, mathematical operations, logic, numbers, formulae, linearity, analysis, words of a song and relationships. The right is associated with forms and patterns, spacial manipulations, rhythm and musical appreciation, images and pictures, imagination, daydreaming, tune of a song and dimension (Rose 1989).

The functioning of the two brains has been demonstrated by measuring the electrical impulses

---

Kwabena Anyane-Ntow is Professor of Accounting at North Carolina Central University.

of the brain during various activities. The brain is known to show alpha (i.e., waves of 8 to 12 cycles per second) brain wave rhythm during state of relaxation.

Ornstein (1977) showed that subjects engaged in solving mathematical problems showed increased alpha brain wave in the right hemisphere, with beta (13 to 25 cycles per second) in the left hemisphere, indicating that the right side was relaxed whilst the left side was active. Conversely, subjects engaged in artistic activities showed alpha brain wave in the left hemisphere and beta brain wave in the right hemisphere, respectively.

The left brain is known to specialize in serial or sequential thought (i.e. rationalizes), whilst the right brain is known to process several pieces of information at a glance into one overall thought (synthesizes). Despite the apparent specialization of the two brains, each complements and improves the performance of the other (Diamond 1979).

The brain chemistry of a positive parasympathetic autonomic nervous-system state is different from that of a negative state characterized by fear, anger or anxiety. In a state of security, confidence and joy, the brain hums, and learning is efficient and effortless (Rose 1989). Learning in the positive relaxed state takes place in expansive global context that allows for connection of the curriculum material previously leanred and to positive applications (Schuster 1976; Lazanov 1975, 1981).

BASIC COMPONENTS OF THE SALT SYSTEM

The main aspects involved in the system are

1. Self-imposed limitations are desuggested and replaced with powerful and positive suggestions that learning is in fact easy, fun and enjoyable.

2. Relaxation is encouraged or induced because this state is known to create an ideal condition of stress-free alertness when information is quickly and easily assimilated.

3. Students are encouraged and/or aided to create mental maps of material or information to be learned in relation to its applications in the various environmental contexts.

4. Integration of "Active Concert" with the material presentation. This involves presentation of the contextual material in a dramatic manner to the accompaniment of a classical (or appropriate) musical background.

Some researchers have suggested that Baroque classical music (Corelli, Telemann, Haydn, Bach, Abinoni, Vivaldi, composed between 1700 and 1750) works better because it is precise and symmetrical. Others suggest that classical romantic music (Haydn, Mozart, Handel, Beethoven, Tchaikovsky, Brahms, Chopin) works better. With the musical background, the instructor's voice blends in the rhythm of the music in a natural manner as if the voice were an instrument in the orchestra. The students follow the sound while looking at the key concepts (words) of the text related to the material being discussed. The music which tempo approximates the rate of heartbeat at between 60-70 beats per minute works to activate the right brain while the sight of key words activates the left brain. Thus, the process independently activates the entire brain. With sound and visual stimuli, both the conscious and the subconscious minds are each involved to accelerate the information into the memory in a positive and enjoyable environment. Since the brain is known to store information in a rhythmical manner, the technique conforms with how the brain operates (Brislan 1987).

5. A rest period or break is recommended after the "Active Concert." This is followed by "Receptive Concert." In this phase no effort is required on the part of the students even though a great deal of mental activity takes place. Prior to the concert, students are instructed to relax, close their eyes and simply concentrate on the music. The music becomes a dominant factor and the text of material is only just audible to the conscious mind, and at the same time perfectly comprehensible to the subconscious mind. Thus, the barriers of the conscious mind are unobstructively bypassed. This concert also eliminates fatigue that normally follows attention to enormous amounts of information. This is followed by another break or intermission before the final phase.

6. The final phase, which may be referred to as "Activators," may consists of business games, case discussions and analyses as well as role, playing in contextual related materials. The purpose here is to review and apply the principles and materials previously learned.

THE ROLE OF MUSIC IN THE SALT SYSTEM

Brislan (1987) states that music has long been recognized as a "harmonizer of the spirit," as a healing and therapeutic agent and as a backdrop — often unconsciously perceived — to many aspects of daily life. Historically, music has been a part of various mystical, physical, psychological, spiritual, medical and cultural events and rituals. The ancient Hebrews, for instance, regularized the use of song as enhanced speech for religious incantations (Brislan 1987). The Hebrews later developed choral and instrumental music as part of their religious life, known as prophesying in the Bible as evidenced by several references to the phrase "to the chief Musician" in the book of Psalms, and David's curing of Saul's depression by playing the harp as the most notable.

African traditional priests, Asian, Polynesian and European shamans, Indian gurus and Native Americans often used music to accompany their rituals. In more recent times, music and rhythm have been used to encourage people to walk unscathed on hot charcoal, to increase worker productivity in factories, in hospitals to increase the healing process and recovery rates of patients and in planetariums to stimulate the growth of plants. No one knows for sure how music accomplishes all these. One thing is indisputable: rhythm and pattern are central and natural to the way our universe and all that is in it operates. According to Lazanov (1981), rhythm is a basic biological principle, a reflection of the rhythms in nature. He suggests that music has been observed to have the useful effect of a "placebo" with durable memorization, creating suspense and positive expectation as well as reduction in fatigue.

Brislan (1987) gives an account of two groups of subjects where one group was instructed in material without musical background and the other with musical background. The groups were pretested and posttested before and after the instructions. The test scores of the group with musical background was observed to be significantly higher than the other group.

SOME POSSIBLE APPLICATIONS OF THE SALT SYSTEM IN ACCOUNTING EDUCATION

Successful application of the technique in accounting programs will require some adjustments on the part of accounting educators and administrators. In addition, some modifications in the environment within which the teaching and learning experience takes place will be called for. The modified classroom environment may include increased use of audiovisual techniques to emphasize the contextual material being presented. It may include increased development and use of accounting-related business games, case studies and role playing in the classroom.

The use of appropriate types of music (with tempo of approximately 60 beats per minute) should be explored and its effects on the efficiency of accounting education examined. In addition, the use of relaxation techniques and positive reinforcement in the classroom should be encouraged and their effects examined in an effort to improve accounting education.

CONCLUDING REMARKS

With SALT systems, the material to be learned is always related to the overall goal of the subject matter and hence to real-world applications. Attention cylces during class requires the instructor to shift the activity level with preplanned brain-grabbing games several times per session. Some SALT instructors throw cushion balls at students to catch while expecting them to answer questions related to the material just learned. The system involves the engagement of the whole brain in the learning process through a balanced use of both right and left brain hemispheres. SALT and other similar peak performance learning systems may represent the new paradigm and classroom practice of the future. These techniques are reported to produce achievement results far beyond the old norms for instructional setting (Palmer 1990). The system is now being used in several classrooms around the world in subjects other than accounting. The effectiveness of this learning system has been officially acknowledged by UNESCO (United Nations Educational Scientific and Cultural Organization) as an important advance in education. It has been described as the key to 21st Century education.

Several major corporations (see appendix) are using the technique to enhance their training programs.

In an era when knowledge is growing at an exponential rate, a technique or system such as SALT that could help accounting students (and professionals) effortlessly assimilate information and comprehend rules, principles and techniques within a short period whilst leaving more time for educators to concentrate on real-world applications is priceless. The SALT system is known to make learning easier and up to five or more times faster than conventional teaching methods (Edwards 1980). The SALT system is being suggested as a possible viable alternative method that could enhance accounting education process as the profession is ushered into the 21st century. Empirical research of its application in the accounting curriculum needs to be undertaken in order to provide some guidance to accounting educators and professionals.

APPENDIX

Some of the major corporations and agencies using the SALT system:

ARAMCO
AT&T
Bell Telephone
Deloitte Touche
Delta Airlines
General Motors
Hilton Hotels
The US Department of Commerce
The US Department of State
The US Department of Defense
Shell Oil
NASA (to train astronauts)
British Airways
ICI
Kodak
Marconi Defence
British Airports Authority
Ciba-Geigy
Unigate 1st Ivel
Mann Egerton
Volkswagen Audi Group
British Coal
Dow Chemical
Metal Box
Lucas Aerospace
British Aerospace
Standard Telephones & Cable
Whitbread Ple

Source: *The Journal of the British Association for Commercial and Industrial Education*, February 1989.

REFERENCES

Accounting Education Change Commission. 1990. *Objectives of Education for Accountants.* Position Statement No. 1 (September).

Brislan, P. S. 1987. Music and Accelerated Learning: Some Historic and Current Applications. *Journal of the Society for Accelerated Learning and Teaching* 12(3&4): 115–139.

Cooter, S. 1980. Brain Lateralization and Lazanov Concerts. *Journal of the Society for Accelerative Learning and Teaching* 5(4): 261–266.

Diamond S. 1979. *Neuropsychology, A Textbook of Systems and Psychological Functions of the Human Brain.* London: Buttersworths.

Edwards, J. 1980. The Effects of SALT on Creativity. *Journal of the Society for Accelerative Learning and Teaching* 5(4): 235–253.

Lazanov, G. 1975. Suggestopedia in Primary Schools. *Suggestology and Suggestopedia* 1(2): 1–14.

———. 1981. *Suggestology and Outlines of Suggestopedy.* New York: Gordon and Breach.

Ornstein, R. 1977. *The Education of the Intuitive Mode, The Psychology of Consciousness.* London: Harcourt Brace.

Palmer, L. 1990. Education's Ecstasy Explosion: The Joyful Experience of Super-Accelerative Learning and Teaching. *Holistic Education Review* (Fall): 47–51.

Rose, C. 1989. *Accelerated Learning.* Aylesbury, Bucks, England: Accelerated Learning Systems Ltd.

Schuster, D. H. 1972. *Evaluation of the Lazanov Method for Teaching Beginning Spanish.* Unpublished manuscript, Iowa State University.

———. 1976. A Preliminary Evaluation of the Suggestive-Accelerative Lazanov Method in Teaching Beginning Spanish. *Journal of Suggestive-Accelerative Learning and Teaching* 1(1): 41–47.

Extraterrestrial Transport, Inc. (ET²): An Out-of-this-World Instructional Innovation for Teaching Management Accounting

Cathleen S. Burns and Sherry K. Mills

INTRODUCTION

The year is 2008. ELSIE, a lunar outpost constructed three years ago near the lunar south pole, has developed sufficiently to date to earn the "colony" status. Projects at the colony include the study of environmental issues in a closed-system biosphere, alternative energy supplies, and astronomy using telescopes located on the farside of the moon....

These words introduce an instructional innovation developed at New Mexico State University to prepare business students for the cost-conscious, quality-focused, team approach to 21st century technology management. As reflected in the accounting, education, management, and engineering literature, continuous improvement of business and project management education using innovative teaching is required for businesses to remain competitive in an increasingly global marketplace.

A list of concerns was assembled after reviewing literature critical of professional education. These concerns provided a foundation for the development of the instructional innovation:

1. Students must develop competence in managing **unstructured problems** in **unfamiliar settings** [Dewey, 1938; Bloom and Debessay, 1984; Cheit, 1985; Jaedicke, 1989].

2. Students should discover connections across the total college curriculum. Life is **interdisciplinary** and business problems do not come in single functional packages [Association of American Colleges, 1985; Boyer, 1987; Porter and McKibbin, 1988; Jaedicke, 1989].

3. **Writing across the curriculum** programs should not be isolated to the college of arts and sciences [Behrman & Levin, 1984; Association of American Colleges, 1985; Boyer, 1987; Porter and McKibbin, 1988]. **Reading and writing together prompt critical thinking** [Olson, 1984; Tierney, Soter, O'Flahavan and McGinley, 1989].

4. Students are not **challenged** by most of the business curriculum [Pierson, 1959].

5. Learning should be seen as a verb and not as a noun. **Active learning** is preferable to passive learning [Boyer, 1987; Porter and McKibbin, 1988; Sundem, Williams, and Chironna, 1990].

6. **Classroom techniques** that involve students include seminars, cases, simulations, and role-playing [Porter and McKibbin, 1988; Arthur Andersen & Co., Arthur Young, Coopers & Lybrand, Deloitte, Haskins & Sells, Ernst & Whinney, Peat Marwick Main & Co., Price Waterhouse, and Touche Ross, 1989; Sundem, Williams and Chironna, 1990].

7. Education in a **group process** teaches mutual accommodation and adaptation [Dewey, 1938; Boyer, 1987].

8. More emphasis needs to be placed on **quality cost systems** and **quality control** in the curriculum [Johnson and Winchell, 1988; Bateson, 1988; Guiffrida, 1990].

STATEMENT OF PURPOSE

The purpose of this paper is to describe an instructional innovation that can improve accounting and management skills of university business students. The innovation was designed to increase the students' knowledge of

- The importance of **cost accounting** in the decision-making process.

- The skills necessary to synthesize contributions by interdisciplinary project **team** members.

- **Critical thinking** about situations and **written** responses to questions.

- The importance of preventive planning and conformance to requirements for safety and high **quality** products and services.

- The **commercialization** of **space**.

Cathleen S. Burns, C.P.A., doctoral student and Sherry K. Mills, Ph.D., C.P.A. are both at New Mexico State University.

To increase the students' appreciation of potential 21st century managerial challenges, a lunar base setting was selected. The setting provides a stimulating, future-focused scenario rich in uncertainties and technology issues that should inspire university educators as well as their students. The experiences of a fictitious business, Extraterrestrial Transport, Inc. (ET²), act as catalysts for achieving the course objectives.

The remainder of the paper is divided into four sections. The first section includes an overview of the instructional innovation. The second section describes, in detail, the instructional innovation. The third section discusses future plans to expand the instructional innovation. The last section suggests an action plan to integrate instructional innovations into the college curriculum.

OVERVIEW OF THE INSTRUCTIONAL INNOVATION

This innovation was used in a required management accounting course for approximately 400 nonaccounting business majors. The college administration requested changes in teaching style and course requirements because the course had been problematic for both the students and the instructors. Historically, the students considered the course to be irrelevant to the anticipated roles they would assume after graduation. The students' negative attitudes diminished the instructors' willingness to teach this course. In addition, the content and traditional teaching style of the course failed to communicate the strategic role that accountants play in project team management. Instead, the students became lost in the calculations normally performed by professional cost accountants.

With this in mind, the authors developed the following mission statement for the course:

> The mission of the course is to **challenge** students with innovative classroom processes to **actively develop critical thinking**, using **group processes** and **reading and writing** assignments. **Management accounting** and **quality cost** topics will provide the content area for the development of these skills.

The desired outcomes for the course included the **personal**, **academic**, and **professional** growth of each student. Students should gain the increased confidence that they can handle the **interdisciplinary, unstructured problems** of tomorrow's **unfamiliar organizational settings**.

The experience-driven curriculum for the course established an interactive classroom learning environment. The format of the course was less formal, more unstructured. The instructors participated as coaches guiding students in the active learning process. Students succeeded in the course by reflecting on knowledge gained through their personal learning experiences and by researching open-ended, loosely structured questions that required an understanding of business process issues. Reworking assignments was encouraged for partial credit. Exams included problem solving and written responses; multiple choice questions were not used. Students and instructors received frequent feedback from each other throughout the semester.

THE INSTRUCTIONAL INNOVATION

This section is divided into two subsections. The first subsection describes the two phases of the innovation. The second subsection provides some preliminary indicators of success in achieving the objectives of the innovation and some of the authors' perceptions.

The Two Phases of the Instructional Innovation:

There were two phases to the project. The first phase provided experiences to prepare students for the ET² cohesion case. The first phase was necessary because the learning process in this course was different from most courses. Different skills were required for students to be successful. The second phase of the course was the ET² cohesion case. The cohesion case provided a single, flexible context in which students could understand the consequences of their decisions in an organizational setting.

The discussion that follows will be presented in two phases:

Phase One—Preparing Students

- Developing student teams.
- Developing a sensitivity to quality issues.
- Developing an understanding of manufacturing excellence.

Phase Two—Cohesion Case

- ET², a fictional manufacturer of lunar transportation vehicles in the year 2008.

Phase One—Preparing the Students

Developing student teams. The authors assumed that the students' past experiences in group work in academic courses were limited. The instructors formed student teams reflecting a balance of past academic performance, work experience, age and gender. A commercially available survival situation (Human Synergistics 1987) provided an introduction to group thinking and interpersonal skills. The relative importance of survival items was ranked individually by team members. These same survival items were ranked several different times by the team. Audiotapes of the team decision-making sessions were evaluated for potential improvement of the team's thinking and interpersonal skills. A memo summarizing the team development process was prepared by each team. Students provided feedback on evaluation forms to the instructors about the ways in which the survival experience developed them personally, academically, and professionally.

A sensitivity to quality issues. The authors believed that students should appreciate the role of quality in their personal, academic and professional lives as a result of their undergraduate learning experience. Students were required to read selections from *Quality without Tears* and *Quality Is Free*, by the popular American quality expert, Phillip B. Crosby. The role of the accountant in developing a quality cost system emerged in the course of the readings.

A series of three Public Broadcasting Service (PBS) programs, "Quality...or Else," provided an independent reinforcement of Crosby's philosophy. The PBS programs reflected the need for corporations competing in the global marketplace to achieve quality in all their business functions. Students prepared essays on the Crosby readings and a written summary of one of the PBS programs. After being sensitized to quality issues, students prepared a self-evaluation about the ways in which this experience developed them personally, academically, and professionally.

Manfacturing excellence. Videos on manufacturing excellence in leading-edge companies reinforced the concepts of teamwork quality, and updating cost management systems to reflect technological progress. Students prepared short summaries of the video programs as well as questions appropriate for informational interviewing.

In conclusion, the authors believe that using a developmental team exercise, readings, and video programs prepared students for the quality and production process issues they would confront individually, and as a team, in the cohesion case that followed.

Phase Two — The Cohesion Case, Extraterrestrial Transport, Inc. (ET²)

The lunar base setting was created by extrapolating relevant information about the moon from the proceedings of Space 88 [Johnson & Wetzel, 1988] and Space 90 [Johnson & Wetzel, 1990], NASA publications and other popular space-related publications. Extraterrestrial Transport, Inc. (ET²), a fictional company, was established to design and manufacture lunar construction and transportation vehicles. Three vehicles were constructed by ET² in two assembly plants located in two different cities.

The cohesion case included seven, 75-minute classes:

1. Introduction to the lunar base setting and ET²'s products.
2. Product costing elements and how the product costs enter the accounting system.
3. Master budgeting process and performance reports.
4. Variance analysis.
5. Product profitability.
6. Short-term decision making.
7. Long-term decision making.

Students purchased a 66-page cohesion case guide that included

1. Background information on ET² written in a narrative describing various product attributes that reflect factual aspects of the harsh lunar environment.
2. Plant layouts for two assembly plants.
3. Product cost information for three products;
4. Additional quantitative information necessary for budgeting, reporting and decision-making.
5. Calculations of basic management accounting concepts.

An essential component of the experiential learning process was the construction of the lunar transportation vehicles using LEGO[R] building blocks. Blocks representing standard and nonstandard material were used to illustrate cost and quality concepts.

Each of the seven classes is outlined below. The description of each class includes the accounting concepts or quality issues addressed, any experiential exercises employed, and individual student or team assignments.

Class one: An introduction to ET². Business students should understand the environments in which organizations, such as ET², compete, and in which their products, such as lunar vehicles, perform. During the first class, a slide presentation of artists' renditions of the lunar base visually introduced the students to the lunar base setting. The slides emphasized the moon's harsh environment and the many opportunities for businesses to create products and services required by a lunar base.

At the completion of the slide show, students built the short distance transport (SDT) product with LEGO[R] building blocks while the instructor reviewed cost elements, inventories, and potential causes of variance. At the end of class, students summarized their learning experiences for the day on a 3 × 5" index card.

Class two: Elements of product cost and the accounting system. Before the second class, students were asked to review the bills of material, operations sheets, and a summary of how direct labor and materials costs were determined. At the beginning of class two, each student received an unassembled SDT with pictorial instructions to be used with their ET^2 packet of information. Using a discussion format, the instructors reviewed how materials were purchased, inventoried, and delivered to the production floor. At each step of the process, the class decided which paperwork flow and detail were necessary for the product cost accounting system to be updated properly. A discussion of the effects of errors and omissions on the quality of the accounting information ensued.

Then, students used visual and written instructions to partially assemble a SDT. The students completed a job cost sheet for the SDT using the partially assembled product, the bill of material and the operations sheet. Additional information about labor and overhead was provided. A three-sentence summary card was prepared by students to provide the instructor with feedback about their learning experiences.

Class three: The master budget. Included in the ET^2 packet are sales, direct materials, direct labor, other expenses, and cash budgets for the three products and two plant locations. The flow of expenses from one budget to the next was illustrated.

The teams prepared a budgeted income statement with all the supporting schedules for one of the production plants that manufactured two products. The teams had to reconcile differences about what types of expenses were included in each account and under what classification the accounts could appear on an income statement. The income statement provided cost classifications to be used later in the class on decision-making.

Class four: Variance analysis. To gain a better understanding of the production process, a production line was created in the classroom to assemble

ten SDT products with zero defects. The students participated as assemblers, material handlers, and inventory control. The instructors assumed the roles of supervisor and quality control. The remaining students timed the assembly operations and kept track of the numerous problems that occurred. Broken, missing, duplicate, and incorrect materials were introduced into the production process at various times. The production area was poorly laid out on purpose and workers were poorly trained. Zero-defect yield rates for the production lines ranged from a low of 30 percent to a high of 60 percent.

The teams were required to write a report explaining the types of variance that were generated, whose reponsiblity it would be to correct the material and process problems, and what role accounting could play in facilitating future zero-defect production. The students individually prepared price and usage variances for the substitution of a cheaper transport part that consistently broke when the product was assembled.

Class five: Product probability. Students prepared a budgeted direct costing income statement from the absorption income statement prepared as a team in class three. Contribution margins and break-even points were calculated for two products manufactured in one plant. One of the products was intentionally designed to contribute much more to the fixed cost coverage than the other product. Students were directed to the role of product contribution margins in decision-making.

Class six: Short-term decision making. The instructors reviewed six short-term decision making problems in class. The problems included whether to make or buy materials, how to handle capacity constraints, alternative segment margin scenarios, and whether to accept a special sales order at a price less than the standard price. The students identified three short-term decisions that might confront ET^2's management. Reports were prepared by the students that listed the quantitative and qualitative information needed for the decision, sources of that information, and the context in which ET^2 would make such a decision.

Class seven: Long-term decision making. The ET^2 packet includes a capital budgeting illustration involving the recommendation of an automated materials handling system as a substitute for the direct labor material handling demonstrated in class four. Both qualitative and quantitative aspects of the capital budgeting project were emphasized. The role of automatic material handling systems to prevent damage was stressed.

Preliminary Indicators of Success and Instructors' Observations

Preliminary indicators of success have been limited to the instructors' observations and frequent student feedback.

Positive feedback received from the students included the following:

- The team experiences helped improve interpersonal skills.

- The visualization of accounting concepts by using the LEGO[R] construction blocks improved comprehension.

- The recognition of the "big picture" where accounting, quality, production and engineering were interrelated was valuable.

- Preparing the budgeted income statement aided understanding of the total budgeting process.

Negative feedback received from the students included the following:

- The difficulty in finding an acceptable meeting time or managing an apathetic teammate in the group assignments.

- Intentional uncertainty built into some instructions for assignments.

- Lack of a standard text that illustrated explicitly how to do the assignments.

- The significant amount of time taken by writing assignments.

Compared to the authors' past experience teaching this course, class attendance was higher, course withdrawals were fewer, and an open, active learning environment was maintained in the classroom. The authors noted a higher personal commitment by the students to achieve quality in their overall academic performance.

The combination of the lunar base setting and the transportation vehicles assembled from LEGO[R] construction blocks aroused student curiosity. The personal involvement of constructing the vehicles helped students to "see" variances being created, and to "see" the activities that drive the variances.

The authors developed a writing-intensive course to improve students' communication and thinking skills. The cognitive skills that were addressed in assignments included deductive reasoning, abstract reasoning, reading comprehension, argumentation, and data analysis. Frequent writing assignments, specific and detailed instructor or peer critique feedback, and rewrite opportunities provided a process for the continuous improvement of students' writing skills. The amount of time required by the authors to provide this feedback was extensive despite page limitations for assignments.

The authors decreased the structure of assignments as the semester progressed in order to give students a sense of the uncertainty in assignments that can exist in the marketplace. This approach, combined with the retention of very little knowledge from a prerequisite course (a 45 percent average pretest score), caused anxiety and frustration in the students. Students were referred to pages in a supplementary textbook but seemed burdened by using a textbook as a resource, not as a learning process. The instructors had to generate supplemental information and show students how to use the textbook as a resource, not as a book of examples to be mimicked with different numbers.

One other observation made by the authors is that students' success in accounting is often dependent upon their attitude towards accounting and its role in organizations. Students commented that as a result of the course, they understood the important role of accounting and wished they could retake their earlier accounting courses. The authors recommend that additional time be spent in introductory accounting classes carefully developing an interesting, dynamic role for accounting before presenting accounting techniques.

EXPANSION PLANS

The flexible framework of the ET^2 cohesion case is purposefully designed for expansion. The cohesion case background information introduces the existence of competition, future negotiations for Mars colony transportation contracts, availability of nearby maquiladora industries, and other complex financial and managerial issues.

Other accounting courses could benefit from additional development of the cohesion case. For example, an assignment in a recent accounting systems course required for senior accounting majors was to design a cost reporting system for incoming materials using spreadsheet software. The students met the challenge by submitting projects that reflected a significant time investment in understanding programming code limitations while balancing management's demands on the accounting system.

Using a space technology theme could potentially increase interdepartment and intercollegiate collaboration. Space commercialization issues could be developed by the engineering, physical and social sciences, and business colleges. Traditional business functions and potential topics that could be developed around a space commercialization theme include:

- Marketing — Transportation and distribution.
- Finance — Investment risk and analysis.
- Management — Optimal project scheduling.
- Business Law — Commercial space business law.
- Accounting — Consistent proposal-to-delivery cost management systems.

ESSENTIALS FOR FUTURE SUCCESS

The initial design of this course has taken almost seven months of full-time development work by two individuals. Without the support of university administration for research funding and their encouragement for innovation, this course would not exist. In order for this innovation and other innovations to develop successfully, the authors suggest the following action plan:

- Provide a reward structure that recognizes innovative teaching.
- Provide release time and funding to develop and improve courses.
- Provide funding for instructors to attend conferences about leading-edge issues that can be disseminated among the faculty and in the classroom.

- Provide grading assistance for writing intensive courses.
- Limit class size to 30 students.
- Encourage team teaching.
- Support the development of a curriculum that develops specific thinking and writing skills in all courses.

SUMMARY

Potential employers describe the ideal business graduate as one who possesses not only technical expertise but also leadership abilities, superior communication skills and experience working on interdisciplinary teams [Bedford, 1986; Porter and McKibbin, 1988; Arthur Andersen et al., 1989]. This paper has introduced an instructional innovation for use in management accounting courses. The goals of this course were to increase the student's awareness of the role of accounting and quality in organizations while improving interpersonal, writing and thinking skills through active learning and alternative classroom techniques. The cohesion case, Extraterrestrial Transport, Inc. (ET[2]), encourages the critical thinking of 21st century employees by providing a setting where some of our Earth rules of thumb work, and others do not. The expansion of instructional innovations depends on the commitment of university administrators to quality throughout the business curriculum. This course is a first step.

REFERENCES

Association of American Colleges. 1985. *Integrity in the College Curriculum: A Report to the Academic Community.* Washington, D.C.: Association of American Colleges.

Arthur Andersen & Co., Arthur Young, Coopers & Lybrand, Deloitte Haskins & Sells, Ernst & Whinney, Peat Marwick Main & Co., Price Waterhouse, & Touche Ross. 1989. *Perspectives in Education: Capabilities for Success in the Accounting Profession* (April): 1-15.

Bateson, R. G. 1988. Discovered: Quality's Missing Link. *Quality Progress* (October): 61-64.

Bedford, N. 1986. Future Accounting Education: Preparing for the Expanding Profession. *Issues in Accounting Education* Vol. 1, No. 1: 168-195.

Behrman, J. N., and R. I. Levin. 1984. Special Report: Are Business Schools Doing their Job? *Harvard Business Review* (Jan-Feb): 140-147.

Bloom R., and A. Debassay. 1984. Educating Professional Accountants for the Twenty-first Century: A Point of View. *Journal of Business Education* (January): 159-162.

Boyer, E. L. 1987. *College: The Undergraduate Experience in America.* NY: Harper & Row.

Cheit, E. F. 1985. Business Schools and Their Critics. *California Management Review* Vol. 27, No. 3: 43-62.

Crosby, P. 1984). *Quality Without Tears.* New York: McGraw-Hill.

————. 1979. *Quality is Free.* New York: McGraw-Hill.

Dewey, J. 1938. *Experience and Education.* NY: Collier Books.

Guiffrida, A. L. 1990. QA Education in the Business School: Practitioners' Views. *Quality Progress* (May): 87-89.

Human Synergistics. 1987. Cascades Survival Situation. Plymouth, MI: (313)-459-1030.

Jaedicke, R. K. 1989. *Presentation to the AACSB*, Annual Meeting, (April 16-19).

Johnson, R. H., and W. O. Winchell. 1988. Education for Quality: A Different Approach. *Quality Progress* (September): 48-50.

Johnson, S. W., and J. P. Wetzel. 1988. Engineering, Construction and Operations in Space. *American Society of Civil Engineers Space ('88) Proceeedings.* New York.

————.(1990. Engineering, Construction and Operations in Space. *American Society of Civil Engineeers Space ('90) Proceedings.* New York.

NASA. 1990. *Report of the Advisory Committee on the Future of the U.S. Space Program.* Washington, D.C.

Olson, C. B. 1984. Fostering Critical Thinking Skills through Writing. *Educational Leadership* Vol. 42, No. 3: 28-39.

Pierson, F. 1959. *The Education of American Businessmen.* NY:McGraw Hill.

Porter, L. W., and L. E. McKibbin. 1988. *Management Education and Development: Drift or Thrust into the 21st Century?* New York: McGraw-Hill, Inc.

Shenkir, W. G. 1990. Forces for Change in Business Education: Accountability, Diversity, and Breadth. Charlottesville, VA: University of Virginia: 1-20.

Sundem, G. L., D. Z. Williams, and J. F. Chironna. 1990. The Revolution in Accounting Education. *Management Accounting* (December): 49-53.

Tierney, R. J., A. Soter, J. F. O'Flahavan, and W. McGinley. 1989. The Effects of Reading and Writing upon Thinking Critically. *Reading Research Quarterly* Vol. 24, No. 2: 134-169.

Teaching Abroad: How to Develop a Summer International Accounting Program

Michael F. Cornick

The American Accounting Association and the AACSB have both called for the increased internationalization of accounting curricula in order to better prepare students for careers in the global business environment. Schools have usually addressed the international question by either introducing international topics in all accounting courses or by creating a specific international accounting course. While both approaches have advantages and disadvantages, they have as a weakness the lack of exposure to a foreign setting, both culturally and in a business sense. To eliminate this weakness, schools can develop international accounting courses to be taught abroad. While a study abroad program can take several forms such as summer, semester, or year long, the summer program offers several advantages such as limited disruption of normal activities for both students and faculty directors, allowance of enough time for students to become familiar with the host country without suffering severe homesickness, and the availability of host school faculties because many possible host schools are on break during much of the summer. Thus, because of its advantages, it is the purpose of this paper to describe how to establish a summer international accounting course abroad.

Development of an overseas accounting program begins with a well-thought-out proposal which should include

(a) Information regarding the targeted audience

(b) Course and program descriptions

(c) A listing of reference material for the course

(d) The place of study

(e) The dates of the program

(f) Estimated program costs

Information regarding the targeted audience is the starting point because this determines the course content. If, for example, only accounting majors are to be in the course, then it can be rather technical in nature. However, if business majors are to be included, then a more general approach would be appropriate.

Creating the course and program descriptions, while considering the target audience, should include details such as the accounting course syllabus, business field trips, business lectures by host school faculty, and the cultural aspects of the course. One method of including the cultural areas of the program is to offer two courses: an international accounting course and a second course which could be a history/culture or language/culture course, depending on the program's location.

In reviewing the course location, one should consider several factors:

(a) Facilities

(b) Proximity to business community

(c) Proximity to cultural activities

(d) Availability of public transportation

(e) Ease of traveling to and from the program site

(f) Host site faculty

When appraising facilities, one must consider housing, dining areas, and classroom space. Housing can essentially be one of three types: dormitory, hotel, or a host family. Dormitory space is usually available and reasonably priced because foreign schools are often closed during part of the summer for vacation. However, if complete cultural immersion is a goal, then having students live with host families may work well. As stated earlier, many schools are closed for part of the summer. Consequently, use of the host school dining facilities may be limited or not available. Thus, the director should make every effort to locate good but reasonably priced restaurants. Classrooms will probably be a basic college lecture room with a small chalkboard. If computers are needed, the director should investigate the availability of such equipment.

Michael F. Cornick is an Associate Professor at the University of North Carolina at Charlotte.

Since the program is business oriented, proximity to the business community is important. Major international accounting firms are excellent resources for lectures, office visits, and the arranging of visits to manufacturers. These firms are eager to assist the academic community and a call to the local domestic office will begin the process. Finally, visits to business or accounting offices will be easier to arrange if the program is in a major business center.

Along with proximity to business, proximity to cultural activities is also important. Seeing the sights and being able to participate in cultural activities are two of the main reasons for offering the study abroad program. If students do not have access to cultural events, or if they must travel long distances to the events, then a study abroad program loses much of its appeal.

While seemingly trivial, the availability of public transportation is important. Most students will want to do some traveling and if the program location is in a rural area, public transportation may not be readily available which will, in turn, result in students renting cars for travel. Needless to say, this practice can be dangerous and a real worry for the director.

The host location should be one where travel time to and from the United States location to the host location is kept to a minimum. The greater the overland travel time as well as the number of transfers, then the greater is the risk of losing baggage or equipment as well as the increased likelihood students will be overly tired and irritable.

Finally, if the program is located at a foreign college or university, one should meet and work with the host faculty. These people can be a valuable resource for lectures, community information, and in this day of higher research expectations, colleagues with whom one can conduct research.

After the preliminary program development, one should meet with the campus study abroad coordinator to learn of schools with relationships with the United States school and to work out specific details of the program and budget.

Relationships with schools can range from the relatively informal to those having specific written agreements. It is quite likely that one of the schools where a relationship exists will become the host school for the accounting program. If no foreign school relationships exist at the United States school, or if those that do exist are inappropriate for a business program, then the study abroad coordinator can provide assistance in establishing a suitable relationship.

The study abroad coordinator can also explain specific budgetary details and method of payment for the director. Some schools may opt to pay the program director a salary while other schools prefer to have the director's expenses paid directly from program fees. If the latter is the case, then the program must have 12 to 15 students for the program to be financially feasible for the director. Additionally, the study abroad coordinator will explain the duties and responsibilities of being a director. Finally, the study abroad office will be happy to assist in the marketing of the program.

With specific program details finalized, one can begin marketing the program. Marketing activity, including the preparation of brochures, should begin early in the Fall semester. This early activity provides students with time to plan their summer schedule, consult with parents, and obtain financing. Various techniques can be used including study abroad fairs, class announcements, program presentations to student groups, letters to students in the target group, and contacts with faculty at neighboring schools. One valuable marketing resource will be the use of students who have participated in study abroad programs. These students are usually quite excited about study abroad and are very willing to tell others about their study abroad experiences. Moreover, these students can provide prospective participants with the "student" perspective.

Regardless of the marketing technique adopted, students will want to know about finances. To help reduce student costs, scholarship money should be made available. Various departments or colleges in the United States school as well as federal and state agencies may be able to provide scholarship money. A commitment for scholarship money should be obtained as early as possible so students can be made aware of scholarship availability and application procedures.

After student fees and applications have been received and it has been determined the program will be offered the director then will be concerned with three areas of student support activities. These activities consist of the pre-departure orientation, in-country support, and the re-entry orientation.

First, all outgoing study abroad participants should attend a pre-departure orientation, usually conducted by the program director and, if possible, the study abroad coordinator. This activity includes culture-specific information: details on travel, housing, meals, medical care, finances, communication with home, course registration, credit transfer, academic expectations, books and information on culture shock and culture — general adjustment tips.

Second, while abroad, students should be provided with on-site support by the program director and/or a designated individual at the host institution. This person should be available to assist with academic expectations, local housing, meal and travel arrangements, medical emergencies, and adjustment problems. In addition to teaching, this person should also attend group functions such as field trips to business and cultural sites.

Finally, there should be some form of re-entry orientation. For summer school students, this may be nothing more than obtaining program evalua-

tions and finalizing administrative details such as the reporting of grades.

In conclusion, the study of international accounting abroad can be an exciting and interesting experience for both the students and the director. Studying accounting abroad enriches students culturally while better preparing them for careers in the competitive and demanding world of business. Directors also will find the program worthwhile as they have the opportunity to travel and teach abroad while at the same time developing contacts for international research.

Gute Reise, Bon Voyage, Buon Viaggie, Have a good trip.

Teaching "The Language of Business" as a Language: An Audio Approach to Elementary Accounting

Curtis L. DeBerg

If the "attrition rate" in a course is defined to be the sum of the students who withdraw and who receive grades of D and F, and then dividing this total by the number of students enrolled in the course at the beginning of the term, many elementary accounting instructors likely would calculate an attrition rate of 40 percent or more. Such has been the case at the three universities where I have taught, namely Oklahoma State University, Arizona State University, and now California State University, Chico. This should be a troubling statistic in an era in which accounting educators have expressed concern that many of the best students enrolled in introductory accounting courses — potential accounting majors — are choosing other disciplines. This paper provides strong evidence that the teaching materials used in elementary accounting, and the manner in which these materials are used, are not effective in (1) preventing students from withdrawing from the course or receiving failing grades and (2) stimulating bright students who might choose to major in accounting if presented in a livelier and more interesting way.

This paper describes a supplementary instructional resource that has potential to reduce the attrition rate and attract students into the accounting major. Specifically, an audio approach is described that attempts to relate "the language of business" as a language. The high attrition rate usually observed in the first accounting course at community colleges and universities make it clear that many students view accounting as a *foreign language*. My experience with this approach indicates that the audio medium can be effective in reaching students who learn best with an auditory approach.

The remainder of this paper is organized into five sections. The first section describes the need for new materials at the elementary level. Results of two surveys demonstrate that innovative, improved instructional materials are badly needed. The second section reviews literature from other disciplines which shows that the audio medium can be helpful to certain students.

The third section describes my response to the documented need for new and improved materials. I have authored, edited, and produced an audiotutorial entitled *How to Pass Principles of Accounting I.*[1] This section describes the tutorial and provides examples of narrative and supplementary printed materials as excerpted from Topic 1. The fourth section describes how the audio tutor has been received in its first semester of publication. Finally, section five concludes the paper.

THE NEED FOR NEW MATERIALS

Jensen (1990, p. 172) criticized the major participants in the instructional materials market—namely, authors, publishers, and the educators who choose to use extant materials without questioning their effectiveness. He said, "Perhaps it is the fault of authors who refuse to accept the risks of innovation. Perhaps it is the fault of publishers who homogenize their textbooks by reference to shallow or short-sighted marketing strategies. Perhaps it is the fault of instructors who do not demand new and innovative material. The explanation for the failure of the market to provide the needed instructional materials may be a combination of all these factors."

Jensen encouraged individual educators to develop innovative ideas and materials for meeting the crisis in instructional materials. His concerns are shared by the Accounting Education Change Commission (AECC 1990). One of the primary charges of the AECC is to serve as a catalyst to bring about demonstrable improvements in the education of accountants through curriculum restructur-

[1]Though the title may suggest that students may use the audiotutorial as a substitute for going to class, it is emphasized on the tapes that the audiotutorial is not a substitute for going to class. Further, students are informed that the only way to master accounting is to always attend class, take good notes, and do the homework.

Curtis L. DeBerg is Associate Professor of Accounting at California State University, Chico.

ing, alternative education processes, and *development of new and different education materials.* Special focus was given the introductory courses (AECC 1990, 309): "The introductory accounting course should be given special attention. It must serve the interests of students who are not going to enter the profession as well as those who are. The broad approach recommended in these objectives serves the interests and needs of both groups."

Further evidence supporting the need for change comes from public accounting firms. In its April 1989 white paper, the (then) Big Eight public accounting firms issued *Perspectives on Education: Capabilities for Success in the Accounting Profession* (Arthur Andersen et al. 1989). This paper discussed changes in the current curriculum as follows: "Basing pre-entry education on capabilities will mean fundamental changes in the curriculum. The current textbook-based, rule-intensive, lecture/problem style should not survive as the primary means of presentation. New methods, both those used in other disciplines and those that are totally new to university education, must be explored. Creative use of information technology will be essential" (p. 11).

The "Market" Survey

My initial response to the call for new materials was focused on the course I was teaching at the time— Intermediate Accounting II. In previous semesters, I had noticed a trend in my classes. More and more students were bringing hand-held tape players to class to record the lectures. As a result, several 30-minute, polished lectures were produced on the more difficult topics (e.g., bonds, leases, pensions, deferred taxes, cash flows) to supplement the required textbook and instructor handouts. Student response was favorable. Approximately half the intermediate students came to my office, borrowed the master tapes, and recorded them at home.

Encouraged by the initial response to the audiotutorial at the intermediate level, I conducted a survey of 745 students enrolled in introductory financial and managerial accounting in the Spring 1990 semester at Arizona State University. This survey asked students the following four questions (among others):

1. What materials or services did you purchase for this course, other than the textbook (circle those that you bought)?

    a. Study guide

    b. Scorebuilder

    c. Working papers

    d. Lecture/Discussion notes

    e. Hired a personal tutor

    f. Other

2. Which of the above materials were the most helpful?

3. Assume that there were a product on the market called *How to Pass Principles of Accounting I* consisting of four 60-minute audiocassette tapes which covered all major topics covered in this course [a description of the product followed]. If such a product existed, please check the statement which best applies to you:

    _____ I would strongly consider buying it, no matter what the price.

    _____ I would strongly consider buying it, if the price were reasonable.

    _____ I would consider buying it, but I would need to see the product first.

    _____ I would not consider buying it.

4. What grade do you expect to receive in the course?

Results of the survey showed that

*   The average student bought just over two additional study items but responded that he/she found *less than one* of them to be very helpful.

*   63 percent of the students bought the textbook study guide, with only half these students responding that they found it to be very helpful.

*   31 percent of the students bought scorebuilder, but only one in five of these students found it to be very helpful.

*   7.5% of the students hired a personal tutor.

*   51 percent of the students said they would strongly consider buying an audiocassette study guide. This percentage increases to 88 percent when including students who responded that they would consider buying if they first saw the product.

*   Even though the title of the album is *How to Pass Principles of Accounting I*, the single largest category of buyers who would strongly consider buying the audio study guide were making a B grade (21 percent). Table 1 provides a table comparing "buying decision" with "expected grade."

TABLE 1
A Comparison of "Buying Decision" to "Expected Grade"

Buying Decision	Expected Grade					Not Reported	Totals (%)
	A	**B**	**C**	**D**	**F**		
Strongly Consider — Price No Consideration	1	18	18	2	0	3	42 (5.64)
Strongly Consider — Price a Consideration	43	141	123	7	1	34	349 (46.85)
Consider — Must See First	55	97	85	6	0	23	266 (35.70)
No Consider	38	22	12	1	0	15	88 (11.81)
Totals (%)	137 (18.39)	278 (37.32)	238 (31.95)	16 (2.15)	1 (0.13)	75 (10.07)	745 (100.0)

It should be noted that the survey was taken on the last day of regularly scheduled classes, indicating that the survey results are biased *downward*. That is, the survey does not include students who had withdrawn from the course. These students potentially could have benefited the most from the audiotutor.

Results of the market survey should send two powerful messages to introductory accounting instructors, as well as authors and publishers of the supplemental materials accompanying textbooks. First, most introductory accounting students are not benefiting from current supplementary materials. Second, even the good students are seeking improved study materials.

A Second Survey

A survey by Adams et al. (1991) emits alarming signals for accounting education and practitioners. The longitudinal study involved the administration of the AICPA aptitude test to 256 beginning accounting students at California State University, Chico during the Fall 1988 and Spring 1989 semesters. At the end of the semester, a questionnaire was administered. Results indicate that

- Introductory accounting students selecting accounting as a major scored very high on the aptitude test, indicating that accounting is initially attracting "quality" students.

- Although accounting is attracting high-aptitude students, only about **17** percent of the students scoring in the top quartile on the aptitude test

select accounting as their major, indicating a possible quantity problem.

- The accounting program tends to lose high-aptitude and attract lower-aptitude students during the junior and senior years, substantiating the concerns of many that the current curriculum may be attracting a lower-aptitude student.

- Students selecting the accounting major are far more concerned with the availability of jobs in the area of their major than are the rest of the introductory accounting students. In contrast, nonaccounting students scoring in the top quartile place far more emphasis on pursuing a major of genuine interest to themselves than do either accounting majors or other majors scoring lower on the aptitude test.

Overall, the results of this survey suggest that the accounting profession may be able to attract larger numbers of "quality" students if the accounting curriculum and faculty are able to portray accounting as an interesting and intellectually stimulating profession. Clearly, this is not currently the case.[2]

---

[2] Doyle Williams, who was on campus in late September, 1990, is president of the AECC. He recounted a story about a principles of accounting student who was enrolled in his class a couple years ago. She had done well in the class— so well, in fact, that she made the top score in his class. But she did not continue on in accounting. "Why?" Williams asked. Her reply: "I sat through a whole semester of accounting and, even though I did well, I refuse to do that to myself again. Quite frankly, I'd rather have my wisdom teeth pulled."

A REVIEW OF EDUCATION LITERATURE FROM OTHER DISCIPLINES

Kozma (1991) reviewed research on learning with books, television, computers, and multimedia environments. The main advantage of books as a learning medium, of course, is that orthographic symbols are fixed. Audiotapes and lecture media (e.g., speech) may convey the same linguistic information but utilize a different symbol system in a transient way. It is the stability of text that allows readers to slow their rate of progression or reread certain passages, something that is difficult or impossible to do with audio.

Research about learning from text with pictures, rather than from straight text is in general agreement that the use of pictures with text increases recall, particularly of poor readers. For example, a study by Kuntz et al. (1989) used university students majoring in either geography or social sciences to test whether visual aids helped comprehension of concepts and rules on meteorology. Results showed that students with little prior knowledge benefited most from the pictures, while students with sufficient prior domain knowledge relied instead on their own well-developed mental models to help them understand the text.

A study by Greeno (1989) described a framework whereby mental representations, or mental models, are derived from symbolic notations that "correspond to real world objects and events and their abstractions" (Kozma, p. 187). Kozma (p. 188) agreed with this framework. "Too often, in school learning, these mental objects and operations have little correspondence to real world objects, events, and their abstractions and map only onto the symbolic domains from which they were derived.[3]

Learning with television combines audio and video symbol systems, but because these systems are transient, students may process this information very differently than the book medium. Most studies showed that the combined use of visual and auditory systems resulted in more recall than visual-only and audio-only formats. Though the visual component is usually more memorable, the audio component carries information about sounds and expressive language that helps interpret visual information. When auditory systems are used alone, learners must draw primarily on prior knowledge for a construction of the situation model.

Kozma suggested that people who are very knowledgeable about a particular domain would probably find textual material sufficient. However, novices to a domain are more likely to benefit from the ability to slow the rate of information processing with a text supplemented with pictures. But what about learners moderately familiar with a topic? Audio and video symbol systems "can supply complementary information particularly useful in constructing a situation model, and its normal pace will accommodate comprehension" (Kozma, p. 195).

Kozma also reviewed studies of learning with computers and multimedia (e.g., videodiscs), whose interactive capabilities can be integrated with textual, audio, and video media to help learners connect their knowledge of their domain.

The overall question posed by Kozma was: Do media influence learning? Based on his extensive review of the literature, he concluded:

> Some students will learn a particular task regardless of delivery device. Others will be able to take advantage of a particular medium's characteristics to help construct knowledge. . . . Some learners rely on pictures to help construct a textbase and map it onto a model of the situation; others can provide the model form information in memory and do not need pictures or find audio presentations sufficient (p. 205).

The audiotutorial instructional technique has been successful in helping students learn in other disciplines. Four articles and one book are reviewed here to show how these techniques are being used.[4] The first two articles present the results of audiotutorial experiments with animal biology students. The last two articles discuss the use of instructional video and videodisc technology, respectively. Finally, a book by Page Smith is briefly addressed.

Audio Studies — Studies by Rowsey and Mason (1975) and Khan (1980) were similar in that both investigated whether the audiotutorial (A-T)

---

[3]The Scheiner et al. (1988) database of education research abstracts was used to search the education literature related to audio and audiovisual instructional aids. I searched under the keywords "auditory," "audio," "audiovisual," and "video." Three of the four articles reviewed in this section were found through this search. The fourth article (Kumar 1990) was found by manually searching the relevant journals, as suggested in the database search, from 1987 to August 1991.

[4]Some critics of the "traditional" elementary accounting sequence in place at most universities have argued that much of what is taught at this level has little or no external validity. For example, Baldwin and Ingram (1991, p. 5) stated that "currently, a great deal of time is spent on trivial issues that have little effect on the use of accounting information. Moreover, they argued that "a whole host of managerial accounting issues are proving to be of little value or to be dysfunctional in many organizations."

method of instruction (i.e., the experimental group) resulted in improved student learning as compared to the conventional lecture-laboratory method (i.e., the control group).

Rowsey and Mason (1975) used introductory animal biology students at Auburn University as subjects. The experimental group was composed of 134 students, and the control group contained 190 students. Subjects in the experimental group received an A-T approach to the course. This approach was based on the normal lecture/lab components of the course, but topics were integrated into 18 separate exercises. Lectures and directions to students were prepared and recorded on standard cassette tapes.

An achievement test developed by qualified experts in biology was used to compare student learning in both groups. This test was administered three times: at the beginning of the course, near the completion of the course, and 11 weeks after the course had ended. The second test was administered to measure immediate achievement and the third test was administered to measure *retention*. A *t*-test comparison between experimental and control group test scores on the first test showed no significant differences between groups.

T-test comparisons between the first and second test scores and the first and third test scores, however, yielded significant results (p < .01). The group taught by the A-T method made significantly higher scores than the traditional lecture group in both cases.

Khan (1980) tested a small sample of 16 student teachers of introductory biology classes at Goulburn College in Australia. The students were randomly assigned to two groups of eight, with the experimental group receiving audio instructions and the control group receiving the traditional lecture instructions. Because such variables as cognitive style, gender, attitude toward science, socioeconomic status, prior grades, and IQ were not controlled in the experiment, Khan employed an analysis of covariance methodology. Results showed that a significant higher level of cognitive achievement was recorded for students receiving the audio instructions. Kahn was cautious in his conclusions, however: "The implications of the A-T method seems effective in some cases, but is obviously not the appropriate for all cases and all situations" (p. 51).

Video Studies — Similar studies have been conducted using a video emphasis rather than audio. Fisher et al. (1977), in an extensive study involving students in three California universities, employed a video-autotutorial (video-AT) method of instruction which fully utilized illustrated tele-vision modules in introductory genetics. Experimental and control groups were compared using pretest-posttest results from objective tests.

The video-AT course was characterized by several features: (1) fully illustrated instructional modules on video tape, each about 25 minutes in length and devoted to a single topic of genetics; (2) frequent quizzes; (3) lectures for motivation; (4) easy access to a viewing room; (4) instructors and tutors available for individual instruction; and (5) a detailed syllabus keyed to the video modules. Overall results of the tests provided "strong evidence for the effectiveness of the video-autotutorial instructional approach in the setting in which it was used in contrast to the more conventional approaches to large-group university instruction in the science field" (p. 493).

A recent study by Kumar (1990) used videodisc technology to teach introductory biology and nursing students at Seton Hall University. The videodisc approach is comparable to video-AT in that both approaches allow students to proceed at their own pace and to review individually or in small groups for cooperative learning. Videodisc differs, however, in its hands-on tutorial benefits. Students can read a short textual passage on the computer monitor and then ask for more details by retrieving related slides or movies. In short, the videodisc system combines both visual and verbal learning. Its potential benefits are compelling in that "the student is able to immediately connect the verbal and visual information during the formation of his or her personal representation of the concept. . . . Thus, the videodisc tutorial may help in conceptual development" (p. 86).

Kumar (1990) concluded that most students liked the interactive videodiscs. Students reported that their attention level was higher than in the conventional lecture format. Nonetheless, many students said that they were annoyed that the tutorials took laboratory time away and would have preferred them to be used outside of the lab for review purposes.

Page Smith's Book — Smith (1990) taught at UCLA and was founding provost at the University of California at Santa Cruz. In his critique of the university system, he said: "I came away convinced from my years of teaching on the college and university level with a conviction that enactment, performance, dramatization are the most successful forms of teaching. Students must be incorporated, made, so far as possible, an integral part of the learning process. The notion that learning should have in it an element of inspired play would seem to the greater part of the academic establishment merely frivolous, but that is nonetheless the case" (p. 210).

Summary — The literature reviewed in this section suggests that audio and video instructional methods have strong potential to help students learn new materials and/or review materials learned earlier. Given that most of today's students are children of a society in which radio and television communication is pervasive, it would seem intuitive that audio and video approaches would appeal to them. Kozma's (1991) literature review supports this reasoning.

DESCRIPTION OF THE AUDIO STUDY GUIDE

A primary motivation for an audiocassette study guide and accompanying study booklet is my dissatisfaction with the way accounting principles is currently presented in textbooks and, hence, taught by most instructors. The literature reviewed in the previous section showed that the audio medium can be helpful to elementary accounting students, most of whom are novices to the domain of accounting. The audio study guide described below (1) is conceptually driven, (2) encourages students to create "mental models" of the real-world situations which are often enhanced by a dialog between two "peer" accounting students, and (3) is supported by textual material and visual aids that are included in the study booklet accompanying the audio tapes.

The audio study guide contains four audiocassette tapes and a comprehensive study booklet.[5] The narration on the tapes is organized as follows:

- A lively, professional introduction by a professional voice who introduces the professor.

- The professor describes the contents of the audio tapes and the accompanying study booklet.

- The professional voice reads the topic title (there are 14 topics).

- Each topic contains the professor's narration (from script) and at least one conversation by two fictional characters, "Arnie Asset" and "Lola Liability."[6]

- The second half of the last tape is devoted to a discussion of the 40 "final exam" questions presented in the final section of study booklet.

Exhibit 1 contains excerpts of the narration and dialog from Topic 1.[7]

The study booklet contains three sections. Section I provides several study tips on how to do better in the course. For example, two of the tips read as follows:

- Don't be afraid to rip up your textbook and start a "filing system," with each file consisting of the chapter, your notes, and homework. This may well save you doctor or chiropractor bills in today's world of 25-lb. textbooks. If you can't bring yourself to rip up your book, consider making a photocopy of each chapter. But make sure you use (1) both sides of the page and (2) recyclable paper (save a tree!).

- If your teacher lists "Working Papers" as a required item for the course, politely ask him or her if you can use 4-column and 8-column

---

[5] I chose the audio medium rather than video for several reasons, but one of the most compelling reasons is accessibility to students. Donovan (p. 43) reported that 80 percent of the households in the United States have cassette recorders and 60 percent of the automobiles are equipped with cassette recorders. Donovan (p. 43) also reported "most people listen to a tape when they are alone in their cars or in the solitary sound world a Walkman creates. . . . A book on tape seems to offer the same solitary enjoyment that reading does. It awakens the same visual imagination and requires the same concentration to enjoy. In fact, many people find themselves circling the block or parking in the driveway with the tape player running so they can hear the end of a particularly compelling chapter . . . . Television and recorded music simply don't demand that kind of attention." The Department of Education (1990, p. 6) is also looking for more ways to involve commuting students in the university lifestyle: "It is especially hard for part-time and commuting students to sustain their commitment to academic pursuits. Research has linked these students' difficulties to their detachment from the informal intellectual life of the institution—snack-bar debates, guest lectures, campus theater, and the like. How can these part-time and commuting students be better integrated into the academic community?" Though my tapes do not address these issues directly, I do try to create scenes which attempt to capture the college atmosphere for students who are physically constrained from taking an active part in traditional campus activities.

[6] Some people have questioned the names "Arnie Asset" and "Lola Liability" as being sexist. After producing the tapes, I realized that the names might be offensive to some. In retrospect, I agree that the names appear to be sexist and I apologize to anyone who may have taken offense (it is interesting to note that the original idea for the names of these characters came from my master's student, Susan King). Anyone who listens to the tapes soon discovers, however, that Lola does not play a secondary role to Arnie. And to add intrigue to the stories, students are often left to wonder if Arnie and Lola might have more than just a common interest in learning financial accounting.

[7] Students have reported that one of their favorite topic titles is Topic 13, "The Statement of Owners' Equity, or Only Your Mama Thinks You Have a Positive Net Worth!"

EXHIBIT 1
Excerpts from Topic 1: Soaking Up the Basics at the Beach

Introduction
(fade in Beach Boys-type beach music)

Accounting can be exciting. Don't laugh! Once you start to understand the basic concepts, you will realize that accounting is nothing more than classifying and measuring—two skills you use in your everyday life. And it doesn't have to be hard as long as you continue to relate accounting rules and concepts to familiar things.

Why do we need accounting anyway? Well, *accounting information* is important to the *economic decisions* that businesses must make on a daily basis. Just as it is important for you to know how much money you make versus how much money you pay out over the course of time, so, too, must businesses keep track of such things. Businesses, government agencies, and charitable organizations all must keep track of, or *account for*, the amounts they will receive and the amounts they owe. This *financial information* represents accounting information.

Discussion of the Balance Sheet and Income Statement
I mentioned the term financial statements earlier. These statements are the culmination of all of the work which accountants do and are the tool used by all kinds of decision makers as mentioned earlier. But what are these statements anyway?

First, the *balance sheet* reflects the financial position of the company at a *specific point in time*. Think of it as a *snapshot*. In contrast, the *income statement* reports revenues and expenses for a given *period of time*; think of it as a *moving picture*. These differences are noted in the heading of each statement. For example, the heading of the balance sheet might include the date—December 31, 1990, while the heading of the income statement would be "for the period ending December 31, 1990." Please note the difference.

It might be useful just for a moment to think in purely conceptual terms. For example, assume your mother takes a picture of your teenage sister on January 1, 1990, and then again on December 31, 1990, she takes another picture of your sister. Also assume that both pictures are taken with your sister standing against a wall with a measuring stick taped to it. If your sister grew one inch over the course of the year, this inch would be measured in her income statement showing other interested people (like your relatives, for example) that one inch has been added to her personal entity over the course of the year.

The pictures taken at the beginning of the year and the end of the year represent her balance sheets on these dates because, on each date, the snapshot shows how tall she is on each of these dates. And she's certainly taller at the end of the year. How much taller? One inch.

Are you beginning to get the picture? The balance sheet shows what is owned at any point in time and the income statement represents how an entity's net assets grew over time.

Transition to the First Dialog
Well, the sun is rising high in the sky, and it's about time I introduced you to two of my more adventuresome students, Arnie Asset and Lola Liability. Arnie and Lola are beginning their tour of the world of financial accounting on the sunny beaches of French Polynesia. Today, they are soaking up the sun on the white-sand beaches of Tahiti. Let's listen in on them as they discuss some of Topic 1's key points.

---

working papers purchased from an office supply store. Instead of $17, you'll pay $3 or $4. Not a bad cost savings!.

Section II of the study booklet contains a detailed study guide broken down by each of the 14 topics. For each topic I present (1) a list of key concepts and definitions, (2) visual study aids related to the material discussed on the cassettes, and (3) several "quiz" multiple choice questions and answers. Exhibit 2 provides Topic 1's visual aids.

The third and last part of the study booklet contains a 40-question "final exam." As an additional aid, Side 2 of the last tape is devoted entirely to a detailed discussion of each even-numbered final exam question.

While the topics in the audio study guide follow the "traditional" financial sequence, it is a significant step in the direction suggested by Baldwin

and Ingram (1991).[8] For example, this semester I am currently teaching one section of the first elementary accounting course. But rather than adopt a traditional textbook for the course, I have completely transcribed the audio script into "text" form. The visual aids contained in the audio study booklet have been incorporated into the "text." The result is a set of printed materials which (1) are about

---

[8]Baldwin and Ingram (1991) recommend a complete reengineering of the elementary accounting sequence based on the concept that these courses should be the last courses in the business major rather than the first courses in the accounting major. Consistent with this concept, they suggest banishing the distinction between financial accounting and managerial accounting. In its place, Baldwin and Ingram argue that "accounting at the elementary accounting level should be taught as an integrated process

(Continued on next page)

EXHIBIT 2
Excerpts from Topic 1: Soaking Up the Basics at the Beach

Arnie and Lola's Dialog from Topic 1

Lola: Arnie, am I ever glad you and I saved enough money to come to this South Pacific getaway. The coral reefs are beautiful. By the way, how were you able to afford this trip?

Arnie: Well, before my freshman year at State U., my father gave me $10,000 in cash. Also, I borrowed $5,000 from the bank. With the $15,000 total I invested in 130 dorm-sized refrigerators that cost $100 each. In other words, I used $13,000 of the $15 grand to buy an inventory of refrigerators.

Lola: Okay, then according to Professor Jones, your balance sheet immediately after buying the inventory would show only two assets, cash and inventory. The only liability is the note payable to the bank. What's the name we give to the difference between assets and liabilities?

Arnie: That's what is called owners' equity. In my case, I had $2,000 in cash and $13,000 in inventory, so total assets were $15,000. Then, if you subtract my $5,000 liability to the bank, that leaves owners' equity of $10,000.

Lola: I see. That means on the first day of Year 1 your owners' equity equaled your initial investment in the business entity. So how well did your business do in the first year?

Arnie: Great! I collected $5,000 in rent revenues, but I incurred $2,000 of repair expenses. So I ended up with net income of $3,000 my very first year.

Lola: Do you remember what financial statement you would have reported your revenues and expenses?

Arnie: Sure do. It's called the income statement, otherwise known as the statement of operations.

Lola: I remember now. And let's look at your balance sheet at the end of the year. Your cash should have gone up from $2,000 to $5,000 when you added in the $3,000 net income. If you didn't buy or sell any more refrigerators, your refrigerator inventory should still have been $13,000. That makes total assets $18,000. Subtracting $5,000 of liabilities gives you owners' equity of $13,000.

Arnie: Hey, you're right. Notice how owners' equity is increased by the first year's net income. But I forgot to answer your original question about how I could afford this trip. You see, I took $2,500 cash from the business in the form of a withdrawal at the end of the year. Therefore, my cash balance wasn't $5,000 but $2,500. And my owners' equity wasn't $13,000 but $10,500 on December 31.

Lola: Hey, but your balance sheet still balanced. Assets of $15,500 minus liabilities of $5,000 equals $10,500. And I remember something about the statement of owners' equity. It would start with $10,000, then you'd add net income of $3,000 and subtract your withdrawal of $2,500.

Arnie: Oh, Lola, you're so articulate! And by the way, when net income is added to owners' equity, the income statement is said to be articulated to, or linked to, the balance sheet.

Lola: Thank you for the compliment, Arnie. But I've had all the basics I can stand for now. Let's go snorkeling. Last one in is a rotten accountant! (fade out — beach music)

---

two-thirds the thickness of a traditional textbook, (2) are three-hole punched to facilitate adding and deleting material as the semester progresses, (3) cost less than $10, and (4) are supplemented by the audio study guide that can be checked out free of charge at the Student Learning Center at the library. With less material and more media available to learn it, instructors have much more time to pursue an introductory sequence as recommended by Baldwin and Ingram (1991).

PERCEIVED USEFULNESS: STUDENTS, PROFESSORS, AND BOOKSTORES RESPOND

Since the audio study guide's release in August of 1990, it appears that two separate groups of students are using them: the introductory students and, more surprisingly at first, Intermediate Accounting I students. Upon greater reflection, however, this probably is not surprising in light of the traditional financial/managerial sequence used at many universities. For intermediate students in this sequence, it's been at least six months or more since they have thought in "financial" terms.

While it is too early to conduct a formal test of the audio guide's usefulness to date, sample responses indicate that it is being favorably received by students, professors, and bookstores:

Footnote 8 Continued

related to the information needs of those who make decisions about an organization. Some decision makers are inside the organization and others are outside, but all need information that is generated by a common data base—the accounting information system" (pp. 8–9).

EXHIBIT 3
Topic 1's Visual Aids

Arnie's Balance Sheet, January 1, Year 1

Assets		Liabilities	
Cash	$ 2,000	Payable to Banker	$ 5,000
Inventory	13,000		
		Owners' Equity	
		Arnie, Capital	10,000
	$15,000		$15,000

Arnie's Income Statement, For the Year Ended December 31, Year 1

Revenues: Rental revenue		$ 5,000
Expenses: Repairs expense		(2,000)
Net Income		$ 3,000

Arnie's Balance Sheet, December 31, Year 1

Assets		Liabilities	
Cash	$ 2,500	Payable to Banker	$ 5,000
Inventory	13,000		
		Owners' Equity	
		Arnie, Capital	10,500 #
	$15,500		$15,500

Arnie's Statement of Owners' Equity, December 31, Year 1

Arnie, Capital, January 1, Year 1	$10,000
Add: Net income, Year 1	3,000
Less: Withdrawals, Year 1	(2,500)
Arnie, Capital, December 31, Year 1	$10,500 #

This sign is known as a cross-referencing "tickmark."

Examples of student responses

- "The audio study album is a wonderful tool for reviewing and reminding."

- "I especially liked the coverage of adjusting entries and inventory."

- "It has been two years since I took principles. The audio study album was a tremendous help for my review of accounting."

Examples of professor responses

- "I share your concern about the introductory accounting course, and especially its approach for non-accounting majors. . .. I applaud your initiative, and wish you success."

- "Anything that can help students through this difficult process is certainly welcome."

Example of the response from a bookstore's purchasing manager

- "An agreement to purchase 300 copies of any title [of *non-required* materials] is almost un-heard in this industry. . . but I have observed the unusually high numbers of students enrolled in these courses trying to obtain additional help, but it seems they aren't finding much success. The audio tutor approach is innovative, and it's reasonably priced."

CONCLUSION

My motto in preparing the audio study guide has been, "Who says accounting has to be boring?" Unfortunately, too many accounting instructors often contribute to the stereotype that accounting is a dull or uninteresting subject because of the pedantic manner in which they teach their courses. If instructors don't seem interested in the subject, how can students be expected to perceive it as anything but dry and boring? And if our finest students are turned off by accounting at the outset, how can we expect them to consider it as a career option?

Based on the attrition rate in the beginning course, accounting is obviously a foreign language to many students. In the preface or first chapter of almost every accounting book, accounting is billed as the "language of business." The very nature of language makes learning through listening more productive than merely wading through sometimes confusing and difficult text. Language educators have known this for many years and have made extensive use of records and audio tapes as learning tools.

The goal of the audio study guide described in this paper was to provide elementary accounting students with an alternative learning tool which some students have found beneficial. As mentioned in the introductory material on the tapes, the approach is simple: to help students *learn*, have fun, pass, and *remember*, not *cram*, hate the subject, (maybe) pass, and *forget*.

While the audio approach has not yet been subjected to empirical scrutiny,[9] it is one step in the direction suggested by the Accounting Education Change Commission. The AECC stated that accounting programs should focus on learning to learn by "developing both an understanding of underlying concepts and principles and the ability to apply those concepts and principles in a variety of contexts and circumstances. A focus on memorization of rules and regulations is contrary to the goal of learning to learn" (AECC, p. 310). The content of the audio study guide emphasizes concepts, visual imagery, and intuition while de-emphasizing rules memorization.

While an audiocassette study guide may be considered unorthodox, feedback from students who have used the guide has been positive. They have found the approach to be innovative and refreshing, especially in light of today's impersonal learning environment often characterized by mega-lecture sections and limited instructor availability.

---

[9] A controlled experiment with the test group using the audio study guide and a control group precluded from using it would be one way to test the effectiveness of the audio approach. But such an experiment has at least two major drawbacks. First, students in the test group would be *required* to use the audio materials, which defeats the purpose of making them available only to those who need them. Second, the current state of accounting education is such that there is no consensus on *course content* let alone how best to deliver it.

REFERENCES

Accounting Education Change Commission. 1990. Objectives of Education for Accountants: Position Statement Number One. *Issues in Accounting Education* (Fall): 307–312.

Adams, S. A., L. Pryor, and S. L. Adams. 1991. Quality and Quantity of Accounting Profession Entrants: Aptitudes and Determinants of Accounting Majors. Working Paper, California State University, Chico (February).

American Accounting Association, Committee on the Future Structure, Content, and Scope of Accounting Education (The Bedford Committee). 1986. Future Accounting Education: Preparing for the Expanded Profession. *Issues in Accounting Education* (Spring): 168–195.

Arthur Andersen, Arthur Young, Coopers & Lybrand, Deloitte Haskins & Sells, Ernst & Whinney, Peat Marwick Main & Co., Price Waterhouse, and Touche Ross (The "White Paper"). 1989. *Perspectives on Education: Capabilities for Success in the Accounting Profession* (April).

Baldwin, B. A., and R. W. Ingram. 1991. Rethinking the Objectives and Content of Elementary Accounting. *Journal of Accounting Education* (Spring): 1–14.

Department of Education, Fund for the Improvement of Postsecondary Education. 1990. Comprehensive Program, Information and Application Procedures Fiscal Year 1991. Washington, D.C.: Department of Education.

Donovan, R. J. 1988. The Writer's Guide to Books on Tape. *Writers's Digest* (December): 41–45.

Fisher, K. M., H. Guenther, B. Macwhinney, P. Sorensen, and D. Stewart. 1977. Does Video-Autotutorial Instruction Improve College Student Achievement? *Journal of Research in Science Teaching* (June): 481–498.

Greeno, J. 1989. Situations, Mental Models, and Generative Knowledge. *Complex Information Processing* (Hillsdale, New Jersey: Lawrence Earlham Associates): 285–318.

Jensen, D. L. 1989. Crisis in Instructional Materials. Editorial, *Issues in Accounting Education* (Spring): 172–173.

Khan, A. G. 1980. Effects of Audiotutorial and Conventional Instructional Techniques on Cognitive Achievement. *Journal of Research in Science Teaching* (January): 47–53.

Kozma, R. B. 1991. Learning with Media. *Review of Educational Research* (Summer): 179–211.

Kumar, L. 1990. Does Learning Improve with Videodisc Tutorials? *Journal of College Science Teaching* (November): 85–89.

Kuntz, G. C., U. Drewniak, and F. Schott. 1989. On-line and Off-line Assessment of Self-Regulation in Learning from Instructional Text and Picture. Unpublished Working Paper. San Francisco: American Educational Research Association (April).

Rowsey, R. E., and W. H. Mason. 1975. Immediate Achievement and Retention in Audio-Tutorial Versus Conventional Lecture-Laboratory Instruction. *Journal of Research in Science Teaching* (October): 393–397.

Scheiner, J. H., M. G. Tiller, H. C. Herring, J .R. Williams. 1988. *A Framework for the Development of Accounting Education Research User's Guide*, Accounting Education Series Volume No. 9. Sarasota: American Accounting Association.

Smith, P. 1990. *Killing the Spirit: Higher Education in America.* New York: Viking.

Experiential Learning Theory: An Application with Individualized Problems on Foreign Currency Restatement

Orapin Duangploy and Guy W. Owings

The accounting profession has called for accounting education reform, reflecting the profession's dissatisfaction with traditional instructional methods. Computer applications have been used to supplement chalkboard demonstrations, and spreadsheets are replacing worksheets. However, it appears that the learning process of accounting students has not been enhanced despite the integration of computer applications into the accounting curriculum. This phenomenon may be due to the fact that the computer has been used primarily as a computational tool rather than as learning aid.

Awards and grants have been established to encourage faculty to implement innovative methods which enable students to be more actively involved in the learning process.[1] According to the *Accounting Education Change Commission Position Statement No. One,* "The focus should be on developing analytical and conceptual thinking, not on memorizing professional standards."[2] Evidence from recent studies indicate that American students lack the ability to apply knowledge to new situations.[3] If students have not developed the ability to think logically, certain questions must logically follow. What is wrong with our teaching methods? Is it because we, the accounting educators, rely too heavily upon lectures and textbooks?

The purpose of this paper is to present an alternative to the traditional note-taking and rote problem solving. It introduces the application of individualized foreign currency accounting problems based on the experiential learning model. The model serves as a conceptual framework for the student's learning process.

LITERATURE REVIEW

Several studies on learning theories have been conducted. A Willingham et al. study[4] introduced the conceptual relationship between the study and teaching of accounting at each learning level. The authors classified learning into stimulus/response and cognitive learning. The cognitive theory stresses the "understanding of complex concepts,

generalization, synthesization, and problem solving."[5] Factors that facilitate the learning process were also identified in this study. Relating facts and concepts combined with clarification of concepts were considered the primary factors for accounting educators in their role as learning facilitators. Finally, the authors concluded that many methods exist whereby students and instructors alike can enhance the learning process.

Shute did an experiment based on his belief that a lack of reasoning ability was the major factor for lack of success in the accounting profession.[6] The results of his experiment revealed a weak correlation between academic success and reasoning abilities. Shute, therefore, suggested that the existing testing methods, in particular multiple choice exams, failed to promote abstract reasoning.

Kolb presented the experiential learning theory and indicated that specific learning styles dominate specific professions.[7] According to the experiential learning model, an effective learner needs four kinds of abilities. They are (1) concrete experience abilities, reflective observation abilities, ab-

---

[1] Report of the Committee on the Future Structure, Content, and Scope of Accounting Education (The Bedford Committee). 1986. Future Accounting Education: Preparing for the Expanding Profession. *Issues in Accounting Education* (Spring): 168-195.

[2] *Accounting Education Change Commission Position Statement No. One*, p. 2.

[3] *Reader's Digest*, June 1991, p. 140.

[4] Willingham, Mc Neil, and Collins. 1974. Learning Theories and Accounting. *Accounting Education: Problems and Prospects.* AAA: 173-180.

[5] Ibid., p. 174.

[6] G. Shute. 1979. Accounting Students and Abstract Reasoning: An Exploratory Study. American Accounting Association.

[7] D. Kolb. 1984. *Experiential Learning.* Englewood Cliffs, NJ: Prentice Hall.

Orapin Duangploy is Professor of Accounting at the University of Houston, Downtown, and Guy W. Owings is Professor of Accounting at Pittsburg State University.

stract conceptualization abilities, and active experimentation abilities.

> Concrete experience (CE) means that a person must be able to involve oneself fully, openly, and without bias in new experiences; reflective observation (RO) is the ability to reflect on and observe those experiences from many perspectives; abstract conceptualization (AC) is the capacity to create concepts that integrate one's observations into logically sound theories; and active experimentation (AE) is the skill to use those theories to make decisions and solve problems.[8]

Briefly stated, learning occurs as observations are drawn from experience, rationalized, reflected upon and conceptualized. Newly developed theories then serve as the basis for decision making and problem solving.

Learning, according to Kolb, is a holistic process whereby knowledge is created through the transformation of experience. The process involves the integrated functioning of the total organism — thinking, feeling, perceiving, and behaving.[9] Learning, therefore, is composed of comprehension and transformation of information.[10] Comprehension ranges from concrete experience to abstract conceptualization whereas transformation ranges from reflective observation to active experimentation. Each individual has his or her own preferred combination of the two dimensions.

In 1981, Kolb developed the Learning Style Inventory (LSI) which measures an individual's learning style. Participants were asked to rank nine sets of four words that describe the four modes of learning. The total scores were paired with their difference and plotted along the CE-AC continuum and the RO-AE continuum. The corresponding map is shown in the four quadrants displayed in Figure 1. Each quadrant represents a combination of two learning modes. Kolb named the four quadrants which represent the four learning style types Diverger, Assimilator, Converger, and Accommodator.

Divergers learn by observing and gathering information. They prefer concrete experiences and reflective observation.

Assimilators approach learning by concentrating on logical soundness. They prefer abstract conceptualization and reflective observation.

Convergers emphasize solving problems by using deductive reasoning and active experimentation. They prefer abstract conceptualization and active experimentation.

Accommodators learn best by concrete experience and active experimentation.

---

[8]B. A. Baldwin and P. M. J. Reckers. 1984. Exploring the Role of Learning Style Research in Accounting Education Policy. *Journal of Accounting Education*, Vol. 2, No. 2 (Fall): 63-76.

[9]Kolb, op. cit., p. 21.

[10]S. P. Agrawal, and P. H. Siegel. 1989. Introduction to Accounting: An Experiment in Experiential Learning Theory (Unpublished Paper): 3.

FIGURE 1
Experiential Learning Model

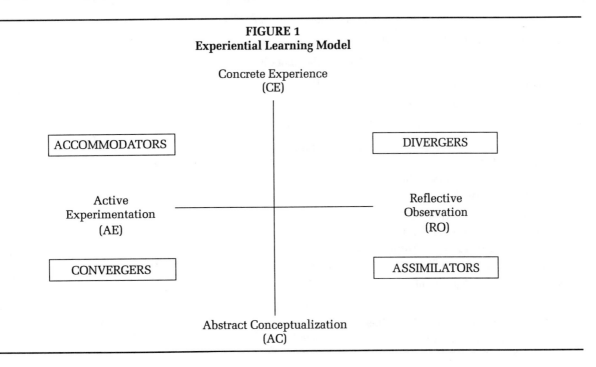

Kolb's LSI has been used in several studies on learning styles of college students and professions.[11] In 1987, J. Collins and V. Milliron concluded that accounting practitioners and accounting majors tend to be convergers, after assessing the learning styles of practicing accountants in both large and small CPA firms and a large industrial company. In fact, 53 percent of their subjects were classified as convergers.

In 1984, R. Baker, J. Simon, and F. Bazeli conducted a similar study. Once again convergers were the most commonly observed learning style among accounting majors, with strong preferences for active experimentation and abstract conceptualization experiences. Thus, early findings suggest that the most effective approach for teaching accounting majors is the incorporation of deductive reasoning and practical applications of concepts into the learning process.

INDIVIDUALIZED ACCOUNTING PROBLEMS

Learning occurs when the student perceives the message the instructor communicates. To be effective, the communication media should be adapted to the interest of each student. To increase involvement by the student in the process, this experiment includes unique accounting problems which are created using criteria specified by the student.

A *Lotus 1-2-3* template was developed to accept variables specified by students. The software has the capability to generate a unique foreign currency accounting set of problem data. Students are asked to provide an amount for total assets and total stockholders' equity for their individualized foreign currency subsidiary. They are also asked to provide an assumed income tax rate and a direct exchange rate, and are asked to make an assumption as to whether the U.S. dollar (the reporting currency of the parent) is weakening or strengthening. (Figure 2 exhibits the display of the input screen.) A unique set of financial statements under the selected translation method is then automatically generated by the computer for the students to apply *SFAS 52* to translate the foreign currency financial statements to US dollars, as shown in Figures 3 and 4.

The software allows the students to view the problem they have generated before printing and to select one of the two translation methods. Students are required to think analytically how the strengthening or weakening of the US dollars affects the translated net asset position of the subsidiary under the current rate method. In the event of their selection of the temporal method, the results generated from their remeasurement will

---

[11]For example, G. Sadler, M. Plovnick, and F. Snope. 1978. Learning Styles and Teaching Implications. *Journal of Medical Education* (Vol. 53): 847-849.

FIGURE 2
IAP Input Screen

Individualized Foreign Currency Translation Problem

To Create Your Own Problem, Enter the Following:

Total Assets of Your Company in Year 19A (200000-900000):	$400,000
Total Stockholders' Equity in 19A (80000-600000):	$120,000
Tax Rate for Regular Income (.30–50):	40.00%
Direct Quotation of Current Exchange Rate (0.01 – 9.99):	2.00

Indicate Whether Dollar Is Strengthening or Weakening by Placing in Cell D17:
   1 If the Dollar is Strengthening or 2 If
   the Dollar is Weakening
	1

Exchange Rate in Effect when the Equipment Was Purchased (Automated):	2.2
Common Stock Was Issued (Automated):	2.2
Inventory Was Acquired Prior to 12/19A (Automated):	2.4
Average of Exchange Rates (Automated):	2.1
Prior Year Translated Retained Earnings (Automated):	$143,660.00
Prior Year Cumulative Translation Adjustment (Automated):	$10,056.20
Prior Year Translated Beginning Inventory (Automated)	$0.00

prompt them to think whether the change in exchange rate will generate a favorable effect on the net monetary asset/liability position.

An inherent disadvantage of having individualized accounting problems is the time to correct each assignment having different answers. This disadvantage has been taken into consideration in the development of the software. Thus, in addition to the individualized problems, the program also generates individualized solutions. However, the solution is accessible only by the instructor after typing a password.

FIGURE 3
Automatically Generated Financial Statements—Current Rate

M.Y. Company
Balance Sheet
12/31/19A

	Local Currency	Exch. Rate	US $
Cash	26,670		
Accounts Receivable	80,000		
Inventory:			
Acquired in 12/19A	0		
Acquired before 12/19A	106,680		
Equipment	213,320		
Accumulated Depreciation	−26,670		
Total Assets	400,000		
Accounts Payable	123,840		
Accrued Liabilities	48,470		
Income Taxes Payable	107,690		
Total Liabilities	280,000		
Common Stock	52,180		
Retained Earnings			
Prior Years	65,300		
Current Year	2,520		
Cumulative Translation Adj.:			
Prior Years			
Current Year			
Total Equity	120,000		
Total Liab. & Equity	400,000		

M.Y. Company
Income Statement
For the Period Ended 12/31/19A

	Local Currency	Exch. Rate	US $
Sales	14,400		
Cost of Goods Sold	−4,000		
Selling and Admin. Expense	−900		
Depreciation	−1,700		
Operating Expense	−3,600		
Income before Income Tax	4,200		
Income Tax Expense	−1,680		
Net Income	2,520		

FIGURE 4
Automatically Generated Financial Statements—Temporal Rate Method

M.Y. Company
Balance Sheet
12/31/19A

	Local Currency	Exch. Rate	US $
Cash	26,670		
Accounts Receivable	80,000		
Inventory:			
Acquired in 12/19A	0		
Acquired before 12/19A	106,680		
Equipment	213,320		
Accumulated Depreciation	− 26,670		
Total Assets	400,000		
Accounts Payable	123,840		
Accrued Liabilities	48,470		
Income Taxes Payable	107,690		
Total Liabilities	280,000		
Common Stock	52,180		
Retained Earnings			
Beginning Balance	65,300		
Current-year Transaction	2,520		
Total Equity	120,000		
Total Liab. & Equity	400,000		

M.Y. Company
Income Statement
For the Period Ended 12/31/19A

	Local Currency	Exch. Rate	US $
Sales	14,400		
Cost of Goods Sold			
Beginning Inventory	80,000		
Purchases	30,680		
Goods Available for Sale	110,680		
Ending Inventory	106,680		
Cost of Goods Sold	− 4,000		
Selling and Admin. Expense	− 900		
Depreciation	− 1,700		
Operating Expense	− 3,600		
Income before Income Tax	4,200		
Income Tax Expense	− 1,680		
Income before Transaction			
from Remeasurement	2,520		
Transaction Gain/Loss-Remeasure.			
Net Income	2,520		

APPLICATION OF INDIVIDUALIZED ACCOUNTING PROBLEMS

Utilizing Kolb's experiential learning model, courses were designed so that each of the four stages of the learning cycle identified by Kolb are completed. The practical application of the four stages using the individualized accounting problems is being implemented in the classroom as follows:

Stage 1. Concrete Experience

Students are assigned to read Chapter 5 of AlHashim and Arpan's *International Dimensions of Accounting*. In addition, sample worksheets demonstrating the translation of foreign currency into US dollars under the current rate method and temporal method are distributed prior to lectures. Students are told to assume that it is their first day of work and their supervisor has requested that they take over a former colleague's work. The sample work sheets represent accurate work previously completed by the colleague.

Students are required to create their own accounting problem and solve it independently. Upon completion and submission of their solution, the instructor attaches a solution sheet to each attempt made by the student. The observation of sample work sheets (representing previous work), creation and solving the foreign currency translation problems provide a concrete experience.

Stage 2: Reflective Observation

Students have deductively formulated the translation concepts. The pertinent instrument at this stage is to provide small group deductive discussion on the concepts of the translation methods.

Stage 3. Abstract Conceptualization

Students are encouraged to question the complexity and logic of the current rate and temporal translation methods after group discussions. At this stage, students are encouraged to clarify and generalize the comprehension of the foreign currency translation concepts through active participation in class discussion. The role of the instructor at this stage is to clarify and generalize the key concepts and answer students' questions. In this stage of the learning process, students should be involved in order to learn as much as possible before the active experimentation.

Stage 4: Active Experimentation

Students at this stage synthesize information and solve problems provided by the instructor. In addition, students have to make decisions on the appropriate exchange rate to apply for each financial statement account. They are also required to apply their knowledge to determine the impact of fluctuating exchange rates on the financial position and performance of the firm. Performance at this stage inevitably depends upon the comprehension of the concepts acquired in the first three stages.

DEVELOPMENT OF MEASURES OF EFFECTIVENESS

Measures of effectiveness were developed to test the recommended innovative pedagogical methods based on two indicators. These indicators include attitude towards the application of the individualized foreign currency restatement problems and scores on class examinations.

Students' attitude can be measured by means of a short questionnaire survey polling their degree of agreement on a five-point Likert-type scale for each question. The following attitude statements were included in the questionnaire:

1. Using the Individualized Accounting Problem (IAP) was an enjoyable experience.

2. Using the IAP enhanced my learning of foreign currency translation.

3. IAP should be incorporated in other accounting topics.

Demographic information was also requested relative to sex, GPA, class standing, and competence in using *Lotus 1-2-3*.

Test of Pedagogical Methods

Measurement methods were developed to be used in evaluating the experiments. The experiments used control and experiment groups, with the same instructor for both an experiment group and a control group. Two schools participated in this study; one is an urban university located in the southwest and one is a regional state university located in the midwest.

At the southwestern university, two sections of Intermediate Accounting II were used for the study, both sections being taught by the same instructor. The morning section was used as the treatment group, whereas the evening section was used as the control group.

The control group was taught using the traditional methodology of lecturing and textbook assignments, while the treatment group was taught by following the four different stages of learning identified by Kolb. The treatment group was further subdivided into study groups assigned by the instructor. Members were assigned to study groups based on their performance on previous examinations. An effort was made to ensure that each group was well balanced with both strong and weak students.

At the midwestern university, a similar approach was taken for the test group, but not with the control group. The control group, an intermediate accounting class in the first semester of the academic year, was taught using the traditional methodology of lecturing and textbook assignments, just as the university in the southwest, with one exception. Students were also assigned problems using the Individualized Accounting Problem (IAP) similar to the way textbook provided spreadsheet software might be used. In the second semester, the treatment group was instructed using the same format as at the university in the southwest.

The southwestern school made a comparison between its two groups based on the total instructional difference, which included the use of innovative software only in the treatment group. The midwestern school compared its two groups based on differences in instructional technique. By comparing each set of groups, the researchers hoped to isolate whether any differences in learning might be due to the innovative software, or be due to the experiential learning process.

RESULTS

Comparisons of test scores between the test groups and the control groups were inconclusive for both schools. At the southwestern university, the students who enrolled in the section designated as the control group were predominately part-time evening students employed full-time. At least 17 percent of the students in the control group had already completed an undergraduate degree and were taking the course in preparation for the CPA examination. The grade point average for this group (A = 4.0) was 2.70, while the grade point average for the test group was 2.53. Students who enrolled in the section designated as the test group were predominately full-time students, who while also interested and motivated, were not nearly the quality of the evening students. At the midwestern university, where the control group was taught in the

fall semester and the test group was taught the following spring, the instructional materials were substantially changed from one semester to the next, such that treatments using IAP and experiential learning could not be isolated. As a matter of fact, the control group performed slightly better than the test group on a common examination. However, the examination was somewhat geared to the textbook which was used in the fall. Therefore, a definitive study of actual performance remains to be accomplished. Nevertheless, an analysis of questionnaires completed by the students in the test group revealed several interesting implications and provided encouragement for continuing the experiments.

As previously stated, at the conclusion of the segment on foreign currency restatement, students were asked to complete a brief questionnaire which asked for demographic information: class standing, sex, GPA, and competence in *Lotus 1-2-3*; and valuative information relative to students' enjoyment using IAP, belief IAP enhanced learning of the subject, and belief IAP should be incorporated in other accounting courses. Responses to the valuative questions were phrased such that students answered agreed to disagreed on a six-point Likert scale. In order to increase statistical validity, questionnaire responses from both universities were combined. A summary of the characteristics of the students in the test groups is provided in Figure 5, and a summary of students' attitudinal responses is provided in Figure 6.

Approximately 63 percent of the students surveyed enjoyed using IAP in varying degrees and approximately 72 percent believed it enhanced their learning and should be used in other courses, again in varying degrees from slightly agreed to strongly agreed.

Cross-correlations for all of the variables were computed (see Figure 7). Encouragement for the use of instructional software such as IAP is provided both by low correlations for certain variables and by high correlations in others. Based on this survey, except for a moderate correlation between GPA and students' enjoyment in using IAP, and between competence in using *Lotus 1-2-3* and students' belief IAP should be extended to other areas of accounting; class standing, sex of students, GPA and competence in using *Lotus 1-2-3* had very little to do with whether students enjoyed IAP, believed IAP enhanced their learning of the subject or that IAP should be extended into other areas of accounting. Therefore, it would seem that these methods would have general applicability.

FIGURE 5
Characteristics of Test Group (N = 67)

Sex		**GPA**		**Class Standing**	
Male	23	3.5 – 4.0	26	Sophomore	2
Female	44	3.0 – 3.49	24	Junior	10
Total	67	2.5 – 2.99	15	Senior	51
		2.0 – 2.49	2	Other	4
		Total	67	Total	67

I Am Competent in *Lotus 1-2-3*

	No.	%
1. Strongly Disagree	3	4.4
2. Disagree	4	6.0
3. Slightly Disagree	6	8.9
	13	19.3
4. Slightly Agree	15	22.4
5. Agree	22	32.9
6. Strongly Agree	17	25.4
	54	80.7
Total	67	100.0

FIGURE 6
Summary of Attitude Responses

	Enjoyed Using IAP		IAP Enhanced Learning		IAP Should be Used in other Courses	
	No.	%	No.	%	No.	%
1. Strongly Disagree	7	10.5	6	8.9	5	7.5
2. Disagree	8	11.9	6	8.9	5	7.5
3. Slightly Disagree	10	14.9	7	10.5	9	13.3
	25	37.3	19	28.3	19	28.3
4. Slightly Agree	22	32.8	19	28.3	24	35.9
5. Agree	16	23.9	24	35.9	20	29.8
6. Strongly Agree	4	6.0	5	7.5	4	6.0
	42	62.7	48	71.7	48	71.7
Total	67	100.0	67	100.0	67	100.0

On the other hand, students of both sexes and across all classes, GPA ranges, and *Lotus* competencies, enjoyed using the software, and enjoyment in using the software was highly correlated with students' belief that IAP enhanced their learning. The three variables, enjoyed using, enhanced learning, and should be incorporated, were all highly correlated. In summary, the questionnaire responses indicate that students enjoyed using the software, believed the software enhanced their learning, and would extend such software to other areas in accounting.

Perhaps as a measure of how far academic computing has come, the majority of students stated that they were competent in using *Lotus 1-2-3*, and that competence in the use of *Lotus 1-2-3* is unrelated to class standing, sex, or GPA. A significant relationship between GPA and enjoyment in using IAP was shown, and students who were competent in using *Lotus 1-2-3* were more likely to recommend use of such software in other courses. However, a significant relationship between GPA and enhancement of learning, and competence in *Lotus 1-2-3* and enhancement of learning could not be shown. In similar questionnaires issued to previous classes, lack of competence in using *Lotus 1-2-3* was seen by students as a significant draw-

FIGURE 7
Correlation of Questionnaire Responses

	Class	Sex	GPA	Enjoyed IAP	Learning Enhanced	Use IAP in Other Courses
Sex	.032					
GPA	−.097	−.126				
Enjoyed IAP	−.242	.002	.413			
Learning Enhanced	−.087	−.001	.174	.705		
Use in Other Courses	−.061	−.100	.267	.664	.772	
Competent in *Lotus*	−.141	.193	−.007	.161	.195	.302

FIGURE 8
Chi-Square Test of Significance of Relationships

Variables	Chi-Square Test Statistic	Significance Level
Learning Enhanced vs Use Should be Extended	28.975	.000
Learning Enhanced vs Enjoyed Using	24.937	.000
Enjoyed Using vs Should be Extended	19.654	.000
Enjoyed Using vs GPA	9.621	.002
Competent in *Lotus* vs Use Should Be Extended	5.158	.023
Competent in *Lotus* vs Sex of Student	2.726	.099
Enjoyed Using vs Class Standing	2.664	.103
Competent in *Lotus* vs Enhanced Learning	2.514	.113
GPA vs Use Should Be Extended	2.341	.126
GPA vs Enhanced Learning	1.286	.257
Competent in *Lotus* vs Class Standing	1.145	.285
Enhanced Learning vs Class Satnding	0.984	.321
Competent in *Lotus* vs GPA	0.850	.357
GPA vs Sex of Student	0.474	.491
Enjoyed Using vs Sex of Student	0.096	.757
Enhanced Learning vs Sex of Student	0.089	.766
Class Standing vs Use Should Be Extended	0.081	.776
Use Should Be Extended vs Sex of Student	0.074	.786
Competent in *Lotus* vs Enjoyed Using	0.009	.924
Class Standing vs Sex of Student	0.006	.938
Class Standing vs GPA	0.001	.975

back. This problem may have been alleviated somewhat by the practice in this study of assigning students to projects in teams and attempting to pair up good students with less gifted students as a mentoring process.

CONCLUSION

This paper has presented two innovative approaches in teaching a difficult topic in accounting. The central points of focus are experiential learning and the individualized accounting problems as a vehicle for instruction. The main departure from the traditional teaching methodology is the requirement that students be active learners rather than passive learners. In order to acquire the required knowledge, students are required to create their own accounting problems with the facility of getting prompt feedback. Further, they are forced to move through the four stages of the learning cycle. They are involved in thinking, feeling, perceiving, and behaving. They are expected to have productive thinking, better reasoning abilities, and better handling of holistic accounting problems.

Application of Technology in Accounting Instruction

Linda Garceau and Robert Bloom

OVERVIEW

This paper conveys ideas on the application of technology to accounting instruction. One definition of "technology," provided by *Webster's New Collegiate Dictionary* (Merriam), is

the totality of the means employed to provide objects necessary for human sustenance and comfort.

A great deal of technology exists in various forms, both traditional and state of the art, for use in the classroom, but precious little is actually applied for that purpose. Nevertheless, considerable technological support tends to exist on American university campuses for research and administration. In this paper, we offer suggestions on reducing the technology gap in the classroom and provide a list of technological resources toward that end.

This paper is motivated by the critique of accounting education, its static and uninnovative nature, found in the Bedford Report (1986) as well as the Big Eight White Paper (1989). The latter report observes (p. 8):

Given the rapid pace of change in the business world, public accountants must understand the methods for creating and managing change in organizations. The professional environment is also characterized by rapidly increasing dependence on technological support. No understanding of organizations could be complete without attention to the current and future roles of information technology in client organizations and accounting practice.

While the accounting profession has changed dramatically in the last 50 years, partly because of significant changes in technology, that has not been the case in the education of accountants. Both the Bedford Report and Big Eight White Paper call for a significant reorientation of accounting education, to include more emphasis on the creative application of high technology in accounting.

Technology can be used as a means to enhance the teaching-learning process, serving to stimulate students' interest in particular subject matter through capturing and holding their attention on the subject. "It takes advantage of the fact that

people retain about 25 percent of what they hear, 45 percent of what they see and hear, and 70 percent of what they hear, see and do."[1] By providing a mechanism for conveying vicarious experiences to students in a discipline such as accounting, technology facilitates instruction. For a consideration of different kinds of experiences to which students can be exposed, we refer to Dale's "cone of experience," which encompasses the "abstract," "iconic" or representational, and "enactive" or direct. According to Dale, learners should first participate in actual experiences, then observe actual events, next observe an event through a particular medium, and finally observe "symbols" representing an event (see Heinrich 1989). In this regard, the Bedford Report (1986, p. 187) recommends:

Faculties should design educational experiences for students that require them to be active, independent learners and problem solvers rather than passive recipients of information.

Simulation and role-playing, as examples, enable students to immerse themselves in real-world situations.

The AAA Committee on Multi-Media Instruction in Accounting (1972, p. 111) has defined "instructional technology" in two senses:

. . . In its more familiar sense, it means that media born of the communications revolution which can be used for instructional purposes alongside the teacher, textbook, and blackboard. . . .

The second. . . definition of instructional technology goes beyond any particular medium or device. In this sense, instructional technology is more than the sum of its parts. It is a systematic way of designing, carrying out, and evaluating the total process of learning and teaching learning and communication. . . .

The former definition describes presentation technology, while the latter defines learning technol-

---

[1]W. A. Kleinschrod, "The Trend to Electronic Training," *Administrative Management*, April 1988, p. 32.

Linda Garceau is Assistant Professor at Cleveland State University, and Robert Bloom is Professor at John Carroll University.

ogy. Presentation technology is used to enhance instruction in the traditional, classroom-lecture setting. It takes advantage of more traditional audiovisual aids, such as charts, chalkboards, and projectors as well as newer media, such as videotapes and disks. The function of presentation technology is to support, not supplant, the instructor.

Learning technology, on the other hand, supports the entire learning process. Such technology may be used to enhance the learning process occurring in the classroom, but it also may support independent learning by the student, occurring in the laboratory or library. In each setting, the educational process can be improved with well-conceived applications of hardware and software.

Some view the introduction of new technology to the learning process as a threat to humanism, envisioning the day will come when people are taught by machines (Scribner 1990). In past years, this belief has inhibited the acceptance of technology as a contributor to the learning process. Whether technology is a threat to humanism actually depends on how it is used. In the classroom, it is the individual instructor who determines how "humanistic" the environment is, regardless of the technology applied. A classroom setting can be dehumanizing with or without technology. How the technology is applied is the key to how humanistic the high-tech classroom of the future will be. Early implementations of poor-quality software have, in some instances, overshadowed course content or impeded the learning process. Many accounting faculty members have had experience with poorly designed practice sets. Problems associated with starting up the system and running it correctly consume valuable instruction time. Students may not learn about the application of accounting principles in an automated environment, but instead about how to manipulate a "toy-like" package, to get the job done.

In no case should technology dictate the nature of curriculum or changes to it. To the contrary, technology should be an aid in the instructional process. Technology ought to be applied to fulfill clearly specified educational objectives and needs. Under no circumstances should the emphasis be on the technology *per se* rather than the particular curriculum objectives.

Conceptually, the educational effectiveness/ineffectiveness of technological applications can be measured on a continuum. Prior to introduction of technology, both course and instructor are in a technology-neutral position. A variety of factors shifts the position of the course/instructor to

the left or right. First and foremost is the appropriateness of technology to the learning objectives. Use of "tutorial-type" software is most appropriate in introductory-level courses, while games and simulations are better used in advanced course work. The quality of software design and implementation also impacts the value of the product. In addition, individual student learning styles may influence the perceived value of technology. Recent research indicates that the perceived value of technology-driven exercises and examples is affected by the student's cognitive style (Ott et al. 1990). Finally, the instructor's familiarity with the basic technology and its application largely determines its effectiveness. The instructor must develop an appreciation of the capabilities of the technology in question and should "preview" its utilization prior to applying it in the classroom or laboratory. Unfortunately, too many faculty are pressed by administrations to introduce technology into their courses, and the faculty do so without adequately assessing the software's pedagogical merits or becoming familiar with its potential pitfalls. It is a major undertaking for instructors to thoroughly evaluate new technology, let alone apply it, involving time that could be spent on research rather than teaching.

Used fundamentally to broaden the students' access and exposure to a host of educational resources, technology can serve various purposes, including the following:

- A guide to assist students in absorbing new information.

- A means to organize students' efforts in the classroom.

- A means to provide remedial instruction.

- A way to convey programmed instruction.

- A means to equalize entry levels among students having diverse backgrounds.

- A way to cover subject matter in an effective and efficient manner.

The well-conceived use of technology in the accounting classroom can have a positive impact upon the quality of instruction. Previous studies have shown that its impact may be greatest among weaker students (Fetters et al. 1986, 76) and when providing instruction in areas of accounting that are conceptually complex (Boer and Livnat 1987, 116). Another study of the effects of technology on instruction indicates that its introduction to the classroom may engender a positive change in student attitudes about accounting (Abraham et al. 1987, 1).

In our judgment, by using technology in accounting instruction, instructors conceivably can improve the development of students' thought processes and retention of basic facts and concepts.

SURVEY OF CURRENT TECHNOLOGY

The range of technological media is quite broad indeed, including cables and satellites, cartridges and cassettes, closed-circuit television, video cameras, and videotapes. Computers, modems (which transfer computer signals across telephone lines), and telecommunications are additional instructional tools. Technology also can be applied to deliver accounting instruction to off-campus sites.

Technology can be used in accounting courses in a variety of ways. Both presentation and learning technology applications are available today that can enhance the presentation and understanding of accounting principles and concepts. Applications of presentation technology that improve instruction in the lecture-oriented classroom setting include the use of electronic transparencies and lecture enhancement videos. Learning technology applications that support the entire learning process consist of integrated practice sets, decision support systems, expert systems, student tutorial videos, CD ROM and hypercard databases, and custom publishing application. Following are descriptions of these technology applications as they are currently implemented.

Electronic transparencies (sometimes referred to as hypergraphics or presentation software) store the transparency image in electronic form. Instead of carrying a box of transparencies to the classroom, the instructor carries a diskette. Using presentation software, the transparency images stored on the diskette can be accessed through a personal computer. Images are projected either on a large screen television or on a liquid crystal screen connected to an overhead projector. Instructors have the ability to use electronic transparencies as they are provided by their publishers, or make modifications to them using software products that are also supplied. The ability to tailor publisher-generated, electronic transparencies and also to add instructor-designed electronic transparencies can enhance the overall quality of the lecture. Another improvement in presentation software that is only now becoming available is the introduction of sound.

Lecture enhancement videos add another dimension to the students' classroom experience. These videos run for 15 to 20 minutes, addressing topics such as accounting history, accounting applications, business operations, and data flows. In many instances, such topics are more easily introduced with visual images rather than language. Lecture enhancement videos are available from many publishers as part of the instructor's textbook package.

Computerized practice sets have been available for more than a decade. Nevertheless, the quality of these packages still varies widely. Within the past several years, integrated practice sets have been introduced. Integrated practice sets can be used in multiple-section courses. "Life-like" software supports financial and managerial accounting as well as auditing applications. The primary advantage of integrated practice sets is that students are required to learn package operations only once. If independent practice sets are used, students will learn to operate one practice set in elementary accounting, another intermediate, and a third in managerial. In this situation, the time spent in and out of class by students and faculty members learning how to manipulate the package increases significantly. Integrated practice sets expose students to computerized accounting applications while minimizing the learning curve.

Decision support systems vary in form from basic software to actual applications. In some instances, students are provided with the basic software, such as LOTUS 1-2-3, and are encouraged to develop worksheet applications to enable them to analyze the case and problem-related data. In other instances, decision support systems and worksheet templates are furnished to the student, who is required to enter the data into the system and analyze the results of processing and the sensitivity of these results to changes in input. Decision support systems encourage the student to understand the underlying economic factors that can influence decision making.

Expert systems provide additional functions beyond the computational and graphical capabilities found in decision support systems. Expert systems incorporate complex decision rules. Using documented "expert" logic, the system guides an inexperienced individual to a correct decision. The expert system not only provides guidance but also tells why the conclusion for a particular line of reasoning has been reached, thus becoming a learning tool. Generally, the greater the quantity of material that must be mastered and the more complex the rules, the more beneficial the expert system application is in guiding the learning process (Boer and Livnat 1987, 10).

Expert systems have not been used to any great extent in accounting education in view of the limited number of suitable programs and the high cost of developing them, not to mention the lack of expertise and incentive that faculty members have in developing their own systems (Dorr et al. 1988).

Student tutorials evaluate students' understanding of the material and identify their strengths and weaknesses. This software combines text, questions, and problems previously found in the student workbooks. It presents the material to students and monitors their progress using true-false and multiple-choice questions and computational problems. The software records the number of correct and incorrect answers and identifies areas where additional work may be required. A student may then selectively identify areas for review and be retested on this work.

Tutorial videos may be used in conjunction with PC-oriented student tutorials. These videos, which are provided by several publishers, present the video instructional material in a well-designed lecture format. They are a useful supplement to classroom instruction, particularly if the student is having difficulty understanding a complex topic. On occasion, when the student has to miss a class, tutorial videos may be used as a substitute for time-consuming, one-on-one instruction.

The integration of the student tutorial and tutorial video has been accomplished with the implementation of interactive video disks. This technology has been introduced in courses in the physical and social sciences. Students sitting at a work station may view the lecture and then be tested on their comprehension of the material. It is anticipated that such technology will soon make its debut in the accounting curriculum.

Diskette, CD ROM, and Hypercard databases are frequently used to support instruction in law and taxation. These databases provide nonsequential approaches to accessing information, permitting the compilation of large volumes of original data that can be accessed using the software by case, code section, or topic. In the future, similar databases may grow to support other coursework. These databases may contain background information, such as a discussion of economic and historical events, and original pronouncements not covered in the traditional accounting textbooks. They should prove to be a valuable research and reference tool.

Custom publishing allows the instructor to select educational and professional information from a large current database and literally build a unique textbook from scratch. Using this facility, instructors may select the order of topics covered in the text and the extent of coverage. Relevant problems also may be selected from the database. Additional material that can be incorporated into the printed text include class syllabi, unpublished professor-developed material, chapters from different textbooks (if they are on the database), published financial statements, Harvard Business School cases, and journal articles. Textbooks using custom publishing can be designed to fit the abilities of the audience and the objectives of the class.

APPLICATION TO A SPECIFIC COURSE

It is advisable for an instructor to focus on one course which he/she has taught frequently and to consider how particular technology can be brought to bear on the instructional process in this course. As an example, one might seek new applications in Intermediate Accounting I and II, often considered to be the heart of the accounting curriculum in the United States. A variety of technological applications could be used to enhance learning and instruction in these courses. Videotape tutorials may be used to review such complex topics as dollar-value LIFO, earnings per share, pensions, income tax accounting, and the statement of cash flows. Tutorial tapes provide the student with the opportunity to review lectures on these difficult subjects. While students often experience considerable anxiety in learning these subjects, tutorial tapes that can repeatedly stress key concepts may be just what is needed to build student confidence. A student's understanding and confidence may be further enhanced with the use of student tutorials. These applications provide self-enhancement opportunities — allowing the students to identify their strengths and weaknesses and plan their programs of study. Integrated practice sets are yet another application of learning technology. Used in the first semester of Intermediate Accounting, they can direct the student's review of the accounting cycle and the treatment of basic accounting transactions.

Subsequent instruction in conceptually difficult topics such as leases, pensions, or earnings per share can be improved with the implementation of decision support or expert systems. Use of a decision support system to perform complex pension calculations may enable the student to evaluate the sensitivity of the data to changes in underlying assumptions. An expert system may be effective in guiding the decision-making process that occurs when earnings per share calculations are performed.

Another illustration of how technology can be used in Intermediate Accounting classes is Hypercard. By utilizing Hypercard in Intermediate Accounting, the instructor conceivably could accentuate specific aspects of financial accounting not covered in the conventional textbook, including the influence of factors on the development of generally accepted accounting principles such as historical events, economic and political consequences, and other disciplines such as law. Hypercard is currently in the development stage in selected disciplines.

The use of custom publishing (e.g., textbooks) can complete the integration of technology in the Intermediate Accounting curriculum. From a practical perspective, it allows the placement of student instructions for the use of all technologies in one location. Pedagogically, like Hypercard, custom publishing supports the introduction of additional materials that may not be covered or emphasized in the traditional Intermediate Accounting text.

CONCLUDING COMMENTS

Technology can be used to improve the quality of accounting instruction. The Bedord Report (1986, p. 185) has admonished ". . . accounting faculties... [to] maintain competence in the information technologies and in efforts to develop comprehensive information systems for organizations." Additionally, the Big Eight White Paper (1989) has criticized the gap between technology available in the business environment and that used in accounting instruction in our universities. In the real world of practice, there is increasing dependence on technological support. However, for simplicity of instruction, textbooks and professors tend to overemphasize traditional, manual methods of accounting.

It is important for instructors to utilize technology in attempting to achieve particular course objectives, but in so doing to match specific media with themselves and their teaching styles. Instructors ought to refrain from utilization of technology with which they feel uncomfortable. That is not to suggest that each and every instructor who desires to use particular technology has to display expertise on the mechanics of that technology. Reliance should be placed on others with such expertise to assist in application of the technology. The instructor must develop an appreciation of the capabilities of the technology in question and has to "preview" its utilization prior to applying it in the classroom.

To promote the integration of accounting technology in the college classroom, administrators must amend faculty reward structures. Faculty who wish to use presentation and learning technologies must make a significant investment in the development and/or application of this software. However, most institutions do not recognize or reward this intellectual contribution. Thus, change in this area has been slow.

REFERENCES

AAA Committee on Multi-Media Instruction in Accounting. 1972. Multi-Media Instruction in Accounting. *The Accounting Review*, Supplement to Vol. XLVII.

Abraham, E., C. Loughrey, and H. Whalen. 1987. Computerized Practice Set in Introductory Financial Accounting. *Issues in Accounting Education* (Spring).

American Accounting Association Committee on the Future Structure, Content, and Scope of Accounting Education. 1986. Future Accounting Education: Preparing for the Expanding Profession (Bedord Report). *Issues in Accounting Education* (Spring).

Arthur Andersen, Arthur Young, Coopers & Lybrand, Deloitte Haskins & Sells, Ernst & Whinney, Peat Marwick Main, Price Waterhouse, Touche Ross. 1989. *Perspectives on Education: Capabilities for Success in the Accounting Profession* (The "Big-Eight" White Paper). New York.

Assad, A. A., and E. A. Wasil. 1986. Micro Computers and the Teaching of Operations Research. *Computers and Operations Research*, Vol. 11, No. 2/3.

Avery, C. G., and D. F. Istvan. 1974. The Multi-Media Approach to Classroom Presentation. *Accounting Education: Problems and Prospects.* Ed. by J. D. Edwards. American Accounting Association.

Bloom, R. 1984. Teaching on Television: An Instructional Alternative. *Business Educational Forum* (March).

Boer, G. B., and J. Livnat. 1987. Using Expert Systems to Teach Complex Accounting Issues. *Issues in Accounting Education* (Fall).

Borthick, A. F., and R. L. Clark. 1987. Research on Computing in Accounting Education: Opportunities and Impediments. *Issues in Accounting Education* (Fall).

Burtness, L. 1989. A Look at IBM LinkWay. *HyperLink Magazine* (May/June).

Conklin, J. 1987. Hypertext: An Introduction and Survey. *IEEE* (September).

Dorr, P., M. Eining, and J. Groff. 1988. Developing an Accounting Expert System Decision Aid for Classroom Use. *Issues in Accounting Education* (Spring).

Dyson, E. 1988. Hypertext Isn't Hype. *Forbes* (June 13).

Fauley, F. E. 1983. The New Training Technologies: Their Rocky Road to Acceptance. *Training and Development Journal* (December).

Fetters, M., J. McKenzie, and D. Callaghan. 1986. Does the Computer Hinder Accounting Education? An Analysis of Some Empirical Data. *Issues in Accounting Education* (Spring).

Harker, S. J. 1989. Hypertext: Technology for Managing Information. *Internal Auditor* (October).

Heinrich, R., M. Molenda, and J. D. Russell. 1989. *Instructional Media,* 3rd ed. New York: MacMillan.

Kleinschrod, W. A. 1988. The Trend to Electronic Training. *Administrative Management* (April).

Lehman, M., and C., 1988. Interactive Spreadsheet Models Reinforce Accounting Principles. *Journal of Accounting Education* (Vol. 6).

Ott, R. L., M. H. Mann, and C. T. Moores. 1990. An Empirical Investigation into the Interactive Effects of Student Personality Traits and Method of Instruction (Lecture or CAI) on Student Performance in Elementary Accounting. *Journal of Accounting Education* (Spring).

Roussey, R. S. 1986. The CPA in the Information Age: Today and Tomorrow. *Journal of Accountancy* (October).

Sakamoto, T. 1987.Computers in the Japanese Educational System. *Business Japan* (March).

Saunders, C., and J. Heyl. 1988. Evaluating Educational Computer Conferencing. *Journal of Systems Management* (April).

Scribner, E. 1990. A Glimpse into an Accounting Department in the Year 2000. *Issues in Accounting Education* (Spring).

Sherman, C. 1990. Buying Smart: Training Technology and Competitive Advantage. *Bulletin of the American Society for Information Science* (August/September).

Thompson, B. 1987. Hyping Text: Hypertext and Knowledge Representation. *AI Expert* (August).

Tucker, M. 1987. Business Goes to School. *Computerworld* (October 7).

Watkins, B. T. 1991. The Electronic Classroom. *The Chronicle of Higher Education* (September 4).

Webster's New Collegiate Dictionary. Springfield, MA.: Merriam, 1977.

Expert System-Driven Accounting Education: A Summary of Empirical Findings on the Reduction of Professorial Control

Paul M. Goldwater and Timothy J. Fogarty

Many believe that accounting education currently faces a crisis. While all would not agree on the nature of this situation, or its causes, most would concur that it involves the opportunity cost of training students in an ever-expanding body of substantive knowledge. While this information remains important (see Mautz 1974), many have suggested that the well-prepared accounting professional requires much more (see Wyer 1984; Subotnik 1987 and many others). The challenge to accounting educators to do all they have been doing, plus much more, would seem to require a superhuman expansion of effort in an era also marked by a decline of relative career rewards for quality teaching (see Campbell, Gaertner, and Vechio 1983).

Many solutions for the crisis of accounting education have been proposed. The better ideas recognize that human effort cannot be infinitely redoubled, that zero-sum constraints exist, and that good intentions will not suffice. A great deal of attention has then focused upon the computer as the locus of solutions, since its use involves the conservation of scarce resources. A bevy of early articles detailed the elementary applications. Before and after then, professional associations have endorsed the use of computers, citing a plethora of benefits (AICPA 1968; AAA 1970). Furthermore, accrediting bodies have institutionalized this trend with the blunt dictate "students are expected to use the computer in accounting classes" (AACSB 1986, 44). Not surprisingly, many surveys have indicated that computer use in the accounting classroom has increased dramatically (e.g., Klein and Cerullo 1990).

Yet the crisis in accounting education continues. This paper addresses this paradox. While a solution to the crisis of the accounting education is not purported, a small step in that direction is offered. In order to do so, the notion that the computer contains the promise of academic progress is extended. However, the nature of its use is distinctly recast in a manner that challenges the pre-cept that the exercise of professional control by accounting educators is unproblematic.

The remainder of this paper is organized into four sections. A literature review introduces the themes that motivated this study. This is followed by the description of an educational innovation and a summary report of results from several studies pertaining to its implementation. The paper continues with a discussion of the issues raised by this innovation.

DIMENSIONS OF THE PROBLEM

The review of previous work in accounting education is organized around a simple and intuitive description of the educational process depicted in Figure 1. Although no formal means of cause and effect are attempted in the illustration, the model suggests an exogenous set of accounting student characteristics and the confluence of a joint throughput initiated by both teachers and students. However, interposed between these throughputs and outcome are media that may have an influence on the process. The media or technology of education provides the greatest opportunity for constructive change.

Inputs

Many accounting educators have studied the role of accounting student characteristics in the production of educational outcomes. Particularly popular choices for these purposes have been gender and learning style. Other characteristics with equally intuitive influences that have not been adequately studied are locus of control, tolerance for ambiguity, need to achieve, and work ethic. Beyond its selectivity, the major flaw with this research tradition is its inability to conceptualize process. Fig-

---

Paul M. Goldwater is an Assistant Professor at the University of Central Florida. Timothy J. Fogarty is an Assistant Professor at Case Western Reserve University.

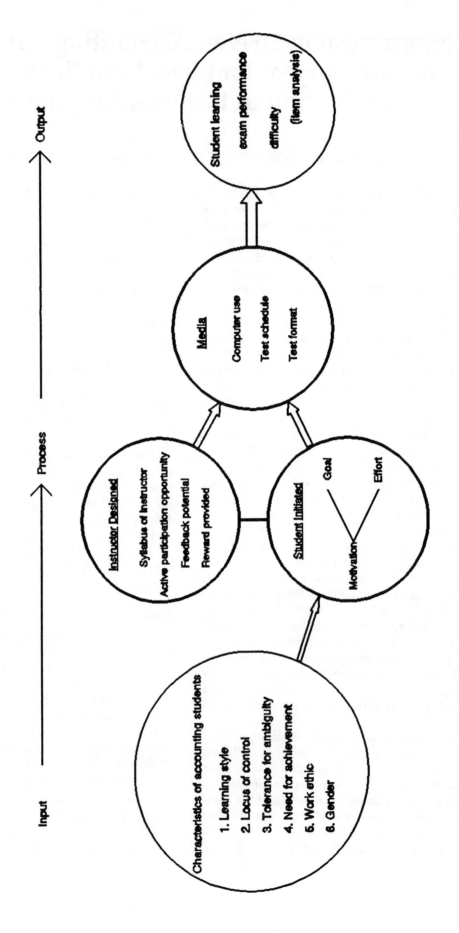

Figure 1
Elements of Accounting Education

Input   Process   Output

Characteristics of accounting students

1. Learning style
2. Locus of control
3. Tolerance for ambiguity
4. Need for achievement
5. Work ethic
6. Gender

Instructor Designed

Syllabus of instructor
Active participation opportunity
Feedback potential
Reward provided

Student Initiated

Goal
Effort
Motivation

Media

Computer use
Test schedule
Test format

Student learning
exam performance
difficulty
(item analysis)

ure 1 shows that this research is an attempt to join inputs and outputs by holding throughput and media constant. The important question that involves accounting student characteristics pertains to the neutrality of educational technology. Since the method of education is more flexible than the profile of the students, accounting student characteristics should be given a secondary role. Only a few studies involving the use of computers have recognized this priority (see Lightner and Hartman 1985; Dickens and Harper 1986).

Throughput

Not much research attention has been extended to the throughput variables shown in Figure 1. A high level of normative agreement, particularly on the student-initiated side, has obscured the research use of these variables.

Effort by students would appear to have a logical and monotonic impact on educational outputs. Educators consistently stress that hard work is the only reliable means of achieving mastery. Ibrahim (1989) documents the positive correlations between self-reported study time and grade earned. The research use of effort, however, has been hampered by the dubious value of self-reports. A second student throughput that has recently gained attention is the extent of active involvement. Very few would suggest that passive learning equals active engagement in its educational potential. Several accounting researchers have found that students are more likely to be actively involved when computer uses are implemented into courses (Briner, Pearson, and Gaunett 1987; Crosby 1984).

The professor's contribution to the educational throughput involves constructing an environment that encourages active learning opportunities, ensuring the presence of ample feedback and attaching sufficient reward to student throughput. The first dimension has gained recent attention through the growing recognition that lecture, as the exclusive means of communicating with students, is inadequate (see AECC 1990). However, how active learning can be structured in the accounting classroom remains problematic. Feedback has been cited as a key learning mechanism in several studies of accounting education (see Wright 1986; Borthick and Clark 1986). Helleloid (1989) provides one of the few studies that shows *how* feedback can be used and be misused. The general thrust of this literature indicates that current levels of feedback are inadequate. Despite a long tradition in psychology, the phenomenon of reward has been over-looked as a variable in the professor-initiated aspects of educational throughput. While several studies can be interpreted as support for the importance of reward, Elikai and Baker (1988) is one of the few studies that find that the level of reward offered by the instructor is correlated with grade attainment.

Media

Growing disenchantment with the use of the computer in the accounting classroom is the product of several factors. An initial review of the literature would prove the performance enhancements attributable to the computer are limited in scope, short in duration and of questionable reliability (see Borthick and Clark 1987). However, this conclusion may be the product of the limited way that research has sought for effects. This literature, as a rule, considers only media and outcomes, from the larger model outlined in Figure 1. The failure to model process also condemns these studies to limited relevance since education *is* process. Another problem pertains to the general way computers have been used in accounting education. Instructors, in deference to accreditation dictates, generally have appended a limited computer exercise, and attached to its successful accomplishment a small grade element. This foray leaves the non-computerized elements of the course essentially unaffected. Second, by stressing the vocational necessity of computer training, teachers fail to provide students with an appreciation of the computer as a powerful learning tool. In short, the computer must become the process of the course to influence outcomes. The current limited usage of computers in accounting education may fail to provide justification for their cost.

Examinations are pivotal moments in the life of students. For many students, the achievement of good grades takes priority over more esoteric notions of learning. Therefore, the arrangement of grade-determining elements acts as a media that cannot be ignored in understanding the production of outputs. Ideally, this measurement process should not itself create outcome effects. However, prior accounting research has identified test-scheduling effects (Reed and Holley 1989), test organization effects (Paretta and Chadwick 1975; Howe and Baldwin 1983; Baldwin and Howard 1983; Gruber 1987), and test format effects (Collier and Mehrens 1985; Frakes and Latham 1985). This research suggests that the specifics about the examination process cannot safely be ignored in accounting education.

Outputs

Scarcely an accounting educator would dispute that student learning is the proper output of accounting education. Although the content of this learning may involve more than that contained by the popular texts (see Arthur Andersen & Co. et al. 1989), it also must include comprehension and application of a wide body of technical material. Therefore, exam grades can be taken as a reliable, albeit imperfect, measure of learning.

Although less often recognized than exam performance, difficulty levels constitute a critical dimension of learning. Without some assumptions about difficulty, exam grades cannot proxy learning. Education must prepare students to face the levels of uncertainty and complexity demanded by their profession. Therefore, difficulty must be set at a level that will adequately prepare students for these challenges. In addition to serving as a dimension of learning, difficulty levels construct vital feedback to the instructor for subsequent course revisions. Surprisingly, virtually nothing is known about the difficulty of accounting courses (cf. Baldwin 1984). One contributing factor to this situation is the fear that reliable data do not exist.

Professorial Control: An Integrating Focus

The model in Figure 1 provides a valuable conceptualization of accounting education. However, this depiction itself does not create an obvious agenda for improvement. This may be provided by the recognition that exclusive professorial control over the media variables (and to a lesser extent, the throughput variables) may create a bottleneck in the production of valued outcomes. If professors could transfer media control to students, improvement might be forthcoming. This, however, would have to be done in a way that would allow the instructor to maintain equity among students and to acquire reliable information about relative student performance. Professorial control, for most an invisible taken-for-granted assumption about how education has to be, needs to be put to the same test that is applied to innovation. If positive results are produced in its absence, the rationale for high levels of professorial control is seriously challenged. Contrariwise, an environment of high student control may contain previously unrecognized advantages that cannot be realized within current arrangements.

THE EXPERT SYSTEM SOLUTION

The computer can be used as a mechanism to empower students and thereby substitute student control for professorial control. An expert system was constructed that essentially converted test bank materials into an inexhaustible resource for structured self-study. The expert system also administered examinations, recorded grades and provided feedback to students. The instructor, in addition to copying the materials provided by the textbook publisher in its test bank, supplemented the total number of questions with most published professional examinations. The core processing of the expert system is the randomization of the numeric values involved in the questions' computations. This program represents a qualitatively unique enhancement that preserves the integrity of the original question and allows students a similar thought sequence in the pursuit of correct responses. The randomization greatly expands the total number of questions available, converting a constrained instructors' aid into a teaching tool of immense flexibility, through the nearly instantaneous performance of thousands of computations.[1] This represents a large break from earlier attempts to use the computer to generate multiple exam forms (see Burton, McKeown, and Shlosberg 1978: Fuglister and Murdock 1988).

Students were informed of the availability of the expert system on the first day of the semester, and were given the appropriate access information. Students were told that there would be no graded homework, but that they could use the automated test bank as a means of evaluating their understanding of the material and preparing for their exam. Students were able to select particular sections of the course (organized by chapter number) for these purposes. Students were also able to select different types of questions (quantitative multiple choice, qualitative multiple choice, true/false). Correct answers were displayed to students only after the students provided their answer. Students could elect to be informed of incorrect responses and have the opportunity to select responses until they chose the correct one. The program also tallied the students' composite success rate by comparing inputted responses to correct responses. Since the test bank was installed on the business school's PC network, students were able to access the materials through the ample computer lab on the business school's premises. Students with their own PCs were given the data base and operating programs on a single floppy diskette, allowing them

---

[1] A more technical version of the design, processing and operation of the expert system can be found in Fogarty and Goldwater 1992a.

to work off premises. In addition, students without their diskettes were able to teleconnect into the network system from their remote locations. In addition to being highly available, the system was very "user friendly." Students, several of whom lacked computer familiarity, reported almost no technical problems in using the system. At the beginning of the semester, students were informed about the number and coverage of the examinations. Although they were given target dates for these exams, they were informed that they could take exams whenever they wished during the semester. A schedule of open exam times was established. When a student wished to take an exam, he or she informed the instructor or his assistant and were given access to a designated PC station at which conventional test security procedures could be maintained. The student received an exam with a similar structure of questions, but with unique numerical solutions. The exam required the selection of the appropriate menu items designating it as a test, but otherwise had a very similar user interface to the study sessions. Students usually faced a testing system that would reward multiple attempts to find the correct answer. Partial credit was awarded on a logarithmic scale that penalized multiple guesses.[2] One difference, however, was that the student saw questions that were reserved in the test section of the data base. Albeit similar, these exact questions had not been previously seen by the student. Following completion of the exam, the system immediately informed students of their grade and the correct answers to all questions.

Students were allowed to retake exams as often as they chose. In the event of a retake, the students' original exam grade would be replaced by the more recent exam grade if such was higher but within ten points of the original exam grade. This one-tailed approach encouraged retakes (as well as the additional studying that would precede them). However, to avoid less serious attempts to shop for higher grades, each retake automatically added five questions to the examination. This feature did not act as a conventional penalty since it did not necessarily reduce a students' score. However, it did escalate the total effort that students were expected to put forth if they were to exceed their ratio of correct responses on the previous exam. In order to add to the gravity of the initial exam attempt, grade increases of more than ten points would result in an exponential combination of the retake grade and the original grade.[3] Retaken exams also randomized the structure of the questions to de-

feat enhancing grades through the brute force memorization of a small number of question formats.[4]

In addition to functioning as a grade book, the instructor's computer program comprehensively monitored the student interface with the system. The instructor was able to track the number of exams taken, the number of study problems answered, the relative success of students in their study sessions, and the total time spent in the study mode for each student. Although these measures are not perfect metrics, they did much more closely approximate student effort than the anecdotal evidence available to most instructors. While studying together was not discouraged, the ease of individual access to such a powerful teaching tool made collaboration less necessary. Furthermore, the disabling of all printing options for security purposes precluded off-line use of the data base that would make this monitoring less reliable.

This innovation is consistent with the model of accounting education sketched in Figure 1. Insofar as it provides an active learning experience that is highly structured and precisely focused, the innovation is harmonious with the prevalent learning style of the largest group of accounting majors (see Baker, Simon, and Bazeli 1986). While question bank access and automated testing may not equally facilitate all learning style preferences, it is no more selective than more conventional procedures. This innovation provides for additional participation of students in the learning process. This student opportunity to interface with the computer on an active basis directly connects with the core knowledge expected of accounting students. One of the main advantages of the innovation is its concern with, and belief in, the value of student effort. Students are imbued with the belief that since the tests will be very similar, they ought to

---

[2]Points were awarded as follows for correct responses: First try = 16, second try = 8, third try = 4, fourth try = 2, fifth try = 1, more than 5 tries = 0.

[3]The following function was used: (First score + 10) + [(Maximum Score − First score − 10) x $e^{0.863}$]. This was designed to give more of the incremental points to students who performed reasonably well on their first attempt. Thus a student first earning a 79 and later earning a 93 would receive a score of 92, whereas a student going from 0 to 100 would receive only 50.

[4]Test questions faced by students on a retake were a random sample of the questions reserved for testing. As such, the degree of difficulty for any particular exam could have varied. No systematic differences were intended or detected.

study. They are also given the opportunity to improve upon their results primarily through the incremental effort of exam retakes. The expert system generates immediate feedback that provides students with a realistic assessment of their command of specific material. This compares very favorably to the conventional provision of homework solutions and *post facto* exam discussion. The computer-generated results, albeit more immediate, require students to actively pursue the rationale for the correct answers. Since success on the exams constituted the only component of the students', course grade, the provision of a reward sufficient to motivate students is undeniably present. Again, the nexus between effort and success is the underlying mechanism. This compares favorably to the more conventional practices of a minor grade component specifically attached to the completion of homework.

Testing on a schedule of student-initiated demand effectively negates some serious, and often ignored, interference effects. Scheduling problems created by both academic and personal interruptions can be overcome when the student determines the timing of the exam. Order effects can be reduced by the random nature of the test generation. Any residual effects are further mitigated by unlimited test retake opportunities.

Finally, the described innovation effectively and efficiently uses the computer as a tutorial supplement in a manner that does not duplicate the contributions of the text or the instructor. Its advantages can be obtained with very little specialized skills on the part of students. The onus for learning remains with the students, although the computer alleviates some of the artificialities induced by the conventional instructional delivery and retention evaluation procedures. Additionally, this computer application is firmly integrated with the substantive knowledge of accounting. As such, students are more likely to approach it as a learning tool, rather than as a loosely connected and incidental toy whose use happens to be a course requirement.

SUMMARY OF RESULTS

The purpose of this section is to provide some description of the main outcomes generated by the ongoing use of the data bank access and test bank-based automated testing application. To provide a broader perspective on the research agenda surrounding the issue of professorial control within the context of Figure 1, research results from sev-

eral different projects will be summarized in this section. Readers interested in more detailed information about particular hypotheses are directed to solicit the particular cited papers from the authors.

Primary Results

Although standards are difficult to formulate, students devoted large amounts of time to work with the expert system. Typical semesters showed an average of 2,600 minutes in the system in which over 2,000 questions were answered. Although great variation among students existed in effort levels, the system appeared to extract higher levels of effort from the average student. Surprisingly, students in summer session courses, despite extreme time compression, did not study less (see Fogarty and Goldwater 1992b).

In the average semester, approximately 73 percent of the students would take advantage of the opportunity to retake exams. The modal case involved a single retake per student, although some students took up to six retakes. In total, the retake provision involved an average of 47 percent more exams than would have been given without this stipulation.

Other descriptive statistics revealed the normality of grade distributions, the lack of grade inflation attributable to partial credit scoring[5] and the approximate similarity of practice and test scores. Therefore, the expert system managed accounting class resembles a traditional accounting class in its tangible results. The key difference is process and control.

Figure 1 invites the linkage of student effort levels and grades earned as part of the impact of a student-controlled environment. Invariably across semesters, study effort, denominated in terms of minutes or questions, is significant at $p < .01$ in the explanation of grade attained (see Fogarty and Goldwater 1992c).

A reduction of professional control might cause a reduction in equity among students. For example, if students were able to achieve higher grades by random chance, allowing infinite retakes of examinations would be a cause for concern. However, grade improvement cannot be associated at $p < .05$ with frequency of reexamination under the rules described in the previous section (see Goldwater and Fogarty 1992a). Along similar lines, allowing students relief from an instructor-imposed sched-

---

[5]This result is not robust over all scoring algorithms. For example, awarding 5, 4, 3, 2, 1 points instead of 16, 8, 4, 2, 1 points will produce higher grades.

ule for exams might provide those that delay additional (and unfair) opportunities. However, the results suggest that exam taking delay is instead statistically associated with lower grades (Goldwater and Fogarty 1992c).

The primary results suggest that the lowering of professional control is feasible. Students work hard, grade inflation does not occur and equity among students is not eroded. Furthermore, students gain by being able to study and be assessed at their own pace. These results suggest that current levels of professorial control might not be as necessary to accounting education as some believe.

The Role of Accounting Student Characteristics

Survey instruments were distributed to students to assess the psychological characteristics listed in Figure 1.[6] Using student grade point average as a covariate, no direct psychological effects on exam scores or effort levels could be found. Furthermore, psychological differences were not associated with test scheduling or test retake requests. However, an important indirect role for most psychological variables was discovered when psychological profiles were considered to moderate the primary relationships. The personality variables were highly associated with the strength of the effort-grade relationship, the scheduling-grade relationship and the incremental grade effect of retakes (see Goldwater, Fogarty, and Lopez 1992)

Beyond specific psychological trait differences lie general differences between the sexes. While many papers have addressed gender effects in the accounting classroom (see Mutchle, Turner, and Williams 1987; Lipe 1989), none have considered the expert system–driven environment. Furthermore, previous gender studies have been limited by unreliable data and extraneous variation introduced by instructor or grading policies. No direct gender effects were found in the subject classes exposed to this expert system. However, females did tend to use the expert system more extensively than males and as a result tended to earn higher grades (Roush, Fogarty, and Goldwater 1992). This finding would seem to challenge further research for an exploration of why female students work harder in accounting classrooms.

Difficulty Assessments

The output files created by student use of the expert system offered a unique window to view the attempts to reach correct answers over thousands of repetitions. The relative success of students in their attempts to answer cost accounting questions supported the existence of distinct difficulty differences by topical area, question format and by specific learning objective (Goldwater and Fogarty 1992b). Furthermore, incremental difficulty apparently unrelated to the materials exists when the exercise is denoted a test rather than a practice. These conclusions were robust over partial-credit and dichotomous scoring alternatives.

Another attempt to evaluate difficulty involved the dimension of question source. Since questions came from several sources (the text test bank, the CPA exam and the CMA exam) an opportunity to evaluate the relative difficulty of these materials existed. Cost accounting questions from the CMA exam proved more difficult than those from the CPA exam, which, in turn, proved more difficult than test-bank questions. Difficulty in these comparisons was not uniform over topical areas nor over question format (see Goldwater and Fogarty 1992a).

Difficulty analysis work in process involves an attempt to evaluate the positioning of cost accounting questions according to Bloom's taxonomy (Bloom 1956). This will entail an assessment of whether accounting students have more trouble correctly responding to questions from more challenging learning objectives.

DISCUSSION

This paper has used an expert system to evaluate professorial control. The general conclusion supported by the results of several papers is that viable educational results are possible without high levels of professorial control in an expert system environment. Figure 2 depicts the general parameters of such a process as a counter distinction to Figure 1. The principal difference between the two figures is the removal of instructor hegemony over the media of education in Figure 2. The use of the computer as the primary process of education facilitates the unique reiteration of learning depicted in that figure.

Accounting educators no doubt aspire to professional status, both organizationally and psychologically. Part of that claim necessarily involves the exertion of control over some critical delivery of valued services (Child and Fulk 1982). Accounting professors exert this control primarily through their dominion over students, both through the

---

[6]More information about the conduct and instrumentation of the survey exists in Goldwater et al. (1992).

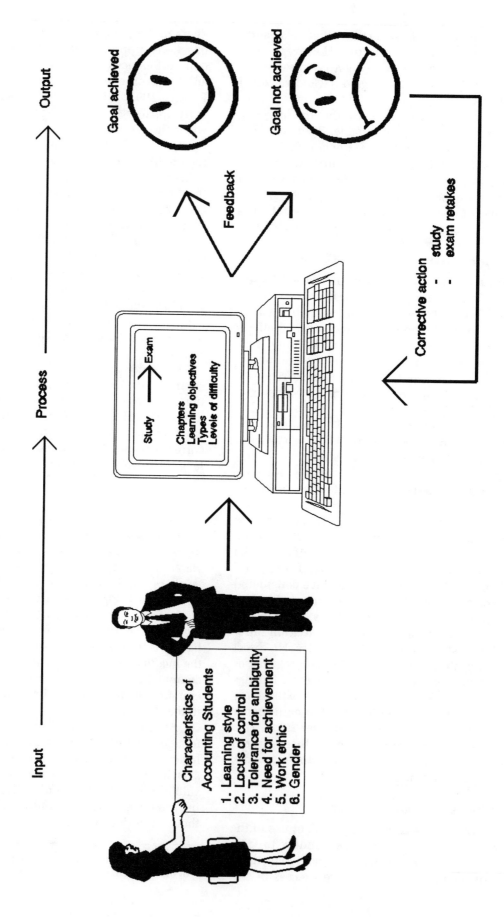

Figure 2
Accounting Education in an Expert System Environment

design of curriculum and by the exercise of authority within the classroom. To some extent, this is necessary since there is an undebatable need for structure and organization. However, elements of the authority are not necessary or even desirable if they contradict the primacy of the students' responsibility for their education and introduce undesirable side-effects inconsistent with an educative purpose.

Extensive control by faculty may induce the belief that faculty must shoulder the brunt of the educational effort. While it is desirable for faculty to aspire toward superior performance and refined technique, faculty effort derives its importance from its contribution to student learning. Faculty effort cannot substitute effectively for student effort for this purpose. Advocating the use of an inexhaustible bank of questions communicates the message that the responsibility for education remains with the student. Allowing unlimited retakes of the exam drives across the point that adequate preparation is the only means to success. Students in conventional homework and testing modes are much more likely to critique the relevance of the assignments to the exams, to blame the instructor for an unfair exam, and to attribute the deficiency in their outcomes to bad timing (the "had-a-bad-day" phenomenon). To the extent that conventional practices add to the credibility of these perceptions, students are able to psychologically transfer responsibility to the instructor.

Professional control that dictates the minutia of classes, however well-intentioned, can be worse than paternalistic in its unintentional consequences. Requiring homework for its own sake (i.e., without a believed tie to the exam) implicitly encourages dishonesty insofar as copying the assignments of others becomes expedient and nearly foolproof. Imposing an inflexible schedule of assignments and evaluations may contribute to test anxiety and perceptions of interpersonal threat (Crosby 1984). Whereas conventional methods involving the denial of access to educational materials and the limited provision of evaluation are justified by some as lessons for the "real world," they also involve substantial elements of faculty convenience.

In several ways, the excesses of control in the classroom are inconsistent with the role of the professor as educational facilitator. Should not a facilitator, where possible, allow students to determine for themselves the extent of effort they expend? Conventional study (particularly assigned homework) establishes a contractual arrangement

that tends to psychologically act as a maximum for student exam rehearsal. Should a facilitator allow students a wealth of opportunities to demonstrate the extent of their achievement? Typical exam practices close the book on a percentage of the final grade after a single take-it-or lose-it chance. The innovation described in this paper attempts to rectify this faculty role confusion. By transferring the work to the computer, the constraints on the true facilitator role are removed. Whereas tight professional control of these aspects of education was once technologically necessary, to continue them in the computer age seems anachronistic.

Ultimately, professors exert control over students through their ability to confer grades upon them. Good grades can be conceived as scarce reasons that students should value for their ability to be translated into other, more tangible resources. Understandably, students tend to focus upon the attainment of grades as the *sine qua non* of their efforts. Contrariwise, many professors think of grades as the natural outcome of evaluations that are neutral measures of accomplishment. This perspective contributes to an artificial separation between the examining process and the teaching process for faculty. The failure to appreciate the continuity between the two elements may contribute to the unwarranted mystification of the examining process. In turn, this may unnecessarily interfere with the relationship between educators and students. The expert system allows examinations to be perceived as more naturalistic parts of the class and more substantively integrated with its subject. Insofar as they are tested by the machine, students no longer need fear that the exam will be a product of the professors' idiosyncratic priorities and values. The instructor can then truly become the students' ally in the studying process.

As technological capabilities advance, educators must assume the responsibility of knowing how to properly exploit these new strengths. Part of this has to be the recognition that the purpose of computers in accounting classes is not limited to the provision of vocational skills, about which there appears to be little consensus (Bean and Mediwitz 1987). Now that students no longer have to be introduced to the computer, the machine can be a source of untapped efficiency gains when it is forced to be a supplementary teacher in a quasi-interactive mode. This expert system works well in this vein because it is applicable to a much wider set of courses than other prepackaged alternatives, it forces students to master the material by not automating too much of the processing, and it allows the student unlimited flexibility in the devotion of time to the project. The computer is not a panacea, for it will not learn for people. However, it can make human learning more efficient, more convenient and a more engaging experience.

An unappreciated consequence of conventional testing methods is the opportunity cost of this use of time. Educators in accounting complain about the explosion of content in their courses, yet unthinkingly give over a nontrivial portion of their contact hours to testing. Taking examinations out of the classroom would result in additional time

for other purposes. The system put forth in this paper holds the promise of conserving time. This advantage is only as good as the value created in the alternative use of this time. There appears to be no shortage of ideas for multidisciplinary, creative problem solving as applied to accounting education. Allowing the machine to establish the important procedural basics might allow the instructor more freedom to establish a sense of community with students about the central dilemmas of the subject (see Wyer 1984) and to inject the economic reality of transactional uncertainty (see Subotnik 1987) into the course.

REFERENCES

Accounting Education Change Commission (AECC). 1990. *Objectives of Education for Accountants* (September).

American Academy of College of Schools of Business. 1986. *Accreditation Council Policies, Procedures and Standards.* AACSB.

American Accounting Association. 1970. *Report of the 1968–1969 Committee on the Role of the Computer in Accounting Education.* AAA.

American Institute of Certified Public Accountants. 1968. *Educational Requirements for Entry into the Accounting Profession: A Statement of AICPA Policies.* AICPA.

Arthur Andersen & Co. Arthur Young, Coopers & Lybrand, Deloitte Haskins & Sells, Ernst & Whinney, Peat Marwick Main & Co., Price Waterhouse, and Touch Ross. 1989. *Perspectives on Education: Capabilities for Success in the Accounting Profession.* Arthur Andersen & Co., Arthur Young, Coopers & Lybrand, Deloitte Haskins & Sells, Ernst & Whinney, Peat Marwick Main & Co., Price Waterhouse, Touch Ross (April).

Baker, R., J. Simon, and F. Bazeli. 1986. An Assessment of the Learning Style Preferences of Accounting Majors. *Issues in Accounting Education* (Spring): 1–12.

Baldwin, B. 1984. The Role of Difficulty and Discrimination in Constructing Multiple Choice Examinations: With Guidelines for Practical Applications. *Journal of Accounting Education*: 19–28.

———, and T. Howard. 1983. Inter-topical Sequencing of Examination Questions: An Empirical Evaluation. *Journal of Accounting Education* (Fall): 89–95.

Bean, V., and J. Medewitz. 1987. Computer Education: A Survey of Accounting Graduates. *Journal of Accounting Education* (Fall): 243–258.

Bloom, B. 1956. *Taxonomy of Educational Objectives.* D. McKay Company.

Borthick, F., and R. Clark. 1986. The Role of Productive Thinking in Affecting Student Learning with Micro-computers in Accounting Education. *The Accounting Review*: 143–157.

———. 1987. Research on Computing in Accounting Education: Opportunities and Impediments. *Issues in Accounting Education* (Fall): 173–192.

Briner, R., D. Pearson, and J. Gaunett. 1987. Microcomputer Application for Attribute Sampling. *Journal of Accounting Education*: 161–166.

Burton, E. J., J. McKeown, and J. Shlosberg. 1978. The Generation and Administration of Examinations on Interactive Computer Systems. *The Accounting Review*: 170–178.

Campbell, D., J. Gaertner, and R. Vecchio. 1983. Perceptions of Promotion and Tenure Criteria: A Survey of Accounting Educators. *Journal of Accounting Education* (Spring): 83–92.

Child, J., and J. Fulk. 1982. Maintenance of Occupational Control: The Case of Professions. *Work and Occupations* (May): 155–192.

Collier, H., and W. Mehrens. 1985. Using Multiple Choice Test Items to Improve Classroom Testing of Professional Accounting Students. *Journal of Accounting Education* (Fall): 40–51.

Crosby, L. 1984. Experiences with the Personalized System of Instruction to Teach Elementary Accounting. *Journal of Accounting Education* (Spring): 139–143.

Dickens, T., and R. Harper. 1986. The Use of Micro Computers in Intermediate Accounting: Effects on Student Achievement and Attitudes. *Journal of Accounting Education* (Spring): 127–146.

Elikai, F., and J. Baker. 1988. Empirical Evidence on the Effectiveness of Quizzes as a Motivation Technique. *Issues in Accounting Education*: 248–255.

Fogarty, T., and P. Goldwater. 1992a. *The Development of an Expert System for Accounting Education.* Unpublished paper.

———. 1992b. *Increasing Student Control Through an Expert System: An Academic Accounting Innovation and Field Test.* Unpublished paper.

———. 1992c. Instructor Control in an Automated Environment: A Reconsideration with Empirical Evidence. *Accounting Education*: 293–310.

Frakes, A., and W. Latham. 1985. A Comparison of Multiple Choice and Problem Examinations in Introductory Financial Accounting. *Journal of Accounting Education* (Spring): 81–89.

Fuglister, J., and R. Murdock. 1988. Use of the Computer in Preparation of Multiple Choice Examinations: A Multiple For Generating Programs. *Issues in Accounting Education*: 174–180.

Goldwater, P. and T. Fogarty. 1992a. *The Comparative Difficulty of CMA Examination Questions.* Unpublished paper.

———. 1992b. *An Empirical Evaluation of Difficulty in Cost Accounting: An Inductive Approach.* Unpublished paper.

———. 1992c. *Giving Students More Control Over Education with an Expert System: A Description and Field Test in Cost Accounting.* Unpublished paper.

———, and P. Lopez. 1992. *Psychological Differences and Student Behavior with an Expert System: A Management Accounting Application.* Unpublished paper.

Gruber, R. 1987. Sequencing Exam Questions Relative to Topic Presentation. *Journal of Accounting Education* (Spring): 77–86.

Helleloid, R. 1989. Providing Answers to Self-Study Questions: An Experimental Investigation of Possible Effects. *Issues in Accounting Education* (Spring): 94–119.

Howe, K., and B. Baldwin. 1983. The Effects of Evaluative Sequencing on Performance Behavior and Attitudes. *The Accounting Review*: 135–142.

Ibrahim, M. 1989. Effort-Expectation and Academic Performance in Managerial Cost Accounting. *Journal of Accounting Education* (Spring): 57–68.

Klein, L., and M. Cerullo, M. 1990. Problems of Integrating Microcomputers into Accounting Education, Again. *Kent/Bentley Journal of Accounting and Computers* (Fall): 59–75.

Lightner, S., and M. Hartman. 1985. Inventory of Computer Software Designed for Use in the Accounting Curriculum: Student Materials and Test Banks. *Journal of Accounting Education* (Spring): 15–36.

Lipe, M. 1989. Further Evidence on the Performance of Female Versus Accounting Students. *Issues in Accounting Education*: 144–155.

Mautz, R. 1974. Where Do We Go From Here? *The Accounting Review*: 353–360.

Mutchler, J., J. Turner, and D. Williams. 1987. The Performance of Female Versus Male Students. *Issues in Accounting Education*: 103–111.

Paretta, T., and L. Chadwick. 1975. The Sequencing of Examination Questions and Its Effect on Student Performance. *The Accounting Review*: 595–600.

Reed, S., and J. Holley. 1989. The Effect of Final Exam Scheduling on Student Performance. *Issues in Accounting Education* (Fall): 327–344.

Roush, P., T. Fogarty, and P. Goldwater. 1992. *An Analysis of Why Female Accounting Students Outperform Male Accounting Students.* Unpublished paper.

Subotnik, D. 1987. Accounting Can Learn from Legal Education. *Issues in Accounting Education* (Fall): 313–324.

Wright, A. 1986. On the Use of an Available Prior Examination Policy. *Issues in Accounting Education* (Spring): 24–33.

Wyer, J. 1984. Conceptual vs. Procedural: A Developmental Approach. *Journal of Accounting Education* (Spring): 5–18.

Innovations in Accounting Education

John W. Hardy, Jay M. Smith, and Larry A. Deppe

"Accounting education in the 90s" has been a common idea discussed by accounting educators. There have been studies of accounting education over the last several years. The Bedford Report in 1986 considered the future structure, content and scope of accounting education.[1] Ralph Estes did a survey of practitioners on the present and future importance of selected knowledge skills for accounting professionals of the future.[2] Another significant study was done by the Big Eight CPA firms which has come to be referred to as the "White Paper."[3] These and other studies have raised questions about the current methods used to teach accounting to university students.

In response to many of these concerns, the American Accounting Association created in 1989 the Accounting Education Change Commission (AECC). It was funded with $4,000,000 by the Big Eight CPA firms. "The commission's charge was essentially to facilitate implementation of the recommendations of two documents:" (1) AAA Bedford Committee report, "Future Accounting Education: Preparing for the Expanding Profession" and (2) Big Eight firms White Paper, "Perspectives on Education: Capabilities for Success in the Accounting Profession."[4]

Brigham Young University's School of Accountancy and Information Systems (SOAIS) made a proposal to the AECC and was selected in the first round of grants given. The purpose of this paper is to identify the status to date of the BYU School of Accountancy and Information Systems on this project and the innovative approach it has taken to improve the accounting education process.

THE BYU COMPETENCY SURVEY

Brigham Young University's approach has been to identify the competencies accounting graduates should possess upon entry into the profession and to design a curriculum for the junior core year that effectively imbues accounting students with these competencies. The goal of the School of Accountancy and Information Systems is to implement the newly designed curriculum during a three-year time period (1990–1992). Following this effort, steps would be taken to measure the effectiveness of the new curriculum and share our findings and experience with other interested institutions.

A study was done to determine what competencies were relevant for an accountant to have.[5] A survey of the literature was made. There were seven major competency categories identified with the number of specific competencies noted:

1. Communication skills (5).
2. Information development and distribution (3).
3. Decision-making skills (3).
4. Knowledge of accounting, auditing, and tax (4).
5. Knowledge of business and environment (3).
6. Professionalism (3).
7. Leadership development (6).

Once the competencies were identified, a questionnaire was developed. Table 1 shows the questionnaire which was used to survey accounting practitioners with the relevant competencies identified. The 27 competencies identified were the ones which the BYU committee felt were the most relevant to consider. An instructional science consultant assisted in the competency identification process.

A survey of 873 practicing accountants was done. The sample selected represented graduates from 158 colleges and universities and included

1. Employees of Big Six public accounting firms in Southern California.

[1] American Accounting Association, Committee on the Future Structure, Content and Scope of Accounting Education (The Bedford Committee), "Future Accounting Education: Preparing for the Expanding Profession," *Issues in Accounting Education* (Spring 1986), 160–195.

[2] R. Estes, "The Profession's Changing Horizons: A Survey of Practitioners on the Present and Future Importance of Selected Knowledge and Skills," *The International Journal of Accounting Education and Research*, Spring 1979, 47–70.

[3] *Perspectives on Education: Capabilities for Success in the Accounting Profession* (New York: Arthur Andersen & Co., Arthur Young, Coopers & Lybrand, Deloitte Haskins & Sells, Ernst & Whinney, Peat Marwick Main & Co., Price Waterhouse, and Touche Ross, 1989).

[4] *Accounting Education News*, American Accounting Association, June 1990.

[5] Larry A. Deppe, E. O. Sonderegges, J. D. Stice, D. C. Clark, and G. F. Streuling, "Emerging Competencies for the Practice of Accountancy," *Journal of Accounting Education* (1991, Vol. 2).

John W. Hardy is Professor, Jay M. Smith is Professor, and Larry A. Deppe is an Assistant Professor, at Brigham Young University.

TABLE 1
Professional Accounting Education Questionnaire

Part II. Sources of impact on your education and professionalism

Directions: Below is a set of professional competencies you have developed in varying degrees. We are interested in where you developed them: (A) your precollege experiences, (B) your college undergraduate program, (C) your college graduate program, or (D) your after-college employment experiences. Rank each of the four sources according to its contribution in helping you develop a given competency. For example, if your ability to "listen effectively" had been developed primarily in after-college employment experiences, it would be given a ranking of "1." If this ability was also developed to a lesser degree in any of the other three categories give additional rankings down to "4." If there is a competency that has not been significantly developed in any of the four categories write "not developed" or "N/D."

Competency	Precollege	Under-graduate Program	Graduate Program	After College Employment
COMMUNICATION SKILLS				
1. Ability to present views in writing.				
2. Ability to present views through oral presentations.				
3. Read, critique, and judge the value and contribution of written work.				
4. Listen effectively.				
5. Understand interpersonal and group dynamics.				
INFORMATION DEVELOPMENT AND DISTRIBUTION SKILLS				
6. Understand the role of information technology in solving business and accounting problems.				
7. Understand the system development life cycle to plan, design, implement, and evaluate an information system.				
8. Effectively apply fundamental programming skills to typical business problems.				
DECISION-MAKING SKILLS				
9. Solve diverse and unstructured problems in unfamiliar settings.				
10. Induce general conclusions from specific situations.				
11. Select and assign priorities within restricted resources.				
KNOWLEDGE OF ACCOUNTING, AUDITING, AND TAX				
12. Possess a knowledge of the purpose and elements of financial statements and how to prepare them.				
13. Understand the fundamentals of accounting, auditing, and tax.				
14. Know methods of gathering, summarizing, and analyzing financial data.				
15. Apply decision rules embodied in the accounting model.				
KNOWLEDGE OF BUSINESS AND ENVIRONMENT				
16. Understand the economic, social, and cultural forces in the world.				

(Continued on next page)

TABLE 1 (Continued)

Competency	Precollege	Under-graduate Program	Graduate Program	After College Employment
17. Know how typical business organizations work and are managed.				
18. Possess a knowledge of financial markets and funding institutions.				
PROFESSIONALISM				
19. Identify ethical issues and apply my own values to them.				
20. Motivation to continue lifelong learning.				
21. Deal effectively with imposed pressures.				
LEADERSHIP DEVELOPMENT				
22. Work effectively with diverse groups of people.				
23. Organize and delegate tasks.				
24. Motivate other people.				
25. Resolve conflict.				
26. Understand methods of creating and managing change within an organization.				
27. Use data, exercise judgments, evaluate risks, and solve real-world problems.				
OTHER COMPETENCIES (Please identify and rank other competencies important to professional accountants.)				

2. Graduates of BYU's SOAIS not employed in Southern California.

3. Employees of Phillips Petroleum in Bartlesville, OK.

4. Employees of Marriott Corporation in Landover, MD.

The conclusion BYU reached was that its list of competencies appeared to be representative. The respondents agreed that the expanded list of competencies needed to be taught but were undecided as to where the competencies should be taught — in the university or on the job.

CURRENT PROGRAM AT BYU

Currently, BYU has a five-year integrated program with two years of general education and business core courses followed by a one-year junior core to which a student must be admitted. The junior year is an entry point for all accounting majors and has a series of common core courses. After the junior year, a student applies to enter the two-year program which enables him or her to obtain a B.S. or master's degree. This approach is identified as the 2-1-2 approach. Students may opt to get their bachelor's degree after the junior year instead of seeking the master's degree. Because the junior year was the common core year for all accounting majors, the SOAIS decided to focus its efforts for innovative changes in accounting education in the junior year.

INNOVATIVE CURRICULUM DESIGN

BYU's SOAIS is in the midst of implementing its innovative integrated accounting core. After extensive study in the first grant year 1990–91, BYU began implementing its new program in Fall 1991. The BYU program includes the following innovative features:

1. An integrated faculty team of eleven, two from each area of accounting specialization plus one

from business law, were selected which represented systems, audit, financial accounting, managerial accounting, and tax. One faculty member from international accounting is also involved. At times there are two faculty teams teaching a given subject area.

2. To provide all students with the same common educational experience, the Accounting Core (first year in the SOAIS) is required of all accounting students. The core has 24 hours of credit and is taught four to five days a week in three hour blocks (8 to 11am or 1 to 4pm). There are two blocks of course material per semester with a grade given to the student at the end of each block. There are five faculty members assigned to each section with 55 students per section or 225 students in total. The students in the junior core have gone through an admission process to enter the first year of the accounting program.

3. A content structure that establishes accounting as an information system that provides information from a database environment to meet the needs of various users as a value added benefit. The program begins with a broad systems and environment content, includes laboratory experiences where students use their own computers and a laboratory to improve their skills in the use of DOS and spreadsheets, and learn to live in a world of networking and databases. Students learn to use a relational database (Paradox) and use it throughout the integrated program.

4. A program organization built around five basic business cycles, (1) sales and collection, (2) acquisition and payment, (3) conversion, (4) personnel, and (5) financing. Each cycle begins with the systems faculty members setting the stage for the cycle by identifying the entities and relationships that exist for that cycle. The auditing professors then discuss the controls needed in the system to establish and maintain the integrity of the database. Professors from each functional area then discuss issues affecting that cycle important for their users. In some cases where two functional areas have in the past taught the same material in different courses, they are now taught together at one time and any differences are highlighted (e.g., LIFO inventory in the conversion cycle taught by tax and financial accounting faculty; legal liability of auditors in a foundation cycle by the law and auditing faculty. Although this approach has been used for the past several years to teach auditing, it is a significant change for financial, managerial and tax. Material from existing textbooks is used where feasible. In other cases, new material is being developed specifically to fit this structure.

5. An introductory eight-week foundation phase that precedes the business cycles and builds a framework for each accounting area that establishes the foundation for the integration into the cycles. Besides the systems orientation in this phase, financial accounting stresses the conceptual framework and the general financial statements, managerial accounting presents the view of quality management and the role of information to achieve improved quality, tax presents an overview of taxation at all levels of government and basic taxation principles, and auditing discusses the role of the auditor, the audit risk model, and the types of reports issued by all types of auditors. In all of these areas, a research orientation is captured as students are introduced to the accounting and business periodicals, the tax library, professional standards and business databases including NAARS and LEXUS.

6. A recognition that there are competencies students need to acquire in their accounting besides knowledge and content. As already noted, in the first part of our study, 27 competencies were identified as important for success in various fields of accounting. These include competencies in communication, interpersonal skills, group activities, analytical reasoning, and leadership skills, We selected nine of these competencies (identified as expanded competencies to distinguish them from content competencies) to intertwine throughout the junior core. The nine expanded competencies selected are (1) present views in writing; (2) present views through oral presentations; (3) read, critique, and judge the value and contribution of written work; (4) listen effectively; (5) understand and work effectively with groups of people; (6) solve diverse and unstructured problems in unfamiliar settings; (7) deal effectively with imposed pressure; (8) organize and delegate tasks; and (9) resolve conflict. The basics for these competencies are taught to the students in the foundation segment of the junior core by experts in organizational behavior, educational psychology, and communications. Experience is then given the students through-

out the year by the functional faculty in a variety of ways to develop these competencies. Students' progress is documented and evaluated by faculty, graduate student observers (including video), and by their peers. Evaluation procedures and forms have been developed to measure the achievement of these competencies.

7. A significant alteration of the teaching pedagogy has occurred because of the emphasis on competencies such as developing communication skills, ability to work in groups with diverse types of people, learning to solve unstructured problems, and ability to work under pressure. Student involvement in case presentation, written papers, oral presentations, and group in-class activities is significantly altering the lecture format many professors have used. Group work has been stressed from the first day, and student participation in groups and in the larger class is the norm.

8. A team approach to developing curriculum. Eleven professors spent eight months in developing 112 teaching plans to deliver the content and develop the competencies. Each teaching plan covers three hours and includes the topics to be covered, the content learning objectives, the expanded competencies to be stressed, the preclass assignment, the in-class activities, any postclass assignments, and the evaluation methods to be used for the expanded competencies. The framework for the year has provided a basis for delegating the workload, and has involved all the faculty in approaching their functional specialties in new and innovative ways.

9. The gathering of extensive data during the implementation year under the direction of our measurement expert. Teaching assistants are present in the classrooms as observers to make field notes and to assist in the evaluation of the students' performance. Students and faculty are providing continuous feedback of what is working well and what is not. This is leading to an adaptive program that changes as the need arises. We are discovering the strengths and weaknesses of such an integrated program from the viewpoint of faculty and students. Since the teaching assistants went through our more traditional program, they are able to provide significant comparative feedback.

It can be noted from the above innovative steps that the focus of BYU's program is on first, an integration of accounting areas and second, a heavy information systems focus. This approach which includes building competency-based students skills for the student in addition to getting accounting knowledge should provide a student with preparation to meet today's professional accounting needs.

Table 2 illustrates an overall calendar for our Winter 1992 program. The number of days spent on the foundation and business cycles is also shown.

In order to facilitate team teaching by the faculty, as well as to provide consistency of topic coverage between different sections, a teaching plan is prepared by the faculty members which each uses. Table 3 illustrates a typical teaching plan. The area illustrated is from the foundation section for

---

TABLE 2
Accounting Junior-Year Core Overall Calendar

	# Days
FOUNDATION	
Orientation and environment	7
Teaching of concepts—group work	1
Financial conceptual framework	5
Tax framework	4
Examination #1	1
Managerial framework	4
Teaching of concepts—listen effectively	1
Auditing framework	5
Teaching of concepts—oral communication	1
Examination #2	1
BLOCK #1 (30 days)	
BUSINESS CYCLE ANALYSIS	
Organizing an entity	3
Systems framework for business cycle analysis	5
Examination #3	1
Sales—Collection cycle	12
Career choices	5
Examination #4—Final time	0
BLOCK #2 (26 days)	
END OF FALL SEMESTER	
Acquisition/Payment cycle	13
Examination #5	1
Personnel and performance evaluation	12
Examination #6	1
BLOCK #3 (27 days)	
Conversion cycle (Part II)	12
Examination #7	1
Financing cycle	13
Investment in other entities	3
Examination #8—Final time	0
BLOCK #4 (29 days)	
END OF WINTER SEMESTER	

TABLE 3
Teaching Plan

CYCLE: Foundation   **PERIOD:** 26   **DATE:** Oct. 17, 1991

MAJOR TEACHING RESPONSIBILITY: Audit

TOPICS:
Business and inherent risk
Materiality
Control structure

COMPETENCY FOCUS
Oral
Groups
Conflict
Critique
Unstructured
Listen

CONTENT LEARNING OBJECTIVES
1. Identify the business and inherent risks of a specific entity and evaluate the acceptability of the company as an audit client.
2. Define the concept of materiality as used in auditing and contrast it with materiality as used in the conceptual framework.
3. Describe how materiality relates to detection risk and sampling risk, and explain why a preliminary estimate of materiality is necessary.
4. Describe the elements of a company's internal control structure and recognize weaknesses and strengths of representative systems.
5. Explain how control risk affects audit risk, detection risk and the type of auditing to be done.

EXPANDED COMPETENCY LEARNING OBJECTIVES
1. Group members will demonstrate how they can work together to resolve conflicts and produce case solution. (Both in and out of class)
2. Group members will critique the work of another group.
3. Groups will demonstrate ability to present views orally through presentation of case solution on video tape outside of class.

PRECLASS ASSIGNMENTS
1. Read Arens Chapter 9.
2. Read "Practical Application of SAS 55," *CPA Journal*, May 1990, pp. 14–27. (Packet)
3. Read "The Case for Risk Driven Audits," *Journal of Accountancy*, March 1989, pp. 55–61. (Packet)
4. Read and prepare initial analysis of Diamond Battery Case. (Packet) Groups
5. Problems 8:28, 8:33, 8:34; 9:25, 9:29

IN-CLASS ACTIVITIES
20 min. Lecture and discussion on business risk and inherent risk.
20 min. Review of homework
40 min. View Dermaceutics video (Act I)
10 min. Listening quiz based on video
30 min. Group work on Dermaceutics in class. Identify risks 20 minutes. Share ideas with another group.
40 min. Lecture and discussion of control structure (Ch. 9)
20 min. Review P. 9:25, 9:29

POSTCLASS ASSIGNMENT
10 min group tape video of Diamond Battery solution. Due date: Tuesday, Oct. 22

COMPETENCY EVALUATION METHODS
1. Homework that deals with unstructured situations
2. Quiz to test listening skills
3. Observation of group activity. Critiques of other teams.
4. Evaluate oral taped presentations of Diamond Battery

---

the area of auditing. The content learning objectives are based on Bloom's taxonomy levels.

The integrative approach to accounting topics has been achieved by identifying several key areas

in the business cycle. Table 4 illustrates the approach used to integrate the teaching of the acquisition and payment cycle. It can be seen from Table 4 that all of the accounting areas are involved in teaching this subject area. It is anticipated that the student will be better prepared and may more easily remember the concepts of this business cycle because the systems, management accounting, tax, financial accounting, and auditing aspects of the topic are integrated.

SUMMARY AND CONCLUSION

Brigham Young University received an Accounting Education Change Commission Grant in 1990. Brigham Young University's approach to innovative accounting education we feel makes a useful contribution for accounting educators. Its unique features include (1) a heavy systems orientation with a database which can be drawn upon by all accounting disciplines; (2) an integrative approach in teaching accounting subjects based on a business cycle approach; and (3) the integration of various competencies into the skill base of the students while learning accounting subject material. These features are achieved through the use of well-developed teaching plans, a cooperative faculty, specific calendaring of teaching days, and specific topical coverage identified for each business cycle topic area.

TABLE 4
Acquisition and Payment Cycle

M	Jan	6	Description of cycle and the management issues surrounding the cycle (Day #1)	Systems
T	Jan	7	Data model for acquisition, pmt., controls over event (Day #2)	Systems
Th	Jan	9	Audit of controls (Day #3A)	Audit
			MANAGEMENT AND TAX VIEW—Planning	
Th	Jan	9	Federal and state tax rates (Day #3B)	Tax
F	Jan	10	Depreciation concepts and methods (Day #4)	Tax
M	Jan	13	Capital budgeting (Day #5)	Managerial
			FINANCIAL AND TAX VIEW—Acquisition	
T	Jan	14	Tax issues in acquisition, capital asset definitions (Day #6A)	Tax
T	Jan	14	Financial accounting—asset cost for various tangible and intangible assets. Lump-sum purchase, nonmonetary asset exchange. (Day #6B)	Financial
Th	Jan	16	Self-construction, interest capitalization, R&D, software, repairs, betterment,	Financial
F	Jan	17	improvements. (Day #7)	
F	Jan	17	Contract formation, risk of loss, nonconforming goods, remedies. (Day #8)	Law
Th	Jan	16		
M	Jan	20	HOLIDAY	
			TAX VIEW—Disposition	
T	Jan	21	Capital asset issues, special asset definitions. (Day #9A)	Tax
T	Jan	21	Exchanges and abandonments, involuntary conversion. (Day #9B)	Tax
			FINANCIAL VIEW—Disposition	
Th	Jan	23	Differences between tax and financial view (Day #10A)	Financial
Th	Jan	23	Asset impairment, abandonment (Day #10B)	Financial
F	Jan	24	Contract formation, etc. (Day #11-Followup from Day #8)	Law
M	Jan	27		
			AUDIT VIEW	
M	Jan	27	Audit of fixed assets, intangibles.	Audit
F	Jan	24	Use of analytical review, contract review, physical observation (Day #12A)	
M	Jan	27	Audit of liabilities, confirmation, lawyer letter, contingencies (Day #12B)	Audit
F	Jan	24		
			INTEGRATIVE CASE	
T	Jan	28	Acquisition and Payment Case (Day #13)	Financial
Th	Jan	30	Examination #5	

Designing, Writing, and Implementing Courses for an IT-Integrated Professional Accounting Program

David Harrison

The purpose of this paper is twofold. The first aim is to review the major elements of the systematic design of instruction and to revisit some recurring issues in instructional design that will be of particular interest to accounting educators in the current climate of curriculum renewal. Second, this paper will describe the program of studies of the Certified General Accountants' Association of Canada, with a focus on the design and implementation of its courses. The paper comprises the following sections:

1. Curriculum renewal and the design of instruction

2. Canadian accounting education and the CGA Program of Studies

3. Overview of the CGA Program of Studies

4. Resolving design issues in the accounting program

5. Looking ahead in instructional design

CURRICULUM RENEWAL AND THE DESIGN OF INSTRUCTION

The accounting curriculum is fertile ground these days for the seeds of renewal. The initiatives for curricular reform that were set in motion by the American Accounting Association (AAA 1986), the Accounting Education Change Commission (AECC 1990), and the American Institute of CPAs (AICPA 1990) are now yielding a sizeable return of attention to the way we are delivering professional accounting education to students across North America.

Appropriately, the cycle of curriculum renewal has begun with broad statements of educational aims and intentions and has been followed by discussion at the level of "models." For example, Needles and Powers (1990) compared 17 models of accounting education published by seven U.S. organizations since the 1967 AICPA report *Horizons for a Profession* (Roy and MacNeill 1967); they attributed the slow pace of change to the consistent emphasis on the content of the curriculum — the body of knowledge — rather than on the process by which the curriculum is delivered, learned, and evaluated. They indicated that this emphasis only began to change with the 1986 Bedford Committee report.

Indication, however, that accounting educators are now shifting their baseline is evident from the range of topics highlighted in the published papers of the *Models of Accounting Education* symposium at Dallas in March 1991 (Sundem and Norgaard 1991). These topics included (in addition to models):

- ways to deal with the knowledge explosion;

- ways to measure the depth of knowledge;

- education for lifelong learning;

- recognition and funding of scholarship that supports teaching;

- ways to classify student capabilities and instructional methods;

- approaches to integrating information technology; and, not least,

- redefinition of the accounting profession.

In two years, the AECC has awarded some $2.5 million of grant money to 11 U.S. universities to implement improvements in accounting education (Williams and Sundem 1990, 1991).

The AECC/AICPA curriculum initiative promotes the concept of a five-year university education requirement, overlaying professional accounting subjects on a broad liberal arts base, with an overall emphasis on problem solving and related

David Harrison is an Assistant Director of Education at the Certified General Accountants' Association of Canada.

The writer acknowledges the contributions made to the development of the CGA program of studies by all those who have participated in its design and implementation over the last 40 years, including several generations of students who have put the curriculum to the real test in their subsequent careers.

higher-order thinking skills. The enthusiasm for these proposals is not universal. Barefield (1991), for instance, takes the AECC to task for inadequate consultation with all sectors of the profession, a hastily implemented grants program, and "wishful thinking" about the value of a liberal arts education.

Accounting educators in Canada have been fortunate to be able to look across the border to this massive surge of attention to the curriculum. In any period, U.S. trends may be reflected (after some cultural filtering and mutation) some years later in parallel Canadian trends. Currently, the United States–Canadian Free Trade Agreement has given even greater incentive to compare notes and exchange ideas across the United States–Canadian border.

In summary, curriculum change is in the ascendant. It is timely, then, to review some of the well-established principles of instructional design and to revisit some of the key design issues that must be faced by anyone who designs or delivers a professional curriculum. This paper takes as its context the program of studies of the Certified General Accountants' Association of Canada (CGA–Canada).

CANADIAN ACCOUNTING EDUCATION AND THE CGA PROGRAM OF STUDIES

A person seeking to become an accountant in Canada has different choices than in the United States. In Canada, the three national professional accounting bodies (with minor regional variation) each has a distinct identity:

- The Certified General Accountants' Association of Canada (CGA designation) has members engaged in all areas of professional accounting. A university degree is generally not required, but many CGA graduates do have at least a baccalaureate.

- The Society of Management Accountants (CMA designation) focuses particularly but not exclusively on managerial and management accounting practice. A university degree requirement has only recently been imposed in some regions.

- The Canadian Institute of Chartered Accountants (CA designation), the largest and oldest-established group, the majority of whose members are in public practice, with the strongest representation in the large public accounting firms. A university degree has been required since 1970 and a five-year degree requirement is now under discussion.

All three organizations have members and students in public practice across the country, and regulate professional affairs and education through their affiliates in the provinces and territories. While there are restrictions on audit rights for CGAs and CMAs in some provinces (notably Ontario), the majority of jurisdictions allow full or partial rights to all three designations and remaining barriers are likely to fall.

It is in the approach to education that the three Canadian bodies most clearly differ. While the CAs and the CMAs both stipulate (in most regions) a university degree requirement, the Certified General Accountants provide several alternative access routes. Students can become CGAs either

(a) by pursuing full-time or part-time university degree courses and taking the final CGA courses and examinations, or

(b) by following a rigorous six-year cooperative program of part-time, university-equivalent courses and practical accounting experience.

CGA finalist examinations and experience requirements are the same for degree and nondegree routes.

At present in Canada, therefore, it is not necessary to have a university or college degree to enter the accounting profession. Nor is it necessary for a prospective student to give up full-time employment in order to attend university full-time or to have to work toward a master's degree in accounting. Through its commitment to distance education, for example, CGA–Canada can deliver the program to students anywhere in Canada (or even to students in other countries). Figure 1 illustrates the concept of a parallel system of accounting education that reflects the alternative access routes to the profession currently facilitated by the CGA program of studies in Canada.

Partnership with Higher Education

Notwithstanding the CGA open-access philosophy and the independence of its curriculum from that of the universities, the CGA program of studies has established a unique partnership with higher education. In the CGA model, overall responsibility for the program of studies and control over its nationally determined curriculum and examinations rests within the CGA profession. However, the Association enlists the expertise of university faculty through joint professional-academic advisory councils and through an extensive network of course authors and examiners.

FIGURE 1
Parallel Systems of Accounting Education

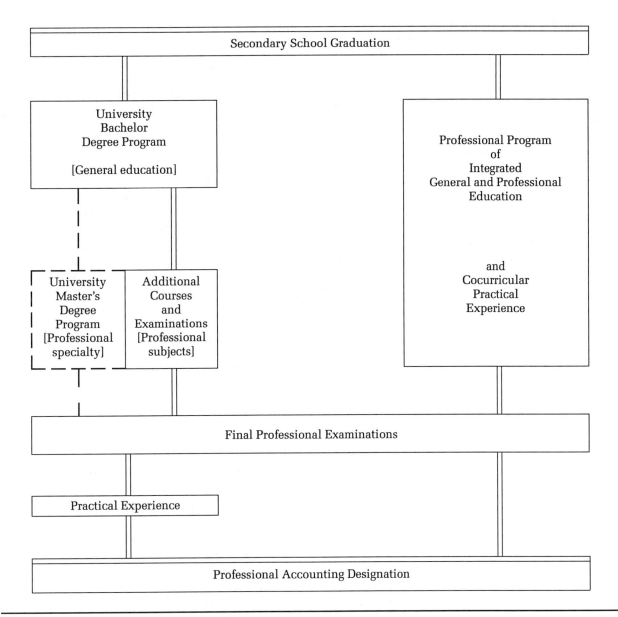

For example, the CGA roster of course authors includes leading academics from the University of British Columbia, Carleton, Dalhousie, Laurentian, Manitoba, McMaster, Queen's, Saint Mary's, Sherbrooke, Simon Fraser, Victoria, Waterloo, Western, Wilfrid Laurier, and Windsor. University faculty are regularly involved in the design and review of CGA courses, while lecture and review sessions are held on many campuses.

At the same time, in specialized professional areas such as taxation, management auditing, and information systems, the CGA Association can call on expertise from both the academic and professional accounting communities. Other links with higher education are established through CGA support for research.

Cooperative Approach to Curriculum Renewal

The fact that CGA had independent control over its own professional curriculum, plus well-established links with higher education, enabled the Association to make bold steps in curriculum renewal in the period of 1984–1991. This major curriculum review resulted from a 1984 CGA task force study entitled *Knowledge Requirements of a Professional Accountant in the 1990s*. The study required extensive consultation with the academic, business, and professional communities across Canada, as well as a review of accreditation developments in the United States, Britain, and Australia.

The outcome of this cooperative effort in curriculum renewal was a revised program of studies, completely implemented at all program levels by the fall of 1991. It was a massive seven-year curriculum development exploration for which no map or guidebook had been written. Through the efforts of CGA program development staff and the university-based faculty who rewrote some 20 courses and tutorials, the new program upgraded the body of knowledge, reshaped the content to provide a more managerial emphasis, and through the design of the study materials placed new emphasis on the learning process.

Furthermore, through its implementation of hands-on illustrations, case scenarios, and assignments in information technology (IT), CGA–Canada became the first professional accounting association to fully integrate the hands-on use of the technology into its courses.

OVERVIEW OF THE CGA PROGRAM OF STUDIES

Between 1984 and 1991, the *Syllabus* of the CGA program was updated to bring it in line with latest developments in accounting standards and information technology, and with the knowledge base of accounting, auditing, finance, taxation, management, and related subjects. All courses were extensively rewritten and the use of the microcomputer integrated wherever appropriate to the content. This section of the paper provides an overview of the program in its revised form (see Figure 2).

FIGURE 2
CGA Program of Studies

Foundation Levels

Level 1	Financial Accounting 1 Economics 1 Law 1
Level 2	Microcomputer Tutorials (noncredit) Financial Accounting 2 Quantitative Methods 2 Management Accounting 1
Level 3	Financial Accounting 3 Finance 1 Management Information Systems 1

Professional Levels

Level 4	Management Accounting 2 Taxation 1 Auditing 1
Level 5	Financial Accounting 4 Finance 2 Auditing 2
Professional options (2)	Financial Accounting 5 Management Auditing 1 Management Information Systems 2 Taxation 2 Strategic Management 1

Cocurricular Requirements

- Practice sets in accounting (2)
- Practice set in auditing
- Business communications and public speaking
- Integrated studies in ethics
- Integrated studies in microcomputer applications and
- Monitored professional experience in accounting (at increasing levels of responsibility)

Mission

The primary mission of the CGA education program is the identification, development, and delivery of the body of knowledge necessary for professional qualification in the field of accounting and related areas.

Emphasis on Abilities

The CGA program of studies emphasizes the development of the key abilities required of accountants and senior financial managers. These include

- effective communication, management, and leadership skills

- development of interpretive, judgmental, and analytical skills

- competence in the use of the computer as a management and accounting tool

- management of change in the technologies, processes, and structures of organizations

- use of information systems as a resource for decision making

Computer-Integrated Studies

The CGA program is designed to ensure that graduates are fully literate in computer technology as it is currently applied in business, industry, and government. Through a carefully crafted strategy of instructional design, course authors identify where computers would likely be used in the profession to gather, analyse, or present data. These illustrations and hands-on exercises are woven into the fabric of the course material. The integrative approach means that the IT curriculum is "added in" to the professional curriculum, rather than "added on" as stand-alone technical courses. Ideally, the technology is applied directly to the professional problem it is designed to solve.

All CGA students at or above the second level are required to have access to a microcomputer for their course work. The majority of these students, in fact, purchase their own microcomputer for the purpose. Typically, students accumulate well over 400 hours of computer time. They work with commercial-equivalent versions of software, including spreadsheets, and programs in accounting, statistical and audit analysis, database management, system analysis and design, and word processing. Each item of course software is selected for its suitability for the real-world accounting or management-related task (Yu 1987).

A consistent objective is to illustrate concepts and practices that a professional accountant or financial manager is expected to understand or personally use. This extensive IT–integration is unique among the education programs of professional accounting organizations, and it exceeds current levels of integration in other Canadian institutions of higher learning.

Structure and Content

The CGA program contains 17 required courses, structured in six levels. Each of levels 1 through 5 contains three mandatory courses, and in the sixth year two advanced professional options are required. The core Level 5 courses are delivered in both English and French. In addition, students must demonstrate microcomputer competence, and fulfill cocurricular requirements in oral and written communication, ethics, and a supervised period of practical experience. Students generally take upwards of six years of concurrent part-time study and work experience to complete the program.

The program structure, as shown in Figure 2, consists of

- A three-year sequence of **foundation studies** in accounting and related subjects, including the **general education** components of economics, law, information systems, and quantitative methods;

- A two-year sequence of **professional studies** in financial and management accounting, auditing, finance, and taxation;

- A sixth-year set of **advanced professional options** chosen from financial accounting (theory and issues), management auditing, management information systems, taxation, and strategic management.

- Cocurricular studies in **general education** and experience in **professional practice**.

A fundamental design concept of every course in the CGA program is that it must be written for independent guided study. The rationale for this is both logistical and educational. Logistical, because independent study materials open up learning access to those who, for reasons of time, distance, or duty cannot attend formal courses given on fixed schedules. Educational, because independent study material, when properly delivered, fosters the growth of independent learning skills and strategies that carry forward well beyond certification, improving the cognitive base for lifelong learning (Verduin and Clark 1991).

Delivery System and Student Enrollment

The CGA courses consist primarily of self-instructional, independent learning packages. While they are specifically designed to fit the constraints of distance education, the CGA materials are increasingly being used as resource materials on university and college campuses. The course packages themselves are sizeable. A CGA course consists of texts, readings, lesson notes, computer software, assignments, and practice examinations. In larger centers of population, lectures and other learning media are available. Student assignments are submitted weekly on a strict schedule and are marked and returned so that students can measure their progress. They must maintain a 65 percent average to qualify for the final end-of-course examination.

The majority of CGA students are employed and therefore are part-time learners. They are expected to commit 15 to 20 hours per week to study. Because of its distance education format, the program is available to students living anywhere in Canada; it has also been successfully implemented in other regions such as the Caribbean and East Asia. The basic entrance requirement is secondary school graduation or equivalent, and there is provision for mature students with acceptable work experience. Upwards of 70 percent of students enter the program with a partial or complete postsecondary degree or diploma. Exemptions may be granted for appropriate courses which have been completed at universities and colleges or courses offered by other professional associations. Course content, standards, and grades of transferable courses from other institutions must meet association guidelines.

Each year, approximately 3,500 new students enter the CGA program at the first and fourth levels, and there are in any year about 20,000 students enrolled. A major point of entry for students transferring from postsecondary institutions is the beginning of Level 4 of the program. Over 1,500 new CGAs graduate each year.

Hands-on Professional Experience

Each student is required to obtain practical experience in the accounting and financial management fields. This provides the opportunity to apply the concepts and skills learned in the program. As students move to higher program levels, they must be employed and their performance evaluated in positions of increasing responsibility. The range of practical experience is verified by employers and evaluated by the Association on a formative and summative basis. While the minimum practical experience is two years, students often have over six years' work experience behind them when they attain the CGA designation.

Examinations

Student performance on every course is evaluated by means of a comprehensive national examination. The required pass mark is 65 percent. All students, regardless of their entry point to the program, are required to satisfy the minimum graduating requirements evaluated by the finalist professional examinations in accounting, auditing, finance, and taxation.

RESOLVING DESIGN ISSUES IN THE ACCOUNTING PROGRAM

When CGA–Canada set out eight years ago to completely revise its whole program of studies, the staff and faculty involved knew that it was a massive undertaking. The existing program had been in place and served well since 1951. However, while course structure and content had been frequently updated for use with new texts and to reflect changes in legislation, standards, and professional practice, the changes had been mainly incremental. Now, a new program with new priorities demanded a redesign and rewrite of every single course.

Curriculum Planning and Development

Whether one is designing a whole curriculum or a course within it, there is a certain, well-proven sequence of phases to the project, and each phase has a set of critical questions for the course designer. Systematic design models have a lineage going back at least to Bobbitt's *The Curriculum* (1918) and Tyler's *Basic Principles of Curriculum and Instruction* (1949); more recent renditions are those of Briggs (1977), Pratt (1980), and Diamond (1989) — the latter addressing his ideas specifically to instruction in universities and colleges. Mock, Pincus, and Andre (1991) have described the application of the systems approach to accounting education at the University of Southern California.

In planning and developing CGA courses, we identify distinct phases in the process of bringing a course onstream. Some phases are specific to the writing of self-instructional materials for distance education (see Figure 3).

Needs Assessment. At the program or course level, we have to answer these kinds of questions: What are the possible goals that this educational unit should meet? How shall these goals be prioritized and checked for feasibility? Where are the data and how can they be assessed?

CGA uses three sources to help identify and update its curriculum goals: the expertise of its own practicing professionals, the faculty of the university business schools, and the feedback circuit from current students taking the courses. As the program is a national one, it has the advantage of being able to draw on ideas from the professional accounting membership across the country through a network of regional education committees; these practicing professionals are the former students of the program. The nationwide spread also enables the Association to establish continuing relationships with many university business schools and to tap into a diversity of views about where the curriculum should be going and why. The third source of curriculum goals is the students, who only recently in higher education institutions (including CGA) have been appreciated in this evaluative role.

Development and Review of a Program Structure or a Course Outline. Again the process is similar at program or course level. The building blocks of curriculum are identified, grouped, and sequenced in some form that makes good sense in itself, but which also makes sense for learners. The instructional design decisions made in this phase have proven time and again to be long lasting, for curriculum flexibility is an extremely difficult trait to incorporate in any program with more than a few courses. As described in Figure 2, the CGA program struc-

ture strongly mirrors the traditional curriculum of the accounting major at a university business school. This similarity of structure is a notable advantage for students making the bridge from the university to the profession and hoping to obtain credit for previous learning. At the level of the course outline, however, the instructional design of a CGA course is usually much more explicit than a university counterpart. A CGA course outline, for instance, is not considered complete until it has resolved, in advance, design issues such as these:

- What is the purpose of the course and what is its place in the program of studies?

- What are the assumed prerequisite knowledge and competencies of people beginning the course?

- What specifically will be expected of students during the course and on completion of it?

- What is the scope and sequence of major topics in the course?

- What is the relationship between lesson notes, readings, microcomputer work, and examinations?

- How are microcomputer applications integrated into the course?

- Are there study techniques that are particularly helpful for this particular subject (such as a method of working through case analysis, or a method for developing spreadsheets for decision purposes)?

- What is the course author's approach to this subject or discipline?

FIGURE 3
Phases of Curriculum Development

Needs assessment	Development of structure/outline	Development of learning objectives and priorities	Review of instructional design

WRITING THE COURSE	Review of content [academic]	Review of learning [instructional]	Hands-on tests and copy edit

Pilot testing	Full implementation	Evaluation and revision

Development of Learning Objectives and Priorities. An educator could be excused for believing that the emphasis on defining learning objectives began with Benjamin Bloom and associates who in 1956 published the landmark *Taxonomy of Educational Objectives: Cognitive Domain*. The idea of defining learning in terms of what competencies the student should be able to demonstrate, rather than what the instructor should "present," was one known to many a good teacher through the ages, especially (dare it be said) in vocational education. Presumably, it must have long been the case in medical and legal education. But even in the 1960s and 1970s, Bloom's renewed focus on the learner was slow to catch on in disciplines outside the behavioral sciences; indeed, many business schools seem to be only discovering in the 1990s that there are definable levels of student performance and cognitive skills.

What Bloom and associates demonstrated so cleverly, and other educators like Mager (1975) demonstrated more practically, was that defining learning in this way was a really useful curriculum design tool. And as we have become more knowledgable about cognitive approaches to learning, writers of learning materials — even textbook writers — increasingly make more precise definitions of what we expect of students beyond the warm fuzzies of "appreciating" and "understanding."

In CGA courses, therefore, each lesson and each microcomputer illustration are prefaced by a list of learning objectives written in terms of what they should be able to do or demonstrate at the end of this study unit ("calculate," "describe," "explain," "analyse," "compare," "evaluate," and so on). To help students further, the subtopics of each lesson are assigned a priority using a three-level system also related to the Bloom scheme and shown in Figure 4. We call these **levels of competence.** The adoption by CGA of these levels of competence reflects the current academic emphasis on the development of skills in the higher levels of the taxonomy. Yet the scheme also recognizes the need to ensure that accountants develop competence in the technical areas of the profession where public expectations are especially high.

One of the interesting effects we have discovered at CGA about specifying learning outcomes more accurately and learning priorities more explicitly is that these design tools are just as valuable to course authors as they are to students. Many students tell us that, while each form of guidance is appreciated, the learning objectives are most useful when it comes time to review for examinations; we have also realized that there is a broad spectrum of individual

FIGURE 4
CGA Levels of Competence

At This Level:	Students are Required to
LEVEL 1 *Mastery*	• attain in-depth understanding of concepts and principles; • develop a sound conceptual and comprehensive technical knowledge of procedures; • become proficient in applying theoretical knowledge to practical situations; • become proficient users of reference documents and sources. On examinations, students are expected to demonstrate mastery of both the conceptual and technical aspects of a topic, including specific detail. Skills developed and examined at this level are comprehension, application, analysis, synthesis, and evaluation.
LEVEL 2 *Comprehension*	• attain a broad understanding of concepts, principles, and procedures; • develop a working knowledge of procedures; • identify common reference documents and sources. On examinations, students are expected to demonstrate understanding of the conceptual aspects of a topic and to apply technical skills. Skills developed and examined at this level are comprehension and application.
LEVEL 3 *Background Knowledge*	• acquire a general knowledge of broad topic areas; • identify common reference documents and sources. On examinations, students are expected to demonstrate general knowledge of a topic. They are not required to answer in-depth questions. Skills developed and examined at this level are recall and general knowledge.

learning styles — students vary enormously in how much structure they need and expect. In general, if we are successful in helping them "learn to learn," students will need progressively less structure as they progress toward graduate level.

Writing the Lesson Notes. The lesson notes have many purposes, and the author will judge the requirements for the course based on the components selected to provide the learning tools for the course. A course which does not have a comprehensive textbook must be presented quite differently from one in which the lesson notes lead students through a textbook which covers all the topics for the course. The emphasis is always on providing a **self-contained** learning package for the course. The lesson notes assist students to develop a sound understanding of the subject and to prepare for the examination. As general guidelines, course authors use the lesson notes to

- clarify and enhance concepts covered in the textbook;

- supplement or replace the textbook for topics not covered there;

- provide supplementary reading, such as key articles from journals, to enhance and clarify a subject;

- present alternative approaches to topics of study;

- provide perspective for students who are without benefit of lectures and discussion groups;

- introduce microcomputer work in contexts where computers would be used in the profession;

- provide a range of review exercises, model solutions, and weekly assignment questions so that students can check the effectiveness of their learning and evaluate their own progress.

In summary, the author's task in the lesson notes is to integrate all components into the best possible composition from which motivated students can learn without benefit of face-to-face classroom interaction.

Working with a Curriculum Development Team. To assist CGA authors bring distance education courses from idea to implementation, we provide a support team with roles defined in Figure 5.

How do our academic and professional course authors respond to all this teamwork, and in particular to the relentless structuring, critiquing, and shaping of their words and ideas? What do they think about giving up their traditional classroom

---

FIGURE 5
CGA Course Development Responsibilities

Course author	As subject matter expert, structures course content into lessons and topics, writes lesson notes to integrate all course components into effective learning units, and creates performance evaluation tasks.
Manager of curriculum development	Contracts with author and manages course development resources so course is implemented on time at optimum quality.
Instructional designer	Works with author and consultants on initial outline, scope, sequence, and presentation aspects of instructional design.
Project editor	Coordinates course development tasks and liaises with author and reviewers to implement all improvements to the draft manuscript.
Education development/ IT specialist	Integrates microcomputer work and liaises with author and reviewers to implement content improvements.
Academic reviewer(s)	Evaluates course for academic content and integrity.
Instructional reviewer(s)	Evaluates course for instructional effectiveness.
Translator	Translates and redevelops course content into French or English.
Copy editor	Performs final copy edit for house style, language, and general clarity.
Word processor	Implements changes within a page design that promotes readability.

autonomy to take their place as just "the most important member of the team?" Well, as researchers often say, there is no clear pattern. Many academics, perhaps because of previous experience with distance education, immediately come to terms with the systematic design of instruction; they accept the collective responsibility to develop a course that can stand before students without a professor in the room. Other course authors, however, are initially uncomfortable with this incursion of others into the professor's domain. Some of these set out, for instance, conceiving their main task as producing a written version of previously delivered lecture notes — the lectures from which their campus-based students have been learning effectively for some years. However, as even these authors soon discover, the spoken word of the lecture and the interaction of the lecture theatre make for a totally different teaching environment than the confines of the self-instructional or distance education course.

For course author and development team alike, the creation of a distance education course is itself a major learning experience. They often emerge with a new set of instructional strategies and expertise that will benefit students, whether in classrooms or elsewhere. The recent Smith Commission on Canadian University Education (1991) made these comments on the undervalued teaching scholarship that went into the production of self-instructional materials:

> To reorganize the material of a given subject so that it can be learned "by objectives" in a self-teaching situation, to develop innovative learning materials for that purpose, and to produce instruments of evaluation appropriate to that learning requires an enormous expenditure of time, a thorough grasp of the breadth and depth of one's subject matter, hours of research in the journals to develop learning materials, and a generally innovative and original approach to intellectual issues. In other words, it is a scholarly activity of prime importance and should be recognized as comparable to the completion of a controlled experiment in a particular sub-discipline. (p. 50)

The CGA curriculum staff who help authors develop the courses are very aware that this is a new and often daunting experience for most academics. Over the years we have learned, for instance, to anticipate the signs of overconfidence, resistance to change (such as improvements suggested by reviewers), and lack of attention to detail, and in such circumstances to gently prompt the academic toward workable solutions. For both parties, it takes a lot of time, patience, and effort to produce a well-crafted course that can work in a distance learning setting and which can be implemented time and again with confidence to thousands of students across a nation.

Quality Control in Course Development

The development timeline for a course extends over about 18 months, and at least half of this time is devoted to quality control. The quality control procedures for course materials are rigorous, including a systematic sequence of reviews for content, method, and presentation. Reviewers are required to scrutinize many different aspects of the learning materials, often "hands-on," and to make detailed written reports on their findings. The criteria for this formative evaluation are derived from established models of curriculum evaluation and based on proven principles of adult learning and distance education. Assignments and examinations follow a similar method of development and review.

Course Development. Review of a course manuscript consists of these (often concurrent) phases:

- instructional design review and developmental editing by CGA–Canada curriculum specialists;

- content review by independent academics;

- instructional review by lecturers or instructors;

- computer materials review and hands-on testing by information technology specialists; and

- copy editing by an instructional writing specialist.

The results and recommendations of the in-house and external reviews are discussed with the course author(s) and revisions made to meet the educational and publishing standards of CGA–Canada.

Pilot Testing. In addition, every new course is intensively pilot tested by a small group of students taking the course for credit. This pilot-testing project is carried out one semester prior to the implementation of the course. Each week, along with their regular written and computer assignments, the pilot project students submit detailed responses and ratings to questionnaires evaluating the course from the perspective of the learner. They also meet periodically, as a group, with the CGA instructional designers. As a result, further fine-tuning of the course materials is made before delivery to the main cohort of students. After implementation of the new course, a system of annual course monitoring takes over.

Information Technology

Two critical decisions have guided the integration of information technology into the CGA program of studies: the access policy and the design for integration.

Access Policy. In order that microcomputer course materials could be standardized, and that the local CGA education offices could provide technical support to students, CGA–Canada adopted the IBM PC industry standard, with DOS as the operating system. From the second level of the program, all students are required to have access to a microcomputer and printer. To provide the start-up knowledge necessary for course work using the latest commercial software, CGA developed self-instructional microcomputer tutorials in the operating system, spreadsheet, word processing, and accounting general ledger software.

Design for Computer Integration. The primary aims that CGA–Canada has achieved by integrating computer use in the program of studies are

1. To provide students with hands-on technical knowledge of how to use microcomputers to solve business problems they may encounter in their professional careers as accountants.

2. To illustrate and illuminate concepts and practices that otherwise cannot be easily taught manually.

3. To bring students to a sufficient level of mastery in computer technology that enables them to adapt more readily to technological changes.

4. To enable students to decrease the time spent on routine data entry and processing, and spend proportionately more time and energy on interpreting and analysing information.

In considering how microcomputer technology was to be integrated into accounting education, CGA–Canada considered several alternatives. These included

- *Computer-assisted instruction.* This is typically a set of on-line or on-diskette tutorials that take students step-by-step through a learning sequence. This option was rejected as impractical, given the cost and amount of development time required to produce quality programs of this type.

- *Computer-managed instruction.* By this method, instructors at a central location keep track of students' progress through units of study, which are typically also computerized and require a network. The emphasis is on management of learning events and does not fit the CGA method.

- *Separate microcomputer courses* on the use of software applications. These are distinct from the mainstream courses of accounting, auditing, finance, and taxation, which continue to be restricted to pencil-and-paper procedures. The CGA program designers concluded that this alternative would teach required skills but would not teach them in the full context of the subjects. If used alone, the courses would be add-ons, not directly integrated into the curriculum. CGA decided to use this design only for a set of "start-up" tutorials to bring students up to an entry level of computer literacy.

- *IT–integrated courses.* This has become the primary CGA design. The computer is used as a tool in appropriate parts of all courses where the technology might typically be used in the business context. Students are presented with practical hands-on examples using the microcomputer and standard commercial software to solve problems that are naturally part of the mainstream accounting education courses. The technology is used to illustrate concepts and practices that a professional accountant is expected to understand and apply.

Cycle of Course Revision

Curriculum development at CGA is conceived as a continuing cycle; the discernible stages include planning, writing, quality control, implementation, feedback from students and academics; then, a return to the beginning of the cycle and the redesign of the course outline to fit changing needs. The content of each course in the program is monitored from year to year and updated as needed in response to changes in the accounting and general business environment. These changes include new accounting and auditing standards, tax laws and regulations, and international standards.

The scale of actual revision must be tailored to fit the pace of change in the body of knowledge for each course. For example, in financial accounting, recent changes in accounting standards as well as an increased conceptual emphasis have required regular annual updates to the original course, and in 1992–1993, a completely redesigned and rewritten edition of the first-year course. Similarly, the taxation courses require substantial annual updates. In courses where microcomputers are used, material is periodically updated to take advantage of new versions of software that students will encounter at work. For example, courses are currently being updated to *Lotus 1-2-3* version 2.4 and *ACCPAC/GL* accounting software version 6.0. The possibility of moving to the Microsoft *Windows* environment is already close.

LOOKING AHEAD IN INSTRUCTIONAL DESIGN

As accounting educators look to the future development of the accounting curriculum, a number of issues suggest themselves. The following is offered as a starter list of such issues.

Curriculum Renewal and Program Design Issues

- What sources should we look to, with how much confidence, when we are redefining the goals of a program or a course? Employers? University faculty? The "Big Six" public accounting firms? Government agencies? Professional associations? Recent graduates? The clientele of the profession?

- How are we to assess the validity of the stream of statements on the accounting curriculum released in the United States since 1986? In particular, where is the new equilibrium in the age-old tussle of (often false) polarities: A liberal general education or a professional specialization? Substantive in-depth knowledge or a broad foundation of transferable intellectual and social skills? Courses organized along discipline or inter-disciplinary lines? Learning for a livelihood or learning to learn?

- How much of what kind of education does a professional accountant need at the time of certification? What kinds of education would be better reserved for postcertification studies?

Performance Evaluation Issues

- What is the validity of the closed-room, closed-book, limited-time examination as a measure of student achievement? Would it be any better if we relaxed any of these three constraints?

- Is a single "comprehensive" or multi-subject examination superior to core subject examinations?

- If the most important change in accounting education is the emphasis on problem solving, decision making, working as a member of the management team, and general communication skills, how are these competencies to be evaluated?

Information Technology Issues

- What is the most effective and economical model for integrating computer applications? How realistic is it to expect instructors to implement it?

- How do we monitor the match between learning objectives, learning activities, and examinations? What difference does technology make to this basic educational design issue?

- How do we assure technical compatibility and reliability?

- What are low-cost, high-efficiency ways of using the electronic media to the delivery of courses to students? How do we ensure that technology does not drive the content and process of education?

Hardware and Software Issues

- How can we improve student access to computer hardware (at a time of budget restraint)? Should students be expected to bear some of the responsibility and cost?

- What is the impact of laptop and notebook computers on course and examination design?

- How important is it to use the most current versions of commercial software packages (such as *Lotus 1-2-3*, *dBASE* IV, *ACCPAC*)? Why?

- How essential is it to keep up with every new development in the technology (386/486/586 machines, Windows environment, CD-ROM) and to synchronize these developments with course material?

This demanding array of issues makes clear the growing impact of information technology, where new inventions and applications will affect not only course content but also methodology and delivery.

REFERENCES

Accounting Education Change Commission (AECC). 1990. Objectives of Education for Accountants: Position Statement Number One. *Issues in Accounting Education* (Fall): 307–312.

American Accounting Association (AAA), Committee on the Future Structure, Content, and Scope of Accounting Education (The Bedford Committee). 1986. Future Accounting Education: Preparing for the Expanding Profession. *Issues in Accounting Education* (Spring): 169–190.

American Institute of Certified Public Accountants (AICPA). 1990. *Education Requirements for Entry into the Accounting Profession.* 3rd ed. AICPA.

Barefield, R. M. 1991. A Critical View of the AECC and the Converging Forces of Change. *Issues in Accounting Education* (Fall): 305–312.

Bloom, B. S., ed. 1956. *Taxonomy of Educational Objectives: Cognitive Domain.* David McKay Company.

Briggs, L. J., ed. 1977. *Instructional Design: Principles and Applications.* Educational Technology Publications.

Certified General Accountants' Association of Canada. 1984. *Report of the Task Force on Qualification Requirements for CGA Graduates in the 1990s.* CGA–Canada.

Commission of Inquiry on Canadian University Education. 1991. Stuart L. Smith, Commissioner. Association of Universities and Colleges of Canada.

Diamond, R. M. 1989. *Designing and Improving Courses and Curricula in Higher Education.* Jossey-Bass.

Mager, R. F. 1975. *Preparing Instructional Objectives.* Fearon.

Mock, T. J., K. V. Pincus, and J. M. Andre. 1991. A Systems Approach to Accounting Curriculum Development. *Issues in Accounting Education* (Fall): 178–192.

Needles, B., Jr., and M. Powers. 1990. A Comparative Study of Models of Accounting Education. *Issues in Accounting Education* (Fall): 250–267.

Pratt, D. 1980. *Curriculum: Design and Development.* Harcourt Brace Jovanovich.

Roy, R. H., and J. H. MacNeill. 1967. *The Common Body of Knowledge for Certified Public Accountants: Horizons for a Profession.* American Institute of Certified Public Accountants.

Sundem, G. L., and C. T. Norgaard, eds. 1991. *Models of Accounting Education.* Accounting Education Change Commission.

Tyler, R. W. 1949. *Basic Principles of Curriculum and Instruction.* University of Chicago Press.

Verduin, J. R., Jr., and T. A. Clark. 1991. *Distance Education: The Foundations of Effective Practice.* Jossey-Bass.

Williams, D. Z., and G. L. Sundem. 1990. Grants Awarded for Implementing Improvements in Accounting Education. *Issues in Accounting Education* (Fall): 313–331.

———. 1991. Additional Grants Awarded for Implementation of Improvements in Accounting Education. *Issues in Accounting Education* (Fall): 315–330.

Yu, J. W. 1987. *Selecting Microcomputer Hardware and Software.* World Congress of Accountants.

Open Learning for Accountancy Education

Michael G. Harvey, Anthea L. Rose, and Stephen Wellings

TRENDS IN PROFESSIONAL ACCOUNTANCY EDUCATION

Accountancy education has been undergoing some far-reaching changes recently, with all the main U.K. accountancy bodies announcing major syllabus reviews. One of the powerful impetuses behind these changes has been the *competences* movement, which promotes the view that qualified accountants should not only have a grasp of the theoretical aspects of their discipline, but also be able to put theory into practice. This proposition has been supported by various attempts to devise assessment methods which test not only knowledge but also performance.

The idea behind *competences* is that qualifications should reflect what individuals can *do*, not simply what they *know*. For instance, while students might know the theory behind financial statements, can they actually do the work necessary to prepare and present financial statements to a satisfactory standard? In measuring the competence of individuals, it is not enough just to test their technical knowledge; it is also necessary to check that they can cope with the normal work environment. Most people can expect to work in offices where they have to deal with occasional crises, difficult clients, overwork, ethical problems and changes in rules and regulations. Being *competent* means people are capable of juggling with all these pressures and still produce work of an acceptable standard, on time.

The implications of these changes for the education process are very significant. First, there will obviously be a shift from an emphasis on inputs (rote learning, years of experience) to outputs (performance and outcomes). The emphasis will move away from evaluating what students have learned towards what they can actually do, and testing whether this is at the appropriate standard.

Second, and related to the above, there will be a shift away from knowledge acquired to knowledge applied. The test will be whether an individual can put theory into practice, rather than whether s/he just knows the theory.

Third, there will be a change in the type of learning activity which will be appropriate. For instance, there will be a greater linkage between place of work and place of learning and a greater recognition of learning acquired in the work place. Learning will have to do with doing and achieving outcomes and less to do with learning by rote. The result should be a system which produces and rewards competent accountants, rather than just those who have learnt the theory but are not actually able to put it into practice very well.

Finally, in a general sense, there will be a shift from a teacher-centred to a learner-centred model of learning. Learners will be far more in charge of their own learning experience, which will be more closely linked to their work experience. This is also very much the approach adopted by the open learning programme which is the main subject of this paper. The role of teachers will also change more to that of supporters and advisers, rather than just instructors.

OPEN LEARNING

This paper focuses on an educational initiative undertaken by the Chartered Association of Certified Accountants (CACA), the first open learning programme designed for professional accountants. It is not the result of a research study but is an informal review of an important new educational development. It considers the principles underlying the open learning programme, describes how and why it has been introduced and demonstrates its application and effectiveness.

Background to the Open Learning Programme

The CACA had been concerned for some time that its worldwide student body (numbering some 85,000) did not always have access to high-quality learning materials. Teaching of a consistently good quality could not be guaranteed throughout the world either. About four years ago, the CACA decided to provide its own learning materials specifically designed for its own examinations. The result has been the open learning programme, de-

Michael G. Harvey is Professor of Accountancy at the City of London Polytechnic, Anthea L. Rose is Deputy Secretary at The Chartered Association of Certified Accountants, and Stephen Wellings is Publisher at the Certified Accountants Educational Projects Ltd.

veloped in conjunction with the United Kingdom's Open College.

When the CACA made this decision, there was no model to build on. Although distance learning courses had existed for many years, no serious attempt had ever been made to apply modern open learning techniques to the professions. This meant that, to some extent, the CACA was feeling its way on style, structure and receptiveness of the market. Nevertheless, it believes that its new open learning programme has considerable potential for improving education provision, and indeed it is already proving very successful in the marketplace. It will also have a substantial impact on the future of accountancy and business education in all its aspects.

THE KEY CHARACTERISTICS OF OPEN LEARNING

The main objective of open learning is to give the student maximum *control* over the learning process — control over
- *where* the learning happens;
- *when* the learning happens;
- *how* the learner learns;
- *what* is learned; and
- *who* is involved supporting and helping.

To help the learner achieve this, open learning materials must be capable of taking the place of all aspects of traditional courses. The materials have to motivate the learner and to present information authoritatively. They have to make the learner practise skills, to test the learner and to provide feedback. The challenge in open learning materials design is to make all this happen when the teacher may not be present.

The materials must be *effective*. The key to ensuring this is encapsulated in an old, possibly Chinese, proverb:

> "I hear, and I forget;
> I see, and I remember;
> I do, and I understand."

Getting the student *actively* engaged in the process of learning — not just the passive recipient of information — is at the heart of all good education, especially open learning. Open learning does not expect the learner to learn only from reading; it shows him/her how to apply what s/he has read and ensures s/he has absorbed it. It represents the very newest approach to studying and learning.

CACA OPEN LEARNING

The CACA materials do not restrict themselves to purely technical education. While appropriate accounting and auditing expertise is clearly essential, accountants in a modern commercial environment are increasingly seen as the providers of a wide range of business advisory services. The materials reflect this by providing coverage in the areas of financial management, information technology, management skills and business development.

Information is presented in carefully structured, modular units, of about one to two hours study time, in which the content is precisely matched to the syllabus and to what the learner is ready to learn. Practice in applying knowledge or skills is provided through the activities, which students are encouraged to complete, before they move on to the next steps, by writing in the spaces provided in the workbooks. The authors have given a high priority to these activities because they are at the heart of the learning process. Self-assessment questions (SAQs) also appear at frequent intervals to help learners check their progress. So that students can correct any errors or misunderstanding, feedback on both right *and* wrong answers is provided after every activity or SAQ.

Study material aims throughout to fulfill a dual function: on the one hand to give learners practical help in acquiring the *skills* they need to work effectively as accountants; on the other hand, to give them a clear *understanding* of the techniques and skills they are using. So, while the workbooks are full of practical activities, the text also encourages learners to analyse and question why and how they use these skills. While it is important for learners to become fluent in the technicalities of the subject matter, it is just as important for them to develop a critical understanding of the topics.

What is in the programme? Physically there is a separate open learning package for each of the CACA's 18 examinations. Each package contains all study material needed to pass the examinations. No further reading is required, other than one reference book on accounting standards and an encouragement to advanced students to read widely in the financial press. Each package contains four, five or six two-colour, A4 format workbooks, one or two audio cassettes, and four accompanying booklets (giving study and revision guidance, tutor and computer-marked assignments, a glossary and an index). The average length of each workbook is about 200 pages, so each package contains from 900 to 1,300 pages of text as well as one to two hours of audio material. The total programme represents well over 18,000 pages of text and more than 30 hours of audio.

Students buy each package as they need it and can use it in a variety of ways, whether for home study, distance learning, or as part of a college or company-based programme. However, it was assumed that a high proportion of students would want to study without tutorial support, so this placed great demands on the design of the materials and the way they were developed.

The student support system which supplements the materials comprises a network of regional centres, approved by the CACA. Students can telephone or attend open access centres to discuss with specialist advisers problems they have encountered in their study, aspects of the course which particularly interest them, or simply for general study guidance or counseling.

The CACA is extending this network of support outside the United Kingdom by entering into arrangements with educational organisations in various locations around the world. To facilitate this, another strong feature of the material is the care which has been taken to ensure that the language level is appropriate for students for whom English may not be the first language.

The open learning materials are also expected quickly to find a place as important teaching aids in colleges. Colleges which want to use the materials in this way will find that they need to adapt their teaching to the new approach to learning and assessment. The programme is likely to have an important influence on the future style and structure of all kinds of accountancy education.

DEVELOPMENT

Two central factors guided the thinking on how to develop these materials. First, they had to be of very high quality and as *effective* as possible, to improve examination pass rates. Second, it was decided to publish the whole series in three roughly annual phases between autumn 1989 and summer 1991. The first phase was launched in autumn 1989, the second between autumn 1990 and spring 1991, and the third in summer 1991. The separate phases overlapped, but each had a maximum of eighteen months' development and manufacturing time. Both these decisions have imposed challenges quite unlike those faced by traditional textbook publishing or even by educational programmes.

Curriculum Development

Before it could begin, it was necessary to identify the most appropriate approach and medium of learning to use. For two main reasons — cost, and the fact that CACA students are assessed by *written* examinations — it was decided that a preponderance of text materials, with audio in support, would be best. The various features of the packages — text design, use of language, activities, SAQs, audio sequences, and so on — were designed according to best current practice and piloted with actual students.

Then, each individual package had to be designed within the resulting framework. This was done by assembling, for each package, a team of consultants, all of whom currently teach the subject to CACA students. Each team's brief was to develop a complete set of learning objectives from the CACA syllabus. The learning objectives had to be unambiguous, achievable and measurable. This process involved two or three workshops for each package and several drafts of the resulting curriculum specification documents. As well as specifying in great detail the structure and content of the workbooks, and the individual units they comprised, these documents set out the assessment strategy for each package. This process lasted some two to three months and resulted in a course specification document, for each package, of 25 pages or more.

Text Development

Only after these course specifications had been agreed were authors recruited. A team of authors could be as few as two in number, or as many as ten. The individuals were chosen for their knowledge of the subject and their experience of teaching it. Because few of them had written open learning materials before, they had to be trained in the relevant skills and thoroughly briefed. To ensure that the materials they produced were technically accurate, each package was assigned two subject consultants, who read and commented on every word written, and a mathematics checker. The effectiveness of the materials was assured by open learning editors, who guided the authors and edited or rewrote as necessary to ensure that the materials matched, and enabled learners to achieve, the learning objectives.

The authors were asked to submit their successive drafts in small batches, so that weaknesses in writing style or approach could be identified early. Authors would submit a 30 to 40 page batch of materials and then receive feedback on it (from the two subject consultants and their open learning editors) about three weeks later. They would be expected to work on their revisions straight away. This ensured that differences in approach or understanding were tackled as early as possible. While authors and editors found this a tough discipline, all agreed that the regular interaction was an invaluable stimulus. Towards the end of each author's assignment, only minimal feedback and revision was usually necessary.

The text was finally prepared for typesetting by copy editors, who checked and corrected grammar, punctuation, consistency, and so on. The same people also acted as proofreaders during the typesetting stage. There were always at least two proofreads, to eliminate error as completely as possible. All authors were obliged to work on a common wordprocessing package — *Microsoft Word* 5 running on IBM hardware — which facilitated the editorial process and greatly speeded up the typesetting stage.

Since there was often a large throughput of typesetting at any one time, the typesetting requirements were spread among several suppliers. Their familiarity with the materials, and the working relationship which developed with them, were important factors in ensuring the materials were produced to the right quality, and on time.

Audio Development

While the text was being written, an audio production company was briefed and commissioned to produce one or two audio tapes per package. A high degree of integration with the text was not attempted — because it was felt to be inappropriate for most subjects — but the audios do perform a very important role within each package. They contain interviews with examiners and authors, and feature practising accountants or managers discussing the materials' relevance to business and the accountancy profession. Some also contain dramatised fictional case studies. The audio master tapes were timed for duplication and delivery as the text materials were in the final stages of manufacture.

Manufacture

Full-quality linotronic typesetting output to camera-ready copy (CRC) was used throughout the programme. Manufacture of the workbooks involved the first known use in Britain of the Rachwal print platemaking system for two-colour work. This system involves photographing the CRC onto a reduced size 70mm film instead of the normal full-size film. Imposition and platemaking are then con-

trolled automatically by computer and involve re-enlarging the image on to the printing plate. The system had been well tried for black and white printing but not on two-colour work where close registration counts. The system had major advantages in terms of both origination costs and time and produced excellent-quality material.

Managing the Process

Obviously, none of this could have been achieved without a very carefully worked out management structure. For each of the three phases of the programme, a Commissioning Editor would have a small team of Managing Editors (MEs), an editorial assistant and a production specialist. Each ME would be responsible for no more than two packages. All other contributors to the programme — authors, editors, proofreaders, subject consultants, and of course typesetters and manufacturers — were external, usually freelance, suppliers. At one stage during Phase 3 of the programme, there were over one hundred people working on the project. Managing such a large number of specialist suppliers, spread across the country, was no easy task. A monthly tailor made newsletter kept them in touch and disseminated information. For part of the time, a project management software package was also used to assist the monitoring and control the very tight schedules.

Keeping to Schedules

The timescale pressures involved working methods which are rarely applied in conventional textbook publishing. Three main factors above all others helped to achieve the publication target on Phase 3 of the programme:

- the detailed course specification documents were produced and approved by author teams at the very beginning, before any writing began. This reduced delays caused by disagreement between authors and consultants or the kind of structural changes which often occur at the writing stage.

- the common wordprocessing package used by all authors reduced typesetting timescales dramatically. The typesetters turned round significant batches of workbook materials in under three weeks, including two thorough proofreads.

- project management skills were foremost among the requirements of the in-house team. Whether the project was monitored and controlled "manually," or by using the project management software, the critical path determined at the design and planning stages was the subject of the editorial team's constant attention.

There were of course other important factors, not least of which was the determination and expertise of the editorial team, but these are the ones which stand out as being critical to the project's success.

Keeping the Programme Up To Date

Now that the full programme is available, the problem of updating is a prime concern. Some packages (those on management accounting, or management decision making, for example) require little updating while others (taxation, law and financial accounting, for example) require a great deal.

A small editorial unit will commission and produce revisions to the packages and time the introduction of new pack components, balancing two (sometimes conflicting) requirements: ensuring that new student purchasers are getting the most up-to-date information and reducing the wastage of out-of-date stock.

Measuring the Programme's Effectiveness

The key success criterion which the CACA had in mind when it decided to go ahead with the open learning programme was to give its students access to reliable, high-quality learning materials. Results from recent examination sittings suggest that students who have studied with the open learning packages are achieving higher than average examination results. This applies to students in the United Kingdom and overseas. The results are not *significantly* higher, but they do suggest that the programme compares favourably with the full range of alternative methods of study, from full-time taught courses, to home study using other distance learning packages or textbooks.

CONCLUSION

Although traditionally an examining body, the CACA has now developed its own educational materials designed primarily — but not solely — for its own students. Because it makes extensive use of practical, work-based examples, and the student's own experience of these, the open learning programme provides a natural link with the other major development being undertaken by the CACA: the move towards a competence-based accountancy qualification.

The programme has achieved a number of firsts in educational provision. It is the first complete open learning route to a full professional qualification. It is also probably the largest ever single open learning programme, providing over 2,700 hours of learning. It took less than four years to develop and produce, and the largest phase of it, the final phase, took just 14 months from beginning to end. Early feedback from the market suggests too that it is the best, in terms of quality and effectiveness, among its competitors.

The programme represents an entirely new approach to accountancy studies. It represents a system of learning materials which will make professional level accountancy examinations accessible to a much wider range of people on a worldwide basis.

Computing in Introductory Financial Accounting Courses: A U.K. Example

Ruth King and John Whittaker

INTRODUCTION

This paper reviews the progress made thus far in integrating computing more explicitly into introductory financial accounting courses at Loughborough University Business School. Two courses are used to characterise the process and potential developments. These are the first-year undergraduate financial accounting course on the Accounting and Financial Management (AFM) degree and part of the finance module for post-experience management development programmes.

The paper first presents the context in which the developments should be seen and the constraints within which they occur. Subsequent sections describe the progress made and the experiences gained,[1] and in particular the practical problems and pitfalls encountered in integrating computing elements within the courses. The paper concludes with an outline of the planned further work.

CONTEXT

The Business Environment

The authors are not alone in holding the view that credible management courses cannot be delivered without appropriate reference to information technology (IT) and specifically, the use of computing (see, for example, Helmi 1986; Lehman and Lehman 1988; Oglesbee Bitner, and Wright 1988; Staubus 1975; Sangster and Wilson 1991). Furthermore, there is an expectation from employers, professional bodies and funding bodies that all our courses (undergraduate, postgraduate and post-experience) should include appropriate elements of IT. The management task has been greatly affected by developments in this area, and this is likely to continue apace for the foreseeable future. Its effects are manifested in all areas of planning, decision making, control and communication, on a day-to-day basis and at the strategic level. Accounting information, as an integral part of the organisational decision-making database, is naturally affected by and included in these developments. It may be observed that the decision-oriented nature of the field of mana-

gerial accounting lends itself more readily to the integrated use of IT in its teaching, and it has been the experience of the authors that there have been many more developments in this field than that of financial accounting. Nevertheless, the authors believe that beneficial use of IT can be made in the teaching of financial accounting.

IT developments in accounting education must be addressed to meet the needs of our students as they move on from their university learning. However, this must be seen in the context of the broader objectives and the academic integrity of our courses. Students must continue to develop the ability to think and question, rather than simply to operate procedures. The integration of computing into accounting courses must therefore be seen as facilitating the teaching and learning processes, not as an end in itself.

Classification of the Teaching of Computing in Accounting Courses

The teaching of computing in accounting courses has been classified by different writers in a variety of ways. The classification devised by Seddon (1987), as quoted in Shaoul (1989), has been used by the authors in relation to their teaching, and can be summarised as follows:

(i) **Computer literacy** — teaching about computers, how they work and how to use them, including their use as a computational tool in, for example, statistical analysis and modelling.

(ii) **Accounting information systems** — issues in information management and the demonstration of specific systems examples.

---

[1]Experiences have been shared in a similar way by other writers, for example Gallagher (1990): 40–41; Hill and Payne (1990): 42–45; McElroy et al. (1989): 8–16; Sangster and Wilson (1990): 26–35.

Ruth King is Lecturer in Accounting and Financial Management and John Whittaker is Director of Management Development, both at Loughborough University Business School, England

(iii) **Demonstration of accounting principles and concepts**, which can be subdivided into computer assisted teaching (CAT) and computer assisted learning (CAL).

The potential advantages of using CAT and CAL to enhance educational effectiveness were summarised in King and Whittaker (1991). Briefly, CAT can be used to demonstrate accounting-specific uses of industry standard software and to demonstrate more clearly and interactively complex accounting examples. CAL, if considered as lecture or textbook substitution, is generally not considered to be cost effective in mass use (Er and Ng 1989; Bhaskar 1983). However, if used as a tool to reinforce both computing and accounting learning, it may be effective for "remedial" or revision work in private study. (See for example, Fetters, McKenzie, and Callaghan 1986; Sangster 1992.)

The authors believe that changes in teaching methods, including the use of CAT and CAL, should have explicit purpose, that being either to improve the course content or to make more effective the delivery of the material. It was the view of the authors that opportunities existed for enhancing the content of some courses by a more extensive use of IT, and that teaching effectiveness could be improved by the use of computerised demonstrations of accounting principles and by encouraging students to apply their computing knowledge in solving accounting problems.

The following paragraphs apply the above classification to the current educational inputs to the AFM degree and post-experience work, to provide the context within which the developments are taking place.

The Accounting and Financial Management Degree

(i) *Computer Literacy*

First–year students on the AFM degree take a combined course in Quantitative Analysis and Computing. The objectives of the computing element are

(1) To develop the confidence to use microcomputers and standard packages.

(2) To give a working knowledge of what computers are, including the practicalities of file handling and storage.

(3) To provide a sound introduction to industry standard software for word processing, spreadsheet and statistical work.

This basic grounding is consolidated in later years with practical experience of standard packages in other courses.

(ii) *Accounting information systems*

Students take a Business Information Systems course in their second year which considers broad issues relating to business management information systems, one element of which is the financial information system. This second-year course provides a foundation for the Financial Information Management option in the final year. That course is primarily directed towards computerised systems and addresses the behavioural, strategic, and practical aspects of financial information management in its widest sense. It includes hands-on practical sessions in the school's Computing Resource Centre, and certain course work involves case study work on the computers.

(iii) *Demonstration of accounting principles and concepts*

Individual members of staff use the computer facilities in their teaching to varying extents, and our students are exposed to considerable practical use of PCs at different points during their studies in accounting and other subjects. However, the demonstration of accounting principles and concepts, particularly in relation to financial accounting, was an area where there had been limited use made of computing. The authors identified this as an area where opportunities existed for the effective use of IT.

Post-Experience Finance Modules

The Management Development Centre (MDC) of Loughborough University Business School provides a wide range of management development and consultancy services to both individuals and corporate clients and is particularly specialised in the provision of tailored executive programmes. Courses in computer literacy and accounting information systems may be offered to clients of the MDC, and they can form part of an integrated programme. However, for the most part, and so far as affects the integration of computing into accountancy teaching, it is the demonstration of accounting principles and concepts which is of primary concern.

A major feature of tailored executive programmes is the use of material directly related to the client's industry and environment. Case material is often constructed using data and information provided by the client. In the area of finance, many courses involve providing delegates with an understanding of financial statements and their interpretation, and invariably the client's own accounts are used for this purpose. The level of the delegates' prior knowledge often necessitates the simplification of their own company's accounts for instructional purposes. The use of information technology is seen as a way of providing a more effective teaching medium for displaying in a dynamic manner the relationship between the elements shown in the financial statements.

Facilities

The Business School has IT facilities available for undergraduate use in its Computing Resource Centre. This room is currently equipped with 20 stand-alone Olivetti PCs (IBM compatible) and the resources are heavily utilised for timetabled classes. The school also makes significant use of the University Computer Centre for formal classes and for students' private study. The school has on its staff a computing resources manager and a part-time assistant. In the past, postgraduate students have assisted with the evening supervision of the Centre, but pressure on funding has forced the withdrawal of this facility and there is now no technical help available from the school outside office hours. The provision of resources is currently under review. A Nimbus network, which was rather dated and working to its full capacity, has recently been removed. It is intended that the Olivetti machines should be networked and linked to the University Computer Centre's facilities. However, constraints on funding, consistent with those being experienced throughout the UK universities, have led to a delay in the implementation of this project. As a result, the school's undergraduate computing resources have been halved since the developments described in this paper were originally set in hand. Furthermore, the situation envisaged by Armitage and Boritz (1986) that "Soon, every student will own his or her own computer" (p. 98) and Ijiri (1983) "By the end of the 1980s, personal computers . . . will be as popular in the classroom as calculators are now." (p. 168), is far removed from the UK experience.

The MDC's post-experience work is carried out in facilities which are available exclusively for post-experience, postgraduate and specialist diploma teaching. A significant proportion of the MDC's earnings have been reinvested in order to provide enhanced facilities, including computer equipment. Computing resources are therefore available in some conference and syndicate rooms for use by lecturers and delegate groups.

CONSTRAINTS

The ability to change methods and materials must inevitably be viewed against the constraints imposed by a scarcity of resources, and increasing competition for existing resources. In particular, consideration must be given to restrictions on staff and student time, the availability of equipment and funds to provide additional facilities, and other constraints which necessarily operate in any diverse academic department. The constraints can apply to both mainstream and post-experience teaching, particularly in respect to development time.

Restrictions on Time

Changes to existing teaching material inevitably take time. Reviewing available software can absorb many hours (Helmi 1986), as can the design and testing of applications (Anderson 1976). This must be viewed in the context of increasing pressures on staff time from other sources, and in particular that demanded by research work. In the UK, this applies notably to younger and probationary lecturers who may well also be the staff with active interests in developing the use of information technology.

Additional time is also required immediately preceding a lecture in order to set up the equipment and to ensure that it is functioning properly. In the case of mainstream teaching, the lecture theatres available to the Business School are not equipped with computer facilities, which necessitates a personal computer being moved from the lecturer's office to the appropriate room for use. The ideal solution of computer equipment installed in all, or even a selected number of lecture theatres, is not a development anticipated in the foreseeable future. Although this is not generally a problem for post-experience work, there is in either case the possibility of equipment failure. Most lecturers have dealt with the experience of an overhead projector which fails to function. However, a malfunction of the computer equipment is much less easily overcome, particularly as the lecture in this case is likely to be much more dependent on the technology.

For undergraduate teaching, work done in a lecture or tutorial is usually restricted to that which can be accomplished in 50, or at most, 55 minutes. If set up time is required, or immediate removal of equipment at the end of the session to make way for the next class, the effective time available is soon eroded. Further, as noted above, equipment failure is a possibility, and even the most temporary fault can lead to considerable loss of time.

Finally, tutorial or syndicate preparation work and course work need to be planned so as to be realistically manageable within the time and other resources available to students outside timetabled sessions, in terms of both their own time and access to the requisite computer equipment.

Availability of Funds

An increase in the use of information technology is likely to involve substantial investment in hardware, software and site licences and a need for additional floor space to accommodate equipment. These demands must be seen against the background of the current funding restraints in UK higher education, and in an environment where universities already pressed for space are being expected to accommodate increasing student numbers.

There may also be a requirement for additional technical help. Ideally, an increase in the use of facilities outside timetabled classes should be supported by the availability of technical assistance. As noted above, such support during evening use of the school's Computing Resource Centre has had to be withdrawn.

Other Constraints

There is a need to achieve a balance between the teaching of principles and ensuring that students have a thorough understanding of them, and relieving students of the tedium of repetitive calculations. The latter can be accomplished by using computing facilities, whilst the former may in fact be reinforced by working manually through those calculations. Helmi (1986) and Ijiri (1983) both allude to this factor.

Coordination problems can arise where a computing course is separately taught, as is the case with the AFM degree. These can be compounded where students from other departments are included with the school's own students for the teaching of accounting. There is a need to ensure that the expectations of staff teaching the accounting component, as regards extent of student knowledge arising from computing component, are met by the appropriate scheduling of teaching.

There may still be a reluctance on the part of some staff to become involved in computing. This requires careful handling in order to encourage participation, particularly where senior and respected members of staff are concerned.

Furthermore, those supervising the computing resources cannot be expected to answer account-

ing queries. This means that software must be carefully chosen and exercises drawn up so as to minimise the potential queries which may arise whilst students are working in their own time.

Many of the constraints outlined in the preceding paragraphs, not least the limited staff time available, apply in the Business School. This led the authors to conclude that gradual change would be necessary. The two elements of accounting teaching referred to earlier were identified as appropriate for initial revision. These were the first-year financial accounting course, and part of the finance module for post-experience management development programmes. Assessment of the success (or otherwise) of the changes was planned,[2] with a view to making more extensive changes to these and other courses as resources become available. The following sections describe the initial developments and outcomes which resulted from this decision.

DEVELOPMENTS AND OUTCOMES — FIRST-YEAR FINANCIAL ACCOUNTING

The approaches taken to increase the utilisation of IT in the teaching of financial accounting on undergraduate courses in a number of other institutions were reviewed by the authors, together with those illustrated in various texts. The methods and texts considered include those of Gray and Nicholson (1990); Groomer (1987); Ivy Educational Publishing plc (1991); Marriott and Simon (1990); PEER (1989); Throckmorton and Talbot (1978); Wildey (1990); Wilkinson-Riddle and Barker (1988). None were found to be exactly suited to the requirements of the course under consideration. The reasons for this are amplified in King and Whittaker (1991) and relate in the main to the differences in course content and emphasis found between individuals and institutions.

The adaptability of spreadsheets to numerous applications was seen to offer considerable scope for the integration of computing into the existing introductory financial accounting course. Marriott and Simon (1990) has been adopted as a supplement to the main course text, in order to provide guidance on the spreadsheet approach to solving financial accounting problems.

---

[2]Students within the school are asked to complete an evaluation schedule for each course studied. This procedure covers all types of studies, including undergraduate, postgraduate and post-experience work.

Two specific areas of change are described below. These are followed by comments on the practical outcomes, based on the personal observations of the member of staff primarily involved with the revisions to the financial accounting course and comments received from the students and from other members of staff.

Demonstration of Principles in Lectures

CAT is employed to demonstrate certain accounting principles in lectures. The approach involves the adoption of spreadsheets for explaining double-entry bookkeeping and for showing in a dynamic manner the impact on ratios of changes in accounting numbers.

Students are first introduced to double-entry bookkeeping using traditional methods, the balance sheet equation and "T" accounts. An alternative recording system is then introduced, whereby transactions are recorded on a spreadsheet, essentially using it as electronic analysis paper. This is seen to be an effective way of reinforcing the principles of double-entry bookkeeping, using a methodology which some students seem to understand more readily, whilst also demonstrating a practical use of information technology. The spreadsheet is in essence developed into a simple accounting package.

In the case of ratio analysis, a simple spreadsheet has been developed which allows demonstration of the effect on certain key ratios of accounting changes to a set of financial statements. An outline balance sheet and profit and loss account are shown, with the key ratios listed below. Adjacent columns are then used to adjust the accounts and show the potential effect on the ratios of accounting adjustments, changes in policies or methods, and "what if?" scenarios. (For example, an issue of share capital or debt, a revaluation of freehold land and buildings, or bringing "off balance sheet finance" back onto the balance sheet.) Such an interactive demonstration successfully brings home some of the problems of comparability and consistency which can occur in analysing company accounts.

Staff time has been required in the initial design of the new material, and setup time is required in the lecture theatre each time it is used. Although there is an increase in "front-end" time, the volume of material covered in the lectures can be increased, thereby arguably increasing teaching effectiveness. In addition to the material which the lecturer would otherwise have included by alternative means, a wider range of scenarios can be demonstrated in the time available. This applies particularly to ratio analysis and the inclusion of certain "creative accounting" techniques.

Several observations may be made as to the practical outcome of the adoption of these teaching methods.

Most important, there is a clear need for the objectives of using the computer as a teaching medium to be explicitly specified to the students. The primary objective of the spreadsheet approach to double-entry bookkeeping was to reinforce their understanding of the principles involved, rather than to revise the use of spreadsheets. However, a difficulty was encountered with some students who felt that more time should have been spent during the lecture in demonstrating the technical aspects of how the spreadsheet had been constructed and was being completed, rather than the principles of transaction analysis. It is evident that the purpose of a session in which CAT is adopted as the teaching medium needs to be more explicitly communicated to the students.

Further, it was observed by using a computer for ratio analysis that students' attention was readily retained by the dynamic demonstration of the effect of "creative accounting" on financial statements and certain fundamental ratios. The interest may have been due to the topical subject matter as much as the method of delivery. However, without the use of the technology, the same quantity of material could not have been covered in the time available.

Tutorial Package

The financial accounting tutorial package offers possibilities for students to use the knowledge gained in their computing course to solve accounting problems, and this can be classified as CAL.

The tutorial package has been developed over a number of years to suit the structure of the financial accounting course, and it was considered desirable to leave this intact. Students are issued with a package of questions and are required to complete examples on specific topics before each tutorial. The package has now been modified such that students are required to use spreadsheets to prepare the solutions to some of the exercises. Essential data are held in spreadsheet files in the school's Computing Resource Centre, without which the questions cannot be completed. The students are given specific instructions in the tutorial package as to how the data can be accessed and suggestions as to the manner in which the problem could be tackled, using commands and techniques with which they are familiar from their computing work. This process is designed to reinforce the link between what the students learn separately as "computing" and "accounting," to demonstrate the use of information technology and standard software in solving accounting problems, and to give additional hands-on experience with specific packages.

The tutorial exercises are designed to be compatible with existing facilities in accordance with the school's IT policy and the content of the students' computing courses. Liaison between the members of staff responsible for the computing and accounting components is necessary in order to minimise practical difficulties. The timing and content of the computing courses are discussed to ensure that the teaching of spreadsheets links satisfactorily with the accounting tutorials. There is no additional input required from the members of staff who are involved solely in the financial accounting tutorials, as they are not expected to answer questions relating to the computing element of the exercises. The accounting tutorial time is spent as before on discussion of the underlying logic of the computations and the results.

Again, observations may usefully be made as to the practical outcome of this use of CAL.

There is once more a need to specify for the students the purpose behind using computers in this way in tutorial exercises, and that it extends beyond simply answering the accounting questions. Some students said that they considered the exercises had taken a disproportionate amount of time to complete; the difficulties referred to below relating to knowledge of the software will clearly have exacerbated this problem. It is apparent that the wider purposes and longer term benefits which will accrue from the additional computing practice (for example enhanced keyboard skills and competence in spreadsheet use) need to be emphasised more clearly to the students.

Students have complained of lack of access to the computer facilities because the Computing Resource Centre is heavily used for timetabled classes. Whilst acknowledging this as a difficulty, it is considered to be partly a problem of access at times which are most convenient to students. (A similar problem is identified by Sangster 1992.) However, it is clear that this will become a major constraint on future developments on this and other courses unless funding can be made available for expansion of facilities, particularly in the light of the expectation of increased student numbers.

A significant number of students appeared to have insufficient knowledge of the software to complete the exercise fully. For example, a considerable number claimed not to have been taught how to print the finished spreadsheet. One or two students simply accessed the data through the network and produced the answer manually and there was evidence that a few students had copied answers saved onto hard disc by other students. On investigation, it was confirmed that the exercises worked in computing tutorials include all the basic facilities required by the accounting exercises. It was concluded that either the students had failed to complete the exercises set in computing tutorials and had therefore not learned all that had been expected of them, or that they had simply forgotten, in the space of a week or so, the techniques they required. Further liaison has recently taken place in order to minimise this problem for the future. Alternatively, certain of these problems may be manifestations of the apprehensiveness observed of some students in relation to the use of computers (Bentz 1979; Sangster and Wilson 1991).

Having listed their complaints, the students were asked if, despite the difficulties, they considered that they now had a better working knowledge of spreadsheets, and the majority answer was affirmative. For this reason, it is felt to have been a worthwhile exercise and it is intended to repeat and extend it as described below, taking into account the experiences encountered thus far. It will be impossible to eliminate some of these problems completely, but steps can be taken, as noted above, to minimise their occurrence, and any residual problems can be looked upon as additional learning points for the students, if treated appropriately.

DEVELOPMENTS AND OUTCOMES — POST-EXPERIENCE FINANCE MODULES

Interactive Company Accounts Software

The MDC commissioned the development of the Interactive Company Accounts Software from a graduate of one of the school's MBA programmes. The software was constructed for use primarily as a teaching tool by the accounting and finance staff involved in such programmes.

Software Structure

The software is a series of spreadsheets constructed using *EXCEL*; this spreadsheet package was chosen as it was considered desirable to develop the software within a *Windows* environment, and to make use of its fully 3-dimensional capabilities. It provides the instructor with three sets of accounts, based upon the same data, but varying in their detail and complexity. The first level contains a highly simplified profit and loss account and a balance sheet in the format of the accounting equation. The intermediate level contains the same documents but in considerably more detail and in UK companies act format. Only one year's accounts are shown at both these levels. The final level contains a full set of accounts with comprehensive accompanying notes, recognisable as the published financial statements of the client company. The instructor may select the level appropriate to the prior knowledge of the audience.

It is intended that the first two levels be used for conveying an understanding of the content and logic underlying financial statements to an audience with little or no prior knowledge of the subject. These two levels, the simple and the intermediate, comprise four files within one workspace and they may be accessed together. Each of the four spreadsheets are headed up with three columns: Original, Increase/Decrease By, and Revised. The profit and loss account and balance sheet at each level are linked only via the retained profit figure. Thus, any change made will affect only the specific item selected, without any effect on the other variables. For example, an increase in sales will not automatically alter the cost of sales. Furthermore, any changes made to the profit and loss account will cause the balance sheet to become out of balance. This allows the instructor to alter a figure in the accounts and ask the delegates to analyse what other impact such an alteration would have on the accounts as a means of reinforcing the learning process.

The final level is a fully automated package consisting of nine files held within one workspace, accessed and activated by a macro. The files are as follows:

    Balance Sheet — accounting equation format;

    Balance Sheet — UK companies act format;

    Profit and Loss Account;

    Source and Application of Funds — *SSAP 10* format;

    Source and Application of Funds — alternative format;

    Notes to the Accounts;

    Key Ratios — abbreviated;

    Operating Ratios and Investment Ratios;

    Decision and Change Screen —- "What if."

The programme is entered through the decision screen allowing the instructor to immediately proceed with any changes he wishes to make. Delegates are supplied with a hard copy of the original screens so that the impact of changes may be monitored. The decision screen and the screens containing financial statements have a key ratio screen at their foot. This key ratio screen comprises six items. The original values are permanently displayed and new values are displayed for comparison whenever changes are made to the accounts. The decision screen determines the results of all the other spreadsheets; changes are passed through the notes to the accounts, where the appropriate formulae drive the data in the remaining spreadsheets, eventually into the ratio spreadsheet.

The final level may be used for the same purpose as the simple and intermediate, that is, for explaining the logic and structure of accounts and showing in a dynamic way the relationships between items. A reasonable level of prior knowledge by the delegates is desirable, however, since the financial statements presented at this level are more comprehensive. However, this level is primarily designed to deal with more advanced aspects of company accounts and in particular to explain the funds flow statement, to highlight the difference between cash flow and profit and for the interpretation of accounts.

Practical Experience with the Software

Delegate reaction to the use of the package as an aid to understanding and interpreting financial statements has generally been favourable. The software has, however, perhaps fallen short of the expectations of the staff involved in its conceptual design and development, and further modifications may be made to it in the future.

It had been anticipated that the software would provide a more effective means of tailoring data to a client's needs in terms of both time and presentation of material. In practice, there has been no time saving over the previous method of manually simplifying the accounts and having them word processed. The spreadsheet accounts were intended to act as a proforma into which any client's accounts could be entered, whilst retaining the information in a similar form to the published accounts. In the event, the package has proved to be less flexible than had been hoped and some modifications to the spreadsheets are necessary to accommodate each individual client's published accounts. Data have thus to be input by lecturing staff and cannot be delegated to support staff as had been hoped. In addition, the material will need to be updated in the light of any future changes in the regulatory framework, as for example with the recent replacement of funds flow statements (*SSAP 10*) with cash flow statements (*FRS1*).

The presentation of material in hard copy form has met expectations, but screen presentation has presented a problem insofar as the whole of a financial statement cannot be displayed at one time. This is not too serious a drawback given that delegates have a hard copy of the original material, nor is this problem unique when seeking to display detailed information on a PC and overhead projector.

At the design stage, the major objective of the detailed ratio screen was seen as being able to demonstrate the impact of "what if" adjustments on the ratios. The ratios presented thus relate to a single year's data and show the original current year information and the revised figures resulting from the changes to that data via the decision screen. Both instructors and delegates have expressed a desire for the ratios to be presented for the two years of data contained at the final level.

Finally, it should be noted that to make any interactive model work, a number of assumptions have to be made in constructing the formulae. For example, what happens to closing stock and debtors if sales are increased? Unquestionably some of the assumptions made in constructing the final level model are open to criticism. For example, an increase in sales alters the purchases/production costs but stocks are not automatically changed as a result of the sales increase. The lack of realism in some of these assumptions is not problematic for the educational purposes for which the programme was designed so long as the instructor is fully aware of them. In practice, they can be used to gauge the delegates' understanding of the financial implications of transactions and as discussion issues.

WHAT NEXT?

First-Year Financial Accounting

A formal feedback mechanism is planned so as to elicit from students their views on the inclusion of computerised material in their financial accounting course, and their experiences in handling it. Work of a similar nature has been carried out by Marriott (1991). He conducted an experiment in an attempt to monitor the effectiveness of using the spreadsheet approach of Marriott and Simon (1990) to teaching financial accounting. First, his study showed that there was apparently no difference in performance in an end-of-term accounting test be-

tween those students who had been taught using the spreadsheet approach and those who had been taught using traditional methods. This, he concluded, showed that the spreadsheet approach had been successfully integrated into the accounting teaching. In a second strand to his work, Marriott notes from the writing of others (Austin 1990; Borthick and Clark 1986) that "... there is evidence to suggest that computer integration can have a detrimental effect on students' attitudes towards using computers in general." All Marriott's students were exposed to computing as a separate element of their studies, and he concluded from his experiment that a "... decrease in attitude ..." took place, but that it was less significant amongst the students who had used the spreadsheet approach to financial accounting. His work is continuing.

It is the authors' intention to carry out further work in monitoring the effectiveness of the developments undertaken. In particular, it is planned to attempt to measure whether there is any difference in students' perceptions of their learning experiences, comparing the use of spreadsheets with other teaching and learning media. The authors believe that there may be advantages in using spreadsheets, particularly for those students who have previously had no accounting tuition. The direction of further developments will be shaped by the outcome of this monitoring.

Interactive Accounts Software

The package as developed has, in the main, fulfilled its initial objective, which was to provide an interactive and dynamic demonstration of certain basic accounting principles. It has provided an alternative means of tailoring material for client companies and a more effective learning medium for the subject matter. So far as the authors are aware, no other such software exists in the UK.

It is intended to experiment with the development of a simplified, combined version of the "what if?" and "key ratio" screens, which would lend itself more readily to use in a classroom situation. In addition, there is considerable scope for using the package, with minor modification, for syndicate group work.

For the longer term, the package would lend itself readily to adaptation for distance learning. There is a need for some refinement of the teaching material content as noted in Developments and Outcomes section above, and for improvement to the user friendliness of the display and input screens. A short accompanying text is also required.

Additionally, the package would need to be available for industry standard software to make it accessible to a wider range of students.

Continued development of the computing content of our accounting courses is required. Although there is scope for improvement in the elements introduced thus far, they have met with sufficient success to justify their continuance and further development.

REFERENCES

Anderson, J. J. 1976. Computer-Supported Instruction in Managerial Accounting. *The Accounting Review* (July): 617–624.

Armitage, H., and J. Boritz. 1986. Integrating Computers into the Accounting Curriculum. *Issues in Accounting Education*. (Spring): 86–101.

Austin, W. W. 1990. *A Study into the Effects of Integrating Microcomputers into the Introductory Financial Accounting Course*. Unpublished Ph.d. thesis.

Bentz, W. F. 1979. Computer Extended Reciprocal Allocation Methods. *The Accounting Review* (July): 595–603.

Bhaskar, K. N. 1983. Computers and the Choice for Accountancy Syllabuses. *Accounting and Business Research* (Spring): 83–93.

Borthick, A. F., and R. L. Clark. 1986. The Role of Productive Thinking in Affecting Student Learning with Microcomputers in Accounting Education. *The Accounting Review* (January): 143–157

Er, M. C., and A. C. Ng. 1989. The Use of Computers in Accountancy Courses: A New Perspective. *Accounting and Business Research* (Vol. 19, No. 76): 319–326.

Fetters, M., J. McKenzie, and D. Callaghan. 1986. Does the computer Hinder Accounting Education? An Analysis of Some Empirical Data. *Issues in Accounting Education* (Spring): 76–85.

Gallagher, D. 1990. Accounting with Sage. *Account* (Volume 2, No. 3): 40–41.

Gray, R. H., and A. H. S. Nicholson. 1990. *Introductory Financial Accounting: A Systems Approach with Spreadsheets*. Paper presented to the CTI Annual Conference, University of East Anglia, March 26–27.

Groomer, S. M. 1987. *Solving Financial Accounting Problems Using Lotus 1-2-3*. John Wiley and Sons Inc.

Helmi, M. A. 1986. Integrating the Microcomputer Into Accounting Education — Approaches and Pitfalls. *Issues in Accounting Education* (Spring): 102–111.

Hill, G., and N. Paine. 1990. Integration of Freeway Accounts into Courses — A Discussion Paper. *Account* (Volume 2, No. 3): 42–45.

Ijiri, Y. 1983. New Dimensions in Accounting Education: Computers and Algorithms. *Issues in Accounting Education*: 168–173.

Ivy Educational Publishing plc. 1991. *Understanding the Profit & Loss Account and the Balance Sheet; How to Compile a Profit & Loss Account and Balance Sheet; How to Analyse Funds Flow Statements; Analysing Financial Statements*. Ivy Educational Publishing plc.

King, R., and J. Whittaker. 1991. Integrating Computers into Accounting Courses. *Account* (Vol. 3, No. 2): 27–35

Lehman, M. W., and C. M. Lehman. 1988. Interactive Spreadsheet Models Reinforce Accounting Principles. *Journal of Accounting Education* (Vol. 6): 131–137.

McElroy, T. et al. 1989. Computing on an Accounting Degree — The Ealing Experience. *Account* (Volume 1): 8–16.

Marriott, N. 1991. *The Effectiveness of Using Spreadsheets to Teach Financial Accounting*. Paper presented to the British Accounting Association Annual Conference. Salford University, April 3–5.

———, and J. Simon. 1990. *Financial Accounting, A Spreadsheet Approach*. Prentice-Hall International.

Oglesbee, T, L. Bitner, and G. Wright. Measurement of Incremental Benefits of Computer Enhanced Instruction. *Issues in Accounting Education* (Fall): 365–377.

PEER. 1989. *Financial Accounting Course*. PEER/System Dynamics Limited.

Sangster, A. 1992. Computer-Based Instruction in Accounting Education. *Accounting Education* (Vol. 1, No. 1): 13–32.

————, and R. A. Wilson. 1991. Knowledge-Based Learning within the Accounting Curriculum. *British Accounting Review* (Vol. 23, No. 3): 243–261.

————. Teaching Accounting Standards: An Experiment with Intelligent Computer Assisted Learning. *Account* (Volume 2, No. 3): 26–350.

Seddon, P. 1987. Computing in the Undergraduate Accounting Curriculum: Three Distinct Goals. *British Accounting Review* (Vol. 19): 267–276.

Shaoul, J. 1989. Teaching Accounting with Computers — Before and After CTI. *The CTISS File* (February 1989): 36–42.

Staubus, G. J. 1975. The Responsibility of Accounting Teachers. *The Accounting Review* (January): 160–170.

Throckmorton, J. J., and J. Talbot. 1978. Computer-Supported Instruction in Financial Statement Analysis. *The Accounting Review* (January).

Wildey, E. 1990. *A New Model for the Design of First Year Accounting Courses in the 1990s.* Paper presented to the CTI Annual Conference, University of East Anglia, March 26–27.

Wilkinson-Riddle, G. J., and B. E. Barker. 1988. *Accounts Trainer* and *Balance Sheet Analysis.* Pitmansoft.

The Process of Academic Quality Improvement the Accounting and Business School of the National Autonomous University of Mexico

Salvador Ruiz-de-Chávez and Alfonso Orozco

THE NATIONAL AUTONOMOUS UNIVERSITY OF MEXICO (UNAM)

In 1553, King Philip II of Spain decreed the establishment of the Royal University of Mexico.

During the Mexican War of Independence from Spain (1810–1821) the University was occupied by the Mexican army. Several years later, the University was closed according to a government decree, which was later revoked.

In 1910, the Congress granted approval for the Minister of Education to create the National University of Mexico. Nineteen years later, the President of Mexico declared the University to be an autonomous institution, separate from the federal government, hence its current name: National Autonomous University of Mexico (UNAM).

UNAM has more students than any other University in the world. Currently, it has enrolled 122,000 high school students, 130,000 undergraduate students and 35,000 graduate students. There are 29,000 faculty members, of which 13,000 work full-time, and 27,000 employees.

UNAM boasts 14 schools with both graduate and undergraduate programs, and nine schools with only undergraduate programs. In addition to 65 different undergraduate majors in science, technology, liberal arts, economy and health, UNAM offers 138 master programs and 49 Ph.D. programs.

UNAM has on-going studies in 15 centers of scientific research and nine liberal arts research centers. The Scientific Research Program in UNAM is made up by 1,900 members and develops approximately 2,500 scientific and technological projects. This program publishes 32 periodicals, as well as many books and specialized articles.

The liberal arts research program has 900 members, who publish 31 periodicals and a variety of books related to their fields. UNAM's editorial office publishes an average of 1200 books per year, in addition to an estimated one hundred periodicals.

UNAM's annual budget is approximately $800 million U.S., of which 90 percent is subsidized by the federal government.

THE ACCOUNTING AND BUSINESS SCHOOL (FCA)

FCA was founded in 1929. Currently it has the largest enrollment of all the UNAM schools. There are almost 16,500 students (Figures 1 and 2) registered in our three undergraduate programs, with 428 credits (50 courses) each: Accounting (Figure 3), Business Administration, and Management Information Systems. In addition, there are 730 students in the Graduate Division of the school (Figure 4).

There are 1,150 faculty members, only 150 of them are full time professors (Figure 5). The Dean of the school coordinates 300 administrative employees of 12 separate divisions: Accounting, Business Administration, Management Information Systems, Graduate, Open University, Continuous Education, Academic Quality Improvement, Associate Dean, Exchange Programs, Extracurricular Activities, Students' Affairs and Administration.

The FCA has 12 buildings, including its own library, with nearly 80,000 volumes related to the multidisciplinary areas of study.

THE PROCESS OF ACADEMIC QUALITY IMPROVEMENT (PAQI)

Since October 1989, when Ruiz-de-Chávez started his four-year term as Dean of FCA, we initiated a process of academic quality improvement, based on Philip Crosby's philosophy. By then, we had already completed the first diagnostic that we prepared as part of the school's plan for the academic years 1990–1993. As a result of the needs reflected on the analysis, we have implemented the following changes at the undergraduate level. We considered that the FCA's inputs are students, faculty, administrative personnel, curricula and infrastructure. The outputs of the system are graduate students, community services (i.e., journals, tax consulting, continuing education), and general image of the school.

Salvador Ruiz-de-Chávez is Dean and Alfonso Orozco is Associate Dean of the Accounting and Business School of the National Autonomous University of Mexico.

FIGURE 1
Accounting and Business School
Total Undergraduate Students by Sex in 1991*

	Number	%
First Year		
Men	1,554	10
Women	1,999	12
	3,553	22
Second to Fifth Years		
Men	5,919	36
Women	7,000	42
	12,919	78
Total	16,472	100
Men	7,473	45
Women	8,999	55

*Includes Open University
Data: Agenda Estadistica UNAM.

FIGURE 2
Accounting and Business School
Students from Second to Fifth Years by Program and Sex in 1991*

Program	Number	%
Accounting	8,738	68
Men	4,017	31
Women	4,721	37
Business	3,874	30
Men	1,778	14
Women	2,096	16
MIS	307	2
Men	124	1
Women	183	1
Total	12,919	100
Men	5,951	46
Women	7,000	54

*Includes Open University
Data: Agenda Estadistica UNAM.

In this paper we will go over some measures taken to improve quality through preventive actions with students, faculty and curricula.

Students

Classes were reduced from 85 to 75 students. This was accomplished by increasing the number

FIGURE 3
Accounting and Business School
Structure of the Curriculum
(concentration in accounting)

Area	Credits Num.		(Courses) %
Accounting	84	(8)	19.7
Cost Accounting	24	(3)	5.6
Control	32	(4)	7.5
Finance	40	(5)	9.3
Auditing	24	(3)	5.6
Taxation	32	(4)	7.5
Total Core Courses	236	(27)	55.2
Administration	48	(5)	11.2
Information Systems	24	(3)	5.6
Mathematics	32	(4)	7.5
Economics	32	(4)	7.5
Law	24	(3)	5.6
Research Methodology	8	(1)	1.8
Sociology	8	(1)	1.9
Optionals	16	(2)	3.7
Total Support Courses	176	(23)	41.1
Total	428	(50)	100%

FIGURE 4
Accounting and Business School
Graduate Students by Program and Sex in 1992

	Number	%
Speciality		
Men	280	38
Women	167	23
	447	61
Master		
Men	182	25
Women	95	13
	277	38
Doctorate		
Men	5	0.7
Women	1	0.3
	6	1.0
Total	730	100
Men	467	64
Women	263	36

Data: Administracion Escolar FCA.

of available groups from 175 to 215 for each 18-week academic term (figure 6) and by hiring 282 additional professors (figure 5).

FIGURE 5

Number of Faculty by Program and Academic Term

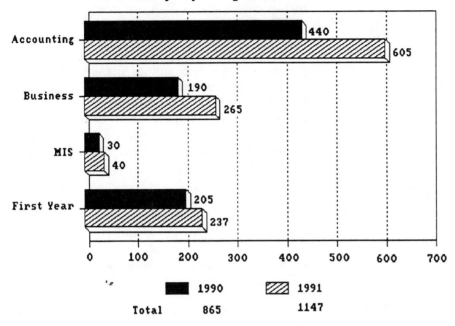

Data: Administracion Escolar FCA.

FIGURE 6

Number of Groups by Program and Academic Term

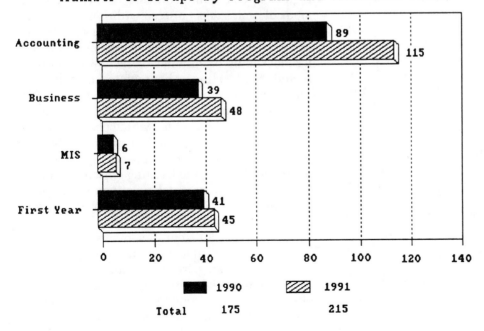

Data: Administracion Escolar FCA.

A program was created to reward students who were able to get an "A" in a minimum of ten required subjects (84 credits) within an academic year. The awards are PCs, and 57 students won them during 1990 and 66 in 1991.

Within the premises of the FCA we initiated extracurricular courses for computer skills and English as well as, courses to improve written and oral skills in Spanish.

Currently, research is carried out in order to find out

1. The causes of attrition, in order to improve our entrance process, and

2. The variables that affect the students' academic performance.

We also participate in an advisory group, working to improve the three-year curriculum of UNAM's High School System. Ninety percent of FCA's freshmen are from this UNAM track.

Each year many students try to get enrolled in the FCA program, much more than at any other school in the UNAM. More than 15,000 students apply annually for one of the coveted 3,400 available slots. Due to this high demand we are able to attract many of the best freshmen to our school.

Faculty

Each new faculty member has to take a minimum of two 30-hour courses of teaching skills, during their first two teaching terms at the FCA.

We also initiated our own optional program of faculty development, which includes 210 hours of courses that are focused on the skills necessary to teach effectively in accounting and business programs. In 1991, 40 professors finished this program, and 460 faculty members attended our training courses. In 1992, we have 26 faculty in our development program.

These courses are designed as a result of the information provided by the student evaluations of teaching skills. This is a 50-item questionnaire which was developed eight years ago and is currently being reevaluated.

Professors have 20 minutes of tolerance for each two hour class. In 1991, considering the 1,150 faculty members, we had an average of attendance of 91.5 percent which is lower when compared to 94.2 for 1990, but in the former year, we had almost 300 professors more.

Curricula

Our curricula are under a continuous process of improvement with the help of two academic councils. The External Academic Council is formed by 20 distinguished alumni working in a wide variety of fields. The Council has met bimonthly since November of 1990 and has been working on strategic planning for the FCA.

The Internal Academic Council combines the talents of the heads of our six academic divisions, as well as the chairpersons of our 16 academic departments: Basic Accounting, Advanced Accounting, Auditing, Finance, Cost Accounting, Taxation, Law, Basic Management, Advanced Management, Manufacturing, Economy, Marketing, Personnel Management, Basic Information Systems, Advanced Information Systems and Mathematics. The dean presides over their monthly meetings and manages the PAQI.

In August 1991, the Internal Academic Council finished a 14-month effort to evaluate our three undergraduate curricula, as well as the profile of the accountant or manager that is being formed within the FCA program. Using Bloom's taxonomy of learning objectives, we found congruence between these profiles and the general objectives of the curricula and the general objectives of the subjects being taught. However, we identified a high level of incongruence between the general objectives of the subject matter and its topics' specific objectives.

Each chairperson of our academic departments worked in teams, made up by faculty members and high-achieving senior students, to review the syllabus of each subject offered within his or her department. A survey carried out among professors in each department allowed us to identify the topics that should be eliminated; the new topics to be included; allocation of hours to teach each topic; selection of bibliography; and other related matters. Each team reviewed the results of its departmental survey and decided which changes should be implemented. Supported by our specialists, the teams also established higher levels of Bloom's taxonomy for the specific learning objectives of each topic. Some departmental examinations are used to evaluate whether these learning objectives were really met.

More than 250 faculty members participated in this process: 30 of them are full-time professors. The remaining are part-time lecturers, with an average of four to eight teaching hours per week. It is our belief that this combination has allowed us to keep a good balance between the theoretical and practical worlds.

In August 1991, taking the evaluation described as a base and with almost the same people, we held a methodology workshop to prepare new curricula. We also carried out a forum, with the participation of 45 distinguished representatives of the government, industry and services. They helped us to develop an expanded profile for our bachelor students (Figure 7).

In the period between each academic term, the administration meets with the faculty, once, in our 600 seat auditorium and once more in their respective departments. Discussions are focused on PAQI and on our respective roles within the University. The chairpersons of each department have meetings with faculty members to discuss specific topics about the on-going curriculum development, results of student evaluations of teaching skills and other matters related to FCA or UNAM.

It is our observation that the more faculty members and students participate in PAQI, the more they support the ensuing changes and endorse these changes among their peers.

SUMMARY AND CONCLUSIONS

In October 1989, the Accounting and Business School (FCA) of the National Autonomous University of Mexico (UNAM) initiated the PAQI with support and guidance of our dean. FCA has an enrollment of 17,000 students in three of the five-year undergraduate programs and 730 students in the Graduate Division.

Using Crosby's Total Quality principles, in order to improve the teaching-learning process, we have implemented various strategies for students, faculty, administrative personnel, curricula and facilities.

The External Academic Council has been working on strategic planning and the Internal Academic Council is directly in charge of the curricula improvement. This process involves 250 professors and 20 senior students.

For the most part, implementation of the reviewed curricula has been a painless process because it is the result of a participative project. Due to the success of PAQI, with the expanded profile of our bachelors in mind, the Internal Academic Council has already finished the new curricula for our three undergraduate programs. We expect to implement these curricula for the term starting October 1992.

One of the problems we have faced is that we initiated PAQI one year before we began with our strategic planning process. Right now, we are working hard to coordinate both projects.

FIGURE 7

Expanded Profile of Bachelors in Accounting, Business Administration and Information Systems

Attitudes to	Skills to	Knowledge
- Criticize life and profession	- Implement theoretical knowledge into practice in a creative way	- The career itself (SOUND)
- Serve	- Analyze and summarize information	- Quantitative methods
- Participate in the learning-teaching process	- Handle interpersonal relations	- Culture general
- Succeed	- Research	
- Commitment	- Make decisions without receiving precise instructions	
- Daily improvement	- Get adjusted to the organizational environment and to new technologies	
- Continuous learning	- Handle computer programs	
- Have entrepreneurial initiative	- Negotiate	
- Ethics (personal and professional)	- Carry out team work	
	- Learn (how to learn)	
	- Have a correct oral and writing communication in English and Spanish	

Data: Conferences organized at FCA, UNAM between July and November 1991

Another problem is that people, generally speaking, do not like to use manufacturing terms that were transferred to service areas. During training courses and lectures, we have to use terms like "outcomes" instead of "finished products," and "source of freshmen" instead of "supplier."

Since we have a strong labor union, with a long tradition of confrontation with the authorities, we have not been able to have enough interaction with the 300 administrative employees.

In March 1992, the committee for waste management improvement began its biweekly meetings. This committee is made up by various areas: faculty, students, administrative workers and personnel from the dean's office.

We acknowledge that PAQI is not an easy task. However, with coordinated efforts of various members of the school, we are sure that we will reach our goal, and that is, to form accountants and managers of the highest quality in Mexico and Latin America.

Using BITNET for International Accounting Education: A Japan-U.S. Study

Ichiro Shiina, M. Susan Stiner, and Frederic M. Stiner, Jr.

INTERNATIONAL EDUCATION REFORM IN JAPAN

Introduction

In the past, Japan had a nationally planned university curriculum for all majors. On July 1, 1991, the Ministry of Education abandoned a required national curriculum and replaced it with guidelines. University accounting curricula can now be decided at the university level. One emphasis of the new guidelines is international education. This paper reports on apparently the first use of electronic mail to have American accounting professors correct Japanese students' accounting homework. This paper describes an experimental class in the accounting department of Chuo Gakuin University (Chiba, Japan), where student papers were corrected by American accounting faculty. The paper also discusses some current issues in international accounting education in Japan and presents some thoughts for future research.

Japan has been a student of other societies throughout its history, having absorbed culture, social systems, religion, and language from China for over 1,500 years until turning its attention, after the Meiji Restoration (1867), to the West. Today, this cultural mix is shown by Japan's polytheistic religious culture and its multiple writing systems. In administration and law, Japan absorbs important messages from other cultures.

Because Japan is a mosaic of international elements, international education is an important theme in every educational field. Foreign languages, especially English, are stressed in university entrance examinations, and students entering university accounting departments find English or other languages used as part of general studies courses. In addition, most accounting curricula require that juniors and seniors read untranslated material from the United States, Great Britain and Germany. Some universities have introduced lecture courses dealing with subjects such as "German and International Accounting," while students in regular financial statement theory classes are lectured on the history of American accounting principles, German static and dynamic theories of accounting, and other theories which have influenced Japanese accounting.

A demographic constraint is that Japan faces an "academic winter." With the nation's population of 18-year-olds peaking at two million in 1992 and forecast to decline to 1.5 million by 2000 and 1.3 million by 2008, the present ceiling on university enrollment will face a shortage of 55,000 students in the year 2000, and this means a new era of bankruptcy and consolidation of universities (Daigaku Shingikai 1991). Therefore, each university must think of international education as a means to survival. To bolster enrollments, Japanese universities are increasing the number of students admitted from other Asian nations.

Reforms after July 1, 1991

When the new university system was established in Japan after World War II, there was a uniform requirement for each major in each university. On July 1, 1991, a sweeping reform of the "Standard for University Establishment" was instituted by the Ministry of Education (Daigaku Shingikai 1991). This reform has three aspects important for accounting education in Japan:

1. The detailed regulation of accounting curricula and credit requirements are abolished. Each university is free to determine its own educational content and curriculum within broad guidelines.

2. To balance this independence, universities now have "self-evaluation" in which they are subject to peer review for the first time.

Ichiro Shiina is Associate Professor of Accounting at Chuo-Gakuin University, Chiba, Japan, M. Susan Stiner is Assistant Professor of Accounting at Villanova University, Villanova, Pennsylvania, and Frederic M. Stiner, Jr. is Associate Professor of Accounting at the University of Delaware, Newark, Delaware.

Acknowledgements: Hironori Sato, Associate Director of the Computer Center at Chuo Gakuin University, provided technical assistance. Dr. Diane Ferry and Dr. Christine Kydd of the University of Delaware provided very useful comments. Any errors are the responsibility of the authors.

3. Universities which have traditionally targeted students of 18 to 22 years of age are now expanding continuing education, with the establishment of night classes and part-time study for the first time.

The reform of the central curriculum control is of particular importance. Under previous ministry standards, the courses in Principles of Accounting, Financial Accounting Theory, and Managerial Accounting were required for accounting majors. Cost Accounting and Auditing Theory were highly recommended courses. Optional courses were Tax Accounting and Corporate Financial Analysis. The new standards require a minimum of eight terms (the equivalent of 124 total credits) required for graduation. Curriculum content is the responsibility of each university. Each university is now forced to clarify its educational philosophy regarding the study of accounting and then develop its own curriculum for required, elective and major courses in line with this philosophy.

Underlying the university's educational mission there must be concrete policy. To implement this, the universities and the Ministry of Education agree that the intent of that policy is best expressed in the following three concerns:

1. Individual education

2. International education

3. Practical computer education

Stating educational philosophy and developing a curriculum based on the above three issues will not alone assure the Japanese university of survival in the coming academic winter. Individual education, rather than group education, has not been emphasized. A professor at a blackboard with passive students is still typical in Japanese classrooms. Japanese student participation is rarely encountered, except in seminars. Student evaluations and required office hour consultation are unknown. Accordingly, we find that problems of reforming teacher consciousness and improving teaching methods are critical for Japanese curriculum development, more critical than even reformation of the mechanism of curriculum (Shiina, Stiner, Stiner 1991). More flexible classroom approaches are needed. Instead of preparing lectures that will satisfy student expectations, or giving pragmatic lectures that can prepare students for actual practice, Japanese accounting professors emphasize principles and theory. Classes where textbooks of basically the same content have been used for ten years are not rare. A typical course in Japan is a lecture

for one 90-minute session each week. The Japanese author of this paper doubts that this is the most effective means of instruction.

Traditional Japanese international education can be described as follows:

1. Broad cultural exposure to foreign languages through the study of the languages of industrialized nations.

2. The reading of important foreign accounting literature in their original versions in major studies.

3. Introduction of students in regular accounting classes to the theories that have most influenced Japanese accounting in major studies. For example, W. A. Paton, A. C. Littleton, and E. Schmalenbach are read in the original language.

Finally, the revision of the computer component of the curriculum must not be rote learning. Knezak, Miyashita, and Sakamoto (1990) describe how the United States leads Japan strongly in the use of microcomputers in elementary and secondary education. Terada et al. (1990) present the Japanese Curriculum Supported by Computer concept as applied to the mathematics curriculum in secondary schools. They believe that the goal of computer education in Japan is to foster creativity, logical and analytical expression, and "the continuous attitude to demand reasons."

Against this background in Japan, the Japanese author of the paper began to investigate ways in which to use the computer in his accounting classes, while increasing the international content of the course.

USING BITNET FOR INTERNATIONAL EDUCATION: AN EXPERIMENT

BITNET, which began in 1981 as a means for interuniversity computer communication (Fuchs 1983), has a goal of communication with minimum cost in programming and time. The program has been very successful in connecting 3,500 nodes worldwide as of June 1991 (BITNETJP 1991); as of May 1992, 116 of these nodes were in Japan. These nodes include over 1,000 universities (Hazari 1990). Japanese use of BITNET has risen sharply: U.S.-bound traffic on BITNET has risen from less than 1,000,000 records in June 1990 to over 2,000,000 records in June 1991 (BITNETJP 1991).

Chuo Gakuin University began its participation in the Japan BITNET Association in 1990 with the objectives of promoting international student education, exchanging information within Japan, and aiding international research for professors. In support of its BITNET program, Chuo Gakuin established in its Information System Center a "Computer Education Division" attended by three specialists which now facilitates a broad variety of activities, from assisting students and guiding student and teacher computer education to offering information to the public by way of computer.

In September 1991, the 31 of the 52 Japanese universities now participating in BITNET were surveyed on their use of electronic mail education.[1] Of the 11 respondents, only two have electronic mail education (in engineering and liberal arts). This suggests the limited degree to which electronic mail education has progressed in Japanese universities. Other countries have used E-mail for education for some time. For example, Jones (1990) describes Britain's Campus 2000 project that links 60 percent of U.K. secondary schools to over 20 other countries. Paulsen (1987/88) describes a "virtual school" from a Norwegian perspective. Such a school is a classroom without walls, where the relationships between faculty and students exist through computer linkages.

We believe that the elements that are essential for success with this method of overseas communication are (1) the desire and effort of the students, (2) a relationship of trust between the Japanese and overseas instructors, (3) preparatory education for the Japanese instructors, (4) knowledge of Japanese culture by the American instructors, and (5) a host computer operation staff able to instruct students and teachers.

BITNET was used for international accounting education when seven students at Chuo Gakuin University in Chiba, Japan, took a one-year experimental course from April 1991 to March 1992.[2] The experimental accounting class was "Reading Foreign Accounting Material." The course fused the three elements of individualized, international, and computer education through the use of English-language readings in Japan and tutorial by American faculty. This created a "virtual classroom." We believe this is the first Japanese-American accounting education class. While it is certainly possible for Japanese teachers to teach American accounting, American accounting professors are better acquainted with the language and accounting principles. While independent electronic mail exchanges between students and clubs and with acquaintances overseas are not unusual at Japanese universities, we believe this is the first Japanese accounting class to receive direct instruction from teachers abroad by way of electronic mail as part of the course.

There are advantages to the use of electronic mail (Losey 1985). Although communication through any E-mail is not as immediate as a lecture or a telephone conversation, it does allow students to communicate at their own pace. A student has time to consult a dictionary for the proper word. Given the time differences between students and professors, the ability to work when one pleases is especially important.

Also, if the number of students is small, the American instructor can provide tutoring based on each student's English ability and understanding of accounting. The American faculty communicated with students individually, correcting their English while discussing accounting. They can discuss topics of mutual interest. The Japanese goal of individual, international computerization is achieved.

The role of the American professors was, first, to determine the direction and objectives of the class and each student's development in English; second, to advise students on details in their overseas communications, preparing reference materials and handling preparatory education; and third, to evaluate the students.

The one-year syllabus, which represents 25 weeks of instruction, follows. (A complete discussion of the syllabus is found in Shiina, Stiner, and Stiner 1992.) For the sake of this experimental class, the junior- and senior-year students were given the same educational content. In broad outlines, the schedule was

- seven lessons for preparation
- three E-mail lessons for introduction
- three E-mail lessons on the accounting profession in America
- four E-mail lessons on the accounting profession in Japan
- four E-mail lessons on accounting regulation and
- one E-mail lesson summarizing the course.

For "Reading Foreign Accounting Sources," the students read foreign source materials which have shaped Japanese accounting. The students prepared by translating the text into Japanese before class, and in class the Japanese teacher provided a

---

[1]The other 21 were colleges without business programs.

[2]April 1 to March 31 is the Japanese school year.

context and discussion. The student then transmitted a paper on the topic to America. The American professor provided comment on each area covered.

Results

Three seniors and four juniors enrolled in the class. Their primary motivation for joining the class was given as follows:

- desire to study living (American) English with overseas teachers (five students)
- interest in this kind of new teaching method (one student)
- desire to increase language ability gained by prior overseas study (one student)

One American professor assumed responsibility for the three senior-year students, and another for the four junior-year students. The syllabus was oriented to the Japanese system, wherein a class is held once a week for 90 minutes in the school year. In response to English work sent by the students once a week, the American professors replied in one or two days, correcting the students' English, making comments on student opinions, offering advice, and raising questions. The students received these replies independently, noted the English corrections in their notebooks and corrected their compositions. They then replied to the professors' questions and suggestions.

The students spent an average of 3.5 hours of preparation for their final replies, which they mailed on the next day of class. The results show that much of the Japanese students' effort went into English composition. The students had almost no time or energy left for learning American accounting. Since English is an international language, and indispensable to Japanese students, a steadily increasing ability with English took precedence over accounting.

Some of the student impressions of the course follow:

Juniors

- have achieved greater speed in writing English,
- are able to express personal opinions in English,
- feel more confident about using English,
- have grasped my level of English for the first time,
- have made valuable acquaintance with a professor who can advise me on my [graduation] thesis,

- understand now the difference between British and American English, and
- the United States has become more familiar to me.

Seniors

- have come to grasp the situation in the United States,
- find that preparation for this course takes three times longer than for the usual course, but the time is well spent for much is learned,
- since the comments are detailed, am able to understand the material well,
- have come to see the importance of a good vocabulary,
- have learned the value of good preparation.

From the perspective of the American professors, the students had various levels of ability in English. Grammar, particularly verb usage, is essential for understanding any language. Questions related to both life in America and American accounting were asked. The students were interested in what American accounting professors do, as well as in their personal lives (family, hobbies, etc.). They were interested in how American undergraduates find jobs, and in the American accounting curriculum.

Specific accounting questions were not asked as often as broad economic and business questions on the structure of the tax system, government spending, and ethics on Wall Street. The continuing savings and loan problem seemed to be beyond the comprehension of the students.

The American professors found that the students were far more expressive via computer than Japanese students met elsewhere, perhaps due to lack of status cues or other nonverbal behavior. There is a rich literature on how E-mail changes communication because of a changed social context (e.g., Sproull and Kiesler 1986).

This was an excellent method for students to practice English composition, word order, sentence construction, and common phrases. The students received quick feedback from a native speaker who is expert in accounting. We met our objective of providing a wider understanding of America. Students chose this course as an elective, so their enthusiasm was high. The improvement in foreign language ability and foreign accounting knowledge may not be as fast in less highly motivated students. It may be useful to compare improvement in foreign language and accounting ability in other students similar to those in the experimental class, but who have not been exposed to the BITNET experience.

Limitations of this method were that weekly lessons in English are not sufficient for fluency. Some students were able to absorb feedback and incorporate it into succeeding messages faster than others. There was no increase in ability in spoken English. Students are unfamiliar with a QWERTY keyboard and spend time searching for English symbols.

With the experience of this international course, we can speculate on the role that E-mail might play in international accounting.

FUTURE INTERNATIONAL EDUCATION USING ELECTRONIC MAIL

Future Possibilities

Beyond just sending electronic mail, the use of BITNET means transmission of files, message exchange, and using various servers (NETSERV, LISTSERV). Of these computer applications, it is message exchange that relates most directly to internationalization. For Japanese students who wish to study American accounting, having direct guidance from American university faculty, as in this experimental class, means enjoying an intimate involvement with the subject that is unattainable through a book. The willingness of these seven students to put three times more effort into preparing for class, as indicated in the survey of their impressions, shows just how interested in and motivated they felt by its format.

In the future this method of study can be used by international accounting students from different nations discussing their own nations' accounting systems and what accounting should mean, through electronic mail. Accounting thus becomes a means for technology transfer (Stiner 1988). If a school has an accounting club, electronic mail will prove useful to the students' research. Students will also derive benefit from using it for their private communications, while Japanese students studying foreign source material will be able to contact authors directly with their questions. The development of a BITNET directory of addresses will make this easier.

Along with these applications to students, the universities can expand the framework of their full and part-time lecture staff, establishing faculty throughout the world who are tied together by electronic mail. It is most beneficial to learn account-

ing directly from a professor of accounting in that country (e.g., Chinese accounting from a Chinese professor). A student is able to use a host country resource without visiting the country. Electronic mail can also facilitate accounting conferences and discussion between geographically distant faculty. Perhaps the time is coming when multimedia will bring the factor of entertainment into these projects.

In order to promote further development of international accounting education using electronic mail, we suggest that there are specific areas that require research. They are (1) reconstruction of curriculum; (2) faculty understanding; (3) development of supporting staffs; (4) the students' motivation; and (5) the effect of the medium on accounting education. These are discussed further below.

Reconstruction of Curriculum

Japanese foreign language education traditionally places emphasis on reading original works while treating writing and oral skills as secondary. When it comes to their weakest subject, English composition, Japanese students face severe difficulty. Freshman and sophomore foreign language education should be applied in international education in students' majors. It was from a similar rationale that Japan's new Standard for University Establishment removed the boundaries between general and major studies and targeted four years of progressive education.

Faculty Understanding

A new undertaking is bound to generate conflict between faculty who are enthusiastic about its promotion and faculty who adhere to the established methods. For university faculty to truly serve the students' educational needs, it is important that a position of understanding and cooperation be taken. Another factor of importance, one revealed by this experimental class, was that of friendship between the Japanese and Americans. The American professors got to know several Japanese technical support staff, emphasizing that E-mail has indeed created a global village.

The American professors got to know the Japanese students more than many American students in a traditional classroom. The American professors both corrected the students' English and guided them in their study of accounting, so considerable interaction was required of them. Education that responds to each student's ability with English and understanding of accounting is essential, so enthusiasm is also a quality required of instructors in this type of project.

Supporting Staffs

Besides such departmental support as payment of foreign instructors and provision of computers, a support staff is necessary. Chuo Gakuin University's Computer Education Division is necessary to maintain the operation of hardware, provide daily assistance to students, and aid teachers. The Japan BITNET Association must also function as an information base, offering information on overseas university personnel willing to participate in this kind of education, and overseas students who wish to be involved in exchange of communication. It is thus desirable that a system be set up that will mesh the Association's functions with the activities of the university.

Student Motivation

Many Japanese students are interested in learning foreign languages but hesitate to enter this realm due to insecurity arising from past experience. It is necessary to reconsider the character of foreign language studies at the university while bringing to the students an awareness of the role of language in internationalization efforts. Toward this, development as recommended above is fundamental. Reformation of university-level education, taking individualized, international, and computer education as components of its basic philosophy, has begun in Japan.

Effects of E-mail on International Accounting

Feldman (1987) has suggested that since E-mail is a low-cost way to find people of similar interest, communication arises between people who would not otherwise be in contact. These are new communications, rather than a substitution of E-mail for another way to communicate. One future development for international accounting could be electronic conferencing or electronic bulletin boards. A critical mass of users might be necessary to make this successful (Rice et al.1990).

As a factor in the future university environment, internationalized accounting education using electronic mail has much to offer.

REFERENCES

BITNET Association. 1991. *BITNETJP News.* Japan BITNET Association (Summer).

Daigaku Shingikai. 1991. *Concerning Reorganization of Higher Education after 1993.* Ministry of Education.

Feldman, M. S. 1987. Electronic Mail and Weak Ties in Organizations. *Office: Technology and People* (Vol. 3): 83–101.

Fuchs, I. H. 1983. BITNET—Because It's Time. *Perspectives in Computing* (March): 16–27.

Hazari, S. 1990. Using E-mail Across Computer Networks. *Collegiate Microcomputer* (August): 210–214.

Jones, G. 1990. Communication in the Curriculum. In A. McDougall and C. Dowling, eds. *Computers in Education.* North-Holland: 983–987.

Knezak, G., K. Miyashita, and T. Sakamoto. 1990. Computers in Education: Japan vs. the United States, in A. McDougall and C. Dowling, eds. *Computers in Education.* North-Holland: 775–780.

Losey, C. L. 1985. Electronic Messaging Systems for More Effective Management. *IEEE Transactions on Professional Communication* (September): 35–39.

Paulsen, M. F. 1987/88. In Search of a Virtual School. *Technological Horizons in Education Journal* (December/January): 71–76.

Rice, R. E., A. E. Grant, J. Schmitz, and J. Torobin. 1990. Individual and Network Influences on the Adoption and Perceived Outcomes of Electronic Messaging. *Social Networks* (Vol. 12): 27–55.

Shiina, I., F. M. Stiner, Jr., and M. S. Stiner. 1991. *The Accounting Profession in America.* Chiba, Japan: Chuo Gakuin Research Foundation.

————, M. S. Stiner, and F. M. Stiner, Jr. 1992. Syllabus for "Reading Foreign Source Material" at Chuo Gakuin University. In T. J. Burns, ed. *Accounting Trends: Innovative Accounting and Information Systems Course Outlines* (Vol. 26): 51–53.

Sproull, L., and S. Kiesler 1986. Reducing Social Context Cues: Electronic Mail in Organizational Communication. *Management Science* (November): 1492–1512.

Stiner, Jr., F. M. 1988. Accounting Education as Technology Transfer. In K. Someya, ed. *Accounting Education and Research to Promote International Understanding.* Greenwood Press: 566–573.

Terada, F., T. Shakushi, N. Nakamura, M. Takeya, and N. Kanda. 1990. Curriculum Supported by Computer (CSC) — Basic Concept, Trial and Evaluation. In A. McDougall and C. Dowling, eds. *Computers in Education.* North-Holland: 311–316.

Accounting Internship: Expectations and Actual Experience

Susan Teo and Joanne Tay

FORMAL INTERNSHIP: THE BUSINESS ATTACHMENT PROGRAMME

Rationale

Accounting education at the tertiary level has become established worldwide, as rapid growth in the areas in which accountants must be knowledgeable has made it highly unlikely that on-the-job training alone can provide the level of competence required for professional performance of duties. However, the emphasis on classroom teaching and evaluation by examinations means that would-be accountants often graduate with little or no practical experience. In the past, the School of Accountancy and Business (SAB) at Nanyang Technological University (NTU) addressed this imbalance with an active but voluntary vacation training placement service. Beginning in the 1991–1992 academic year, however, a compulsory internship programme — the Business Attachment Programme (BAP) — was introduced as a nonexaminable requirement for SAB's Bachelor of Accountancy (B.Acc) degree.

In view of the importance of the BAP, NTU made the decision to organise a pilot, non-compulsory programme for second-year undergraduates in the 1990–1991 academic year, scheduled over 10 weeks from March to May 1991. This period spanned the months between the undergraduates' main and supplementary examinations, and was deemed adequate to provide both students and participating organisations the opportunity to begin and complete meaningful assignments or projects. Students who completed this voluntary programme were issued Certificates of Participation.

Organisation

The pilot BAP and all future programmes were administered by NTU's Industrial Liaison Unit (ILU). However, SAB's academic staff acted as tutors to the students during their attachment. In this capacity, staff were required to visit the participating organisations prior to the commencement of the BAP to discuss and evaluate the programmes submitted by the organisations. They also visited midway through the BAP to discuss the students' progress, monitor the organisations' adherence to the planned programmes and review the students' logbooks. Based on this meeting, SAB staff provided feedback to students to help them improve their performance, and/or amended the organisation supervisors' evaluation of the students' performance in circumstances where the evaluations appeared biased. The SAB staff also had to grade the students' final reports, which were submitted to them at the end of the BAP.

RESEARCH OBJECTIVES AND QUESTIONNAIRE

The purpose of this paper is to evaluate the perceptions of past and future student participants of the BAP, as well as the academic staff who served as tutors in the pilot project. These participant perceptions will help to assess the contribution of the BAP to the B.Acc degree, as well as enable the ILU to identify areas where the BAP has met expectations, and areas where changes may be needed.

A two-part questionnaire was used to survey SAB staff and second- and third-year students. The first part was more structured, focusing on the objectives of the BAP, the comprehensiveness of the instructions issued by the ILU and the contributions of the tutors and supervisors. A 5-point Likert scale was employed, with respondents asked to evaluate very important/successful items as 5, and unimportant/unsuccessful items as 1. The second part requested comments on the need for students to meet with the NTU tutors before the commencement of the BAP, the grading of students by the tutors before the commencement of the BAP, the grading of students by the tutors and organisation supervisors, and the requirements for keeping a logbook and writing a final report.

Survey questionnaires were given to 62 SAB staff, 650 second-year students and 600 third-year students (those who did not take part in the BAP were excluded from the survey). The response from the three groups was as follows: staff, 31 percent

Susan Teo and Joanne Tay are faculty members at Nanyang Technological University.

(19/62); second-year students, 17 percent (109/650); and third-year students, 25 percent (148/600). Feedback from the second-year students suggested that their particularly low response rate was due to lower awareness of the BAP. At the time of the survey (August 1991) these students had not been briefed on any aspect of the BAP and therefore found it difficult to understand, let alone answer, some of the questions asked.

Eighty-one percent of the third-year students who responded, and 89 percent of the second years had had some working experience prior to the BAP, mostly on a part-time basis.

SURVEY RESULTS

Objectives of the BAP (Table 1)

Second-year students rated the objectives of the BAP from 4.36 to 2.74, while third-year students' and staff ratings ranged from 3.51 to 2.35 and 3.71 to 2.17, respectively. This difference may indicate that the objectives of the BAP, while important, were not met very successfully by the actual programme. In particular, the second-year students ranked the objective of providing the students with practical training as most important, followed by increasing the students' awareness of the business environment, and providing the students with the opportunity to relate theory to practice. Both staff and third-year students thought that only the first two of these objectives ranked amongst the three most successfully met objectives. It is possible that participating organisations perceived and used the students as "cheap labor," thus denying them the opportunity of relating theory to practice.

Second-year students also expected the BAP to be relevant to third-year course material, but third-

year students and staff indicated that the experience gained was more relevant to first- and second-year course material. This is underlined by a suggestion made by third-year students that the BAP would be of greater benefit if implemented in the first rather than second-year of the B.Acc programme.

In view of the differences in the students' responses, NTU may need to take steps to reduce the students' "expectation gap," in order to avoid student dissatisfaction at the end of each BAP. In particular, it may have to reevaluate the BAP's objectives to see if they are realistic, and possibly prioritize them.

Comprehensiveness of Instructions (Table 2)

Instructions issued to students were generally rated as satisfactory, with the exception of those for the logbook and final report. Unlike the progress report and summary of training forms, these two documents are less structured and require the students to write more. The differences in the responses of the second-year and third-year students probably reflects the fact that the latter had actually used the instructions, and had encountered problems in doing so.

SAB staff rated the comprehensiveness of the instructions much lower than the students. Staff indicated that guidance was given on the format rather than the contents of these documents, with the result that students did not seem to know what material to include. As a result, they tended to focus on their feelings and perceptions during the BAP, rather than on what they had learnt.

Tutors are required to evaluate the student's logbook and final report, as well as the organisation supervisor's evaluation of the student's performance. The responses indicate that the basis of

TABLE 1
Importance/Fulfillment of the BAP Objectives

BAP Objectives	2nd Year	3rd Year	Staff
Practical training	4.4	3.5	3.3
Relate theory to practice	3.9	2.8	3.1
Relevance to Year 1 course	2.7	2.7	2.8
Relevance to Year 2 course	3.6	2.9	3.2
Relevance to Year 3 course	3.8	2.4	2.2
Awareness of profession	3.9	3.1	3.6
Awareness of business environment	4.1	3.5	3.7
Sense of professionalism	3.5	2.7	2.7
"Right" work attitude	3.3	3.0	2.8
Career choice	3.7	3.2	2.9
Effectiveness and productivity	3.3	2.7	2.7
Relationship between NTU and industry	3.0	2.8	3.2
Assessment of potential employees	3.2	3.1	3.0

TABLE 2
Comprehensiveness of BAP Documents

BAP Documents	2nd Year	3rd Year	Staff
Mid-attachment progress report	0.71	0.68	0.71
Summary of training/experience	0.80	0.71	0.65
Students' logbook	0.87	0.74	0.53
Students' final report	0.85	0.72	0.47

these evaluations is not clear. However, the second-year students appear to understand the evaluation criteria better than the third-year students and the staff themselves! Again, this is probably due to their lack of first-hand experience of the BAP.

Overall, it appears that the ILU should try to set clearer criteria for the required contents of the logbook and report, and the evaluation process to be carried out by staff members.

Contribution of the NTU Tutor (Table 3)

While second-year students have high expectations of the NTU tutors, third-year students and the staff members themselves do not perceive that the tutors contribute much to the BAP. There are two main problem areas: the screening of programmes submitted by participating organisations and the review and evaluation of student performance, logbooks and final reports. In addition, although the timing of the tutor's visits to the students at the organisations was regarded as acceptable, there were suggestions that the number of visits should be increased in view of the role tutors play in student evaluation.

One factor which undoubtedly contributed to the apparent failure of the screening function was the nonadherence by the participating organisations to the programmes originally submitted and screened. This however, was a problem which tutors had difficulty dealing with on an individual basis and should more properly be resolved at the University level.

Another contributory factor could be the assignment of SAB staff in nonaccounting as well as accounting disciplines, due to the large number of students involved (an average of about 10 stu-

dents was assigned to each tutor). Nonaccounting staff inevitably experienced difficulties in performing screening and supervisory functions. Furthermore, the amount of time all tutors were able to spend with each student was limited, because other administrative and academic commitments continued during the period of the BAP.

In the light of these factors, more serious consideration could be given to the suggestion that specialised NTU staff be assigned to administer all aspects of the BAP, with SAB staff serving as consultants or advisers where accounting knowledge is necessary. An alternative would be to redefine the role of staff members from evaluator to mentor. Staff would then still be responsible for liaising with the students and organisations, but would not have to review performance, logbooks and final reports.

Organisation Supervisor's Duties

There is a general agreement that the organisation supervisor's duties include supervision and evaluation of students. In practice, however, it appears that supervisors in different organisations had different levels of involvement in designing the programme and liaising with the NTU tutors. Whether supervisors should be responsible for the design and administration of the organisation programme is an issue which is best left to the discretion of the participating organisations. However, NTU should clarify that the supervisor's duties should include liaising with the tutor about the student's progress and any difficulties encountered, as these will affect the evaluation of the student. Since the tutor is required to moderate the supervisor's evaluation, it is important that both parties understand the basis of the evaluation.

TABLE 3
NTU Tutor's Contribution to BAP

Tutor's Duties	2nd Year	3rd Year	Staff
Screening of organisations	4.2	2.5	2.7
Visits to students	3.6	2.4	2.9
Review of logbook	3.0	2.4	2.0
Evaluation of supervisors' report	3.3	2.4	2.4
Evaluation of final report	3.4	2.5	2.1

Duration of the BAP

The majority of the students and staff feel that the 10-week period is adequate. However, one suggestion is that the BAP could vary in duration, taking into account the nature and volume of work and training the organisations plan for the students. For example, a range of 8 to 12 weeks could be set, with the exact period left to the organisations and the students to work out.

The BAP as a Compulsory Programme

The responses on this issue were totally nonconclusive: 55 percent of the second-year students, 52 percent of the third-year students and 47 percent of the staff think that the BAP should be compulsory.

Factors that Affected the Students' Choice of Firms (Tables 4 and 5)

The students were asked to list the five most important factors that affected their choice of firms. These factors were allocated points — 5 for the most important factor, and 1 for the least important.

Second-year students cited pay and location most often, but the average scores (2.73 and 2.77, respectively) indicate that they were not ranked very highly. Factors which were cited relatively often, and also had high total and average scores were nature of organisation (public accounting firm, manufacturing, etc.), training provided and nature of work (auditing, cost accounting, taxation, etc.). Of these, nature of organisation appeared to be the most important.

Third-year students also cited pay and location most often, but also ranked these factors low (average scores were 2.77 and 2.73, respectively). There were only two factors which were cited relatively often, and also had fairly high total and average scores: nature of organisation and reputation of organisation. While specific factors and rankings obviously differed between the two groups of students, the most important factors identified are quite similar. The emphasis on the organisation rather than on pay and location may be interpreted as a willingness on the part of students to take a more long-term view on the benefits to be gained from the BAP.

Comments Made by Students and Staff

Meeting Prior to Commencement of BAP

About 20 percent of the third-year students expressed disappointment that no such meeting was arranged for them. The majority of second- and third-year students (about 75 percent) felt that such a meeting, between the student and the tutor, would be beneficial in building rapport between the parties. It would also help students to find out more about the organisations they would be attached to, and their tutors' requirements of their logbooks and final reports.

However, a substantial minority of third-year students (19 percent) felt that such a meeting is not necessary, because the information which is needed about the attachment can be better provided by the ILU.

Staff comments supported the need for a meeting prior to commencement of the programme, but

---

TABLE 4
Factors for Second-Year Students' Choice of Firms

Factors	Total Points	Times Chosen	Average Points
Location	166	60	2.77
Pay	169	62	2.73
Nature of organisation	155	35	4.43
Reputation	65	21	3.10
Training	89	21	4.24
Size	45	15	3.00
Environment	108	31	3.48
Nature of work	110	28	3.93
Relevance	59	14	4.21
Career	23	6	3.83
Programme	77	17	4.53
Organisation's requirement	28	8	3.50
Working hours	26	10	2.60
Number of vacancies	10	4	2.50
Organisation's commitment	15	3	5.00
Organisational structure	14	4	3.50
Allocation method	21	6	3.50
Others	20	7	2.86

TABLE 5
Factors for Third-Year Students' Choice of Firms

Factors	Total Points	Times Chosen	Average Points
Location	314	98	3.20
Pay	218	79	2.76
Nature of organisation	191	44	4.34
Reputation	186	51	3.65
Training	111	26	4.27
Size	102	26	3.92
Environment	99	32	3.09
Nature of work	98	24	4.08
Relevance	82	20	4.10
Career	70	16	4.38
Programme	38	10	3.80
Organisation's requirement	27	8	3.38
Working hours	19	9	2.11
Number of vacancies	18	7	2.57
Clientele	18	5	3.60
Big-6	13	3	4.33
Friends	12	5	2.40
Others	17	6	2.83

stipulated that staff should not be involved, due to heavy administrative and academic commitments.

Grading by Organisation Supervisors

Most second- and third-year students admitted the necessity for some form of assessment, in order to motivate students, ensure a minimum level of supervision by the organisation, and provide feedback to the University. However, many expressed reservations as to whether the assessment should form part of the grading process. Their main concern was that the assessment could be subjective and inconsistent among organisations and supervisors.

The comments of third-year students were more detailed, reflecting their personal experience of the BAP. Factors mentioned as adversely (and unfairly) affecting the assessment included personality clashes between the student and the organisation supervisor; insufficient interaction between students and supervisors; working for more than one supervisor over the attachment period, with none being able to give an overall assessment; and the assignment of repetitive and mechanical tasks which would not be a good basis for evaluation. On these grounds, students suggested that assessments should be done by the organisation supervisors, but should not weigh heavily in the grading process.

Students also felt that the assessment criteria and the assessment should be made known to them, and that they be allowed to defend themselves, especially in cases when the original organisation programme has not been followed.

Staff comments reflected all of the above views. In particular, staff felt that the assessment criteria given to organisation supervisors were too general, and that giving feedback to the students was probably more important than simply grading them.

Grading by the NTU Tutor

Staff and students all felt that it would be difficult for the tutor to evaluate the student's performance because of the very limited interaction between them over the course of the BAP. Most of the tutors only visited the students once (and a minority did not visit at all). Moreover, some tutors have insufficient accounting knowledge. There is thus almost no basis for tutors to evaluate their students' work performance and work attitude.

Students were in general uncertain about the criteria on which they are evaluated by tutors. Most concluded that they are evaluated on the basis of their organisation supervisor's assessment, logbook and final report, which they felt were unsuitable for evaluation purposes. For example, students could exaggerate their working experiences to try and improve their grades. Students with language problems or personality clashes with their supervisors would also be penalised.

In general, students would prefer tutors to play the role of mentor, and liase between them, NTU and the organisations by acting as a balance against biased supervisors and ensuring that both organisations and students fulfill their obligations. If it is necessary for the tutors to evaluate them, then the weight placed on such evaluations should be lower, or the number of tutor's visits increased. As in the case of the organisation supervisor's evaluation, the criteria used and the results should also be made known to them.

Logbook and Final Report

Third-year students had mixed views about these documents. Only a minority felt that each has separate purposes and were useful. Many considered them irrelevant, redundant and time consuming, with only one, preferable the final report, being necessary. Logbooks could, however, still be kept at the discretion of students, as they form a good basis for the preparation of the final report.

Students also commented on the need for more explicit guidance on the required content of logbooks and final reports. A number pointed out that the requirement that logbooks and final reports be reviewed by the organisation supervisor restricted their freedom of expression, and introduced bias. The evaluation criteria — presentation, content or grammar — is unclear to them, and some students resorted to exaggeration and plagiarisation (from textbooks) to make their reports more interesting. Finally, the deadline for submission of the final report (a few days after the end of the BAP) was viewed as being too tight.

Second-year students made similar, though less detailed, comments. A noteworthy point was a comparison made between the logbooks and final reports required for the BAP, and those required for the six-month Industrial Attachment programme for NTU engineering students. Given the difference in duration and nature of work, the students questioned the feasibility and the need to have the same requirement in the BAP. Finally, some students suggested that SAB make available to them the exceptional final reports submitted in previous years, to indicate the content and quality required.

Many staff members commented that logbooks should not be evaluated at all. More guidelines are also required on the content of final reports, as students do not seem to know what should be included and tend to focus on feelings and perceptions rather than on what they have learnt. Thus, the final report often deteriorates into a channel for expressing their complaints.

Additional Comments

Survey respondents were also asked to comment on any aspect of the BAP. Their responses touched on a number of common areas and themes.

Information and Feedback

A number of students felt that they were not given enough information on pay, number of vacancies available for each organisation, working hours and the nature of the work involved. In addition, students' complaints during the BAP were not well handled, return envelopes for the student feedback forms were not provided, and the results of the feedback exercise were not made available to them.

Staff agreed that students should be given more information, both about the organisations and the nature of work, as well as the evaluation process. They also felt that the BAP was too bureaucratic, involving too much form filling in evaluating organisations and students.

Timing

Third-year students commented that the BAP increased examination stress in several ways: the examination period was reduced from three to two weeks; the attachment began immediately after the last examination and it ended only a few weeks before the beginning of the supplementary examinations, reducing the preparation period for the students affected (generally the weaker students). All these factors were thought to put the students at a disadvantage.

The second-year students were mainly concerned that lessons would end two weeks earlier than in previous years, with the examinations commencing two weeks earlier. They felt quite strongly that timetabling and teaching hours should not be changed simply to accommodate the BAP.

The students suggested that the BAP period be made more flexible, or that supplementary examination leave be granted to affected students. More radically, a number proposed that the entire B.Acc programme be lengthened to incorporate a longer, more formal and structured BAP, if the attachment is regarded as a vital part of accountancy education.

Participating Organisation Programmes and Working Conditions

The most common comments about the programmes offered by the participating organisations were that they were vague and not properly thought out, and very often not adhered to. Perhaps because the minimum allowance stipulated by the ILU was even lower than the market rate for regular clerical staff, students were treated as cheap labour and made to do routine, repetitive clerical work involving little or no training. Organisations' programmes thus need to be evaluated and monitored more strictly by the NTU tutors or the ILU. Additionally, organisations should be informed that students should not work overtime without compensation. In cases of proven exploitation, organisations should be blacklisted and the students transferred to another organisation.

Some students felt that they could have obtained better working experience and pay elsewhere and should have been allowed to look for alternative employment on their own. This is especially important for the poorer students, who often use the long vacation to earn enough to support themselves through the academic next year.

Tutors

In general, students felt that the role of the NTU tutors was not well defined. They commented on the varying levels of individual tutors' interest and involvement in the BAP, and suggested that only staff with genuine concern should be involved. They also wanted tutors to have some working knowledge of accounting and the BAP.

Staff suggested that administrative rather than academic staff be used to organise and implement the BAP.

CONCLUSION

The responses to the questionnaire appear to indicate that there is some gap between the expectations of the second-year students and the experiences of their seniors, in relation to what they can achieve through the BAP and what to expect from their NTU tutors.

There were, however, some areas which concerned both past and future participants of the BAP. One of these was the need for more and better information about the participating organisations. Students were also clearly concerned with how participating organisations are vetted, and how they can be made to adhere to the programmes offered.

While students seem fairly unhappy about being evaluated by either their organisation supervisor or NTU tutor, they concede that such evaluation is necessary. More information is required about the evaluation process, and more explicit instructions are necessary regarding the contents of the logbooks and final reports.

Finally, students appeared rather uncertain about the role of the NTU tutor in the BAP. This may have been exacerbated by the different perceptions of the staff involved, and the varying levels of individual interest and involvement.

These results will be of interest to the ILU as it seeks to streamline and improve the BAP in future years. They will also be of interest to other institutions which are considering implementing accounting internships on such a large scale. There are some suggestions which can be acted on quite easily — for example, the provision of more information and feedback. Other concerns, such as the perceived exploitation of students, may only be capable of being addressed in the future, when the BAP becomes more established and more organisations are willing to participate. Still others, such as the interest and commitment of NTU staff, may ultimately lie beyond the ability of the ILU to control or affect.

The Use of a Computer Competency Exam Requirement in Undergraduate Accounting Programs: The Experience of University of Hawaii

David C. Yang

INTRODUCTION

The rate of development in information technology is accelerating. Our society is becoming more information based as computers become cheaper, smaller and faster and as software and communications technology improve. Accounting is one of the disciplines that is most affected by the new and emerging environment of information technology. Accounting educational institutions must immediately develop educational strategies for their curricula that will incorporate the exposure, the literacy, and the functional expertise of computers. Several studies (see Bedford et al. 1986; Graham 1990; Ingram 1988; and Mock et al. 1987) which focus on coping with this issue have been published in recent years. The American Assembly of Collegiate Schools of Business accreditation standards also emphasize the integration of the computer into accounting courses.

In response to the impact of information technology in accounting and the disparities in students' computer background when entering the college, the faculty at the College of Business Administration (CBA), University of Hawaii at Manoa (UHM) has instituted the requirement of successfully completing the Computer Competency Exam (CCE) as a prerequisite for entering its undergraduate business program (School of Accountancy is part of the CBA). UHM students enter the undergraduate business curriculum at the beginning of their junior year, typically having completed about 55 credits of college-level work. This requirement for admission to the undergraduate business program became effective in the Spring of 1984.

THE DEVELOPMENT OF THE COMPUTER COMPETENCY EXAM

Prior to 1983, the students took a course in computer fundamentals during their junior or senior year, which introduced business data processing and problem solving using the BASIC programming language. With this limited computer background, which at times was not acquired by the students until their last semester, it was very difficult for other business courses to integrate computer related topics into the curriculum.

In 1983, the faculty of the CBA made a major change in their undergraduate curriculum. Starting in the Spring of 1984, all business students were required to take during their first semester at the CBA, an intensive course: Computer-Based Information Systems (DS350). This course introduces them to word processing (*WordPerfect*), spreadsheets (*Lotus 1-2-3*), data management (*Rbase*) and modeling tools (*IFPS*) and provides insights into the current use of data processing in business. Both the microcomputer and the mainframe computer are utilized.

In order to ensure that students entering the CBA were properly prepared to assimilate this information, a demonstration of their computer competence was required. A literature search, including contacting the Princeton Testing Service, disclosed that there were no instruments available that could meet the CBA's needs. A CCE was then developed which tested the candidates in their knowledge of computer concepts and required that they demonstrate their ability to read and write programs in the BASIC programming language. This exam was first offered in the Fall of 1983.

In the Fall of 1986 and the Spring of 1987, a review was made to determine the efficacy of using the BASIC language. Considering that "computer proficiency" has moved away from requir-

David C. Yang is Director and Associate Professor of the School of Accountancy at the University of Hawaii.

The author appreciates assistance from Professor Hiram Tompkins.

ing computer language programming skills, the faculty agreed that starting September 1987, the CCE should be reoriented to the microcomputer with a spreadsheet being used to demonstrate computer problem-solving skills. This exam has been reoriented toward the following goals:

Goal 1: The student should have a good understanding of the microcomputer environment. This includes the major components, their functions, and how they relate to each other.

Goal 2: The student should demonstrate an excellent knowledge of the Microsoft Disk Operating System (DOS version 2.1 or later). This includes its conceptual basis as well as how specified functions can enhance the performance of the user.

Goal 3: The student should be able to perform problem-solving abilities with a spreadsheet in an efficient and effective manner. Students may demonstrate their knowledge with either *Lotus 1-2-3*, *Twin*, or *VP-Planner Plus* spreadsheet software.

THE COMPUTER COMPETENCY EXAM

The CCE exam is made up of two parts. Part I (Written) held in the classroom takes two hours. Part II (Program) held at the microlab takes 40 minutes. Part I and Part II count for 60 percent and 40 percent of the final score, respectively.

Examination Content

Part I consists of multiple choice, matching, and true and false questions covering microcomputers, DOS and spreadsheets. Part II is a hands-on exercise on the use of DOS/spreadsheets. Students need to demonstrate their knowledge with either *Lotus 1-2-3*, *Twin*, or *VP-Planner Plus* spreadsheet software. In order to ensure that all the candidates understand explicitly what is expected of them in taking the CCE, a list of references is provided (see Appendix A) and is used to specify minimum requirements for candidates.

Administration

The CCE exam is offered five times (i.e., March, April, June, October and November) each year. This exam is administered by the Center of Computer Resources of the CBA. Exam questions are reviewed and updated for every exam. Passing requires that students demonstrate competence on the computer.

A passing grade of 70 points (out of 100 points) is set for entrance into the CBA. Students are allowed to take the exam any time and can retake the exam if they fail. More than 1,300 students pay $15 each to the state to take this nonprofit basis exam every year at the CBA.

Preparation for the Computer Competency Exam

There are several ways that students can prepare for this exam. One is self-study, but this requires a great deal of discipline. Another is to take an introductory computer course at the high school or college level. A third way is to take the Computer Competency Course offered by the College of Continuing Education and Community Services. This nonrequired, noncredit course is specifically geared to the exam. A Study Guide (see Appendix A) providing CCE information is available for students to prepare for the exam.

THE EFFECTIVENESS OF THE COMPUTER COMPETENCY EXAM

In spite of the reorientation of the CCE toward the use of spreadsheet/DOS, the faculty still identified a great disparity in students' spreadsheet/DOS skills when entering the CBA. To examine the effectiveness issue of the CCE, an experiment was conducted in Fall 1988. Two hundred eighty-eight students who passed the CCE exam after September 1987 and registered for the Fall 1988 DS350 classes were notified that a quiz would be given on spreadsheets and DOS. A four-hour review workshop designed as preparation for this quiz was held one week before the test. One hundred seventeen students took this review workshop and 171 students did not.

A multiple regression analysis was performed to examine which variables contributed to the different scores of the test results of these 288 students. The regression model follows

$$Y = a\,X_1 + b\,X_2 + c\,X_3$$

Y: score of quiz,

a,b,c: coefficients of the corresponding independent variable,

X_1:   take review course or not (a dummy variable),

X_2:   the elapsed time between when the student took the CCE and entered DS350, and

X_3:   score on the CCE.

Figure 1 shows that the adjusted R^2 is 0.21 and the F ratio is significant at the 1 percent level. The re-

FIGURE 1
Results of Multiple Regression Analysis on 288 students

Variable	Mean	Standard Deviation
Y	73.02	12.72
X_1	0.41	0.49
X_2	3.25	1.27
X_3	83.58	6.95

Y:	score of quiz,
a,b,c:	coefficients of the corresponding independent variable,
X_1:	take review course or not (a dummy variable),
X_2:	the elapsed time between when the student took the CCE and entered DS350, and
X_3:	score on the CCE.

Dependent Variable: Y

Independent Variable	Regression Coefficient	Std. Error	T (DF = 285)	Prob.
X_1	6.36	1.3784	4.614	0.00001
X_2	0.56	0.5345	1.051	0.29433
X_3	0.71	0.0961	7.402	0.00000
Constant	9.16			

Adjusted R^2 = 0.21
F Ratio = 26.77   PROB = 6.000E-14

sults indicate that differences among students' scores can be explained by how high the student scored on the CCE (X_3) and whether the student took the review course (X_1). Both independent variables (X_1 and X_3) are significant at the 1 percent level. The elapsed time between when the student took the CCE and entered DS350 (X_2) did not affect results significantly. However, if the students demonstrated through the CCE that they had acquired the spreadsheet/DOS skills, these skills could quickly be brought back to acceptable levels by a review workshop regardless of when the CCE was taken. Furthermore, the one-way ANOVA shows that students who took the review course did better than students who did not; that is significant at the 1 percent level. Average scores for students who took the review course was 76 points and those who did not was 70 points.

The results show that CCE scores and their attendance at the review workshop were the main contributors, in that order, in bringing skills back to acceptable levels. Given the above results, students who are to enter future DS350 classes, the first course for CBA students, have been notified that they will have a graded quiz during their initial classes. A review workshop early in the semester will be offered, supplement to the CCE, to re-

duce the disparities in students' spreadsheet/DOS background.

CONCLUDING REMARKS

It is the goal of CBA at UHM that every accounting faculty integrate computer technology into his/her courses. With the requirement of the Computer Competency Exam, computer education in accounting may become more effective and easier because students come in with a baseline competence. Accounting courses with computer-related assignments can become more user friendly to accounting students.

Furthermore, with the increasing influence of information technology in accounting and the continued popularity of accounting as a college major, establishment of appropriate admission standards for limiting enrollments and selecting good prospective accounting students will continue to be a serious concern for many accounting faculties. The experience of a CCE requirement at UHM should also provide useful information to those with such concerns, especially for those campuses which are thinking of introducing the CCE standard in their programs.

APPENDIX A
Portion of Computer Competence Exam Study Guide

Goals of Computer Competence

Goal 1: The candidate should have a good understanding of the microcomputer environment. This includes the major components, their function, and how they relate to each other.

Goal 2: The candidate should demonstrate an excellent knowledge of the Microsoft Disk Operating System (DOS version 2.1 or later). This includes its conceptual basis as well as how specified functions can enhance the performance of the user.

Goal 3: The candidate should be able to demonstrate problem-solving abilities with a spreadsheet in an efficient and effective manner. Candidates must demonstrate their knowledge with either *Lotus 1-2-3* version 2.0, *Twin*, or *VP-Planner Plus*.

In order to ensure that all students understand explicitly what is expected to be covered by the Computer Competence Exam, the following listed references will be used as minimum requirements for students.

1. Any *Microsoft Disk Operating System Manual* (version 2.1 or later).
2. Pitter, K. (1990) *Using VP-Planner Plus*, McGraw Hill, Inc.
3. Computer Competence Course, Spring 1991, *Lab Exercises, Practice Exercises, DOS Commands and Slides from Lectures*, Revised March 1991.

Disk Operating System

The candidate is responsible for understanding the function and be able to use the following:

binary files
ASCII (text) files
TYPE
CHKDSK
CLS
COMMAND.COM (Command Processor)
SORT
COMP
data files
DATE
DIR (includes /W & /P)
DISKCOMP
DISKCOPY
ERASE (DEL)
floppy disks
BATCH (.BAT) files
MORE
FORMAT (includes /S & /V)
RENAME
TIME

CONFIG.SYS
AUTOEXEC.BAT
PROMPT PG
COPY (includes CON & COMBINE)
VER
PAUSE
Cold boot (start)
Internal Commands
External Commands
Default Drive
function keys
K Bytes
Hidden files
Scrolling
MS-DOS Boot Sequence
Piping Symbol |
sectors
tracks (cylinders)
File Allocation Table (FAT)
WILDCARDS (*/?)

Spreadsheets (Pitter)

Students must be familiar with the following:

absolute address
applications
point mode
macros
template
cells
function keys
@DATE
external storage medium

bits
expansion slot
CALC
cell cursor
CIRC
column
format
peripherals
command line

directory
data table
database
default
edit mode
extension
field names
file
filename

@VLOOK
@PMT
ASCII
memory board criterion
@VERSION
recalculation
graphing
bin
help key
hercules emulation
@IF
import
input
insert mode
keyboard macro
kilobyte (K byte)
label
legend
line graph
logical function
microprocessing unit
margin
monochrome
mixed reference
window
mode indicator
NUM LOCK
Objectives of DOS
output

command mode
condensed print
copy right
@SUM
criterion table
currency format
data commands
File Combine
percent format
pie chart
protected cell
range justify
range name
ready mode
row
relative address
RAM
ROM
SCROLL LOCK
setupstring
sorting
stacked bar
status line
monitor
synchronized
table
template
tilde ~

financial functions
fixed format
floppy disks
formatting
function keys
general format
goto key
graph key
offset
WKS, PIC, PRN, BAK
extensions
Mother (system) board
firmware
main memory
volatile
terminal
backup
daisy wheel
dot-matrix
hard disk
keyboard
laser printer
menu
statistical functions
pixel
numerical keypad
resolution
directory

REFERENCES

Bedford, N., E. E. Bartholomew, C. A. Bowsher, A. L. Brown, D. Davidson, C. T. Horngren, H. Knortz, M. M. Piser, W. G. Shenkir, J. K. Simmons, E. L. Summers and J. T. Wheeler. 1986. Future Accounting Education: Preparing for the Expanding Profession. *Issues in Accounting Education* (Spring): 168–190.

Graham, C. 1990. Computing in Accounting Educaiton. *Management Accounting* (September): 54–59.

Ingram, R. W. 1988. *Computer Integration into the Accounting Curriculum: Case Studies.* American Accounting Association.

Mock, T. J., E. C. Barry, G. B. Davis, M. A. Vasarhelyi, C. E. White and J. W. Wilinson. 1987. Report of the AAA Committee on Contemporary Approaches to Teaching Accounting Information Systems. *Journal of Information Systems* (Spring): 127–156.

Using International Data Sources to Assess Audit Risk

Douglas E. Ziegenfuss

BACKGROUND

The accounting department at Old Dominion University is currently resurrecting a dormant graduate accounting degree program to implement the AICPA's 150-hour requirement. As a result, a graduate-level auditing course, Advanced Auditing, will be developed. The undergraduate auditing course will also be offered and will be a prerequisite to the graduate course.

The Advanced Auditing course will be case study intensive and geared toward applying the principles and standards learned in the undergraduate auditing course. It will also address new areas such as internal auditing, governmental auditing, auditing an international company, etc. The case study presented here was developed for this course. It gives the U.S. auditing student an understanding of the problems faced by a practitioner in servicing a non–U.S. company wishing to issue financial statements in the United States.

DEVELOPING THE CASE STUDY

The traditional case study approach in which all students solve an identical case has several drawbacks. First, it is nearly impossible to keep students from working together on the cases. Second, students usually obtain solutions to the cases after one semester. The use of a case study in subsequent semesters becomes a clerical rather than a learning exercise. Third, students have a hard time relating to "fictional" companies even if the facts of the case are based on "real" companies. Last, students have interests in some companies either because they or their relatives have worked there or own stock in the company.

Despite these shortcomings, the case study approach is still the best manner in which to expose the auditing student to such complex issues as audit risk, materiality, and analytical review procedures (ARP). For this reason, the traditional case study approach was altered to allow students to choose their own company (as long as it was not chosen by another student) for which they are required to obtain background data (from Disclosures database, annual reports, and financial literature) and perform a fluctuation analysis on a non–U.S. company seeking to issue its financial statements in the United States. The student then uses the background data to write an audit planning memo. This approach was also selected because it can easily be revised for use on students of other countries by changing the identity of the domestic country from the United States and revising the appropriate auditing standards.

Developing the case study required identifying issues to be addressed in the planning memo, and sources for that information. The first task was accomplished by reviewing *SASs 51*, "Reporting on Financial Statements Prepared for Use in Other Countries," *47*, "Audit Risk and Materiality in Conducting an Audit," and *56*, "Analytical Procedures." The second task was accomplished by examining the various international data sources for information on non–U.S. companies.

THE PLANNING MEMO

The instructions for the case study are shown in Table 1. They are given to the students after the lecture on auditing the international company and a case study requiring them to assess audit risk for a U.S. company. This case builds on the earlier one by exposing the student to audit risk factors associated with international companies.

The factors listed under client company general background information and audit risk are more fully described in auditing textbooks by D. Guy et al. (1991), O'Reilly et al. (1990), Wallace (1991), and Robertson and Zlatkovich (1990). They correspond to those in *SAS 47*, "Audit Risk and Materiality in Conducting an Audit." The factors under client country background were identified by examining requirements of *SAS 51*, "Reporting on Financial Statements Prepared for Use in Other Countries."

Each student is required to review appropriate financial literature and report the results of the review in the form of an annotated bibliography in the literature review section of the planning memo.

Douglas E. Ziegenfuss is Assistant Professor at Old Dominion University.

TABLE 1
Case Study Directions

Auditing
Fall 1992
International Auditing Planning Project

<u>Purpose</u>: This project is designed to give the U.S. auditing student an understanding of the problems faced by a practitioner in servicing a non–U.S. company wishing to issue financial statements in the United States.

<u>Directions</u>: The student will select a company from those listed in the DISCLOSURE DATABASE. After obtaining approval of the selection from the course instructor, the student will use the DISCLOSURE DATABASE, INFOTRAC, the annual report and other materials (see "Sources" below) to gain an understanding of the auditing issues affecting the company. A planning memo will then be prepared and submitted using the following format/outline.

Cover Memo:

    From you to in-charge accountant telling the in-charge that you have completed a review of the company's financial statements and other appropriate material and that your findings are included in the attached report.

Title Page:

XYZ Company
Results of Financial Statement Review

By
Your Name
Submitted: Date Submitted

Table of Contents:

    I.   Client Company Background Information
          Business
          Industry
          Control Environment
          Accounting System
          Control Procedures
          Management Integrity

    II.   Client Country Background Information
          Business Environment
          Regulatory Environment
          Business Entities
          Audit Requirements and Practices
          Accounting Principles and Practices
          Taxation

    III. Audit Risk
          Operating Environment
          Management Attitudes or Credibility
          Special Accounting Problems
          Management Fraud
          Related Party Actions
          Illegal Acts
          Business Failure

    IV. Literature Review

    V.   Financial Statement Analysis
          Fluctuation Analysis
          Common Size Financial
          Ratio Analysis

TABLE 1 (Continued)

VI. Overall Assessment of Audit Risk

VII. Opinion to be Issued

Sources
- Sample Report Attached
- Library Resources:
>   Disclosure — World Scope
>   Annual Report
>   Price Waterhouse — Doing Business in Series
>   *International Accounting and Auditing Trends*
>   *International Accounting* by Choi and Mueller
>   Major Financial Periodical of Client's Home Country
>   *Business Periodicals Index*
>   *Wall Street Journal Index*
>   Predicasts F & S Indexes
>   *New York Times Index*
>   *Infotrac General Periodicals Index*

This will allow the student to assess the overall business reputation of the company being studied.

The financial statement analysis section will report on the results of analytical review procedures normally associated with audit planning — fluctuation analysis, common size financial, and ratio analysis. The purpose of this section is to give the auditing student practice in applying ARP to an international company. Determining an appropriate currency translation rate and appropriate industry ratios are issues unique to international companies.

Once the students have summarized the information gathered for the above factors, they are required to describe their conclusions concerning the audit risk of the subject company. This is documented in the Overall Assessment of Audit Risk section of the report. This is the key section of the report as far as demonstrating the ability of the student to analyze the information gathered and described above, and to clearly communicate the results of that analysis.

Once the assessment of audit risk has been done, the student describes how the audit is to be accomplished (by the firm itself, or by a subcontracted non–U.S. firm), what additional audit procedures are required by foreign GAAS, and the form of the opinion to be issued (see *SAS 51*, "Reporting on Financial Statements Prepared for Use in Other Countries," paragraphs 14 and 15).

Completed memos will be evaluated for clarity and completeness of expression, and evidence of successfully synthesizing information gathered from diverse international sources.

INTERNATIONAL FINANCIAL DATA SOURCES

The chief obstacle in implementing the case study method described above was locating appropriate information sources on actual companies. Several computer databases (NAARS, Global Vantage, and Disclosure Worldscope) were examined because they allow students to easily and quickly review financial data for numerous companies in selecting one for the case.

NAARS (National Automated Accounting Research Center) is part of the Lexis\Nexis online database. Users are charged based on the number of searches performed and online time. It was not selected for use on the case because it contains information on very few non–U.S. companies, and its costs are prohibitive and cannot be easily controlled.

Global Vantage is produced on a CD-ROM format by Standard & Poor's Compustat Services, Inc. It contains financial information for 6,758 companies from 31 countries for the past 12 years. Although costs of using Global Vantage could be controlled by the fixed fee contract, its data elements are more suited for the financial analyst than the auditor. Thus, it too was rejected.

Disclosure Worldscope too is on a CD-ROM format. It is produced by Disclosure Information Service, and contains more comprehensive financial statement information (such as footnotes and other textual fields) than Global Vantage for more companies (7,000 plus), but for only the past 10 years. The costs of using Worldscope are also controlled by a fixed fee arrangement. For these reasons it was chosen for the case.

All of the databases discussed above are good starting points for researching the audit risks of an international company, but each lacks essential information on the subject company and country which must be supplemented by additional sources.

Additional financial and operating information concerning the client company can be gathered from the annual report (Old Dominion University uses a microfiche service "Q File" by Q Data Corporation). Information about the subject company's reputation can be gathered from the financial literature. It can be accessed by reviewing the major business publication of the subject company's home country (for example, *The Economist* in Great Britain) or numerous indexes such as *The Wall Street Journal Index*, *Business Periodicals Index*, *Infotrac General Periodicals Index*, or the *New York Times Index*.

Information concerning the client company's home country can be gathered from The Price Wa-

terhouse Doing Business in series of books, *International Accounting and Auditing Trends*, and *International Accounting* by Choi and Mueller.

The relationship of these sources to specific risk factors is presented in Table 2. Students are encouraged to find additional sources.

EVALUATION

Final evaluation of the case study will not take place until the Fall 1992 semester when it will be assigned to graduate students for the first time. Meanwhile, copies of the case study are being reviewed by fellow academicians and practitioner members of the accounting department advisory committee who service international clients. Preliminary reactions are very positive and supportive with only minor revisions proposed. Similar results were obtained for a similar audit planning case study.

TABLE 2
Sources for Risk Factors

Risk Factors	Sources
Background Information:	
Business	DW, AR
Industry	DW, AR
Control Environment	DW, AR
Accounting System	AR
Control Procedures	AR
Management Integrity	AR
Client Country Background Information:	PW
Business Environment	PW
Regulatory Environment	PW
Business Entities	PW
Audit Requirements and Pracitices	PW, IAAT, IA
Accounting Principles and Practices	PW, IAAT, IA
Taxation	PW, IAAT, IA
Audit Risk:	
Operating Environment	AR, MFP
Management Attitudes or Credibility	AR, MFP
Special Accounting Problems	AR
Management Fraud	AR, MFP
Related Party Transactions	AR
Illegal Acts	AR, MFP
Business Failure	AR, MFP
Literature Review	AR, MFP, BPI, WSJI, PFS, NYTI, IGPI
Financial Statement Analysis:	
Fluctuation Analysis	DW, AR
Common Size Financial	DW, AR
Ratio Analysis	DW, AR

Legend:
    DW = Disclosure - Worldscope
    AR = Annual Report

TABLE 2 (Continued)

PW = Price Waterhouse - Doing Business in Series
IAAT = *International Accounting and Auditing Trends*
IA = *International Accounting* by Choi and Mueller
MFP = Major Financial Periodical of Client's Home Country
BPI = *Business Periodicals Index*
WSJI = *Wall Street Journal Index*
PFS = Precasts F & S Indexes
NYTI = *New York Times Index*
IGPI = *Infotrac General Periodicals Index*

REFERENCES

American Institute of Certified Public Accountants. 1990. *AICPA Professional Standards —Volume I.* Commerce Clearing House, Inc. Section 312: 231-7–232.

———. 1990. *AICPA Professional Standards —Volume I.* Commerce Clearing House, Inc. Section 534: 801–806.

———. 1990. *AICPA Professional Standards —Volume I.* Commerce Clearing House, Inc. Section 329: 323–327.

Bavishi, V. B. 1989. *International Accounting and Auditing Trends.* Center for International Financial Analysis & Research, Inc.

Choi, F. D. S., and G. G. Mueller. 1984. *International Accounting.* Prentice-Hall Inc.

Guy, D. M., C. W. Alderman, and A. J. Winters. 1990. *Auditing.* Harcourt Brace Jovanovich, Publishers: 157–158.

———, ———, and ———. 1991. Harcourt Brace Jovanovich, Publishers.

O'Reilly, V. M., M. B. Hirsch, P. L. Defliese, and H. R. Jaenicke. 1990. *Montgomery's Auditing.* John Wiley & Sons.

Robertson, J. C., and C. T. Zlatkovich. 1990. *Auditing.* Homewood, IL: BPI/Irwin.

United Nations Centre on Transnational Corporation. 1985. *International Accounting and Reporting Issues: 1984 Review.* United Nations.

Wallace, W. A. 1991. *Auditing.* PWS-Kent Publishing Company.

Performance Evaluation in Accounting Education

The conference program included six papers that focus on methods for evaluating students and student performance. The papers examine the cognitive complexity and competency of students attracted to the accounting major, whether performance in the introductory courses is a function of overall academic performance, criteria for evaluating writing assignments, comparability of performance on exams with different formats, and the use of a capstone course as a measurement and diagnostic tool. Suggestions include improvements in teaching methods, performance evaluation, and future research relevant to performance evaluation.

UNT Accounting Change Program Evaluation: Empirical Examination of Baseline Competencies

Frieda A. Bayer, William A. Luker, Robert H. Michaelsen, and Neil Wilner

Accounting education in the United States is currently faced with a dilemma. Several large public accounting firms have stated that most students that matriculate from a four- or five-year accounting curriculum do not possess all the skills necessary to begin a successful accounting career (Arthur Andersen et al. 1989). Deficiencies include communication, interpersonal, critical thinking, and lifelong learning skills. Academic accounting programs may not even be attracting the students who show the most promise of these skills (Inman, Wenzler, and Wickert). Finally, debate continues on the value of a 150-hour program versus a more traditional four-year program in enhancing these skills (Alford, Strawser, and Strawser 1990). These questions revolve around the type of curriculum offered at our nation's postsecondary institutions. Insights which may lead to a resolution of the continuing debate require the collection of data related to the nature of the students attracted by accounting programs and the degree to which alternative accounting curricula enhance the skills demanded by the accounting profession in the entry-level accounting professional. Currently, accounting programs do not systematically collect and evaluate the data necessary to assess the success of their curriculum in these areas.

The University of North Texas (UNT) has received an Accounting Education Change Commission (AECC) grant to implement an experimental professional accounting program designed to develop several of the nonknowledge-based competencies defined by the accounting profession (University of North Texas 1990). An important component of the UNT program is an explicit commitment to measure the success of the program in graduating students with enhanced professional skills.

After a literature search and extensive discussion with AECC measurement experts,[1] a UNT measurement committee, established in conjunction with the curriculum change program, concluded that the constructs defined in the College Outcome Measures Program (COMP) provide the best match with a number of "global competencies" defined in the program evaluation experimental design (Luker et al. 1991). The COMP instrument was developed by the American College Testing Program (ACT) (American College Testing Program 1976). It assists colleges in assessing their effectiveness at promoting skills deemed necessary for graduation and functioning in society after graduation. The test is designed to measure growth in achieving these skills from the freshman to senior years. Six outcome constructs are identified in the COMP. These constructs are (1) solving problems, (2) clarifying values, (3) communicating, (4) functioning within social institutions, (5) using science and technology, and (6) using the arts. The COMP constructs are not identical to the experimental program competencies nor do they measure all the competencies envisioned in the UNT program. However, of the six, four approximate UNT's five global competencies of critical thinking (solving problems), complex thinking (solving problems), professional ethics (clarifying values), written communication (communicating), and social responsibility (functioning within social institutions).

The COMP was administered to 263 UNT students during fall 1990 and 1991 to gather baseline data for the assessment study. Students tested included those entering the UNT experimental program and in various stages of UNT's traditional program (freshmen, juniors, seniors and graduate students). Demographic information was also collected. ACT provided COMP scores for two national norm-reference groups. A cross-sectional analysis of this baseline data was performed as a part of UNT's experimental program evaluation and to gain insight into the questions facing accounting education.

This research contributes to the accounting education debate in two ways. First, most accounting assessment studies have focused on technical knowledge evidenced by scores on class tests, and

---

[1]For an example of the direction offered by the AECC, see Stark (1990).

Frieda A. Bayer is Assistant Professor of Accounting, William A. Luker is Professor of Applied Economics, Robert H. Michaelsen and Neil Wilner are Associate Professors of Accounting at the University of North Texas.

so on. The results of this study provide empirical support for the contention that senior accounting students do not compare favorably with a national sample of seniors from nonaccounting programs in the skills considered valuable by the accounting profession when controlling for other relevant student characteristics, for example, ACT (SAT) scores. In addition, offering an experimental program designed to increase these skills does not appear to attract different students than the traditional accounting program. Finally, fifth-year graduate accounting students do exhibit higher levels of communication and problem-solving skills than senior accounting majors. These findings sug-

gest that the concerns of the profession, that is, how to attract students with relevant aptitudes to nontraditional accounting programs and how to change the curriculum to develop important skills among its graduates, are valid. Second, although these research results are initially helpful at a local level, that is, to educators at UNT implementing its curriculum change program, the results of this study are relevant to all accounting education programs. Other universities anticipating curriculum change or concerned about the outcomes of their current program may wish to adapt all or a part of the UNT assessment approach for their own use.

REFERENCES

Alford, R. M., J. R. Strawser, and R. H. Strawser. 1990. Does Graduate Education Improve Success in Public Accounting? *Accounting Horizons* (March): 69–76.

American College Testing Program. 1976. *College Outcome Measures Program.* American College Testing Program.

Arthur Andersen & Co., Arthur Young, Coopers & Lybrand, Deloitte Haskins & Sells, Ernst & Whinney, Peat Marwick Main & Co., Price Waterhouse, and Touche Ross (The Big Eight). 1989. *Perspectives on Education: Capabilities for Success in the Accounting Profession.*

Inman, B. C., A. Wenzler, and P. D. Wickert. 1989. Square Pegs in Round Holes: Are Accounting Students Well-Suited to Today's Accounting Profession? *Issues in Accounting Education* (Spring): 29–47.

Luker, W. A., F. A. Bayer, B. A. Coda, Jr., A. G. Mayper, and R. H. Michaelsen. 1991. Curriculum Change in a Professional Accounting Program: An Evaluation Model. Working Paper (October).

Stark, J. 1990. Potential Plan for Evaluating Achievement of Outcomes. AECC Task Force on Measurement. AECC, March 1 draft.

University of North Texas Department of Accounting. 1990. *A Proposed Five-Year Accounting Program Incorporating Liberal Arts into a Professional Learning Core and a Professional Business Foundation.* University of North Texas.

Integrating Communication Skills into the Accounting Curriculum: Evaluating Writing Assignments

Edward A. Becker and Thomas G. MacLennan

INTRODUCTION

For many years accounting practitioners have been emphasizing to accounting educators the severe lack of communication skills among accounting graduates. In addressing the perceived problem, accounting pedagogues have responded in several ways: (1) they maintained that the weakness is not the fault or the problem of the Accounting Department, (2) they recommended including more liberal arts courses (e.g., English) as part of the required curricula, (3) they tried including an occasional writing assignment in an occasional accounting course, or if all else failed, (4) they buried their heads in the sand and hoped the problem would disappear.

All four responses are inadequate. First, response 1 is not true. It is our problem. Second, response 4 resolves nothing. The problem persists. Third, response 2 is difficult to implement in the typical four-year accounting program because of the ever-expanding accounting body of knowledge. Furthermore, placing the blame and the burden on the English department sends the wrong message. It suggests that communication skills and accounting skills are mutually exclusive.

Finally, response 3 only minimally addresses one communication skill: writing. There are four traditional communication skills: reading, writing, speaking, and listening. Today's and tomorrow's accountants and accounting leaders need to be proficient in all four. In addition, in today's highly technical and complex business environment, a fifth communication skill should be added to the list: computers.

This paper recommends that accounting professors make a commitment to integrate the teaching of each of the communication skills into the total accounting curriculum. It suggests that writing assignments be the starting point. This monograph proposes writing assignments with varying degrees of difficulty corresponding to the students' year (e.g., junior, senior). Finally, this paper presents some easily applied grading criteria with varying grading schemes.

BACKGROUND

All sectors of the accounting community are stressing that current and future accountants need to be comfortable with all of the communication skills.

The accounting educators are saying so. The Bedford Committee (American Accounting Association 1986) made 28 recommendations that accounting educators should implement if accounting education is to keep pace with the predicted expansion in the accounting profession. Several of those recommendations mentioned communication skills. Integrating communication skills within the accounting curriculum has been a major topic of discussion in many articles and conferences (e.g., Becker 1988).

The industrial accounting practitioners are saying so. Their report (NAA 1987) lists communication skills as the most important skill for managerial accountants.

The AICPA is saying so. In its 1988 policy statement, it devoted one section to communication skills (AICPA 1988).

The public accounting practitioners are saying so. A report signed by each of the chief executives of the Big 8 (*Perspectives on Education* 1989) specifies communication skills as the most important capability necessary to practice accounting.

The Accounting Education Change Commission is saying so. In its *Position Statement No. 1* (AECC 1990) it suggests that communication skills are the number one set of skills that accounting students should be learning. Interestingly, it listed all four traditional communication skills.

Edward A. Becker is a faculty member at Nova University, and Thomas G. MacLennan is a member of the faculty at University of North Carolina at Wilmington.

The desirability of incorporating communication skills into the teaching of accounting courses is undeniable. The next question is, where to begin?

GETTING STARTED

Writing assignments are the most frequently suggested starting point for teaching communication skills. Recent examples those by include Griffin (1989) and Wygal and Stout (1989). However, even this initial step is resisted by many accounting pedagogues. Their expressed argument is that the ever-expanding body of accounting knowledge does not leave them with enough class time to teach the accounting that must be taught. There is no time available for nonaccounting subjects. This objection is easily overcome by making the writing assignment an outside assignment and by budgeting a small amount of class time to discuss the assignment and the grading criteria.

Accounting educators may have a hidden agenda for not including writing assignments as part of the normal course work. For example, (1) the accounting instructors may be unwilling to spend the extra time required to assign and grade writing assignments or (2) the accounting instructors are uncomfortable with grading writing assignments, because they either do not have criteria with which to grade them, or they are unsure of their own English skills.

For those in group one, this article offers no solace. For those in group two, this article offers some easily applied criteria for grading writing assignments. Furthermore, one does not have to be an English expert to utilize the criteria.

WRITING ASSIGNMENTS

There are, at least, three good reasons for incorporating writing assignments into the accounting curriculum. First, if writing assignments are solely the province of the English Department, then students may get the impression that once they have finished their English requirements they are through learning and using writing skills. Second, by including writing assignments in accounting courses, students get additional practice in using their writing skills. They learn that good writing skills and success in accounting are inseparable. Most important, writing assignments force students to analyze, synthesize, and think about accounting topics while they organize, structure, word, and reword their thoughts until a logical and sequential flow of ideas is produced. The exercise becomes

one of the most worthwhile learning experiences. In essence, writing skills become thinking skills.

Writing assignments should not only be included in every accounting course, but they should be progressively more difficult. For example, the principles of accounting course assignment might be between 250 and 500 words on "Accounting and My Future" or "The Definition of an Asset." An intermediate accounting assignment could be 1,000 to 1,500 words on "The History of Accounting for _____" or a discussion of some current "hot topic," Senior-level course assignments can be full-blown research papers in some area of accounting theory. Assignments for the tax courses might be some interesting tax research. The auditing course assignments could be an in-depth discussion of some ethical situation(s).

Not all writing need be as formal as essays. Accounting instructors may choose informal writing exercises. For example, students could use Zinsser's (1988) technique, by keeping an informal writing journal of daily class learning experiences. At the next class meeting, they could present the contents of their journal for classmates who missed the previous class, or submit a short paper with each previously discussed accounting principle condensed into one complex sentence. If students have difficulty with this, it might be a message to the instructor that they did not understand the material. Additionally, journals could be turned in from time to time for a dichotomous grading, noting whether they were acceptable (+) or needed improvement (–). Maintaining a journal often raises questions in the students' mind that they might not otherwise have asked.

Other techniques that might be considered are (1) allowing rewrites and substituting the higher grade and (2) grading or critiquing each others' papers.

THE GRADING CRITERIA

The grading criteria developed in this paper were derived from Diederich (1974, 53–59). He noted that inexperienced graders seldom realize how routinely English teachers disagree in their judgments of writing ability unless there is some predetermined criteria.

Spandel and Stiggins (1990) argue that instructors should have explicit, written criteria for evaluation. They also add that evaluators who work from criteria that exist solely in their heads are liable to make the most impulsive judgments, even as they attempt to persuade everyone that their grading system is logical and defensible. With a little practice and the available criteria, accounting educators can overcome the problem of what to do with students' writing assignments.

Exhibits A and B show the recommended grading criteria. The criteria are easily applied because there is a range within each area: high, middle and low. If a paper is high in a given area, it gets high credit. If it is middle in that area, it gets middle credit. If it is low for that area, it gets no credit. If it falls in between a given area, it gets in-between credit. The criteria are flexible because they allow each instructor to change the grading scheme according to his/her personal preference or to accommodate the difficulty of the assignment or the sophistication of the students (freshmen vs. seniors).

Following Diederich's (1974) scheme, the grading criteria are divided into two classifications: "content" and "mechanics." The flexibility is provided for along a continuum from high content to high mechanics. Exhibit C provides three illustrations of scoring within that continuum.

The grading criteria shown in Exhibits A and B have been used by an accounting professor (who had only moderate English skills), an English instructor (who did not have any accounting knowledge), and a noneducator. All three reported complete satisfaction with the criteria. They stated that the criteria were easy to apply. In addition, when using the criteria, they were able to differentiate among the good, average, and poor papers.

Students should be given a copy of Exhibits A and B when they receive the writing assignment. They should also be told what scoring scheme will be used (e.g., content high = ____, mechanics middle = ____) (see Exhibit C). Graded papers should be returned to the students with a set of grading criteria with their actual scores for each area.

SUMMARY

Good communication skills are critical to your students if they are to achieve the degree of success in accounting that is our *raison de etre*. For many accounting professors, the first step towards incorporating communication skills in their accounting courses is to assign formal or informal writing assignments. However, they are reluctant to give writing assignments because they are unsure how to grade them.

This article provides some flexible, easily applied, nontechnical criteria for grading writing assignments. Is the subjectivity in grading removed? No, that is probably not possible. Is adding writing assignments going to mean more work for the accounting instructor? Yes. So what else is new?

EXHIBIT A
Evaluation Criteria for Grading Accounting Writing Assignments
Content

1. Ideas

High   Each idea is supported with examples or details. Points are clearly related to the topic and the main idea of the piece. No necessary points are overlooked and there is no padding.

Middle   There is evidence of thought. However, some points are not clearly illustrated with examples or details. There is an uneven quality to the points presented. Some cogent points are made, but others are omitted.

Low   Ideas are not explained or expanded. Assertions are made without support, or they are erroneous assertions.

2. Organization

High   The paper has an underlying plan that the reader can follow. Main points are treated at greatest length or with greatest emphasis, while minor points are treated in proportion to their importance.

Middle   Organization is standard and conventional. Some trivial points are treated in greater detail than important points, and there may be some superfluous material.

Low   Main points are not clearly separated from one another, and they are unfolded in a disorganized manner. The paper starts in one direction and then moves in other directions, until the reader becomes lost.

3. Wording

High   The writer uses words correctly and with sophistication. The paper includes language that indicates mastery over the technical nuances of accounting. The wording demonstrates a thorough knowledge of the discipline.

Middle   Although the writer uses correct wording, there is a tendency to depend upon common uses of technical language. The writer may be occasionally misusing the language of accounting.

Low   The wording is inexact and there are many errors. Writing may demonstrate a lack of awareness of technical terminology.

4. Manuscript Appearance

High   The manuscript is clear, attractive, well-spaced, and the rules of manuscript form have been observed.

Middle   The manuscript is fairly legible. There are some violations of the prescribed format.

Low   The manuscript is difficult to read. The prescribed format is not utilized. The writer may even give the impression that the manuscript was hastily prepared.

EXHIBIT B
Evaluation Criteria for Grading Accounting Writing Assignments
Mechanics

1. Usage, Sentence Structure

High   There are no errors in usage by current standards of formal written English. The sentence structure is usually correct, even in varied and complicated sentence patterns.

Middle   There are a few errors in usage and several that obscure meaning. The sentence structure is usually correct in simple sentence patterns but there are occasional errors in complicated patterns: errors in parallelism, subordination, consistency of tenses, and pronoun reference.

Low   There are so many errors in usage and sentence structure that the paper is difficult to understand.

2. Form

High   The prescribed format, including footnoting and bibliographic references, has been followed.

Middle   Although there may be a few errors in form, the prescribed format is followed.

Low   There are so many errors in form that the paper is difficult to understand.

3. Punctuation

High   There are no serious violations of rules governing punctuation, capitalization, abbreviations, or numbers.

Middle   There are several violations of rules and it causes the reader some difficulty with meaning.

Low   There are so many violations of rules that the paper is difficult to understand.

4. Spelling

High   There are no misspelled words in the paper.

Middle   There are several spelling errors in technical words and some basic inconsistency: spelling a word correctly in one sentence and incorrectly in another.

Low   There are so many spelling errors that they interfere with comprehension.

EXHIBIT C
Possible Numerical Grading Schemes

	High Content/ Low Mechanics	EqualContent and Mechanics	Low Content/ High Mechanics
CONTENT (each area)			
High	20 points	12.5 points	5 points
Middle	10 points	7 points	3 points
Low	0 points	0 points	0 points
Perfect Score For Content	80 points	50 points	20 points
MECHANICS (each area)			
High	5 points	12.5 points	20 points
Middle	3 points	7 points	10 points
Low	0 points	0 points	0 points
Perfect Score For Mechanics	20 points	50 points	80 points
Perfect Score For Paper	100 points	100 points	100 points

REFERENCES

American Accounting Association Committee on the Future Structure, Content, and Scope of Accounting Education, Norton Bedford, Chairman. 1986. Future Accounting Education: Preparing for the Future Expansion. *Issues in Accounting Education* (Spring): 169–195.

Accounting Education Change Commission. 1990. *Objectives of Education for Accountants.*

American Institute of Certified Accountants. 1988. *Education Requirements for Entry Into the Accounting Profession.*

Becker, E. A. 1988. Integrating Communication Skills with the Teaching of Auditing. *Proceedings of the American Accounting Association's 1988 Mid-Atlantic Regional Meeting*, J. E. Ketz, ed. (March): 24.

Diederich, P. B. 1974. *Measuring Growth in English.* Urbana, Illinois: National Council of Teachers of English.

Griffin, L. 1989 Communication Skills and the Accounting Curriculum: A Survey. *Collected Papers and Abstracts of the American Accounting Association's Southwest Regional Meeting* (March): 23–24.

National Association of Accountants. 1987. *Education for Careers in Management Accounting.*

Perspectives on Education: Capabilities for Success in the Accounting Profession. 1989. Arthur Andersen & Co., Arthur Young, Coopers & Lybrand, Deloitte Haskins & Sells, Ernst & Whinney, Peat Marwick Main & Co., Price Waterhouse, and Touche Ross.

Spandel, V., and R. J. Stiggins. 1990. *Creating Writers: Linking Assessment and Writing Instruction.* Longmans.

Wygal, D. E., and D. E. Stout. 1989. Incorporating Writing Techniques in the Accounting Classroom: Experience in Financial, Managerial, and Cost Courses. *The Proceedings: A Collection of Papers and Abstracts 1989 Mid-Atlantic Regional Meeting* (April): 82.

Zinsser, W. 1988. *Writing to Learn.* Harper & Row.

An Innovative Assessment Tool in the Accounting Curriculum: An Accounting Capstone Course Focusing on the Public Sector

Steven C. Dilley and Susan C. Kattelus

A nationwide call for change in accounting higher education was sounded in the 1980s. At the same time, oversight bodies called for accountability by institutions. The academic accounting profession is spending the 1990s extensively reexamining the accounting curriculum and proposing innovative responses to these calls. An effective method of assessing the success of the innovations will ensure that college and university accounting education in the 21st century will not only be substantially different from that of the last 100 years, but sufficiently effective in preparing students for a dynamic, global business environment. The calls for change in accounting higher education have come from industry, the public accounting profession, the academic community, and the public at large. The consensus is that students need the ability to think critically and creatively, know "how to learn," thrive on uncertainty, integrate ethics into their decisions, and effectively communicate with an international business community using professional interpersonal skills.

One potential response to the calls for change is a return to a broad-based, liberal arts education. However, an obstacle to such an approach is the dramatic change in the technology of information. That technology is driving a demand for greater specialization within accounting. In the 21st century, the demand for accountants who can effectively integrate complex information systems with the specialized needs of a diverse set of users will be greater than ever before. The call for innovative change is coupled with a call for accountability by institutions of higher learning. The taxpaying, tuition-paying public and elected oversight agencies, faced with tight budget constraints, are holding colleges and universities "accountable" for efficiently and effectively using the scarce resources allocated to them.

The purpose of this paper is to propose an integrating capstone accounting course to help meet this call for change and accountability. The innovation is that the course will test the student's ability to apply functional accounting tools learned in the commercial, business setting to the public and nonprofit sectors. The assessment tool will be a capstone course. The course will be toward the end of the student's "undergraduate" accounting curriculum. Students entering the course will be enrolled in a five-year, 150-hour accounting curriculum. They will have completed accounting major courses in accounting information systems, intermediate financial accounting, management accounting, auditing, and tax. The course will assess the students' ability to effectively extend and apply their accounting background in a related subject area.

The remainder of the paper is organized as follows. First, stakeholders and their calls for change in the accounting curriculum are identified. Second, the universities' "assessment plans" response to meet the demand for accountability is discussed. Third, the focus on the nonprofit entities in a capstone course is justified. Fourth, implementation of the capstone course is described. Finally, conclusions and implications of the proposal are identified.

CALL FOR CHANGE IN THE ACCOUNTING CURRICULUM

Dissatisfaction with higher education in the United States has become a national issue. Academics in accounting were among the first in the accounting profession to recognize that our "product" will only be consumed by a public that demands it and is satisfied with the results. The American Accounting Association (AAA) established a committee in 1984 to study the future of accounting education. The Bedford Committee (1986) reported that accounting education required major reorientation between now and the year 2000. Recommendations included

Steven C. Dilley is a Professor at Michigan State University and Susan C. Kattelus is an Assistant Professor at Eastern Michigan University.

1. approaching accounting education as an information development and distribution function for economic decision making, and

2. emphasizing student's learning to learn as the primary classroom objective (p. 169).

The (then) Big 8 accounting firms' White Paper entitled "Perspectives on Education: Capabilities for Success in the Accounting Profession" (1989) followed. Their observation was that the existing accounting curriculum did not produce students well prepared to operate in a complex, rapidly changing work environment. Accounting researchers also found that the academic caliber of students attracted to accounting had declined and those students that did complete an accounting program have had little emphasis on the ambiguities and uncertainties encountered in the business world.

The American Institute of Certified Public Accountants also studied the issue of accounting education and concluded that today's professional needed an extra year of coursework in order to acquire the skills necessary for a dynamic business environment. The AICPA proposed expanding the CPA educational requirements to a 150-semester- hour academic program. This "fifth year" should be used to increase students' general knowledge and broaden their scope rather than to give them a more narrow look at only one aspect of accounting. More than 25 states have now mandated a 150-hour academic program (AICPA 1992).

The Accounting Education Change Commission (AECC) was created in 1989, inspired by the reports of the AAA and the (then) Big 8 CPA firms and funded by the firms themselves. The 18 members of this commission represent a broad range of constituencies and are charged with "... fostering changes in the academic preparation of accountants consistent with the goal of improving their capabilities for successful professional careers." The AECC's mission includes stimulating change through a grant program and through dissemination of information. The Commission's Issues Statements #1 (1990) and #2 (1991) and Position Statements #1 (1990), #2 (1992) and #3 (1992) articulate objectives for the education of accountants that include elimination of the focus on certifying exams in the curriculum (e.g., CPA, CMA, CIA). As with the law and medical professions, preparation for certifying exams is a task the student should undertake after the academic requirements are met.

The American Assembly of Collegiate Schools of Business (AACSB), one of the accreditation bodies, has called for instruction directed toward an understanding of the environment in which accounting operates. A revised accreditation process (AACSB 1991) recognizes that programs will have different missions. However, the AACSB clearly calls for the study of governmental and not-for-profit organizations.

Table 1 summarizes the calls for change in the accounting curriculum as well as particular references to the study of the public sector.

Although quality education has always been the mission of all institutions of higher learning, recent financial incentives have stimulated the search for innovation. The AECC awards grants to universities that have proposed accounting curriculum innovations. Ten universities have received grants.[1]

Other clear signals of support for teaching innovation now exist. The AAA has initiated an "Award for Innovation in Accounting Education" for innovations which are transferable and useful to other accounting programs. The AAA established a section on Teaching and Instruction. New journals such as *Issues in Accounting Education* (AAA) and *Accounting Education: An International Journal* (Chapman and Hall, United Kingdom) provide an outlet for academic studies on accounting education. On a smaller scale, the Faculty Center for Instructional Effectiveness at Eastern Michigan University presents eight $1,200 awards a year for innovations in teaching and curriculum.

CALL FOR ACCOUNTABILITY: ASSESSMENT ISSUES

In the wake of inflation and recession in the 1980s, the public demanded accountability for the scarce resources that it had entrusted to institutions of higher education. At least 36 states either require or have considered mandated "assessment programs" (Herring and Izard 1992). Without defining the term "assessment," these states have called for colleges and universities to design a plan to document student learning and quality of educa-

---

[1] In 1989–90 these schools were Brigham Young University, Kansas State University, The University of Massachussets at Amherst, The University of North Texas, and Rutgers University. In 1990–91 awards went to Arizona State University, University of Chicago, University of Virginia, University of North Carolina, and the University of Illinois and University of Notre Dame in a combined project. More recently, community and two-year colleges have received awards.

TABLE 1
Call for Change and Focus on Public Sector

ACADEMIC
American Accounting Association (AAA)
"Future Accounting Education: Preparing for the Expanding Profession" *Issues in Accounting Education.* (Spring 1986)

"The essential components of the general professional accounting education should include: . . . Decision problems and information in organizations, including: . . . Knowledge of the functional activities of business, governmental, and not-for-profit organizations . . ." (p. 182)

INDUSTRY
Large CPA firms
"Perspectives on Education: Capabilities for Success in the Accounting Profession (White Paper)" (1989)

"Individuals seeking to be successful in the diverse world of public accounting must be able to use creative problem-solving skills in a consultative process . . . They must be able to comprehend to solve diverse and unstructured problems in unfamiliar settings." (p. 6)

"The development of an efficient curriculum requires attention to integration. Re-engineering the curriculum should include a careful evaluation of topical coverage in all subjects . . . Emphasis should be placed . . . on the compounding of learning by appropriate combination across course and departmental lines." (p. 12)

American Institute of CPAs (AICPA)
150-hour requirement to be a member by the year 2000; 25 states have adopted legislation of this nature

JOINT VENTURE
Accounting Education Change Commission (AECC)
Issues Statement #1, " AECC Urges Priority for Teaching in Higher Education" (August 1990)

"The importance of effective teaching and innovative curriculum and course development cannot be over emphasized."

AECC *Position Statement #1,* "Objectives of Education for Accountants" (September 1990)

"The Commission defines the accounting profession broadly. It includes career paths in . . . government and nonprofit accounting" (p. 1)

"An attitude of accepting, even thriving on, uncertainty and unstructured situations should be fostered." (p. 6)

AECC *Issues Statement #2,* "AECC Urges Decoupling of Academic Studies and Professional Accounting Examination Preparation" (July 1991)

AECC *Position Statement #2* (June 1992)

AECC *Position Statement #3* (September 1992)

ACCREDITING ORGANIZATIONS
American Assembly of Collegiate Schools of Business (AACSB)
Final Report — The AACSB Accreditation Project (April 1991)

"Education in accounting should prepare students for a wide range of careers including: . . . (3) government, (4) not-for-profit organizations . . ." (p. 33) "Accounting faculty members should be involved in ongoing processes to ensure that accounting education programs reflect the current needs of the profession, business and other organizations, and society." (p. 39) "Topics such as not-for-profit/governmental accounting . . . should be offered" (p. 41)

Federation of Schools of Accountancy (FSA)
"150-hour Requirement — Report of the Implementation Issues Committee." (December 12, 1988).

North Central Association of Colleges and Schools (NCA)
Memorandum on Assessment Plans (September 9, 1991)

National Association of State Boards of Accountancy (NASBA)

GOVERNMENTAL AND NONPROFIT SECTOR
AAA – Governmental and Nonprofit Section
"A Model Program for Accounting Education for Governmental and Not-for-Profit Organizations" (presented to AECC March 1991)

"GNP Accounting and the AECC." *Government & Nonprofit News* 15 (Winter 1991): 3.

tion. Components of an assessment plan, as outlined by the North Central Association of Colleges and Schools (NCA — an organization accrediting virtually all 81 schools in Michigan and other states), are shown in Table 2.

Always an integral part of each faculty member's relationship with a student in a particular course, assessment has now taken on the meaning of a systematic, comprehensive, continual plan for monitoring students using multiple measuring techniques. This assessment plan will acknowledge that the department, college, and university have joint assessment responsibility with the accounting faculty member. The effectiveness of the academic curriculum must be documented for the many stakeholders and constituents of the university.

An exemplary assessment plan, according to the NCA, will employ multiple methods to assess students' progress in a conceptually sound program that is linked to the mission of the school. A key element of an assessment plan is documenting that students can integrate and apply the knowledge gained in their academic curriculum.

Methods of integrating a student's learning in a culminating experience that have been used over time include an integrative seminar course, thesis, comprehensive examination, completion of a de-

velopment project, recital or showing, portfolio, internship experience, or certifying examination. Traditionally, business schools have used a capstone policy course towards the end of the bachelor's program to integrate and demonstrate the interdependence of the functional areas of business (e.g., accounting, finance, law, management, marketing, operations, and systems). Instructional methods are designed to develop the student's critical thinking skills in analysis and synthesis. Whether labeled as an assessment tool or not, this capstone experience tests the student's ability to identify issues in a "real-world" case, apply appropriate technical skills to solve the problems, simulate group decision making, and communicate the results of the analysis orally and in writing to a client/teacher. Theoretically, successful completion of this course is a signal to potential employers that the student has attained a certain level of competency in areas essential for effectively functioning in business.

The diversity and complexity of the functional areas within accounting call for a similar integration. Dramatic technological advances have moved our society into "The Information Age" from the Industrial or Agrarian Ages (Elliott 1990). Accountants, as producers of information for decision

---

TABLE 2

Components of an Assessment Plan

1. Is linked to the mission, goals, and objectives of the institution
2. Is carefully articulated and is institution-wide in conceptualization and scope
3. Leads to institutional improvement
4. Is being implemented according to a timeline
5. Is administered

Characteristics of an Assessment Plan

1. Flows from the institution's mission
2. Has a conceptual framework
3. Has faculty ownership/responsibility
4. Has institutionwide support
5. Uses multiple measures
6. Provides feedback to students and the institution
7. Is cost effective
8. Does not restrict or inhibit goals of access, equity, and diversity established by the institution
9. Leads to improvement
10. Has a process in place for evaluating the assessment program

The North Central Association of Colleges and Schools, Memorandum September 9, 1991.

makers about economic events, have been thrust into a very dynamic environment in the last 20 years. Computers have virtually eliminated the technological constraints on information. Now an expanding and diverse set of decision makers demand useful information about global economic events. The accounting industry's response to the diverse demand for information, like the law and medical professions, has been to specialize. CPA firms develop industry expertise, individual sections of the accounting associations such as the AAA and AICPA have been established, new journals target different segments of the accounting audience, accounting "tracks" are offered in many university curriculums, and professional certifications for special areas have been developed (e.g., Certified Management Accountant, Certified Internal Auditor, Certified Information Systems Auditor).

All of the documents calling for change reflect a common theme. Students must develop their intellectual, communication, and interpersonal skills, as well as the ability to monitor their own progress. A capstone course integrating the tools and functional components of the accounting curriculum can serve as a forum for the student to practice these skills, and for the professor to assess the student's mastery of these skills.

CALL FOR STUDY OF THE PUBLIC SECTOR

Each of the documents calling for accounting education reform specifically include the public sector (governmental and other nonprofit organizations) in the recommended sphere of study. Even the general call for internationalization of the business curriculum suggests that the public sector is a logical setting for exposing students to the complexities of providing information about entities which operate in a global environment.

Many accounting programs include a course on Governmental and Nonprofit Accounting. The status of such courses varies significantly across colleges and universities.[2] We propose that a public sector course is a strong candidate for the capstone accounting course. Seniors have substantially completed many tool courses. A real test of critical thinking skills is to ask the student to apply these profit sector tools and concepts to the often unfamiliar and unique public sector. The contrast between profit and public sector environments allows the student to critically compare different systems, principles, and reports designed to meet diverse user needs.

The typical required courses in an accounting curriculum cover five functional areas: accounting information systems; financial principles, markets, and reporting; managerial accounting; auditing; and taxation. Technical tools and processes learned in each of these areas can be applied to issues that arise in the public sector. What is sometimes not appreciated is that these nonprivate sector entities face supply and demand forces, oversight by regulatory bodies, technological constraints, and accountability to diverse users that are quite similar to those issues faced by commercial for-profit enterprises. The public sector is not just a specialized industry. Often, nonprofit entities directly compete with the private sector business for labor, capital, and other economic resources.

The following section describes some issues facing governmental and nonprofit entities to which the accounting tools developed in the five functional areas of accounting could be applied.

Accounting Information Systems

Public sector entities use a fund accounting system. The fund accounting system, often computerized, is designed to meet the unique needs of a broad base of users who have provided financial resources to the entity. In addition, the accounting system must be able to classify revenues and expenses/expenditures by fund, function or program, organizational unit, activity, character and object in order to account for the use of these financial resources (NCGA *Statement #1*).

The system must incorporate various component entities which may be geographically independent but functionally dependent upon an oversight entity. For example, the Michigan comprehensive annual financial statement of the City of Ann Arbor, includes the Ann Arbor Building Authority and Housing Commission but not the Transportation Authority or Economic Development Corporation. The financial statements of the component entities are either blended or discretely combined into one reporting entity.

---

[2]The relative commitment to the course differs across universities. Teaching-oriented colleges often require the course. Research-oriented universities may offer only a one credit course to ensure that students are qualified to sit for the CPA exam in their state. Some research universities with graduate programs in the public sector, such as Harvard and Yale, offer graduate courses focusing on the unique managerial and budgeting issues in governmental and nonprofit entities.

Financial Principles, Markets, and Reporting

Double-entry accounting principles apply to each fund (an accounting and fiscal entity) and to each group (only an accounting entity). The basis of accounting and concepts of realization and recognition are applicable to these entities. In particular, Governmental Accounting Standards Board (GASB) *Statement #11* on measurement recognition relates to principles of financial accounting.

Interfund transactions play an important role in the conduct of business in a governmental entity. Many entities are beginning to report on a consolidated basis, making elimination of interfund transactions necessary. Currently, generally accepted accounting principles for governments require that the total columns are captioned "Memorandum Only" because differences in the methods of accounting used among funds make the total columns misleading.

The GASB shares equal standing with the Financial Accounting Standards Board (FASB) under the umbrella of the Financial Accounting Foundation and is charged with promulgating generally accepted accounting principles for governmental entities. The GASB follows the same "due process" as the FASB. Recent GASB statements have addressed issues quite similar to those studied by the FASB, for example, deferred compensation plans, repurchase agreements, pensions, defeasance of debt, depreciation, risk financing and related insurance, measurement focus and basis of accounting, postemployment benefits, and operating leases.

Also, comprehensive annual financial reports include concepts of combining statements and general-purpose financial statements. Footnotes are critical and several GASB statements (#3, #5, #7, #12) relate to adequate disclosure.

The Government Finance Officers Association (GFOA) offers a certificate of excellence in financial reporting for completeness and clarity. There is some evidence that receipt of a certificate in this voluntary program may result in higher bond ratings, and consequently, a financial gain to the municipality (Grossman 1984). Municipal bonds, bond-rating agencies, and the financial markets are a significant component of the financing tasks of a government's finance officer and treasurer. Also, risk of default on municipal debt is a sensitive political issue with public costs.

Managerial Accounting

The budget is formally incorporated into the accounting system in order to report on the variance between actual and budgeted expenditures for governmental-type funds. In Michigan, there are legal sanctions against a finance officer who spends more than what was appropriated. Economic concepts such as scarce resources, public goods, supply and demand, and monopoly position play an important role in the public sector. Managerial tools can help analyze these issues. Political and agency concepts relate to the role the finance officer and elected officials of governments play as agents to the principals and stewards of the public's resources.

Auditing

Governments are subject to a complex set of laws and auditors must express an opinion about whether there has been compliance with those laws. For example, municipal bond covenants and legal sanctions for spending more than what was appropriated require auditing tasks not commonly done on a commercial audit. Also, the use of volunteers and dependence upon cash transactions often pose internal control problems.

The Single Audit Act passed by Congress in 1984 changes the way audits are conducted for recipients of federal funds. OMB Circular A-133 extends the provisions of this act to nonprofit organizations such as colleges and universities. Compliance with GAAP requires that the auditor be familiar with the statements of the National Council of Governmental Accountants and the GASB. Audits conducted by the Governmental Accounting Office have an expanded scope. They include efficiency and effectiveness objectives as well as fairness with respect to GAAP and compliance with laws. Governments may receive qualified opinions for the omission of the General Fixed Asset Account Group, a violation of GAAP.

Taxation

The Internal Revenue Code has strict guidelines for the issuance of tax-exempt bonds. Nonprofit entities exempt from income taxation under IRC §501 are subject to an "unrelated business income tax" on business activities not related to their exempt purpose. Nonprofit entities must maintain their exempt status or donors will not be allowed charitable deductions contributions. Governments can also levy state and local taxes based on use, property, and income.

Accounting is the process of producing information about economic events for decision makers. The complexity of economic events faced by governmental and nonprofit entities has dramatically increased over other times. Consequently, the demand for information about the public sector has also grown. The decision makers using the financial statements of governments and nonprofits are more diverse and demand timely and thorough information. An accounting education should prepare a professional to meet these increased demands. A capstone course is an ideal place to meet the calls for more knowledge about the public sector, assessment of students' abilities to think critically, and innovative change in the accounting curriculum.

IMPLEMENTATION OF THE CAPSTONE COURSE

The capstone accounting course should be in the fourth year of a five-year program. Like a senior intern experience, the course can be used as a measurement assessment tool. In addition, though, a capstone course in the fourth year of the five-year curriculum can also be used as a diagnostic tool. Identification of students' weaknesses can result in the implementation of specialized plans for improvement, followed by monitoring of students' progress during the remaining one year of the program.

The purpose of this capstone course is to provide an integrating course suitable for all accounting majors, regardless of their area of concentration. Accounting issues arise across organizational functions. The emphasis in this course is on developing an understanding of the many interrelated applications of accounting. One of the objectives of the course is to expose the accounting student to the unique environment and issues facing governmental and nonprofit entities in order to increase his or her competence as an auditor, finance officer, accountant, and/or taxpayer.

Other objectives include developing students' appreciation and understanding of the social implications of the various aspects of accounting, the interconnectedness of the various facets of accounting, and the ethical issues involved in the production and presentation of accounting information.

The primary instructional approach is the case method. The focus is on student involvement in the process of learning "how to learn." Cases which have multiple threads are used — threads involving the functional accounting areas. For instance, a nonprofit art museum is conducting a fund-raising activity for the first time. The activity requires analysis and decisions on financial accounting

(profitability reports), managerial accounting (cost allocation), accounting systems implications (reprogramming of the financial reporting software), and tax implications (Is the fund-raiser an unrelated business activity subject to income tax?). Another example, described in Table 3, identifies some of the issues a college may face when it is also in need of resources. The case method also involves bringing in practicing accountants to share their current critical issues with the students. The practicing accountants will lead discussions of those critical issues and interrelate the issues to the students' course work.

One underlying theme of the course will be ethics. Students are asked to work in groups to evaluate the ethical consideration in the practice issues and the cases. A term paper/project is also required. It must be cross-functional — the students cannot focus only on their area of specialization. Another theme of the course is the development and/or refinement of critical thinking skills. Table 4 presents the nine critical thinking themes. In a fast-paced, technological environment, critical thinking is even more necessary than ever. The critical thinking themes are integrated into the case analyses and become second nature to the students. One of the early critical thinking assignments requires its application to the following questions: Are integrative skills required of accountants? How can accountants acquire integrative skills? The framework for the course is the multifaceted role of accounting in society, with an emphasis on the ethical and social implications of accounting applications. The course begins and concludes with a section on ethical/social implications of accounting applications. During the course, five main skill areas are used to help students develop a better understanding of the role these accounting functions serve in a broad organizational and social context: accounting systems, financial, managerial, auditing, and taxation.

The course integrates the functional areas of accounting and applies them to the public sector. Students work in teams and are ranked on their performance. The course includes projects that require students to "respond to clients" with accounting problems. Students must present their findings and recommendations both verbally and in writing.

In the spirit of preparing students for a dynamic environment, the content of this course must be continually assessed. An informal advisory board of professionals in both accounting and governmen-

---

TABLE 3
Example Case

A university's administration wants to solicit funds for the explicit purpose of advertising and promoting the passage of a much needed millage. The university currently has a deficit in the fund balance of the General Fund and is in need of operating funds. As the CPA in charge of the annual financial audit, you have been asked for advice.

What is the best way "to account for" this contribution to ensure that donors will be eligible for a charitable deduction from their income? What are the alternative ways to handle transactions such as this; that is, in what account should donations be deposited?

Functional Area and Issues Involved in This Case

SYSTEMS — Fund Accounting
- Should a restricted fund be established for this purpose?

FINANCIAL — Financing
- What alternative means are there to fund this operating deficit?

FINANCIAL — Reporting
- Is the selected entity (e.g., Friends of ABC College) to be included as a component within the reporting entity?

MANAGERIAL — Budgeting
- Is there proper monitoring of actual expenditures budgeted to prevent future problems?

AUDITING — Disclosures
- Does the auditor have a responsibility to disclose the nature of this solicitation?

TAX — Individual
- Will the donor be eligible to take a charitable deduction from income?

TAX — University
- Will the university risk its tax-exempt status (IRC §501(c)(3))?

LAW
- Should a separate nonprofit entity be established for this purpose?
- Is there a state law which prohibits this activity, and consequently impacts the appropriation for the University?

TABLE 4
Nine Critical Thinking (CT) Themes

1. CT is a productive and positive activity.
2. CT is a process, not an outcome.
3. Manifestations of CT vary according to the contexts in which it occurs.
4. CT is triggered by positive as well as negative events.
5. CT is emotive as well as rational.

Components of CT

6. Identifying and challenging assumptions is central to CT.
7. Challenging the importance of context is crucial to CT.
8. CTers try to imagine and explore alternatives.
9. Imagining and exploring alternatives leads to reflective skepticism.

Source: S. D. Brookfield. 1987. *Developing Critical Thinkers*. San Francisco.

---

tal and nonprofit accounting is asked to review the content of the course, cases, and exercises for relevance and timeliness of the issues selected.

Incremental faculty costs are substantial. First, the faculty member expends significant time designing cases which integrate the functional accounting areas in the context of the public sector.

Second, time will be required to evaluate students' written assignments in a thorough and timely manner. Third, extensive materials are developed to serve as a text. Also, substantial time is spent coordinating the presentations by practicing accountants.

CONCLUSION AND IMPLICATIONS

Those involved in accounting education have the responsibility to respond to criticism of higher education in a truly innovative way. This paper proposes a required capstone accounting course whose objectives include teaching the student to use high-order thinking skills to integrate the various functional areas of accounting, communicate effectively, and appreciate the dynamic and global environment in which the accounting profession operates. The course Governmental and Nonprofit Accounting is due for an overhaul and offers a tremendous setting for students to apply their technical skills learned in the functional areas of accounting to the public sector.

The end result of a course which demands written and oral presentations of cases can be a student who leaves the accounting undergraduate program with the confidence of knowing how the accounting pieces fit together and, consequently, has a basis upon which to continue the process of becoming an accounting professional.

Even if accounting education is not a homogeneous product, academic programs at other universities can benefit from the experiments and successes of innovative curriculum proposals. However, the mission and constituencies of each university will be an important factor in the successful implementation of any proposal. Assessment of any curriculum change will remain a challenge.

It may be said that the test of a true innovation may be measured by the amount of resistance put forth to prevent its implementation. We expect the following roadblocks from our accounting colleagues to implementing a course such as the one proposed:

- reluctance by accounting faculty to focus on the public sector; many people consider it a specialized industry, such as banking or insurance.
- logistical problems if team teaching is used; for example, pay and scheduling
- scarcity of effective materials (including cases) integrating functional accounting areas and study of the public sector
- difficulty in identifying the best accounting teacher to teach this course, for example, one who is broadly versed (excited and challenged) in all the subdisciplines
- burden of grading and providing constructive comments on the many writing assignments required of the students
- lack of consensus about positioning the course in the curriculum (e.g., at the end of the fourth or fifth year)

Like the many assessment plans that are being developed today by colleges and universities, it is hoped that this paper contributes to the debate leading to a better quality of higher accounting education.

REFERENCES

American Accounting Association, Committee on the Future Structure, Content, and Scope of Accounting Education (The Bedford Committee). Future Accounting Education: Preparing for the Expanding Profession. 1986. *Issues in Accounting Education* (Spring): 168–195.

American Institute of CPAs. 1992. *The CPA Letter* 72 (September): 2 (updated).

Elliott, R. K. 1990. *Accounting Education and Research at the Crossroad*, remarks at the Plenary Session at the Annual Meeting of the American Accounting Association (August 11).

Government Accounting Standards Board. 1991. *Measurement Focus and Basis of Accounting — Governmental Fund Operating Statements.*

Grossman, H. C. 1984. The CAFR as a Tool in Credit Evaluation. *GAAFR Review* (September): 2.

Herring, H., III, and C. D. Izard. 1992. Outcomes Assessment of Accounting Majors. *Issues in Accounting Education* (Spring): 1–17.

Inman B., A. Wenzler, and P. D. Wickert. 1989. Square Pegs in Round Holes: Are Accounting Students Well-Suited to Today's Accounting Profession? *Issues in Accounting Education* (Spring): 29–47.

National Council of Governmental Accountants. 1979. *Statement #1,* Governmental Accounting and Financial Reporting Principles.

BIBLIOGRAPHY

American Assembly of Collegiate Schools of Business (AACSB). 1988. *Strategic Thrusts for the Future: Report of the Strategic Planning Committee.* AICPA.

Beyer, B. K. 1987. *Practical Strategies for the Teaching of Thinking.* Allyn and Bacon.

Brookfield, S. D. 1987. *Developing Critical Thinkers.* Jossey-Bass.

Committee C. 1990. Mandated Assessment of Educational Outcomes. A Report of Committee C on College and University Teaching, Research, and Publication. *Academe* (November-December): 34–40.

Cross, K. P., and T. A. Angelo. 1988. *Classroom Assessment Techniques.* National Center for Research to Improve Postsecondary Teaching and Learning.

Deppe, L., D. R. Hansen, and S. Jenne. 1988. The 150-Hour Educational Requirement: The History and Message of the Utah Experience. *Accounting Horizons* (June): 53–57.

Draughdrill, J. H., Jr. 1988. Point of View. *The Chronicle of Higher Education* (January 17): A52.

Johnson, D. W., and R. T. Johnson. 1987. *Learning Together and Alone: Cooperative, Competitive and Individualistic Learning.* Association for Supervision and Curriculum Development.

Keeley, S., and M. Browne. 1988. Assignments That Encourage Critical Thinking. *Journal of Professional Studies* (Winter): 2–11.

Macer-Simmer, A. P. 1990. Substance and Strategy in the Accounting Curriculum. *Issues in Accounting Education* (Spring): 129–140.

Marquette, P. 1990. Chair's Message. *Government and Nonprofit News* 14 (Summer). American Accounting Association.

Needles, B. E., Jr., and M. Powers. 1990. A Comparative Study of Models for Accounting Education. *Issues in Accounting Education* (Fall): 250–267.

———, and H. R. Anderson. 1991. A Comprehensive Model for Accounting Education. Working paper presented to the AECC Symposium (March).

Patten R. J., and D. Williams. 1990. There's Trouble—Right Here in Our Accounting Programs: The Challenge to Accounting Educators. *Issues in Accounting Education* (Fall): 175–179.

Perspectives on Education: Capabilities for Success in the Accounting Profession. 1989. Arthur Andersen & Co., Arthur Young, Coopers & Lybrand, Deloitte Haskins & Sells, Ernst & Whinney, Peat Marwick Main & Co., Price Waterhouse, and Touche Ross.

Rankin, L. J. 1991. Student Capabilities and Instructional Methods: A Framework for Curriculum Development, Assessment, and Research. Working paper presented at the AECC Symposium (March).

Subotnik, D. 1988. What Accounting Can Learn from Legal Education. *Issues in Accounting Education* (Fall): 313–324.

Wallace, W. 1990. One Educator's View of How to Respond to the Challenges Faced by Higher Education in Business. *Issues in Accounting Education* (Fall): 302–306.

Williams, J. 1988. *A Framework for the Development of Accounting Education Research.* Coopers & Lybrand Foundation and American Accounting Association, Accounting Education Series, Volume 9.

Williams, J. R. 1990. Invited Editorial: Curriculum Innovation and 150 Hour Legislation: Friends or Foes? *Issues in Accounting Education* (Spring): 1–6.

Zeff, S. 1989. Does Accounting Belong in the University Curriculum? *Issues in Accounting Education* (Spring): 203–210.

Cognitive Complexity and Accounting Education

Robert L. Hurt

INTRODUCTION

The purpose of this paper is to discuss cognitive complexity, an essential characteristic for success in the accounting profession in the 21st century. The paper is divided into five parts: changes in the profession creating the need for cognitively complex individuals, the nature of cognitive complexity, measuring cognitive complexity with the Paragraph Completion Test (PCT), assessing the relationship between PCT score and performance on first-year accounting problems, and recommendations for further research.

CHANGES IN THE PROFESSION

A pressing need exists to attract more independent thinkers into the accounting profession in light of the changing character of the profession. According to Seidler (1985, 12),

> The accounting profession has reacted to the increasing complexity of the business environment in the last thirty years by redesigning its written technology, but not by making any significant changes in the personnel charged with implementing that technology.

In current practice, the need to go beyond the rudiments of accounting procedure and make sound recommendations using professional judgment is expanding. According to Stallman (1974, 203),

> The accountant must be able to think independently, to relate what he sees to what he knows, to modify his notions of how things relate in the light of new information, to draw implications from changing conditions, to creatively seek solutions to new problems, and to evaluate the ideas which he generates.

A recent article ("The Big Eight Focus on Systems Integration," *Computers in Accounting*, February-March 1989, p. 8) stated: "Most Big Eight firms are establishing strategies for breaking into systems integration. *They no longer want to be known as simply accountants and tax consultants.*" (Emphasis added.)

A survey conducted by Schneider (1988) provides evidence of the changing abilities required of the professional accountant. According to his study, "the range of services [provided by professional accountants] has expanded, requiring expertise and skills far removed from the accounting and auditing knowledge sets" (p. 27). Further, he stated, "technological change has not only had a tremendous impact on what is done and the way it is done, but also on the knowledge and skill demands placed on people" (p. 59). Schneider's survey revealed that management advisory services have become a major source of revenue for public accounting firms. Yet in contrast to the traditional auditing services provided by public accounting firms, no standards exist as to what professionals should know about management advisory services, which require expertise in such areas as finance, statistics and quantitative methods, marketing, human resource management, psychology, and information systems (Schneider 1988).

Sathe (1982) conducted a study which further supports the need for better decision-making skills among accounting professionals. Looking specifically at the involvement of corporate controllers in organizational management, he made the following comments:

> The notion of active controller involvement in this study thus encompasses not only the presentation of information and analysis to aid management in business decision making but also the recommending of courses of action to be taken and the challenging of plans and actions of operating executives. . . It is one thing to be able to make recommendations and challenge management in the areas of accounting policy or internal control where defined rules and procedures exist. It is quite another thing to be able to recommend and question business decisions and actions in areas where clear guidelines or answers do not exist. (p. 10)

Thus, he expressed the need for controllers to be actively involved in business decision making to be effective, attributing this new role to "the advent of computers which presumably allowed a

Robert L. Hurt is an Assistant Professor at California State Polytechnic University–Pomona.

refocusing of effort from the prediction of numbers to their analysis and use in decision making" (p. 11).

In today's dynamic professional accounting environment, practitioners are called upon to sort, analyze, and integrate enormous volumes of information to solve accounting and management problems (see Schneider 1988). The call from the professional arm of accounting to accounting educators has been and is to train students who possess the skills necessary to function effectively in an increasingly complex and rapidly changing workplace. According to the American Institute of Certified Public Accountants' Committee on Educational Standards (Carey 1965, 266–267):

> Professional education should have as one of its goals the development of the ability to analyze and solve independently problems and situations of a diverse nature. Sound solutions require the use of knowledge, reasoning, and judgment. Accounting educators . . . must do their best to develop this kind of ability in their graduates, insofar as it can be developed through education.

In their discussion of cognitive learning theory, Willingham, McNeill and Collins (1974) point out that learning can be defined as moving closer to the goals of the learner. In addition, they state that "understanding of complex concepts, generalization, synthesization, and problem solving" are important factors in learning accounting (p. 175). In terms of the previous discussion, then, individuals equipped to respond to the increasingly complex, abstract situations faced in the practice of accounting must be attracted into the profession.

THE NATURE OF COGNITIVE COMPLEXITY

Cognitive complexity, also known as conceptual level, can be thought of as the degree to which an individual is equipped to deal with ambiguity in processing information. According to Hunt et al. (1978, p. 3),

> The general definition of conceptual level is in terms of (1) increasing conceptual complexity as indicated by discrimination, differentiation, and integration and (2) increasing interpersonal maturity as indicated by self-definition and self-other relations.

In other words, the cognitively complex individual is one who can look at a wide array of available information and select those pieces which are germane to solving a particular problem.

Miller and Gordon (1975) discuss the differentiation and integration components of cognitive complexity, elaborating on them as follows (p. 260):

Conceptual level, also known as the level of cognitive complexity, refers to two basic features of the cognitive system: the number of dimensions taken into account in formulating a judgment (i.e., the degree of differentiation) and the nature of the rules used to combine these dimensions in arriving at a final decision (i.e., the level of integration).

Cognitive complexity is a concept distinct from IQ/ability/achievement (Hunt et al. 1978, 45). However, a relationship *does* exist between cognitive complexity and IQ/ability/achievement variables. Specifically, "persons very low in ability/achievement are almost always also low in (cognitive complexity); however high ability/achievement persons vary enormously in (cognitive complexity)" (Hunt et al. 1978, 45).

PARAGRAPH COMPLETION TEST

The Paragraph Completion Test (PCT), developed by Hunt et al. (1978), is designed to assess a subject's conceptual level (also known as level of cognitive complexity). The PCT consists of six open-ended questions regarding subjects' opinions and reactions to a variety of topics. The six questions include:

1. What I think about rules . . . .
2. When I am criticized . . . .
3. When someone does not agree with me . . . .
4. What I think about parents . . . .
5. When I am not sure . . . .
6. When I am told what to do . . . .

For the purpose of the current study, question four ("What I think about parents") was excluded. A precedent was set for this procedure by Amernic and Beechy (1984), who felt that feelings about parents were not appropriate measures of conceptual level for adult samples.

The test is easily administered in a group setting, as long as subjects have adequate facility with English. According to Hunt et al. (1978), the test is inappropriate for subjects whose first language is not English. Each of the five questions included in the test is written on a separate sheet of paper. Subjects are instructed *not* to look at the questions until instructed to do so by the test administrator. About three minutes are allotted for responding to each question, depending on the educational level of the subjects. More time is recommended, for example, for subjects in high school than for subjects at the university level (Hunt et al. 1978). Subjects are asked to write at least three sentences in response to each question as a way of ensuring that the cognitive processes motivating responses can be adequately assessed. Oral administration is recommended for samples of learners with deficient written communication skills (Gardiner and Schroder 1972, 960).

Scoring of the PCT is necessarily subjective. Therefore, PCT responses in this study were scored by both the researcher and an assistant. If the correlation between the researcher's scores and the assistant's scores was less than .7 (the minimum level recommended by Nunnally 1978, 245–246), both scorers discussed the evaluations on a case-by-case basis and achieved a compromise in cases where the overall PCT scores differed by more than 0.5. This comparison improved the overall correlation between the two sets of scores, eliminating potential bias in evaluating individual responses. Responses to each question are scored on a continuum from zero to three; the general characteristics of each level are summarized below (Hunt et al. 1978):

0   Respondents react impulsively or defensively to questions.

1   Subjects are concerned with socially acceptable behavior. Cognitive processes are polarized or dichotomous.

2   Statements indicate an openness to others. Individuals at this level are open to the feelings and opinions of others. They listen to others' ideas, but fail to integrate them into their own cognitive and decision-making processes.

3   People at this stage weigh all the alternatives when confronting a problem or conflict situation. The subject will choose the optimal solution, considering the feelings of all parties involved.

Scores of .5, 1.5, and 2.5 may be given for intermediate responses which demonstrate the characteristics of more than one level. Thus, the test recognizes seven different levels of cognitive complexity for each question.

After scoring a subject's responses in all five areas, the two lowest scores are discarded. The rationale for this procedure is clear when one considers the "dispositional" and "situational" aspects of cognitive complexity discussed previously (also see Hunt et al. 1978). The basic notion is that subjects do not always function at their highest conceptual level because of situational influences. The arithmetic mean of the three scores retained constitutes the measure of an individual's conceptual level.

PCT SCORE AND ACCOUNTING PERFORMANCE

To establish the relationship between PCT score and accounting-related cognitively complex

behavior, student performance was assessed in a first-year accounting course on two problems during Winter 1990; the problems selected appear in the appendix to this paper. The subjects of the experiment were students enrolled in sections of an introductory financial accounting course at California State Polytechnic University Pomona (n = 70).

The first problem, "Effects of Journal Entry Errors," was part of the first midterm examination in the course; the second problem, "Financial Statement Preparation," was given as a non-graded in-class quiz. In solving the exercises, students were required to draw on information presented in class; however, solutions were not merely rote repetitions of lecture material. Rather, students had to utilize decision-making skills to determine *how* topics discussed in class could be applied to solve the problems. Thus, the problems measured each student's ability to distinguish relevant information from irrelevant information, applying the former to obtain a solution to the problem. In terms of the previously cited comments by Miller and Gordon (1975, 263), the two problems selected represent interdependent cognitive complexity; students are presented with sufficient data to require decision making, but not so much as to overload their cognitive capacity.

In the first problem, the responses to individual items were independent of one another. Thus, a student could demonstrate cognitively complex reasoning in obtaining a correct response to one element of the problem, while responding incorrectly to another part. Therefore, all parts of the problem were weighted equally. Students were required to identify the effect of five accounting errors on each of six accounting elements, a total of thirty responses. However, if the original scaling had been used as an independent variable, its magnitude would have far outweighed the second supplementary problem, which was scored on a scale from zero to three. Therefore, the original score on the first problem was divided by ten to make its relative weighting equal to that of the second problem.

The second problem, however, required a different scoring procedure. The primary element of complex thinking measured by the second problem was the *rationale* for making adjustments to the accounting elements, not the *arithmetic* involved in doing so. Thus, to achieve a maximum score (three) on the problem, students had to compute the correct figures for the balance sheet *and* explain correctly the reason(s) for making the required adjustments. If a student failed to give adequate explanations but correctly computed all the figures for the problem, a score of two was given. In order to compute all figures correctly, students had to apply their knowledge about the basic nature of double-entry accounting. The only balance sheet element which required adjustment not specifically mentioned in the problem was the owner's equity account. Therefore, if students simply adjusted the accounts listed in the text of the problem but failed to adjust the equity accordingly, they were given a score of one. Finally, students who were unable to complete the required arithmetic computations were given a score of zero.

The interitem correlation between the scores on each of the two supplementary problems was 0.76, indicating that approximately 58 percent of the variance in the score of the first problem could be explained by knowing the score of the second problem. According to Nunnally (1978, 245–246), the minimum acceptable correlation for research of this type is 0.7; the two supplementary problems, then, are within the prescribed limit, indicating that both problems measure the same construct.

In addition to interitem reliability, the correlation between scores on the problems and level of cognitive complexity as determined by the PCT was important to the study; that is, some indication that the supplementary problems and the PCT were measuring the same psychological construct (cognitive complexity) was needed. Unlike the interitem correlation for the supplementary problems, however, the correlation between the supplementary problems and PCT score was 0.11, indicating that only about 1 percent of the variance in PCT score is explained by knowing the scores on the supplemental problems.

Given the nature of the application problems, measurement validity is of some concern; that is, the construct validity of the application problems may be so low as to preclude their use as a measure of cognitive complexity. Because of the way responses to the problems were structured and scored, students could have responded in a cognitively complex fashion by random chance; that is, because the questions were given in multiple choice or similar formats, students may have arrived at correct responses through incorrect reasoning. Sufficient information was presented in the application problems to enable students to manipulate figures to obtain correct responses that would have been judged high on the cognitive complexity scale. Thus, students with relatively low PCT

scores could have, by random chance, achieved a relatively high score on the application problems.

As stated previously, the measurement of cognitive complexity is a subjective task, requiring the researcher to examine the cognitive processes of the respondent. Given the format of the application problems, detailed examination of students' cognitive processes was precluded; thus, some question exists as to the validity of the problems for measuring cognitive complexity. In other words, because subjects' detailed methods of solving the application problems could not be observed directly, one cannot be certain that the application problems provide a realistic measure of cognitive complexity. Potential future behavioral accounting research may improve the measurement of cognitive complexity in accountants and accounting students by developing applied measures of cognitive complexity specific to the accounting profession and validating them with practicing accountants. For example, experienced accountants could be made familiar with the general concept of cognitive complexity. Then, drawing on their experience in the profession, they could suggest situations from practice requiring the application of cognitively complex reasoning skills. Working in concert with accounting educators and curriculum designers, appropriate instructional materials could be developed for each level of the accounting curriculum to assess and potentially enhance accounting students' cognitively complex reasoning abilities.

RECOMMENDATIONS FOR FURTHER RESEARCH

The measurement of cognitive complexity in practicing accountants and the inclusion of instructional materials which appeal to the cognitively complex student in the accounting curriculum are important areas for further research. Possible research questions along these lines are the following:

1. What is the exact nature of cognitive complexity as applied to the accounting profession? That is, what types of decisions do practicing accountants face that require cognitively complex decision-making abilities?

2. Is the Paragraph Completion Test (the measure of cognitive complexity used in this study) an appropriate measure of cognitive complexity as applied to accounting? The results of this study indicate that the PCT is a weak measure of cognitively complex behavior as applied to accounting. Therefore, more valid, reliable measures should be developed for the accounting domain.

3. What additional pedagogical techniques can be employed to demonstrate to *first-year* accounting students the importance of abstract reasoning and analytical decision-making skills in the study and practice of accounting? What, if any, role should computer-assisted instruction play in the process?

4. What specific instructional techniques and materials should be incorporated *later* in the accounting curriculum to allow students to exercise and/or develop cognitively complex reasoning and problem solving skills?

In most cases, accounting instructors assign a series of problems and then spend substantial time in class reviewing them and explaining their solution. However, cognitively complex students may prefer to wrestle with problems on their own, seeking out additional help only if they cannot solve the problems independently. This characterization is congruent with the picture of the cognitively complex learner presented by Hunt et al. (1978) since individuals with higher conceptual levels are open to the feelings and opinions of others and weigh multiple alternatives when confronting a problem.

In addition, when problems are discussed in accounting courses, instructors should remind students consistently that the primary objective of accounting is to provide information for making business decisions. Even at the earliest levels of accounting training, instructors should make a concerted effort to discuss potential managerial decisions which are based on the accounting data students are learning to generate; that is, even in fundamentals courses, students should be taught *more* than how to arrive at a given figure or use a specific accounting procedure. Rather, after explaining the technical, procedural side of a topic, accounting instructors should move on to examine the impact of alternative accounting policies and procedures on human behavior and management decision making in organizations.

For example, a common topic covered in first-year financial accounting courses is the valuation of merchandise inventory. Rather than simply explaining the mechanics of FIFO, LIFO, and weighted average inventory valuation, accounting instructors should demonstrate to students the impact each method has on profitability and the resultant change in the perception of a firm's financial position. Rather than being "spoon-fed" by the instructor, students in financial accounting courses (as well as all other courses in the accounting curriculum) should be expected to reason through common problems, explaining their rationale for a given point of view.

Basic case studies, for which no single correct response exists, are an additional pedagogical tool which should be exploited by accounting instructors. Even at the most fundamental levels of accounting, students should be able to construct *and interpret* a conventional income statement and balance sheet. For a case study which would appeal to the cognitively complex learner, the accounting instructor could present comparative income statements and balance sheets for two firms or for two years in a single firm's history, and ask students to respond to questions involving abstract reasoning. For example, students could be asked about the advisability of borrowing money, expanding the firm's physical facilities, holding inventory in the warehouse, and/or issuing additional capital stock. Such questions would not have a single correct response, thus giving the instructor an opportunity to interact with students on a more cognitively complex level. Computers could be used in such a scenario to facilitate calculations and "what-if" situations.

CONCLUSION

As accountants and accounting educators move into the 21st century, they must work in concert to meet the expanding needs of the profession. Identifying ways to measure cognitive complexity and to attract cognitively complex individuals into the profession should be high on the agenda of tasks to complete.

APPENDIX

Problem 1: Effects of Journal Entry Errors

Indicate the effect of the following errors on each of the following accounting elements: (1) Total Revenue, (2) Total Expenses, (3) Net Income, (4) Total Assets, (5) Total Liabilities, and (6) Owner's Equity. Use the following symbols: O = Overstated; U = Understated; NE = No Effect.

a. Recorded collection of an account receivable by debiting Cash and crediting a revenue account.

b. Failed to record depreciation.

c. Purchase of typewriter for cash recorded by a debit to an expense account and credit to Cash.

d. Recorded payment for rent as debit to Salaries Expense.

e. Recorded payment of an account payable by debiting Accounts Payable and crediting an expense account.

Scoring for Problem 1:

As noted in the directions, students were to indicate the effect of each error on six accounting elements. Thus, the problem required thirty responses. The number of correct responses was divided by ten to obtain the score used for analysis (maximum score = 3).

Problem 2: Financial Statement Preparation

Hollywood Scripts is a service-type enterprise in the entertainment field, and its owner, Brad Jones, has only a limited knowledge of accounting. Jones prepared the balance sheet on the following page, which, although arranged satisfactorily, contains certain errors with respect to such concepts as the business entity and asset valuation.

By talking with Jones and inspecting the accounting records, you find the following:

1. One of the notes receivable in the amount of $700 is an IOU which Jones received in a poker game about two years ago. The IOU bears only the initials B.K. and Jones does not know the name or address of the maker.

2. Office furniture includes an antique desk purchased November 29 of the current year at a cost of $2,100. Jones explains that no payment is due for the desk until January and therefore this debt is not included among the liabilities.

3. Also included in the amount for office furniture is a typewriter which cost $525 but is not on hand, because Jones gave it to a son as a birthday present.

4. The "Other assets" of $22,401 represents the total amount of income taxes Jones has paid the federal government over a period of years. Jones believes the income tax law to be unconstitutional, and a friend who attends law school will help Jones recover the taxes paid as soon as he completes his legal education.

5. The land had cost $34,000, but was increased to $70,000 when a friend of Jones offered to pay that much for it if Jones would move the building off the lot.

Instructions:

1. Prepare a corrected balance sheet at November 30, 19__.

2. For each of the five numbered items above, use a separate numbered paragraph to explain whether the treatment followed by Jones is in accord with generally accepted accounting principles.

Hollywood Scripts
Balance Sheet
November 30, 19__

ASSETS		LIABILITIES & OWNER'S EQUITY	
		Liabilities:	
Cash	$ 940		
Notes receivable	2,900		
Accounts receivable	2,465	Notes payable	$ 67,000
Land	70,000	Accounts payable	29,800
Building	54,326		
Office furniture	6,848	Total liab.	$ 96,800
Other assets	22,401		
		Owner's equity:	
		B. Jones, Capital	$ 63,080
Total	$159,880	Total	$159,880

Scoring for Problem 2:

This problem was scored from 0 to 3, depending on the sophistication of the student's analysis. Specifically, the following scale was used:

All figures and all explanations correct	3
All figures correct; no explanations	2
All figures except Capital correct; no explanations	1
One or more figures incorrect	0

For correlation with the PCT score, each student's total score from both problems was used (maximum possible = 6). All problems were taken from Meigs and Meigs (1987).

REFERENCES

Amernic, J. H., and T. H. Beechy. 1984. Accounting Students' Performance and Cognitive Complexity: Some Empirical Evidence. *The Accounting Review* (April): 300–313.

The Big Eight Focus on Systems Integration. 1989. *Computers in Accounting* (February–March): 8.

Bottenberg, E. H. 1969. Instrumental Characteristics and Validity of the Paragraph Completion Test (PCT) as a Measure of Integrative Capacity. *Psychological Reports* (February): 437–438.

Carey, J. L. 1965. *The CPA Plans for the Future.* AICPA.

Gardiner, G. S., and H. M. Schroder. 1972. Reliability and Validity of the Paragraph Completion Test: Theoretical and Empirical Notes. *Psychological Reports* (August): 959–962.

Hunt, D. E. 1971. *Matching Models in Education: The Coordination of Teaching Models with Student Characteristics.* The Ontario Institute for Studies in Education.

———, L. F. Butler, J. E. Noy, and M. E. Rosser. 1978. *Assessing Conceptual Level by the Paragraph Completion Method.* The Ontario Institute for Studies in Education.

Kemp, J. E. 1977. *Instructional Design: A Plan for Unit and Course Development.* Fearon-Pitman.

Meigs, W. B., and R. F. Meigs. 1987. *Financial Accounting.* McGraw-Hill Book Company.

Miller, D., and L. A. Gordon. 1975. Conceptual Levels and the Design of Accounting Information Systems. *Decision Sciences* (April): 259–269.

Nunnally, J. C. 1978. *Psychometric Theory.* McGraw-Hill Book Company.

Sathe, V. 1982. *Controller Involvement in Management.* Prentice-Hall, Inc.

Schneider, W. B. 1988. *Certified Public Accountants: A Profession in Crisis.* Unpublished doctoral dissertation. The Claremont Graduate School.

Schroder, H., and P. Suedfeld. 1971. *Personality Theory and Information Processing.* Ronald.

Seidler, L. J. 1985. Adding Up the Change in Accounting. *The CPA Journal* (July): 12–16.

Stallman, J. C. 1974. Inquiry in the Accounting Classroom, in James Don Edwards, ed. *Accounting Education: Problems and Prospects.* American Accounting Association: 203–210.

Weigle, C. B., C. R. Christensen, and J. W. Rosenblum. 1972. *Prelude Corporation.* President and Fellows of Harvard College.

Willingham, J. J., I. E. McNeill, and E. F. Collins. 1974. Learning Theories and Accounting, in James Don Edwards, ed. *Accounting Education: Problems and Prospects.* American Accounting Association: 173–180.

Performance of Students in Introductory Accounting Courses: A Case Study

Can Simga Mugan and
Gulnur Muradoglu Sengul

As a developing country, Turkey witnesses an increasing number of students enrolling in business administration programs in all universities. During the last five years, the number of business schools increased from 14 to 19, which brought an increase of 20 percent in the number of business majors. The present study concentrates on the business school of the only private university in Turkey. Bilkent University was established in 1986 with emphasis on engineering and business programs. Students are admitted to the program based on their performance in the university entrance examination which is similar to the ACT in the United States. Another unique aspect of the program is that the curriculum is English in a country where the native language is Turkish.

A survey of literature on the determinants of performance of accounting students reveals several opinions. The results of earlier studies suggest that past grades and grade point averages are positively associated with student performance (Eckel and Johnson 1983; Hicks and Richardson1984; Ingram and Petersen 1987). In more recent studies, researchers used regression models to explain the variation in student performance in the first- and second-level accounting courses (Eskew and Faley 1988; Doran, Bouillon, and Smith 1991; Booker 1991). The findings of these studies demonstrate the importance of factors such as academic aptitude, cumulative college grade point average, and having had bookkeeping courses in high school in addition to the factors identified in the earlier studies.

A few studies addressed the gender issue as well. Previous research in this area tried to determine whether the female students outperform males, and they also examined the association between the sex of the instructor and the sex of the student (Mutchler, Turner, and Williams 1987; Lipe 1989; Tyson 1989). The authors tend to suggest that female students perform better than males in female instructed classes and vice versa. However, the results are not conclusive.

The study presented in this paper attempts to validate the determinants of student success in the first and second semesters of introductory accounting courses in terms of overall performance and background of the students.

Present study differs from the previous ones in the following aspects: Most of previous research mentioned earlier report results obtained in the United States — a developed country and at universities where the medium of instruction is the native language. This paper presents a case study conducted at a university in a developing country where the medium of instruction is not the native language.

If the results of this case study are consistent with the results of the previous research, then it may serve to confirm universal traits in determining success in introductory accounting courses. Furthermore, it may be of general interest to similar universities and to foreign student admission departments of the universities in the United States.

DETAILS OF THE STUDY

This study was conducted at Bilkent University where the medium of instruction is English. Therefore, all students are required to take an English placement test before they register. Based on their English placement test scores, they either enroll in first-year courses or go to the preparatory language school. Upon successful completion of the language school, the students are permitted to register in the regular program. Presently, there are around 8000 students in the university (up 3000 from last year). The number of students registered in the Faculty of Business Administration is around 400. Course requirements of the business program are similar to those of most other business school programs (presented in the Appendix).

At Bilkent University, Accounting Principles I and II are taught during the sophomore year in fully coordinated sections. Both courses are taught in small lecture sections ranging from 20 to 40 students meeting for three hours a week. Each section is instructed either by a permanent or an adjunct faculty member.

Can Simga Mugan and Gulnur Muradoglu Sengul are faculty members at Bilkent University, Turkey.

All business and economics majors are required to take both principles courses. Occasionally, students from other departments, especially from industrial engineering, take the courses as electives. Three examinations including the final are given in each class during the semester. Approximately 90 percent of the semester points are derived from free response problems, and 10 percent from homework assignments. During the first semester the first 10 chapters, and during the second semester chapters 13-20 of *Accounting for Business Decisions* by Meigs and Meigs (1990) are covered.

Data for this study were obtained from the files of 140 business majors who have taken both principles courses. Sixteen of those students are excluded from the study because of missing information. Students from other departments are excluded from the study in an attempt to homogenize the sample. No attempt was made to collect data on work habits of the students, or to establish the association between the sex of the student and the instructor. Descriptive statistics relating to the students are presented in Table 1.

Despite the increasing number of female students in business programs in recent years, the total number of female students is still less than the number of male students. The sample under study consists of 65 percent male and 35 percent female students.

Although exploration of the gender issue is not within the scope of this paper, it will be appropriate to include some information about the performance differences between the two sexes: General academic performance of female students measured by cumulative grade point average is better than that of the male students. Tests of the means show that female students perform significantly ($p < .01$) better in both accounting courses, and they also have significantly ($p < .01$) higher grade point averages than males. This finding supports the results of an earlier study (Tyson 1989). A test of analytical abilities measured by the grade received in calculus exhibits similar findings. However, their university entrance exam scores are not significantly different.

METHOD

This study attempts to validate the determinants of student performance in introductory accounting courses. Performance in introductory courses is hypothesized to be related to the overall performance and the analytical background of the student.

It is reasonable to assume that overall performance is a reflection of the general attitude and work habits of the student. Therefore, in this study overall performance is used as an independent vari-

TABLE 1
Profile of Sample Students

Gender	Male	81	Female	43

Performance in Accounting Courses:

Principles I:

Grade range:		Frequency	%
	$0 \geq 1$	13	10.5
	$1 \geq 2$	32	25.8
	$2 \geq 3$	43	34.7
	$3 \geq 4$	36	29.0
average (out of 4)	2.56 (st.dev.0.96)		

Principles II:

Grade range:		Frequency	%
	$0 \geq 1$	19	15.3
	$1 \geq 2$	41	33.1
	$2 \geq 3$	43	34.7
	$3 \geq 4$	21	16.9
average	2.20 (1.06)		

General Academic Performance:

GPA I (grade point average in the semester when the first accounting course is taken)

Grade range:		Frequency	%
	$0 \geq 1$	1	0.8
	$1 \geq 2$	24	19.3
	$2 \geq 3$	72	58.1
	$3 \geq 4$	27	21.8
average	2.51 (0.67)		

GPA II (grade point average in the semester when the second accounting course is taken)

Grade range:		Frequency	%
	$0 \geq 1$	7	5.6
	$1 \geq 2$	48	38.7
	$2 \geq 3$	52	41.9
	$3 \geq 4$	17	13.7
average	2.16 (0.78)		

CGPA (cumulative GPA at graduation or as of the last semester)

Grade range:		Frequency	%
	$0 \geq 1$	0	5.6
	$1 \geq 2$	16	38.7
	$2 \geq 3$	86	41.9
	$3 \geq 4$	22	13.7
average	2.50 (0.52)		

Analytical Background Variables:

Calculus I

Grade range:		Frequency	%
	$0 \geq 1$	17	13.7
	$1 \geq 2$	32	25.8
	$2 \geq 3$	31	25.0
	$3 \geq 4$	44	35.5
average	2.52 (1.16)		

University Entrance Examination Score (maximum points 700)

Range:		Frequency	%
	<400	10	8.1
	400-450	85	68.5
	450-500	27	21.8
	500 +	2	1.6
average	430.74 (28.33)		

able to explain success in introductory accounting courses. Overall performance of the student is measured by using three variables:

(1) his\her GPA during the semester the student took the first principles course (MAN 211) (C5),

(2) his\her GPA during the semester the student took the second principles course (MAN 212) (C6), and

(3) his\her cumulative GPA at graduation (C9)

The analytical background of the student is designated to be an appropriate preparation for an introductory accounting course. The university entrance examination in Turkey mainly measures the analytic abilities of the student and hence is included as the first (C8) and calculus (MATH101) grade obtained at the freshman level is included as the second background variable (C10) to reflect analytical background. Furthermore, MAN211 grade is assumed to be a predictor of MAN212 and is used as the third background variable (C3).

Multiple regression models are employed to test the validity of the hypothesized relation between the grades received in introductory courses in accounting and overall performance and analytical background variables. The general formulation and specification of the regression models are presented below in Table 2.

RESULTS

The results of models 1 and 2 are presented in Table 3. The regression results reveal that the hypothesized independent variables explain a significant portion of the variation of student performance in MAN211 ($R^2 = 0.6$: $p < .01$), and MAN212 ($R^2 = 0.7$: $p < 0.01$).

The two significant variables ($p < 0.01$) that are positively associated with student performance in MAN211 (C3) are the student's GPA during the semester he/she is enrolled in MAN211 (C5) and the university entrance examination score (C8). Student performance in MAN212 (C4) is significantly ($p < 0.01$) related to student grade in MAN211 (C3), and student GPA during the semester the student is enrolled in MAN212 (C6).

CONCLUSION

The findings of this study support the results of previous research conducted in developed countries. In a developing country and in an institution where the medium of instruction is a foreign language, academic performance in introductory accounting courses is found to be a function of over-

---

TABLE 2
General Formulation and Specification of Regression Models

Model 1: Introduction to Accounting I (MAN211)
$$C3_i = b_0 + b_1 C5_i + b_2 C6_i + b_3 C8_i + b_4 C9_i + b_5 C10_i$$

Model 2: Introduction to Accounting II (MAN212)
$$C4_i = b_0 + b_1 C3_i + b_2 C5_i + b_3 C6_i + b_4 C8_i + b_5 C9_i + b_6 C10_i$$

Dependent Variables

C3 = student grade in MAN211
C4 = student grade in MAN212
Range = 0-4 (A - F)

Independent Variables

Academic performance:
C5 = student GPA during the semester the student was enrolled in MAN211
C6 = student GPA during the semester the student was enrolled in MAN212
C9 = cumulative GPA of the student at graduation
Range = 0-4

Background of the student:
C8 = University entrance examination score
range = 340 - 550
C10 = student grade in MATH101
Range = 0-4 (A - F)

---

all academic performance and general aptitude, suggesting universal support for the relevance of those variables.

The results of this study suggest that student performance in both introductory accounting courses depends on the overall success\effort of the student, which is measured by the student GPA during the semester the student is enrolled in the course. This implies that student performance in introductory accounting courses can be improved by increasing the average hours devoted to the course. Thus instructors are encouraged to increase homework assignments and classroom participation. Since at Bilkent University both courses are fully coordinated, we do not have a chance to test the effect of the homework assignments and classroom participation, but further research should emphasize that.

The significant analytical background variable for the first principles course is the university entrance exam score; and in the second principles course student performance in the first principles course becomes the significant variable. Thus, based on the findings, one can state that benefits of high university entrance examination score (i.e., high general aptitude) lasts only for one semester. The results are similar to those of Doran et al. (1991) where the benefits of early exposure to accounting

TABLE 3
Regression Results

Model 1: Dependent Variable = C3 (first accounting grade)

Independent Significance Variables	Coefficient	St.Deviation of Coefficient	T value	$p < ..$
	− 2.20	0.86	− 2.56	
C5	0.97	0.14	6.80	0.0005
C6	0.19	0.12	1.59	NS
C8	0.01	0.002	2.67	0.005
C9	− 0.22	0.22	− 1.03	NS
C10	0.05	0.06	0.82	NS

Adj. R^2 = 0.59
F = 34.78
$p < 0.0001$

Model 2: Dependent variable = C4 (second accounting grade)

Independent Significance Variables	Coefficient	St.Deviation of Coefficient	T value	$p < ..$
	− 1.56	0.84	− 1.85	
C3	0.23	0.09	2.49	0.005
C5	− 0.19	0.16	− 1.18	NS
C6	1.06	0.11	9.30	0.001
C8	0.003	0.002	1.75	NS
C9	− 0.08	0.021	− 0.37	NS
C10	0.03	0.06	0.43	NS

Adj. R^2 = 0.68
F = 45.29
$p < 0.0001$

does not last long. Advisers are encouraged to direct students with low performance in introductory courses to majors other than accounting. Instructors are also encouraged to inform students with low performance during the first semester to consider their position after the first examination and persuade them to put forth more effort or withdraw from the course.

Students from other departments, especially engineering, choose accounting courses as electives because of the increasing demand to employ those who are exposed to accounting systems. Therefore, advisers are encouraged to examine academic measures in their counseling services and to encourage only the students with above-average GPAs to enroll in accounting courses as electives.

APPENDIX

Curriculum:

	Courses	Credit Hours
First Semester:	Calculus I	4
	Sociology	3
	English I	3
	History of Civilization I	3
	Economics I	3
Second Semester:	Calculus II	4
	Psychology	3
	English II	3
	History of Civilization II	3
	Economics II	3
Third Semester:	Introduction to Business	3
	Linear Algebra	3
	Principles of Accounting I	3
	Computers & Info. Processing I	3
	Probability	3
Fourth Semester:	Organizational Behavior	3
	Principles of Accounting II	3
	Computers & Info. Processing II	3
	Decision Sciences	3
	Statistics	3
Fifth Semester:	Corporate Finance	3
	Marketing	3
	Production Management	3
	Business Law	3
	Organization Theory	3
Sixth Semester:	Business Forecasting	3
	Cost Accounting	3
	Money and Banking	3
	Marketing Strategy	3
	Production Planning, Scheduling and Control	3
Seventh Semester:	Business Communication	0
	Managerial Economics	3
	International Business	3
	3 Electives	
Eighth Semester:	Business Policy	3
	Investment Analysis	3
	3 Electives	

REFERENCES

Booker, Q. 1991. A Case Study of the Relationship betweenUndergraduate Black Accounting Majors' ACT Scores and Their Intermediate Accounting Performance. *Issues in Accounting Education* (Spring): 66–74.

Doran, B. M., M. L. Bouillon, and C. G. Smith. 1991. Determinants of Student Performance in Accounting Principles I and II. *Issues in Accounting Education* (Spring): 74–84.

Eckel, N., and W. A. Johnson. 1983. A Model for Screening and Classifying Potential Accounting Majors. *Journal of Accounting Education* (Fall): 57–65.

Eskew, R. K., and R. H. Faley. 1988. Some Determinants of Student Performance in the First-Level Financial Accounting Courses. *The Accounting Review* (January): 137–147.

Hicks, D. W., and F. M. Richardson. 1984. Predicting Early Success in Intermediate Accounting: The Influence of Entry Examinations and GPA. *Issues in Accounting Education* (Spring): 61–67.

Ingram, R. W., and R. J. Petersen. 1987. An Evaluation of AICPA Tests for Predicting the Performance of Accounting Majors. *The Accounting Review* (January): 215–223.

Lipe, M. G. 1989. Further Evidence on the Performance of Female Versus Male Accounting Students. *Issues in Accounting Education* (Spring): 144–153.

Meigs, R. F., and W. B. Meigs. 1990. *Accounting: Basis for Business Decisions*, 8th Edition. McGraw-Hill.

Mutchler, J. F., J. H. Turner, and D. D. Williams. 1987. The Performance of Female Versus Male Accounting Students. *Issues in Accounting Education* (Spring): 103–111.

Tyson, T. 1989. Grade Performance in Introductory Accounting Courses: Why Female Students Outperform Males. *Issues in Accounting Education* (Spring): 153–160.

Accounting Students' Performance Evaluation: Does the Examination Format Matter?

Mahmoud M. Nourayi

Accounting faculty are commonly concerned with the philosophical, practical, and behavioral issues relevant to preparation of examinations. First, educators do not agree, philosophically, as to the *primary* objectives of the testing process. Some believe that examinations are teaching devices and an additional step in the learning process. Others view examinations as performance measurement instruments. Second, educators have to make trade-offs due to facilities/exam scheduling constraints and the ripple effect of time limitation on the structure and the length of examinations. Furthermore, the grading time requirements cause concern for meeting the grade submission deadlines. The grading time is especially relevant for larger classes. Finally, the examiners' decisions about the topics included in an exam, extent of topical coverage, sequencing questions, and form of questions are subjective ones.

The purpose of this study is to examine this last issue regarding the effect of examination formats on students' performance. I will maintain that the primary purpose of the testing process is performance evaluation, where the individuals are given the opportunity to differentiate themselves on the basis of their abilities and mastery of an academic subject, as a part of a more substantial educational program. By no means does this view of the testing preclude students from enhancing their knowledge by recognizing their own deficiencies and shortcomings.

To ensure that the time allotted is sufficient for administering and grading examinations, one may limit exam coverage by reducing the number of questions and problems, thereby reducing the written answers and solutions required. The "limited coverage" of the subject matter seems incompatible with both views of the examination process. An alternative to the "limited coverage exam" is an exam with a number of predetermined answers. The students choose an answer for each question with no requirement to demonstrate the process of arriving at such an answer. Consequently, the grading process is not as time consuming since the choice process is not evaluated and only the final choice is classified as either correct or incorrect.

BACKGROUND AND PREVIOUS STUDIES

Previous studies have evaluated the effect of sequencing of multiple choice questions on student performance. Paretta and Chadwick (1975) found that sequencing examination questions in order of difficulty level of questions affected student performance while Howe and Baldwin (1983) did not observe such an effect. Baldwin and Howard (1983) ordered examination questions by topic presentation order and found a significant interaction effect of sequencing and student ability on the test scores. Gruber (1987) presented questions in the reverse order of presentations and observed a positive effect on the test scores across all students.

On March 16, 1987, the AICPA Board of Examiners, in an Exposure Draft entitled *Proposed Changes in the Uniform CPA Examination*, suggested in part that the CPA examination consist of an all-objective question format. The Board indicated that the change in the format, together with other changes, enhance the content coverage, reduce examination time, provide more consistent coverage, and increase grading accuracy.[1] Advocates of the all-objective test approach believe the method is both efficient and adequate in the evaluation process. Frakes and Lathen (1985) concluded, "there were no significant differences in scores on multiple-choice versus problem examinations." Sedaghat and Martin (1988) surveyed 400 faculty members regarding proposed changes by the AICPA Board of Examiners. Their results indicated "of the 398 faculty members responding, only 48 members supported an all-objective examination." Martin and Sedaghat's (1990) survey of 520 practitioners also revealed that about 90 percent of respondents were opposed to an all-objective question format.

---

[1]On April 28, 1989, the Board of Directors of the National Association of State Boards of Accountancy (NASBA) adopted changes that basically increase the objective questions on the uniform CPA examination to 80 percent and reducing the examination time from 19 1/2 to 16 hours. New types of "objective" questions appeared on each section of the May 1992 examination.

Mahmoud M. Nourayi is an Associate Professor at Loyola Marymount University.

Many studies have indicated that accountants posses distinctive personality characteristics (Belkaoui 1989). Holland (1973) identifies public accountants as the "investigative type" who are precise, unassuming and rational. Holland's theory, in the field of vocational psychology, has been used to examine the relationship between accountants' personality type and commitment to work (Aranya, Meir, and Bari-Ilan 1978; Aranya, Barak, and Amernic 1981; Aranya and Wheeler 1986).

Theory of psychological type, advanced by Carl Jung (1923), provided the foundation for Kolb's Learning Style Inventory (LSI) that was developed to measure the theory posited by his experiential learning model (Kolb 1974). Myers-Briggs Type Indicator (MBTI), suggested as a career counseling tool (Jacoby 1981; Huber 1983), is also based on Jung's theory.

Students' learning styles or personality types, together with the examination format, may impact performance evaluation. LSI studies classify the majority of accounting students as "Convergers" (Baldwin and Reckers 1984; Baker, Simon, and Bazel 1986; Brown and Burke 1987; Collins and Milliron 1987). Convergers are individuals with a preference for practical application of ideas, who do best in conventional intelligence tests where there is a *single correct solution* to a problem, and prefer dealing with technical tasks.

Researchers using MBTI have concluded that the accounting profession has generally attracted individuals who are factual with preference for objectivity (Myers 1980; Jacoby 1981).

RESEARCH DESIGN AND DATA COLLECTION

This study is based on the final examination scores earned by 169 students in eight different classes and over three semesters. The sample consists of 99 junior-level accounting majors, in the Cost Accounting Course, and 70 sophomore business majors, taking their Managerial Accounting Core Course. Examinations, prepared by the same instructor, were designed to include both multiple choice and essay/problem type questions. One-half of possible points were equally divided among 30 multiple choice questions. The other half of the credit was distributed among three problems and one essay question.

In order to prevent information leakage, the analyses of this study were limited to the final examination scores for the accounting/nonaccounting groups. Even though the tests given the accounting (juniors) and nonaccounting (sophomores) students were not the same, the similarity in the subject matters, instructional approach, type of questions, grading policies, and length of examinations should allow some intergroup comparison in this study.

In order to examine the effect of personalty differences, an MBTI questionnaire was used to identify students' personality types. Students were grouped based on four bipolar dimensions, i.e., Extraversion (E)/ Introversion (I), Sensing (S)/ Intuition (N), Thinking (T)/ Feeling (F) and Judging (J)/ Perceptive (P).

Indicator questions deal with the way individuals like to look at things and the way they make decisions. Figure 1 shows what each preference signifies.

FIGURE 1
Myers-Briggs Type Indicator

EXTROVERSION
Relate more easily to the outer world of people and things than to the inner world of ideas.

SENSING
Rather work with known facts than look for possibilities and relationships.

THINKING
Judgment more based on impersonal analysis and logic than personal vales.

JUDGING
Like a planned, decided, orderly way of life better than a flexible, spontaneous way.

INTROVERSION
Relate more easily to the inner world of ideas than to the outer world of people and things.

INTUITION
Rather look for possibilities and relationships than work with known facts.

FEELING
Judgment more based on personal values than on impersonal analysis and logic.

PERCEPTIVE
Like a flexible, spontaneous way of life better than a planned, decided, orderly way.

ANALYSIS AND RESULTS

To examine the importance of the question format in the evaluation process, the analysis of variance (ANOVA) techniques and descriptive statistics are used in this research. First, the test scores for different question formats will be examined. Initial analysis will be done for total sample and then for two sets of analyses, accounting and nonaccounting, will be completed. Next, the effect of the test format on the performance of students with different personality types will be studied. Table 1 shows the sample distribution.

The ANOVA results of the all-students sample, Table 2, did not reveal any significant difference, $F = 0.25$, in the mean test scores for answers/solutions and multiple choice answers.

The analysis of variance, for the two different test formats, Table 3, disclosed that accounting (cost) students scored higher in both multiple choice and essay/problem parts. The results were statistically significant, at 95 percent confidence interval, for multiple choice and essay/problem based on the F-statistics of 148.10 and 9.16, respectively. The analysis of accounting/nonaccounting students' test scores

TABLE 1
Sample of Distribution

Type	All Students		Non-Accounting		Accounting	
	No.	%	No.	%	No.	%
Introversion	33	19.5	8	11.4	25	25.3
Extroversion	119	70.4	56	80.0	63	63.6
Intro/Extro*	17	10.1	6	8.6	11	11.1
Total	169	100.0%	70	100.0%	99	100.0%
Intuition	53	31.4	24	34.3	29	29.3
Sensing	93	55.0	32	45.7	61	61.6
Intuit/Sens*	23	13.6	14	20.0	9	9.1
Total	169	100.0%	70	100.0%	99	100.0%
Feeling	76	45.0	36	51.4	40	40.4
Thinking	79	46.7	30	42.9	49	49.5
Feel/Think*	14	8.3	4	5.7	10	10.1
Total	169	100.0%	70	100.0%	99	100.0%
Perceptive	24	14.2	16	22.9	8	8.1
Judging	140	82.8	52	74.3	88	88.9
Percept/Judge*	5	3.0	2	2.8	3	3.0
Total	169	100.0%	70	100.0%	99	100.0%

*Balanced individuals with no marked preference for either ends of the scale.

TABLE 2
Analysis of Variance of Students' Scores by Test Format

Source	DF	SS	MS	F
Test	1	93	93	0.25
Error	336	125317	373	
Total	337	125410		

Level		N	Mean	STDEV
Essay/Problem		169	59.79	21.09
Multiple Choice		169	58.74	17.36
Pooled STDEV				19.31

"Test" is the test format variable.

TABLE 3
Analysis of Variance of Test Scores by Student Groups

Source	Multiple Choice				Essay/Problem			
	DF	SS	MS	F	DF	SS	MS	F
Major	1	23794	23794	148.10	1	3884	3884	9.16
Error	167	26830	161		167	70808	424	
Total	168	50625			168	74692		
Level	**N**	**Mean**	**STDEV**		**N**	**Mean**	**STDEV**	
Accounting	99	68.72	11.88		99	63.82	19.62	
Nonaccounting	70	44.63	13.73		70	54.09	21.89	
Pooled STDEV			12.68				20.59	

demonstrated significant differences, for both student groups, between the mean scores of multiple choice and essay/problem. Table 4 shows F-statistics of 9.37 for the nonaccounting group and 4.52 for the accounting group. These results are significant at 95 percent confidence interval. The fact that nonaccounting students' mean scores on the essay/problem questions were higher than that for the multiple choice and the opposite for accounting students was true explains the earlier results of Table 2.

To compare the performance of students based on their overall abilities in the course, students were divided into three categories, above average, average, and below average. The grouping was based on the total points earned in the course.[2] Mean test scores for each format/category are shown in Table

[2]One student, in the nonaccounting group, was omitted randomly in order to achieve equal number of observations in each category, desired for analysis of variance.

TABLE 4
Analysis of Variance of Test Scores by Test Formats & Student Groups

Source	Nonaccounting Students				Accounting Students			
	DF	SS	MS	F	DF	SS	MS	F
Test	1	3130	3130	9.37	1	1188	1188	4.52
Error	138	46088	334		196	51551	263	
Total	139	49218			197	52739		
Level		**N**	**Mean**	**STDEV**		**N**	**Mean**	**STDEV**
Essay/Problem		70	54.09	21.89		99	63.82	19.62
Multiple Choice		70	44.63	13.73		99	68.72	11.88
Pooled STDEV				18.27				16.22

"Test" is the test format variable.

TABLE 5
Mean Score by Student Categories and Test Formats

Students Group: Category	Test Format	
	Multiple Choice	Essay/Problem
A. Nonaccounting Students		
Above Average	54.70	73.04
Average	42.09	57.17
Below Average	37.00	33.39
Group/Format Mean	44.63	54.09
B. Accounting Students		
Above Average	76.79	78.76
Average	67.36	65.15
Below Average	62.00	47.55
Group/Format Mean	68.72	63.82
C. All Students		
Above Average	69.37	77.21
Average	59.20	61.13
Below Average	47.86	40.55
Group/Format Mean	58.74	59.79

FIGURE 2
Student Group Means by Category and Test Format as a Percentage of Group/Format Mean

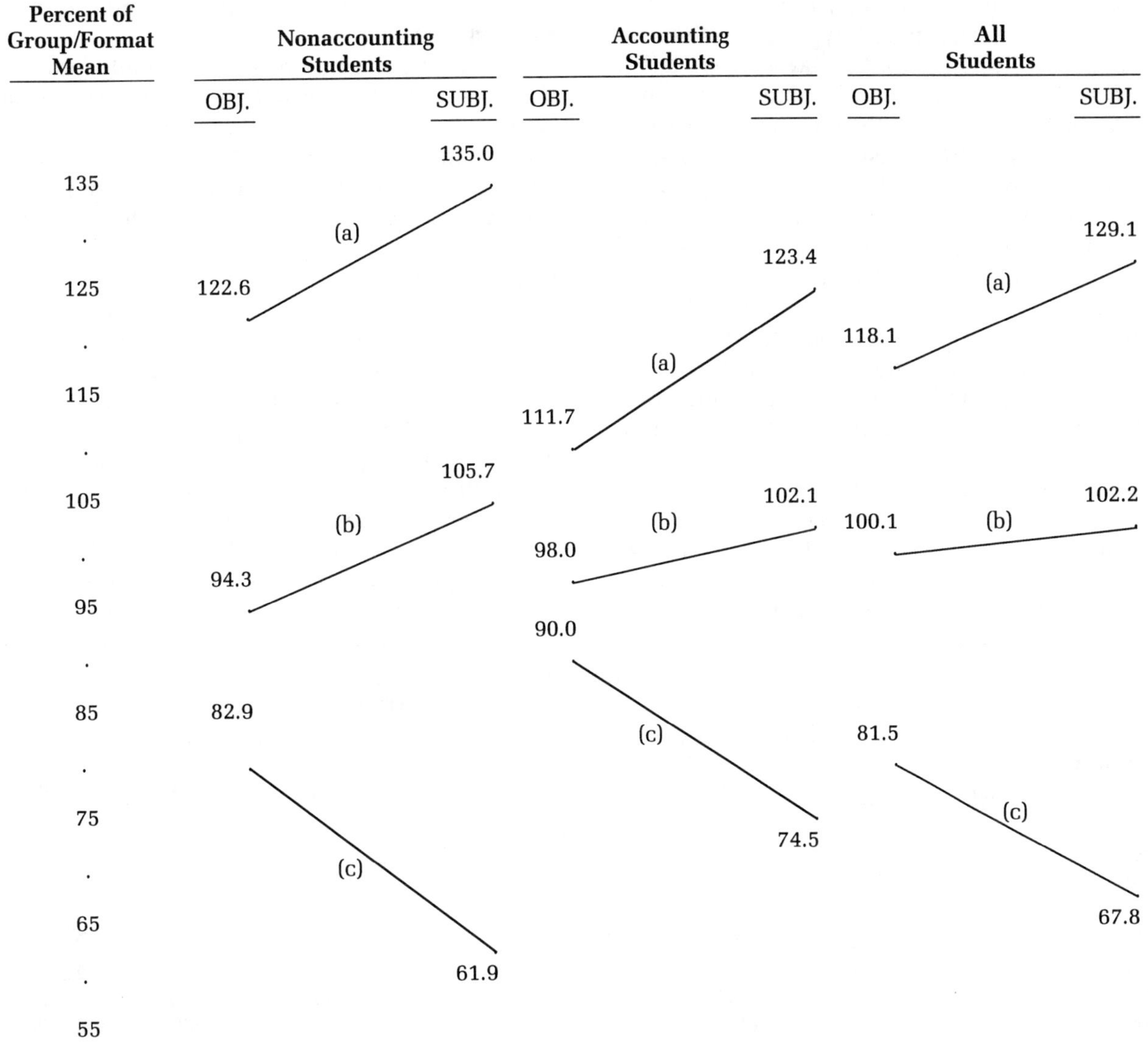

Percent of Group/Format Mean	Nonaccounting Students		Accounting Students		All Students	
	OBJ.	SUBJ.	OBJ.	SUBJ.	OBJ.	SUBJ.

Chart data points:
- Nonaccounting: (a) 122.6 → 135.0; (b) 94.3 → 105.7; (c) 82.9 → 61.9
- Accounting: (a) 111.7 → 123.4; (b) 98.0 → 102.1; (c) 90.0 → 74.5
- All: (a) 118.1 → 129.1; (b) 100.1 → 102.2; (c) 81.5 → 67.8

Vertical axis: 135, 125, 115, 105, 95, 85, 75, 65, 55

"OBJ." is the Multiple Choice format and "SUBJ." is the Essay/Problem format.
(a) Above Average, (b) Average, (c) Below Average.

5. The course total points are made up of class credit (e.g., assignment, participation, and projects, as well as credit for quizzes and examinations).

The effect of test formats on the average students' test scores was not as large as the other groups. It is clear that, in both nonaccounting and accounting groups, only below-average students benefited from the multiple choice format and above-average students differentiated themselves, more effectively, with their answers to essay/problem questions. The mean score of student categories for each type of question format as a percentage of the format/group mean was computed. The results were plotted. Figure 2 shows that the essay/problem testing format provides a much wider range for measuring students' performance.

The extrovert individuals find their energies externally and desire interaction with people and environment. On the other hand, concentration and pursuing the solitary activity intensively seem to be a preferred approach for an introvert. Written examinations require concentration and pursuit of concepts and, unlike group projects or the work environment, do not allow for individuals' interaction. Therefore, the setting of a written test is much preferred by the introverts.

The analysis of the data for introvert/extrovert partitioning, Table 6, indicated superior performance by introverts, on both type of questions, in the nonaccounting group. Similar analysis failed to differentiate performance of accounting students.

As shown in Table 6, the scores for extroverts and introverts in the nonaccounting group were different, at 5 percent significance level, regardless of the type of question, based on F-statistic 2.89 and 2.94 for the multiple choice and the essay/problem questions, respectively.

An individual's approach in collecting information may be reflected on one's test score. For individuals with a preference for factual information (sensing), the written accounting examination setting may be more desirable than for intuitive individuals who are more imaginative and innovative and look for possibilities, meaning, and relationship in the data and events.

The results of test score analysis for sensing/intuitive dimension are shown in Table 7. As expected, in both accounting/nonaccounting groups,

sensing individuals performed better than intuitive students in dealing with multiple choice questions. The difference was significant, at 95 percent confidence interval, for the accounting group based on F-statistic 2.62.

Open-ended essay questions should provide intuitive students with an opportunity to use their comparative advantage in theoretical work. Table 7 shows the mean score of intuitive students in the accounting group, though not statistically significant, was higher than sensing students. This condition did not hold for the nonaccounting group, that is, sensing students had a higher mean (57.88) on the essay/problem part of the examination than the intuitive students with the mean score of 47.29.

Analysis of students' scores, considering individuals' decision-making modes, did not reveal any significant difference in the performance of thinking and feeling types. This is true for either group, accounting or nonaccounting, and for either examination format. The results are presented in Table 8. It should be pointed out that rationality of the decision process is not the issue in question, for both types of decision-making modes are rational.

TABLE 6
Analysis of Variance of Test Scores for Introvert/Extrovert by Test Formats

Multiple Choice	Nonaccounting Students				Accounting Students			
Source	DF	SS	MS	F	DF	SS	MS	F
Type	2	1033	517	2.89*	2	157	79	0.55
Error	67	11977	179		96	13663	142	
Total	69	13010			98	13820		

Level		N	Mean	STDEV		N	Mean	STDEV
Introvert		8	55.12	20.89		25	63.82	19.62
Balanced		6	45.67	18.57		11	72.27	14.55
Extrovert		56	43.02	11.44		63	68.33	12.00
Pooled STDEV				13.37				11.93

Essay/Problem								
Source	DF	SS	MS	F	DF	SS	MS	F
Type	2	2672	1336	2.94*	2	72	36	0.09
Error	67	30405	454		96	37659	392	
Total	69	33077			98	37731		

Level		N	Mean	STDEV		N	Mean	STDEV
Introvert		8	65.87	27.96		25	65.12	19.62
Balanced		6	67.17	12.94		11	64.45	14.45
Extrovert		56	51.00	20.93		63	63.19	20.61
Pooled STDEV				21.30				19.81

"Type" is the variable for personality indicator.
* Significant at 5 percent level.

TABLE 7
Analysis of Variance of Test Scores for Intuitive/Sensing by Test Formats

Multiple Choice Source	Nonaccounting Students				Accounting Students			
	DF	SS	MS	F	DF	SS	MS	F
Type	2	88	44	0.23	2	716	358	2.62*
Error	67	12922	193		96	13104	137	
Total	69	13010			98	13820		
Level		**N**	**Mean**	**STDEV**		**N**	**Mean**	**STDEV**
Intuitive		24	43.42	13.87		29	64.86	12.51
Balanced		14	46.57	9.04		9	67.11	13.94
Sensing		32	44.69	15.48		61	70.79	10.93
Pooled STDEV				13.89				11.68
Essay/Problem Source	DF	SS	MS	F	DF	SS	MS	F
Type	2	1692	846	1.81	2	413	207	0.53
Error	67	31385	468		96	37318	389	
Total	69	33077			98	37731		
Level		**N**	**Mean**	**STDEV**		**N**	**Mean**	**STDEV**
Intuitive		24	47.29	24.82		29	63.90	16.74
Balanced		14	57.07	17.28		9	70.11	20.91
Sensing		32	57.88	20.74		61	62.85	20.80
Pooled STDEV				21.64				19.72

"Type" is the variable for personality indicator.
* Significant at 5 percent level.

The only difference is that there is a greater reliance on interpersonal and social relationships by the feeling types and trust in the mind's abilities by the thinking types. The results are somewhat surprising because the thinking types were expected to demonstrate some comparative advantage in an examination setting.

The final set of analysis of scores was completed to determine the effect of life style on test score. The Judging individuals, with a systematic and decisive approach, were compared to the Perceptive types with a spontaneous and flexible manner who allow for impulse and are adaptive to life's events.

The results are presented in Table 9. These results indicate that one's life style preference has no bearing on his /her performance on an accounting examination. These results should be interpreted with caution however because of a disproportionately large number of Perceptive types in the business student population.

CONCLUSION AND DISCUSSION

The findings of this study justify the concerns of accounting faculty and practitioners regarding the proposed changes in the uniform CPA examination format (Sedaghat and Martin 1988; Martin and Sedaghat 1990). The analyses of this research indicate that the essay/problem question format is a finer measure of student performance than the multiple choice question format. More importantly, the multiple choice format penalizes the above-average and, to a lesser degree, average students and rewards the below-average students. For the below-average accounting major, multiple choice scores were higher than their essay/problem scores and had a dominating effect on the averages. Therefore, an evaluation process based solely on a set of all-objective questions may be distorted and unfair.

The final exam scores may be affected by other factors such as final examination scheduling and preparation for other examinations given during

TABLE 8
Analysis of Variance of Test Scores for Feeling/Thinking by Test Formats

Multiple Choice	Nonaccounting Students				Accounting Students			
Source	DF	SS	MS	F	DF	SS	MS	F
Type	2	18	9	0.05	2	85	43	0.30
Error	67	12992	194		96	13735	143	
Total	69	13010			98	13820		
Level		N	Mean	STDEV		N	Mean	STDEV
Feeling		36	44.94	15.04		40	68.15	11.95
Balanced		4	42.75	11.79		10	71.40	14.77
Thinking		30	44.50	12.68		49	68.63	11.36
Pooled STDEV				13.93				11.96

Essay/Problem								
Source	DF	SS	MS	F	DF	SS	MS	F
Type	2	757	379	0.78	2	54	27	0.07
Error	67	32320	482		96	37677	392	
Total	69	33077			98	37731		
Level		N	Mean	STDEV		N	Mean	STDEV
Feeling		36	56.50	22.29		40	63.08	18.56
Balanced		4	60.00	20.70		10	65.50	18.34
Thinking		30	50.40	21.69		49	64.08	21.03
Pooled STDEV				21.96				19.81

"Type" is the variable for personality indicator.

TABLE 9
Analysis of Variance of Test Scores for Perceptive/Judging by Test Formats

Multiple Choice	Nonaccounting Students				Accounting Students			
Source	DF	SS	MS	F	DF	SS	MS	F
Type	2	257	129	0.68	2	140	70	0.49
Error	67	12753	190		96	13680	143	
Total	69	13010			98	13820		
Level		N	Mean	STDEV		N	Mean	STDEV
Perceptive		16	46.50	15.26		8	64.75	12.06
Balanced		2	53.50	4.95		3	70.00	18.68
Judging		52	43.71	13.46		88	69.03	11.73
Pooled STDEV				13.80				11.94

Essay/Problem								
Source	DF	SS	MS	F	DF	SS	MS	F
Type	2	258	129	0.26	2	390	195	0.50
Error	67	32819	490		96	37341	389	
Total	69	33077			98	37731		
Level		N	Mean	STDEV		N	Mean	STDEV
Perceptive		16	52.50	22.17		8	67.37	19.39
Balanced		2	64.50	26.16		3	54.00	12.77
Judging		52	54.17	22.03		88	63.83	19.88
Pooled STDEV				22.13				19.72

"Type" is the variable for personality indicator.

the same day/week, etc. The students' total points earned, on the other hand, represent the students' performance over a semester. Total semester points were correlated with students' final exam scores. The correlation between the total points and essay/problem scores was larger than the correlation between total points and the multiple choice scores. These results are consistent with the claim that essay/problem format is a more complete measure of one's ability.

The data in Table 4 do not confirm the conclusion by Frakes and Lathen (1985) that there was no significant difference in scores on multiple choice versus problem. Frakes and Lathen (1985) did not observe significant change in students' rankings based on the test format. These inconsistencies could be attributed to the fact that Frakes and Lathen studied introductory accounting students, probably with different majors, and did not control for the student majors.

Although the sequence of questions was not changed, this study and that by Baldwin and Howard (1983) have common constructs and are complementary. Baldwin and Howard discovered that above-average and average students performed better on the "ordered" questions and below-average students did better on the "scrambled" version of the multiple

choice examinations. Baldwin and Howard's findings about "ordered" and "scrambled" multiple choice tests are similar to the results here for the essay/problem and multiple choice formats, respectively.

The results indicate that the Introvert and Sensing types are relatively more comfortable in a written accounting examination environment. These individuals prefer solitary activities and depend on factual information provided. It is also shown that the decision-making mode and individuals' life style do not have any significant effect on the test scores.

The study, however, does not examine the consequences of the traditional accounting tests on the overall learning process. Furthermore, it is not clear if the performance evaluation process should incorporate a measure for individuals' decision-making modes. Other interesting question are whether failure of a written accounting examination to measure and evaluate decision-making modes and life style preferences discourages individuals who are unable to demonstrate their comparative advantage and whether individuals with characteristics other than those attributed to the stereotypical accountants would perform satisfactorily in an accounting and auditing environments.

REFERENCES

Aranya, N., A. Barak, and J. Amernic. 1981. A Test of Holland's Theoryin a Population of Accountants. *Journal of Vocational Behavior* (February): 15–24.

———, E. I. Meir, and A. Bar-Ilan. 1978. An Empirical Examination of the Stereotype Accountant Based on Holland's Theory. *Journal of Occupational Psychology* (June): 139–145.

———, and J. T. Wheeler. 1986. Accountants' Personality Types and Their Commitment to Organization and Profession. *Contemporary Accounting Research* (Fall): 184–199.

Baker, R. E., J. R. Simon, and F. P. Bazeli. 1986. An Assessment of the Learning Style Preferences of Accounting Majors. *Issues in Accounting Education* (Spring): 1–12.

Baldwin, B. A., and T. P. Howard. 1983. Intertopical Sequencing of Examination Questions: An Empirical Evaluation. *Journal of Accounting Education* (Fall): 89–95.

———, and P. M. Reckers. 1984. Exploring the Role of Learning Style Research in Accounting Education Policy. *Journal of Accounting Education* (Fall): 63–76.

Belkaoui, A. 1989. *Behavioral Accounting: The Research and Publication Issues.* Quorum Books: 129–130.

Brown, H. D., and R. C. Burke. 1987. Accounting Education: A Learning Style Study of Professional, Technical and Future Adaptation Issues. *Journal of Accounting Education* (Fall): 187–206.

Collins, J. H., and V. C. Milliron. 1987. A Measure of Professional Accountants' Learning Style. *Issues in Accounting Education* (Fall): 193–206.

Frakes, A. H., and W. C. Lathen. 1985. A Comparison of Multiple-Choice and Problem Examinations in Introductory Financial Accounting. *Journal of Accounting Education* (Spring): 81–89.

Gruber, R. A. 1987. Sequencing Exam Questions Relative to Topic Presentation. *Journal of Accounting Education* (Spring): 77–86.

Holland, J. L. 1973. *The Psychology of Vocational Choice.* Prentice-Hall.

Howe, K. R., and B. A. Baldwin. 1983. The Effect of Evaluative Sequencing on Performance, Behavior, and Attitudes. *The Accounting Review* (January): 135–142.

Huber, G. 1983. Cognitive Style as a Basis for MIS and DSS Design: Much Ado about Nothing? *Management Science* (May): 567-579.

Jacoby, O. F. 1981. Psychological Types and Career Success in Accounting Profession. *Research in Psychological Types:* 24–37.

Jung, C. J. 1923. *Psychological Types.* Pantheon Books.

Kolb, D. A. 1974. On Management and the Learning Process, in *Organizational Psychology: A Book of Readings,* 2nd ed. Prentice-Hall.

———. 1985. *Learning Style Inventory: Technical Manual.* McBer and Company.

Martin, C. L., and A. M. Sedaghat. 1990. Proposed Changes in the Uniform CPA Examination: A Survey of Accounting Practitioners. *The Accounting Educators' Journal* (Summer): 134–148.

Myers, I. B. 1962. *Manual: The Myers-Briggs Type Indicator.* Consulting Psychologists Press.

———. 1980. *Gifts Differing.* Consulting Psychologists Press.

Paretta, R. L., and L. W. Chadwick. 1975. The Sequencing of Examination Questions and Its Effects on Student Performance. *The Accounting Review* (July): 595–601.

Sedaghat, A. M., and C. L. Martin. 1988. Perception of Accounting Faculty Regarding Proposed Changes in the CPA Examination. *Issues in Accounting Education* (Fall): 409–422.

Shackleton, V. 1980. The Accountant Stereotype: Myth or Reality? *Accountancy:* 122–123.

Ethics and Professionalism in Accounting Education

The conference program included three papers that examine issues involving ethics. The papers report that there has been limited response to societal demands for integrating ethical issues or discussions into accounting courses in Australia and New Zealand. A role play approach is suggested as a possible solution to the dilemma of how to integrate ethical considerations into accounting courses. But one research paper found a by-country difference when practitioners were asked their opinions about factors involving marketing and advertising among public accountants and ethics relating to providing accounting services.

Integrating Ethics into Financial Management Courses: A Role-Play Approach

Kate M. Brown

An increasing need for incorporating more explicit attention to ethical elements of business decision making in business education programs has been expressed by both corporate (Saari et al. 1988) and academic (Kullberg 1988) sources. Research (e.g., Henderson 1988) has indicated that new graduates, especially, suffer from "ethical naivete" — a generally low level of appreciation for the complex moral questions that often underlie business decisions which are formulated and evaluated in purely profit terms. If ethics is to be integrated into business education, the question arises as to the pedagogical methods that might be employed. The purpose of this paper is to suggest the particular method of role-play, presented in the context of (but by no means limited to) financial management education.

The recent rash of highly publicized white collar crime by Wall Street giants has highlighted the deterioration of ethical standards within corporate settings (Sender 1986). While studies indicate that managers have individual value preferences comparable to those of the general population (Frederick and Weber 1987, reported in Frederick 1988), corporate cultures emphasize and reward pragmatic behaviors that ignore or evade ethical considerations (Frederick 1988). Justification for such moral myopia is derived from such respected economists as Milton Friedman (1962), who stated, as if it were unquestionably true, that "there is one and only one social responsibility of business—to use its resources and engage in activities designed to increase its profits so long as it stays within the rules of the game, which is to say, engages in open and free competition, without deception or fraud" (p. 133). In so doing, the argument goes, jobs will be created, income will be distributed throughout an entire economy, and society will be best served. It is not, in Friedman's view, the business of businesspeople to get involved in doing good in any sense other than running their businesses well. Any negative effects on society or the environment, real or potential, accomplished without fraud are acceptable if profitable.

The position that business should not concern itself with social issues beyond profit making is ultimately pragmatic. The implication is that business decision makers are not in a position to determine what is good for society, and therefore should not meddle with noncorporate concerns. Most of the recent literature in the area of business ethics recognizes that this pragmatism is an oversimplified, shortsighted view of the role of the corporation in society, and that the ethical implications of business decisions are relevant factors for decision makers (Nash 1982; Wilson 1989; Cooke and Ryan 1988). The question for these and other writers is not whether ethics should be taught as part of the business curriculum. Gandz and Hayes (1988) summarize the general sentiment when they say "(a)s a socially responsible organization, a business school has a moral obligation *to contribute to the ethical development of students*" (p. 659). The main focus in this portion of the literature is the question of how best to incorporate ethics into a business education.

One of the debates that emerges from the literature is over the value of teaching the fundamental philosophical positions on ethics (Bahm 1982) The two primary schools of philosophy devoted to ethics are teleology, which is based on the consequences of actions, and deontology, which is based on *a priori* concepts of right actions. Presentation of the fundamentals of these two schools of thought are unquestionably appropriate for a dedicated business ethics class, but probably should not be included in the actual content of other courses (Nash 1982; Cava 1990). This is not to suggest that the two approaches to a situation cannot be made part of the analysis in any class, and indeed, the teaching technique of role-play provides a strong vehicle for introducing and discussing both in a structured if contrived context. The teleological point of view would suggest that business ethics "seeks the greatest good for the greatest number for the greatest length of time" (Henderson 1988, 53), and, consequently, that all decisions

Kate M. Brown is a faculty member of the University of Otago, New Zealand.

The author would like to thank Markus Milne, Michael Metcalfe, and Alan Stent for their valuable comments.

must be debated openly by all concerned to even approach that goal. The deontological argument is that certain underlying principles are right by reason of being universally applicable, and therefore do not require debate. Role-play allows these fundamental positions to be examined without ever using the words "teleological" or "deontological," as long as the instructor understands the basic concepts. The philosophical and logical merits of these positions have occupied philosophers for centuries, from Aristotle through J. S. Mill and Immanuel Kant and into the current decade, and will not be resolved in any business course. The purpose of raising the issues in the role-play, with as much detail as the instructor chooses to include, is to increase the students' awareness of the relevance of ethics to business decisions.

One theme that does seem to have universal acceptance in the business ethics literature is that all courses should include some element of ethics (Murray 1987; English 1990; Gandz and Hayes 1988; Cooke and Ryan 1988; Baxter and Rarick 1987), and that this element is probably best incorporated as consciousness raising. Strong and Hoffman (1990) assert that "the Ethics classroom should be used as a consciousness raising tool and as awareness training" (p. 603). Nash (1982) says that "what is needed is a process of ethical inquiry that is immediately comprehensible to a group of executives and not predisposed to the utopian, and sometimes anticapitalistic, bias marking much of the work in applied business philosophy today" (p. 199). Cava (1990) suggests that "the more productive starting point in ethics education would seem to be finding a way to stimulate critical thinking in decision making" (p. 10). The premise of this paper is that role-play is an effective teaching method for accomplishing these goals. Two of the advantages of role-play articulated by van Ments (1983) are changing attitudes and providing portrayals of generalized social problems. Chesler and Fox (1966) suggest that students can achieve insights into themselves, others, and motivations for actions which "can aid students in clarifying their own values and in effectively directing or changing their own behavior" (p. 13).

Role-plays have the advantages of creating low-risk conditions for expressing extreme opinions, requiring limited interference from an instructor, thus avoiding preaching by the authority figure. Situations can be created that allow numerous aspects of a decision to be exposed and challenged, forcing the participants to expand their perceptions from within themselves (Chesler and Fox 1966).

The same attributes are inherent in the asking of ethical questions. Castro (1989) suggests that "ethical questions are intended to lead to confrontation with whatever underlying issues are faced by the organization or individual asking them. The power or ethical inquiry lies in its ability to force such a confrontation and, through it, to achieve enhanced self-understanding" (p. 463). The marriage of ethics and role-play as a method of teaching appears likely to be fruitful.

By its nature, a role-play has no ultimate solution contained within it, and so emphasizes the indeterminate elements of decisions. Included in the activity of the play is the ability to take nothing for granted, to question all of the statements and their implications of all of the actors. The freedom afforded by playing a stranger, and attributing extreme positions to that individual, allows the players tremendous scope of exploration into the nuances and conflicts inherent in any complex situation, without exposing the players' own beliefs. However extreme or absurd the development of the scenario, each individual is allowed to evaluate and question all positions within themselves. The culmination of the role-play is not intended to be a public confession of wrongly held views that have been enlightened, but rather a private reflection on the issues raised that will go beyond the particular class and degree program.

THE NEW ZEALAND ROLE-PLAY

The actual role-play included here was created for a financial management course, and has worked well in both undergraduate and graduate classes ranging in size from 17 to 50. The evaluation of success for the role-play is purely subjective, and is supported only by anecdotal comments from students.[1] The situation was designed to be real enough to illustrate principles of finance as well as raise serious ethical questions. It also contains a deliberate element of fantasy, the reference to the science fiction saga of *Star Trek*. The fantasy is included to enhance the nonthreatening nature of the exercise, rather than relying on students accepting the instructor's word that they are not being judged on their contributions. Other approaches might work as well, but this adds

---

[1]Once an instructor is committed to the technique, the perceived positive outcomes effectively preclude conducting any experiments in which one group is not exposed to the role-play. Further research might include attempting to evaluate the results, possibly by designing a questionnaire asking students to evaluate the aspects of the role-play, as outlined above.

to the theater aspect of the event and does seem to relax most students.

New Zealand Metals, Limited

NZM Ltd. has just discovered a (probable) substantial pocket of dilithium crystals during routine exploration for aluminum. The crystals are embedded in a cliff near a popular vacation spot on the coast near a small city. If the estimates by the geological expert are correct, NZM stands to make a 200 percent return on the extraction. Dilithium is required for the warp drives on the latest class of space vehicles, and the limited supply of natural crystals coupled with the exorbitant cost of synthetic ones makes the find very significant to NZM's future. The company is currently facing declining earnings in the light of worldwide recycling efforts reducing the value of new aluminum.

The management team at NZM is naturally very excited about this find. The managing director calls in the functional managers to discuss the potential costs and benefits of the project. NZM had been given permission by the New Zealand government to make preliminary exploratory tests for aluminum, but the company is well aware of the opposition to mining any ores near the coastline. The management team knew that they would have to come up with very convincing arguments to get past the environmentalists and tourist industry forces, to say nothing of the colony of penguins nesting 100 meters from the crystal site.

This particular role-play builds on several aspects of life in a particular corner of New Zealand. Its coastline has one of the few remaining mainland yellow-eyed penguin nesting areas, and residents are continually working to safeguard the habitat of the world's rarest penguin. Adding to the reality of the situation is an ongoing controversy surrounding a quarry, which has been extracting basalt from a coastal location, with devastating impacts on a particularly spectacular rock formation.

The ambiguity of the time frame is intentional, as it allows the players considerable freedom in the creation of their characters and potential solutions. The total size of the project and its obvious economic impacts are also left deliberately vague, and good players will quickly learn to use whatever values support their position the most.

The number of players can vary, although the original scenario was created for 17 primary characters. All characters are intended to represent stakeholders in the situation, so more may easily be envisaged beyond these 17. The first group is the management team, which (in New Zealand par-

lance) are the managing director, the financial manager, the production manager, the marketing manager, and the geologist. Also involved in the company side of things is a chairman of the board of directors and a labor union leader. Representing the local community are a member of the City Council, a member of the local merchant's association, a travel agent, and an unemployed mine worker. Representing the activist groups are a member of the Save the Peninsula Trust, an investigator for the Ministry of the Environment, a conservationist, and a penguin lover. Rounding out the field are roles for Paul Holmes, a real television interviewer, and Mr. Spock, a character in the *Star Trek* saga.

RUNNING THE ROLE-PLAY

Just as the writing of the role-play has its dangers, the actual running of the exercise can be daunting, especially the first time through.[2] The instructor deliberately gives up control, usually to a group of total strangers (i.e., new students). The success of the exercise is dependent on the willingness of the majority of the students to participate in the spirit of a play, the ability of the instructor to provide guidance only when absolutely necessary to get all of the important issues into the discussion, and usually the talent of the first few players to set the tone of what will follow. Nevertheless, the advantages of the method for teaching things like the ethics of complex economic decisions are too numerous to ignore, and the mechanisms (tricks) for guiding a successful role-play are reasonably well established (van Ments 1983).

The first mechanism available to the instructor is the introduction of the exercise. The words and tone of voice used in the description of the role-play, with mention of the roles to be played, will provide strong signals of support for the creativity of each player, and an indication that the exercise is meant to be nonthreatening, interesting, stimulating, and actually fun. Calling for volunteers may require some cajolery, but again provides an opportunity for the instructor to send out signals that all will be supported in their efforts.

The second guiding mechanism available to the instructor to get the role-play off to a good start is the setting of the stage. In this particular role play, asking the management team to move into a group facing the main group will allow them the secu-

---

[2]See Chesler and Fox (1966) or van Ments (1983) for full discussions of the role-play technique.

rity of a team, and tend to make the logistics of the room more conducive to discussion. The instructor can then suggest that the managing director has called a meeting to discuss the proposed mining operation and turn the action over to that player. If the actor has any feel for the role-play at all, the "meeting" is likely to move quite naturally from that point. The normal course of events would be that each functional manager is asked for his or her input into the decision, with the geologist making up something technical sounding, and finance and marketing making up projections, and the production manager making up new ways of extracting dilithium from cliff faces. The tenor of the handout included above is clearly aimed at capitalistic, short-term greedy decision making, and most groups pick up on that direction. The instructor should just have to keep things moving with a few words of encouragement.

When the "meeting" has come to a consensus, the instructor can suggest that word of NZM's plans has leaked to the outside and then just stand back. Some groups will wait for indications of when each player should speak, but most will just jump in at will. The various controversies are obvious, and students have little trouble expanding the roles with great inventiveness. The instructor can attempt to provide some balance, or act as devil's advocate if a particular role or group seems weak or timid, but may have to do very little at all.

THEORETICAL CONSIDERATIONS

The role-play is purposefully designed to start from the ultra-capitalist solution of investing without any regard for the costs to the environment and the community.[3] The development of the situation and the introduction of players representing the noncorporate concerns is aimed at getting the students to examine other relevant interests and perspectives. Essentially all of the issues raised in this scenario have both ethical and economic implications. The players naturally develop these implications, and they and the audience come to the realization that some compromise is probably necessary. Moreover, the actual outcome is likely to depend on the relative strengths of the parties involved.

Students are encouraged to examine their own feelings about the situation as it unfolds but are not required to express those feelings as their own. The remaining members of the class who do not actually participate can be involved at the conclusion as observers. When the actual play has drawn to an end, the instructor should go through a debriefing process (van Ments 1983). This involves summarizing the events as they developed and discussing the implications. The instructor can dissipate any tensions remaining from the confrontations that may have occurred, thus removing any anxiety on the part of players that they will be associated with the positions they took during the play. The primary focus in a financial management course will be on the financial aspects of the play, but the instructor can reemphasize the ethical considerations as well.

The debriefing portion of the role-play also allows for greater examination of the theoretical bases for ethical decision making. The entire class can discuss the problems from the point of view of the greatest good for the greatest number, and from the concept of *a priori* universal principles. The solutions proposed within the role-play can be examined within these perspectives. If the group decided that the greatest number includes all those new civilizations that dilithium is required to reach (continuing the *Star Trek* motif), then the access to this ore might be seen to be paramount. Alternatively, the group could decide that the only relevant greatest number is the penguins, and no commercial enterprise should be allowed. If universal principles are applied, the group is more likely to decide in favor of the environment than the capitalists, but this outcome is certainly not guaranteed. Part of the analysis of the actual role play, therefore, can be the introduction of the theoretical foundations of ethics, but entirely related to the events rather than as a separate and fairly esoteric discussion.

CONCLUSION

The ultimate aim of the role-play is to get students to come to a decision, both as the players they represent, and as individuals. This exercise is used as the introductory lecture for a case course in financial management and sets the stage for continued exploration of all aspects of financial decision making, including ethical questions. The role play also provides a reference point for discussion throughout the course (Brown 1990), and as such has continued benefits beyond actual play.

Throughout both the role-play and the remainder of the course, the instructor can adjust the amount of emphasis given to ethics, and avoid

---

[3]The instructor can suggest to the management team that the generally accepted goal of financial management is the maximization of shareholder wealth to forestall any highly environmentally sound conclusion at the outset.

preaching without avoiding the fundamental ethical issues encompassed by corporate decision making. While role-play is not the only method of accomplishing this goal, it does have the inherent advantages of a low risk, high interaction activity that can capture the students' imaginations and allow significant freedom of expression. This forum seems ideally suited to the task of raising the moral consciousness of business students in the context of functional area courses.

REFERENCES

Bahm, A. J. 1982. Teaching Ethics Without Ethics to Teach. *Journal of Business Ethics*, Vol. 1: 43–47.

Baxter, G. D., and C. A. Rarick. 1987. Education for the Moral Development of Managers: Kohlbergs's Stages of Moral Development and Integrative Education. *Journal of Business Ethics*, Vol. 6: 243–248.

Brown, K. M. 1990. The Use of Role Play in the Teaching of Corporate Finance. *Financial Education* (Fall): 37–43.

Castro, B. 1989. Business Ethics and Business Education: A Report from a Regional State University. *Journal of Business Ethics*, Vol. 9: 479–486.

Cava, A. 1990. Teaching Ethics: A Moral Model. *Business and Economic Review*, Vol. 36, No. 3: 10–13.

Chesler, M., and R. Fox. 1966. *Role-Playing Methods in the Classroom*. Science Research Associates.

Cooke, R. A., and L. V. Ryan. 1988. The Relevance of Ethics to Management Education. *Journal of Management Development*, Vol. 7, No. 2: 28–38.

English, L. 1990. The Teaching of Ethics. *Australian Accountant*, Vol. 60, No. 1: 22–25.

Frederick, W. C. 1988. The Culprit Is Culture. *Management Review* (August): 48–50.

Friedman, M. 1962. *Capitalism and Freedom*. University of Chicago Press.

Gandz, J., and N. Hayes. 1988. Teaching Business Ethics. *Journal of Business Ethics*, Vol. 7: 657–669.

Henderson, V. E. 1988. Can Business Ethics Be Taught? *Management Review* (August): 52-54.

Kullberg, D. 1988. Business Ethics: Pace Provides Lessons from "Real Life." *Management Review* (August): 54–55.

Murray, T. J. 1987. Can Business Schools Teach Ethics? *Business Month*, Vol. 129, No. 4: 24–26.

Nash, L. L. 1982. Ethics Without the Sermon. In *Doing Ethics in Business*, ed. D.G. Jones. Gelgeschlager, Gunn and Hain, Publishers, Inc.

Saari, L. M., T. R. Johnson, S. D. McLaughlin, D. M. Zimmerle. 1988. A Survey of Management Training and Education Practices in U.S. Companies. *Personnel Psychology*, Vol. 41, No. 4: 731–743.

Sender, H. 1986. What the Scandals Wrought. *Institutional Investor*, Vol. 20, No. 10: 243–245.

Strong, V. K., and A. N. Hoffman. 1990. There Is Relevance in the Classroom: Analysis of Present Methods of Teaching Business Ethics. *Journal of Business Ethics*, Vol. 9: 603–607.

van Ments, M. 1983. *The Effective Use of Role-Play*. Kogan Page.

Wilson, J. Q. 1989. Adam Smith on Business Ethics. *California Management Review*, Vol. 32, No. 1: 59–72.

Integration of Ethics into Tertiary Accounting Programmes in New Zealand and Australia

F. C. Chua, M. H. B. Perera, and M. R. Mathews

INTRODUCTION

Over the years, the economic, political and social fabric of civilised communities has been characterised by confidence placed by their members on one another. Confidence is based on trust. Both confidence and trust are societal norms that are regulated not only by the law but also by certain unwritten standards such as honesty, integrity, fairness and good faith. Though fragile, these are valuable underpinnings of a stable society as they are necessary in promoting a bonding relationship among the various individuals and groups of individuals in fulfilling their roles in society. For example, each profession, inclusive of accounting, has been entrusted with the responsibility for providing the specialist skills needed to resolve the conflicts that arise within its jurisdiction.

In order to preserve the confidence that society has placed in it, the accounting profession has initiated a code of ethical conduct for self-regulation over many years. However, during the last decade, there have been renewed calls from many directions for improved standards of ethics. The accounting profession is therefore under pressure to restore its image as a group of "ethical" people (Armstrong and Mintz 1989). The key issue is whether society's value system in general is properly geared towards preparing people to act ethically in their careers. Naturally, attention has been directed towards the educational system. The sharemarket crash in 1987 has not only brought financial distress to many people but also unveiled distressing numbers and kinds of illegal and unethical activities on the part of those in business, many of whom are business and/or accounting graduates (Hurley 1988; Mace 1989). Questions have been raised about whether the business schools are inculcating a sense of ethical behaviour in their students (Smith 1990).

Many business schools in the United States have intensified their efforts to instill ethical behaviour among students headed for a business world tainted by scandal. The move to integrate ethics into the accounting curriculum has already been recommended by the Anderson Committee (1986), the Bedford Committee (1986), the Treadway Commission (1987), and the American Accounting Association's (AAA) "Project on Professionalism and Ethics" (1988, as reported by Langenderfer and Rockness 1989). There has also been an increasing number of articles on the topic, e.g., Armstrong (1987), Loeb (1988), Armstrong and Mintz (1989), Langenderfer and Rockness (1989), and Scribner and Dillaway (1989). However, this issue has not been examined in detail in either New Zealand or Australia, hence the present study.

The objective of this research project is to determine the extent to which the study of ethics is integrated into the curriculum within the accounting departments of universities and colleges of advanced education in Australia and New Zealand at both the undergraduate and postgraduate levels. An empirical study in the form of a questionnaire survey was carried out to ascertain the coverage, the resources, research and publications, and future plans in this area. The "Directory of Accounting Academics in Australia and New Zealand 1990" (Wiley) was used as the means of identifying participants. As a result, the chairpersons of 56 accountancy departments of Australasian tertiary institutions were approached to take part in the study.

The present paper is organised as follows: the second section attempts to provide a definition of accounting ethics. The third section describes previous research conducted on business and accounting ethics education. Research results are analysed and presented in the fourth section and the fifth section draws the conclusions.

DEFINITION OF ETHICS

Ethics is the study of standards of conduct and moral judgment. *General ethics* comprises a code of principles (written and unwritten) about what

---

F. C. Chua is a Lecturer, M. H. B. Perera is an Associate Professor, and M. R. Mathews is a Professor, all at Massey University, New Zealand.

is right and what is wrong, which is aimed at clarifying the kind of conduct necessary to promote human welfare (Powers and Vogel 1980). As occupational groups aspire to professional status, they have historically made the development of a code of ethics one of their foremost concerns, testifying to the public that their obligation to society transcends economic self-interest (Smith and Bain 1990).

Professional ethics is also concerned with moral behaviour, but is more restrictive in the sense that it encompasses the expected ethical pattern unique to a certain profession. Furthermore, as the circumstances of professional practice change, the specific responsibilities of the practitioner change as well. As a result, some principles take on a new meaning or importance whereas some others decline in importance. However, the purpose of a profession remains unchanged and it acts as a "normative filter" (Powers and Vogel 1980).

Ethics as such is *normative* in nature because its purpose is to guide action toward human welfare. *Applied ethics* is a species of the genus of normative ethics. It focuses on the tools, concepts, and concerns of normative ethics to help specify and clarify the obligation of agents who regularly encounter ethical issues in particular sectors or spheres (Powers and Vogel 1980). In other words, it involves the use of ethical theory and moral rules to arrive at concrete moral judgments in specific circumstances.

Accounting ethics is a subclass of professional ethics which is also normative in nature. It can be defined as the study of those decisions of accountants which involve moral values and actions which might differentially affect various parties such as clients, competitors, colleagues, members of the community or the broader society (as adapted from Gandz and Hayes 1988).

PRIOR STUDIES

This section begins with a review of previous empirical studies which may be expected to provide some guidance on the results expected from the present study. A few articles have addressed the issue of ethics courses in the business curriculum. Among these are studies conducted by Hoffman and Moore (1982), George (1987), and Singh (1989). Studies that have specifically examined the issue of ethics coverage in the accounting curriculum include those carried out by Loeb and Bedingfield (1972), Karnes and Sterner (1988), Cohen and Pant (1989), Armstrong and Mintz (1989), and Mintz (1990). The remainder of this

section is a brief summary of some of the results of these studies.

Ethics Courses in the Curriculum

Hoffman and Moore (1982) conducted an extensive survey of over 1,200 colleges and universities concerning the teaching of ethics courses in business schools. They found that of the 655 schools that responded, 317 stated that they offered at least one course in ethics. They also found that the majority of business courses (83.4%) were developed after 1973 with a trend towards increased coverage over time. However, they did not examine the degree to which ethics was being integrated within existing functional area courses.

George (1987) conducted a survey among 225 deans of undergraduate and/or graduate programmes accredited by the AACSB. At the undergraduate level, it was found that 46.8% of the respondents offered a special course in ethics and 35.5% offered the subject in other required courses, whereas at the graduate level, 33.9% offered ethics as a special course and 39.5% offered it in other required courses. Approximately half of these courses were compulsory for business majors.

Singh (1989) conducted a survey of Canadian Schools of Management and Administrative Studies in 1987 to establish the status of ethics in their existing curricula. It was found that 55 percent of the responding schools offered courses in ethics and 80 percent of the 25 courses offered were electives. Singh remarked that since most of the ethics courses offered were electives, it raised serious doubts about whether the offering of business ethics in Canadian business schools was "mere tokenism."

In the accounting field, it was found that ethics received limited coverage in the curriculum. This was first confirmed by the survey conducted by Loeb and Bedingfield (1972) of the department chairmen of 141 universities which had AACSB–accredited undergraduate programmes. The data they received indicated that there was little support for a separate ethics course. Even when ethics was taught in other functional courses, it received only minimal coverage, with most ethics education taking place in auditing courses, and to a lesser extent in taxation courses. This is further supported by Karnes and Sterner (1988), Cohen and Pant (1989), and Armstrong and Mintz (1989) more than a decade later.

Karnes and Sterner (1988) conducted a survey on 281 accounting chairpersons listed in the Accounting Faculty Directory 1987 (U.S.) to elicit information about the extent to which ethics was taught in business and accounting programmes. Their findings indicated that only 8.5% of the accounting programmes and 33.3% of the business programmes provided a separate course in ethics. The remaining 58.2% of the programmes integrated the coverage of ethics into auditing and other accounting courses.

The Cohen and Pant (1989) study was an extension of the Hoffman and Moore (1982) study focusing on some 445 U.S. colleges and universities that were offering an undergraduate degree in accounting. They did not address the issue of separate ethics courses in accounting. However, they reported that ethics was covered in other accounting courses, receiving the most coverage in auditing and to a much lesser extent in taxation and accounting theory.

Armstrong and Mintz (1989) reported results similar to the previous studies in that only 7.3% of their respondents indicated that they had a separate course in accounting ethics, mainly at the graduate level. Information was also obtained about the inclusion of ethics in other courses, by course and by level of offering. It was found that in both undergraduate and graduate programmes, auditing received the most coverage (95.6%). The other accounting courses having a reasonable coverage of ethics were taxation and accounting theory at the graduate level and introductory accounting and business law at the undergraduate level.

Time Devoted to Ethics Teaching

The time devoted to accounting ethics was also found to be minimal. Loeb and Bedingfield (1972) found that the number of hours reportedly devoted to ethics in the various courses ranged between zero and nine class hours. For instance, when taught in taxation courses, generally between one and three class hours were devoted to ethics. On reviewing the course outlines of auditing and other accounting courses, Armstrong and Mintz (1989) found that, on average, one and a half weeks of an auditing course were spent on accounting ethics and related topics. Similarly, one session of other accounting courses was found to be devoted to the coverage of ethics in.

Teaching Resources

Cohen and Pant (1989) attempted to obtain information about the qualifications of accounting faculty involved in teaching accounting ethics. The results indicated that the respondents perceived the

accounting faculty to be relatively well qualified. As such, teacher competence was not an impediment. However, it was found that the reward structure of universities had failed to provide sufficient tangible incentives to encourage academic staff to devote time to developing ethics modules in the accounting curriculum. This finding was also supported by Armstrong and Mintz (1989) and Mintz (1990).

As for other resources such as teaching materials and techniques, it was found that a variety of resources was employed but that traditional approaches still prevailed. Loeb and Bedingfield (1972) found that most of their respondents used a chapter in the text (mostly auditing works) and that a large proportion made use of the codes of ethics. Not many used journal articles in their courses. However, Armstrong and Mintz (1989) found that the most popular course materials were selected readings from journals, followed closely by a book on accounting ethics and a book on the SEC, the codes of ethics and cases. In his study of ethics coverage in management accounting, Mintz (1990) found that the codes (especially the NAA code) were the favourite source. Other materials include journal articles, the NAA ethics video, and written case studies. Textbooks, however, were generally light on ethical issues and were therefore not used very often.

Similarly, a variety of teaching techniques was employed. However, all the studies found that the lecture approach was the most popular. For instance, Loeb and Bedingfield (1972) found that 82 percent of their respondents used lectures, with written papers, guest lectures, case studies and class discussions being used to a much lesser extent. Armstrong and Mintz (1989) also found that the lecture approach was the predominant teaching method, especially when it was integrated with guest lectures and case presentations.

Future Plans

When questioned about the future plans for ethics coverage, Hoffman and Moore (1982) found that 48 of their 655 respondents had plans to offer an ethics course, whereas 144 had an interest in developing a business ethics course. Based on the structure of the Hoffman and Moore study, Singh (1989) attempted to examine the number of business schools planning to offer a course or courses in business ethics. He also requested his respondents to provide reasons for not offering such courses. It was found that about 42 percent of the respondents who did not offer such courses at the time of the survey intended to do so by 1989. However, he also detected that there was an underlying resistance to the teaching of business ethics in business schools. In the same vein, Mintz (1990) investigated constraints that would limit the amount of class time in ethics integration and found that curriculum constraints were the most serious (40.2%). Others included the lack of subject matter/materials, the lack of ability/knowledge required to integrate ethics, and the lack of interest/desire to integrate ethics. The Karnes and Sterner (1988) study also found that a number of constraints affected the ethics coverage in accounting, namely, financial constraints, lack of subject matter and faculty and curriculum constraints.

RESEARCH RESULTS

Questionnaires were returned from 45 of the 56 schools, representing a response rate of 80 percent. All 45 responses were usable. This high response rate may be assumed to be indicative of a high level of interest among the respondents in the subject matter of the survey.

Current Coverage of Ethics in Accounting

The first section of the questionnaire dealt with the coverage of ethics at both the undergraduate and postgraduate courses. The results (see Table 1) show that 82.3% of the responding schools offer courses that contain an ethics component. Of the 45 respondents, 30 (66.7%) had an ethics component in their undergraduate programme and only seven (15.6%) had such a component in their postgraduate programme. Overall, the current coverage is limited and far from encouraging. The results indicate that some ethics is taught at both the undergraduate and postgraduate levels. The research instrument did not identify any explanation for the difference in ethics coverage in undergraduate and postgraduate courses.

Type of Coverage

Those respondents who provided an affirmative answer to ethics coverage in accounting were asked whether their institutions had a separate paper/course/unit in accounting ethics or whether ethics constituted part of other papers/courses/units in the accounting curriculum. As shown in Table 2, at the undergraduate level, only two of the respondents (4.3%) indicated that they offered separate courses in accounting ethics whereas 29 (63.1%) included ethics teaching in other courses within the accounting curriculum. It must be noted that of the 30 respondents indicating that they had an ethics component in their accounting curricula, one of them offered ethics both as a separate course as well as in other courses. At the postgraduate level, all of the seven schools included ethics as part of other papers/courses/units.

The research results in Table 2 show little support for a separate course in accounting ethics. Ethics was taught as a separate course in only two undergraduate programmes (4.3%) and none of the postgraduate programmes had ethics as a separate course. One of the undergraduate courses was a first-year compulsory course, with 52 class hours per semester devoted to it. The other was a third-year elective, involving three class hours per week. Developing separate ethics courses requires not only teacher competence and dedication but also time. At a time when there are very few tangible incentives, it is encouraging to see two Australian universities providing a separate ethics course in accounting.

Ethics as Part of Other Accounting Courses

Ethics components were generally incorporated in to other accounting courses. As shown in Table 2, 29 (63.1%) undergraduate programmes and seven (15.6%) postgraduate programmes incorporated some elements of ethics in their accounting courses. Because many of the offerings were

TABLE 1
Ethics Coverage in Accounting
(n = 45)

| | Undergraduate | | Postgraduate | |
	Number	Percentage	Number	Percentage
Ethics component	30	66.7	7	15.6
No ethics component	15	33.3	38	84.4
Total	45	100.0	45	100.0

TABLE 2
Type of Coverage
(n = 45)

	Undergraduate		Postgraduate	
	Number	Percentage	Number	Percentage
Ethics as separate course	2	4.3	0	0.0
Ethics as part of other courses	29	63.1	7	15.6
Ethics not in curriculum	15	32.6	38	84.4
	46*	100.0	45	100.0

*One school taught ethics both as a separate course and in other accounting courses.

courses of a similar nature, they were grouped into 14 categories to facilitate analysis.

Table 3 shows that at the undergraduate level, ethics was most frequently taught in auditing (42.6%), followed by accounting theory (9.8%). The differential treatment is obvious from the percentages. Other accounting courses that had some ethics content included financial accounting, business law, taxation, management accounting, and internal auditing. At the graduate level, auditing and accounting theory received the same amount of coverage, followed equally by financial accounting, taxation, current issues and accounting information systems.

Depth of Coverage

The results in Table 3 indicate a significant difference in the perceived coverage of ethics among the courses. For instance, auditing, at both the undergraduate and postgraduate levels, was the course that provided the most coverage of ethics. However, a question needs to be raised about the thoroughness of this integration. The coverage of ethics was minimal with the class hours devoted to the actual teaching of ethics ranging between zero and ten hours at the undergraduate level (see Table 4) and zero and 15 hours at the postgraduate level. It must be noted that some respondents stated the percentage without providing the total class

TABLE 3
Courses in Which Ethics Was Taught

	Undergraduate			Postgraduate		
	Number	Percentage	Rank	Number	Percentage	Rank
Auditing	26	42.6	1	4	33.3	1
Accounting Theory	6	9.8	2	4	33.3	1
Financial Accounting	5	8.2	3	1	8.3	2
Business Law	5	8.2	3	—	—	—
Variety of courses*	3	4.9	4	—	—	—
Introductory Accounting	3	4.9	4	—	—	—
Taxation	3	4.9	4	1	8.3	2
Internal Auditing	2	3.3	5	—	—	—
Management Accounting	2	3.3	5	—	—	—
Professional Accounting	2	3.3	5	—	—	—
Business Policy	2	3.3	5	—	—	—
Intermediate Accounting	1	1.6	6	—	—	—
Accounting Info Systems	1	1.6	6	1	8.3	2
Current Issues	—	—	—	1	8.3	2
	61	100.0		12	100.0	

*This includes Economics, Behavioural Accounting, and Accounting Workshop.

TABLE 4
Time Devoted to Accounting Ethics (Undergraduate Level)
(n = 45)

Number of Class Hours Devoted to Ethics	Percentage Responding												
	Courses*												
	A	B	C	D	E	F	G	H	I	J	K	L	M
None	13.0	93.3	90.0	97.0	83.3	80.0	93.3	90.0	97.0	93.0	93.0	83.3	90.0
1	3.0	—	—	—	3.3	—	—	—	—	—	—	—	—
2	10.0	—	3.3	3.0	3.3	3.0	3.3	7.0	—	—	—	6.7	—
3	13.0	3.3	3.3	—	3.3	3.0	—	—	—	—	—	3.3	3.3
4	27.0	—	3.3	—	3.3	7.0	—	3.0	3.0	7.0	—	3.3	—
5	7.0	—	—	—	—	—	—	—	—	—	—	—	—
6	7.0	3.3	—	—	—	—	—	—	—	—	—	3.3	3.3
7	—	—	—	—	—	—	—	—	—	—	—	—	—
8	7.0	—	—	—	—	—	—	—	—	—	—	—	—
9	—	—	—	—	—	—	—	—	—	—	—	—	—
10	7.0	—	—	—	3.0	—	—	—	—	—	—	—	—
unclear	6.0	—	—	—	—	7.0	3.3	—	—	—	7.0	—	3.3
	100.0	100.0	100.0	100.0	100.0	100.0	100.0	100.0	100.0	100.0	100.0	100.0	100.0

*Courses:
A - Auditing
B - Internal Auditing
C - Introductory Accounting
D - Intermediate Accounting
E - Financial Accounting
F - Accounting Theory
G - Management Accounting
H - Taxation
I - Accounting Information Systems
J - Professional Accounting
K - Business Policy
L - Business Law
M - Variety of courses

hours of the subject(s) while some indicated the total class hours without giving the actual hours spent on ethics.

For the postgraduate courses, the average class hours devoted to ethics teaching were as follows: 4.7 for auditing, 3.7 for accounting theory, 3 for accounting systems, 4 for both financial accounting and current issues, and 15 in one programme in taxation. Similarly, at the undergraduate level, an average of 4.6 class hours of auditing was devoted to ethics, 3.25 in accounting theory, 3.8 in financial accounting, and 4 in accounting systems. This indicates that the time devoted to ethics at both undergraduate and postgraduate levels was about the same.

Course Status

The majority of the courses listed by the respondents were compulsory courses at the undergraduate level. Generally, the course status depended on the requirements of the professional bodies. As a result, auditing, financial accounting, and accounting theory were more likely to be compulsory courses. At the postgraduate level, an equal number of com-

pulsory and elective courses were offered, seven compulsory and seven electives. However, at the undergraduate level, 46 of the courses were compulsory and 16 were elective courses. These figures indicated that 53 (69.7%) of the 76 courses offered were compulsory (see Table 5).

However, 62.9% of the 61 courses incorporating ethics at the undergraduate level were courses offered at the third-(or final) year level, 22.5% at the second-year level, and 8.1% at the first-year level. Four respondents (6.5%) indicated that they offered such courses in the fourth year since their institutions had a four-year degree structure.

Resources

This section on resources concerned the qualifications of the teaching staff, course materials and teaching techniques.

Qualifications of Teaching Staff

Respondents were requested to answer two questions concerning the qualifications of those involved in the teaching of ethics. As shown in Table 6, all the responses in this section (30 undergradu-

TABLE 5
Status of Courses Incorporating Accounting Ethics

Level		Compulsory Number	Elective Number	Total
Undergraduate:	1st Year	5	0	
	2nd Year	13	1	
	3rd Year	26	13	
	4th Year	2	2	62*
Postgraduate		7	7	14*
Total		53	23	76

*One of the courses can be either an elective or a compulsory course.

TABLE 6
Teaching Staff

Qualifications	Frequency of Responses	
	Undergraduate	Postgraduate
Accounting academics	30	7
Others:		
(1) Accountants from other university departments	—	—
(2) Accounting practitioners	4	1
(3) Nonaccountants such as ethicists or philosophers	3	1
(4) Lawyers	2	1

ate programmes and seven postgraduate programmes) indicated that departmental academic staff were the main people who taught ethics. Twenty-nine of the 30 undergraduate responses indicated the number of staff involved. The majority of them used only one staff member (41.3%). Some used two to three staff members (20.6% for each case). Others used more than three, and one school had 12 staff involved. For the postgraduate programme, the number of staff involved ranged from one to four, with three the most common.

Other participants in the teaching of ethics included practising accountants, nonaccountants such as ethicists and philosophers, and lawyers. This can be regarded as a positive development in utilising those who have specialist skills to offer.

Course Materials

The course materials are an important means of imparting knowledge and transmitting skills. As Table 7 shows, codes of ethics were the favoured choice at the undergraduate level (29%), followed by selected readings from journals (22%), general accounting texts (17.4%) and case studies (16.3%). However, at the postgraduate level, codes of ethics, selected readings and case studies were on an equal footing (21% each). Some respondents answered the open-ended portion and provided in-

formation on what other course materials were being utilised, such as the AAA videos and items from the financial press.

The popularity of the codes of ethics, with auditing being the favourite course, was not unexpected. Most of the students will pursue their career paths within accounting/auditing and it is imperative that they know the various codes of ethics. This finding also highlights the fact that what they learn will be code bound. According to Mintz (1990), the code approach is the second best to the case approach, that is, if ethical dilemmas introduced in the classroom are related directly and flexibly to the codes, which can then be used as a framework for the discussion of problems by drawing on standards of expected conduct.

Teaching Techniques

Table 8 shows the predominant teaching method in accounting ethics at the undergraduate level to be the lecture approach (34.2%), followed by both case studies (20.2%) and seminar discussions (20.2%). The least favoured approach employed was the use of tutorial questions, an additional item provided by one of the respondents. At the postgraduate level, both the lecture approach and seminar discussions were the forerunners

TABLE 7
Teaching Materials Used in Ethics Courses

Materials	Undergraduate		Postgraduate	
	Frequency	Percentage	Frequency	Percentage
General accounting texts	15	17.4	2	10.5
Case studies	14	16.3	4	21.0
Codes of ethics	25	29.0	4	21.0
Selected readings from journals, etc.	19	22.0	4	21.0
Books on accounting ethics/policy	9	10.5	3	15.8
Others: AAA Video	1	1.2	1	5.3
Books on accounting	1	1.2	1	5.3
Financial press	1	1.2	—	—
Videos (not specified)	1	1.2	—	—
	86	100.0	19	100.0

(40% each). Comparatively, the case approach was not as frequently employed (20%).

Research and Publications

A question was asked about the number of staff members at the respondent's department who were currently pursuing ethics research interests within the accounting department. In addition, a list of publications was requested. Responses to this question indicated that out of the 45 responding institutions, only 17 had some staff members researching in this area. The number of researchers per department ranged from one to four, with one the most common.

Plans for the Future

Respondents were requested to choose amongst three alternatives in regard to future plans — expand, contract, or no change, at both the undergraduate and postgraduate levels. All respondents but one attempted to answer this question. The majority provided explanations to justify their choices, as requested. In total, 29 respondents indicated that there would be some expansion in their respective programmes. Of these, 21 were at the undergraduate level whereas eight were at the postgraduate level. However, 18 respondents at the undergraduate level and 15 at the postgraduate level stated that no changes were contemplated. There was some "overlap" in the responses to both programmes. In addition, a few responses clearly expressed some uncertainty about the future development of their institutions. It must be noted that none of the institutions indicated that the existing programmes would be contracted.

Reasons given for the inclusion of ethics in the curriculum varied, ranging from a response to worldwide trends to education, a response to societal demands, to fostering an understanding of expected behaviour. A few institutions indicated that some full or part units of accounting ethics would be offered in 1991. About eight others stated that such an expansion had been contemplated and

TABLE 8
Teaching Techniques Employed in Ethics Courses

Technique	Undergraduate		Postgraduate	
	Frequency	Percentage	Frequency	Percentage
Lectures (including guest lectures)	27	34.2	4	40.0
Role-playing	5	6.3	—	—
Case studies	16	20.2	2	20.0
Case studies with videos	7	8.9	—	—
Workshops	7	8.9	—	—
Seminar discussions	16	20.2	4	40.0
Others: Tutorial questions	1	1.3	—	—
	79	100.0	10	100.0

would be operational in the near future. Some respondents remarked that given additional curriculum time, for example, with an expansion into a four-year degree structure, ethics would definitely be included.

Among the reasons cited for not making any change to the existing programmes, the most often cited was that the present coverage was adequate. There were other priorities besides ethics and an inclusion of the ethics component would necessarily stretch departmental resources. However, there were some respondents who took the view that the teaching of ethics was a highly philosophical issue beyond the capability of accounting academics.

Constraints on Institutional Development of Ethics Education

In connection with future plans of the institutions, all respondents were asked to identify which factors they considered were hindering the development of their ethics programmes. The results are shown in Table 9.

The most frequently mentioned impediment to developing ethics courses is that it was not a priority relative to other subjects. Others included the lack of properly qualified staff, time constraints, lack of interested staff, lack of student interest, lack of relevance to the curriculum, and budgetary constraints in curriculum development. It must be noted that about six percent of all respondents stated that there were no impediments at all. It was

also evident that the existing three-year degree structure posed the greatest constraint on class time and curriculum development.

Institutional Support

Respondents were also asked about institutional support in the development of ethics programmes. Thirty-two affirmative responses (71%) were received, indicating that support from their institutions would be forthcoming. Eight respondents (18%) stated that they did not anticipate such support. The remaining respondents, five in all, did not answer this question. Thirty-five respondents commented on why there would or would not be institutional support.

Potential Limitations

The authors share the sentiments of Karnes and Sterner (1988) that the results of surveys of this nature should be interpreted with caution. With regard to the present study, a number of potential limitations can be mentioned.

First, some problems were encountered during the process of identification of research participants because it took place at a time when some Australian colleges of advanced education had just merged to become universities or were in the process of merging with existing universities. Results may have been biased by the existence of courses of study which had not been changed to take account of the changed status of the institution. Sec-

TABLE 9
Impediments to Developing Ethics Programmes

Constraints	Those Integrating Ethics		Those not Integrating Ethics	
	Frequency	Percentage	Frequency	Percentage
Lack of student interest	3	4.5	1	4.0
Lack of interested staff	8	11.9	4	16.0
Lack of properly qualified staff	11	16.4	5	20.0
Not a priority relative to other subject(s)	21	31.3	11	44.0
Not relevant to the curriculum	2	3.0	—	—
Others:				
*Time constraints (three-year undergraduate degree)	10	14.9	3	12.0
*Lack of materials	1	1.5	—	—
*Budgetary constraints	2	3.0	—	—
*Not an academic subject	1	1.5	1	4.0
*Not priority relative to other departmental matters	2	3.0	—	—
*Not function of accounting departments	1	1.5	—	—
*Not required by industry and profession	1	1.5	—	—
No impediments	4	6.0	—	—
	67	100.0	25	100.0

ond, the interpretation of the open-ended questions in the questionnaire may lead to some generalised categorisations. Third, the class hours allocated to the teaching of ethics are estimates because many accounting papers have integrated ethics into their syllabi. Fourth, because the questionnaire is limited to one respondent per institution, it is possible that the respondent might not be completely aware of what his or her colleagues are doing in relation to the subject of ethics. Some respondents might have different interpretations of what is meant by ethics coverage; consequently, different sets of answers would result from differing definitions of ethics.

CONCLUSIONS

In view of the weakening of professionalism (Briloff 1990; Parker 1987; Sack 1985), it is time that the accounting profession take stock of the various factors affecting its status. Otherwise, the decline in public confidence will never be reversed. This is the reason that individual researchers and accounting professional bodies are searching for a "body of knowledge" that would encompass ethics education.

Contemporary notions of accounting education rest on a commitment to training in a technical sense, to transmit specific skills that are job and profession oriented. With the increase in business and accounting graduates, it is imperative that business/accounting educators should nurture ethical values in their students. Since there is an increased realisation that appropriate ethical awareness as well as technical competence is important in a complex, pluralistic business environment, it is important that business and in particular accounting majors at least acquire some ethics competence at university. Now more than ever, there have been attempts to redress the balance by introducing a consideration of ethical values into the accounting curriculum.

The present survey was conducted with a view to obtaining a general profile of the current state of accounting ethics education in New Zealand and Australia. Research findings, however, are not particularly encouraging. Except for two Australian universities, accounting ethics has not been isolated and treated as a separate subject. The coverage of ethics in the other accounting courses is also limited. These combine to show a marginal response to current societal demands. Nevertheless, this study will contribute to the extant empirical literature as evidence from New Zealand and Australia of the need to strengthen the ethics component in accounting education.

REFERENCES

American Institute of Certified Public Accountants, Committee on Standards of Professional Conduct (The Anderson Committee). 1986. *Restructuring Professional Standards to Achieve Professional Excellence in a Changing Environment.* AICPA.

American Accounting Association, Committee on the Future Structure, Content, and Scope of Accounting Education (The Bedford Committee). 1986. Future Accounting Education: Preparing for the Expanding Profession. *Issues in Accounting Education* (1): 168–195.

Armstrong, M. B. 1987. Moral Development and Accounting Education. *Journal of Accounting Education* 5: 27–43.

———, and S. M. Mintz. 1989. Ethics Education in Accounting: Present Status and Policy Implications. *Association of Government Accountants Journal* 38 (2): 70–76.

Briloff, A. J. 1990. Accountancy and Society: A Covenant Desecrated. *Critical Perspectives on Accounting* (1): 5–30.

Callahan, D., and S. Bok. (Eds.) 1980. *Ethics Teaching in Higher Education.* Plenum Press.

Cohen, J. R., and L. W. Pant. 1989. Accounting Educators' Perceptions of Ethics in the Curriculum. *Issues in Accounting Education* 4 (1): 70–81.

English, L. 1990. The Teaching of Ethics. *The Australian Accountant* 60 (1): 22–25.

Gandz, J., and N. Hayes. 1988. Teaching Business Ethics. *Journal of Business Ethics* 7 (9): 657–669.

George, R. J. 1987. Teaching Business Ethics: Is there a Gap between Rhetoric and Reality? *Journal of Business Ethics* 6 (7): 513–518.

———. 1988. The Challenge of Preparing Ethically Responsible Managers: Closing the Rhetoric-Reality Gap. *Journal of Business Ethics* 7 (9): 715–720.

Hoffman, W. M., and J. M. Moore. 1982. Results of a Business Ethics Curriculum Survey Conducted by the Centre for Business Ethics. *Journal of Business Ethics* 1: 81–83.

Hurley, G. 1988. The Decay of Business Ethics. *Management* (November): 27–28, 30–31, 34.

Jones, T. M. 1989. Ethics Education in Business: Theoretical Considerations. *The Organizational Behaviour Teaching Review* 13 (4): 1–18.

Karnes, A., and J. Sterner. 1988. The Role of Ethics in Accounting Education. *The Accounting Educators' Journal*: 18–31.

Langenderfer, H. Q., and J. W. Rockness. 1989. Integrating Ethics into the Accounting Curriculum: Issues, Problems, and Solutions. *Issues in Accounting Education* 4 (1): 58–69.

Loeb, S. E. 1988. Teaching Students Accounting Ethics: Some Crucial Issues. *Issues in Accounting Education* 3 (2): 316–329.

———, and J. P. Bedingfield. 1972. Teaching Accounting Ethics. *The Accounting Review* 47 (4): 811–813.

Mace, J. 1989. Taking Stock of Business. *Chartered Accountant of Australia* 60 (4): 8–10, 12.

Mintz, S. M. 1990. Ethics in the Management Accounting Curriculum. *Management Accounting* 71 (12): 51–54.

National Commission on Fraudulent Financial Reporting (Treadway Commission). 1987. *Report of the National Commission on Fraudulent Financial Reporting.*

Parker, L. D. 1987. An Historical Analysis of Ethical Pronouncements and Debate in the Australian Accounting Profession. *Abacus* 23 (2): 122–140.

Powers, C. W., and D. Vogel. 1980. *Ethics in the Education of Business Managers.* The Hastings Center.

Sack, R. J. 1985. Commercialism in the Profession: A Threat to be Managed. *Journal of Accountancy* 160 (4): 125–134.

Scribner, E., and M. P. Dillaway. 1989. Strengthening the Ethics Content of Accounting Courses. *Journal of Accounting Education* 7 (1): 41–55.

Singh, J. B. 1989. The Teaching of Ethics in Canadian Schools of Management and Administrative Studies. *Journal of Business Ethics* 8 (1): 51–56.

Smith, L. M., and C. Bain. 1990. The Challenge of Professional Accounting Ethics. *Internal Auditing* 5 (4): 20–31.

Smith, R. B. 1990. Ethics in Business: An Essential Element of Success. *Management Accounting* 71 (12): 50.

Comparing Accountants' Perceptions Towards Marketing and Advertising in Hong Kong and Malaysia: A Preliminary Study

Thomas C. H. Wong, Oliver H. M. Yau,
Abdul Latif Shaikh Mohamed Al-Murisi and Abdul Aziz Abdul Latif

INTRODUCTION

The existing literature on attitudes toward advertising and marketing has progressed along two distinct streams of research. Studies in the first stream explore attitudes towards marketing and advertising from the viewpoint of consumers (Barksdale and Deaden 1972; Hite and Bellizzi 1986; Hite and Kiser 1985). Overall, two types of results were obtained. First, it was found that consumers had negative attitudes towards advertising and marketing in general. Criticisms mainly focused on advertising, deceptive advertising, insufficient information and proliferation of advertising. Second, consumer attitudes about professional advertising were generally favorable. Consumers believed that advertising would not lower professional image (Hite and Bellizzi 1986).

The second stream of research comprises a number of studies that explore professionals' viewpoints of advertising and marketing (Honeycutt and Marts 1990; Yau and Wong 1987; Yau 1987; Hite and Schultz 1987; Hite, Schultz, and Weaver 1988; Hite and Fraser 1988; Jackson and Tod 1991; Stevens, McConkey, and Loudon 1990; Yau and Sin 1985). It was found that professionals tended to be more conservative than consumers. Most studies indicated that professionals still held negative attitudes towards advertising their services.

Studies in the above two streams were mostly conducted in the United States. Yau and Wong (1987) have indicated that economic and cultural forces would have impacts on professionals' attitudes toward advertising. However, little has been done comparing professionals' attitudes toward advertising. Hence, this article attempts to examine how CPA firms in different countries perceive the concepts of advertising and marketing. More specifically, the main points are (a) to better understand how accountants perceive the effects of advertising and marketing of their services on pro-

fessional ethics and (b) to compare Hong Kong accountants' perceptions towards marketing and advertising with those in Malaysia.

BACKGROUND

Professional accounting associations were established during the late 19th century. Like other professional bodies, a feature of their structure is self-discipline. A code of ethics is imposed upon members in order to protect the interests of the public and the reputation of the profession. Since the earliest years, one of the tenets of that code has been restriction on self-promotion through advertising or publicity. This restriction has gained virtually universal support from the public and the profession until the 1970s. Nowadays, professional accounting bodies in most English-speaking countries have relaxed restrictions on advertising and other marketing activities to varying degrees.

Reasons for Development

The development of marketing, especially advertising, by professional accountants in most developed or developing countries followed more or less the same pattern as the United States, profession whose members initiated the change. The driving force behind the change came mainly from government. The United States accounting professions were challenged by the Federal States Commission and later by the Justice Department on the issues of price fixing, anti-trust law, and conspiracy in restraint of trade. The British accounting professions were challenged by the Monopolies Commission, and by the Office of Fair Trading on restrictive trade practices.

Thomas C. H. Wong is at Griffith University in Australia, Oliver H. M. Yau is at University of Southern Queensland, Australia, and Abdul Latif Shaikh Mohamed Al-Murisi and Abdul Aziz Abdul Latif are both at Universiti Utara Malaysia, in Malaysia.

In the 1970s the British accounting professions presented a united front against the arguments of the Monopolies Commission's view that restrictive trade practices resulted from prohibition of promotional activities. In 1983, the Council of the Institute of Chartered Accountants in England and Wales changed its attitude towards advertising and agreed that the present rules were unsatisfactory in many respects and that publicity and advertising should be permitted. This line of thinking was shared and supported by large accounting firms. One of the possible reasons which brought about this drastic change was that large accounting firms, which are major international enterprises, were heavily hit by stagflation in the 1970s. Suffering from a combination of lower earnings and rising overheads, these major firms had to look for opportunities to increase market share. The territory of the smaller practice did not escape attention. The large firms saw that liberalization of advertising and some marketing activities was the surest way of gaining much of the smaller firms' business. Another reason for the change of attitude was the competition from nonaccounting sectors, such as banks and financial institutions, which had provided services traditionally rendered by chartered accountants. Nonaccounting firms were able to use all media to advertise their services whereas professional accounting firms were not allowed to compete equally. Thus, professional accountants found that there was a need to inform the general public of all services which their profession was able to offer and thereby to ensure that the profession did not lose ground to those without professional qualification or professional responsibility.

The Accounting Profession in Hong Kong

The Hong Kong Society of Accountants (HKSA) was established in 1973 by the Professional Accountants Ordinance. There are three classes of membership: student, associate, and fellow. In addition, practicing certificates were issued to those who have obtained appropriate experience and passed the required examinations. In December 1988, HKSA had about 12,000 student members, 4,500 associate and fellows, and 400 accounting firms. Among these accounting firms, 95 percent have fewer than 50 staff. All the Big Eight firms have offices in Hong Kong. The largest of them has about 800 staff. The average size of the Big Eight firms is around 400 staff.

Since the 1970s, Hong Kong has built herself into one of the major financial and industrial centers of the world. The success of Hong Kong is largely attributed to the "nonintervention" policy of the government. As such, business is able to operate under minimum government regulation. Nevertheless, accountants in Hong Kong are not allowed to advertise within this environment of free trade and free competition. Statement 1.205B, Professional Ethics: Advertising, of the Hong Kong Society of Accountants states, "A member should not advertise his professional services or skills." A member of the HKSA may be restricted from placing an advertisement under these situations. The development of accounting standards in Hong Kong was or has been very much in line with their development in the United Kingdom. The direction of the HKSA is no doubt influenced largely by its counterpart in the United Kingdom It would be surprising therefore to see that both institutes have different views on the issue of advertising and marketing.

The Accounting Profession in Malaysia

Malaysia was formerly a colony of the United Kingdom. The development of the accounting profession in Malaysia was also very much influenced by the professional accounting associations in the United Kingdom. A well-organized accountancy profession started in Malaysia, when a group of qualified accountants returned from the United Kingdom in pre- World War II and established the Association of Chartered and Incorporated Accountants (ACIA). However, their activities were stopped in 1940 to 1945 during the World War II.

In 1958, twenty local accountants who were members of the ACIA incorporated the Malaysian Association of Certified Public Accountants (MACPA) and the Malaysian branch of the Association of Certified and Corporate Accountants (ACCA). The MACPA is responsible for controlling accounting standards in Malaysia. The Accounting and Auditing Standards Committee of the MACPA has been assigned the responsibility of studying every standard issued by the International Accounting Standards Committee (IASC). The approved standards will then become mandatory to all MACPA members. However, as a private body which was hampered by its relatively small membership, MACPA was unable to address many issues faced by the accountancy profession.

In 1967, recognizing the need for legal regulation, the Government, through the Accountants Act 1967, established the Malaysian Institute of Accountants (MIA). However, for the first twenty years of its incorporation, the MIA was dormant except in the activity of registering its members.

Since 1973, the idea of integration to strengthen the profession had been deliberated by the Councils of the MACPA and the MIA. Unfortunately, in July 1985, the Amendment Bill to the Accountants Act 1967 to effect the merger of the two bodies was rejected by the Cabinet. Despite this setback, the MACPA and the MIA continued to work towards unification of the profession.

April 1987 saw a new dimension in the accounting profession in Malaysia when the joint working committee's proposed cooperation arrangement was accepted by the Council of the two bodies. Under this arrangement, all technical standards for the accountancy profession in the country would be jointly developed by them and issued as joint statements to members of both bodies. Through the consolidation of resources and efforts, the two bodies will minimize duplication of effort and work together for the good of the accountancy profession in Malaysia.

THE STUDY

The Samples

The Hong Kong sample was drawn from the Hong Kong *Yellow Pages* telephone directory which provided a list of 360 CPA firms. One hundred twenty firms were drawn by systematic sampling. Eighty successful interviews resulted, a response rate of 75 percent. This response rate is acceptable when it is compared with those in similar studies in Hong Kong (Sin, Cheng, and Yau 1986). The CPA firms in the sample were largely small firms with only one partner (68.75%). Only 6.25% of them had four or more partners. Results also indicate that 93.75% of them were small firms with 50 or less staff and only 6.25% had more than 50 staff. These findings are very close to those of the population.

The Malaysian sample was drawn by using a systemic 1 in 3 sampling technique using the Directory of Accountants, Tax Consultants and Tax Advisers (as at 30 September, 1988) as the sampling frame. Structured questions were sent to the senior partners of 416 CPA firms. Out of the 416 questionnaires posted, 68 envelopes marked moved or no such person were returned. Eighty-six successful responses were received which give an acceptable response rate of 20.67% (Kerlinger 1973).

Measurement Instrument

Apart from the demographic profile of respondents, 27 statements were tailored to analyze the CPAs' perception of marketing and advertising. These 27 statements were classified into five categories: (1)

promotion, (2) products/services, (3) price, (4) customers and (5) ethics of accounting services, and were evaluated by respondents on a 5-point Likert scale, ranging from strongly disagree (1) to strongly agree (5). To make the analysis simple, responses on all statements were recoded in three categories: "agree," "uncertain" and "disagree."

FINDINGS

After eliminating the uncertain responses, each statement of the 27 items was subject to a two-tailed z-test. For the two samples, the hypothesis was tested at the alpha level of 0.05. The result shows that all statements are significant at 0.05, except for statements 3 and 8 for the Hong Kong sample. In order to compare the perceptions of the two samples employed in the analysis, a T-test was used to compare their mean scores. At the level of 0.05, 14 out of the 27 statements were found to have significant difference between the two samples.

Attitudes Towards Promotion

Accountants in both countries showed a significant difference in opinion on statement 1, "all accounting firms should be allowed to advertise." In Hong Kong, 71.25% of the respondents disagreed with this statement whereas in Malaysia only 44.7% disagreed. In addition, the Hong Kong respondents disagreed more strongly that "accounting firms should not have marketing departments" than their counterparts in Malaysia. In the same vein, Hong Kong accountants agreed more than the Malaysian accountants that "advertisements will ruin our company's (accounting firm's) goodwill." Being professional, these two groups of respondents all agreed very strongly that "our service quality is the best promotional tool."

Attitudes Towards Product/Services

A total of 94.2% of the Malaysia respondents agreed that "accounting firms tailor their services according to the needs of the clients" whereas 82.5% in Hong Kong agreed to this statement. In the same direction, Malaysia accountants showed much stronger disagreement to the statement, "differences between the quality of competing firms are insignificant and unimportant," than their Hong Kong counterparts.

Attitudes Towards Pricing

The two groups of respondents showed a significant difference in opinion in four out of the six

TABLE 1
Attitudes Towards Promotion

Statement	Mean Score		
	Hong Kong (N=80)	Malaysia (N=85)	*T*-Value
1. All accounting firms should be allowed to advertise.	2.088	2.810	−3.40**
2. We will not advertise even if it is allowed.	3.150	3.024	.53
3. Sales turnover can be increased through aggressive advertising campaigns.	2.962	3.048	−.39
4. Our company needs a marketing department.	1.788	2.424	−3.18*
5. Advertisements will ruin our company's goodwill.	3.175	2.602	2.60*
6. Sponsoring academic exhibitions or contests can improve goodwill.	3.825	3.512	1.66
7. Our service quality is the best promotional tool.	4.663	4.702	.39
8. Direct mailing is the best way to make our company known to the public.	2.900	2.602	1.44
9. Personal selling will have a limited effect on promotion of our services.	2.575	2.655	−.37

* significant at the level of 0.05.
** significant at the level of 0.01.

TABLE 2
Attitudes Towards Product/Service

Statement	Mean Score		
	Hong Kong (N=80)	Malaysia (N=85)	*T*-Value
10. We need to increase the provision of a variety of services.	3.738	4.024	−1.49
11. We tailor our services according to the needs of our clients.	4.138	4.518	−2.59*
12. Quality of services is not important.	1.563	1.235	1.93
13. Differences between the quality of competing firms are are insignificant and unimportant.	2.413	1.624	4.13**

* significant at the level of 0.05.
** significant at the level of 0.01.

TABLE 3
Attitudes Towards Pricing

Statement	Mean Score		
	Hong Kong (N=80)	Malaysia (N=85)	*T*-Value
14. Lower price cannot attract more customers.	2.713	3.323	−2.40*
15. Higher-quality services deserve higher prices.	4.200	4.698	−3.65**
16. Customers in general pay more attention to price than quality.	3.300	3.577	−2.03*
17. We always revise our prices.	3.025	3.518	−2.33*
18. When we price our services we consider our competitors' pricing policy.	3.113	3.259	−.67
19. We price our services after considering our market position.	2.925	3.329	−1.89

* significant at the level of 0.05.
** significant at the level of 0.01.

statements in this section. The Malaysian accountants showed much stronger agreement than the Hong Kong accountants towards the statement, "higher quality services deserve higher price." In addition, they tended to believe more that "customers in general pay more attention to price than quality," (62.8%) and also "accounting firm always revise their pricing policy"(52 percent). However, a contradiction was shown in that the Malaysian accountants agreed more than the Hong Kong accountants that "lower prices cannot attract more customers."

Attitudes Towards Customers

This section shows a very significant difference in opinion between the two groups of respondents. Three out of the four statements showed significant difference at the level of 0.01. It was found that both groups had mixed feelings about their primary objective, whether to make money or to provide services to satisfy customers. However, the Malaysian accountants seemed to be more customer-oriented than their Hong Kong counterparts. A total of 95.3% of the Malaysian respondents indicated that "they will try their best to effect a satisfactory remedy when their clients complain about their service," whereas only 70 percent of respon-

dents in Hong Kong agreed to the statement. However, they all disagreed with the statement that "customers are always right" and significant differences were not shown in this regard. However, most Hong Kong respondents (76.25%) indicated that they disagreed to statement 23 with, which was concerned with the provision of marketing training courses to the accountants of their firms, whereas only 62 percent of their Malaysian counterparts showed disagreement. Although it appears that in general, Hong Kong accountants are less customer oriented, 72.5% of the Hong Kong accountants agreed that the primary objective of their accounting firm is to make money whereas only about half of the Malaysia accountants agreed to this statement. Hong Kong accountants, therefore, tended to be more profit oriented than their counterparts in Malaysia.

Attitudes Towards Ethics

The findings show that accountants in both countries in general are ethical. A total of 92.8% of the Malaysian respondents disagreed with the statement that "in order to satisfy our customers, we may do something that they request, even though it is unethical," whereas 80 percent of the

TABLE 4
Attitudes Towards Customers

Statement	Mean Score		
	Hong Kong (N=80)	Malaysia (N=85)	T-Value
20. The primary objective of our company is to make money.	3.875	2.843	4.87**
21. Customers are always right.	2.275	2.386	−.57
22. When clients complain about our services, we try our best to effect a satisfactory remedy.	3.825	4.643	−5.79**
23. We provide marketing training courses to our accountants.	1.850	2.725	−4.35**

* significant at the level of 0.05.
** significant at the level of 0.01.

TABLE 5
Attitudes Towards Ethics

Statement	Mean Score		
	Hong Kong (N=80)	Malaysia (N=85)	T-Value
24. If we are too aggressive in promoting our services, there will be undesired effects upon our professional image.	3.575	4.048	−2.33*
25. MIA/HKSA should relax the rules against advertising and promotion.	2.638	2.940	−1.39
26. Word of mouth is not enough to inform customers about our services.	2.775	3.012	-1.04
27. In order to satisfy our customers, we may do something that they request, even though it is unethical.	1.675	1.268	2.91*

* significant at the level of 0.05.
** significant at the level of 0.01.

Hong Kong accountants showed disagreement. However, only 63.25% agreed to the statement that "if we are with too aggressive in promoting our services, there will be undesired effects upon our professional image," whereas more than 70 percent showed agreement with the same statement. On the other hand, only 28.75% agreed that the HKSA should relax the rules against advertising and promotion whereas 41.7% of the Malaysian accountants agreed that the MIA should relax the rules against advertising and promotion.

DISCUSSION AND IMPLICATIONS

The findings of the comparison between the opinions of accountants in Hong Kong and Malaysia on marketing and advertising suggests several broad conclusions:

1. In general, accounting firms in Malaysia are more aggressive in marketing their services.

2. Accounting firms in Malaysia are more market oriented because they recognized the fact that there are significant and important differences between competing firms.

3. Accounting firms in Malaysia are price conscious; therefore, they revise their pricing policy in order to remain competitive.

4. Accounting firms in Malaysia in general are more customer oriented. They will try their best to effect a satisfactory remedy when clients complain about their services. In order to remain competitive, they would provide marketing training to their accounting staff.

5. In general, accountants in both countries are ethical, and they are not particularly in favor of the idea of relaxing the rules against advertising and promotion.

In general, the success of Hong Kong in becoming one of the financial and industrial centers of the world is largely attributed to the "nonintervention" policy of the government. Business is able to operate under minimum government regulations. Under this kind of business environment, business firms enjoy a very high degree of freedom in conducting their business. Likewise, professionals there should be very market and customer oriented. However, the findings show that the Malaysian accountants are in fact more market and customer oriented in all aspects.

There are several possible reasons that explain why Hong Kong accounting firms were not more market and customer oriented as their counterparts in Malaysia.

First, Hong Kong has been lacking the necessary catalyst to facilitate changes of attitudes towards marketing and advertising. During the 1970s and 1980s, Hong Kong enjoyed a very steady economic growth, which has made CPA firms complacent with their present situations. CPA firms have been enjoying steadily flourishing business since the People's Republic of China opened its doors in 1978.

Second, because of the fast expanding market in Hong Kong and China, it is apparent that Big Eight (now Big Six) firms do not need to cannibalize market share from small CPA firms in order to maintain their huge operating expenses.

Third, it seems that the business of large CPA firms in Hong Kong has not been affected by competitors such as banks, financial companies and other management consulting firms, which offer many of the services traditionally provided by CPA firms. This may be due to the rapidly expanding market potential as a result of the economic growth in Hong Kong and China. Hence, there has been no pressure for change of the advertising and promotion rules.

Traditionally, Hong Kong has been regarded as more liberal than Malaysia because of the government's laissez-faire policy. The findings indicate that Hong Kong accountants were not as market oriented, which may be attributed to the factors of a buoyant economic environment, absence of government pressure and absence of competition from nonaccounting companies. Further research should operationalize these constructs and relate them to accountants' attitudes towards advertising across a number of countries. Also, the cultural values of accountants can be incorporated as a predictor variable to explain differences in accountant's perceptions among countries.

REFERENCES

Adbdul Latif, S. M. A., and A. L. Abdul Aziz. 1990. Perceptions of CPAs Towards Marketing and Advertising: A Malaysian Experience. *Proceedings of the Second Asian-Pacific Conference on International Accounting Issues.* Vancouver, B.C. Canada (October 11–13): 88–91.

American Institute of Certified Public Accountants. 1988. Rule of Conduct 502 — Advertising and Other Form of Solicitation.

Barksdale, H. C., and W. R. Deaden. 1972. Consumer Attitudes Towards Marketing and Consumerism. *Journal of Marketing* (36): 28–35.

Hite, R. E., and J. A. Bellizzi. 1986. Customers Attitudes Toward Accountants, Lawyers and Physicians with Respect to Advertising Professional Services. *Journal of Advertising Research* (June/July): 45–54.

———, and C. Fraser. 1988. Meta-Analysis of Attitudes Toward Advertising by Professionals. *Journal of Marketing*, 52 (July): 95–105.

———, and E. Kiser. 1985. Consumers' Attitudes Towards Lawyers with Regard to Advertising Professional Services. *Journal of the Academy of Marketing Sciences* (Spring): 321–339.

———, and N. O. Schultz. 1987. A Survey of the Utilization of Advertising by CPA Firms. *Journal of Professional Services Marketing* (3:1/2): 231–245.

———, N. O. Schultz, and J. A. Weaver. 1988. A Content Analysis of CPA Advertising in National Print Media From 1979 to 1984. *Journal of the Academy of Marketing Science* (16: 3/4): 1–15.

Honeycutt, E. D., and J. A. Marts. 1990. Marketing by Professionals as Applied to CPA Firms: Room for Improvement. *Journal of Professional Services Marketing* (6: 1): 29–42.

Hong Kong Society of Accountants, Statement 1,205B. 1986. Professional Ethics: Advertising.

Institute of Chartered Accountants in England and Wales. 1986. Revised Guidelines on Publicity and Advertising. *Accountancy* (September).

Jackson, M., and A. Tod. 1991. Attitudes Towards Marketing: The Case of Queensland Solicitors. *Asia Pacific Business: Issues and Challenges*. Proceedings of the Academy of International Business Southeast Asia Conference. National University of Singapore: 254–260.

Kerlinger, F. N. 1973. *Foundation of Behavioral Research*. Holt, Rinehart and Winston.

Oliver, D. D., and C. L. Posey. 1980. National vs Local Accounting Firms: What Are their Differences of Perception Concerning Advertising. *Arkansas Business and Economic Review*, 14 (Fall): 1–5.

Schweikart, J. A. 1987. Attitude Measurement and Instrumentation in International Accounting Research. *International Journal of Accounting* (Spring): 131–141.

Sin, L. Y. M., D. W. L. Cheng, and O. H. M. Yau. 1986. Occupational Stress of Managers in An Oriental Culture: A Causal Analysis. Proceedings of the Academy of International Business Southeast Asia Regional Conference: 664–778.

Stevens, R., C. W. McConkey, and D. L. Loudon. 1990. A Comparison of Physicians' and Attorneys' Attitudes Toward Advertising. *Journal of Professional Services Marketing* (5: 2): 115–125.

Yau, O. H. M. 1987. Consumer Rights: The Perception of Business Managers in Hong Kong. In J. M. Hawes, and G. B. Glisan, eds. *Developments in Marketing Science* (Vol. X): 146–150.

———, and L. Sin. 1985. Attitudes Towards Advertising Among Executives in the People's Republic of China. In *Proceeding of the Annual Conference of the European Marketing Academy*: 248–256.

———, and T. Wong. 1990. How Do CPA Firms Perceive Marketing and Advertising? A Hong Kong Experience. *European Journal of Marketing* (24:2): 43–54.

International Accounting Standards

The conference program included four papers that examine problems involving international accounting standards. The central question is: To what extent should standards be harmonized internationally? These papers offer several suggestions for addressing the harmonization issue, both in practice and in the classroom. For example, the numerous competing environmental factors and theories are organized into intellectually manageable groups, global and segmented models are presented, and greater cooperation is urged. One solution offered is to replace the emphasis on harmonization with an emphasis on synchronization with the use of trading blocs similar to the EEC. Another solution is to focus efforts on the most important differences such as disclosure by the largest publicly-traded companies.

IASC and Globalization: Can the Problem of Noncompliance be Overcome?

Fouad K. AlNajjar

INTRODUCTION

In general, there seems to be an agreement about many of the environmental factors that influence accounting practices worldwide. These factors usually shape the accounting practices in different countries. This article discusses these factors and then focuses on the nature of the accounting differences themselves. A score is then assigned to every country on each factor and is carried in a section at the end of the paper to measure the development of accounting standards in these countries. Eight countries from different parts of the world were selected for this study. These are four western European countries, the United Kingdom, France, Germany, and Belgium; two communist countries, Commonwealth of Independent States (Commonwealth of Independent States—CIS—is used to refer to the former Soviet Union) and Poland; and two developing countries, Iraq and Egypt. Later, the United States and China are briefly referred to.

The research methodology involved sending questionnaires, conducting personal interviews with partners of major accounting firms[1] as well as with academics in many of the examined countries. Responses to questionnaires and personal interviews are shown in Table 1.

Following the stock market crash of October 1987, globalization of the capital markets as well as the accounting rules became inevitable. This raises several questions: Is globalization of accounting rules possible? Do national accounting systems have to remain different? Should the international accounting standards change? This paper tries to address these questions and to propose a model for the international standards.

CAUSES OF DIFFERENCES

Accounting practices differ substantially from one country to another. Several factors explain this. The most likely characteristics which influence accounting development include differences in political systems, nature of economic laws, providers of finance, taxation rules, legal systems, and strength of the accounting profession. These factors are examined first.

POLITICAL SYSTEM

Internationally, political systems differ and range from democracies (e.g., United States, United Kingdom, Germany) to totalitarian oligarchies (e.g., China). In the former, companies of the private sector play an important role in running the economy while in the latter, the state owns almost all means of production with very little roles for the private sector. In some of the socialist countries, this case still exists despite the long-awaited intention of these governments to open their economy and introduce free market systems. In fact, these countries, like the CIS, are having difficulties in privatizing their economies due to the fact that communism was enforced in these countries for 70 years. Under a planned economy, accounting principles, procedures and measurements are rigid and centrally controlled, and auditors are government employees. Accordingly, an accounting system which is suitable for a free market economy is different from another system that is optimal for a centrally controlled one.

Furthermore, political systems export and import accounting systems. For instance, CIS accounting has influenced the accounting practices of many countries. Examples are Poland, Czechoslovakia, and some Middle Eastern countries. British accounting rules were exported to most of the Commonwealth and colonial countries. In addition, the French accounting plan was exported to many French colonies in Africa and Asia. Examples of such colonies include Algeria and Tunisia.

---

[1]While visiting these countries, valuable insight, opinions and materials on the accounting practices were collected. Those firms which were particularly helpful with this and in arranging for interviews were Arthur Andersen, Arthur Young, Ernst & Whinney, Peat Marwick and Price Waterhouse. The author is grateful for their help.

Fouad K. AlNajjar is an Assistant Professor at Wayne State University.

TABLE 1
Summary of Questionnaire Responses and Personal Interviews

Country	Questionnaires Sent	Completed Responses	Response Rate %	Personal Interview
Western Countries				
Belgium	18	10	55.5	5
France	12	5	41.7	4
Germany	27	13	48.0	7
United Kingdom	24	11	45.8	8
Subtotal	81	39	47.8	24
Other Countries				
Egypt	31	5	16.0	5
Iraq	24	11	46.0	6
Poland	10	7	70.0	2
CIS	2	2	100.0	2
Subtotal	67	25	58.0	15
Total	148	64	52.9	39

NATURE OF ECONOMIC SYSTEMS (NATURE OF BUSINESS OWNERSHIP)

World economic systems also vary from almost total reliance on free market forces (e.g., Switzerland) to almost complete central control (e.g., China). Along this spectrum, the degrees of central government involvement in controlling the economies differ and this led to differences in accounting systems (different degrees of standardization). In the free market system, market prices are the powerful factors that guide economic decisions and the allocation of scarce economic resources. Free market systems make possible the preservation of private property rights, individual freedoms and orderly economic organization. It has been suggested that "the accounting standards and principles needed to assure the discipline's utility in market-oriented economic systems rest on such key concepts as transactions and events measurements, systematic and periodically complete accumulation of data, measurement of periodic business income, and the entire process of periodic financial reporting, full disclosure, and outside review of accounting reports presented by management" (Choi and Mueller 1978, 35).

Under controlled economies, however, the role of accounting seems larger and more important.

The entire system of prices and costs is established through accounting procedures rather than through market processes. In the CIS, enterprises once had and still have access to new resources through a planning and control process rather than through past performance. This case still exists even with the introduction of *Perestroika* in 1986. In these countries, accounting and statistical records and reports are all typically kept within a uniform system. Accounting rules and procedures are very formalized and subject to uniform central control. The purpose of such a rigidly constructed accounting system is to facilitate planning and control. Accounting reports are used for evaluating enterprises' performance and resource allocation.

PROVIDERS OF FINANCE (USERS OF ACCOUNTING INFORMATION)

Acquisition of all or most means of production by the government has resulted in producing a rigid and compulsory uniform accounting system since the government is the main user of accounting information (e.g., the CIS, China, Poland). This also still applies to many other Eastern Bloc countries and many developing countries. On the other hand, in the United States and the United Kingdom, the widespread private ownership of corporate securities has resulted in a tremendous need for financial reports and disclosure. This has led to the introduction of many accounting standards and rules by the accounting profession.

In between, however, Germany has a heavy bank ownership of corporate equities which resulted in banks being the main user of accounting information. In France, the relative absence of private participation in corporate equities has limited effective financial communications largely due to "insider" communication channels.

TAXATION

This factor reflects the extent to which taxation rules determine the accounting measurements found in financial statements. The degree to which tax regulations determine accounting measurements varies. In some countries the figures included in financial statements are strictly determined by tax laws and other government legislation. Germany is an example where tax rules have considerable influence on accounting. In this country, the tax regulations are the accounting rules and hence the published reports are the same as the tax accounts. This case still exists in the CIS, Poland, Iraq and Egypt. In these countries, the tax laws require that any allowances which are to be claimed for tax purposes must be charged to the published reports. In addition, depreciation methods and rates are prescribed. In Germany, tax regulation requires the use of the double declining balance method, but this may be changed to the straight-line basis when the latter results in a higher charge.

Another example of the overriding influence of taxation on accounting measurement is the valuation of fixed assets. In fact, according to the latest French Finance Acts of 1978 and 1979, revaluation is obligatory for listed companies and for those which receive funds from the state. It is optional for others. This is done by using government indices and the credit is carried to an undistributable revaluation reserve. The purpose of such revaluation is to show current value of the assets. For depreciable assets, an amount equal to the extra depreciation due to revaluation is credited to the profit and loss account and debited to the revaluation account. Thus, the effect of revaluation on profit and tax is neutralized. This move from no revaluations to compulsory revaluations was due to the change in tax rules in France.

As far as the remaining countries of this study are concerned, taxation rules have little or no impact on the content of the published reports. Figures

from these reports are subsequently adjusted for tax purposes. In the United Kingdom, for instance, which has an older tradition of published accounting and where commercial rules have come first, there is no degree of separation between tax and financial accounting. Taxation authorities in the United Kingdom have to adjust the published accounts for their own purposes.

LEGAL SYSTEM (SETTING ACCOUNTING RULES AND STANDARDS)

Internationally, the nature of the legal system varies. The legal systems have been divided into many groups, but the most common are two: common law and *Romano-Germanic* law. The former system depends on a limited amount of statute law which is interpreted by courts to build up large amount of case law to supplement the statutes. Its rules seek to provide answers to specific cases rather than to formulate general rules for the future. The common law was formed in England primarily by postconquest judges acting on the king's behalf (David and Brierley 1978).

This, of course, has an effect on accounting through company law. In the United Kingdom, for instance, until the introduction of the 1981 and 1982 Companies Acts, the law did not prescribe large numbers of accounting details, but rather established general rules covering companies' behavior and how they should publish their financial accounts. This is mainly due to the strength and influence of the accounting profession in the United Kingdom. After 1982, however, accounting, specifically financial reporting, began to be more dependent upon law because of the introduction of the EEC 4th Directive.

Other countries have *Romano-Germanic* law which was based on the *Romanius civile* as compiled by Justinian in the sixth century and developed by European universities since the twelfth century (Kagan 1955; Derrett 1968). Under this legal system, rules are linked to ideas of justice and morality which then become doctrine. This difference in law has an important effect on company laws and commercial codes which set accounting rules and reporting standards in greater detail. In Germany, for example, to a large extent company accounting is a branch of company law. In some other countries, *dirigisme* is compounded with centralization and a desire to control the economy. This may be found in the CIS and other socialist countries and to some extent in France and Egypt where an accounting plan or chart of accounts exists.

Accordingly, in the United Kingdom with its common law tradition, the accounting profession finds room to introduce accounting standards, as the law in the past has provided only general rules for financial reporting. On the other hand, where the legal system is based on the *Romano-Germanic* tradition, accounting rules are rigid and set in greater detail. Therefore, the profession has no room or it is too weak to play any important role in setting accounting standards. This case exists in the CIS, China, Poland, Iraq, Egypt, and to some extent in France, Germany and Belgium.

ACCOUNTING PROFESSION

The strength, size, competence and age of the accounting profession in a country may follow to a large extent from the various factors outlined above and from the type of accounting system they have helped to produce. For example, the lack of a substantial body of private shareholders and companies of the private sector in some European countries (e.g., France, Belgium) meant that the need for auditors is much smaller than it is in the United States or the United Kingdom. More specifically, in France, the youth and the absence of a private professional accounting body may be explained by the fact that the government dominated early and set accounting and auditing rules which led to the unimportance of auditing.

The governments of many European countries require certain types of companies to be audited, thus setting certain restrictions on who shall carry out the audit. In Germany and France, for instance, memberships in the accounting bodies overlap with auditing bodies. Membership in the accounting body usually enables membership in the auditing association (AlNajjar 1991a, 7).

In the CIS, a totally different case exists. There is no professional accounting body similar to those of the Western countries. There is, however, a union for each ministry for all workers and employees, regardless of their profession. In Poland, the profession plays no role in setting accounting standards or in making any recommendations.

In the developing countries, accounting skills are relatively low. Generally speaking, there is no security market and even where there is one, it is usually underdeveloped and there is little need for financial reporting and disclosure. In these countries, accounting practices are expressed by law. Accounting rules and principles were previously felt to be the responsibility of the companies concerned. In Egypt, for example, the accounting function was monopolized in the past by foreign companies who operated in that country. However, since the government took control over the economy, influences started to come from the Eastern Bloc. Consequently, in most of the developing countries, an accounting profession either does not exist or has barely developed. For instance, in Egypt it was not until 1958, and in Iraq until 1968, that the profession was organized by the government.

OTHER INFLUENCES

In addition to the above, many other factors may also shape accounting practices. Some of these include, stage of economic development, language, geography, organization of capital market, status of accounting education, speed of business innovation and differences in size, complexity and level of sophistication of both business management and the users of accounting information. Culture is another significant factor that influences the accounting practice.

As far as the developing countries are concerned, influences may also come from the importation of accounting systems from the developed nations. The French Plan, the United States GAAP, the British Companies Acts, and the international accounting standards have been adopted by many developing countries. Some developing countries blindly adopt accounting systems of developed countries irrespective of environmental differences. In this case, the borrowed accounting system does not succeed in the developing country.

NATURE OF DIFFERENCES (ELEMENTS OF STANDARDIZATION)

Having discussed the environmental factors which shape the accounting systems, some of the differences themselves are examined below. To a certain extent, the nature of some of the differences in accounting has already been discussed. Taxation rules, for example, are not only influences towards differences but amount to the differences themselves.

BOOKKEEPING PROCEDURES

This element includes source documents, journals, ledgers, and subsidiary books (their format, content, classification), journalizing and posting accounting transactions and the remaining steps of the accounting cycle. Standardizing the bookkeeping procedures is one of the most essential steps in the process of standardizing an accounting system. The need for consistent and comparable data would certainly start at the very initial stage of the accounting cycle. Standardizing an accounting system would basically require a uniform system of bookkeeping in which accounting transactions are classified and recorded in the books according to the chart of accounts.

With the exception of the United States, the United Kingdom and Germany, all the remaining countries of this study pay considerable attention to this factor. In these countries, the law stipulates format, content, and circulation of primary documents as well as all necessary instructions for carrying out the procedures of journalizing and posting transactions. Content and format of accounting records are also standardized and are classified according to the chart of accounts. In fact, in many of these countries, a certain ministry or agency prepares and prints uniform forms of the required accounting documents, books and financial reports accompanied with instructions for their completion.

Furthermore, in the CIS, the law specifies how accounting documentation and accounting records are to be made up, what is to go into them, how they are to be drawn up and by whom they are to be approved. Such rigid uniform procedures are to ensure that accounting data are ready for the next stage of the accounting cycle in a uniform manner and comparable form.

CHART OF ACCOUNTS AND DEFINITIONS OF ACCOUNTING TERMS

This is another essential element of standardization. In fact, when a country seeks to standardize its accounting system, a chart of accounts is usually first prescribed. A uniform chart makes it easy to classify accounting transactions, enabling government or management to have classified, up-to-date and quick access to data for different purposes. The chart is also important for comparisons because it classifies and defines uniformly all accounting terms. The Russian chart, for example, follows the cycle of business activities with emphasis on cost accounting. This is basically carried out for the purposes of planning and control, setting prices and for resource allocation. In such a country, it was found necessary to explain, for instance, how receipt and issuance of materials are to be recorded in the accounts allotted to this purpose in the chart of accounts, and how they are to be valued.

In France, on the other hand, the chart is mainly concerned with financial accounting with only one class (class 9) assigned for cost accounting. This is because the French government is concerned primarily with financial reporting.

As far as definitions of accounting terms are concerned, in some countries, it is still common to find different words used for the same concept, and differences between concepts confused by the use of the same word for more than one of them. Therefore, accounting terms too are regulated by law in many countries so as to ensure uniformity. The law gives standard definitions for every accounting term included in the chart and gives mutually consistent definitions for such different items as might be brought together in the course of economic and financial analysis. With the exception of the United States, the United Kingdom and Germany, this has been carried out by all countries of the study.

HISTORICAL COST

It seems appropriate for several countries not only to establish uniform formats of financial statements but also to ensure that all displayed items are uniformly valued and measured in order to enable comparisons within and between industries, and for control purposes.

Although historical cost accounting is used widely, the concept is adhered to in varying degrees around the world. In the CIS, China, Poland, Egypt, Iraq and Germany, for example, there is a rigid adherence and consistent use of unsupplemented historical cost accounting. In the United Kingdom, on the other hand, there is a rather relaxed attitude toward revaluation within "historical cost" accounts coupled with steps towards replacement cost. The cases of France and Belgium are different with the organized and compulsory revaluation. But despite this, the distinction between the Western countries in this context remains unclear. For example, even when concentrating on large companies in these countries, it is still very difficult to define the relative positions of these countries. Another example is that it is also difficult to tell which country is more affected by replacement cost: Is it France with the compulsory revaluation of the late 1970s or Britain with relatively considerable use of replacement cost?

DEPRECIATION

Methods and rates of depreciation are also subject to legislation in many countries due to their influence on the results of the year. Some countries rigidly prescribe rules for allocating and calculating depreciation. In the CIS, the straight-line method is widely used and rates of depreciation are fixed by law according to the nature of assets. The rates also depend on the quantities of work done by the assets per day. This is believed to be justified on the grounds that cost stability is necessary for pricing and interperiod cost comparisons. To some extent, this is the case in the other countries with the exception of the United States and the United Kingdom, where the law allows flexibility.

CONSERVATISM

Conservatism applies to an accounting practice that tends to produce "lower values for assets and profits" than would the application of another acceptable practice. It is a basic accounting concept. The strength of conservatism differs from one country to another. This is due to the different users of accounting information. For example, the importance of government as a user of information in the CIS, China, Poland, and Egypt explains the greater conservatism in reporting. In these countries, it is widely known that government officials are more concerned with base figures in order to ensure that the "public funds" are in safe hands.

In Germany, banks play a dominant role in the capital market and the economy. This results in greater conservatism compared, for instance, to the United Kingdom. The reason for this is that banks have to be sure that their long-term investments are safe. Consequently, the accruals convention is less important and there is less interest in the British "true and fair view" concept. The "true and fair view" means the disclosure of all significant information necessary for a reader's understanding of the financial position and the results of operations of an enterprise. Applying the "true and fair view" modifies conservatism.

In the United Kingdom, on the other hand, accounting standards are the compromise treaties which settle a battle between conservatism and the accruals concept. For instance, allowing the capitalization of any development expenditure as allowed in *Statement of Standard Accounting Practices* (SSAP) 13 is not fully conservative, but it may still be prudent. Similarly, the partial accounting for deferred tax in *SSAP 15*, or the taking of profit on long-term contracts as in *SSAP 13* may indicate the same point (Nobes 1984b, 18).

Consequently, when comparing a German company's figures with those of a U.K. company, for example, a series of adjustments to increase the German company's profit figures are always car-

ried out by financial analysts before carrying out the comparison.

CONSISTENCY

Consistency is necessary for the standardization process so as to show as accurately as possible the final results of the year. In the CIS, China, Poland, and Egypt consistency is rigid and compulsory. This is found to be necessary to avoid misuse of the "public funds." In countries like the United Kingdom, France and Belgium, consistency is less adhered to compared to those discussed above. In Germany, the degree of adherence to consistency is even less than that of the latter countries where shifting from one rule or measurement to another may be found in subsequent financial statements of German companies.

UNIFORM FINANCIAL YEAR-END

In order to provide uniform accounting information for users, uniformity is prescribed. Therefore, standardizing financial years for all enterprises becomes necessary for these data to be especially useful for planning and control. Annual figures need to be accumulated at the same time each year. This case exists in the CIS, Poland, and Egypt, where the law prescribes the calendar year as a compulsory financial year with the exception of Egypt where the compulsory financial year is July 1 to June 30 each year.

In France and Belgium, most companies voluntarily (some for fiscal purposes) use the calendar year as a financial year. In addition, this study shows that about 70 percent of companies in each of Germany and the United Kingdom adopt the same financial year.

CONTENT AND FORMAT OF FINANCIAL STATEMENTS

The final and essential phase of the accounting cycle is the task of preparing financial statements. Standardizing financial statements is important because they are used as a basis for comparison. For example, for the CIS, China, Poland, and Egypt, and to some extent for France and Belgium, financial statements are the devices used to express actual operations and to inform the central government about the operations of the enterprises. For financial statements to be as useful as possible, a certain degree of uniformity is needed. Without comparable accounting information, it would be impossible for a central government to find out which sector of the economy is lacking efficiency and productivity. This explains why there is a tendency for uniformity whenever a government of a nation is in control of the economy.

In other countries where the government is less involved, standard formats of financial statements are also found to be necessary. In Germany, for example, standard formats and contents of financial statements have been in force for a long time. This, however, was more emphasized with the introduction of the Corporation Act of 1965 and the Company Act of 1986. In the United Kingdom, the 1981 and 1982 Companies Acts prescribe for the first time in compliance with the requirement of the EEC Fourth Directive obligatory formats and contents of financial statements, but still allows some flexibility. As a result, one may note that both content and format of financial statements are prescribed in all the countries examined.

MODEL FOR THE IASC

Having examined the accounting environment of a number of countries with various degrees of economic freedom, we now turn to focus on the international standards. This paper attempts an in-depth investigation of the major causes which shape accounting rules. For IASC standards to be complied with, those causal factors must be studied seriously. Recently, even the CIS, China and many other former socialist countries have opened their economic doors to the West and are seeking help to develop their economies, including their accounting systems, and learning from "capitalistic" accounting. Some of the IASC standards have been looked at or used by some of the aforementioned countries including a few developing countries. However, IASC standards were rejected or problems arise from their application due to differences in the underlying structures of the accounting environment. To overcome these problems and the problem of noncompliance, this study suggests that the IASC standards to attempt to suit various countries with different environments by issuing them at three levels. For example, each standard should be set not only at its current status, but rather at three levels:

Level 1 (all details of how to apply the stds. are provided)	To suit those countries which have controlled economies (e.g., the CIS, Poland, Yugoslavia, and some developing countries).
Level 2 (many details	To suit those countries with less government involvement com-
provided on the standard)	pared to Level 1 (e.g., France, Belgium, countries of North Africa).
Level 3 (IASC current status)	To suit countries with mainly private enterprises (U.S., U.K.).

Noncompliance with international standards is a big issue for the IASC. The above proposal may provide a base for better adoption of the international standards and may pave a new avenue for the IASC.

CONCLUSION

Internationally, factors that influence the development of accounting practices are many. Clearly, the mix of users of accounting information is crucial to the emergence of the dominant source of rules for accounting practice. In many countries, the importance of the government as a controller of the economy, user of accounting information, and collector of taxes has resulted in the dominance of laws, commercial codes and tax rules. On the other hand, in the United Kingdom and to a great extent in the United States, the effective control over the process of developing the accounting rules has been mainly exercised by the accounting profession. This has resulted in the issuance of detailed accounting standards which give scope for flexibility and the use of judgment. The interest of the private shareholders as the main user of accounting information has been a continuing background pressure on the profession as it develops the standard. This article shows that the environment shapes the accounting practices of many countries. Economic and political systems, legal laws, tax rules, and culture as well as the accounting profession are the foundations for the accounting systems in many countries.

Addressing the questions raised at the beginning of this paper, this article shows that despite the pressure for international harmonization, it would be very difficult, if not impossible, to harmonize the accounting practices of the world. This is basically because of the obvious differences in the underlying structures of the various countries. This paper shows that there are sufficient reasons for differences in accounting systems and that national systems were developed to suit the different needs of the various countries and that they have to stay different. International harmonization may be attempted at regional levels where economic, political, social, cultural and other environmental factors set common boundaries. This paper proposed a model for the IASC.

REFERENCES

AlNajjar, F. K. 1991a. The Dilemma of the Accounting Profession in Germany. *The CPA Journal* (February): 7.

Choi, F. D., and G. G. Mueller. 1978. *Essentials of Multinational Accounting, An Anthology.*

David, R., and J. E. Brierley. 1978. *Major Legal System in the World Today.* Stevens.

Derret, J. D. M. 1968. *An Introduction to Legal System.* Sweet and Maxwell.

Kagan, K. K. 1955. *Three Great Systems of Jurisprudence.* Stevens.

Nobes, C. W. 1984a. *International Classification of Financial Reporting.* Croom Helm,

———. 1984b. An Insight Into U.S. Accounting. *Accountancy* (February).

BIBLIOGRAPHY

Accountancy. 1983. IASC Comes of Age — and Its Only 10 (July).

AlNajjar, F. K. 1991B. Accounting and Society: The Soviet Experience. *Advances in International Accounting Journal* (Vol. 4): 39–64.

———. 1986. Standardization in Accounting Practices: A Comparative International Study. *The International Journal of Accounting* (Vol. 21, No. 2): 161–176.

AICPA. 1975. *Professional Accounting in 30 Countries.*

Benny, J. H. 1975. *European Financial Reporting — West Germany.* ICAEW.

Berlioz, G. 1988. Defeasance Comes to the French Scene. *International Financial Law Review* (Vol. 7, No. 4): 17–18.

British Government. various years. Companies Act 1948, 1976 and 1981. Her majesty's Stationery Office.

Bromwich, M. 1985. Accounting Standard Setting: Can Self Regulation Survive. Paper presented at Strathclyde University (May).

Dewhurst, Charles S., et. al. 1988. Accounting for International Operations. *The CPA Journal* (August): 77–79.

Ernst & Whinney. 1984. *A Guide to Generally Accepted Accounting Principles and Generally Accepted Auditory Standards — The Continental Practice.* Ernst & Whinney.

Forrester, D. A. R. 1977. *Schmalenbach and After, Strathclyde Convergencies.*

Garner, P. 1984. The Development of International Accounting Standards and Conventions. *Research Bulletin of the Institute of Cost and Work Accountants of India*, Vol. III (January).

Gray, S. J. 1985. Cultural Influences and the International Classification of Accounting Systems. Paper presented at EISAM Workshop. Amsterdam (June).

International Accounting Bulletin. 1984. French Bodies Reach Accord on Joint Peer Review (November).

Metcalfe, B. K. 1988. The New Prophets of Profit. *CA Magazine*, Vol. 121 (March): 34–44.

Needles, B. E. 1985. Auditing Standards in Eleven Countries: Similarities, Differences and Possibilities for Harmonization. Paper presented at the 8th EAA Congress. Brussels.

Nobes, C. 1985. Is the IASC Successful? *The Accountant* (August): 20–21.

———. 1986. New Laws for Old: Germany Leads. *Accountancy* (December): 20–21.

———. 1987. Financial Reporting in the EEC: Why and How It Differs. *Management Accounting* (April): 34–35.

Swinson, C. 1988. Towards the European Accountant. *The Accountant's Magazine* (January): 18–19.

Wallace, W. A. 1987. International Accounting and Likely Approaches to Future Inquiry: An Overview of Research. *Management International Review* (Vol. 27, No. 2): 4–25.

Synchronizing International Accounting Standards through Expert Systems

Man C. Maloo and Motichand Maloo

INTRODUCTION

This paper is a continuance of three earlier papers presented/published in the proceedings of American Accounting Association's regional meetings and in the professional journals. They are interrelated and provide the background material for this paper. They are briefly summarized below.

The central thesis of this paper is synchronization of global accounting standards through the expert systems. With communism in eclipse and capitalism taking roots everywhere from St. Petersburg to Shanghai, nations with close cultural and business ties are busy forming trading blocs. These blocs can be used as vehicles to promote synchronization through the use of expert system methodology.

The international accounting standard-setting organizations, especially the International Accounting Standards Committee (IASC) and the blocs, have tools, techniques, and resources to promote global accounting standards through the design and development of a computer-based information system (CBIS) using expert systems. There will be two such systems — one for each bloc and another for global reporting for achieving comparability of financial statements. Being able to provide the global investor with timely, accurate, reliable and comparable information is essential for efficient working of capital markets around the globe.

The First Paper

In the first paper, the researcher was concerned with the identification and analysis of barriers to the development of global accounting standards. The barriers identified in the paper include (1) general disagreement on the objectives of global reporting; (2) level of sophistication of the accounting profession in each country; (3) varying tax laws; (4) national pride and priorities; (5) cultural diversities; (6) level of economic developments; (7) rate of inflation; (8) currency fluctuations, sophistication of national capital markets; (9) inconsistencies permitted or promoted by national professional bodies suited to national needs; (10) emphasis of company laws on form rather than economic substance; (11) fundamental reporting differences; and (12) associate members of the IASC (Maloo 1989). Because of these barriers, it may not be possible to harmonize international accounting standards, and hence capital markets around the globe may not be integrated for free flow of capital (Maloo 1990).

The Second Paper

In the second paper, the researcher continued his focus on the need for synchronization of global accounting standards and integration of global capital markets (Maloo 1991). The focus of attention was on new efforts and strategies employed by international accounting standard-setting bodies who changed their underlying philosophy for global reporting. Specifically, the International Accounting Standards Committee (IASC) changed its philosophical emphasis from flexibility to uniformity along with other efforts and strategies initiated by the International Organization of Securities Commission (IOSCO).

The Third Paper

In the third paper, the researcher discussed and analyzed international accounting standards with the emergence of United Europe of 1992 and beyond (Maloo 1992). The paper concludes that we are one step closer to synchronization with the emergence of many trading blocs around the globe. The European Economic Community (EEC) may play a catalyst role in gradually supplanting national accounting standards. It may create an atmosphere encouraging exemplary behavior for other blocs to follow. Each trading bloc may be looked upon as a vehicle for synchronization of global reporting within the bloc and between blocs with an eventual goal of synchronization of global reporting.

Man C. Maloo is an Associate Professor at Towson State University and Motichand Maloo is a faculty member at Poddar College in India.

The Present Paper

This is an important time for all organizations — countries, trading blocs and international accounting bodies — to recognize that this is the age of teamwork and technological advances. The paper explores the relationship of teams and technologies which may help solve some problems related to international financial reporting. Teams supported by advanced computer technology and communication technology are proving their superiority every day in every walk of our lives. Let us capitalize on them to improve global reporting. Therefore, this paper focuses on integration of team efforts on the part of countries within various trading blocs and advanced or advancing technologies for improving global financial reporting. A computer-based information system (CBIS) using the expert system methodology is suggested in the paper. The CBIS may help improve comparability of financial statements regardless of who and where they were prepared. Such comparable financial statements may help international investors.

The paper does not purport to present the design and development of the expert system. It does not deal with specifics of expert system methodology, nor even with use or growing importance of expert systems where the problem is unstructured. The focus is rather on the global standard-setting organizations and trading blocs who may borrow from the emerging discipline to improve global reporting. Hence, the paper reflects the spirit, if not substance, of the expert systems.

The central thesis of the present paper is synchronization, not harmonization, of global accounting standards which may be possible if all trading blocs national and international accounting standard-setting bodies cooperate. If congruence of goal of global reporting is accepted as *sine quo non* for all involved, it may be possible to achieve synchronization of global accounting standards and financial reporting through synergism. Before we expect the synergistic effect, we have to recognize the diversity and complexity in the global arena which are discussed next.

What are the imperatives beneath the need for synchronizing international accounting standards? Four major imperatives are (1) defining and/or modifying objectives of international reporting; (2) identifying organizations interested in achieving global comparability in financial statements; (3) teamwork by trading blocs; (4) exploring and exploiting expert system methodology and technological advances; and (5) building an expert system for international reporting.

Diverse Objectives

It would be more appropriate that we make every attempt to define international accounting objectives well before we attempt to formulate international accounting standards. How can we make progress on setting global standards without agreeing on the objectives of global financial reporting? All international accounting standards (IAS) developed so far are based on an ad hoc basis or a piecemeal approach rather than conscious and consistent application of accounting theory. The reasons that explain this phenomenon are the complexity of the international environment, social, economic and political differences among nations.

The global accounting standards are set under the influence of the United Nations (UN), Organization of Economic Cooperation and Development (OECD), among others. Global investors and financial statement users have different needs and concerns than national users. Risks inherent in global financial statements are quite different. Measurement of income and valuation concepts used in preparation of financial statements are flexible and differ widely. Flexible financial standards allowed in different countries provide considerable freedom of choice in global reporting. Reliance on an ad hoc change of accounting standards cannot be in the best interest of the accounting profession. Therefore, we should focus on specific global objectives of financial reporting as outlined in Figure 1.

Why can the international accounting organizations not accept the three principal objectives of the Financial Accounting Standards Board (FASB) instead of switching from flexibility to uniformity in global rejoining? According to the FASB's statements of *Financial Accounting Concepts No. 1*, the three principal aims of financial accounting are to

1. provide information that is useful to present and potential investors and creditors and other users in making rational investment, credit, and similar decisions;

2. provide information to help present and potential investors and creditors and other users in assessing the amounts, timing, and uncertainty of prospective case receipts from dividends or interest and the proceeds from the sale, redemption, or maturing of securities or loans;

3. provide information about the economic resources of an enterprise, the claims to those resources, and the effect of transactions, events and circumstances that change resources and claims to those resources.

FIGURE 1
Hierarchy of Elements in a Conceptual Framework for International
Accounting Standards and Reporting

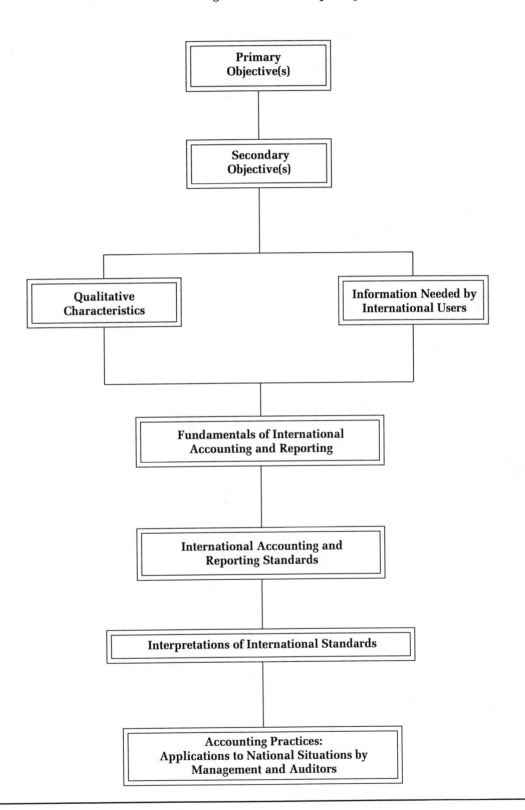

Basic to these objectives is reporting data in terms of economic reality. The FASB also emphasized that the accounting data should be relevant, and noted:

> Information is relevant if it has the capacity to make a difference in decisions. To be recognized, the information conveyed by including an asset, liability, or change therein the financial statements must be relevant (*SFAC No. 5*, 211).

International Diversity

Once Donald J. Kirk, a former chairman of the Financial Accounting Standards Board said, "Harmonization even within the United States is difficult, so I have to be pessimistic about international prospects." In the similar view, Jeau-Claude Paye, the Secretary-General of the OECD said, "Given the complexity of the subject and the weight of the past, the goal of harmonization still seems to be a rather long way off" (Hemp 1985, 34). The notion of harmonization is more myth than reality.

One reason for the synchronization bias in the development of international accounting standards has been due to the far-fetched goal of harmonization. Widely varying national tax and company laws, national priorities and pride still are stumbling blocks in global financial reporting. Some of the differences in accounting standards and practices are justified by economic circumstances and these differences will continue to exist. Because of the national rationale, accountants and professional organizations in these countries resist the wholesale "imperialistic" imposition of U.S. standards. Therefore, each nation should be allowed to use its national accounting standards best suited to its laws and priorities.

The paper proposes synchronization, not harmonization, of international accounting standards through close cooperation among nations and trading blocs which have more similarities than differences. Some trading blocs are more organized than others. What, then, is needed for synchronization? What can a trading bloc such as the EC do to create an atmosphere encouraging exemplary behavior for other trading blocs to emulate? Synchronization is relatively easier than harmonization, and it has become a necessity for those nations who want to raise capital. Global accounting standards for achieving comparability are more important than national accounting standards, necessary though they are for national consumption and priorities.

International accounting standard-setting and reporting environments are quite diverse because of differences in cultures, languages, taxation policies, national priorities, needs and pride. Some authors (Beazley 1968; McComb 1979; Maloo 1992; Harrison and McKinnon 1986; Soeters and Schreuder 1988) have recognized that countries' cultures have decisive effects on their financial reporting. Even if foreign financial statements are restated to U.S. generally accepted accounting principles (GAAP), they may be misleading (Choi and Mueller 1984, ch. 8; Evans, Taylor, and Holzman 1988, ch. 2). While explaining how cultural differences affect financial statements, some authors (Nair and Frank 1990; Gray 1988; Karnes et al. 1989; Rhia-Belkaoui and Pincur 1991) have isolated and identified common factors of culture which affect the financial reporting.

HOMOGENEITY AMID DIVERSITY

A trading bloc is an entity operating as a foreign trade functionary that unites heterogeneous cultures into a relatively homogeneous group of nations for protecting its trade, commerce and industry. The United Europe of 1992 is a patent fact now. In late 1991, the EC agreed to establish a single European currency by no later than 1999. European leaders celebrated this as a high step toward greater unity. The trouble is that creating a European currency requires individual countries to meet stringent conditions such as (1) lowering budget deficits, (2) achieving similar inflation rates, and (3) curbing interest rates, among others.

East Asian Economic Caucus is in the process of forming to give Southwest Asia a more powerful voice as a potential trade bloc. At an Association of Southeast Asian Nations (ASEAN), a summit held recently proclaimed that Brunei, Indonesia, Malaysia, the Philippines, Singapore and Thailand will be at the center of this caucus. The 25-year-old economic and political grouping expressed strong support for launching a new common market comprising more than 320 million people in response to "perceived" trends toward greater protectionism and economic regionalism" elsewhere in the world (Branigin 1992).

In January 1992, ministers of the 20 nations known as the Preferential Trade Area (PTA) of Eastern and Southern Africa met to review the past decade and chart ways of achieving their aim of a common market by the year 2000. The talks of a possible merger with the 10-nation Southern African Development Coordination Conference (SADCC) established in 1980 are under way (Richardson 1992).

What about the United States–Canada (and possibly Mexico) Free Trade Agreement? Very recently, this agreement has reached the final stage of negotiations (Auerbach 1992). A free trade trade zone from Canada to Argentina is also being widely discussed and explored (Belli 1991). Japan is busy forming a web of trading and economic alliances throughout the Pacific Rim. The collapsed communist bloc and its impoverished new democracies of Eastern Europe may also form new trading relationships. The formation of trading relationships and economic alliance has become an economic and financial necessity for the very survival of countries around the globe. It allows a free flow of capital necessary for economic growth.

Historically, nations within proximity form trading blocs. This proximity may be in terms of geography, demography, linguistics or culture. They form and bind themselves in economic ties in order to protect their vested interests in terms of trade, commerce and industry. Because of some similarities in their tradition, customs and level of economic growth, they want to solidify and affirm their economic ties in order to achieve some common goals. Nations within a trading bloc have common needs, national priorities, laws, import-export barriers, tariffs and traffic. In sum, they have many socioeconomic similarities and minimal differences.

Basic to each trading bloc is the feeling that they work together as partners, not competitors (Oliva 1991). They share common concerns and problems related to trade, traffic or tariffs. Mutually, they agree to abolish all economic barriers and improve goodwill among themselves. This helps promote trade, commerce and industry germane to their economic growth. Each trading bloc promotes free flow of capital among its members which in turn demands uniformity in financial reporting.

Formation of trading blocs have become an economic necessity for growth and development of nations. The broad question is how long the United States can act as a big engine of growth for other countries? Volcker and Gyohten (1992) trace the postwar world's changing economic fortunes. In the 1980s the massive U.S. trade deficits (which peaked in 1987 at $159.5 billion) provided a powerful economic stimulus for the rest of the world. The real advantages the newly industrialized countries and Japan have enjoyed unlimited access — for entirely political reasons — to the enormous market of the United States, as well as relatively huge aid programs. When the deficits began to fall — as they have for the last four years — export

dependent countries began to feel a tremor in their economic growth. Last week a wider threat of persisting global stagnation caused nervousness in stock markets around the globe.

In 1990, EEC, Japan and the United States represented about two-thirds of total global economic output. Effectively they have closed or are about to close doors for imports by forming trading blocs. These three largest economies have been experiencing very slow (U.S. negative in 1991) growth rate since 1987 and this will hurt the nations dependent upon exports to these economies. Therefore, there is little, if any, choice for newly industrialized economies to form economic alliances for their survival.

Global Investors' Needs

It is so easy to list stumbling blocks and limitations of global reporting that we tend to forget the substantial achievement so far made by the International Accounting Standards Committee (Maloo, 1983). It's fair to say that seldom has a committee achieved so much and perceived its achievement as so little, given the scope and problems it faces in the development of global accounting standards for the international user.

In a global investment environment, the international investor needs user-oriented financial statements which are comparable within a nation, a trading bloc and on a global level. We know international accounting standards set by the IASC are often in conflict with the national reporting standards within trading blocs. Even the national reporting standards are sometimes in conflict with trading blocs' policies and directives. For any given international corporation, creating comparable financial statements according to both trading bloc and international reporting standards would be difficult, if not impossible, and cost prohibitive.

One basic assumption is that heterogeneous nations are grouped into homogeneous trading blocs which also demand comparability on trading bloc level, also assuming that economic growth, level of development, rates of exchange and inflation are similar within a trading bloc. Therefore, one may expect that the financial statements prepared in accordance with national standards are relatively comparable for all nations within each trading bloc. Such arrangements permit usage of national standards for local consumption of financial statements and at the same time comparable financial statements are prepared to meet policy requirements of a trading bloc.

Nature of Information

Expert systems have the most potential in those situations where explicit rules are difficult or impossible to construct, and the system must be able to learn by example (of each trading bloc), developing its own hidden rules of behavior as it learns. Expert systems have been touted for their apparent ability in this regard to facilitate language processing, data compression, problem solution, pattern recognition, data classification, signal filtering, forecasting and predicting, and a number of other tasks.

The knowledge of most domains may be divided into factual or hard and heuristic or soft. Heuristic knowledge is problem-solving knowledge about a domain. In most cases, there is no consensus among experts about how this knowledge should be organized, what constitutes this knowledge, its activation and so on. In contrast to heuristic knowledge, factual knowledge reflects the way things are. The knowledge that a pathologist has about the human body clearly falls within this category. These two types of knowledge are not dichotomous, but rather there is a rich interrelationship between them. The heuristic problem-solving knowledge of a diagnostician may have need of the factual knowledge, especially in those cases in which the solution of a problem cannot be obtained directly by applying straight rules.

Building the Expert System

It is unrealistic to expect nations to give up their national accounting standards or sovereignty in favor of harmonization of global accounting standards imposed by the IASC. However, one may expect nations within a trading bloc to compromise or to go along with accounting "directives and policy" statements issued by their trading bloc. In fact, member countries may be obligated to comply with the requirements imposed by the bloc. Thus, each nation will enjoy full freedom in national reporting for local consumption and synchronize their financial statements for achieving comparability at the bloc-level. Such arrangement will also eliminate the problem of compliance with the IASC's international accounting standards (IAS) issued so far.

At this point we must realize that the international investor is not interested in small or medium-size companies. Rather, he or she is interested in multinational companies (MNCs) that normally provide above normal returns on their investment.

Since corporate characteristics are common denominators of all MNCs regardless of their origin, one can think in terms of designing and developing expert systems for those multinationals. To some extent, their corporate disclosure may be positively corrected with corporate characteristics such as (1) asset size, (2) number of stockholders, (3) listing status on national and/or international stock exchange(s), (4) earnings per share, (5) rate of return, (6) CPA/chartered accountant firm size and so on. Therefore, our focus of attention on designing and developing expert systems is related to large multinationals to save cost, time and efforts involved in such venture.

Expert systems are interactive knowledge-based computer information systems which emulate human thinking processes within a specified domain. The term "expert" implies a highly specialized and competent individual or group in the specified domain. Designing and developing such a system is a resource-intensive and expensive proposition. Many expert systems have been developed. Why can these trading blocs and the IASC not design and develop such systems for global reporting in order to achieve comparability? What are the opportunities and difficulties associated with developing such a system? What role, if any, can such systems have on the bloc level and on the global level? What steps are to be followed in developing global reporting systems? Conventional accounting techniques generally are inadequate for representing these heuristics, especially when the various factors interact simultaneously.

Global reporting domain seems suitable context for exploring expert systems methodology. Expert systems have four basic components such as (1) knowledge base, (2) interference engine, (3) user interface and (4) explanation mechanism. The knowledge base deals with facts in a specialized area and "rules of thumb" for using these facts. The rules are generally presented in form of "if...then" propositions developed by the human expert(s) from his or her accumulated experience in the field. Knowledge engineers extract "rules of thumb" from experts who place them into the knowledge base.

A computer program is an interference engine which uses the information (facts and rules) in knowledge base. Combination of user-supplied facts and rules creates a chain in which the "then" part of one rule creates another link to the "if" part of the next rule and so on. This process ultimately leads to a desired solution. The goal of the system is to stimulate a user's thinking, knowledge, and intuition by providing some expert tips in a systematic and organized way for the user's needs.

Expert systems provide solutions, conclusions and judgments. They capture and disseminate expert knowledge. In making judgments, they apply accumulated experience and expertise in a selective and heuristic way. In order to provide judgment, expert systems need the user interface which is the bridge between the inference engine and the user. Therefore, the user interface is a facilitator between the CBIS and its user(s). Last, the explanation component of expert systems helps the user understand logically why such judgment or conclusions are arrived at.

At this stage the IASC may play a catalyst role of coordination which would involve close cooperation with each trading bloc. The designing and developing of expert systems should be broken down into two simultaneous projects. One project should be on a trading bloc level and the other on a global level. The level of coordination between these projects needs to be high so that in the end the two completed expert system projects may be combined into one integrated expert system.

On a trading bloc level, an expert system project may generate financial statements in accordance with national reporting standards. It would be a smaller and manageable task than the megasystem. The knowledge base would consist of only one set of standards based on accounting "directives" and accounting policy of that bloc, making it easier to create and maintain. By coordinating efforts, the miniexpert systems (of each bloc) could be designed and developed in compatibility with an international expert system.

The second project would be an international expert system carried out and maintained by the IASC. Using the same input data as the bloc-level expert systems and applying international standards, the international expert systems would generate comparable global financial statements for the use by the global investor. By coordinating efforts, the miniexpert systems could be designed and developed in compatibility with the megasystem. This may reduce overall cost of expert systems in the long run which in turn may help both borrowers and lenders in terms of lower cost of capital.

First, the expert system should be an open one. Second, the systems need to be highly interactive user interface. The input data would be somewhat structured, narrative or explanatory in nature. Third, in order for the systems to properly structure the data into acceptable accounting records, the CBIS should be able to ask the user for additional information

needed over and beyond the initial data entry. The user in turn should be able to imagine or question the treatment of a data record to ensure that proper accounting standards are applied.

The first problem encountered is designing an expert system in that of proper knowledge representation, i.e., how to encode knowledge so that it is an honest reflection of what the expert knows and it can be manipulated by the CBIS (Forsyth 1986). Next, international accounting standards set by the IASC can be reduced to "Horn clause" subsets (Vasarhelyi 1989). The Horn clauses are in a form of predicate logic on which Prolog is based and with which the Prolog system can perform inferences.

The second problem is how to approximate the reasoning process in determining the proper application of IAS to specific transactions. Inference engines follow one of two reasoning strategies — forward chaining and backward chaining. Forward chaining involves working from evidence to conclusion. Backward chaining begins with an hypothesis and select data to support or refute it. Both strategies are important for manipulation of data by the CBIS using expert system methodology.

Prolog system will search the knowledge base of Horn clauses in a sequential order. That is, the inferences engine will have to check each standard in sequence until the applicable standard is found. To alleviate this problem and to insure against application of the wrong standard, backward chaining should also be used. The hypothesis in this case will be the structured accounting entry made in accordance with national accounting standard. From this hypothesis, the expert system will check for compliance with IAS located within the knowledge base. Because of the need for full compliance to the IAS for achieving comparability, the user interface will have to be highly interactive, which will allow for a discourse between the accountant/security analyst and the expert system.

By allowing the accountant to interact fully with the expert system, the probability for errors may be greatly reduced. In cases where national accounting standards do not agree with IAS, the expert system will be able to alert the accountant for further details of the transaction, if they are needed, to determine the proper disclosure according to the IASC's IAS. Also, the accountant would be able to ask the computer to explain the reasoning behind any decision, as well as cite the IAS being applied in that transaction.

The last problem in designing an expert system is that of knowledge transferring from the human expert into a computable form. One of the ways to overcome this is to allow the computer to generate rules from preclassified examples by induction. Since the application of IASs has been steadily increasing, the IASC is the logical choice for the expert to turn to interpret any voids, ambiguities or internal inconsistencies within the IAS.

CONCLUDING REMARKS

Let every nation enjoy its sovereignty and flexibility in using national accounting standards for local reporting. Rather than imposing global ac-

counting standards, accountants around the globe should strive for synchronization of international accounting standards through use of expert system methodology. Belonging to a trading bloc is a matter of economic necessity; the member nations have no choice but to follow membership agreement. The member nation has to follow accounting "directives" and policy statements issued by the bloc, which will force compliance and comparability in financial reporting on the bloc level. The paper suggests designing and developing two expert systems — one on each bloc level and another on the IASC level.

REFERENCES

AlHasim, D. D. 1973. Accounting Control through Purposive Uniformity: An International Perspective. *International Journal of Accounting, Education and Research* (Spring): 21–32.

Auerbach, S. 1992. Overcoming a Continental Divide: North American Free-Trade Pact Reach Tough, Final Stage. *The Washington Post* (July 25): F1.

Beazley, Jr., G. G. 1968. An International Implication for Accounting. *International Journal of Accounting Education and Research* (Spring): 1–10.

Belli, P. 1991. Globalizing the Rest of the World. *Harvard Business Review* (July-August): 50–55.

Branigin, W. 1992. Southeast Asian Leaders Support Plan to Form Regional Free-Trade Bloc. *The Washington Post* (January 28): 12.

Choi, F. D., and G. G. Mueller. 1984. *International Accounting*. Prentice Hall.

Evans, T. G., M. E. Taylor and O. Holzman. 1988. *International Accounting and Reporting*, 2nd ed. PWS Kent Publishing Company.

Forsyth, R. 1986. *Machine Learning: Application of Expert Systems*. Hasted Press.

Gray, S. J. 1988. Towards a Theory of Cultural Influence on the Development of Accounting Systems Internationally. *ABACUS* (Vol. 1): 1–15.

Harrison, G. L. and J. L. McKinnon. 1986. Culture and Accounting Change: A New Perspective on Corporate Reporting Regulation and Accounting Policy Formulation. *Accounting Organizations and Society* (Vol. 11): 232–252.

Hemp. P. 1985. Where Boards and Governments Have Failed, The Market Could Internationalize Accounting. *The Wall Street Journal International* (May 8): 34.

Karnes, A., J. Sterner, R. Walker and F. Wu. 1989. A Bicultural Study of Independent Auditors' Perceptions of Unethical Business Practices. *The International Journal of Accounting* (24): 29–41.

Maloo, M. C. 1992. Global Accounting Standards with the Emergence of United Europe of 1992 and Beyond. *Chartered Accountant* (May): 921–926.

————. 1992. Synchronization of International Accounting Standards: Can an Expert System be Designed and Developed in the Trading Block Level? In the *Proceedings of the 1992 Northeast Regional Meeting of the American Accounting Association* (April 25).

————. 1991. One Step Closer to Synchronization of International Accounting Standards with the Emergence of United Europe of 1992 and Beyond. In the *Proceedings of the 1991 Mid-Atlantic Regional Meeting of the American Accounting Association* (April 13).

————. 1990. Synchronization of Global Accounting Standards and Integration of Capital Markets: New Efforts and Strategies. In the *Proceedings of the 1990 Northeast Regional Meeting of the American Accounting Association* (April 26).

————. 1989. Barriers to Development of Global Accounting Standards. In the *Proceedings of the Mid-Atlantic Regional Meeting of the American Accounting Association* (April 8): 118.

————. 1983. The Need for International Accounting Standards: Development and Analysis. *The Singapore Accountant* (Volume 16): 25–34.

McComb, D. 1979. International Harmonization of Accounting: A Cultural Dimension. *The International Journal of Accounting Education and Research* (Spring).

Nair, R. D., and W. G. Frank. 1990. The Impact of Measurement Practices on International Accounting Classification. *The Accounting Review* (July).

Oliva, L. 1991. *Partners not Competitor: The Age of Teamwork and Technology.* IDEA Group Publishing.

Riahi-Belkaoui, A., and R. D. Pincur. 1991. Cultural Determinism and the Perception ofAccounting Concepts. *The International Journal of Accounting* (26): 118–130.

Richardson, M. 1992. In East Asia, a Push for Green Growth. *Herald International Tribune* (January 25-26): 9.

Soeters, J. and U. Schreuder. (1988). Interaction between National and Organizational Cultures in Accounting Forms. *Accounting Organizations and Society* (13:1) : 75–86.

Statement of Financial Accounting Concepts, No. 1: Objectives of Financial Reporting. Richard D. Irwin, Inc.: 1–25.

Turban, E. 1988. *Applied Expert System.* North-Holland Publishing Company: 208.

Vasarhelyi, M. 1989. *Artificial Intelligence in Accounting and Auditing.* Marcus Wiener.

Volcker, P., and Gyohten, T. 1992. *Changing Fortunes: The World's Money and the Threat to American Leadership.* Time Books, Inc.

How are Accounting Standards Justified?
An Anglo-American Perspective

Michael J. Mumford

This paper is concerned with the ways in which accounting standards are justified in the tradition of standard setting common to Britain and America. This need to justify standards has major implications for the way standards are presented and explained in the classroom.

LEGAL BACKGROUND

Britain has no written constitution. Of the three elements of the law, *statute law* and *case law* are both accessible in written form, but the third element, *"common law,"* exists only in the abstract until it is expressed in a statute or in cases decided by the courts. America, too, has a common law tradition augmenting statute and case law. It is made more complicated in America by the fact that there are 50 states, each with its own jurisdiction, as well as a pattern of federal laws and courts and a written constitution overarching the whole. Even so, areas of legal rules can be delegated to nonlawyers to devise and act upon, for the law to endorse or reject subsequently.

Companies are, of course, artificial constructs, with a "legal personality" conferred by the law. The status, capacity and duties of companies both in Britain and in America is not a matter of precision under the law. A lot is left unspecified. There have been a dozen Companies Acts in Britain since 1844, but the current body of company law was restated and consolidated in the 1985 Companies Act, as amended by the 1989 Companies Act. It has been necessary for many years for all companies registered with limited liability to publish financial accounts (by filing with the Registrar of Companies). The Acts have laid down general disclosure headings for display, so that, for example, fixed assets have had to be shown separately from current assets. However, the detailed rules of recognition and valuation in accounts have been left to the accounting profession to determine.

The Securities Act of 1933 and the Securities Exchange Act of 1934 together created a much more formal regulatory framework in America than in most other countries with a common law tradition. However, the Securities and Exchange Commission (the SEC) delegated many of its powers to draw up detailed accounting rules to the accounting profession, in *Accounting Series Release* (ASR) *No. 4*, April 1938, and *ASR 150*, December 1973. The SEC retains power to overturn standards set by the Financial Accounting Standards Board, but it does not usually do the standard setting by itself. A form of partnership is involved, and advocacy forms a significant part of the dialogue. Accounting standards are open to challenge, and they have to be defended. The remainder of this paper is concerned with ways in which such defences are constructed.

WAYS OF JUSTIFYING ACCOUNTING STANDARDS

Accounting standards can be justified in terms of four classes of argument: (a) mutually accepted agency agreements, (b) accounting theory, (c) economic theory, and (d) other arguments. These are examined below.

Mutually Accepted Agency Agreements
Basic Stewardship

Formalised accounting reports originated with the separation of ownership and control well before companies were known as a form of business organisation. Littleton (1933) illustrates primitive relationships between the owners of property and stewards with day-to-day control over it. It may have been unclear just what powers and duties were delegated to the steward (as in the "Parable

Michael J. Mumford is Senior Research Fellow at Lancaster University.

An earlier version of this paper was presented to the Workshop on Accounting in Europe No 2, run by the European Institute for Advanced Studies in Management, Frankfurt-am-Main, 5-6 December 1991. Thanks are due to the participants of this Workshop. The author also acknowledges with thanks the support of the Chartered Association of Certified Accountants (the ACCA), 29 Lincoln's Inn Fields, LONDON WC2A 3EE, England, in particular for grants to enable the paper to be presented first in Frankfurt and now in Arlington, Virginia. The views expressed herein are those of the author, and not necessarily those of the International Centre for Research in Accounting, or of Lancaster University, or of the ACCA.

of the Talents": St. Matthew, 25: 14-30), but customary terms and conditions of stewardship evolved amongst the traditions of agrarian societies. Moreover, when trading was undertaken through agents, the need for agency agreements became even more obvious, to show how the duties had been discharged. Standards would have formed part of stewardship agreements.

A Fair Basis for Comparison

Standard procedures are valuable to compare the performance of different stewards, not just with explicit goals set down by the property owner, but between the activities of one steward and another. Any basis for comparison needs commonality, and the more there is at stake, the more important it is to have explicit, standard rules, binding on all concerned. DR Scott (1931:161) suggests standardisation plays a major role in social development: "Standardization of the terms in which social intercourse runs has always magnified both the possibilities and the actual scope of cooperation within the social group."

Social Contracts

More complex multiparty relations are also possible. Bonding costs will probably be reduced if there are standard ways to set out duties and obligations, and to account for performance. To this extent, what is seen as fair and equitable merges with what is efficient in economic terms. This still begs the question, what forms of analysis will show how to frame such forms of standard agreement. Legal theory is obviously one place to look.

Legal Theory

A basic assumption of most legal theory is the existence of conflicting interests between individuals and groups of individuals. Economics also recognises conflicts of interest, but economic analysis generally takes it for granted that such conflicts are resolved by mutually agreed market transactions. Legal theory acknowledges a much wider range and variety of social relationships.

Rawls accepts in *A Theory of Justice* (1977) that individuals commonly contract with one another as a question of fact; he is concerned with analysing rights under conditions of heterogeneous preferences, incomplete knowledge, and uncertain benefits. He looks for concepts of fairness that will sustain the rights of one member of society as against those of another where these conflict. His theory uses the notion of "reflective equilibrium,"

relying on the internal logic of his arguments rather than any empirical referents. In a recent paper, Michael Power (forthcoming) translates Rawls' theory of justice into a possible conceptual framework for accounting. Standards here form part of agency and contract law.

Accounting Theory

In its study *A Statement of Accounting Theory and Theory Acceptance* (SOATATA) (AAA 1977), the American Accounting Association reviewed the literature then available on accounting theory and identified three theoretical approaches, (1) "classical" models, (2) decision usefulness approaches, and (3) information economics. The authors hoped to be able to find "a sufficient and compelling basis for specifying the content of external financial reports" (p. 39), and they regretted that theory closure was unlikely to be achieved. The first two approaches are considered below: the third appears in the section on economic theory.

"Classical" Models

"Classical" models of accounting theory advance definitions of the basic constructs (assets, liabilities, income, etc.) which are justified by reference to internal rules alone. Accounting is seen as complete and self-justifying, with no need to draw upon other fields of knowledge. "True" income is true by definition, and that definition is the responsibility of accountants using their own experience and insights. As long as accounts are prepared in accordance with accounting rules, they are beyond criticism — the system is complete and there is "theory closure." Standards merely embody the rules for implementing these truths.

The weakness of this argument is that it does not fit clearly with a utilitarian view of accounting. If corporate accounts are supposed to meet the decision needs of users, this provides a further criterion for evaluating accounting practice. And, indeed, this is exactly the source of criticism made of accounting both in Britain and America over much of the present century.[1]

---

[1] It is worth noting that it is possible to reconcile the "classical approach" with a number of decision usefulness criteria. Standards may comprise a single set of arbitrary rules, precisely framed and strictly enforced; indeed, this may well save information processing costs to users. However, it may be possible to do even better than this by demonstrating a single set of accounting standards that will meet other user needs as well.

Decision Usefulness

Theories of decision usefulness in accounting can take either individual decision processes or aggregational processes at the level of the economy or market. The former type of model considers how decisions are structured, and information used, by individuals. The latter type of model recognises that there are many groups of decision maker, each with generalised behaviour patterns.

Many decision-useful models have attempted to base standards upon sets of qualitative characteristics such as "reliability," "relevance," "timeliness" and so on, to evaluate specific reporting practices. The problem with these decision-usefulness theories is that they are short of empirical evidence, they lack the means to resolve conflicts of interest, and they generally also lack theoretical linkage between theory and policy prescriptions. Thus, it remains unclear how sets of characteristics translate into disclosure standards, but the standards exist to help users make their decisions.

Possible Linkage between Accounting and Law

Simon Archer (forthcoming) suggests combining accounting with soft systems methodology. "Classical" theories of accounting are not alone in seeking a set of theoretical propositions which are complete and self-justifying in themselves. Rawls' analytical jurisprudence does the same. Archer shows how Rowe's soft systems "Gross Balance Method" can augment Summers' "New Analytical Jurisprudence" to provide empirical feedback.

Economic Theory

Economic arguments are valuable in analysing accounting issues; however, economics is not a single, coherent body of thought. The basic assumptions of welfare economics, for example, differ from those of industrial economics, finance, or the theory of the firm. Certain common assumptions of economic analysis, such as complete information, homogeneous products, and absence of joint inputs and outputs, are valuable in simplifying the analysis, but they conflict with business experience.

Economists often argue that perfectly competitive market equilibrium represents an ideal market state, towards which markets will tend if left to themselves. Even so, they recognise the existence of "market failure," and of disequilibrium that might or might not tend towards equilibrium. Theorists may disagree over the efficacy of markets and still accept that standards for financial reporting, however set, have a valuable economic role.

Accounting Standards in Unregulated Markets

There may well be demands for standardised information in unregulated markets. Information production and usage are both costly activities, and standardisation will confer economies in information processing and contracting. Benston (1976) argues against any system of government regulation of accounting standards. Nevertheless, he sees scope for standards set under voluntary agreement.

In practice, virtually every country regulates corporate financial reporting (Watts and Zimmerman 1986, Chapter 10). The issue is whether accounting standards lead to appropriate information within a specified institutional context. Proponents of unregulated markets cite Paretian optimality to explain the economic benefits that will result. However, Paretian optimality is based upon satisfying marginal conditions in static equilibrium. In a real world of dynamic uncertainty, financial accounts do not disclose marginal rates of return, *ex post* or *ex ante*, but only total/average returns on total/average capital employed, irrelevant for Paretian analysis. The role of standards would be to convey information about the firm to transactors dealing in all related markets.

Accounting Standards under Market Failure

Baruch Lev (1988) queries whether unregulated markets can produce optimal disclosure by way of voluntary standards. He argues that there are economies of scale in investing, so that wealthy investors have an inbuilt advantage in obtaining and processing information. It is possible for small investors to achieve economies of scale by alliances, but then agency costs are imposed. However, without large numbers of transactors, the efficiency of the market is impaired so that even the wealthy suffer. It is in their interests that smaller investors are encouraged by the prospect of a fair game, ensured by impartial regulators. Lev asserts that state regulators are less likely to be "captured" than private agencies.

Lev does not address the main question which interests the New Institutional Economics school (below), namely the limits which prevent a single economic agent, enjoying economies of scale, from commanding the whole market. Nor does he address the contradiction implicit in a market that is both so efficient that there is no scope for abnormal profits and yet able to attract transactors by prospects of abnormal returns unavailable elsewhere.

Lev's paper seeks to use the arguments of market economics to make the case for mandatory accounting rules, using the reasoning of Watts and Zimmerman but drawing opposite conclusions. His analysis would be more plausible if he formally relaxed some of the assumptions of their model. For example, his case for fairness obviously carries implications about the behavioural response of investors who are not sure who to trust. Watts and Zimmerman work on the assumption that people act as "rational economic men," trusting the law to enforce rights and redress wrongs. Lev's people seem to be subtler, but Lev himself rejects any jurisprudential concept of fairness as too inexact for his purposes. Standards exist to assure investors of a "fair game."

Information Economics

Zecher (1984, 70–73) summarises the special assumptions of information economics in a world which recognises the significance of portfolios, the Capital Asset Pricing Model, and efficient market theory. In modern capital market theory, the role of accounting information is seen in the context of a market with rich alternative sources of nonaccounting information. Once admitted, these factors have profound implications for accounting standards. There may be little point in companies disclosing information about their unique financial characteristics if the returns on their securities are dominated by systematic effects in the market, moderated by a "beta" specific to each security. Perhaps it is only the company's target beta *ex ante*, and its actual value periodically *ex post*, that are relevant to securities investors. At present the linkage is poorly specified between accounting disclosures and the observable returns on securities. Market reaction testing has produced an extensive literature, but so far this does not translate directly into policies for standards, whose role at present remains unclear.

"New Institutional Economics"

Williamson (1986) outlines the development of what he calls New Institutional Economics since 1960; its implications for standard setting have scarcely been noted yet. It stresses interests rather different to those of information economics, although the role of limited information is central to the ideas of bounded rationality, opportunism, information asymmetry and asset specificity. The structure of organisations depends heavily upon the nature of information, and access to that information. Accounting standards are not neutral in this process; they influence organisations as well as reflect them. Similarly, transaction costs do not merely affect the operation of markets, but influence significantly the way business is organised.

A major distinction is made in this literature between economic resources bought from well-traded markets, day-to-day or under longer-term external contracts, and those "core" assets that are difficult to trade and which the firm therefore owns and exploits for itself. This raises doubts about the sense of seeking current market values for core assets on the firm's balance sheet. The balance sheet excludes many of the human and intangible assets critical for the firm's success; conversely, it also includes many of those "core" assets whose market values are particularly difficult to estimate. Indeed, this is a major reason why they are owned as core assets! Standards have a role in helping to reduce transaction costs.

"Legal Tribology"

At present it is generally assumed in economics that legal rights to own property and to engage in contracts are effective and enforceable. But problems can arise from the costs and uncertainties of legal action, particularly in the courts, and this raises interesting questions. For example, property rights do not always confer complete control over property with full and costless redress in the event of breach of contract. Uncertainties over enforcement inhibit market transactions generally; rather as Lev (1988) suggests, they work in financial markets.[2] The nature and authority of (possibly unreliable) standards is now seen as an additional source of uncertainty.

Each of these "economic" arguments makes important assumptions about the institutional environment which need to be recognised in framing policy, and none provides complete support for accounting standards.

Other Arguments

Each of the previous lines of argument has considered theory as supporting accounting standards.

---

[2]An analogy between the study of legal friction in market dealings and the study of friction between moving parts in mechanics suggests the name "legal tribology." In each case, the friction causes results quite different from those which would result from a "friction-free" world.

An alternative set of views sets standards in a broader context, and looks at accounting as a phenomenon to be explained, rather than justified and supported.

Political Power

Explanations of accounting and standard setting may focus upon the general activity of accounting or on the specific activities of regulatory agencies. Examples of both are readily found in the accounting literature. Tinker (1985, 87) takes a broad view of accounting as a product of the social and economic system, using Marxian analysis to provide a critique of current accounting practice. "Value theory and accounting represent sophisticated rationales for resolving exchanges, distributing income and resources, and dividing up the social product." Alternative explanations adopt a framework based upon Foucault.

Horngren (1984) discusses accounting regulation in America by reference to Pfeffer (1981, 70–71). He cites with approval Pfeffer's view that power is the only way to arrive at complex decisions under uncertainty, using analysis that addresses many of the problems familiar to economics (heterogeneous goals and expectations, costly knowledge, uncertain outcomes) but adopting a variety of mechanisms to deal with them.

Professional Power

Watts and Zimmerman (1986) argue that, whatever the effects of accounting in society, the accounting profession dominates the production of accounting information, possibly on behalf of major corporate clients. Regulatory capture is indeed evident in the membership of the British ASB and the American FASB, both staffed largely by (former) auditors trained with the biggest international firms. Peasnell and Williams (1986) are among several authors who point out how Watts and Zimmerman oversimplify a complex picture (they show how implausible is a "market for excuses"). But there is clearly scope for research on professional power and standard setting.

Corporate Power

Just as plausible is the argument that corporations exercise the power that leads to accounting standards. The issues are very similar to those of professional power, but here it is asserted that accountants act merely as agents for corporate clients.

Corporate governance has been an issue for much of the 20th century, certainly since Berle and Means (1932). Empirical work on corporate governance is patchy in Britain. For example, it appears that ownership of shares has become increasingly concentrated in the hands of financial institutions (individual shareholders now own less than 20 percent of quoted shares). But it remains unclear how the concentration of power is used by the portfolio managers who control it, or why this is so.

A recent book by Lazonick (1991) argues, from the point of view of the business historian, that the major feature of industrial economies over the past two centuries has been the rate of dynamic change, first apparent in Britain with the rise of proprietory capitalism from the mid-18th century, then in America with the onset of managerial capitalism from about 1870, and most recently in Japan with the rise of collective capitalism from about 1960. Lazonick is concerned with the processes of innovation — the creation of new products, processes, and organisation structures that allow businesses to overcome the constraints of given resources and technologies.

Economic analysis in America (and Britain) usually takes competitive market equilbrium analysis as its starting point. Still worse, much economic policy has been predicated upon competitive market equilbrium as a desirable ideal, even though in terms of wealth creation this describes conditions incompatible with innovation. (Businesses in acute competition *adapt* in their use of resources, but are unable usually to *innovate*.)

Lazonick regards the form of corporate governance as important for determining the rate of innovation. He finds 19th century patterns of shareholder dominance understandable, given the small scale of firms at that time and the predominence of external economies of scale. But from the start of the 20th century, American firms were able to rid themselves of control by the stockholders, and develop professional management teams with their own long-term strategic goals, free from short-term speculative pressures.[3]

Japanese business history since 1960 has shown a further development of business organisation, with large networks of suppliers adopting very long-term strategies to create and exploit relative advantages in world product markets. These organisations take great care to protect themselves from short-term market pressures, in financial markets no less than in the markets for

---

[3]This line of thought contrasts strongly with that of Michael Jensen, who argues that shareholder control is vital, with takeovers aiding that control (e.g., Jensen 1986).

labour, management, research and equipment. To Lazonick, this is a mark not of "market failure" but of "organisational success."

Lazonick's message for accountants is that disclosing information to the public often amounts to giving away competitive advantage. Indeed, any business that is potentially profitable over the long term has to be innovative, rather than merely adaptive; its most important assets — research results, managerial skills, product strategies and so on — necessarily have to be guarded as secrets of the utmost commercial confidence. Thus the role of information disclosure shifts from external reporting to internal sharing between members of the organisational network. Standards still have a role, but in economising on contracting costs between parties with a variety of long-term relationships. In this context, shareholders are generally seen as insignificant, since they typically take an "adaptive" rather than an innovative role.

Constructing Reality

An issue that has recurred repeatedly amongst writers on accounting theory has been whether, and if so how, accounting can become a science, perhaps like physics. The implication is that once scientific method has been established, cause and effect relations underlying accounting practice will be understood and policy decisions guided by technology.

Accounting as science has been analysed in two recent papers. Murray Lindsey (forthcoming) argues that science is as much about the attitude of the researcher as about the subject matter. Scientific research is characterised by a conscious effort to eliminate bias. Writing as a research physicist, Philip Stamp (forthcoming) also tries to identify the characteristics that mark science from other

forms of knowledge. He denies that experimentation is a necessary feature, and describes physics itself as relativistic. He identifies meteorology as a plausible science, despite the complexity of the open systems it studies, and he suggests that Chomskyan linguistics also "has the feel" of science. This being so, he sees no reason why accounting should not be scientific too —- but probably best viewed as a open system.

Both Lindsay and Stamp urge accountants to be willing to try out different viewpoints, question ideas and test new proposals with creative imagination. This is consistent with the views of James Gaa in his 1988 AAA study *Methodological Foundations of Standardsetting for Corporate Financial Reporting*. Gaa rejects any single theoretical base as sufficient to justify standards; the processes involved in finding evidence are more important than the adoption of a particular theoretical base.

CONCLUSION

Although legal, accounting and economic theory overlap, they typically address different issues. This is right and proper; indeed, it is necessary for theory to be broken down into simple models, without which knowledge is too complex to handle. For those with responsibility for setting accounting standards in an Anglo-American context, it is a challenge to identify arguments that help justify those standards, recognising that the authority of company law itself is not fully sufficient in either country. While it is problematic to expect the student to be able to form an educated judgment about the relative merits of all the issues, rather than simply taking existing rules as a set of facts to be learned, learning about the ways in which standards are justified will give a much richer understanding of their role.

REFERENCES

AAA Committee on Concepts and Standards for External Reporting. 1977. *A Statement of Accounting Theory and Theory Acceptance*. American Accounting Association.

Archer, S. Forthcoming. On the Methodology of Constructing a Conceptual Framework for Financial Accounting. In Mumford and Peasnell, eds.

Berle, A. A., and G. C. Means. 1932. *The Modern Corporation and Private Property*. Macmillan.

Benston, G. J. 1976. *Corporate Financial Disclosure in the UK and the USA*. Saxon House (for the Institute of Chartered Accountants in England and Wales).

Gaa, J. C. 1988. *Methodological Foundations of Standardsetting for Corporate Financial Reporting, Studies in Accounting Research No. 28*. American Accounting Association.

Horngren, C. T. 1984. Institutional Alternatives for Regulating Financial Reporting. In R. H. Mundheim and N. E. Leech, eds. *The SEC and Accounting: the First 50 Years Amsterdam*. North-Holland: 29–51.

Jensen, M. C. 1986. Agency Costs of Free Cash Flow, Corporate Finance, and Takeovers. AEA Papers and Proceedings (May): 323–329.

Lazonick, W. 1991. *Business Organisation and the Myth of the Market Economy*. Cambridge University Press.

Lev, B. 1988. Towards an Equitable Theory of Corporate Financial Reporting. *The Accounting Review* (January): 124–146.

Lindsay, R. M. Forthcoming. Achieving Scientific Knowledge: The Rationality of Scientific Method. In Mumford and Peasnell, eds.

Littleton, A. C. 1933. *Accounting Evolution to 1900*. American Institute Publishing Co., reprinted by University of Alabama Press, 1981.

Mumford, M. J., and K. Peasnell, eds. Forthcoming. *Philosophical Perspectives on Accounting*. Routledge.

Peasnell, K. V., and D. J. Williams. 1986. Ersatz Academics and Scholar-saints: The Supply of Financial Accounting Research. *Abacus* (Vol. 22 No. 2): 121–135.

Power, M. K. On the Idea of a Conceptual Framework. In Mumford and Peasnell, eds.

Rawls, J. 1977. *A Theory of Justice Oxford*. Oxford University Press.

Scott, DR. 1931. *The Cultural Significance of Accounts*. Scholars Book Co. (reprinted 1974).

Stamp, P. In search of reality. In Mumford and Peasnell, eds.

Tinker, A. M. 1985. *Paper Prophets*. Praeger.

Watts, R. L., and J. L. Zimmerman. 1986. *Positive Accounting Theory*. Prentice-Hall.

Williamson, O. E. 1986. *Economic Organisation: Firms, Markets and Policy Control*. Harvester Wheatsheaf.

Zecher, J. R. 1984. An Economic Perspective of SEC Corporate Disclosure. In Robert H. Mundheim and Noyes E. Leech, eds. *The SEC and Accounting: the First 50 Years*. North-Holland: 69–77.

Disclosure Pattern of Japanese Firms and Internalization of Capital Transactions: Education Needs in the Changing Economy

Ellie Okada-Onitsuka

Nowadays Japanese firms are often blamed by foreign countries for the internalized transactions and the lack of transparency in their market practices. The purpose of this paper is to give a theoretical framework for the relationship between the internalized transaction and disclosure pattern of Japanese firms and to argue for the need for strengthening the disclosure regulation in the Japanese style and for the educational needs in the changing environment of the financial liberalization. Disclosure can be one of the effective means for finance, for it lessens capital costs if it is made effectively. If firms' disclosure level becomes higher, the Japanese market will become more competitive, transparent and efficient.

This paper shows that (a) firms whose stocks are held by long-term stockholders are not active for fund-raising in foreign capital markets, (b) those which are not active in fund-raising in foreign capital markets have little motivation to disclose additional information, and (c) those which are active in fund-raising in foreign capital markets are sensitive to strategic behavior[1] in disclosure in the foreign and domestic markets. These results imply that the close relationship between management and long-term stockholders tends to give rise to internalization of capital transaction, and have important effects on the disclosure level of Japanese firms.

This paper is organized as follows: first, the relevant literature is surveyed and hypotheses are introduced; second, analytical framework is discussed; third, results are presented. In the last section, a summary and implications are given.

HYPOTHESIS

Relevant Literature

If financial activities are liberalized completely, how and where fund-raising is made is irrelevant (Modigliani and Miller 1958). However, in reality, capital transaction environments and capital costs vary from country to country. In the 60s, firms be-

gan to raise funds in foreign markets. This new development led to the research in the area of disclosure in foreign markets.

Choi (1973) indicates that firms which entered into the Euro market improved disclosure levels more than those which did not enter, and the improvement was statistically significant. Barrette (1976) showed that the more subsidiaries a firm consolidated in financial statements, the higher was its disclosure level.

The above studies consider disclosure in competitive markets. On the other hand, there are some papers which focus attention on the special characteristics of Japanese market. Okada (1986) extended the research by Choi, and proved that firms which raised funds in foreign capital markets actively showed a higher level of disclosure in the Japanese market than those which did not. Sakurai and Yamaji (1990) showed that firms whose stocks were held by long-term stockholders were less active in timely disclosure.

Framework

From the above, it turns out that the key factor for disclosure level is uncertainty about a firm from the viewpoint of investors, and an information asymmetry between firms and fund suppliers. If a firm is to raise funds in foreign markets or if a firm is large in its scale and has many subsidiaries, the degree of uncertainty is high. In a competitive market, a firm has a motivation to disclose more information than required by the regulation, otherwise the firm cannot obtain funds for a low cost (Mautz and May 1978). Furthermore, the disclosure is a part of bonding activities by firms. Firms make dis-

---

[1]Sakurai and Yamaji (1990) state that the disclosure is a part of a financial PR activity. I extend this idea and conclude that the disclosure must be regarded as a part of financial strategy.

Ellie Okada-Onitsuka is a faculty member at Yokohama National University.

closure voluntarily to eliminate stockholders' suspicion about a firm's moral hazard. However, in Japan, there is a close relationship between management and investors and there is little uncertainty about firms in many cases from the viewpoint of the investors who enjoy a long-term relationship with the firm.

In Japan, fund suppliers have enough information about firms in many cases. In Japan, fund suppliers are often banks. Loans from banks account for a large portion of firms' external funds. Furthermore, on average, more than 70 percent of stocks are held by corporations and more than half are held by banks (Futatsugi 1982). They hold the other corporations' stocks to control them or to cooperate with them. Accordingly, they hold stocks for a long time. There is no information asymmetry, for corporations know about each other through daily commercial trades. Banks even dispatch management to firms, so they can get information about firms privately.

In these cases, fund suppliers and firms are not in equal position. Let us call this context "internalization of capital transaction." This context has a close relationship with the resource allocation mechanism of capital in Japan. In the internalized capital transactions, transactions are made by an order of an authority. Participation in the transaction is limited to those inside the internalized "organization." Furthermore, the relationship between trading partners is long term and almost fixed.[2]

Hypothesis Setting

If a capital transaction is internalized, these firms are not sensitive to the constraints of liquidity (Hoshi, Kashyap, and Scharftein 1991). In this context, firms have little incentive to get funds outside the internalized organization. On the other hand, if there are no strong ties between firms and banks, firms seek as low cost funds as possible. It is more advantageous for noninternalized Japanese firms to raise funds in foreign markets, because the cost of capital is cheaper in the Euro market and firms can become famous worldwide if they list stocks in the U.S. or U.K. markets. Thus the following hypothesis can be set:
Hypothesis 1: If there are no strong ties between firms and banks or other major long-term stockholders, Japanese firms will tend to be active in fund-raising in external markets, including foreign markets.

If firms are to raise funds in foreign markets, they must give a signal to potential foreign investors. Furthermore, in the case of external financing, a considerable number of firms' stocks are held by short-term stockholders, and there is information asymmetry between firms and fund suppliers. Thus, firms have incentive to disclose additional information which investors need. Therefore, the following hypothesis can be set:
Hypothesis 2: Firms that actively raise funds in foreign markets (FRAFM) disclose additional information more than firms which depend on the Japanese market for most of their funds (non-FRAFM).

Even when Japanese firms issue bonds in foreign markets; foreign subsidiaries of Japanese banks underwrite them in many cases. When this occurs, the strong ties that exist between firms and banks in Japan continue in the foreign markets (Okumura 1987). If there are such ties in the foreign markets, firms will have little incentive to disclose additional information.

According to Yunker's research, if an enterprise gives one of its subsidiaries managerial autonomy, the enterprise tends to give autonomy to all of its components (Yunker 1982). We can infer from his finding that, if a firm gives a subsidiary relatively high managerial autonomy, the internalized transaction relationship will be limited in a foreign market.
Hypothesis 3: If a firm gives its subsidiary relatively high managerial autonomy, the degree of internalization is low in the domestic and foreign markets and the firm has incentive to disclose additional information which investors need.

When firms raise funds in foreign markets without an international capital market, they disclose strategically according to the market mechanism. A firm can lower capital costs by disclosure. On the other hand, it may suffer competitive disadvantage. However, if a firm's foreign operation is large enough, a firm may not suffer from competitive disadvantage when it discloses details of its foreign operation.
Hypothesis 4: The larger a firm's foreign scale of operation is, the higher the firm's incentive is to engage in additional disclosure concerning its foreign operation.

[2]See Imai, Itami, and Koike (1982).

RESEARCH DESIGN

Data

In this research, the disclosure level of additional information is analyzed. In Japan, important additional information means that which is recommended by the International Accounting Standards Committee (IASC) and standards recommended by the United Nations (UN) and the Organization for Economic Cooperation and Development (OECD) so long as they are not incorporated in the domestic law. Among these standards, I chose geographic segment information to measure the disclosure level, because it relates to international operation by firms. Furthermore, the geographic segment information was additional information in the Japanese market until March 31, 1991. Even in the U.S. market, foreign firms were not required to disclose this information for many years.[3] Therefore, I consider it appropriate to analyze the disclosure level of this information in the consolidated financial statements for the period after its disclosure was prescribed by IASC, OECD and UN and its disclosure was not required by law for Japanese firms both in the foreign and domestic markets. This is the reason I chose the business year 1982.

The scoring scale for disclosure level was made using the following checklist.

A. Geographical segment information

	Score
1. The analysis of sales or exports	10
2. The analysis of earnings	10
3. The analysis of total assets	10
4. The analysis of capital expenditures, and if applicable, that of depreciation	10
5. The presentation which helps us understand the relation between all the above information and the consolidated figures	10
6. The selection of the appropriate segment	10
7. The disclosure of the policy of transfer pricing	10
8. Other voluntary, useful information	5

B. Information about fund-raising in foreign markets

1. The analysis of fund-raising by geography	10
2. The analysis of currency	10
3. Other voluntary, useful information	5
Total	100

Sample

Sample firms are Japanese firms whose operations are internationalized and whose stocks are listed in the first section of the Tokyo Stock Exchange. The internationalized firms mean (1) ex-

port-oriented firms (EOF), (2) multinational enterprises (MNE) and (3) firms which raise funds actively in foreign markets (FRAFM).

In selecting EOF, I define them as follows:

1. a firm which has foreign sales subsidiaries in more than five countries;

2. a firm which does not have foreign manufacturing subsidiaries in more than five countries.

Then I define a foreign sales subsidiary as follows:

1. a foreign subsidiary which operates neither manufacturing nor resource industries, but engages in exclusively or mainly sales activities;

2. a subsidiary, more than 20 percent of whose capital is owned by its parent company;

3. a foreign subsidiary which was in operation in 1982.

I exclude those firms that are in effect other firms' subsidiaries. Twenty-seven EOFs are selected according to the above criteria.

Next, I define MNEs as follows:

1. a firm which has foreign manufacturing subsidiaries in more than five countries.

Then a foreign manufacturing subsidiary is defined as follows:

1. a foreign subsidiary which operates manufacturing or resource industry;

2. a subsidiary, more that 20 percent of whose capital is owned by its parent company;

3. a foreign subsidiary which was in operation in 1982.

I exclude those firms that are, in effect, other firms' subsidiaries.[4] Seventy MNEs are selected according to the above criteria.

In selecting FRAFM, I chose firms which continuously disclosed consolidated financial statements in the Japanese market according to the SEC rules from the year 1978 to 1982. A certain kind of firm is permitted to prepare consolidated financial statements according to the SEC rules (SEC F/S) in the Japanese market. It is one which disclosed consolidated financial statements in foreign markets

---

[3]The SEC prescribed in November 1982 the reports of F-1, F-2 and F-3 as a new style of filing reports by foreign firms. This is the first time for foreign firms to be required to disclose segment information in the U.S. markets.

[4]As for the method of selecting export-oriented firms and multinational enterprises, see Yoshihara (1979).

when consolidated financial statements were not required in the Japanese market, that is, prior to the year 1978.

Thirty-six FRAFMs are selected according to the above criteria. This group includes 20 companies which are included either in EOFs or in MNEs. In addition to them, I select firms which have experience preparing SEC F/S more than once but not continuously. Fifteen firms are selected according to this criteria. Three companies are included either in EOFs or in MNEs.

In total, 114 companies are selected as the sample.

The total current cost amount of the sample firms' stocks accounts for 29.9 percent of the mar-

ket capitalization of the first market of the Tokyo Stock Exchange on March 31, 1982. This means that the selected sample is significant from the viewpoint of investors.

RESULTS

From the preliminary observation of the sample, evidence exists that Japanese firms have only low motivation to disclose additional information (see List 1). The firms whose disclosure performance was excellent are listed in List 2.

Hypothesis Examination

Examining hypothesis 1, I categorize the sample into two classes: FRAFM and non-FRAFM.

LIST 1
Disclosure Contents Concerning the Foreign Operation

Disclosure Contents	Number of Firms	
1. Disclose information about foreign operation in some form	31	27.2%
1. Geographical segment information	11	
2. Information about export	10	
3. Information about fund-raising in foreign markets	25	
Disclose all of the above	7	
4. State clearly that the scale of the foreign operation is insignificant	1	
2. No disclosure	83	72.8%
Total		100 %

LIST 2
The Top Ten Companies that Show the Highest Level of Disclosure

Rank	Firms' Name	Score	Rank	Firms' Name	Score
1	Toray Industries, Inc.	100	8	Matsushita Electric Industrial Co., Ltd.	30
2	Marubeni Corp.	90		Renown Incorporated	
	Mitsubishi Corp.		9	Asahi Optical Co. Ltd.	25
	Ricoh Com. Ltd.			Olympus Optical Co. Ltd.	
3	C. Itoh & Co., Ltd.	80		Canon Inc.	
4	Kyocera Corp.	70		Kubota Corp.	
	Murata Manufacturing Co., Ltd.			Sanyo Electric Co. Ltd.	
5	Mitsui & Co.	65		Nippon Steel Corp.	
6	Casio Computer Co., Ltd.	50		Sumitomo Metal Industrial	
	Omron Corp.			Sumitomo Heavy Industries, Ltd.	
7	Komatsu Ltd.	35		Toshiba Corp.	
	TDK Corp.			NEC Corp.	
	Nippon Meat Packers Inc.			Fuji Photo Film Co. Ltd.	
8	Sony Corp.	30		Mitsubishi Electric Corp.	
	Pioneer Electric Corp.		10	Komatsu Forklift Co. Ltd.	20
	Honda Motor Co., Ltd.				

For each class, I calculate the average percentage of major long-term stockholders in relation to all stockholders. I examine by *t*-test whether or not the difference of the two average figures are statistically significant. The result is shown in List 3. The result shows that the FRAFM's capital transaction is not so much internalized than that of non-FRAFM.

If we categorize the sample into *Keiretsu* firms and non-*Keiretsu* firms,[5] there is no significant difference statistically. This means that the *Keiretsu* do not necessarily indicate the internalization of the capital transaction.

To examine hypothesis 2, I select matching pairs from FRARM s and non-FRAFMs whose industry and scale are similar. The selected matching pairs are listed in List 4.

I set the null hypothesis that the disclosure level of the FRAFM (Ei) and that of the non-FRAFM (Ci) are similar. The Wilcoxon matched-pair signed-ranks test was used and the null hypothesis was rejected at the one percent level (see List 5).

It can be argued that the difference of Ei and Ci depends on the difference of the content of accounting rules, for FRAFM was defined as firms which prepare SEC F/S. If the disclosure level of firms which raise funds in the U.S. or U.K. market is significantly higher than that of firms which raise funds in other foreign markets, the higher level of Ei may be attributed to the higher level of account-

---

[5]As for the method of categorizing *Keiretsu* and non-*Keiretsu* firms, see Keizai Chosa Kyokai (1981).

LIST 3
Relationship between Internalization of Capital Transaction and Fund-Raising in Foreign Markets

	Number of Firms	Avg.	Stv.	*t*-value
FRAFMs	35	36.60	6.01	
non-FRAFMs	77	41.17	10.40	2.41[*]
Keiretsu firms	62	40.29	9.43	
non-*Keiretsu* firms	50	39.93	9.73	0.001

[*]: significant at 1% level.
Avg.: the average of the rate of major long-term stockholders to that of all the stockholders.
Stv.: the standard deviation.

LIST 4
Matching Pairs Selected for the Wilcoxon's Nonparametric Statistics

	FRAFMs	NON-FRAFMs
Food Industry	Nippon Meat Packers, Inc. (328,039)	Ajinomoto Co. Inc. (444,509)
Fiber Industry	Wacoal Corp. (101,660)	Mitsubishi Kasei Corp. (254,385)
Chemical Industry	Fuji Photo Film Co., Ltd. (587,405)	Dainippon Ink and Chemicals Inc. (408,575)
Electric Industry	Casio Computer Co., Ltd. (166,421)	Tokyo Electric Co., Ltd. (141,297)
Electric Industry	Murata Manufacturing Co., Ltd. (96,931)	Kenwood Corp. (85,918)
Machine and Transportation Industry	Komatsu Ltd. (703,705)	Suzuki Motor Corp. (590,154)
Machine Industry	Sumitomo Heavy Industries, Ltd. (329,216)	NTN Corp. (219,627)
Precision Machine Industry	Asahi Optical Co., Ltd. (84,663)	Nihon Kogaku K.K. (140,115)

The numbers in parentheses indicate consolidated sales proceeds.

LIST 5
Results Derived from the Wilcoxon Matched-Pair Signed-Ranks Test

	Ei	Ci	Di	Ranks of Di	*t*-value
Food Industry	60	0	60	6.5	
Fiber Industry	0	0	0	1.0	
Chemical Industry	25	0	25	3.0	
Electric Industry	60	0	60	6.5	
Electric Industry	80	0	80	8.0	
Machine and Transportation	35	0	35	5.0	
Machine Industry	25	0	25	3.0	
Precision Machine Industry	25	0	25	3.0	
					0[*]

[*]: significant at 1% level.

ing rules, though Japanese firms were not required to disclose segment information in either the U.S. or U.K. markets in 1982.

To clear this point, I categorized the FRAFMs into two groups: firms whose stocks are listed in the U.S. or U.K. markets and firms whose stocks are not listed there. Then I examined the null hypothesis that both groups were selected from the same population. Concluding, the null hypothesis could not be rejected (see List 6). This result suggests that the assertion may not be correct that Ei is higher than Ci because of a higher level of disclosure requirement.[6]

As for FRAFM's disclosure levels, there is a great difference between the highest and the lowest. On the other hand, disclosure levels of non-FRAFMs are uniformly low. Then I looked for the factors which influence the disclosure level of FRAFMs. This leads to the examination of hypotheses 3 and 4.

A multiple regression analysis was used for the examination, assigning the dependent variable to the disclosure score, and the independent variables to the independence of subsidiaries of an organization and the scale of the foreign operation. To express the independence of subsidiaries, I used data of a rate of external sales against the sales of parent company in Japan (RES). Similarly, for the scale of the foreign operation, I used data of the number of foreign consolidated subsidiaries (CNSLD), the net balance outstanding of foreign direct investments (BFDIV), the number of foreign countries in which foreign subsidiaries are located (NFC), the amount of assets (ASSET), and the number of stockholders (NSH).

---

[6]Firms are permitted to adjust the content of disclosure according to the different condition of the markets. For example, Sony and Matsushita Electric Industrial do disclose the segment information in the U.S. market, although, they did not in the Japanese market in 1982.

LIST 6
Results Derived from the Median Statistics

	Number of Firms with Stocks Listed in the U.S. or U.K. Markets	Number of Firms with Stocks Listed in Other Foreign Markets
Firms whose score is:		
Higher than the median	8	10
Lower than the median	3	15

$x^2 = 2.09$; not significant even at 5% level.

At first, CNSLD is selected as an independent variable through the stepwise selection procedure. The *F*-value is 13.89 and is significant at the one percent level. The second, RES is selected. Then the multiple regression equation can be expressed as follows:

Y = 15.29 + 0.96 CNSLD + 0.15 RES

The F value is 7.47 and significant at the one percent level.

Then BFDIV and NFC are selected. However, these variables have a very high correlation with CNSLD (0.738 each); therefore, it is likely that there is no need for additional independent variables. This equation justifies hypotheses 3 and 4.

SUMMARY AND IMPLICATIONS

In this research, the influence of the internalization of capital transactions upon the disclosure level is analyzed. It has become clear that the internalization of capital transactions weakens the incentive for disclosure as a financial strategic means of a bonding activity; on the other hand, a firm whose capital transactions are not so internalized tends to raise funds actively in foreign markets; furthermore, a firm which is active in fund-raising in foreign markets generally shows high level disclosure, even in the Japanese markets; a firm which is active in fund-raising in foreign markets is more sensitive to strategic disclosure, considering both the cost aspect of fund-raising through reduction of uncertainty for investors and the possible competitive disadvantage by the disclosure.

In the process of the liberalization of finance in Japan, the relationship of firms and banks is changing gradually these days. This means that firms whose capital transaction is internalized must change their disclosure pattern. Some firms are now changing their attitudes towards disclosure. For example, Sony makes IR activities a part of stock management.

However, in general, firms are not willing to disclose additional information, because the cost of disclosure for firms tends to exceed the benefit they receive under the present environment including regulatory rules. This is because information is a public good. The wide spread of the internalized capital market has also kept the general level of disclosure low. Under these circumstances, firms are not penalized for their reluctance to disclose information by a high cost of borrowing from suspicious investors.

It is desirable for the standard setters in Japan to strengthen disclosure regulation. However, the strengthened regulations must leave some leeway for firms to choose not to disclose in certain areas in order that the characteristics of the Japanese capital market are taken into account.

If individual investors can get a significant portion of the information which has been made available only to long-term stockholders so far, the market will be able to function more efficiently and stock prices will be formed more appropriately. Furthermore, as the internalized relationship is weakened, Japanese firms will become more sensitive to strategic disclosure and the disclosure level will be brought closer to the Pareto-optimality.

REFERENCES

Barrette, M. E. 1976. Financial Reporting Practices: Disclosure and Comprehensiveness in an Industrial Setting. *Journal of Accounting Research* (Vol. 14, No. 1): 10–26.

Choi, F. D. S. 1973. Financial Disclosure and Entry to the European Capital Market. *Journal of Accounting Research* (Vol. 11, No. 2): 159–175.

Futatsugi, Y. 1982. *Nihon no Kabushiki Shoyu Kozo* (in Japanese) Dobunkan.

Hoshi, T., A. Kashyap and D. Scharftein. 1991. Corporate Structure, Liquidity, and Investment: Evidence from Japanese Industrial Groups. *The Quarterly Journal of Economics* (Vol. CVI): 33–60.

Imai, K., T. Itami and K. Koike. 1982. *Naibusoshiki no Keizaigaku* (in Japanese) Toyokeizai Shinposha.

Keizai, C. K. 1981. *Nenpo: Keiretsu no Kenkyu* (in Japanese) Vol. 22. Keizai Chosa Kyokai, Tokyo.

Mautz, R. K., and W. G. May. 1978. *Financial Disclosure in a Competitive Economy*. Financial Executive Research Foundation.

Modigliani, F., and M. H. Miller. 1958. The Cost of Capital, Corporation Finance, and the Theory of Investment. *American Economic Review* (June): 261–297.

Okada, E. 1986. Nihon no Kaiji Kankyo to Kigyo no Kaiji Kodo ni Kansuru Josetsuteki Kenkyu (in Japanese). *Rokkodai Ronshu* (Vol. 33, No. 2): 14–33.

Okumura, H. 1986. *Nihon no Kabushikikaisha* (in Japanese). Toyokeizai Shinposha.

Sakurai, H., and H. Yamaji. 1990. Kabushiki Anteika ga Kaikei Joho Kokai ni Oyobosu Eikyo (in Japanese). *Kigyo Kaikei* (Vol. 42, No. 7): 72–78.

Yoshihara, H. 1979. *Takokuseki Keieiron* (in Japanese) Hakuto Shobo.

Yunker, P. 1982. *Transfer Pricing and Performance Evaluation in Multinational Corporations — Survey Study —*. Praeger Publishers.

Further Issues in Accounting Education

The conference program included nine papers that explore principally the future direction of international accounting education. Three of these papers deal with planning for the future needs of accounting education and the profession. Two present information about how we can view accounting education differently; e.g., as a portfolio of courses or as an integrated framework. Two papers are concerned about why accounting research articles do not properly communicate their practical value to many practitioners and accounting professors. Another paper proposes that before progress can be made in accounting education a new model of accounting that goes beyond double-entry must be developed. For the individual who wishes to be a visiting scholar in the United States, one paper explores the U.S. tax implications, and finds them to be inequitable and unduly complex.

Accounting Education Changes for the Future

Dale Bandy

The agrarian economy of the 19th century was served by one-room schools that taught basic skills and honed self-reliant individuals prepared to participate in an economy of family farms and small shops. By the 20th century, schools had changed to assembly lines that moved students through grades and schools, toward diplomas and jobs in an industrialized, assembly line economy. During the 21st century, education and business will both change to reflect a service-oriented, technology-based, worldwide economy. Accounting is a part of that changing economy. The mergers of accounting firms and the introduction of technology that ranges from computers and fax machines to expert systems and artificial intelligence mean that accountants are moving toward a role as skilled business advisers.

As a result, accounting education is at a crossroads. The fundamental textbook-based, rule-intensive, lecture/problems style of instruction will not well serve accountants who act as advisers in the emerging world economy. The managing partners in the major accounting firms have offered $4 million of financial support for accounting programs that undertake efforts to improve the educational process. Among other things, the managing partners are concerned that accounting graduates lack problem-solving skills. As the managing partners state, "Individuals seeking to be successful in the diverse world of public accounting must be able to use creative problem-solving skills in a consultative process. They must be able to solve diverse and unstructured problems in unfamiliar settings. They must be able to comprehend an unfocused set of facts; identify and, if possible, anticipate problems; and find acceptable solutions."

A vote by the AICPA membership has prompted several states to adopt a requirement for a fifth year of education. The implementation of the fifth year represents an unique opportunity for curriculum development. The fifth year, however, does not mean that courses must be added to the accounting curriculum in an effort to achieve the impossible goal of encyclopedic coverage of all accounting rules. In fact, such an effort could hinder the effort to advance the profession.

Because of the lack of professional experience, entry-level accountants often face the frustrating problem of dealing with unfamiliar topics. These situations can be grouped into three categories:

- Difficult technical questions not covered in the typical accounting curriculum,

- Determinations requiring professional judgment, and

- Areas of professional ethics involving borderline calls.

DIFFICULT TECHINICAL ISSUES

When professional accountants tackle a problem it sometimes involves only the routine application of familiar rules. Undoubtedly, accounting education trains students well for this situation. Much of accounting, however, involves situations not found in textbooks or covered in college programs. Special and regulated industries, state taxes and taxes of foreign countries, accounting standards of foreign countries, SEC rules, and bankruptcy are typical problem areas that are either not covered or are only briefly covered in accounting texts and accounting classes. Yet accountants must deal with these areas when they are encountered without regard to whether they were covered in accounting classes. Experienced accountants recall situations such as having to prepare a State of Utah tax return when they had not previously known that Utah had a state income tax, or being assigned to an audit of a client with a significant foreign operation when the accountant was completely unfamiliar with the accounting standards of the foreign country. This is not to say that everyone has had precisely these experiences, but everyone has had parallel experiences. In the past, accounting may have been different. At one time it was possible to read everything published in accounting. R. M. Mautz reports that, in 1948, A. C. Littleton stated that "he read everything that was published in accounting. . . . Who could do that now? Or would want to?" Today's world is far different and

Dale Bandy is Knights' Professor of Taxation at the University of Central Florida.

more complicated than that of 1948. No amount of education will prepare someone for every contingency, and even if it were possible to cover every technical issue, the standards and laws would quickly change, leaving the accountant to deal with new rules.

Traditional methods of accounting instruction developed when it was possible to read everything that was published in accounting. The growth of accounting information means that accounting has outgrown the traditional instructional method.

PROFESSIONAL JUDGMENT

Moreover, accountants must learn to exercise professional judgment in difficult situations. Is the going concern assumption still valid for a troubled company? Is an amount sufficiently material to require disclosure? Is an estimated allowance for bad debts adequate? Is the available authority sufficient for a taxpayer to claim a questionable deduction on a tax return? Textbook coverage and classroom discussions seldom are sufficient for students to develop the professional judgment necessary to cope with such problem situations.

To what extent was the savings and loan crisis caused by accounting education? Clearly, a large number of auditors failed to identify troubled savings and loans before the problems reached crisis stage. Did we teach them what accounts to debit and credit, but fail to teach them how to measure uncollectible accounts? Or is it that we failed to teach them how to apply the going concern concept? Or perhaps we failed to instill a sufficient level of professional ethics. I am not sure what it is we did wrong, but I am sure that American accounting education failed.

ETHICAL ISSUES

Learning ethical behavior is more complicated than simply reading ethical standards. There are often close calls requiring precise judgment. Accountants must maintain a confidential relationship with clients yet adequately disclose necessary information on financial statements. Does terminology suggested by a client actually result in misleading financial statements or tax returns? Further, accountants must understand the difference between audit independence and tax advocacy. Ethical and unethical behavior are not two extremes separated by a large vacuum. Instead there are shades of differences between sometimes conflicting standards. It is often the case that ethical behavior involves knowing where a line must be drawn and having the willpower to stand on the right side of the line.

IMPLICATIONS OF CURRENT EDUCATIONAL APPROACH

On occasion, the better graduates of strong accounting programs fail on the job because they failed to learn fundamental accounting rules covered in classes. More often, however, failure is due to an inability to cope with the variety of situations not covered in class.

These ideas are hardly new. The first article in the first issue of *The Journal of Accountancy* states, "The public accountant should be more than a mere manipulator of figures, a sort of half-way detective, an assistant to the lawyer and public prosecutor."

Teaching students to deal with complicated and unfamiliar situations represents perhaps the greatest challenge to accounting education. Students can be taught to deal with these problems only if the focus of accounting education is altered. According to the managing partners of the country's largest accounting firms, "The current textbook-based, rule-intensive, lecture/problem style should not survive as the primary means of presentation." This is not to say that attempts to cover a variety of specific rules should be entirely eliminated. Rather accounting education must be changed so as to reflect the reality that coverage cannot be encyclopedic. Law schools do not attempt to teach law students every law. Rather law schools attempt to provide students with skills needed to conduct legal research. Moot court serves to provide students with simulated courtroom experiences before they serve real life clients.

The knowledge base in accounting is not merely increasing but also is growing exponentially. Intermediate accounting was originally one course at most schools and was expanded to two as the body of rules grew to the point that the information could not be thoroughly covered in just one course. Today, many schools cover intermediate accounting in three courses. But, of course, the three intermediate courses are typically preceded by two principles courses and followed by one or two advanced courses, as well as courses in systems, auditing, and theory.

SUGGESTED CHANGES

Problem-solving skills are important enough that they should be taught, even if it is necessary to reduce coverage of technical topics in existing classes. It is necessarily true that every successful accountant is a problem solver. Yet it is not true that every successful accountant is a technician. Would a successful accountant after a few years out of school want to retake the CPA exam? A successful tax accountant may not have an in-depth knowledge of financial accounting, and the government accountant may not be up to date on recent tax developments. Both, however, will be able to attack accounting problems and resolve them.

What can accounting education do to better prepare students for accounting work? The case method is a promising approach. Instructors can assign cases that cannot be solved by reading the assigned texts. These cases can entail library research, team projects, and consultations with experienced accountants. Classes should discuss what constitutes acceptable sources of accounting authority and what represents a reasonable interpretation of that authority. Thus, a case might provide detailed information relating to a troubled company. Students can then be asked to determine whether the company is a going concern. This case could lead students to read not only accounting and auditing standards but also court cases dealing with litigation relating to accountant's liability. Practicing professionals can be both a source of such cases and participants in classroom discussions of potential solutions. Alternatively, professionals could evaluate case presentations by individual students or teams.

It may be true that these techniques are most useful in advanced courses. In introductory classes, instructors may continue to lecture while students listen and occasionally ask questions. By the time students reach advanced classes, however, the students should be able to make presentations and communicate critical ideas to their peers.

Fundamentals of problem-solving methodology should be discussed in classes. These include identifying issues, gathering facts, locating authority, weighing authority, reaching a conclusion, and communicating the conclusion. Students need to be become familiar with the sources of accounting information such as journals and treatises, as well as professional standards. Databases such as LEXIS, Westlaw, and NARS are becoming routinely used tools in many offices. Although it may be appropriate for students to rely on textbooks early in the educational process, it is essential that they learn to rely on the other sources before they enter the profession. Further, students need to be taught how to use and when to rely on alternative sources.

Artificial intelligence is taking its place in the accounting profession. Just as accounting education had to adapt to computers, it must also prepare students to use artificial intelligence. In time, accounting education may come to realize that expert systems will represent an extraordinary learning tool. Perhaps professional judgment can be learned through the use of expert systems as students can develop answers to cases and match their solutions against those of an expert system.

Internships provide students with real job experience. When interns return to the classroom, they have experienced practical problems and can relate those experiences to the classroom discussion and they can share the real experiences with other students. These practical experiences make interns more pragmatic. They have dealt with the variety of the job situations that require problem-solving skills, and they are ready for discussions that delve into problem solving. Even entry-level experience makes interns more willing to accept answers that are based on facts and circumstances.

OBSTACLES TO CHANGE

Although many will agree that the problems discussed here are real, some will argue that problem-solving and ethical practices cannot be taught, or that there is not room in accounting courses to add problem solving to classes.

Accounting programs attract students with strong quantitative skills and a desire for closure. Accounting students prefer problems with clear-cut answers that can be obtained from the application of rules that entail math-like certainty. For example, students are comfortable with an exercise that entails the application of a specific depreciation method for a specific fact situation, and textbooks are filled with assorted and rarely used methods. Yet the important issues such as selecting the appropriate depreciation method, estimating useful life, and estimating salvage value are discussed only in general terms. Most accounting instructors learn that accounting students are uncomfortable with issues that do not have specific answers. The students will ask, "So what do I do?" They do not like instructors to respond, "It depends on the facts and circumstances. You must learn to exercise your judgment. You have to think."

The accreditation of business and accounting programs and the CPA exam are at the same time both obstacles and incentives to change. Both seek to standardize the common body of knowledge possessed by those who enter the profession. For example, one need only review a few questions on recent CPA exams to observe the emphasis on the recollection of rules and the application of those rules. The tax questions deal with specific tax rules. There is no consideration given to tax research methodology or to the role of advocacy. In the area of auditing, however, the CPA exam has long addressed issues relating to professional judgment. Similarly, accreditation standards encourage the coverage of business policy and ethics. Individual universities, however, are left with the responsibility of seeing to it that graduates have exposure to problem-solving cases.

Managing partners and their front-line staff personnel seem to have different views of accounting education. Seniors and managers note that staff personnel with a traditional four-year accounting education do well in the entry-level jobs and progress just as fast as those staff personnel who hold advanced degrees. They further note that the starting salaries for staff with advanced degrees is higher, and they feel that this may be an unnecessary expense.

Managing partners, particularly those with national firms, have a different perspective. They note that turnover is lower among staff with advanced degrees, that personnel with advanced degrees are more likely to become partners, and that the advantages of the advanced degree become evident as the individual advances through the organization. They are aware of the extremely high cost of recruiting and training new staff, and they note the inefficiency of new personnel. Perhaps most importantly, the managing partners believe that the individuals with advanced degree are more likely to possess the communication skills, the interpersonal skills, and the business savvy necessary to hold advanced positions within the firm.

The interests of national accounting firms are not always the same as those of local firms. Nevertheless, both national and local firms serve as advisers to clients. Clearly, those who serve in a consultative capacity need problem solving skills and perspective. Similarly, professional liability concerns both large and small firms. Liability often stems from situations where accountants failed to address problems instead of situations where rules were intentionally disregarded. Therefore, in the case of both small firms and large one, problem solving is critical to success.

PRESENT EFFORTS

Accounting education has not entirely ignored practical problems and problem solving. One area where accounting has made exceptional progress is in the teaching of tax research. Over 80 American schools offer tax research courses, and there are three leading books available to instructors. These books and courses do an excellent job of explaining tax research methodology, identifying the sources of authority, and outlining how to locate and use published materials. If there is a major weakness in the courses and texts, it probably relates to the fact that limited attention is devoted to dealing with research efforts that produce ambiguous results. Advocacy is an intricate and delicate relationship that balances professional liability, professional standards, taxpayer and tax preparer penalties, client personality, and an understanding of fundamental technical rules. One cannot relate the results of tax research to a practice problem without an appreciation of these factors.

In spite of this weakness, tax research courses are generally well designed. Unfortunately, there are few if any parallels in other accounting subject areas. Moreover, tax education is often encyclopedic in coverage. There are at least a dozen universities that offer two dozen tax courses and one that offers over 40 courses. Such programs cannot be justified in terms of a normal university objective of providing graduates with a well-rounded education along with career preparation, and, in fact, no university expects students to take dozens of tax courses even if they earn a master's degree. Instead, the courses are intended to offer electives to students who do not take all courses while earning a degree and to provide a source of continuing education for professionals who choose to enroll in credit courses.

Case studies are available in tax and other areas. An example of an excellent set of cases is the *Price Waterhouse Case Studies in Tax* edited by Sally Morrow. The Price Waterhouse Foundation published the uncopyrighted cases and has made them available to instructors at no charge. The publication contains several "case studies which are 'true-to-life' situations upon which tax practitioners are asked to consult." These integrative cases combine a variety of issues in a single fact situation and require an estimated 20 hours of research time each.

Perhaps the best-known effort to bring reality to accounting education is the Trueblood Professors' Seminars sponsored by the Deloitte Touche Foundation and the American Accounting Association. These seminars, which began in 1966, provide professors with cases relating to financial accounting and auditing issues. Over one thousand professors have attended these seminars. Cases summarize the facts of real problems not addressed specifically in the professional standards. A panel of faculty and Deloitte and Touche partners and staff discuss the cases and answers are suggested. Faculty are encouraged to utilize the cases in auditing and accounting classes.

One recent effort to explain and evaluate the role of professional judgment is a book entitled *Professional Judgment in Financial Reporting*. This book represents a significant effort to define professional judgment in financial reporting context and to explain the framework in which professional judgment is exercised. This ambitious book is a unique resource for those who wish to study professional judgment.

CONCLUSION

Over the decades, accounting education has developed the approach of providing encyclopedic coverage of extensive topics. This is most true in the area of financial accounting, but the approach can be found in other areas including cost, tax, and auditing. In traditional courses, students are asked to

solve homework problems from the end of the chapter by applying rules explained in the chapter. Subsequently, students are tested with questions that require quick solutions to difficult and intricate problems covering the same rules. This methodology developed because of the fundamental misconception that the objective of accounting education is to teach accounting. One might ask, what could possibly be wrong with this effort? If it is all right to teach history in history classes, why is it not all right to teach accounting in accounting classes? The answer relates to the fundamentally different objectives of history and accounting courses. The purpose of history classes is to teach history. The purpose of accounting classes is not to teach accounting, but rather to teach students to be accountants. Many history classes are aimed at teaching history to individuals who do not plan to be historians, and, as a result, these basic courses do not cover the methodologies used by historians. Accounting, however, is more than just the mechanical application of accounting rules. Accounting education must change to recognize this.

Is Accountancy a Profession? Implications for Education

Tonya K. Flesher and Dale L. Flesher

Is accountancy a profession? Or is it a multiplicity of professions (such as taxation, internal auditing, external auditing, and management accounting)? Alternatively, is accounting only a subset of business (such as is implied by the way it is taught at the Ivy League business schools)? Other more specific questions include these: Is management accounting a subdiscipline of accounting, or a subdiscipline of management? Similarly, is governmental accounting a subdiscipline of accounting or of public administration? It seems that the answer to these questions could reflect on the manner in which accounting is taught, and the organizational structure under which it is taught.

For example, the answer to the question of whether accountancy is a profession leads to the question of whether accounting should be taught in the business school or the accountancy school. The question about whether management accounting is a subdiscipline of accounting or management results in the question of whether a management accountant should hold a master of accountancy degree (MACC) or a master of business administration (MBA) degree. Perhaps governmental accountants should hold master of public administration (MPA) degrees.

First, is accountancy a profession or a subset of business? What are the implications of each answer for the form and structure of accounting education? Exhibit I outlines some of the implications.

These basic issues have been debated for many years. Henry Rand Hatfield addressed the Annual Meeting of the American Association of University Instructors in Accounting (the predecessor of AAA) in 1923 on the topic, "An Historical Defense of Bookkeeping." This address, which was published in the *Journal of Accountancy* in 1924, emanated from remarks which he made to a society of Berkeley scholars on the appropriateness of teaching accounting at the college level. Zeff refers to these defenses in his article in *Issues in Accounting Education* in 1989 entitled "Does Accounting Belong in the University Curriculum?" (which was based on his address to AAA in 1988). This image and identity problem has existed throughout the history of accounting education. In fact, accounting was originally taught under some other designation, such as Political Economy, at most schools.

Accounting education may well be at a critical point in determining its image as the accounting profession's image is at a crossroads. Accounting practitioners and educators need to arrive at an answer to this question, and apparently there is not a consensus. Robert Elliott of KPMG Peat Marwick was asked this question at an Administrators of Accounting Programs (AAPG) meeting, and he said that he did not know whether accounting was a profession or a subset of business. The answer is crucial because the resulting consequences of each answer on accounting education are vastly different, as Exhibit I shows.

Schools of Accountancy

Over the years, those arguing the support of separate schools of accountancy have contended that the business school emphasis on a general management education was not compatible with the needs of the public accounting profession. As cited by Bricker and Previts in their 1990 article on schisms, the need for separate schools of accountancy was noted as early as 1892:

> As a constituent of our educational system, the so-called commercial or business college, however valuable their curriculum, are from their very nature precluded from giving a practicable training in this special subject. . . and bear little or no relation to those broader views characteristic of the public accountant (p. 4).

Similarly, Charles Waldo Haskins observed in 1901 that one of the most important effects of CPA legislation had been to motivate students to pass the CPA examination (Bricker and Previts 1990, 4). More recently, the establishment of professional schools of accountancy at more than 40 major universities has been based upon a perception that accountancy schools could better provide the training needed by individuals who wish to pursue careers in accountancy. It should be noted that sev-

Tonya K. Flesher is Dean and Dale L. Flesher is Arthur Andersen & Co. Alumni Professor, at the School of Accountancy at the University of Mississippi.

EXHIBIT I
Accountancy: Profession or Subset of Business?

	Profession	Subset of Business
Structure	Separate School of Accy.	Dept. within Bus.
Accreditation	Accy. Accreditation Body	Business Agency
Model	Law School	Economic/Management
Undergraduate	Any Major	Business Major
Graduate	Maccy/Mtax or Accy.D.	MBA
Education Base	Liberal Arts-minded Students	Liberal Arts Trained
Governance	Professional School Model	Business School Model
Independence	Yes	No
Image/Identity	Develop New/Separate	Tied to Business Image

eral large private universities (including the Ivy League schools) continue to offer accounting as a subset of the business curriculum. However, this seems to be an anomaly in that major recruiters of accounting graduates do not recruit at most such schools. For instance, Charles Horngren recently stated that none of the Big 6 CPA firms recruited at Stanford (a school which is often cited as the best MBA program in the country).

You would think that the recent growth of professional schools of accountancy would have closed the issue of the best place to educate professional accountants, but such is seemingly not the case. In a recent article, University of Illinois professor Frederick L. Neumann stated that he had heard a public accounting practitioner make the comment that his firm's goal was to hire "businessmen who are also good auditors." Neumann concluded that this comment "signifies to me a shift which could jeopardize the fundamental commitment of the profession—to honor the public trust" (Neumann 1991, 9). More specifically, what the practitioner may have been wanting was a person with both a business degree and an accountancy degree, in other words, a person with more education than the traditional bachelor's or master's degree in either field.

Accreditation

If accounting is a subset of business, then obviously accreditation of accounting programs should be under the auspices of a business accrediting agency. If accounting is a profession, then shouldn't accounting professionals and educators set the standards for accounting accreditation? Accounting accreditation should be conducted by a separate agency just as are other professional schools such as law, medicine, pharmacy and engineering. This is not a new idea. In Scotland, accountancy programs are accredited by a professional organization, and in New York, the State Board of CPA Examiners tried to set accreditation standards in the early 1950s. Similarly, the AICPA and AAA threatened to take over accounting accreditation in the late 1970s.

Pedagogical and Philosophical Model

If accounting is housed in the business school, then accounting educators will have to adopt the economics/management model. As a separate profession, accounting educators might want to look at other professional models. One author (Subotnik) has explored some of these issues in a 1987 *Issues in Accounting Education* article entitled "What Accounting Can Learn from Legal Education." Subotnik said:

> It might be interesting to look at other professions such as medicine which have some features similar to accounting and law, including the premium put on good judgment, to see whether the educational model resembles accounting at one extreme or law on the other. Now it is true, obviously that the purpose of accounting, unlike law, is to report valuable information to users of financial statements. But this objection overlooks the significant respect in which accounting, like law, is designed to regulate economic activities, and penalties for failure to comply with existing rules result in both civil and criminal sanctions that are sometimes quite severe. Like accounting, law is commonly construed in our culture as requiring generally applicable principles and, in the end, a single binding solution. Nevertheless, our conception of law also admits, in its very essence, the existential reality of differences in human interpretation and the consequent unavoidability of discretion—which is to say, subjective judgment in the resolution of those differences [p. 318–319]. Accounting, by contrast, is an unambiguous paradigm in our culture for the clear-cut structure with a bottom line [p. 320].

Subotnik thinks that this tendency contributes to the unenthusiastic response that accounting courses often receive from students. It is difficult to expect any other reaction where the course textbook is so likely to assume a dead, unresponsive world. Subotnik goes on to state:

> Accountants have suffered from a negative image for several generations. To be sure, the lawyer also does not occupy the highest rank in popular consciousness. Yet, the attorney, whatever his or her perceived negative attributes, is at least given credit for a certain kind of craftiness. Accounting may be the only profession around that is not characterized by a single positive stereotype [p. 320].

Maybe these arguments also help to explain why interest in studying accounting has declined nationwide while applicants for law schools are at the highest levels in history. Subotnik is correct in stating that accounting educators need to look at the educational models of other professions in answering these critical questions.

Undergraduate and Graduate Education

Accounting taught as a subset of business would require that a student study the common body of business knowledge and pursue an MBA degree at the graduate level. Were accounting to adopt some of the other professional school models, any undergraduate major would be appropriate preparation for the study of accounting. The college graduate would then enroll in a school of accountancy and pursue a Master of Accountancy or Tax degree or perhaps a professional doctorate (Accy.D.) like law (J.D.) or pharmacy (Pharm.D.).

The education base of the business major will be primarily business with various ranges of liberal arts courses required at different institutions. In contrast, a professional school of accountancy would attract students who are not just trained in liberal arts courses because they were required, but students who elected to concentrate on liberal arts studies because of their mindset. The question is, which background and mindset provide accounting professionals with the best critical thinking and judgment skills? Which does the accounting profession need as specialists — the liberal arts–trained or liberal arts–minded students?

Faculty Governance and Independence

Faculty in a professional school of accountancy would have independence in faculty governance and in setting standards for research, tenure, and promotion. These standards should be set to complement the demands of the profession as they are in other separate professional schools. But if accounting is a subset of business, accounting faculty should be held to the same standards as business faculty members.

Image and Identity

As a subset of business, accounting practice and education will continue to be tied to business. In contrast, accounting could attempt to establish a separate and new identity and image. A separate professional school is a start in that direction. A new degree designation (Accy.D.) would be another. Regardless, everyone in the profession would agree that accountants need to work on an improved image.

Besides questions of where accounting education should be housed, other questions arise with respect to the ever-expanding role of accountants. As the role of accounting expands into management advisory services, personal financial planning, operational auditing, and social reporting, the elements of accounting education must similarly expand, which means either superficial coverage or more time spent on an education.

EARMARKS OF A PROFESSION

If accountancy is a profession, how many accountancy professions are there, and how do educators teach for each of these separate professions? People refer to the profession of internal auditing (Savage 1981, 5; Wesberry 1989, 23) and the profession of management accounting. Taxation and personal financial planning are similarly mentioned as being sufficiently different from "accounting" to be separate professions. If students had to select a career field from external auditing, taxation, management consulting services, managerial accounting, internal auditing, governmental accounting, or personal financial planning—all subfields of accountancy—they would be doing so without knowledge of any of those "professions," and would be limited in their future career moves across boundaries. Thus, spending more time and covering all aspects of accounting during the educational process seemingly would be preferable in the long run (although the Big 6 CPA firms who are the major supporters of university accountancy programs might disagree).

Whenever the subject of professionalism is discussed, the question arises as to what is a profession. Naturally, the thought that immediately comes to mind is that of "the world's oldest profession" (which is presumably not accountancy). There have been many definitions and descriptions of professionals over the years. Many of these descriptions have included lists of attributes which persons must meet before they can call themselves professionals. Unfortunately, some of those lists are so general that they can often be applicable not only to true professionals, but to imitators as well. One list of professional characteristics that seemingly does apply to professionals, and rules out the imitators, is one that was espoused in a 1963 speech by Joseph Glickauf, then the head of the Advisory Services Division of Arthur Andersen & Co. (Glickauf 1971, 93–98). Glickauf listed ten characteristics of a professional person. These are summarized as follows:

1. A professional is a highly skilled person who offers a service in a specialized area in which the general public is untrained (and thus unable to make an evaluation as to quality).

2. A professional is very well educated (particularly breadth of education).

3. A professional holds the ultimate responsibility for his own work.

4. A professional is a person of unimpeachable integrity.

5. A professional practices within the framework of a code of ethics which defines professional standards of conduct.

6. A professional is required to analyze a problem and develop a solution (diagnose and treat).

7. A professional requires a lifetime of self-improvement because professional knowledge continues to expand.

8. A professional is obligated to contribute to the furtherance of the profession through personal effort in pioneering new fields.

9. A professional is not solely motivated by monetary considerations (i.e., provides free services to the needy or to civic organizations).

10. A professional is a member of a group which is banded together into a strong professional organization.

Taken together, these characteristics say that a professional person is one who is broadly educated and highly skilled in an area that is built around a boundless body of broad knowledge. A professional is a person of high integrity who is dedicated and responsible, and deals with concepts and ideas rather than their implementation. This person is altruistic and a member of a professional organization.

Given this structured definition, who in accountancy can claim to be a professional? Who cannot? Certainly, the external auditor working with a CPA firm can meet all of the ten criteria.

But what about an internal auditor? Is internal auditing a separate profession? Probably. Internal auditors have their own code of ethics and professional organization, certification, and a broad level of education is required. In fact, internal auditors have one code of ethics worldwide, with one international professional organization—The Institute of Internal Auditors. Could it be said that the internal auditor is a "purer" professional because there is one profession worldwide? Similarly, the Institute of Management Accountants is a professional organization with a code of ethics defining the professional standards for accountants working in industry. Tax preparers would probably also meet the criteria listed in that they are subject to professional standards of conduct established both by the government and by the American Institute of CPAs. There are several professional organizations for tax preparers.

Given this definition of professionalism (and most others), any accountant can claim to be a professional. Therefore, since accounting is a profession, does it not make sense to educate these professionals in a professional school? Also, given the relationships among the various components of the accounting profession, it seems reasonable to educate these individuals in as broad a manner as possible. A comparison can be made at this point to the education received in American law schools. The field of law encompasses criminal law, civil law, property law, tax law, patent law, admiralty law, and other areas. Despite the broad areas of practice, all lawyers receive the same initial degree—which basically consists of a three-year program beyond the bachelor's degree. Thus, it seems logical to structure a professional degree in accounting in a manner similar to a law degree. That is, every accountant would receive a similar broad education regardless of whether his or her ultimate career objective was public accounting, management accounting, taxation, internal auditing, or whatever. Although specialties within a degree program would exist, prospective accountants would take many of the same courses despite having differences in career objectives. This would be justified because all areas of accounting borrow ideas from other areas, and practitioners would be able to change jobs more readily, particularly to other subfields of accounting, if a broad education was obtained.

A DOCTORATE FOR PRACTITIONERS

The logical conclusion is that accounting practitioners should hold a doctorate—a degree similar to a law degree or a Doctor of Pharmacy (Pharm.D.). Such a degree would be a true professional degree on a comparison with those of other professionals.

An Accountancy Doctorate (Accy.D.) should consist of approximately two years of course work (at least 36 semester hours) beyond the master's degree. Course work would ideally consist of accountancy, business, and liberal arts courses. Those individuals with undergraduate and master's degrees in accounting would take mostly business and liberal arts courses with a few capstone courses in accounting. Individuals with business majors (perhaps an MBA) would take both accounting and liberal arts courses. People with degrees in liberal arts would take primarily accountancy courses. The total time commitment for a master's degree and Accy.D. would be the same as for a pharmacy or law degree. Some might argue that six years is too long to study for a career in accounting, but six years of study is already the norm in some European countries, notably Scotland. As with the law degree and Pharm.D., there would be no dissertation, but a thesis option might be offered for those who wished such an opportunity. Holders of such degrees would be capable of working in any aspect of accounting and perhaps could specialize during the last year of the program. Given the increase in CPA and CMA exam performance by people with master's degrees as compared to those who hold only bachelor's degrees, it is logical that new doctorates would have almost a 100 percent pass rate. No longer would the first two years on the job be devoted to worrying about the professional examinations.

CONCLUSION

Accounting educators need to ask many questions about the direction of the accounting profession and the manner in which accounting professionals are to be educated in the future. Although a few private schools will likely continue to offer accounting as a subset of business, the direction for the future seems to be in separate programs for professional accountants. But then educators must address the question of which segment of the accounting profession students are to be educated toward. Given the desires of recruiters for an individual with both a broad background and technical skills, it seems the direction to go is to broaden the accountancy program. This can be accomplished by offering more superficial coverage of various accounting topics or lengthening the accountancy program to provide thorough coverage of all aspects of the profession. The latter move can be accomplished by the development of a new degree—the Doctor of Accountancy (Accy.D.) for practitioners. In some ways, the development of such a broad degree might help bring the accountancy profession closer together. Presently, some subdisciplines, such as personal financial planning, are almost outside the realm of the accounting profession in that insurance agents and stock brokers are as great a force as accountants. The Personal Financial Planning Section of the AICPA has recently found it necessary to prepare brochures to make college students aware of the opportunities available in personal financial planning. Similarly, internal auditing is almost a forgotten field at many universities as professors presume that a generic auditing course is equally applicable to external and internal auditing. Consequently, the Institute of Internal Auditors devotes a great deal of resources to familiarizing students with the profession (or is it subprofession?) of internal auditing. A degree program with a less superficial treatment of the areas outside of public accounting would result in a better prepared student for all aspects of the profession of accounting.

REFERENCES

Bricker, R. J., and G. J. Previts. 1990. The Sociology of Accountancy: A Study of Academic and Practice Community Schisms. *Accounting Horizons* (March): 1–14.

Glickauf, J. S. 1971. Footsteps toward Professionalism, in *Footsteps toward Professionalism*. Arthur Andersen & Co.: 93–98.

Neumann, F. L. 1991. Businessmen Who Are Good Auditors. *The Auditor's Report* (Fall): 9.

Savage, L. J. 1981. Professionalization of Internal Auditing. *Review of Business* (Spring): 5–6, 22.

Subotnik, D. 1987. What Accounting Can Learn from Legal Education. *Issues in Accounting Education* (Fall): 313–324.

Wesberry, J. P. 1989. The Pursuit of Professionalism. *Internal Auditor* (April): 22–29.

Vocational or Liberal? The Future of Accounting Education as an Analogy for the Higher Education Debate

Victor L. Honigberg

INTRODUCTION

As the accounting and auditing professions endeavour to keep pace with changes in business, technology and the economy in general (American Accounting Association 1986; Elliott 1986), some of the interested parties in education, or stakeholders, are advocating changes in the way accounting students are educated. Many of the professional societies, employers of graduate accountants and accounting academics argue for more education for accounting students, but not for more accounting courses. The changes these stakeholders seek are intended to broaden the breadth of education for accountants by requiring successful completion of more nonaccounting courses prior to receiving a bachelor degree. They also recommend segregating specialised accounting courses to postgraduate study (American Accounting Association 1986; New Zealand Society of Accountants 1984; *Perspectives . . .* 1989). In short, these stakeholders are advocating a change to a more liberal education.

There are other views, however, about the types of changes to be made. Some professional societies, employers and educators seek change aimed at providing more specialised instruction in particular fields, such as internal auditing (Kagle 1987) and international accounting (Stout and Schweikart 1989). These parties advocate the introduction of additional accounting courses, or at least the intergration of their topic into existing courses. Their intentions may be interpreted as seeking a new curriculum which is more relevant to the work done by practising accountants, or a curriculum which is more vocationally oriented.

Due to this schism of views held by its constituents, the university community is experiencing a problem in deciding what, and how, to teach accounting students. Should the curriculum emphasize current accounting standards and rules and prepare students for professional licensure examinations, or should a broader view of education, that of preparing the student for lifelong learning, be employed?

The debate is not new. The university is the nexus through which the discourse of professional education must pass, and for centuries western universities have been trying to find a balance between liberal and vocational education. Accounting education has only recently been included in the discussion, but given the standing and commitment of the stakeholders who have expressed their opinions on the topic, one could perhaps be excused for believing that accounting education has been the focus of the debate, or maybe even its cause, for a long time.

Since Oxford and Cambridge first began the education of future clergymen, doctors, and lawyers, universities have been attempting to find the right combination of education and training which would both enable the graduate to practice his or her vocation immediately upon completion of study and also provide for his or her spiritual, moral and ethical advancement.

This paper will attempt to demonstrate that the current debate as to the future of accounting education is an analogy for the vocational/liberal arts debate which has been going on for centuries. An analogy is useful because it allows certain inferences to be made about the eventual outcome of the debate. To this end, several philosophers' views on the topic of higher education will be presented, and the origins of the current debate will be exposed. Next, the development of western universities will be addressed, and their placement in the vocational/liberal arts continuum will be shown to be a reaction to the world extant at the time of their founding. Theories as to the causes of dissatisfaction with current accounting education will be reported, along with the details of some representative calls for change in accounting education. In so doing, the paper will indicate that the debate about the future of accounting education is a valid analogy for the continuing, and much larger, de-

Victor L. Honigberg is a Lecturer at the University of Otago.

bate on professional education in western colleges and universities.

PHILOSOPHIES OF HIGHER EDUCATION

Beginning the examination of this dilemma for the university with a discussion of philosophy allows two direct questions to be asked: What is higher education? What is higher education for? Through this discussion, an attempt will be made to demonstrate the depths at which the question of a balance between liberal and vocational education has been addressed through the last three millennia.

THE EARLY CHINESE PHILOSOPHERS

Although they were probably not the first to consider the matter, Confucius and Lao-tse offer an insight into the origins of the debate. Confucius (c. 551–479 BCE) believed that education helped socialize the individual, and that the acquisition of knowledge was important for harmony within the society. His theories thus provide the foundation for what is now known as vocational education, or education aimed at making people productive and thereby good citizens (Chaplin 1978, 3205).

Lao-tse (c. 604–531 BCE), the founder of Taoism, held a different view on education. He saw education as part of the cultivation of the individual (Allen 1988, 15), and learning was a step toward understanding and personal growth. This view is in keeping with the modern concept of a liberal arts education. Thus, nearly 2,600 years ago, the debate about what we now call vocational and liberal education had begun.

PLATO AND ARISTOTLE

Plato (427–347 BCE) produced the first comprehensive and systematic philosophy of education in the western world. His view of the importance of higher education was that it both cultivated the individual for the good of the ideal society and also led to inner happiness and harmony of the individual. Higher education was not for everyone, though, only the intellectually elite. In this meritocracy, the state was also a beneficiary of the inner harmony, which was reached through individuals achieving their proper roles in society (Brubacher 1982, 65–66). Those who were capable of advanced study would be given the opportunity to go beyond the discovery that the senses permit; they would be trained in logic and dialectic, and so would be able to discern the truth and the good-

ness, and therefore be qualified to rule (Chaplin 1978, 3206).

Aristotle (384–322 BCE), on the other hand, was critical of education for any purpose save preparing the individual for the active pursuit of leisure. This pursuit was typified through the disinterested search for truth, which should be seen as a worthy activity in its own right and need not be associated in any way with economic or monetary gain.

> Of possessions, those rather are useful which bear fruit; those liberal which tend to enjoyment. By fruitful, I mean which yield revenue; by enjoyable, where nothing accrues of consequence beyond the using. (Brubacher 1982, 75).

THE MIDDLE AGES

The rise of Christianity gave rise to the view that life on earth was a preparation for the afterlife, and education was a means of attaining salvation. The universities of the time were dedicated to the training of scholars and to the advancement of knowledge. In contrast, the humanist philosophies of the Renaissance focused on the development of the individual, and learning was intended to enhance life in this world.

COMENIUS

Though there were many notable thinkers during and after the Reformation, John Amos Comenius (1592–1670) stands out for his tireless search, despite religious persecution and personal tragedy, for perfect teaching methods. Comenius was a believer in the Pansophic view of the world, which in its narrower sense can be said to define experience as "being fundamentally mental since reality itself is for human beings what they perceive it to be" (Sadler 1969, 21).

The study of Comenius, particularly his view of the curriculum, provides an insight into today's debate. Unlike some who teach or propose the teaching of a common body of knowledge, Comenius believed that such learning was not necessary so long as the essentials of knowledge, which would never go out of date, were taught. New knowledge could be integrated through the application of the essentials, and the same essentials would apply to all disciplines. Hence, Comenius saw education as a means through which indefinite further investigations could be undertaken.

NEWMAN

Cardinal John Henry Newman defined a university as "a place of teaching universal knowledge" (Newman 1976, ix). He was anxious to discredit the German notion that a university should be primarily a research centre. Universities, he argued, should be about the diffusion of knowledge, not its advancement.

Newman's view of the purpose of liberal education can be expressed as a method for training the mind.

> (a) habit of mind is formed which lasts through life . . . or what . . . I have ventured to call a philosophical habit (Newman 1976, lvii).

Through liberal education, people will be able to "fill their respective posts in life better" and be "more intelligent, capable, active members of society" (Newman 1976, 7).

> . . . and the man who has learned to think and to reason and to compare and to discriminate and to analyze, who has refined his taste, and formed his judgment, and sharpened his mental vision, will not indeed at once be a lawyer, or a pleader, or an orator, or a statesman, or a physician, or a good landlord, or a man of business, or a soldier, or an engineer, or a chemist, or a geologist, or an antiquarian, but he will be placed in that state of intellect in which he can take up any one of the sciences or callings I have referred to, or any other for which he has a taste or special talent, with an ease, a grace, a versatility, and a success, to which another is a stranger." [Newman 1976, 145]

He pointed out that the aim of the education of professional students was to make them capable and active members of society, but argued against professional education as an end in itself. Newman never opposed the teaching of professional or scientific subject matter at the university, for

> . . . a University teaches all knowledge by teaching all branches of knowledge . . . . (L)iberal education ... which is the proper function of a University ... refuses the foremost place to professional interests, does but postpone them to the formation of the citizen . . . . (Newman 1976, 145-146)

TWENTIETH CENTURY PHILOSOPHERS

The 20th century has seen knowledge increase at such a pace that no one may possess the whole of learning, or Comenius' pansophic or encyclopedic knowledge. What, then, does a liberal education mean in modern times? Has the notion become unattainable?

A single-purpose university was visualised by Ortega y Gasset, a Spaniard whose works were influential after the World War II. Ortega did not believe that research and teaching were irrevocably linked. Like Newman, he saw teaching as the

university's primary function, but he saw the teaching as being intended for the professions and for science (Wyatt 1981, 61).

Karl Jaspers was a German whose book *The Idea of the University* was written in the period between the world wars. Like his countrymen of earlier times, Jaspers believed that research was the central purpose of a university, but unlike others he saw a place for vocational education, too. "The university is simultaneously a professional school, a cultural centre and a research institute" (Jaspers 1960, 53). Jaspers thus delineated the multifaceted approach to higher education which has now become the predominant model of the modern western university.

THE DEVELOPMENT OF WESTERN UNIVERSITIES

If philosophy is, among other things, the study of truth, universities may be said to be the institutions where the study is conducted. National leaders and university councellors and administrators set a course toward their collective view of how the truth should be pursued; but just as philosophers differ as to what the truth is, so the universities differ in their approaches to its pursuit.

Oxford University, founded in 1214, and Cambridge University, founded in 1318, are the earliest establishments of universities in the western tradition. These institutions were founded to promote the training of clergymen, doctors and lawyers: the tradition of the pursuit of truth and learning was thus established. During and after the medieval period, these universities declined in their positions as centres of vocational training, save for the clergy. This retreat was not, however, compensated by advances in other directions. Scott (1981) cites three great intellectual movements, the Renaissance, the scientific revolution and the Enlightenment, as being independent of the university, while the industrial revolution nearly was so.

It was not until the 19th century, when Oxford and Cambridge were seen not to be meeting Britain's needs, that other universities and civic colleges became established and began granting degrees and qualifications. Indeed, the older universities' refusal to admit Roman Catholics and Jews and their reluctance to train students in science applied to industry were seen as powerful arguments for the creation of the new institutions. While Oxford and Cambridge maintained their supremacy as centres of education for the Church of England, and while they still continued the study of law and medicine, the emphasis was not on training for practice.

UNIVERSITIES IN TODAY'S SOCIETY

Higher education in the 20th (and the 21st) century must deal with the problem of the plural thrust, or the needs of a plural culture (Goodlad 1976). In a plural society, no ultimate belief is paramount over another. Therefore, a single world view is not institutionalised, but different views remain open to pursuit, debate and questioning. Many diverse settings may foster this process for a while, such as a corporate boardroom, a city council chamber or a private research laboratory. The university, however, holds this activity as its business (Goodlad 1976, 69).

Just as there is no single world view in a plural society, there is similarly no room for just one model of higher education, be it vocational or liberal. If the specific responsibilities of universities are the creation, interpretation and dissemination of advanced knowledge (Lynton and Elma, 1987), then the mechanisms and institutions must be in place to accomplish all three. The debate, therefore, cannot be framed along mutually exclusive poles, but should provide for a melding of emphases, methods and approaches to accommodate the needs of all those with a stake in higher education. It is likely that institutions which are not prepared or amenable to change will find their students going elsewhere. Such is the threat to the universities posed by some of the stakeholders in accounting education.

ACCOUNTING EDUCATION

The debate about liberal versus vocational education is central to the future of the accounting profession. In a passage that seems to have been written with the discipline of accounting in mind, Lynton and Elman (1987, 1) describe the need for knowledge in the so-called information age as

> ... pervasive, ubiquitous and continuous. Increasingly, data and information have to be aggregated and interpreted before they can become usable knowledge. Knowledge not only needs to be made available to young people but must be updated throughout life. It must reach all sectors of the economy and all parts of government, again on an ongoing basis. The continuous replenishment and reinterpretation of knowledge are crucial.

These beliefs are shared by employers, accounting academics and professional societies; however, different means for their attainment are proposed by members of each group. There is much dissatisfaction with the way accounting students are educated at universities, but before reviewing recommendations to improve the situation, a brief summary of opinions as to the causes of the problem will be presented.

CAUSES OF THE PROBLEM

Opinions as to the sources of the dissatisfaction with accounting education include the relatively low educational requirements for students entering the profession (Higley and Baker 1987), course objectives which narrowly focus on passing the qualifying examinations (Zeff 1989), the abdication of responsibility for the content of textbooks (Zeff 1989), and university policies which channel funds away from accounting departments (Shanahan 1990).

In a review of the educational requirements for entry into six professions (accountants, architects, lawyers, dentists, nurses and physicians) in the United States, Higley and Baker (1987) report that accountants have the lowest educational requirements (equal to nurses), and that only two state licensing agencies require formal education beyond a baccalaureate degree. A different view of the core of the problem is proposed by Zeff (1989), who posits that the focus on passing the licensure examination is one of the most significant causes of poor performance by accounting educators. He identifies the examination's emphasis on detail as the impetus behind the fact-and-method curriculum, or the "unthinking absorption of practice rules in financial accounting education" (Zeff 1989, 207).

He continues, in a second argument, that textbook authors, through their abdication of responsibility over content, are also partly to blame, as the texts seem to present the ideal of proper practice as prescribed by the standard setters, not by academics.

Subotnik's (1987) analysis of the content of accounting texts leads him to the conclusion that every question in accounting has a correct answer which can be discerned through the proper application of rules, and that learning these rules is preferred to developing "a full understanding of underlying accounting principles, on which intelligent rule-making and applications ultimately depend" (p. 315).

In contrast to the above reasons, Shanahan (1990, 77) finds the problems to be more deeply rooted and institutional in nature. First, an accounting degree takes three years (in Australia, where he writes) while,

> . . . even teachers get four years' training when a Dip Ed is added to their basic undergraduate degree. Accountants must be brighter; they don't need as much time at university.

He then cites the "Review of the Accounting Discipline in Higher Education," an Australian study, which asserts that much of the blame lies with university administrations who have diverted to other parts of the university government funds and salary savings from unfilled accounting staff vacancies. Thus, money which could be spent for improvement of staffing levels, equipment, etc., is instead used elsewhere.

Given the many causes of dissatisfaction with the current state of accounting education cited above, it is not surprising that other stakeholders have put forth their own recommendations for improvement. Some of these will now be examined.

THE STAKEHOLDERS' RECOMMENDATIONS

Stakeholders in accounting education include many groups, such as employers and practitioners, academics, professional societies, governments, students, and the universities. This paper will focus on the employers and academics, as they are the constituents who can best see the results of the current shortcomings (employers) and who are able to make the necessary changes most efficiently (academics).

EMPLOYERS AND PRACTITIONERS

The traditional view of improving accounting education is reflected in the results of research by Kanter and Pitman (1987), who surveyed practitioners, and by Schwartz and Stout (1987), who included both academics and practitioners in their survey. The results of Schwartz and Stout (1987) indicate that more than 70 percent of their respondents wanted to include at least two tax courses in the undergraduate program (73 percent of universities require only one course); the practitioners who were of this opinion were willing to give up course work in liberal arts and sciences to create time for the extra course or courses. It is not known whether educators were asked this question. Kanter and Pitman (1987) asked practitioners to give their opinions on a list of topics to be included in the curriculum and what the objectives of an auditing course should be. The findings on the second ques-

tion were split between (1) preparing the student for the licensure examination and (2) preparing the student for the first year in practice. Results were not supplied which would suggest that other objectives were recommended. Based on the survey results, the authors prepared three sets of course outlines, one for the prelicensure objective, one for the preservice objective and a third one combining the two objectives into a two-course program.

The recommendations of another set of employers of accounting graduates, as put forward by the chief executives of the then-Big Eight accounting firms in the United States (*Perspectives . . .* 1989), mark a definite shift in emphasis from the views traditionally attributed to practitioners. This shift in emphasis can be clearly seen by the language used by the authors.

> Education for the accounting profession must produce graduates who have a broad array of skills and knowledge [p. 5]. Passing the CPA examination should not be the goal of accounting education. The focus should be on developing analytical and conceptual thinking — versus memorizing rapidly expanding professional standards. [p. 8]

More examples which signal the change in direction can be inferred by identifying items that are not included in *Perspectives . . . .* There is no Common Body of Knowledge to be taught and learned. Furthermore, specific course content and teaching methods are not prescribed; rather, the particulars are left to the faculty of the universities.

Similar sentiments were expressed in 1984 by practitioners half-way round the world. The New Zealand Society of Accountants cited the need for rising education levels as one of the two "key forces shaping our future" (the other force being automation). They. too, saw that the emphasis should be placed on broader topics, due to the "increasing importance of thinking as compared with knowing, of education for life rather than a particular vocation" (New Zealand Society of Accountants 1984).

ACCOUNTING ACADEMICS

The body charged with designing, implementing and evaluating the curriculum is the faculty of the university. As cited before, some academics see weaknesses in the curriculum caused by insufficient time devoted to their area of specialisation.

Representing a different view is a report by the Committee on the Future Structure, Content, and Scope of Accounting Education, also known as the

Bedford Committee. Their report (American Accounting Association 1986) describes the Committee's views on the expanding profession, the current state of accounting education and the future scope, content and structure of accounting education. The Committee's recommendations for change are aimed at the scope and content of future education (broad scope, learning how to learn, lifelong learning), the structure (liberal education for undergraduates, specialised accounting courses for postgraduate study), and institutional concerns (higher value on teaching as a scholarly activity, support of basic and applied research, educational peer review by nonaccounting faculty and by faculty from other universities).

This report and *Perspectives . . .* provide a clear indication of the views of two significant, mainstream groups which have a vested interest in the education of accountants. In general, they perceive the current process as emphasising rote memorization of rules and problem-solving mechanics (Inman, Wenzler, and Wickert 1989), and this narrow education is perceived as being helpful only as long as the rules do not change and the problems come to the accountant framed in the same manner throughout his or her career. When the inevitable changes in the accounting environment occur, the accountant will not be prepared to adapt and so will cease to be as useful to his or her employer and clients (*Perspectives . . .* 1989).

In the view of these stakeholders, universities should not attempt to inculcate a set of promulgated rules and standards and then call the student an accountant. Education should be redirected toward an emphasis of providing capabilities (*Perspectives . . .* 1989) which will assist the student in becoming successful for his or her working life. In summary, the goal of an accounting education should not be the making of an accountant equipped only for the world extant at graduation.

Rather, one of the goals should be the education of a person who is equipped with tools for lifelong learning, someone who is capable of becoming and remaining an accountant.

The choice, then, appears clear. Future accounting education can produce graduates who are skilled at memorizing a set of rules and answering questions which come neatly stated in terms the graduate understands. On the other hand, the graduate could be prepared with the skills and attitudes which will enable him or her to meet challenges not anticipated by curriculum designers or textbook authors, to uncover problems in a scenario where the question is unstated or unknown, and to provide service to clients in businesses and industries as yet not even contemplated.

SUMMARY

This paper has attempted to identify the debate regarding future accounting education as an analogy for the "liberal versus vocational education" debate which has been argued for nearly three millennia. The ancient, medieval and modern philosophers' works have been explored, and the range of views has been highlighted. The origins and development of western universities have been shown in a similar manner.

Against these philosophical and institutional backgrounds, the views of several groups of stakeholders in accounting education have been presented. Some of these views are aligned with what might be called the vocational school of thought, while others are more in keeping with the so-called liberal tradition. Each end of the continuum is supported by earnest, well-intentioned research. It should come as no surprise, however, that the debate in accounting education has not been resolved. After all, it is part of a three-thousand year tradition.

REFERENCES

Allen, M. 1988. *The Goals of Universities.* SRHE and Open University Press.

American Accounting Association, Committee on the Future Structure, Content, and Scope of Accounting Education (The Bedford Committee). 1986. Future Accounting Education: Preparing for the Expanding Profession. *Issues in Accounting Education* (Spring): 168–195.

Brubacher, J. S. 1982. *On the Philosophy of Higher Education.* Jossey-Bass Publishers.

Chaplin, M. 1978. Philosophies of Higher Education, Historical and Contemporary. In A. S. Knowles, ed. *The International Encyclopedia of Higher Education.* Jossey-Bass Publishers.

Elliott, R. K. 1986. Auditing in the 1990s: Implications for Education and Research. *California Management Review* (Summer): 89–97.

Engle, T. 1985. A New Opportunity to Influence Collegiate Accounting Curricula. *The Internal Auditor* (December): 28–32.

Goodlad, S. 1976. *Conflict and Consensus in Higher Education.* Hodder and Stoughton.

Higley, W. M., and R. E. Baker. 1987. A Comparative Analysis of Professional Education and Licensure Requirements. *Issues in Accounting Education* (Fall): 220–236.

Inman, B., A. Wenzler, and P. Wickert. 1989. Square Pegs in Round Holes: Are Accounting Students Well-Suited to Today's Accounting Profession? *Issues in Accounting Education* (Spring): 29–47.

Irvine, R. 1988. Newman Revisited: The Idea of a University. *New Zealand Journal of Educational Studies* (Vol. 223, No. 1): 3–14.

Jaspers, K. 1960. *The Idea of the University.* Peter Owen.

Kagle, A. R. 1987. A College-level Course in Internal Auditing: Practitioner Perceptions. *The Internal Auditor* (February): 41–43.

Kanter, H. A., and M. K. Pitman. 1987. An Auditing Curriculum for the Future. *Issues in Accounting Education* (Fall): 251–263.

Lynton, E. A., and S. E. Elman. 1988. *New Priorities for the University.* Jossey-Bass Publishers.

Newman, J. H. 1976. *The Idea of a University: Defined and Illustrated.* The Clarendon Press.

New Zealand Society of Accountants. 1984. *Horizon 2000 — and Beyond.*

Perspectives on Education: Capabilities for Success in the Accounting Profession. 1989. Arthur Andersen & Co., Arthur Young, Coopers & Lybrand, Deloitte Haskins & Sells, Ernst & Whinney, Peat Marwick Main & Co., Price Waterhouse, and Touche Ross.

Sadler, J. E. 1969. *Comenius.* Collier-Macmillan Limited.

Schwartz, B. N., and D. E. Stout. 1987. A Comparison of Practitioner and Educator Opinions on Tax Education Requirements for Undergraduate Accounting Majors. *Issues in Accounting Education* (Spring): 112–126.

Scott, P. 1981. Inheritance of the Robbins/Crosland Era. *The Times Higher Education Supplement* 7 (August): 24.

Shanahan, J. 1990. Are Accountants Properly Educated? *Australian Business* 29 (August): 77.

Stout, D., and J. Schweikart. 1989. The Relevance of International Accounting to the Accounting Curriculum: A Comparison of Practitioner and Educator Opinions. *Issues in Accounting Education* (Spring): 126–143.

Subotnik, D. 1987. What Accounting Can Learn from Legal Education. *Issues in Accounting Education* (Fall): 313–324.

Tomlin, E. W. F. 1952. *Great Philosophers of the East.* Anchor Press Ltd.

Wyatt, J. F. 1981. Ortega y Gasset's "Mission of the University": As Appropriate Document for an Age of Economy? *Studies in Higher Education* (Vol. 6, No. 1): 59–69.

Zeff, S. A. 1989. Does Accounting Belong in the University Curriculum? *Issues in Accounting Education* (Spring): 203–210.

The Direction of Accounting and Accounting Education: Raising Crucial Questions in Terms of an Integrated Framework

Hideyuki Kamiryo

INTRODUCTION

Accounting has moved from a view based on revenue and expense to one based on asset and liability, and from stewardship of accountants to decision usefulness for users of accounting information. This may be the current of the times, and one that has been accepted as a consensus and supported by an empirical approach rather than a normative approach.

This paper aims at raising crucial questions on this current tide and its intended direction, particularly from the viewpoint of accounting and financial comparison of the United States and Japan in changing economies.

First of all, the author believes that something must exist between stewardship and information usefulness. This "something" needs a much more robust ideal than service potentials or economic benefits. It is the ideal of the maintenance of the economic value of a firm as advocated by Hicks (1946), but it must be expressed organically (ecologically) throughout an accounting system. Current economic benefits cannot organically express the maintenance of the economic value of a firm. This is because accounting is apt to follow an economic framework which is project-oriented and is in favor of the NPV method and also because accounting does not organically integrate income, assets and capital.

The ideal of the maintenance of the economic value of a firm must be supported by the IRR method, period oriented and in perpetuity, and accordingly by a concept of minimum reinvestment of retained earnings.[1] The concept of minimum reinvestment presupposes that dividends as distributable economic income are paid out after maintaining the economic value of a firm. This theoretical world can be distinguished from the real world represented by current ex-post accounting. The theoretical world itself produces such important parameters for decision usefulness as the theoretical cost of capital as the IRR and the constant growth rate, both in perpetuity.

Current accounting and finance borrow the cost of capital and other important parameters from the capital market. The author perceives the importance of these given parameters since listed firms are in the capital market; however, the author advocates that decision usefulness in accounting will come to pay its own expenses by introducing its own theoretical world into accounting. Then, the capital market becomes a monitor.

U.S. accounting has been dominated by an empirical approach. Japanese accounting seems to be far behind this tide. However, it is certain that a normative approach and an empirical approach must cooperate with each other. Or, after a normative approach has been completed, an empirical approach may be effectively applied. Why did U.S. accounting develop an empirical approach so rapidly? Why could Japanese accounting not move more smoothly to an empirical approach?

Empirical studies in the United States use the economic framework together with mathematical and statistical methodologies. The author does not deny such an approach, but its direction must recognize that the applied economic framework is essentially mathematical and mechanically dynamic. A typical example is the equilibrium framework of the capital asset pricing model. This implies that accounting needs its own normative approach.

---

[1]The author distinguishes the *minimum* reinvestment of retained earnings and the reinvestment of retained earnings. Note that the reinvestment ratio = the retained earnings ratio (= 1 − payout ratio), assuming that reinvestment = retained earnings. The author defines *minimum* as "needed for maintaining the economic value of a firm" in a whole system, and reinvestment as net reinvestment after deducting depreciation, assuming that economic depreciation > accounting depreciation.

Hideyuki Kamiryo is at Hiroshima Shudo University in Japan.

It is true that Japanese accounting after having been influenced by European accounting has mainly followed U.S. accounting for the last half a century. Interpretations and comparisons have been important in Japanese accounting and the modification of its own normative approach has been directed. However, current Japanese accounting studies do not produce as much essential discussion as before, according to Professor Iino's Anniversary Speech at the 50th Annual Meeting (Sept.12, 1991) of the Japan Accounting Association. Moreover, Japanese empirical studies have been pursued by small groups, in contrast with prosperous empirical studies in the United States.

The author, however, believes that a field of accounting studies should be led in advance by a normative approach. Otherwise, empirical approaches both in the United States and Japan will continue forever without effective results. The mechanical economic framework should be reformed basically from the viewpoint of a whole system that denies the automatic reversibility or the swing of the pendulum. The cause will be attributable to the deficits of the economic framework itself.

This paper clarifies such crucial points and presents a productive discussion for accounting and accounting education in the future. Canning (1929) failed to introduce totally the economic concept into his accounting system. We should not repeat these experiences but try to open up a more robust accounting future. Social science such as accounting and finance must be distinguished from natural science such as physics and dynamics.

Double-entry bookkeeping and historical cost accounting are endowed with the character necessary for a social science in terms of a whole system. However, they are still incomplete in terms of an organic whole system. They will become complete, philosophically supported by thermodynamics rather than by dynamics, when they introduce variable-fixed-classification for accounting titles. This classification is that main accounting titles are classified into a proportionately variable part and a fixed part to net sales. As a result, this accounting system will make firms survive steadily and set a normative approach of accounting success, in harmony with an empirical approach.

The economic framework cannot measure and support the above variable-fixed-classification. It will continue to live with a concept of utility and the net present value method which cannot accept a concept of minimum reinvestment. An accounting system with the variable-fixed-classification can introduce a concept of minimum reinvestment and accordingly utilize the IRR method organically.

PROJECT IRR (ROI) IN THE UNITED STATES VERSUS PERIOD ROT IN JAPAN

First, let us review capital budgeting in a broad sense both in U.S. and Japanese firms. Capital budgeting compares the investment rate of return for each project, the project IRR, with a given cost of capital. Or capital budgeting ranks the net present value of each project, NPV, which has a different cash flow pattern under a given cost of capital.

American management is much more project oriented than Japanese management and uses the project IRR, while Japanese management generally uses profitability ratios for a fiscal year. Why does Japanese accounting not accept the project IRR?

The project IRR (ROI) is calculated for a finite term and by cash flow pattern, but it does not usually introduce a concept of reinvestment. The NPV method swallows the difference of cash flow pattern and cannot take into consideration a concept of reinvestment.

However, it was proved by economists that the value of IRR must be unique (Arrow and Levhari 1969, 560–564). Also, it was proved that the term of the IRR must be infinite or perpetual. These two proofs together imply that the IRR used in any project should be changed to the period-oriented IRR, the period IRR.

Incidentally, Myers (1977) finally concludes that the textbook formula gives a valid hurdle rate, at least in certain special cases, if the project j has the same cash flow pattern as the firm. Three conditions, that project j is a perpetuity, that it makes a permanent contribution to the firm's debt capacity, and that the firm in aggregate is a perpetuity, were replaced by a specification of cash flow pattern.

Can capital budgeting be converted from project oriented to period oriented? The answer is yes, by setting a one-period perpetual model, where initial data grow for a predicted year and the data are repeated in perpetuity.

Why did capital budgeting not introduce the above two proofs of the IRR into the project IRR and the NPV method? The answer is traced back to the essence of an accounting framework, which makes it difficult to specify cash flow pattern and accordingly to measure the constant growth rates in perpetuity.

A revolutionary theory has appeared in "the Momentum Accounting and Triple-Entry Bookkeeping" advocated by Ijiri (1989). This triple-entry bookkeeping system, when it is applied to earnings, classifies total earnings into the initial earnings level (= initial momentum × time) and actions during the following year (= impulse × time). The separation of initial earnings may persuade capital budgeting to shift from the project IRR to the period IRR.

A one-period perpetual model based on the financial structure uses initial data which are brought from the ex-post data at the end of a previous year. The financial structure organically integrates income, assets and capital, under the variable-fixed-classification of account titles to net sales.[2] When the actual ex-post data are realized after one year, as in the current accounting system, the accounting rate of return, ARR for the year, assuming a one-period perpetual model, becomes the period IRR which satisfies uniqueness and perpetuity, the period ARR. The rates of return for projects can now be replaced by the period ARR.

Incorrect use of the IRR is not limited to capital budgeting, but also to the conventional economic framework in terms of the valuation of a firm, as will be shown later. The growth stock valuation model sets the growth rate of net income as the product of the investment rate of return for projects and the retained earnings ratio (= 1.0 – the payout ratio). This investment rate of return[3] corresponds exactly to the project IRR used in capital budgeting and assumes no uniqueness and no perpetuity.

In short, a comparison of the project IRR and the cost of capital is common both to capital budgeting and to stock valuation. Accordingly, both capital budgeting and stock valuation have committed the same fault; the two proofs — uniqueness and perpetuity — as the essence of the IRR have been neglected theoretically.

Accounting education must be aware of this typical example. A normative approach in accounting should be improved constantly and its methodology must be brushed up cautiously.

Turning to U.S. and Japanese management, it may now be easier for the author to explain the Japanese ROT criteron. The ratio of net income after tax to total assets, ROT (= Y_A/T), is the product of the ratio of net income after tax to net sales, Y_A/X, and the ratio of net sales to total assets, X/T. These three ratios are usually calculated after confirming ex-post data at the end of a predicted year. The amount of total assets is accumulated under a concept of average, compared with any new investment expressed under a concept of marginal.

Did the Japanese criterion really take a concept of average rather than a concept of marginal? The Japanese criterion may apparently take a concept

of average in terms of conservative behavior, but actually, under heavier competition, Japanese management is more growth oriented and more market share oriented. The future existence of a firm is more important than the profitabilty of its investment and total assets.

The author asserts that the period ROT criterion is not an aim but is needed as a restrictive *minimum* condition. From the viewpoint of technological innovation, the higher the period ROT, the lower in a long run the probability of the existence of a firm. However, the period ROT can be directly converted to the period-oriented accounting rate of return, the period ARR, by setting ex-post total assets as the initial amount at the beginning of a predicted fiscal year and by assuming "a predicted year" as "a one-period repeated perpetually."

On the other hand, American management employs the rate of return on investment, the project IRR, ROI. The higher the ROI, the more effective the management. The project IRR is accepted as a social consensus, but it is rational, only assuming that the IRR be infinite under certain cash flow pattern. This implies that the project IRR should be the period IRR, as stated earlier, and accordingly the same period ARR as above.

It would seem that American management and Japanese management have different philosophies and that neither philosophy has a common consensus as a base, even if the ROT turns to the period ARR in Japanese management and the ROI turns to the same period-ARR in U.S. management.

But, the author rejects this idea for higher ARR in the United States and lower ARR in Japan. The author advocates that the ARR in a one-period perpetual model must reveal a constant growth rate in perpetuity. The ARR assuming infinite periods is still incomplete, unless the ARR reveals its constant growth rate in perpetuity. It implies that the ARR must be connected with the valuation of a firm. Separation of the constant growth rate in perpetuity is necessitated for the ARR comparison in the United States and Japan.

---

[2]Without this classification as a control key, a system cannot work and survive ecologically. A reformed accounting system is eligible for it.

[3]When assets in placement (average) are taken into consideration, using a measure like ROE, "the reinvestment ratio = 1.0" cannot be satisfied.

VALUATION OF A FIRM IN THE ECONOMIC FRAMEWORK VERSUS EARNINGS CHANGES IN ACCOUNTING

Second, let us review the valuation of a firm and clarify the relationship between economic income and acccounting income. This study occupies an important area of empirical approaches both in the United States and Japan. Its methodology is common both in the United States and Japan, since the U.S. studies in this area have always been ahead of Japanese studies. However, the valuation model or the dividend discounting model has its own problem. This is because capital budgeting and the valuation of a firm have been studied closely for many years, and also, according to the author's interpretation, have failed in the sharp specification of cash flow pattern of a firm together with a concept of reinvestment. This will be discussed later.

The dividend-discounting model uses economic income or economic cash flow which is different from accounting income or cash flow. The economic framework defines or assumes economic cash flow as follows:

1. Net cash flow after deducting economic depreciation which is needed for maintaining the economic value of a firm (Beaver 1981).

2. Operating income or free cash flow after deducting economic investment which is needed for maintaining the economic value of a firm (Miller and Modigliani 1961; Jensen 1972).

3. Net cash flow after deducting economic investment which is needed for maintaining maximum market value of a firm (Fama 1976).

However, it is true that economic depreciation must be defined as "the change in the present value of the remaining cash flows at two points in time" (Beaver 1981, 67). It implies that economic depreciation is measured with the valuation of a firm. Economic depreciation must be measured in tautology. Beaver's example shows that economic depreciation *happens to be equal* to accounting depreciation.

Likewise, how can economic investment be measured without using accounting data? The author concludes that both economic depreciation and economic investment cannot be introduced into the economic framework and that each is set as an important assumption.

When the economic framework assumes that the economic value is maintained, it is not necessary for the framework to have the minimum growth rate in perpetuity in order to maintain the economic value of a firm. The economic framework has been tough in the perfect capital market: It has been supported by the utility function, the theorem of separation, investment decison independent from financing decision, and the law of great numbers (in the CAPM). As a result, according to the author's interpretation, the economic framework has been in favor of the net present value method which would not accept a concept of reinvestment.

Therefore, the economic framework cannot consistently accept the constant growth rate in perpetuity.

However, the cost of capital must be the internal rate of return in perpetuity which guarantees the maintenance of the economic value of a firm. The economic framework does not measure this maintenance and leaves it in the hands of the efficient market. Accordingly, the economic framework will survive without being interrupted by differences in cash flow patterns and by the measure of the constant growth rate in perpeuity. The growth rate can be used for "the true growth" (Miller and Modigliani 1961) which is beyond the minimum maintenance of the economic value of a firm.

Asset investment (with the initial assets) and the rate of return (ROI) is used for measuring the growth rate, assuming that economic value of the firm is maintained. Therefore, when the ROI equals the cost of capital, the growth rate is set as zero.

This is a foundation of the valuation of a firm in the economic framework. The empirical approach in accounting has been naturally and strongly influenced by the above economic framework.

Accounting itself has not been related to the ex-ante growth rate, although it can measure various ex-post growth rates for the past fiscal year. Accounting research has predicted earnings changes in the near future, by taking advantage of changes in the future cash flow patterns.

A typical example is the work done by Ou and Penman (1989a, 1989b). They establish "one summary measure" which is integrated using selected predictors nominated after a survey of financial accounting and financial analysis texts. They state (1989a, p. 300) that "let the data speak" is the motto here, and that the predictive ability of the financial statement attributes could have been observed by investors at the end of the estimation period. Their method for measuring one-year-ahead earnings is tested using the ex-post data confirmed after one year.

However, they cannot specify the pattern of cash flow for one-year-ahead. Of course, no one can specify the pattern of cash flow even for the next one year. This implies that the accounting framework cannot easily approach earnings changes even though it is endowed with self-controlled double-account bookkeeping.

Unless the accounting framework becomes successful in specifying the pattern of cash flow, it is hard to predict earnings changes except by way of "let the data speak."

Thus, it is harder to estimate each growth rate to assets and to net income for the predicted year, and it is impossible to estimate each constant growth rate in perpetuity. Nevertheless, the dividend discounting model is required to estimate the constant growth rate in perpetuity as a value to be deducted from the cost of capital.

This is the actual condition underlying the prediction of earnings in the accounting framework. Neither the economic framework nor the accounting framework can introduce the constant growth rate in perpetuity necessary for the valuation of a firm.

The author established a methodology to specify the cash flow pattern by using an initial financial structure under a specified payout ratio and by introducing the IRR method wholly into the financial structure. The trend and tradition using the NPV method has been cut by putting a concept of reinvestment into the financial structure.

CONCEPT OF REINVESTMENT AND CONSTANT GROWTH RATE IN PERPETUITY

Neither the current economic framework nor the current accounting framework can accept the IRR method without contradiction. First of all, the assumption set by the economic framework, the maintenance of the economic value of a firm, must be cancelled and replaced by a new assumption that "economic depreciation > accounting depreciation." Also, the cost of capital must be defined as the minimum hurdle required IRR necessary for maintaining the economic value of a firm.

Then a whole system is expressed as a one-period perpetual model using the ex-ante, initial financial structure which integrates the balance sheet, the income statement, the cost statement, and income distribution at the end of the previous year. The financial structure is only integrated as a whole organic system by classifying main account titles into variable-to-net sales and fixed-to-net sales.

The financial structure as initial condition produces two kinds of asset investments; the ex-ante minimum asset investment necessary for maintain-

ing the economic value of a firm, and the ex-post total asset investment confirmed after a predicted year. "Ex-post total investment" in the financial structure is the sum of the ex-ante minimum asset investment and the ex-post asset investment beyond the minimum asset investment. The minimum asset investment follows the cash flow pattern specified initially, while the ex-post total asset investment is not restricted by the cash flow pattern specified initially, but follows "let the data speak" as Ou and Penman predicted "one-year-ahead earnings."

Even the latest study done by Brief and R.A. Lawson (1992) directly deals with the asset investment and total assets under the reinvestment ratio ≠ 1.0.[4]

The economic framework cannot divide the ex-post total investment into the above two parts, and this total investment results in "the investment rate of return is larger or smaller than the cost of capital."

The financial structure thus distinguishes ex-ante minimum asset investment with ex-post total asset investment. The question now is how can asset investment be converted to the growth rate of assets? The above minimum asset investment is easily converted to the minimum growth rate of total assets supported by the concept of reinvestment. The minimum reinvestment ratio = 1.0 is defined as "the ex-ante minimum net (after depreciation) asset investment equal to the sum of the retained earnings produced from the initial total assets and the marginal retained earnings produced from the minimum asset investment under a one-period perpetual model and without time-lag." The minimum growth rate of total assets is constant and in perpetuity, and is expressed by using the growth rate of fixed assets, assuming that variable assets are proportionate to net sales. The constant growth rate of fixed asset in perpetuity can use a certainty equivalent, CE.[5]

The author does not directly measure the constant growth rate of net income in perpetuity, but

---

[4]The intention expressed by Brief and Lawson (1992, 412) is great: understanding how accounting data can be used in DCF analysis leads to a greater appreciation of the general nature of acocunting and provides a compelling reason to give the ARR a more prominent place in financial statement analysis. The author agrees with their opinion and believes that a concept of minimum reinvestment must be taken into consideration.

[5]The certainty equivalent, CE, is also calculated using the market price as a monitor. The theoretical stock value drawn by the value of CE, say from .5 to 1.0 (no risk), shows a hyperbolic curve as a function.

measures it totally and structurally, after confirming the minimum asset investment.

The ex-ante minimum reinvestment ratio = 1.0 guarantees the economic value of a firm under a specified payout ratio. The minimum constant growth rate of total assets in perpetuity now can be converted to the minimum constant growth rate of net income in perpetuity when the notion of turnover is applied. When the total assets after growth are larger than annual net sales, the constant growth rate of net income in perpetuity is larger than that of total assets, and vice versa. The author uses simply the relativity coefficient, K, for the conversion, where K is the ratio of total assets after growth to net sales.

Back to the project-oriented NPV method, the IRR as the cost of capital must be borrowed from the market. Even for the projects, the IRR = the ARR = the constant growth rate of total assets in perpetuity, g_T, as was first suggested by Solomon (1970) and proved by Livingston and Salamon (1970) under a specified cash flow pattern.[6]

A one-period perpetual model based on the ex-ante financial structure verifies that the g_T = the IRR = the ARR under the reinvestment ratio = 1.0, which implies a complete specification of cash flow pattern. For the IRR method, the g_T = the IRR = the ARR is more robustly proved. Thus, the value of the IRR as a theoretical cost of capital is either measured directly from the ex-ante financial structure or measured as the value, g_T which is equal to the IRR.

Turning to the ex-post total asset investment, the reinvestment ratio ≠ 1.0 is defined as the ex-post asset investment more or less than the sum of the initial retained earnings produced from the initial total assets and the marginal retained earnings produced from the ex-ante minimum asset investment. The difference between the ex-post asset investment and the ex-ante minimum asset investment is funded or refunded by debts and may be funded by new stock issues. Thus, the cash flow pattern cannot be specified in advance and must be confirmed after a predicted year.

Assuming a one-period perpetual model, the ex-post accounting rate of return, the ARR (≠ the IRR) and its constant growth rates to total assets and net income in perpetuity are measured, just like those "under the reinvestment ratio = 1.0." These values are not as stable as those under the reinvestment ratio = 1.0, owing to the release during a predicted year from the cash flow pattern specified initially.

Now here is a serious question. Is the market price of a share decided as the minimum value for maintaining the economic value of the firm? If so, the cost of capital as the IRR and the constant growth rate in perpetuity must be measured under the reinvestment ratio = 1.0. If it is not so, the cost of capital as the IRR and the constant growth rate in perpetuity must be measured under the reinvestment ratio ≠ 1.0. Asset investment under the reinvestment ratio ≠ 1.0 includes the true growth defined by Miller and Modigliani (1961). Even such an empirical approach as that of Ou and Penman (1989a,b) considers the asset investment under the reinvestment ratio ≠ 1.0 and the predicted earnings which are each observed one year later.

They may be right with an assumption that the economic value of a firm is maintained. However, the author asserts that "one-year-ahead predicted earnings" can be replaced by "the initial earnings" and the following constant growth rate in perpetuity, without double-counting. It is hard even to predict one-year-ahead earnings under the reinvestment ratio ≠ 1.0, although Ou and Penman proposed "one summary measure." With the initial earnings, the cost of capital and the constant growth rate in perpetuity are measured easily under the reinvestment ratio = 1.0. The cost of capital includes implicitly the growth rate, which must be the same as the constant growth rate in perpetuity measured separately. As a result, there is no need for predicting one-year-ahead earnings.

The cost of capital and the growth rate included in the cost of capital must be minimum, hurdle and required. In spite of it, the growth rate in the dividend discounting model is calculated as the product of the ROE and the retained earnings ratio. Consequently, this growth rate is not any more minimum, hurdle or required.

The author must stress that the difference between the reinvestment ratio = 1.0 (ex-ante) and ≠ 1.0 (ex-post) for a predicted year is partly absorbed in the initial earnings of the next predicted year.

In short, the specification of cash flow pattern will be successful only under the reinvestment ratio = 1.0, where the cost of capital and the con-

---

[6]Livingston and Salamon (1970, p. 208) prove that if c = 1 then ARR is approximately equal to the IRR for all values of b, where c = the retained earnings ratio and b = the factor which describes the pattern of cash flows generated by the project. The author proves that IRR = ARR = g_T for any value of c (> 0) under b = 1; not approximately but completely.

stant growth rate in perpetuity are measured as values to maintain the economic value of a firm.

CONCLUSION

A one-period perpetual model based on the ex-ante financial structure reveals two kinds of growth rates of total assets, under the reinvestment ratio = 1.0 and under the reinvestment ratio ≠ 1.0. The growth rate of total assets under the reinvestment ratio = 1.0 guarantees the economic value of a firm, where the growth rate of total assets, g_T = the internal rate of return (the cost of capital), IRR = the accounting rate of return, ARR.

Ex-ante minimum asset investment under the reinvestment ratio = 1.0 is expressed as a normative approach in accounting studies. Ex-post asset investment under the reinvestment ratio ≠ 1.0 is expressed as an empirical approach in accounting studies. Total ex-post asset investment under the reinvestment ratio ≠ 1.0 is the sum of ex-ante asset investment under the reinvestment ratio = 1.0 and the ex-post asset investment beyond the ex-ante asset investment under the reinvestment ratio = 1.0.

When asset investment is introduced into a whole system, this asset investment does not need an assumption such as the economic framework had to use. The results and hypotheses derived without the assumption are different from those which are derived from the assumption.

It is clear that a normative approach and an empirical approach must cooperate under the same assumption; economic depreciation > accounting depreciation. The normative approach for asset investment made it possible to reveal and measure the cost of capital, the constant growth rate in perpetuity, and the theoretical stock value. This normative approach needs some help from the empirical approach; market price analysis will help position the theoretical stock value by adjusting the certainty equivalent, CE. Also, asset investment under the reinvestment ratio ≠ 1.0 will clarify the initial earnings in the next predicted year.

The economic framework as a normative approach, however, does not distinguish the growth rate of assets and the growth rates of cash flow and dividends. The economic framework follows linear and homogeneous functions supported by a philosophy of dynamics. It also uses some data from the stock market which absorbs and digests necessary information, assuming that these data are consistent with variables and parameters within the framework. However, it cannot measure the same growth rate as is included in the cost of capital,

owing to the assumption that the initial earnings are those after deduction of economic depreciation or economic investment.

For capital budgeting, the ARR, higher in the United States and lower in Japan, is measured in any one-year perpetual model and is each compared with the cost of capital. But each constant growth rate in perpetuity is not measured, as pointed out earlier.

However, the one-period perpetual model based on the ex-ante financial structure has a key to solve this problem, supported by a philosophy of thermodynamics and ecology.

Asset investment under the reinvestment ratio = 1.0 changes greatly according to the level of dividend payout, and higher asset investment under the reinvestment ratio = 1.0 does not mean higher true growth.

Japanese minimum asset investment at the reinvestment ratio = 1.0 is much higher than in the United States owing to lower payout ratio. However, Japanese asset investment beyond the minimum asset investment is not always higher than in the United States and fluctuates greatly. It means that the true growth is unstable and a one-year-ahead base is weakened.

Moreover, the low level of dividend payout ratio is more capital-gains-oriented and brings lower dividend payout ratio. As a result, the financial structure becomes unhealthy with an endless increase in total assets. This corresponds to the low ARR in Japan.

On the contrary, American management insists on stable payout ratio together with its faster turnover than does Japanese management. These two constraints save the financial structure from irreversible aggravation.

This paper shows a normative approach in accounting research. Asset investment and payout ratio are closely related, as suggested in many empirical approaches and as proved in the financial structure. A normative approach must perceive this fact. The financial structure reveals important results much closer to empirical studies, released from the conventional assumption that the economic value is maintained. In short, Japanese management has grown faster than American management, but has accumulated irreversible aggregation of the financial structure, while American management has always been ready for new chances owing to a healthy financial structure. The current stock markets in the United States and Japan indicate this striking difference. The comparison will be deepened by pursuing a normative approach represented by the asset investment under the reinvestment ratio = 1.0 and also by studying an empirical approach under the reinvestment ratio ≠ 1.0

REFERENCES

Arrow, K. J., and D. Levhari. 1969. Uniqueness of the Internal Rates of Return with Variable Life of Investment. *Economic Journal* 79 (315): 560–566.

Beaver, W. H. 1981. *Financial Reporting: An Accounting Revolution.* Prentice-Hall: 213.

Brief, R. P., and R. A. Lawson. 1992. The Role of the Accounting Rate of Return in Financial Statement Analysis. *Accounting Review* 67(2): 411–426.

Canning, J. B. 1929. *The Economics of Accounting.* Ronald Press.

Fama, E. 1976. *Foundations of Finance.* Basic Books.

Hicks, J. R. 1946. *Value and Capital, An Inquiry into Some Fundamental Principles of Economic Theory,* 2nd ed. Clarendon Press: 172.

Ijiri, Y. 1989. *Momentum Accounting and Triple-Entry Bookkeeping: Exploring the Dynamic Structure of Accounting Measurements,* Studies in Accounting Research #31. American Accounting Association: 151.

Jensen, M. C. 1972. *Studies in the Theory of Capital Markets.* New York: Praeger

Kamiryo, H. 1987. Interrelationships between Growth Rates, Leverage, ARR, and IRR in the Financial Structure Using An Accoundting Approach. Working Paper at University of Louisville: 1-80 (revised).

————. 1991. A New System for Measuring Theoretical Cost of Capital and Stock Value and Clarifying Theoretical Relationships between and among Financial Parameters within a Firm. AAA Paper: 33.

Livingston, J. L., and G. L. Salamon. 1970. Relationship between the Accounting and the Internal Rate of Return Measures: A Synthesis and an Analysis. *Journal of Accounting Research* 8(1): 199–216.

Miller, M. H., and F. Modigliani. 1961. Dividend Policy, Growth, and the Valuation of Theories. *Journal of Business* (October): 411–433.

Myers, S. C. 1977. Reply. *Journal of Finance* 32(1): 218–220.

Ou, J. A., and S. H. Penman. 1989a. Financial Statement Analysis and the Prediction of Stock Returns. *Journal of Accounting and Economics* (11): 295–329.

————, and ————. 1989b. Accounting Measurement, Price-Earnings Ratio, and the Information Content of Security Prices. *Journal of Accounting Research* 27 (Supplement): 111–152.

Solomon, E. 1970. Alternative Rate of Return Concepts and Their Implications for Utility Regulation. *Bell Journal of Economics* (1): 65–81.

Multientry Multiexit Accounting Education

J. E. McLachlan and V. Wood

THE NEEDS OF THE ACCOUNTING PROFESSION

The accounting profession must draw on a wide spread of talent — of differing levels — to satisfy private and public demands for those trained in this discipline. This demand is evident when one looks at the employment vacancies for accountants advertised in most countries.

There is therefore an identified need for the provision of training for a wide spread of ability groups ranging from the school leaver at various levels to the mature student wishing to continue his or her education. Courses must be tailored not only to meet the needs of these students of differing ability, age and experience, but also to meet the requirements of a varied spectrum of employers while at the same time remaining acceptable to the professional accounting bodies.

THE RAW MATERIAL

Students may be

- school leavers of basic ability at school leaving age, with little or no formal qualifications;

- school leavers who have studied accounting as an academic subject and who wish to build on their knowledge to obtain a professional accounting qualification;

- the talented school leavers with the appropriate certificates who choose to attend a vocationally orientated university rather than one of the more traditional universities;

- the school leavers who have gone to university or college to study a discipline other than accounting and who have discovered, before finishing their original course, that accounting has more appeal or more earning potential than their original discipline;

- the graduate in a nonaccounting area who wishes to turn to accounting or who finds that the degree achieved leads to insufficiently challenging employment or to no employment at all;

- the employee who has drifted into a low-level accounting position and who finds that, to rise significantly in the organisation, or to build

protection from the threat of redundancy, an accounting qualification is needed;

- the married woman with family responsibilities decreasing, who wishes to continue her education in an area which could lead to a responsible business career;

- the single parent who requires a fast route to a qualification which can meet both family needs and future economic demands.

No matter which category the student falls into, he/she is aiming for the same goal — to obtain the highest accounting qualification recognised by the accounting professional bodies and commensurate with their academic ability which will lead them to relevant employment.

RECRUITMENT

Given the falling demographic trend and the increasing financial pressures on educational establishments to increase their intake of students, any course offered has to be attractive to the prospective applicant. The need to market one's courses has never been so great as educational establishments vie one with another to increase their fee income and to build up additional full-time equivalent students (FTEs).

Publicity has never been so widespread ranging from careers guidance visits to schools, institution open days and student fayres, advertising through every aspect of the media and in the publications of the professional bodies, close contact with employers and overseas recruitment visits. However, the quantity and quality of the publicity will bear no long-term return if the quality of the product is found lacking.

To the prospective student, the measure of the accounting course on offer is simple:

- Will they be able to obtain a place on a suitable course?

- Will they obtain a qualification commensurate with his/her ability?

- Will the qualification be recognised by the professional bodies?

J. E. McLachlan is Dean at Napier University, Scotland and V. Wood is Administrator at Napier University Business School.

- Will they obtain employment at the end of the day?

THE DEVELOPMENT OF ARTICULATED ACCOUNTING PROVISION

By 1985 there was an identified need for the development of a range of courses, tailored to meet the needs of students of differing abilities, the employers and the professional bodies. However, more so, the need for a portfolio of articulating courses was recognised which would allow good students to progress quickly through the levels of accounting education.

At that time the Department of Accounting and Law offered the following range of accounting courses:

BA Ordinary Degree in Accounting:
Full-Time: Internally examined: Validated by the Council for National Academic Awards (CNAA)

Higher National Diploma (HND) in Accounting:
Full-Time: Externally examined; Validated by the Scottish Vocational Education Council (SCOTVEC)

Higher National Certificate (HNC) in Accounting:
Full- and Part-Time: Externally examined; Validated by SCOTVEC

Chartered Association of Certified Accountants (ACCA)
Full-Time; Partially Internally Assessed; Validated by ACCA
Part-Time; Externally examined; Validated by ACCA.

Chartered Institute of Management Accountants (CIMA)
Part-Time; Externally examined; Validated by CIMA.

These were, in the main, stand-alone courses, with only a few opportunities for students to transfer between them.

The lessening of control by the CNAA and SCOTVEC — leading to the Institution being granted greater autonomy and control of its courses with the advent of CNAA accredited status in 1987 (McLachlan and Wood 1989) and SCOTVEC delegated authority status in 1989 — was a major factor in the development of the articulated accounting provision. Staff now had the power to restructure their courses and amend the syllabi to bring them more into line with the needs of the marketplace and to dovetail one with another.

In addition, some smaller colleges were developing HNC accounting courses with the intention of providing, in a local setting, a course which would attract local young people, thus retaining them in the community for an extra year after leaving school. Without this provision, the better school students were going to the large centres of population —- at an age when they might experience personal problems when settling down in an alien environment and coming to terms with a much more demanding and self-regulating educational experience.

We considered it a part of our social obligation to help those colleges and we have made arrangements with several whereby we take their good HNC students after their first year of study onto our second year HND, and in some cases, onto the second year of the BA in Accounting.

This has reciprocal benefits — we receive a stream of students with a proven examination record at the two different levels and the smaller college can give its staff the experience of a higher level of work than they would otherwise have. This enables these colleges to attract and retain staff who would otherwise go elsewhere, and to attract local students, and keep them for a further year when they can study and mature in their home environment.

THE DEVELOPMENTAL PROCESS

Student Flexibility

As a first step towards increasing flexibility for students, the Business School developed and introduced a common first year across its undergraduate CNAA Degrees in Accounting, Business Studies and Commerce. The development of this common first-year curriculum was a lengthy process and took two years from its inception in September 1985 to its introduction in September 1987 (McLachlan and Wood 1991). During the developmental period, our institution applied for and was granted delegated authority by CNAA in January 1987. Prior to 1987, the ultimate responsibility for academic standards lay with CNAA via a system of validation and review visits carried out by panels of academics and industrialists selected by the Council. The advent of delegated authority status transferred the responsibility for validation and review of CNAA–taught courses to the Institution, with representatives of CNAA in membership of the validation and review panels and it was under these new procedures that this concept of a common first year across a number of degrees — a concept new to the Institution — was validated.

The major issues addressed during the developmental period were

- the need for syllabi that were broad enough to allow students to sample a variety of subjects in business education, in the widest sense, yet would allow them to make an informed choice of the route to choose at the end of their first year of study.

- the need for the syllabi to be specific enough to provide a strong foundation for the later years of each degree — regardless of the student's choice

- the implications of the introduction of the common first year for the structure of those later years

- the need to maintain individual course identity — mainly for marketing purposes.

- the need to ensure that any restructuring still met the requirements of professional bodies for exemption purposes — particularly in the case of accounting students.

This last issue was of particular relevance to the BA accounting degree and this need was a constraining factor on the structure and mix of subjects that could be adopted. The majority of its graduates go into one of three of the main U.K. accounting bodies with the aim of becoming qualified accountants; thus it is vital that any degree is recognised by these three bodies — the Institute of Chartered Accountants of Scotland (ICAS), the Chartered Association of Certified Accountants (ACCA), and the Chartered Institute of Management Accountants (CIMA), each of which assesses accounting degrees for their relevance. It was essential that great care be taken in the renegotiation of the internal content of the accounting degree, to ensure that the move towards a common first year, and the subsequent dilution of the accounting content, with a reduction from five hours per week to 3 1/4 hours per week, did not penalise those students pursuing an accounting qualification, in terms of a reduction in the levels of exemption granted by the professional bodies. The accounting bodies were at first rather hostile to the idea of a reduction in the accounting content in the first year but considerable persuasion was exercised on them, and, given the excellent relations established with them during our years of accounting provision and the good measure of confidence built up between them and the staff and students, following extensive discussion and compromise, the revised structure of the BA accounting degree was finally acceptable to the accounting bodies.

Following an extensive series of scrutiny and validation meetings involving academics from within and outwith the institution and respresentatives from business and commerce, the common first year was approved for introduction in Session 1987-88.

A first step had been taken in extending flexibility of provision for first-year students by allowing them to delay their final choice of course — by one year — thus giving them the opportunity to discover their aptitudes and dislikes and to change their course if they so wished without loss of time and without the need for bridging courses.

Those successfully completing their accounting degree could progress to the full-time ACCA course or could take employment and then return to continue their accounting education via the part-time courses leading to the ACCA and CIMA qualifications.

But what if they discovered that they could not cope with a degree or what if they had enrolled on the HNC or HND course but had more ability than they had at first thought — what then?

Direct Entry

With the change of policy adopted by SCOTVEC in 1987 — and because of our institution's reputation and standing in the academic community, the institution was invited to develop "pilot" courses under a delegated authority scheme with SCOTVEC. Whereas in the past the syllabi had been designed by SCOTVEC, taught by our staff and examined by SCOTVEC we now had the opportunity to update existing syllabi, develop new syllabi and new assessment procedures and examine our own students — with the blessing of SCOTVEC.

This was the opportunity we had been waiting for and no time was lost in restructuring the HNC and HND accounting courses in such a way that students could not only move from one to the other but could also, if they had achieved exceptional results, transfer to the BA accounting degree, again without loss of time and without the need for bridging courses. Extensive discussion took place with the professional bodies to ensure that maximum exemptions would be awarded to students completing their HND qualification with appropriate merits, thus ensuring that they could progress directly to the later stages of ACCA or CIMA professional courses. For those unable to meet the standard required for transfer, agreement was reached that those obtaining the HND without merits could be given complete exemption from the Association of Accounting Technicians (AAT).

Professional Courses

The professional accounting courses offered in our institution are continually being reviewed and updated with the agreement of the relevant professional bodies. ACCA courses are offered on a full-time or day release basis, and CIMA courses on a day release basis only, thus catering to the full- and part-time students alike. Recently, graduate students wishing to attend the full-time ACCA course have experienced problems in obtaining education grants as the government cut back on its allocation of postgraduate grants. This problem does not affect those students progressing to the professional course via the HND qualification as the grants for HND and degree/postgraduate courses are administered by different authorities (i.e., HNC/HND students' grants are provided by local government authorities through their regional education offices, while degree and postgraduate grants are administered by central government via the Scottish Office Education Department (SOED)). Under normal circumstances, a student will be awarded an education grant once only by either authority — thus a graduate has already used up his/her "education grant entitlement" from the SOED and will not be funded to take a second course even though it leads to a higher qualification. This problem is being addressed at present and, meantime, staff, when interviewing prospective students, are advising those expressing the intention of proceeding to the full-time ACCA course to do so via the HND route to ensure financial support throughout their period of study.

THE VALUE OF COMMUNICATION

The value of effective communication in the development of this portfolio cannot of course be overstressed. Only by talking to and listening to those involved at all levels in the accounting discipline — both academically and professionally — was it possible to identify what was required, by whom and for what purpose. Discussions involved academic staff from within and without the institution, employers, representatives from the professional bodies, representatives from CNAA, SCOTVEC and SOED, administrative staff in the institution, and, perhaps most importantly, the students past, present and future. Their views were sought throughout the development process, both formally and informally, via informal discussion with staff; staff/student liaison committees; their elected representatives on the Course Boards of Studies and throughout the scrutiny and valida-

tion processes for the restructuring of the BA accounting degree and the HNC/HND accounting courses. Accounting courses can be successful only if they meet the needs of the students, the employers and the relevant professional bodies and to do so, the needs of all concerned must be identified — through discussion — and met — through persuasion and compromise.

CASE STUDIES

Table 1 shows the progress of four students accepted onto the BA accounting degree with nonstandard entry qualifications.

Conclusions

By any standard, the record of the accounting courses at Napier has been a success — in attracting direct from school students with good grades, mature students with nonstandard entry qualifications, and by the transfer of students who perform well at the certificate and diploma levels to the later years of the degree or the available professional courses.

A SUCCESSFUL OUTCOME

Our portfolio of articulating accounting courses makes it possible for students of all ages and from many varied backgrounds to make the most of their potential and to achieve an accounting qualification relevant to their level of ability — from a certificate at HNC level, via HND and AAT exemption, and degree to the professional ACCA and CIMA qualifications. In addition, successful graduates can pursue other professional courses without our institution leading to the qualifications of the Institute of Chartered Accountants of Scotland; the Institute of Chartered Accountants of England and Wales and the Chartered Institute of Public Finance and Accounting (CIPFA).

Our courses have been designed

- to provide flexibility of entry — catering to school leavers, direct entrants from other educational establishments; mature students, employees, women returners, single parents and overseas students

- to provide flexibility in mode of study by providing full- and part-time day release and evening modes of attendance

- to formally recognise the level of performance achieved by awarding qualifications in the HNC/HND courses at standard or merit level depending on performance, and by negotiating a package of professional exemptions com-

TABLE 1

Name	Mrs J	Mr J	Mrs C	Ms B
Sex	Female	Male	Female	Female
Age on Entry	31	36	33	26
Entry Qualifications	Out of Date Highers but not enough	Theatre Lighting Technician	Housewife SNC Business Studies	Out of Date Highers but not enough
BA Year 1	Average 67	Average 58	Average 47	Average 59
BA Year 2	Average 63	Average 54	Withdrew	Average 42
BA Year 3	Average 62	Average 58	—	Poor results
	Overall Average 64	Overall Average 57		
Result	Degree with Distinction	Degree	—	Fail Failed Resit in 1991
Comment	CA Qualified	ACCA Qualified	Needed to help run family business	Option to Resit until 1993

TABLE 2
Details of Four Students on HND Accounting Who Progressed to BA Accounting.

Name	Mr A	Mr O	Mr D	Mr S
Sex	Male	Male	Male	Male
Age on Entry	18	19	20	17
Applied BA Accounting	Reject	Reject	No	Reject
Other previous course	No	HNC Acc Pass	HND Chemistry Fail	No
Results HND Yr 1	5 Merits	5 Merits	4 Merits	3 Merits
Yr 2			6 Merits	4 Merits
BA Yr 2	Average 58	Average 56		
Yr 3	Average 64	Average 55	Average 60	Average 62
Results	Degree with Distinction	Degree	Degree with Distinction	Degree with Distinction

mensurate with the standard achieved by each student.

ADDITIONAL DEVELOPMENTS

Our intention is to continue to expand our accounting provision. We are at present developing an Honours course for the BA accounting degree which it is hoped will be introduced in September 1993.

Other future developments are

- to bring in a distance learning mode of study for our degree and HNC/D provision, thus enabling students to study outside the university using our materials and being tutored by our staff; and

- to use the credit accumulation and transfer scheme (CATS) devised by CNAA, so that stu-

TABLE 3
Details of Three Students on HND Accounting Who
Progressed to the Internally Assessed ACCA Course

Name	Ms Y	Mr S	Mr M
Sex	Female	Male	Male
Age on Entry	17	31	27
Results			
HND Yr 1	6 Basic Passes	6 Merits	5 Merits
Yr 2	4 Merits	4 Merits	4 Merits
ACCA Level 2 March 92	Pass	Pass	Pass

dents can build up a qualification by studying at different institutions and by accumulating various nationally recognised modules to finish with a nationally recognised qualification; and

- to franchise the common first year to Dumfries & Galloway College of Technology, thus widening the catchment area for prospective BA accounting students.

BENEFITS

The benefits of our accounting provision are many:

- Students recognise the worth of our provision and there are many more applicants than places on our courses each year.

- While student numbers generally are decreasing, the number of students in our Department of Accounting and Law increases each year.

- Our students gain professional recognition for their efforts and only a very few leave the institution with no qualification at all.

- Employers are confident that students, recruited from our institution will make worthwhile employees, with students enjoying an excellent employment record within six months of graduating.

- The professional bodies are confident that those students progressing to take their qualifications have been educated to the exacting standards defined by them.

GLOSSARY

AAT	Association of Accounting Technicians
ACCA	Chartered Association of Certified Accountants
CA	Chartered Accountant
CATS	Credit Accumulation and Transfer Scheme
CIMA	Chartered Institute of Management Accountants
CIPFA	Chartered Institute of Public Finance and Accounting
CNAA	Council for National Academic Awards
FTE	Full-Time Equivalent Student
HNC	Higher National Certificate
HND	Higher National Diploma
ICAS	Institute of Chartered Accountants of Scotland
SCOTVEC	Scottish Vocational Education Council
SNC	Scottish National Certificate
SOED	Scottish Office Education Department

REFERENCES

McLachlan, J. E. 1991. The Tension between Professional and Academic Education. British Accounting Association Annual Conference.

———, and V. Wood. 1989. External to Internal Validation — A Scottish Experience. Eleventh EAIR Forum.

———, and ———. 1991. Three into One *Did* Go — The Development of a Common First Year Curriculum. Thirty-first AIR Forum.

Taxation of Foreign Scholars in the United States: A Barrier Hindering International Accounting Education

Cherie J. O'Neil and Joseph W. Antenucci

The public policy problems of the future are certainly technical and logistical (as well as conceptual), but they are also political and ethical in nature. —Louis Gawthrop[1]

INTRODUCTION

While studying abroad, foreign scholars, teachers, and researchers often earn income subject to taxation in their host country. Taxation of this income may create an unanticipated financial hardship and also generate ill will toward their host country when that tax policy is neither fair nor articulate.

Few foreign scholars who enter the United States comprehend the complicated manner imposed upon them by U.S. tax law. Confronting new forms, requirements, and tax liabilities, they are likely to be confused by the level of tax complexity. Many foreign students, who have never paid income taxes in their home country, will have no first-hand knowledge about how a tax system works.

Referring to U.S. tax laws, the Institute of International Education stated:

> Unfortunately, the tax laws that apply to (foreign students) are often complex and are not generally understood by many independent tax consultants, host institutions, or grantees.[2]

The majority of international scholars visiting the United States mistakenly assume they can file the same tax forms as their American colleagues.[3] The required tax forms for aliens are structured to accommodate foreign businesspeople, not students. The proper form for foreign students is the difficult and tedious Form 1040NR. It is both complex and inequitable in its treatment of international scholars. This contradicts the position advocated by the United Nations Model Treaty, Art.20(2), which recommends that foreign scholars be allowed to be treated for tax purposes as citizens of the country in which they are studying.

The United States, as well as other developed countries hoping to encourage international study should reconsider their tax policies regarding foreign academicians. More severe taxation imposes a hidden barrier to international education while fostering tax noncompliance. Intelligent tax legislation must encourage both compliance and goodwill among foreign visitors.

CURRENT OPEN-DOOR EDUCATION POLICY

The U.S. open-door policy toward international education has encouraged the entrance of large numbers of nonimmigrant foreign scholars.[4] Institutions of higher education are receptive, and indications are that this trend will continue. In 1989, the most recent year for which data are available, nearly 750,000 foreign students, teachers, trainees,

---

[1]L. C. Gawthrop. 1984. *Public Sector Management, Systems and Ethics*. Indiana U. Press, p. 35.

[2]Institute of International Education. 1990. *Grantax Program Memo* (October). Introduction.

[3]The Organization for Economic Cooperation and Development (a 24-member group which includes the U.S.) reported that countries which undertook audits of foreign taxpaying activities, invariably found "clear evidence of noncompliance in this area" [GAO. 1988. *Opportunities Exist for Improving IRS's Administration of Alien Taxpayers Programs*, GAO/GGD –88–54. General Government Division, 15].

[4]Academicians generally fall into this category. According to the Immigration and Nationality Act [§101, 8 U.S. Code §1101(a) (15) (A) – (L) (1980)], a foreign national in the U.S. for temporary purposes only, and not intending to stay is considered a "nonimmigrant."

[5]U.S. Department of Justice, Immigration and Naturalization Service. 1990. *1989 Statistical Yearbook of the Immigration and Naturalization Service*. U.S. Government Printing Office.

Cherie J. O'Neil is Quinn Professor of Tax Accounting at the University of South Florida, and Joseph W. Antenucci is Assistant Professor at Middle Tennessee State University.

and their family members entered the United States.[5] This is an increase of 10.3 percent from 1988.[6] America currently has the largest international student population in the world.[7]

U.S. higher education is rated as the world's best on such criteria as scientific research quality, ingenuity, flexibility of programs, and accessibility to all segments of the population.[8] Elizabeth Hull states:

> Even among developed countries the United States is particularly enticing because of its traditional receptiveness, its accessibility, and its strong and supportive immigrant communities.[9]

Derek Bok, former president of Harvard University, stated that the United States was "the country of choice for students around the world seeking to pursue their education abroad."[10]

The number of international students at the graduate level in the United States has been increasing by 6.5 percent annually.[11] Of total graduate enrollment 12 percent (15 percent at doctoral-granting institutions) are internationals.[12] One of every nine students at Cornell University is foreign.[13] At the universities of Illinois, Wisconsin, California-Berkeley, Ohio State, Stanford, M.I.T., Cornell, Michigan, Texas, and Pittsburgh at least 25 percent of doctorates granted, in the most recently measured five-year period, were awarded to international students.[14] In 1989 over half of U.S. doctorates granted in engineering and half of those in math and computer science were awarded to internationals.[15]

The United States should not feel threatened by this influx of foreign talent to its graduate schools. According to William Carroll of NAFSA: Association of International Educators, the foreign students "are filling slots that are going empty," not depriving Americans of an educational opportunity.[16]

Many U.S. corporations depend on international scholars relocating to this country.[17] At Texas Instruments, employees engaged in research who have Ph.D.s are 25 percent foreign born. This number is 35 percent at IBM and 40 percent at Bell Labs. There is sentiment in private industry that the country should make every effort, including favorable tax policy, to welcome foreign scholars. There is an apparent contradiction, however, between the U.S. open-door education policy and its severe tax treatment of visiting scholars and students.

U.S. TAXATION OF INTERNATIONAL SCHOLARS

The current complicated tax treatment of the United States toward visiting international scholars could act as a disincentive for remaining in the

United States or could foster noncompliance with U.S. tax law, which could cause financial hardship, especially should an IRS audit lead to assessment of additional tax, interest, and penalties. By the guidelines established in the Deficit Reduction Act of 1984 (DRA'84) tax code changes, all foreign teachers (for at least their first two years), 100 percent of all master's degree candidates, and an estimated 90 percent of international doctoral candidates in the U.S. are subject to the form 1040NR filing requirements.[18]

Far from welcoming foreign scholars, experts believe U.S. policies have the "perverse effect of penalizing only those aliens who have resided in the country" for a short period of time.[19]

[6]U.S. Department of Justice, Immigration and Naturalization Service. 1989. *1988 Statistical Yearbook of the Immigration and Naturalization Service.* U.S. Government Printing Office.

[7]G. Leggat. 1991. The Foreign Influence. *Cornell Alumni News* (June): 36–41.

[8]D. Bok. 1990. What's Wrong with Our Universities? *Harvard Magazine* (May-June): 44–59.

[9]E. Hull. 1985. *Without Justice for All: The Constitutional Rights of Aliens.* Greenwood Press, p. 5.

[10]Bok, p. 44.

[11]Institute of International Education. 1990. *Open Doors 1989–1990.* Institute of International Education.

[12]Council of Graduate Schools. 1989. *Annual Survey of Graduate Enrollment.* National Research Council.

[13]G. Leggat. 1991. The Foreign Influence. *Cornell Alumni News* (June): 36–41.

[14]Ibid., p. 11.

[15]S. Lee. 1991. Train 'em here, keep 'em here. *Forbes* (May 27): 110–116.

[16]Ibid.

[17]Congress apparently shares this sentiment. The Immigration Act of 1990 nearly tripled the number of U.S. "green cards" to be granted highly qualified foreigners (Leggat 1991).

[18]§7701(b), added to the Internal Revenue Code by DRA'84 (Public law 98.369, effective January 1, 1985), provides a statutory definition of "nonresident." The distinction between citizen and nonresident is critical. Special nonresident tax laws deny equal treatment. Prior law provided only subjective distinction based on an ill-defined notion of current circumstances and intent to stay. The American Bar Association Committee on U.S. Activities of Foreigners and Tax Treaties, believing "intent" was too hard to verify, encouraged Congress to simplify the filing status rules for foreign businesspersons. In DRA'84 Congress obliged [H.R. Rept. No. 432, part II, 98th Congress, 2nd Sess at 1523 (1984)]. It explicitly intended to simplify the determination of tax filing status for foreigners (U.S. Congress Staff of the Joint Committee on Taxation, 98th Congress, 2nd Session, *General Explanation of the Revenue Provisions of the Deficit Reduction Act of 1984* (Committee Print, 1984) pp. 463–464.) and to provide a "brightline" definition.

[19]Hull, p. 49.

When foreign academicians apply for, receive, or present visas in the United States, there is no organized taxpayer assistance program to provide them with the information needed to comply with U.S. income tax laws.[20] This creates problems because the U.S. has a voluntary income tax system whereby the compliance burden falls on the taxpayer, with periodic auditing by the Internal Revenue Service (IRS).

The proper nonresident federal income tax return, the Form 1040NR, is an imposing document five pages long. In contrast, most U.S. students may file the short, large print Form 1040EZ. The 1040NR must be filed the first five years a foreign student is in the United States. The 1040NR contains unwieldy terms, such as "not effectively connected income," unfamiliar to tax practitioners, let alone recently arrived internationals. Prior tax research has shown that jargon and new terminology contribute to "reading complexity" of the law, which makes compliance difficult.[21]

Tax research also shows that two factors, excessive detail and numerous computations, explain 86 percent of variation in subjects' perception of complexity.[22] Also, time required to file has been used as a surrogate measure for complexity.[23] The detailed and lengthy Form 1040NR (five pages long) meets all these criteria.

According to an IRS estimate of the average time required to complete a tax form, the 1040NR requires over seven hours to complete (which includes reading the instructions, filling in and assembling the form) versus approximately one hour total for the 1040EZ. Three companion publications, ranging from 25 to 38 pages in length, provide additional information needed to complete the five-page form 1040NR. An estimated additional six and a half hours is required for record keeping for the form 1040NR as compared to an estimated five *minutes* for the 1040EZ. Should the international scholar seek the assistance of a paid professional, estimated fees for professional assistance in filing a form 1040NR could top $800!

On the form 1040NR, income is segregated into categories, depending on source and applicable treaty provisions, and taxed at different rates and on different pages. Experts have defined this filing process as "complex."[24] However, true complexity of nonresident filing is not fully revealed by the tax forms. Affiliated requirements exist in addition to all regular U.S. tax rules, which must be followed. The form 1040NR is completed differently depending on visa country. Married couples must file separate form 1040NRs. Benefits such as dependency exemptions are allowed only in limited circumstances. Although foreign students must itemize their deductions, they cannot claim many of most common itemized deductions. Medical expenses, personal property taxes, real estate taxes, and mortgage or personal interest are all *non*deductible.

A CALL FOR CHANGES TO U.S. TAXATION OF INTERNATIONAL SCHOLARS

International educators are anxious for changes to the U.S. system of taxing foreign students. Lobbying efforts have resulted in several proposed pieces of legislation. However, current policy requires any U.S. tax proposal, even one calling for simplification, be "revenue neutral" (i.e., it must be shown the change does not reduce tax revenues). This is unfortunate because the projected tax loss associated with simplification of taxation of foreign scholars would be negligible.[25]

Senators Pryor and Kennedy, along with five cosponsors, introduced in the U.S. Congress The International Scholarship Tax Corrections Act [Senate Bill S.1155, 101st Congress, 1st Session, June 9, 1989] to alleviate the more severe tax laws applicable to foreign scholars.[26] This bill failed to clear the Senate Committee on Finance to come for a floor vote. The bill was not revenue neutral, and no revenue enhancement was proposed to offset anticipated revenue losses.

[20]GAO. General Government Division, Washington, D.C.

[21]V. C. Milliron. 1985. A Behavioral Study of the Meaning and Influence of Tax Complexity. *Journal of Accounting Research* (Autumn): 17–31, refers to this dimension of complexity as "readability." S. B. Long and J. A. Swingen. 1987. An Approach to the Measurement of Tax Lay Complexity. *The Journal of the American Taxation Association* (Spring): 22–36, describes it as clarity in forms. B. S. Koch and S. S. Karlinsky. 1984. The Effect of Federal Income Tax Lay Reading Complexity on Students' Task Performance. *Issues in Accounting Education*: 98–110, term it the "reading complexity" of a tax law.

[22]Long and Swingen.

[23]J. Slemrod. 1989. Complexity, Compliance Costs and Tax Evasion (Chapter 5): 156–181, in J. A. Roth, and J. T. Scholz. 1989. *Taxpayer Compliance Volume 2: Social Science Perspectives*. U. of Pennsylvania Press.

[24]R. M. Lipton and S. G. Filer. 1986. Taxation of Compensation Paid to Aliens Requires Careful Analysis. *TAXES—The Tax Magazine* (July): 444–451.

[25]Dr. Scott Newlon. 1991. International Economist, Office of Tax Analysis, Treasury Department. Personal interview, June 7, 1991, and internal working report, untitled (June 26).

[26]One year earlier a version of this legislation was included in the year-end budget reconciliation, H.3150. During floor debate, however, the Senate dropped this provision.

Senator Lugar and members of the Senate Committee on Foreign Relations attempted to attach relief legislation to the Foreign Relations Authorization Act of 1989, S.1160. However, the proposal was dropped because the Foreign Relations Committee does not have any jurisdiction over tax matters.[27] Two other recent proposals to alleviate the more severe taxation of foreign students have also been discussed in the Congress.[28]

INEQUITY IN TAX TREATIES

Equity, or fairness, in a tax system is a cornerstone for theories of taxation. The principles of equity have been accepted as tenets of a good tax system since the days of Adam Smith.[29] Research shows taxpayers' perception of fairness in a tax system to be a key variable in determining the success of that tax system.[30] Bittker addresses equity:[31]

Traditionally equity has been the standard applied by tax theorists to the structural details of the federal income tax. Equity theorists ask whether existing law treats equals equally (horizontal equity) and whether it differentiates appropriately among unequals (vertical equity).

Those who are at the same earnings position before taxes should be at the same position after taxes (horizontal equity). Those with different levels of income should be taxed differently (vertical equity). Subjecting U.S. taxation of foreign scholars to such a standard reveals it woefully lacking. The problem is inconsistent tax treatment of scholars from different countries.

Principles of international law should also be reflected in the treaties of a country. A nation may distinguish its treatment of various classes of aliens provided the distinctions neither violate international law nor appear irrational given the obligations of the citizens of that nation.[32] Rational tax equity principles form the basis for tax obligations of U.S. citizens. Such is not the case for foreign scholars in America.

Because of inequity in tax treaties, those with equal levels of income often do not end up paying the same tax (a violation of horizontal equity). Those with unequal levels of income may pay equivalent amounts of taxes (a violation of vertical equity principles).

Tax treaties help to defray the tax liability of internationals. A treaty may provide exclusions or reduced rates for specific items of income. Treaties also are "a means of avoiding double taxation of income."[33] Tax treaties between the U.S. and foreign countries may allow for an amount of U.S.

source income to escape taxation.[34] Some treaties exclude the compensation paid for teaching or research, for example.

Since the foreign student or teacher filing a U.S. tax return is denied access to the standard deduction available to citizens, it could be argued the treaty exclusion amount is a substitute for the lost standard deduction. However, the great majority of foreign students in this country, 68 percent, have no treaty benefits to shelter U.S. source income By way of illustration, Table 1 presents the treaty exclusions for foreign students from selected countries.[35]

There are actually several questionable inequities present in the current system of tax treaties. Horizontal equity is lacking for foreign scholars, who hold visas from nontreaty countries, compared to U.S. scholars. Within the population of international academics, horizontal equity does not exist when comparing treaty with nontreaty countries. Also, the possibility of vertical inequity occurs because those with different before-tax incomes may not be taxed differently after a tax treaty is considered.

Beside the exclusion amounts, inconsistent treatment of internationals with children exacerbates tax inequity. According to IRC §152(b)(3) and two spe-

[27]Liaison Group. 1990. *Workshop on Taxation of International Exchange Participants* (June 18). Conference Workbook.

[28]P. D. Morrison, International Tax Council, Treasury Department. Personal interview. May 22, 1991.

[29]A. Smith. 1776. *An Inquiry Into the Nature and Causes of The Wealth of Nations,* Book V, Chapter II, Part II on Taxes. Adam and Charles Black, 1863.

[30]G. Schmolders. 1959. Fiscal Psychology: A New Branch of Public Finance. *National Tax Journal* (December): 340–345, and M. Spicer, and S. Lundsted. 1976. Audit Probabilities and the Tax Evasion Decision. *Journal of Economic Psychology* (No. 2): 241–245.

[31]B. L. Bittker. 1980. Equity, Efficiency, and Income Tax Theory: Do Misallocations Drive Out Inequities? in H. Aaron and M. Boskin. *The Economics of Taxation.* Brookings Institute, p. 19.

[32]B. H. Weston, P. Falk, and A. D'Amato. 1980. *International Law and World Order.* West Publishing Co., p. 687.

[33]M. J. Flaherty. 1990. Foreign Recipients of U.S. Income, and Tax Withheld. *SOI Bulletin* (Winter): 41–56.

[34]IRS Publication 901 summarizes treaties in force. The full text of U.S. tax treaties with other countries can be found in RIA Federal Tax Coordinator, Vol. 20. Six additional treaties were ratified by the Senate in 1990 and will become effective for tax year 1991. These include Finland (replaces existing treaty), Germany (replaces existing one), India (new treaty), Indonesia (new treaty), Spain (new treaty), and Tunisia (new treaty).

[35]All dollar amounts are stated in U.S. currency values.

TABLE 1

Selected Treaty Exclusions for Students and Apprentices (On Income from Personal Services Performed in U.S. in 1990)

Country	Students	Trainees
Argentina	0	0
Canada	0	0
China, People's Republic	$5,000	$5,000*
Ethiopia	0	0
France	2,000	5,000
Greece	0	0
India	0	0
Japan	2,000	5,000
Korea, Republic of	2,000	5,000
Mexico	0	0
Panama	0	0
Pakistan	5,000	5,000
Saudi Arabia	0	0
Spain	5,000	8,000
Taiwan	0	0
United Kingdom	0	0

NOTE: All treaties listed allow a five year exclusion period for students. For trainees the exclusion period is only one year, unless marked by an asterisk, in which case the exclusion period is five years.

cial tax treaties, only foreign nationals from four countries may claim dependency exemptions for their children.[36] In the 15 percent tax bracket, dependency exemptions would save a taxpayer with two children $645 ($2,150 × 2 × .15) in 1991, a not immaterial amount for a scholar on a tight budget.

A more subtle point is that inequity may be intensified by visa status. Different tax law applies to holders of different types of visas, even though they may be from the same country.[37] The first year present, an H visa academician may be able to claim all tax benefits afforded to a U.S. citizen. It is only in the third year, at the earliest, that a fellow citizen J visa holder may take advantage of these same benefits. For F visa scholars, their sixth year present would be the first year to claim equitable benefits.

Should the tax treatment of an individual hinge on factors as inconsequential as visa type? With foreign students, for example, the difference between receiving one type of visa rather than another could be as insignificant as which agency (e.g., U.S. Information Agency or Department of Education) has approved the plan of study.[38]

Difference in taxes for a married academician with two dependents, between an H visa holder from a country with no treaty benefit (but allowed benefits of a U.S. citizen the first year present) or an F

visa holder from the same country, could exceed $10,000 over the five-year period an F visa holder is denied equal treatment (even if all taxable income falls in the lower 15 percent tax bracket). A similar magnitude of differential could be achieved if a treaty country F visa holder's taxes (favorable benefits and dependency exemptions allowed) were compared to a nontreaty F visa holder's taxes.

Perhaps of greater concern is the possibility that perceived inequity in a tax system leads to noncompliance.[39] A tax policy which fosters noncompliance, in a country such as the United States, which has a voluntary tax system, defies logic. One relic of U.S. taxation which fostered noncompliance by international scholars was recently repealed. The so-called sailing permit rules of IRC §6851(d), the name of which represents an anachronism from 1921 when the law was first established, has been repealed with respect to foreign academicians.[40] Its repeal demonstrates that when there is significant noncompliance with a tax law, an alternative to enforcement is to change the law.

RECOMMENDATIONS

In order to increase compliance with U.S. tax law by visiting scholars, a different set of tax rules is needed for scholars as opposed to foreign business persons who are temporarily present in the United States. The foreign businesspersons may have significant income from their home country that they do not want subject to U.S. taxation. A nonresident individual who enters the United States for educational purposes, further training or temporary

---

[36]This depends on country of citizenship. Mexicans, Canadians, Japanese, and South Koreans, provided they have a certain amount of U.S. source income and are present for a minimum part of the year, may claim some portion of their dependency exemptions. The portion depends on which country they are from, how long they have been present, *and* how much earned income they have in the U.S.

[37]§7701 (b) (5).

[38]8 USC §1101(a) (15) (F), (J) and (M).

[39]S. Kaplan, P. Reckers, and S. Roark. 1988. An Attribution Theory Analysis of Tax Evasion Related Judgments. *Accounting, Organizations, and Society* (Vol. XIII, No. 4): 371-379.

[40]Temp. Reg. §1.6851-2T(a) (2) (ii), promulgated by TD 8332, Fed. Reg. January 28, 1991. Effective 1991, foreign academicians need not obtain a sailing permit provided their only U.S. income is (1) an allowance to compensate for study expenses in the U.S.; (2) for services or accommodations furnished incidental to that study; or (3) received in accordance with the employment authorizations applicable to the alien's visa type in 8 CFR §274 (a) (12).

teaching activity rarely has extensive non–U.S. source income. Thus, the person does not benefit from the form 1040NR rules, which permit an exclusion for such income. The majority of foreign graduate students are supported by research or teaching assistantships or financial aid, the maintenance portion of which is now subject to U.S. tax under IRC §117. They would benefit from being able to file a regular U.S. tax form, such as the form 1040A or form 1040EZ.

Present U.S. tax policy, which requires visiting scholars to file the form 1040NR, presents them with confusion and inequalities. For example, it is inconsistent to allow an educational deduction[41] to one individual who briefly practiced a trade rather than to another who pursued his/her education continuously. The complexity of such an allowable deduction may also mean that the majority of those qualified for it fail to take advantage of the opportunity. Also, tax relief from treaty exclusion is fortuitous and political. Different treatment of nationals from the same country, who happen to hold different types of visas but are engaged in substantially the same activity violates tax equity. A more coherent, consistent policy for foreign scholars is needed.

With the goal of offering international scholars fair and uniform income tax treatment, Congressional relief is needed. One alternative would be the addition of a code subsection permitting foreign teachers and students to make a binding election on their first income tax return to file either as nonresident aliens or U.S. residents for the duration of their (F or J) visa classification.[42] Some individuals would choose to file a form 1040NR, perhaps sheltering compensation with treaty exclusions, while others would elect to file using one of the regular U.S. tax forms to take advantage of the standard deduction, the dependent exemption deduction, and possibly the child care credit.

Additionally, for those who choose to file the form 1040NR, some simplification of this form is needed. The fact that a person is from a foreign country with no prior exposure to U.S. tax laws makes the terminology and phraseology used in the instruction booklets just that much more complex to interpret. IRS Publication 901, which summarizes treaty benefits, is a prime candidate for simplification. Many foreign academicians have mistakenly interpreted passages from this publication that seem to support their position that either their income is tax exempt, or that they are entitled to certain deductions or exclusions.

Also, dissemination of information about U.S. tax laws to foreign scholars before they enter the United States by the Department of Immigration and Naturalization and the State Department is recommended. This would help in informing foreign visitors in advance of the complexity of the U.S. tax laws and would encourage compliance by making them aware of their filing requirements at the outset.

Until the above changes have been implemented, the authors will provide on request a further explanation of current U.S. income tax filing procedures for foreign scholars. This document also discusses the limited tax-planning strategies available to the visiting scholar. In addition, names and addresses of organizations concerned with the problems of foreign education in America will be provided upon request.

CONCLUSION

Everyday technological and political changes bring people of the world closer together. Countries once discrete now are receptive to international exchange, a notion deemed an impossibility only a few years ago. Intellectual and academic exchanges are not only frequent occurrences but are also necessities of this new world order. Already much has been gained from scholarly exchange and the opportunity exists for accounting educators to be at the forefront of the continued, mutually beneficial flow of new ideas and information.

It is ironic that even while the more obvious barriers to free intellectual commerce crumble, more subtle barriers persist. The global challenge for accounting educators, indeed educators from all disciplines, is to foster the unimpeded growth of scholarly exchange. If true intellectual freedom is to triumph, then myopic, exclusive policies hindering the flow of scholarship should be eschewed. Accounting educators are well positioned to detect the existence of such conflicting policies, and we believe that the U.S. unfair, more severe, and complex taxation of international scholars is one such policy. As discussed, our recommendation is for simplification of tax treatment of visiting academicians to permit accounting education to better meet the global challenges of the 21st.

---

[41]§1.162-5.

[42]Such a provision is included in the recently ratified tax treaty with India, effective beginning with tax year 1991. Art. 21(2) states in part, ". . . a student or business apprentice described in paragraph (21) 1 shall, in addition, be entitled during such education or training to the same exemptions, reliefs or reductions in respect of taxes available to residents of the State which he is visiting." It is not clear how one will claim these benefits.

The Search for a Better Accounting System: The Overlooked Concern

Martin Putterill, Roger Debreceny, and Darien Kerkin

THE SETTING

There is in the air the scent of change and a growing awareness that accounting must respond to meet new demands. The complexity of global business activities and availability of new information technologies require that external and internal financial reporting must become richer in the production of information helpful to a variety of users.

At the same time, accounting educators are concerned about the relevance of current programmes and large sums of money are being devoted to exploring the options for revitalising course structures and teaching methods. It is a slow process with perhaps a decade or two before the Bedford Committee (Grinyer, Al-Bazzaz, and Yasai-Ardekani 1986) conclusions are actioned. It will be many more years before accountants begin to fully achieve the mission proposed for the American Accounting Association; namely an "intellectual discipline concerned with the measurement, communication and use of decision-oriented information" (Grinyer et al. 1986).

Strong adherence to the prevailing double-entry accounting system inhibits reflection on the nature of accounting in the context of 21st century commerce. This paper offers a modest set of proposals for rethinking the manner in which accounting can be aligned to the needs of the complex business and international environment in the decades ahead.

By posing the unthinkable question (*Should accountants dispense with the double-entry structure?*), the way is opened for discussion about the nature and scope of accounting in a global economy characterised by rapidly changing markets and technologies.

The "new form of accounting" (NFA), which is the focus of this paper, addresses the weaknesses of traditional accounting processes based upon double-entry principles. The paper synthesises prospective requirements of recording, decision making and accountability, with emerging technologies to bring accountants back from their increasingly peripheral status.

Before we can address the matter of change, it is necessary to review the basis of the present model of accounting.

THE DOUBLE-ENTRY SYSTEM—ORIGINS AND PRACTICE

Accounting is less substantial now than as codified by Pacioli in his 1494 treatise *"Sûma dé Arithmetica Geometria Proportioni i Proportionalita"* (Chatfield 1974; Geijsbeek 1914). The journal, ledger and financial statements are still with us but without all the full range of recording processes that 15th century Venetian traders required to manage the complex, international businesses of those days. The systems of Pacioli's day provided a set of multidimensional information. The physical inventory of goods held by a merchant extended to rich descriptions of the merchandise. For example, the "Eighth Item" of inventory comprised

> . . . so many cases of ginger *bellidi,* etc., and so many sacks of pepper, long pepper or round pepper depending on what it is; so many packages of cinnamon, etc, that weigh so much; so many packages of cloves, etc., that weigh so much, with *fusti polvere* and *cappelletti* or without, etc., and so many pieces of *verzini* weighing so much, and so much sandalwood, red or white, weighing so much, and so on entering one item after another (Geijsbeek 1914).

Those accounting systems included the "memorandum book" which regrettably over time has disappeared from modern accounting systems. The memorandum was a "day book" providing a running record of the transactions that the trader has entered into with as much information as possible recorded in the book in a free-form format.

Martin Putterill is Associate Professor at the University of Auckland, Roger Debreceny is at the University of New England–Northern Rivers, and Darien Kerkin is at Auckland Institute of Technology.

Our thanks for comments to Alan McGregor, Sidney Weil, Gary Sundem, Michael Bradbury, Barry Spicer, Murray Wells and Kasi Ramanathan.

Much of that information was nonfinancial in nature. The journal would be written up from the memorandum book and the subsequent posting to the ledger would not repeat the richness of the memorandum book. As Pacioli noted ". . . Here [in the ledger] you do not need to be very lengthy if you have already given the description . . . Try to be very brief" (Geijsbeek 1914, 35).

The accounting systems described by Pacioli were attuned to the management requirements and information technology of the day. In the 15th century, businesspeople were primarily merchants, not manufacturers. They were sole traders, short-term joint ventures and longer-term partnerships all of which were closely and personally managed by owners and the modern-day separation of ownership and management did not exist. Owners could, if necessary, reconstruct outcomes by working backwards from the ledger to the memorandum. In short, there was no separation of "management" and "financial" accounting systems.

The Crisis of Modern Accounting

As recently as the past century, the scale and diversity of business has increased dramatically. The double-entry bookkeeping system described by Pacioli was modified in the wake of developments in mechanical data processing such as accounting machines and punched card systems. These mechanical systems were undoubtedly more efficient in processing data than the preexisting handwritten "books" that Pacioli would recognise but gave rise to sanitised accounting stripped of richness and informational value.

Computerised accounting systems are notable for their slavish adoption of these mechanistic processes. Timidity or sloth on the part of accountants unwilling to come to grips with computing has allowed computer programmers, without any understanding of the historical developments in accounting information needs of users to shackle accounting.

BUSINESS TRENDS—STRUCTURES AND PROCESSES

Modern business is increasingly global and complex. Further concentration of manufacturing production and service output can be anticipated in multi- and transnational corporations (Attaran and Guseman 1988; Attaran and Sahafi 1988). Sanitised and inflexible computerised accounting systems cannot meet the demands of organisations engaged in global commerce. The

alignment of information systems with strategy and short-term objectives is crucial for the success of these large enterprises. A broadening of the definition of relevant information to include such elements as the monitoring of competitors' actions is a necessary requirement of new accounting systems (Howell and Soucy 1987, 1988; Shank and Govindarajan 1989).

Additionally, managers will need to interpret a range of events across legal and national boundaries. These events could include such key corporate phenomena as sourcing in one country, manufacture in a second and realisation in a third.

At the same time as organisations are growing in size and becoming more international, there is a related trend for management structures to become less hierarchical and more flexible with wider delegation of management responsibility (Duncan et al. 1988; Hayes and Jaikumar 1988). Suppliers and customers in the value chain are being increasingly included in the information network for reasons of quality improvement and waste reduction.

Increasing use of automation and robotics will further change the nature of business, particularly on the focus of labour as a key element of cost (Drucker 1990). Management understanding of fixed cost relationships is becoming more important and potentially much more demanding on accounting systems. The current interest in activity-based costing systems is an indication of this concern (Cooper and Kaplan 1988, 1991).

As if this all was not enough, companies are being forced by market pressures to develop new products in a much faster timeframe than might have been required in markets which were not subject to the demands of international competitors. This means that product life-cycle monitoring will be an essential part of business strategy (Brimson 1986; Ferrera 1990; Murphy and Braund 1990; Peavey 1990; Shields and Young 1991).

The strategic demands of fast-lane business direct attention to emerging management and financial accounting systems needs. Figures 1 and 2 provide an outline of the nature and extent of data-gathering and derived information uses and are a useful starting point for this form of review.

The framework incorporates data sources beyond those which accountants traditionally recognise. It shows that within a management planning framework, there are many users of information other than a finance function.

Much information which is vital to the modern corporation is nonfinancial in nature. Smith provides a useful categorisation of nonfinancial indicators (NFIs) by input, work performance, product, market, employees and customer measures (Smith 1990). An example of a "work performance" measure is the number of production units lost through maintenance failures as part of a wider "maintenance effort" indicator. At present the raw data necessary to calculate NFIs are stored on a variety of formal and informal corporate databases and almost always divorced from the financial data which relate to particular occurrences of the activity being measured. NFIs are useful for management of complex organisations but if they cannot be associated with financial results, lose much of their significance.

Information coming into the organisation will come in a variety of formats of increasing complexity. Electronic data interchange (EDI) implies that much financial and nonfinancial information will flow to and from the entity without a single piece of paper being generated. EDI will be very important to organisations that wish to improve the productivity of their relationships with both suppliers and customers (Hansen and Hill 1989; Kalashian 1990).

In the past, data gathering has been alphanumeric. Changes in the nature of information flows into and within the firm will increasingly present challenges to any accounting system. For example, customer orders may be authorised by approved voice patterns of approved customers which are stored in digitally compressed form. Processing such information will severely test financial and management accounting systems. Internal auditors will find that the "paper trail" underlying transactions upon which they have relied may no longer exist (Hansen and Hill 1989).

Modern business management needs to be able to simultaneously understand the impact of decisions taken by one part of the organisation on other elements. The integrated nature of these relationships are emphasised in Figure 1. It is hard to explain the difference in attitudes between production and marketing functions other than to assume that some factor in the accountability process has fostered myopia.

LIMITATIONS OF THE PREVAILING ACCOUNTING APPROACH

In the light of these demands, the appropriateness of prevailing approaches must be questioned. Of particular importance are the following issues.

Concept of Time

As the pace of business intensifies, a new balance will have to be struck between accounting focus on past events and probabilistic future outcomes. Current accounting systems are preoccupied with the past of which a small proportion is relevant to strategic decision making.

Another concern about "time" is calendar-dominated reporting. Neither seasonality nor critical events are allowed to disturb the calendar pattern of recording and reporting. There is a loss of connection between one time period and another. Accounts are "closed" as if knowledge about these events has no place in decision support or trend analysis.

Preoccupation with Digital Recording

The automatic balancing feature of double-entry systems was useful when accounting was undertaken by hand. It is hardly a justification for limiting the system to a two-vector view and only financial vectors at that (Ijiri 1982, 1989; Smith 1990).

Fragmentation

The act of "posting" to the ledger divorces elements of commercial incidents, making it impossible to subsequently reconstruct events. For control and performance measurement purposes, this feature of double-entry accounting has led to a line-item rather than an integrated view. Sales managers, for example, take an interest in the sales accounts without sufficient regard for the product profit contributions.

Lack of Responsiveness

Increasing concentration of business is associated with a high degree of vertical integration across national boundaries (Kumpe and Bolwijn 1988). Entity separation prevents clear understanding of product revenue and cost outcomes.

Accounting systems have also failed to provide the foundation for planning because few automatic procedures have been established to link-related costs and revenues or to reflect trends for simulating future events. The limitations of prevailing accounting systems are in sharp contrast to the anticipated business needs of the 21st century. A case has been established for a new form of accounting.

Finally, notwithstanding the efforts of accounting researchers, the Pacioli-derived accounting pro-

FIGURE 1
Strategic Data Flows

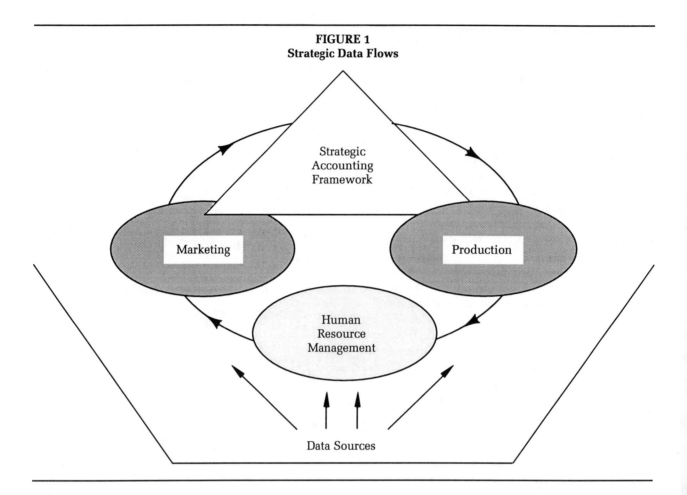

cess has not been satisfactorily grounded in theory (Watts and Zimmerman 1990).

NEW FORM ACCOUNTING (NFA)

Introduction

The new form of accounting can be viewed first as "process" and second as "uses."

Figure 2 describes the broad framework upon which NFA can be built. It shows that an accounting system must deal with a rich variety of data sources, with complex external relationships with stakeholders and interactions with financial and other markets. At the same time, NFA must make possible analysis for planning and control at levels appropriate to the scale and complexity of the issues.

Figure 2 can be amplified to recognise the process requirements of NFA.

The NFA "process" begins with the collection of data in many forms. These will include financial, text, voice, video and graphical components. The responsibility for aligning data gathering with user needs will be on going as will be the mainte-

nance of quality. This is a proactive responsibility requiring close contact between users and the accounting "gatekeeper."

Once gathered in its manifold forms, the data must be stored for subsequent retrieval and analysis. This stage of the "process" might have many of the elements of an "events" view of accounting (Haseman and Whinston 1976; Sorter 1969).

Given the complexity of data types, the database storage mechanisms will need to be equally comprehensive. While it might be that the relational database model may be appropriate as the underlying database methodology (Everest 1986; Everest and Weber 1977; Weber 1986), the object-oriented databases of the future are more likely to provide the appropriate technology for NFA (Cattell 1991; Khoshafian 1990; Kim and Lochovsky 1989; Winblad, Edwards, and King 1990).

Transactions would be stored at an elemental level and the database would provide a mechanism for the construction, as required, of a rich set of accounting processes. The data set could include financial, text, voice, video and graphical components. Attributes of the elements which make up

FIGURE 2
Foundation for New Form Accounting

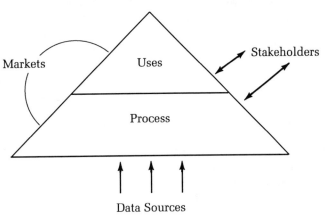

the database might include financial and nonfinancial data, the source of the transaction, the nature of the transmission process which conveyed the data to the database, the time and date of the event and the nature of the originating entity and the entity relationship. Here the accountant will work as the "storeperson" of integrated corporate data.

The database would be open ended but time-based reports would be available from the database on demand. The outcome of some trading events is probabilistic. A database could identify these items and thereby offer managers the

opportunity to weight their impact when producing financial reports. A database which really reflects management actions would be maintained in contingent mode because only in this way can spending levels of the corporation be determined, Contingent elements might include future capital expenditure commitments and back orders from suppliers. A database could be designed to incorporate budget items and appropriate flexing to provide the framework for planning and control. The accountant will become more of a "librarian" providing informed and ready access to information that has been the case in the past where the ac-

FIGURE 3
Broad Foundation for NFA Accounting

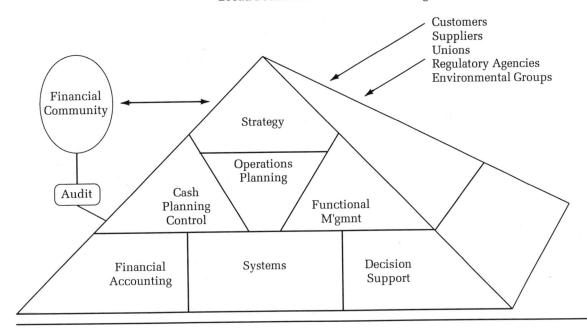

countant has fulfilled a role of "service provider" and "reporter." These latter roles will still be important but less important than in the past as users can be empowered to analyse their own financial and nonfinancial information.

Using the New Form of Accounting

Adoption of an open ended database as the foundation for the new form of accounting would present at least the advantages listed below. Importantly, there would be none of the limitations of calendar-based closure of accounts and the consequent loss of historical information. Given appropriate rights of access, stakeholders may utilise this capacity of a database to select any desired time period for reports.

This break with the calendar will certainly require accountants to be in constant readiness to ensure the reliability and integrity of any statements produced on demand. Because valuation of inventories has been one of the main stumbling blocks to real-time accounting systems, agreement will be needed on procedures for valuation. Fortunately, the widespread adoption of just-in-time (JIT) methodologies are reducing the quantity of inventory in many businesses, thus making some of the elaborate closing off procedures rather academic.

Database methodology will allow financial and nonfinancial characteristics of projects and capital investments to be tracked according to life cycle costing concepts. Furthermore, it would be possible to mark significant events such as the introduction of management changes or the appointment of a new manager and measure outcomes from such points in time. It is also an important management requirement to understand changes in cost and revenue behaviours. Traditional accounting trial balances do not make it easy to establish trends; however interrogation of the database enables rates of change to be measured for particular costs or revenues. As managers become familiar with this analogue form of information analysis, it would not be unexpected to find a growth interest in third-order changes in the rate of change (e.g., the velocity of sales arising from advertising expenditures).

The ability of management to correlate the impact of causes and effects of actions and outcomes has to be enhanced to cope with a more complex, global business environment. Management will seek to associate groups of cost or revenue items in the database by such features as size, time or rates of change. This will have two impacts. It leads towards the development of expert systems to as-

sist the process of association, which is hard for humans to carry out unaided. Second, having identified actual costs and revenues of bundled elements, it is possible to simulate the probability of future outcomes for planning purposes.

An extension of the idea of stakeholder accountability is the potential for a company's database to be made available to stakeholders external to the entity for the purpose of making their own analyses. This empowers of those with interests in the fortune of the entity through a process which gives access to actual information and provides tools for projecting this historical data into the future using whichever assumptions they deem appropriate.

While the traditions of "entity" (AARF 1991) are strong, global trading can be made easier by the capacity to merge databases of different entities. This is a process which could, for example, give a marketing manager information at any time about the location and value of inventory items held by subsidiaries in different parts of the world. The entity concept, further, sets up a barrier which screens out information about events which *accountants* deem not to be part of the entity. Managers, on the other hand, are increasingly pressed to identify externalities in relevant cost studies and the analysis of the impact of actions which impact on the environment. To be effective in the future, each corporate database will contain data which relates both to itself and to other entities. This enlargement offers practical benefits without precluding the presentation of entity specific information.

CONCLUSION

Whether or not it is generally accepted, accounting is in a crisis because the double-entry system has been overtaken by the demands of a global enterprise framework. Management is tired of blunt basic information and reluctant to sanction a proliferation of disaggregated "back-pocket" systems.

A defence against criticism of the "doing" capability of accounting might be that spreadsheets are now being used. Alternatively, some might point to the work of the Accounting Education Change Commission as evidence of changing intention. Something much more radical is needed. This paper has presented the problem and given pointers to new directions. The challenge confronting accountants is whether there is the will to design and make a new accounting mould for the 21st century.

There will be a considerable responsibility for the design and maintenance of the new form accounting computer-based accounting systems including protocol definition and user servicing arrangement. The capacity to meet user needs must exist in future, present and past modes (i.e., simulation, real time and historical). The real-time data focus will encompass transactions as we know them today as well as a range of contingent and uncertain events.

The "process" functions described above of "gatekeeper," of "storeperson" and of "librarian" will require new skills and training for new form accountants who must be competent to fulfill each of these roles.

REFERENCES

AARF, Australian Accounting Research Foundation. 1991. Statement of Accounting Concepts 1 — Definition of the Reporting Entity. In C. Parker, ed. *Accounting and Auditing Handbook 1992*. Prentice Hall: 89–98.

Attaran, M., and D. Guseman. 1988. An Investigation into the Nature of Structural Changes within the Service Sector in the US. *Journal of the Market Research Society*, 30(3): 387–396.

———, and M. Sahafi. 1988. Concentration Trends and Profitability in the U.S. Manufacturing Sector: 1970–84. *Applied Economics*, 20(11): 1497–1510.

Brimson, J. 1986. How Advanced Manufacturing Technologies are Reshaping Cost Management. *Management Accounting* (USA): 25–29.

Cattell, R. 1991. What Are the Next-Generation Database Systems? *Communications of the ACM*, 34(10): 31–33.

Chatfield, M. 1974. *A History of Accounting Thought*. The Dryden Press.

Cooper, R., and R. S. Kaplan. 1988. Measure Costs Right: Make the Right Decisions. *Harvard Business Review*, 66(5): 96–103.

———, and ———. 1991. *The Design of Cost Management Systems: Text, Cases and Readings*. Prentice Hall.

Drucker, P. 1990. The Emerging Theory of Manufacturing. *Harvard Business Review*, 90(3): 94–102.

Duncan, W., P. Ginter, A. Rucks, and T. Jacobs. 1988. Intrapreneurship and the Reinvention of the Corporation. *Business Horizons* (May/June): 16–21.

Everest, G. C. 1986. *Database Management Objectives, System Function and Administration*. McGraw-Hill.

———, and R. Weber. 1977. A Relational Approach to Accounting Models. *The Accounting Review*, 52(2): 342–359.

Ferrera, W. 1990. Contribution Margin Analysis: No Longer Relevant/Strategic Cost Management: The New Paradigm. *Journal of Management Accounting Research*, 2: 1–31.

Geijsbeek, J. 1914. *Ancient Double-Entry Bookkeeping*. Reprint. Scholars Book Co.

Grinyer, P., S. Al-Bazzaz, and M. Yasai-Ardekani. 1986. Towards a Contingency Theory of Corporate Planning: Findings in 48 U.K. Companies. *Strategic Management Journal* 7(1): 3–28.

Hansen, J., and N. Hill. 1989. Control and Audit of Electronic Data Interchange. *MIS Quarterly*: 403–414.

Haseman, W., and A. Whinston. 1976. Design of a Multidimensional Accounting System. *The Accounting Review*, 51 (1): 65–79.

Hayes, R., and R. Jaikumar. 1988. Manufacturing's Crisis: New Technologies, Obsolete Organizations. *Harvard Business Review* (September/October): 77–85.

Howell, R., and S. Soucy. 1987. The New Manufacturing Environment: Major Trends for Management Accounting. *Management Accounting*, 69(1): 21–27.

———, and ———. 1988. Management Reporting in the New Manufacturing Environment. *Management Accounting*, 69(5): 22–29.

Ijiri, Y. 1982. *Triple Entry Bookkeeping and Income Momentum*. American Accounting Association.

———. 1989. *Momentum Accounting and Triple-Entry Bookkeeping: Exploring the Dynamic Structure*. American Accounting Association.

Kalashian, M. 1990. EDI: A Critical Link in Customer Responsiveness. *Manufacturing Systems*, 8(12): 20–26.

Khoshafian, S. 1990. Insight into Object-Oriented Databases. *Information & Software Technology*, 32(4): 274–289.

Kim, W., and F. Lochovsky, ed. 1989. *Object-Oriented Concepts, Databases and Applications*. Addison-Wesley.

Kumpe, T., and P. Bolwijn. 1988. Manufacturing: The New Case for Vertical Integration. *Harvard Business Review*, 66(2): 75–81.

Murphy, J., and S. Braund. 1990. Management Accounting and the New Manufacturing Technology. *Management Accounting* (UK), 68 (2): 38–40.

Peavey, D. 1990. Battle at the GAAP? It's Time for a Change. *Management Accounting* (USA), 71(8): 31–35.

Shank, J., and V. Govindarajan. 1989. *Strategic Cost Analysis*. Irwin.

Shields, M., and S. Young. 1991. Product Life Cycle Management. *Journal of Cost Management for the Manufacturing Industry* (Fall): 39–52.

Smith, M. 1990. The Rise and Rise of NFI. *Management Accounting* (UK), 68(5): 24–26.

Sorter, G. H. 1969. An "Events" Approach to Basic Accounting Theory. *The Accounting Review*, 44(1): 12–19.

Watts, R., and J. Zimmerman. 1990. *Positive Accounting Theory* (2nd ed.). Prentice Hall.

Weber, R. 1986. Data Models Research in Accounting: An Evaluation of Wholesale Distribution Software. *The Accounting Review*, 61(3): 498–518.

Winblad, A. L., S. D. Edwards, and D. R. King. 1990. *Object-Oriented Software*. Addison-Wesley.

Incorporating Practical Significance Results in Accounting Education Research: The Use of Effect Size Information

David E. Stout and Thomas L. Ruble

INTRODUCTION

Over the recent past, there has been a veritable explosion of empirical studies published in the accounting education journals. Rebele, Stout, and Hassell (1991) document this in their review of over 160 such studies published during the period 1985–1991. In general, this research has been concerned with methods or programs to improve the acquisition of relevant knowledge in the accounting field. Thus, the field has a practical concern toward applying the results of empirical research, not merely developing and validating educational theories.

Given a concern for application, the user of accounting education research needs to know whether the results of a particular study are likely to have a "meaningful" (rather than a "trivial" or unimportant) impact on the educational (that is, teaching and testing) process. Unfortunately, results pertaining to studies published in most accounting education journals do not provide information useful for judging the likely impact of those results on the educational process. Thus, the practical significance of the research is often difficult to discern.

In evaluating the results of research, practical significance is not equivalent to statistical significance. Tests of statistical significance are commonplace in behavioral research, including accounting education research. Unfortunately, misinterpretations of the term "significance" in this context are commonplace also.

In everyday language, the term "significance" has a variety of meanings and typically refers to something that is important or meaningful. However, in statistical hypothesis testing, significance has a very narrow technical meaning. Researchers expect to find differences between groups or relationships among variables in samples drawn from certain populations. The observed differences or relationships are evaluated in terms of the probability that they might occur by chance even if no such differences or relationships exist in the population. A low probability level (usually .05) is selected as the standard to judge whether the observed results could reasonably be attributed to chance. If the statistical test indicates a low probability that the observed differences or relationships occurred by chance (say, $p < .05$), the results are termed "statistically significant."

Unfortunately, a test of significance does not indicate that the results obtained are "important" or useful in a practical sense. With a large enough sample, virtually any difference or relationship, no matter how trivial, will yield p-values deemed significant at levels less than .05. (In the extreme, if the researcher is working with population data, inferential statistics become unnecessary. One need only observe whether the reported means under analysis are different.) Games and Klare (1967), among many others, note that statistical significance is a necessary, but not sufficient, condition for an obtained result (difference in means) to be important in a practical sense.

Since statistical significance does not provide sufficient information to judge practical significance, many researchers (across disciplines) and statisticians have recommended reporting effect size information in published empirical studies. In this context, "effect size" refers to the *degree* to which the phenomenon under study is present in the population (Cohen 1988, 9). Oakes (1986, 49) uses the term "size of effect" to mean either the size of the difference between two population means or the strength of association between variables. Others refer to this construct as "magnitude of effects" (Friedman 1968), "strength of relations" (Kerlinger 1986), or "proportion of shared variance" (Hays 1988).

Regardless of the terms used, estimates of effect size provide information considered relevant to assessing the practical significance (or importance) of research findings. With respect to policy decisions, effect size information provides a basis for judging whether the observed difference is large enough to have a meaningful impact. Such infor-

David E. Stout is an Associate Professor at Villanova University and Thomas L. Ruble is a member of the faculty at Rider College.

mation is meant to complement, not supplant, statistical significance tests. Thus, we argue for reporting effect size information in accounting education research.

In the next section of this paper, we present some basic notions concerning measures of effect size. We include popular effect size measures for simple comparisons (one-factor designs) and more complex (factorial) ANOVA research designs. We include in this section a brief discussion of cautions and limitations of effect size measures. This is followed by a review of the disclosure of effect size information in published accounting research (education and noneducation). The paper concludes with a summary a set of recommendations.

BASIC NOTIONS OF EFFECT SIZE MEASURES

Assume we want to examine the effect of aptitude (as measured by SAT score) on the performance of accounting students in their major (measured by GPA in upper-division courses). To assess this relationship, we correlate SAT scores with GPA. Both variables in this model are continuous. The product-moment correlation coefficient (r) expresses the degree of association and (r^2) indicates the proportion of variance in GPA due to SAT. The statistic r^2 can be interpreted as the effect size of SAT on GPA. Thus, correlational studies provide a relatively direct measure of effect size (strength of relations) (Kerlinger 1986).

As a second example, assume we are interested in assessing the relationship between student gender and accounting GPA. In this case, the independent variable is categorical rather than continuous. To assess the effect of gender, we test for differences in mean grades between male and female students. The basic strategy for estimating effect size in this case, and in other experimental designs, is to translate group differences into correlational terms (cf. Friedman 1968; Kerlinger 1986; Oakes 1986). First, t-tests or F-tests are used to determine the statistical significance (i.e., probability of chance occurrence) of the observed group difference. Next, using the t or F-statistic, we can compute the strength of association of the categorical form of the independent variable (gender) with the continuous dependent variable (accounting GPA). This measure can be squared to provide an estimate of the shared variance or effect size. While this approach has some limitations and cautions, the result is information relevant to assessing the practical significance of the observed differences.

We turn now to a more formal presentation of effect size measures for some simple (but commonly used) research designs. Such designs are found in many recent accounting education studies.

Simple Comparisons (One-Factor Designs)

A number of measures have been proposed to estimate effect size in single-factor experimental studies. Of the different alternatives, two measures have received the greatest attention: (1) eta squared and (2) omega squared.

Eta (also known as the correlation ratio) is a rather straightforward index of relations often used with data that are not linear (Kerlinger 1986). Eta squared provides a measure of the proportion of variance shared by two variables in a specific sample.

The general formula for computing eta squared is very simple:

$$\text{eta squared} = \frac{\text{SS}_{\text{between groups}}}{\text{SS}_{\text{total}}}$$

Readers should note that eta squared is included as part of the output for the ANOVA program in *SPSS* (including *SPSS-PC*) and, thus, is readily available to most researchers.

Omega squared is an estimate of the strength of association between the independent variable and the population dependent variable (Kerlinger 1986; Hays 1988). Thus, omega squared is considered as an "inferential" statistic (Maxwell, Camp, and Arvey 1981) which can be generalized beyond the specific sample. Omega squared is included as part of the output for the MANOVA program in *SPSS*, Mainframe Version 5.

For the two-group case (for example, a study of the relationship between accounting grades and student gender), the following formula can be used to *estimate* omega squared using information from a t-test performed on the difference between sample means (Hays 1988, 312):

$$\text{omega squared} = \frac{t^2 - 1}{t^2 + N1 + N2 - 1}$$

In single-factor designs where there are more than two groups ($j > 2$), the following general formula can be used to estimate omega squared (Hays 1988, 375) after a one-way ANOVA is performed:

$$\text{omega squared} = \frac{\text{SS}_{\text{between groups}} - {(j-1)}\text{MS}_{\text{within groups}}}{\text{SS}_{\text{total}} + {}^{\text{MS}}\text{within groups}}$$

It should be noted that the above formula does not provide an unbiased estimate of the population value. As noted by Fleiss (1969) and by Kerlinger (1986), omega squared provides a conservative estimate of the population effect size.

More Complex (Factorial) ANOVA Designs

The procedure for estimating omega squared can be extended easily to two-factor designs. Hays (1988, 453) and Keppel (1982, 204) provide formulas for estimating omega squared based on information commonly available in standard ANOVA tables.

The extension of omega squared to multifactor and multivariate designs is somewhat problematic. The statistical computations may become burdensome in these more complex designs. Moreover, interpretations of relative effect size may become difficult in complex designs (Ronis 1981). While these issues are beyond the scope of the present paper, the interested researcher can consult any of a number of advanced papers in the area (see, for example, Fowler [1987]).

Cautions and Limitations

Both eta squared and omega squared should be used cautiously in estimating effect size. Both of these measures are biased estimators of the population relationship between the independent and dependent variables (Fleiss 1969; Maxwell et al. 1981). Without the adjustment to eta squared (cf. Haase, Ellis, and Ladany 1989), this descriptive statistic tends to overestimate the effect size in the population. Omega squared may underestimate the population effect size (Fleiss 1969). These tendencies may be particularly troublesome if sample sizes are small (i.e., 10 subjects or less) (Keppel 1982; Maxwell et al., 1981). However, Maxwell et al. (1981) note that the bias effect is usually small.

Probably the greatest danger in interpreting effect size measures is the tendency to oversimplify their meaning and overgeneralize from the results of a single study. This problem is similar to the problems of misinterpreting measures of statistical significance (cf. Keppel 1982). Measures of effect size must be interpreted in terms of the context of the particular study under consideration. As O'Grady (1982, 766) notes, optimal use of measures of explained variance can be made when researchers examine the agreement between the magnitude that their theory would suggest and the empirical finding.

Despite the need for caution in interpreting effect size information, the argument for including this information is compelling. According to Kerlinger (1986, 218), from a practical and applied standpoint, eta squared, omega squared, or other measures of association should *always* be calculated and reported in empirical research (emphasis ours).

USE OF EFFECT SIZE INFORMATION IN ACCOUNTING EDUCATION STUDIES

Based on the preceding considerations, we wanted to determine the extent to which published studies in accounting education disclose effect size information. Therefore, we reviewed all empirical studies published in the three major accounting education journals (viz., the *Journal of Accounting Education, Issues in Accounting Education*, and *The Accounting Educators' Journal*) through Spring 1991. We limited our review to those studies that had used a regression or an ANOVA/ANCOVA design. The results of this review can be summarized as follows. One, across all 103 empirical studies included in our sample, only a minority (less than 20%) reported effect size information. Two, an even smaller percentage of studies using an ANOVA/ANCOVA/t-test design reported such information (6.8% of 88 studies). Of the six studies in this category that did report effect size information, five reported R-squared values; only one of the six reported omega squared. Three, of the studies using a regression design, 14 of 15 reported R-squared information; of the 14, only 2 reported incremental R-squared information obtained through a hierarchical (step-wise) approach.

An overall conclusion that can be drawn from this analysis is that empirical researchers in accounting education do not routinely report effect size information. (This same conclusion was reported in literature reviews in management, marketing, and education published in the early 1980s.) As we have argued, inclusion of such information would be informative to paper reviewers, journal editors, and readers as they attempt to discern the practical significance of reported empirical test results.

USE OF EFFECT SIZE INFORMATION IN OTHER ACCOUNTING STUDIES

Also, we wanted to determine the extent to which other areas in accounting routinely report effect size information in published empirical research. Our review of *Behavioral Research in Accounting, The Accounting Review*, and the *Journal of Management Accounting Research* yielded the following three references: Harsha and Knapp (1990), Poe, Shearon, and Strawser (1991), and Beck, Davis, and Jung (1991).

Harsha and Knapp (1990) addressed the general problem of making cross-study comparisons using repeated-measures (i.e., within subjects) versus between-subjects designs in behavioral accounting research. The authors advise (p. 50) that when cross-study comparisons are made, researchers should consider both levels of statistical significance and the strength of association between independent and dependent variables. To the best of our knowledge, this was the first behavioral (albeit nonempirical) accounting paper to include a discussion of the importance of effect size information in published research.

Beck et al. (1991) report experimental test results concerning the effects of income uncertainty and other economic factors (tax rate, penalty rate, and audit probability) on taxpayer aggressiveness as measured by self-reported taxable income. Three separate experiments were performed and the results analyzed using a balanced repeated measures ANOVA design (equal n's per cell).

In deciding on "parsimonious" ANOVAs (i.e., which model tests to report in their paper), the authors state (pp. 545, 548) that some higher order interactions are not disclosed in the paper, even though such interactions were "statistically significant." Their justification for this decision was that none of these effects was predicted theoretically, and that the percentage of variance explained by these omitted effects (i.e., omega-squared statistics) was less than one percent for any individual factor and, in total, was less than three percent in the ANOVA models. This is an interesting application of effect size information in empirical accounting research.

Poe et al. (1991) investigated the effects of managers' perceptions of the style used by supervisors to evaluate their performance on their own personal evaluation styles when accounting information is included in the evaluation process. The authors used ANOVA to test for the statistical significance of the various factors in their model. In addition, they reported estimated omega-squared statistics to identify the most important of these factors.

Our brief review of the noneducation accounting literature can be summarized as follows. First, only three published studies to date have included practical significance (effect size) information. Two, all three of these studies were published recently (1990 and 1991). Three, these studies represent an interesting (though perhaps limited) cross-section of topics and journal outlets. One could expect that reporting of this information in the future may be more commonplace in the noneducation accounting journals we examined.

CONCLUSIONS

Significant resources (time, effort, money) are currently being devoted to the conduct and dissemination of research studies in accounting education. Many, perhaps most, of these studies are empirical in nature, dealing with topics such as the process of teaching accounting and assessing student performance. In short, much of recent empirical research in accounting education has taken a decidedly practical orientation.

Given increasing curricular demands and teaching loads, accounting professors may be relying on this body of published research to provide guidance for ways to improve their own teaching. In evaluating empirical education research, it is important to distinguish sharply between *statistical* significance and *practical* significance of reported results. The magnitude and statistical significance of effects are logically independent features of data from samples. Therefore, we recommend that researchers in accounting education routinely calculate and report measures of effect size (variance explained) along with statistical testing results. This information will allow authors, paper reviewers, and readers to better assess the practical significance (importance) of observed empirical results. In turn, accounting educators will be better able to judge the extent to which published recommendations are likely to lead to meaningful changes in the educational process.

REFERENCES

Beck, P. J., J. S. Davis, and W. Jung. 1991. Experimental Evidence on Taxpayer Reporting Under Uncertainty. *The Accounting Review* (July): 535–558.

Cohen, J. 1988. *Statistical Power Analysis for the Behavioral Sciences*, 2nd ed. Lawrence Erlbaum Associates.

Fleiss, J. L. 1969. Estimating the Magnitude of Experimental Effects. *Psychological Bulletin* (Vol. 72): 273–276.

Fowler, R. L. 1987. A General Model for Comparing Effect Magnitudes in ANOVA Designs. *Educational and Psychological Measurement* (Vol. 47): 361–367.

Friedman, H. 1968. Magnitude of Experimental Effect and a Table for Its Rapid Estimation. *Psychological Bulletin* (Vol. 70): 245–251.

Games, P. A., and G. R. Klare. 1967. *Elementary Statistics: Data Analysis for the Behavioral Sciences.* McGraw-Hill.

Haase, R. F., M. V. Ellis, and N. Ladany. 1989. Multiple Criteria for Evaluating the Magnitude of Experimental Effects. *Journal of Counseling Psychology* (Vol. 36): 511–516.

Harsha, P. D., and M. C. Knapp. 1990. The Use of Within- and Between-Subjects Experimental Designs in Behavioral Accounting Research: A Methodological Note. *Behavioral Research in Accounting*: 50–62.

Hays, W. L. 1988. *Statistics*, 4th ed. Holt, Rinehart, & Winston.

Keppel, G. 1982. *Design & Analysis: A Researcher's Handbook*, 2nd ed. Prentice-Hall, Inc.

Kerlinger, F. N. 1986. *Foundations of Behavioral Research*, 3rd ed. Holt, Rinehart, & Winston.

Maxwell, S. E., C. J. Camp, and R. D. Arvey. 1981. Measures of Strength of Association: A Comparative Examination. *Journal of Applied Psychology* (Vol. 66): 525–534.

Oakes, M. 1986. *Statistical Inference: A Commentary for the Social and Behavioural Sciences.* John Wiley & Sons.

O'Grady, K. E. 1982. Measures of Explained Variance: Cautions and Limitations. *Psychological Bulletin* (Vol. 92): 766–777.

Poe, C. D., W. T. Shearon, Jr., and R. H. Strawser. 1991. Accounting Evaluative Styles and the Contagion Effect in Middle-Managers. *Journal of Management Accounting Research* (Fall): 169–193.

Rebele, J. E., D. E. Stout, and J. M. Hassell. A Review of Empirical Research in Accounting Education: 1985-1991. *Journal of Accounting Education* (Fall): 167–231.

Ronis, D. L. 1981. Comparing the Magnitude of Effects in ANOVA Designs. *Educational and Psychological Measurement* (Vol. 41): 993–1000.

Towards Understanding the Gap between Accounting Research and Practice

Siva Velayutham and Asheq Rahman

INTRODUCTION

There is a growing concern about a gap between accounting research and practice. This gap was, most recently, highlighted in a plenary session at the 1990 Annual Meeting of the American Accounting Association by S. Sunder and R. K. Elliot.[1] Table 1 provides an overview of the nature of the gap as depicted in the accounting literature. This review indicates three major reasons for the gap, namely (1) lack of communication between researchers and practitioners, (2) inappropriate research output for practicing purposes and (3) contradictory views on research lagging behind practice or *vice versa*.

The purpose of this study is to investigate the second reason and determine why research outputs are perceived to be inappropriate for practice. One of the major research outputs identified in accounting literature is the development of accounting theories. In this paper accounting theories are reviewed to understand why they lack the appropriateness as desired by the practitioners.

The second section of this paper adopts a framework on which theories can be classified according to their level of development. In the third section the accounting theories are reviewed and matched with the classification framework of the second section. Based on the understanding acquired in the third section, in the fourth section an attempt is made to identify and provide reasons for the gap between accounting theories and the desired needs of accounting practice.

LEVELS OF THEORY DEVELOPMENT

The word "theory" is normally used as if it has a simple clear-cut meaning when in fact it is a generic term with a range of meanings. Because of this, theories have been classified based on assumptions, methodology and function (for example see Rahman 1989, 2–3). These classifications however fail to take into account the stages of development of a theory.

Smith (1968) put forward a model of theory development based on the uses of the term "theory" and the levels of proposition making. In his model Smith classified theory into five levels. These levels are briefly explained as follows.

Level 1

Theories at level 1 are those that are based on common sense, or on assumptions accepted by the society, or on personal whims. Such beliefs, ideas and preferences have rarely been examined scientifically, that is through systematic analysis or empirical experimentation.

Level 2

Level 2 is a more scientific level, for here a hypothesis, although incorporating a narrow area of knowledge, has been tested empirically, observed and described systematically, and/or analysed logically and conclusions have confirmed the belief.

Level 3

Level 3 comprises theories for which a hypothesis has come to be regarded as a principle or a law through its confirmation from many different sets of experimental tests. Since the principle or law is based on much confirming evidence, it can be accepted as a working fact for the sake of practice.

Level 4

Level 4 theories can be described as a series of interconnected facts, principles, laws and/or hypotheses, forming an integrated explanation of a larger area of man's knowledge — a structured body of knowledge.

Level 5

The fifth sense of "theory" does not grow in a systematised way from the levels before it. Many people have a more or less coherent set of personal

---

[1]See *Issues in Accounting Education* (Spring 1991), 1.

Siva Velayutham and Asheq Rahman are at Massey University.

The authors acknowledge the financial assistance of the Massey University Research Fund. They also thank Associate Professor M. H. B. Perera for reviewing the paper.

TABLE 1

Review of the Literature on the Gap between Accounting Research and Practice

Author/s	Type of Gap	Reasons for the Gap	Proposed Solution
1. Sterling (1973) -A	Research is isolated from practice.	1. Research outputs are not practised. 2. Educators teach accepted practice, not research output. 3. Resistance to reform within the profession.	Educators should teach the research results as the desired state and teach accepted practice as the current state.
2. Mautz (1974) -P	Gap between the real world of the practitioner and the educational world.	Practitioners expect immediate solutions in a complex world. Academics theorise in a simple world.	Education should provide for: 1. Conceptual understanding, 2. Technical skills, 3. Business judgment, 4. Professional responsibilities, 5. Basic virtues of life.
3. Staubus (1975) -A	Research results do not reach the professionals.	Value of research is uncertain and evidence is not well organised.	Teach well-established decision-usefulness approach.
4. Flint and Shaw (1981) -A	Research is not relevant and does not have sufficient authority to lead practice. Communication gap.	Research results are not relevant and not conclusive. Separate academic and practitioner journals.	Improve impact of research on practice. Results of research should have relevance or potential relevance to practice. Accounting research results should be: 1. Authoritative, 2. Relevant, 3. Communicated.
5. Baxter (1988) -A	Gap exists between research and practice.	1. Research is geared towards acquiring new knowledge whereas practice demands solutions for immediate application. 2. Research results are too remote from practice.	Professional bodies should commission more applied research to bridge the gap between academic research and practice.

(Continued on next page)

TABLE 1 (Continued)

Author/s	Type of Gap	Reasons for the Gap	Proposed Solution
		3. Academic researchers have broader background than practitioners.	
		4. Academics look for theories and principles whereas practitioners seek new techniques.	
6. McLean (1988) -P/A	Practice is lagging behind research and development.	1. The lag between theoretical development and practical acceptance.	1. Need for practice-based research and development capable of offering short-term insights into the practice of management accounting.
		2. Many large firms do not even think of management accounting as a tool for expansion. Mergers and acquisitions are in vogue.	2. Both academics and practitioners should research and publish their views.
		3. Management accounting theory is inappropriate for complex problems.	
7. Scapens (1988) -A	1. Mode of communication used by researchers is remote from practice.	Type of research method used did stress the development of techniques but not its usage.	Need for: 1. Case studies in practice environment.
	2. Research has not kept pace with new manufacturing techniques.		2. Broadening the area of research to include noneconomic business practices.
8. Flint (1988) -A	Gap between interests of academics and practitioners.	1. Adds to Baxter's (1988) list unlike other professions, lack of a common comprehensive education for academics and practitioners.	Establish a research council to bring the academic and practitioners together.
		2. Absence of a theoretical intellectual enquiry in professional development.	

(Continued on next page)

TABLE 1 (Continued)

Author/s	Type of Gap	Reasons for the Gap	Proposed Solution
9. Williamson (1989) -A	Mismatch between management accounting theory and practice.	3. The increasing vigour and intensity of research making it less intelligible to nonresearchers.	Partnership between academics/researchers and practitioners to develop research results.
		1. Textbooks are written for passing exams, not for guiding practice.	
		2. Case studies written by academics without input from practitioners.	
		3. Research is devoid of inputs from practitioners and nonaccounting executives.	
		4. Current practice is not reported by practitioners.	
10. Elliot (1990) -P	Accounting practice lagging behind business needs.	Accounting practice is providing for industrial era enterprises, whereas enterprises are in the information era.	Rethink accounting paradigms. Accounting information should help entitles attain goals. Accounting should provide real time information, not just past information. Implicitly, accounting research should help in bridging the gap between practice and business needs.
11. Williamson (1989) -P/A	Education lags behind changing practising needs.	Emphasis on the designing of techniques.	Not just teach techniques but encourage broad learning. Redress the balance between teaching and research.
12. Sunder (1990) -A	Accounting research follows practice. It should lead practice.	Research ideas are not communicated to practioners, or being highly technical, are not adopted in practice.	Teach research output in the classroom so that students take it to the profession. Pursue research to understand the new managerial regime, not just the past.

A = Academic
P = Practitioner

ideas about reality. Theories at this level are a complete statement of beliefs of such people with a view to explaining reality. In other words, these theories are speculative systems that attempt to account for the most general ideas about reality, that is, existence, knowledge, and values.

In Smith's scheme of theory development, level 1 is an elementary level and levels 2 to 4 grow out of the preceding levels. Level 5 theories are above other theories in terms of the scope of the phenomena they attempt to explain. Smith argued that when the term "theory" is used, any one of the above five meanings could be intended. He also felt that when people claimed, for example, that there may never be a theory of education (e.g., Snow 1977) the meaning adopted is the fourth sense. In Smith's classification, level 3 and 4 theories are more attuned to the needs of practice than the theories in other levels.

Fleming (1990) adopted Smith's model to explain conflicting views on the usefulness of theories of education to the practice of education. He reinforced Smith's views and added that research effort directed towards the development and testing of level 3 and 4 theories in education could be counterproductive. Level 3 theories were felt to be an impossibility due the problems associated with the validation of level 2 theories. Fleming felt that in education appropriate instruments for measuring and validating level 2 concepts were lacking, and without the validation of level 2 concepts, level 3 theories could not be established. As for level 5 theories, it is difficult to gain wide acceptance for such theories due to their very nature — personal ideas and views of reality.

THE NATURE OF ACCOUNTING THEORIES

Belkaoui (1985, 11) observed that no comprehensive theory of accounting exists at the present time. He noted that different theories have been and continue to be proposed in the accounting literature. Many of these theories, he felt, arise from the use of different approaches to the construction of a theory or from the attempt to develop theories of a "middle range" rather than one single comprehensive theory.[2] Such middle range accounting theories result from differences in the way researchers perceive both the users of accounting information and the environment in which both the users and preparers of accounting information behave.

Basically, there are two schools of thought in accounting research — the positive-inductive and the normative-deductive (see AAA 1977). The purpose of accounting theory therefore varies according to the perspective of theory development chosen by the respective researcher. There can also be overlaps between the methodology adopted in theories. For example, inductive theories may tend to empirically test hypotheses which have been deductively derived from earlier theories of the same or related disciplines. Therefore, it may not be possible to distinctly classify theories amongst the different schools [see Rahman (1989) for the problems associated with theory classification].

Nevertheless, accounting theories are analysed for the purposes of this paper to understand the level of development of certain broad categories of accounting theories. These categories of accounting theories are listed in Table 2. In Table 2, first the theories are classified according to the intended or underlying purpose behind each theory or class of theories. Second, the basic assumption/s and methodology adopted in each category are identified.

Based on the broad features identified in Table 2 and other aspects as identified in accounting literature, each category of accounting theory is analysed to determine its level of development within Smith's schema (the last column of Table 2 provides a summary of this analysis).

Substantially Descriptive Theories

Descriptive theories in accounting are theories that are derived from "what accounting is." Littleton (1953) reinforced this belief by explaining that accounting theorists must look to accounting to determine why accounting is what it is and then develop theory inductively.

1. Stewardship

    According to Mathews and Perera (1991, 73–74), stewardship is the oldest of the functions of financial accounts. Stewardship in accounting arises due to the separation of ownership and control. Stewardship refers to the relationship between owners and managers under which the function of financial statements is to demonstrate that the resources entrusted to managers have been used in a proper manner.

    Early 20th century authors such as Sprague (1907), Hatfield (1927) and Paton (1922) used

---

[2]Perhaps the *Statement of Accounting Theory and Theory Acceptance,* 1977, was the last aborted attempt at constructing such a theory.

TABLE 2
Types of Accounting Theory

| Purpose | Approaches to Theory Formulation | | | | | Underlying Assumptions | | | | | | | Level on Smith's Classification |
| | Non-theoretical | | Theoritical | | | | | | | | | | |
	Practical	Authoritative	Deductive	Inductive	Eclectic	Economic	Sociological	Ethical	Human	Behaviour	Communication	Theory	
I. Descriptive													
1. Stewardship	X			X					X				1
2. EMH				X		X			X				2
3. Agency				X		X			X				2
4. Behavioural				X				X	X				2
5. Deconstruction			X								X		1
6. Critical			X				X						5
II. Normative													
1. Decision Usefulness			X			X		X	X				5
2. Information Economics			X			X			X				5
3. Accountability			X					X	X		X		1 & 5
4. Professional promulgations		X			X	X	X	X	X		X		1

an inductive approach to develop accounting theory based on the notion of stewardship. They established ideas and preferences for certain aspects of accounting, for example historical cost for quantification, by simply observing the behaviour of accountants within their environment. Since most such early theories were based on ideas derived from practice, much of the beliefs established by them could be seen as pragmatic measures applicable to similar practices but not necessarily all-embracing principles. Therefore, we can classify most stewardship based views as level 1 theories in Smith's classification scheme.

2. Efficient Market Hypothesis

Efficient Market Hypothesis (EMH) may well be called a hypothesis since it is yet to be proven in accounting as well as in economics, from which the notion has been derived. In this class of research, Belkaoui (1985, 122–123) explains, it is generally assumed that the securities market is efficient and the market price of securities always equals the underlying intrinsic values at every instant in time. Intrinsic value is generally regarded as what the price ought to be and what the price would be given that other individuals possess the same information and competence as the person making the estimate. One of the most important implications of this notion to accounting is that if the securities market is efficient, then there is no or very little need for accounting information for those who use it for operating in a securities market.

Belkaoui (1985, 123–133) states a few reasons why EMH can still be regarded as a hypothesis. First, there are several competing definitions of market efficiency. Second, there is anomalous evidence regarding market efficiency. Third, some studies show self-selection bias and omitted variables. Finally, the presence of confounding effects poses a serious threat to the internal validity of EMH studies.

Since EMH is yet to attain the status of theory, we may classify it as a level 2 theory in Smith's schema. The hypothesis in this case has been deduced from economic theories and is still in the process of being refined in accountancy. If proven and accepted, it may be regarded as a level 3 principle.

3. Agency

The premise of agency theory is that the corporation is the locus or intersection of contractual relationships that exist among management, owners, creditors, employees and government. The theory is concerned with the various costs of monitoring and enforcing relations among these various groups. In accounting, agency theory posits a conflict in interest between those groups that is mitigated to some extent by financial reporting. Agency theory has also been used to explain the demand for audits. The auditor acts as an independent verifier of financial reports submitted by managers to owners. Agency arguments all relate to the incentives for the managers to report information about themselves to owners and to other users of financial information in general. Therefore, agency theory is employed to explain that there are private incentives arising through contractual relationships for reliable and voluntary reporting by firms (Wolk, Francis, and Tearney 1989, 42–43, 81–83).

Agency theory is not a new perspective in accounting research. Traditionally, this type of research appeared under the notion of stewardship but was limited to the relationship between the managers as the stewards and the owners as the investors and beneficiaries. The broadening of this stewardship perspective into various other forms of agency relationships is fairly new and intensive research under this theme started only in the late 1970s. Hence, hypothesis development and testing seem to be in the early stages.

The agency perspective, perhaps because of its infancy and also due to some methodological deficiencies, has faced severe criticisms (see Watts and Zimmerman 1990). A more recent and vehement attack on the agency framework by Sterling (1990) [not cited in Watts and Zimmerman 1990] revealed some important deficiencies of this framework and the research done till now under this perspective. Sterling noted that the agency perspective allowed for a study of accountants and others who deal with the selection of accounting methods rather than a research in the discipline of accounting (p. 131). This, he felt, led to the prohibition of the assessment of practice which in turn precluded progress. In his opinion, more generally, the positive accounting literature, of which agency theory is a segment, has failed to provide any thing that was not known earlier.

This and other allegations/shortcomings (some in terms of methodology; see Watts and Zimmerman 1990) indicate that, although the agency theory research has made serious inroads into understanding the nature of financial reporting, the theory is still at the hypothesis development and testing stage. Consequently, in Smith's framework it can be classified as a level 2 theory.

4. Behavioural

The behavioural approach to accounting theory development emphasises the way individuals and groups react to accounting information. According to this approach accounting is assumed to be action oriented; its purpose is to influence action (behaviour) directly through the information content of the message conveyed and indirectly through the behaviour of accountants (Belkaoui 1985, 85). Much of the research in this area has been based on controlled laboratory experiments using student subjects and some field studies (Wolk et al. 1989). This approach also includes human information processing research.

Belkaoui (1985) found, however, that most studies in this area have made little attempt to formulate a theoretical framework to support the problems or hypotheses to be tested. Dickhaut, Livingstone, and Watson (1972) also found the application of studies using surrogates for the broad population of real decision makers highly suspect. Mathews and Perera (1991, 61) in a similar vein argued that this cannot be a complete approach for the development of accounting.

Questions raised about the validity of findings and lack of a theoretical framework therefore limits its usefulness. Therefore, it can only be classified as a level 2 theory in Smith's schema.

5. Deconstruction

This approach mainly draws on the works of Jacques Derrida and its aim is to locate contradictions in a text or theory by examining the process of its production. This, its supporters argue, would open the text or theory to multiple interpretations (Belsey 1980). Macintosh (1989) argues that this would be valuable in understanding why currently accounting seems mired in controversy and disagreement about accounting practices and theory building.

Wolk et al. (1989, 44) point out that deconstruction calls into question the very notion of theory itself. Proponents of deconstruction research set out to develop a coherent idea of reality, and therefore in Smith's schema this approach can probably be considered as a level 1 theory.

6. Critical

Critical theory was developed by a group of philosophers, known as the "Frankfurt School" who argued that most societies are permeated with "objective illusion." This, they believed, caused human beings to suffer from self-inflicted delusion and a fettered existence. The objective then was to effect a transition of society to a state where agents are free from false consciousness and liberated from self-inflicted coercion (Macintosh 1990).

Critical works in accounting have mainly been concerned with the determination of institution's function, and the impact of accounting on economic planning, power distribution, value clarification and political manoeuvring (Macintosh 1990). Critical theorists seldom set out to develop principles, and their role in a democratic and capitalist society is ambiguous (Wolk et al. 1989, 45). This type of theory can only fall into level 5 of Smith's schema because it explains reality using a statement of beliefs of those who propagate it.

Substantially Normative

Normative theories in accounting are theories that are derived from "what should be." Normative theories are usually derived using the deductive approach. Construction of theories using this approach begins with establishing the objectives of accounting. Based on the objectives, a logical structure for its accomplishment is developed (Mathew and Perera, 1991, 58).

1. Decision Usefulness

This approach stresses the relevance of accounting information for particular decisions by a particular user group or groups. The main comprehensive works in this area are by Chambers (1966), Edwards and Bell (1961), Sterling (1970).

These works are good examples of level 5 type theory because each one of them forms a comprehensive speculative system which tends to explain reality but are difficult to be tested in the real world. Accordingly, practitioners have also resisted the introduction of such models.

2. Information Economics

Information economics research, according to Wolk et al. (1989, 43, 220–221), is usually analytical/deductive in nature. Information economics analysis tries to determine the value of specific information for a narrowly defined decision. Whether the benefits of alternative information sets or larger information sets are worth their cost or the question of which are the optimal sets of policies can be analysed through information economics. An important facet of information economics is that it appreciates how accounting information is likely to have value in the decision-making process.

However, Wolk et al. (1989, 221) point out that because of its abstractness and generality, the multiuser setting of information economics has not yielded specific conclusions concerning the value of accounting information. Therefore, the approach is still too general to provide specific answers.

Information economics also draws its basic premise from economics and dwells on the notions of cost benefit and demand supply of information. It offers an explicit individual demand–based analysis of accounting policy questions. Rationality is the major assumption employed. This approach provides a means for examining whether regulatory intervention is desirable for external financial reporting (see AAA 1977 for a detailed review). This analytical scheme, according to Verrecchia (1982, 17) lacks empirical evidence and appears to have no general consensus. Works in this area perhaps can be classified as speculative theories within level 5 of Smith's scheme.

3. Accountability

    The objective of accounting according to this view is to account for actions taken in various marketplaces for products, services, employment and the environment. This view is based on the following thesis:

    > The technology of an economic system imposes a structure on its society which not only determines the economic activities but also influences its social relationships and well being. (Mobley 1970)

    The impact of economic systems on society, employees and environment is generally accepted, but interest in noneconomic information has, however, varied over time and, consequently, practitioner interest has also been mild. Efforts to develop a comprehensive theory in this area has been low as well as measurement of the influence of economic systems on the environment, employees and society is also primitive. Therefore theoretical output of this approach can only be categorised as level 1 or 5 type theories in Smith's schema.

4. Professional Promulgations

    AAA (1977) concluded that there exists in financial accounting literature not a theory of financial accounting but a collection of theories. This situation has led to the development and use of different methods and bases of accounting.

    The use of different methods led to lack of comparability among financial statements and consequently criticisms of the profession. These criticisms have led to the development of standards and conceptual frameworks. The professional promulgations are usually based on consensus and are always changing. Professional promulgations in general are not hypotheses for testing but solutions for immediate problems based on various ideas of reality and therefore can be classified as level 1 type theories.

THE GAP

One of the criteria used for a definition of a profession in a multiple criteria definition offered by Schein (1973) is the following

> The professional makes his decision on behalf of a client in terms of *general principles, theories or propositions*, which he applies to the particular case under consideration i.e. by universalistic standards. (p. 8) [Emphasis added]

All occupations seeking professionalisation have sought to develop a systematic theory, and the accounting profession is no exception (Chambers 1955). Initially, accounting theories consisted of authoritarian principles and "generally accepted accounting principles." This kind of theory is, however, felt to be insufficient for decision making by professionals in any field as argued by Goode (1961) when commenting on the librarian as a professional. According to Goode, such theories have little reference to general scientific principles and are more like rule of thumb regulations (p. 39).

Arguments with a similar view were raised in accounting by Chambers (1955). Flint and Shaw (1981), in addition, argued that an important criterion for determining useful accounting research from the perspective of practice is authority, that is, to arrive at conclusive relationships having a high degree of certainty, which can be used by practitioners as universal standards to make decisions. This is what Sparrow (1981), a practitioner, argued is missing from accounting research and theory. His assertion is also supported in this paper in the review of accounting theories using Smith's model. Only theories in levels 3 and 4 would have sufficient authority to replace "generally accepted accounting principles" as guidelines for decision making. This kind of theory, however, as shown by our review, is nonexistent in accounting.

This then begs the question "Would the development of level 3 and 4 type theories be ever possible in accounting?" Chambers (1972) at the peak of the normative theory period wrote:

> Researchers and practitioners both entertain the expectation that research will lead to advances in practice. But there would be more disciplined research if practitioners refuse to take notice of research work unless or until the products of inquiry had been thoroughly debated by researchers themselves, were substantially supported by evidence and were in the form of tightly constructed and well defined proposals. (p. 73)

Ten years later, noting the lack of impact of research on practice and the failure of the researchers to arrive at a generally acceptable coherent and consistent set of principles, one practitioner noted:

> Since his statement, we have spent practically ten years with practitioners refusing to take notice of research work. Moreover, researchers are not able to reach a consensus on their research results. I believe the time has come for practitioners and researchers to get together and, at least, speak the same language. (Sparrow 1981, 29)

This situation raises the question of why efforts by accounting researchers to emulate their colleagues in the pure sciences to develop level 3 and 4 type theories has not been very successful. Similar records of poor success in areas such as education has led to calls for abandonment of basic research and concentration on applied research (Ebel 1969).

Fleming (1990) points out that research in a young science has two major functions. One is to identify the basic variables, measure them and study their interrelationships, and the other to discover which of the techniques used by practitioners are really successful. He continues that when the basic variables and their relationships, and successful techniques have been identified, then it would be possible to investigate why these techniques are successful. This way, a step towards developing level 3 or 4 type theories could be taken through the determination of the mix of variables needed for successful practice.

Accounting researchers, however, have attempted to take a quantum leap without the development of a sound foundation. Applied research like the works of Sanders et al. (1938) were discouraged and at the same time research on the definition and means of measuring the basic elements (assets, liabilities and income) were not encouraged sufficiently. Instead accounting researchers went ahead to discover "if . . . then . . . ." propositions (see Watts and Zimmerma 1986). In other words, accounting researchers, instead of clearly identifying the basic variables of accounting and their relationships and the successful techniques, have gone into determining the relationship between variables and techniques. This approach, as mentioned earlier in the review of accounting theories, was meant to deliberate the behaviour of contracting parties, not for the determination of a cohesive set of principles.

CONCLUSION

This inquiry into the gap between accounting research and practice indicates that this situation is not unique to accounting but is also common to other disciplines in the social sciences. One of the useful explanations provided for the gap is that by Smith (1968), who argued that the level of theory development has a major impact on the gap. In this paper we have attempted to use his model to show that the practitioners' desired objective of having a coherent set of principles to guide practice is yet to be fulfilled by the researchers. The research indicates that the gap between what the practitioners desire and what the researchers provide is there because of the inability of the researchers to provide a coherent set of principles which is universally acceptable for practice purposes. In this manner, the paper improves the understanding of the nature of the gap in accounting and, it is hoped, will contribute towards identifying ways and means of narrowing the gap.

REFERENCES

American Accounting Association (AAA). 1977. *Statement of Accounting Theory and Theory Acceptance.*

Baxter, W. T. 1988. *Accounting Research — Academic Trends versus Practical Needs.* The Institute of Chartered Accountants of Scotland.

Belkaoui, A. 1985. *Accounting Theory.* Harcourt Brace Jovanovich.

Belsey, C. 1980. *Critical Practice.* Methuen.

Chambers, R. J. 1955. Blueprint for a Theory of Accounting. *Accounting Research* (UK) 6 (1): 17–25.

———. 1966. *Accounting Evaluation and Economic Behavior.* Prentice Hall Inc.

———. 1972. The Anguish of Accountants. *The Journal of Accountancy* (March): 73.

Dickhaut, J. W., J. L. Livingstone, and D. J. Watson. 1972. On the Use of Surrogates in Behavioral Experimentation. In Report on the Committee on Research Methodology in Accounting. *The Accounting Review* (47): 455–470.

Edwards, E. O., and P. W. Bell. 1961. *The Theory and Measurement of Business Income.* University of California Press.

Elliot, R. K. 1990. *Changes in Accounting Education and Research.* Paper presented at Annual Meeting of the American Accounting Association, Toronto.

Fleming, P. G. 1990. *Theory — Practice — Research — Teaching an Integrated View.* Continuing Professional Education Conference, Auckland.

Flint, D. 1988. Academic Research and Accounting Practice. *The Accountant's Magazine* (92): 29–30.

———, and J. C. Shaw. 1981. Accounting Research from the Perspective of Practice. In M. Bromwich and A. G. Hopwood. *Essays in British Accounting Research.* Pitman.

Goode, W. J. 1961. The Librarian: From Occupation to Profession? *The Library Quarterly* (31): 306–320.

Hatfield, H. R. 1927. *Accounting.* D. Appleton & Co.

Littleton, A. C. 1953. *Structure of Accounting Theory.* AAA.

Macintosh, N. B. 1989. *Accounting and Deconstruction: A Postmodern Strategy for 'Reading' Accounting,* Paper presented at the Division of Accountancy, Massey University, New Zealand.

———. 1990. Annual Reports in an Ideological Role: A Critical Theory Analysis. In D. J. Cooper and T. M. Hooper. *Critical Accounts.* Macmillan.

Mathews, M. R., and M. H. B. Perera. 1991. *Accounting Theory and Development.* Thomas Nelson, Australia.

McLean, T. 1988. Management Accounting Education Is Theory Related to Practice? *Management Accounting,* Part 1, 66(6): 44–46.

Mobley, S. C. 1970. The Challenges of Socioeconomic Accounting. *The Accounting Review* 45(4): 762–768.

Paton, W. A. 1922. *Accounting Theory.* The Ronald Press.

Rahman, A. 1989. Theory Closure in Accounting Revisited. *Discussion Paper No.100.* New Zealand: Massey University, Department of Accountancy.

Sanders, T. A., H. R. Hatfield, and U. Moore. 1938. A Satement of Accounting Principles. American Insitute of Accountants.

Scapens, R. 1988. Research into Management Accounting Practice. *Management Accounting* (December): 26–28.

Schein, E. 1973. *Professional Education.* McGraw Hill.

Sparrow, V. P. 1981. *The Objectives of Research Regarding Financial Accounting,* Paper presented at the Accounting Research Convocation, University of Alabama.

Smith, S. L. 1968. The Pattern of Educational Theory. *Australian Journal of Education* 12: 252–264.

Snow, R. E. 1977. Individual Differences and Instructional Theory. *Educational Researcher* 6: 11–15.

Sprague, C. 1907. *The Philosophy of Accounts.* Scholars Book Co.

Staubus, G. J. 1975. The Responsibility of Accounting Teachers, *The Accounting Review* 50(1): 160–170.

Sterling, R. R. 1970. *Theory of the Measurement of Enterprise Income.* University Press of Kansas.

———. 1973. Accounting Research, Education and Practice. *The Journal of Accountancy* 136(3): 44–52.

———. 1990. Positive Accounting: An Assessment. *Abacus* 26: 97–133.

Sunder, S. 1990. *Change in Accounting Research.* Paper presented at Annual Meeting of the American Accounting Association, Toronto.

Verrecchia, R. E. 1982. The Use of Mathematical Models in Financial Accounting. *Journal of Accounting Research:* 1–42.

Watts, R. L., and J. L. Zimmerman. 1990. Positive Accounting Theory: A Ten Year Perspective. *The Accounting Review* 65(1): 131–156.

Williamson, D. 1989. Bridging the Gap between Theory and Reality: The Need for a Partnership. *Management Accounting* 67(10): 34–37.

Wolk, H. I., J. R. Francis, and M. G. Tearney. 1989. *Accounting Theory.* PWS-Kent Publishing Co.

Appendix

Discussant: Anton Egger (University of Economics and Business Administration-Vienna, Austria)

Presenters: "Accounting Education in China," Barry J. Cooper (Royal Melbourne Institute of Technology, Australia), Lynne Chow (Hong Kong Polytechnic, Hong Kong) and Tang Yun Wei (Shanghai University of Finance and Economics, China)

"Accounting Practices and Education in Russia and Other Republics of the C.I.S.," Adolf J. H. Enthoven (The University of Texas at Dallas, USA) and Jaroslav V. Sokolov (Institute of Commerce and Economics St. Petersburg, Russia)

4. ACCOUNTING EDUCATION IN DEVELOPING COUNTRIES-Grand Salon G

Moderator: Annie T.E. Thomas (University of Sierra Leone, Sierra Leone)

Discussant: D. Robert Okopny (Eastern Michigan University, USA)

Presenters: "A Western Accountancy Program for the People's Republic of China," Barry J. Cooper (Royal Melbourne Institute of Technology, Australia) and Anthea L. Rose (The Chartered Association of Certified Accountants, London, UK)

"Accounting, Development and the IFAC Guidelines," Gabriel D. Donleavy (Hong Kong University, Hong Kong)

5. REGULATORY BODIES AND ACCOUNTING EDUCATION-Grand Salon J

Moderator: Konrad W. Kubin (Virginia Polytechnic Institute and State University, USA)

Discussant: Allen T. Craswell (University of Sydney, Australia)

Presenters: "IASC and Globalization: Can the Problems of Non-Compliance Be Overcome?," Fouad K. AlNajjar (Wayne State University, USA)

"How Are Accounting Standards Justified? An Anglo-American Perspective," Michael J. Mumford (Lancaster University Management School, United Kingdom)

6. ETHICS AND VALUES IN ACCOUNTING EDUCATION-Grand Salon K

Moderator: Kyojiro Someya (Waseda University, Japan)

Discussant: Chris Guilding (University of Auckland, New Zealand)

Presenters: "Integration of Ethics into Tertiary Accounting Programs In New Zealand and Australia," F. C. Chua, M. H. B. Perera, and M. R. Mathews (all from Massey University, New Zealand)

"Comparing Accountants' Perceptions Towards Marketing and Advertising in Hong Kong and Malaysia: A Preliminary Study," Thomas C. H. Wong (Griffith University, Australia), Oliver H. M. Yau (University of Southern Queensland, Australia), Abdul Latif Shaikh Mohamed Al-Murisi, and Abdul Aziz Abdul Latif (both from Universiti Utara Malaysia, Malaysia)

7. INSTRUCTIONAL INNOVATIONS AND MATERIALS-Grand Salon E

Moderator: Walter O'Connor (Fordham University, USA)

Discussant: Richard E. Baker (Northern Illinois University, USA)

Presenters: "Some Exploratory Applications of Suggestive Accelerated Learning and Teaching (SALT) In Accounting Education," Kwabena Anyane-Ntow (North Carolina Central University, USA)

"Extraterrestrial Transport, Inc. (ET²): An Out-Of-This-World Instructional Innovation for Teaching Management Accounting," Cathleen S. Burns, and Sherry K. Mills (both from New Mexico State University, USA)

8. VISITING INTERNATIONAL SCHOLARS-Grand Salon F

Moderator: Hanns-Martin Schoenfeld (University of Illinois at Urbana-Champaign, USA)

Discussant: Rajul Y. Gokarn (West Georgia College, USA)

"Taxation of Foreign Scholars In the US: A Barrier Hindering International Accounting Education," Joseph W. Antenucci (Middle Tennessee State University, USA) and Cherie J. O'Neil (University of South Florida, USA)

"Teaching Abroad: How to Develop A Summer International Accounting Program," Michael F. Cornick (University of North Carolina at Charlotte, USA)

10:00 AM   BREAK-Exhibit Area-Arlington I and II

FRIDAY, OCTOBER 9, 1992

10:30- AM -12:00 Noon

1. **HOW TO INCORPORATE ETHICS INTO ACCOUNTING CURRICULUM-Grand Salon C**

Moderator: W. Morley Lemon (University of Waterloo, Canada)

Panelists: Mary Beth Armstrong (California Poly State University, USA)

James C. Gaa (McMaster University, Canada)

Harold Q. Langenderfer (University of North Carolina, USA)

2. **RECENT DEVELOPMENTS AND ISSUES AFFECTING ACCOUNTING EDUCATION IN THE CARIBBEAN AND LATIN AMERICA-Grand Salon H**

Moderator: Ronald J. Patten (DePaul University, USA)

Reporter: W. John Brennan (University of Saskatchewan, Canada)

Panelists: Robertine Chaderton (University of the West Indies, Barbados)

Enrique Gutierrez (Autonomous University of the State of Mexico, Mexico)

Juan M. Rivera (University of Notre Dame, USA)

Keith B. Scott (Certified General Accountants Association of Canada, Canada)

3. **ACCOUNTING EDUCATION IN DEVELOPING COUNTRIES-Grand Salon D**

Moderator: Max Gottlieb (College of Staten Island, USA)

Discussant: Amin A. Elmallah (California State University-Sacramento, USA)

Presenters: "Accounting Education in the Perspective of Economic Development in India: In Retrospect and Prospect," Bhabatosh Banerjee (University of Calcutta, India)

"Future Problems and Challenges of Accounting Education in Small States," Charles A. Francalanza (University of Malta, Malta)

4. **ACCOUNTING EDUCATION AND EXPERT SYSTEMS-Grand Salon G**

Moderator: James A. Schweikart (University of Richmond, USA)

Discussant: Richard Vangermeersch (University of Rhode Island, USA)

Presenters: "An Expert System for Accounting Education: An Empirical Evaluation with Implications for Professorial Control," Paul M. Goldwater (University of Central Florida, USA) and Timothy J. Fogarty (Case Western Reserve University, USA)

"Synchronizing International Accounting Standards through the Expert Systems," Man C. Maloo (Towson State University, USA) and Motichand Maloo (Poddar College, India)

5. **EVALUATION OF PERFORMANCE-Grand Salon J**

Moderator: John T. Ahern, Jr. (DePaul University, USA)

Discussant: Peter Secord (St. Mary's University, Canada)

Presenters: "UNT Accounting Change Program Evaluation: Empirical Examination of Baseline Competencies," Frieda A. Bayer, William A. Luker, Robert H. Michaelsen and Neil Wilner (all from University of North Texas, USA)

"Accounting Students' Performance Evaluation: Does the Examination Format Matter?," Mahmoud M. Nourayi (Loyola Marymount University, USA)

6. **INSTRUCTIONAL INNOVATIONS AND MATERIALS-Grand Salon K**

Moderator: Motichand Maloo (Poddar College, India)

Discussant: Manuel A. Tipgos (Indiana University-Southeast, USA)

Presenters: "Experiential Learning Theory: An Application with Individualized Problems on Foreign Currency Restatement," Orapin Duangploy (University of Houston-Downtown, USA) and Guy W. Owings (Pittsburg State University, USA)

"Designing, Writing, and Implementing Courses for an IT-Integrated Professional Accounting Program," David Harrison (Certified General Accountants' Association of Canada, Canada)

7. **ACCOUNTING EDUCATION IN CHANGING ECONOMIES-Grand Salon E**

Moderator: Robert A. Lyon (University of Dundee, UK)

Discussant: Nazik S. Roufaiel (Ithaca College, USA)

Presenters: "Accounting Education Changes for the Future," Dale Bandy (University of Central Florida, USA)

"Accounting Internship: Expectations and Actual Experience," Susan Teo and Joanne Tay (both from Nanyang Technological University, Singapore)

FRIDAY, OCTOBER 9, 1992

12:00-1:30 PM

Founders' Award Luncheon-Arlington IV

Presiding: Paul Garner (University of Alabama, USA)

Award Presentation: Dhia Alhashim (California State University at Northridge, USA)

Awards: Vernon Zimmerman (University of Illinois at Urbana-Champaign, USA)

Eric Castle (London City College-Retired, United Kingdom)

FRIDAY, OCTOBER 9, 1992

1:30-3:00 PM

1. **RECIPROCITY AND HOW TO HELP UNIVERSITIES IN NEWLY INDUSTRIALIZED COUNTRIES ACHIEVE IT-Grand Salon C**

Moderator: Jane T. Rubin (American Assembly of Collegiate Schools of Business, USA)

Panelists: Amal K. Chakraborty (Chartered Accountant, India)

G. H. Karreman (Netherlands Institute of Registered Accountants, The Netherlands)

David A. Wilson (Institute of Chartered Accountants of Ontario, Canada)

2. **RECENT DEVELOPMENTS AND ISSUES AFFECTING ACCOUNTING EDUCATION IN WESTERN EUROPE-Grand Salon H**

Moderator: Cécil W. Donovan (Deloitte & Touche, Ireland)

Reporter: Giuseppe Galassi (University of Parma, Italy)

Panelists: John Flower (Centre for Research in European Accounting, Belgium)

Giuseppe Galassi (University of Parma, Italy)

Richard M.S. Wilson (University of Keele, UK)

3. **INSTRUCTIONAL INNOVATIONS AND MATERIALS-Grand Salon D**

Moderator: D. Gerald Searfoss (Deliotte & Touche, USA)

Discussant: Linda M. Malgeri (Kennesaw State College, USA)

Presenters: "Innovations in Accounting Education," John W. Hardy, Jay M. Smith and Larry A. Deppe (all from Brigham Young University, USA)

"Open Learning for Accountancy Education," Michael Harvey (City of

London Polytechnic, UK), Anthea L. Rose (The Chartered Association of Certified Accountants of London, UK) and Stephen Wellings (Certified Accountants Educational Projects Ltd. London, UK)

4. EDUCATION AND THE PROFESSION-Grand Salon G

Moderator: Jose A. Gonzalez (Inter-American University, Puerto Rico)

Discussant: Frieda Bayer (University of North Texas, USA)

Presenters: "Customizing the Education Needs of Accounting Professionals: Two Australian Case Studies," Jillian C. Phillips (University of Central Queensland, Australia), Keith Sloan (University of New England-Northern Rivers, Australia) and John Dekkers (University of Central Queensland, Australia)

"Cross-Cultural Influences on Audit Quality: A Comparison of Pacific Rim, European, and North American Audits," James C. Lampe (Texas Tech University, USA) and Steve G. Sutton (Arizona State University, USA)

5. ETHICS AND OTHER ISSUES IN ACCOUNTING EDUCATION-Grand Salon J

Moderator: Jerry E. Trapnell (Clemson University, USA)

Discussant: Linda Savage (University of Central Florida, USA)

Presenters: "Integrating Ethics into Financial Management Courses: A Role Play Approach," Kate M. Brown (University of Otago, New Zealand)

"Multi-Entry Multi-Exit Accounting Education," J. E. McLachlan and V. A. Wood (both from Napier Polytechnic, UK)

6. ACCOUNTING EDUCATIONAL SYSTEMS-Grand Salon K

Moderator: Alvin Carley (University of Pennsylvania, USA)

Discussant: Erik DeLembre (University of Ghent, Belgium)

Presenters: "An International Survey of Accounting Programs," Barbara Powell Reider and Donald N. Hester (both from University of Alaska-Anchorage, USA)

"Implications for Proposed Changes in Accounting Education: The New Zealand Experience," Lawrence A. McClelland (University of Otago, New Zealand) and Kenton B. Walker (University of Wyoming, USA)

7. ACCOUNTING EDUCATION IN CONTRASTING ECONOMIES-Grand Salon E

Moderator: Edward Shoenthal (Brooklyn College of the City University of New York, USA)

Discussant: David Stout (Villanova University, USA)

Presenters: "Aligning Accounting Education and Training to the Skills Needs in Developing Nations—The Case of SADCC," Shabani Ndzinge (University of Botswana, Botswana)

"Disclosure Pattern of Japanese Firms and Internalization of Capital Transaction—Education Needs in the Changing Economy," Ellie Okada-Onitsuka (Yokohama National University, Japan)

3:00 PM BREAK-Exhibit Area-Arlington I and II

FRIDAY, OCTOBER 9, 1992
3:30-5:00 PM

1. THE CHANGING CURRICULUM IN THE NEXT DECADE FOR ACCOUNTING STUDENTS-Grand Salon C

Moderator: Thomas A. Gavin (University of Tennessee, USA)

Panelists: J. Efrim Boritz (University of Waterloo, Canada)

Michael A. Diamond (University of Southern California, USA)

John Hegarty (Federation des Experts Compatibles Europeans, Belgium)

Gerhard G. Mueller (University of Washington, USA)

494

2. RECENT DEVELOPMENTS AND ISSUES AFFECTING ACCOUNTING EDUCATION IN EASTERN EUROPE-Grand Salon H

Moderator: Adolph Enthoven (University of Texas at Dallas, USA)

Reporter: Maureen Berry (University of Illinois at Urbana-Champaign, USA)

Panelists: Istvan Friedrich (International Training Center for Bankers Ltd., Hungary) Alicja Anna Jaruga (University of Lodz, Poland)

Valery V. Kovalev (St. Petersburg Institute of Commerce & Economics, Russia)

TABLE TOPIC DISCUSSION GROUPS - These discussion groups are less formal than the paper presentations with discussants and are meant to encourage interaction among participants. Please join the group which is discussing a topic of interest to you.

3. CORPORATE ACCOUNTING ISSUES-Grand Salon D

Moderator: Jane O. Burns (Texas Tech University, USA)

Presenters: "Accounting for Commonwealth of Independent States-American Joint Ventures: Problems and Applications," Steven D. Grossman, D. Larry Crumbley (both from Texas A&M University, USA) and Sandra T. Welch (University of Texas at San Antonio, USA)

"Who Pays the Most and the Least? A Comparison of Corporation Income Taxes from A to Z (Antigua to Zimbabwe)," Jack R. Fay (Stetson University, USA) and M. E. Rinker (Institute of Tax and Accountancy Deland-Florida, USA)

4. THE USE OF COMPUTERS AND CASES IN ACCOUNTING EDUCATION-Grand Salon G

Moderator: John C. Ford (University of the Witwatersrand, South Africa)

Presenters: "The Investigation of the Status of Accounting Education and the Use of Computers," Muneya Sato (Yokohama City University, Japan)

"An Integrative Case for Principles of Accounting: Donegal Brewing Company," Kimberly J. Smith (College of William and Mary, USA)

5. EDP AND AUDITING EDUCATION-Grand Salon J

Moderator: Thomas G. Evans (University of Central Florida, USA)

Presenters: "The Research of EDP Accounting Education in Japanese Universities," Kazumasa Takemori (Chubu University, Japan)

"Internationalizing Audit Education," James A. Yardley, Gail B. Wright and N. Leroy Kauffman (all from Virginia Ploytechnic Institute and State University, USA)

6. ENVIRONMENTAL REPORTING AND FINANCIAL REPORTING-Grand Salon K

Moderator: William T. Geary (College of William and Mary, USA)

Presenters: "Environmental Disclosure—A Case for Statutory Mandate," Chhote Lal (Banaras Hindu University, India) and Arvind K. Keshary (Associate Chartered Accountant, India)

"An Examination of Patterns of Financial Reporting Practices and Their Relationship to Economic and Educational Development," Stephen B. Salter (Texas A&M University, USA), Jeffrey Kantor (University of Windsor, Canada) and Edward Shoenthal (City University of New York-Brooklyn, USA)

7. ACCOUNTING EDUCATION-Grand Salon E

Moderator: Roger W. Hopkins (Victoria University of Wellington, New Zealand)

Presenters: "Accounting Education in India—An Appraisal," Dr. N. M. Khandelwal (Saurashtra University, India)

"Accounting Education and Practice: The Singapore Experience," Tan Teck Meng, Yang Hoong Pang and See Liang Foo (all from Nanyang Technological University, Singapore)

8. ACCOUNTING RESEARCH AND TEACHING-Grand Salon F

Moderator: Farhad Simyar (Concordia University, Canada)

Presenters: "Research, Teaching, Tenure and Accreditation—Misunderstood Interfaces, Missions and Mixes," Jack R. Fay, William L. Ferrara and Judson P. Styker (all from Stetson University, USA)

"Accounting Research: Its Pedagogical Impact," Andrew Higson (Loughborough University Business School, UK)

9. COST CONTROL AND INTERNATIONAL COORDINATION-Grand Salon B

Moderator: Anastasia Maggina (University of Laverne, Greece)

Presenters: "The Evolution of Cost-Control Systems: A Cultural Phenomenon," Alain Burlaud, Lionel Dahan and Claude Simon (all from Ecole Superieure de Commerce de Paris, France)

"International Harmonization of Accounting Terms with the Use of a Computerized Database," Aiko Shibata (Tezukayama University, Japan)

10. ACCOUNTING EDUCATION ISSUES-Manassas (Second Floor)

Moderator: Claude D. Renshaw (Saint Mary's College, USA)

Presenters: "The Development of Accounting Education and Management in China," Guo Daoyang, Li Guibin, Tao Dexiong and He Mouqing (all from Zhongnan University of Finance & Economics, China)

"Assisting in the Identification and Resolution of Accounting Education Issues in Changing Economies," Hans E. Klein and Joseph A. McHugh (both from Bentley College, USA)

11. ACCOUNTING CERTIFICATION AND ETHICS-Lobby Level

Moderator: Ali A. Peyvandi (California State University-Fresno, USA)

Presenters: "Professional Accountancy Certification in China, Taiwan and the United States," Michael C. Blue and Dennis Hwang (both from Bloomsburg University, USA)

"Teaching Ethics in Accountancy: Responding to the Needs of the Profession," Philomena Leung (Victoria University of Technology, Australia)

FRIDAY, OCTOBER 9, 1992

6:00-8:00 PM

Presidents' Reception-Arlington IV

Hosted by The American Institute of Certified Public Accountants

SATURDAY, OCTOBER 10, 1992

8:30-10:00 AM

1. TEACHING AN INTERNATIONAL PERSPECTIVE IN THE FUTURE ACCOUNTING CURRICULUM-Grand Salon C

Moderator: Sidney J. Gray (University of Glasgow, Scotland)

Panelists: Frederick D. S. Choi (New York University, USA)

G. D. Donleavy (University of Hong Kong, Hong Kong)

Lee Radebaugh (Bringham Young University, USA)

2. RECENT DEVELOPMENTS AND ISSUES AFFECTING ACCOUNTING EDUCATION IN ASIA AND THE PACIFIC RIM-Grand Salon H

Moderator: Seigo Nakajima (Ferris Jogakuin, Japan)

Reporter: Yukio Fujita (Waseda University, Japan)

Panelists: Tan Teck Meng (Nanyang Technological University, Singapore)

Ichiro Shiobara (Waseda University, Japan)

Don G. Trow (Victoria University of Wellington, New Zealand)

Yu Xu-ying (Xiamen University, China)

496

3. **INFLUENCES ON ACCOUNTING EDUCATION-Grand Salon D**

Moderator: Marian Powers (Northwestern University Executive Program, USA)

Discussant: Marvin W. Tucker (Southern Illinois University-Carbondale, USA)

Presenters: "Accounting Education Program for the Twenty-First Century: A Canadian Experience," Z. Jun Lin and Al Hunter (both from The University of Lethbridge, Canada)

"Australian Government Policy on Higher Education: Impact on Accounting Education," Joan D. Wells (Swinburne University of Technology, Australia)

4. **COMPARISON OF ACCOUNTING EDUCATION SYSTEMS-Grand Salon G**

Moderator: Gary K. Meek (Oklahoma State University, USA)

Discussant: T. Sterling Wetzel (Oklahoma State University, USA)

Presenters: "Action and Results Oriented Research and Consultancy Approach to Third World Accounting Education and Professional Development," J. B. Ato Ghartey (University of Massachusetts, USA)

"A Comparison of Accounting Education Systems in Australia, The United States of America, and the People's Republic of China," Yi-fen (Grace) Hu (S W University of Finance and Economics, China) and John A. Marts (University of North Carolina-Wilmington, USA)

5. **ACCOUNTING EDUCATION ISSUES-Grand Salon J**

Moderator: Kathleen Sinning (Western Michigan University, USA)

Discussant: Marshall K. Pitman (The University of Texas at San Antonio, USA)

Presenters: "Cognitive Complexity and Accounting Education," Robert L. Hurt (California State Polytechnic University-Pomona, USA)

"Using International Data Sources to Assess Audit Risk," Douglas E.

Ziegenfuss (Old Dominion University, USA)

6. **INSTRUCTIONAL INNOVATIONS AND MATERIALS-Grand Salon K**

Moderator: Robert B. Sweeney (Memphis State University, USA)

Discussant: Betty S. Harper (Middle Tennessee State University, USA)

Presenters: "Application of Technology in Accounting Education," Linda Garceau (Cleveland State University, USA) and Robert Bloom (John Carroll University, USA)

"The Use of A Computer Competency Exam Requirement in Undergraduate Accounting Programs: The Experience of University of Hawaii," David C. Yang (University of Hawaii, USA)

7. **ACCOUNTING EDUCATION IN CHANGING ECONOMIES-Grand Salon E**

Moderator: Felix E. Amenkhienan (Radford University, USA)

Discussant: Lech Bednarski (University of Gdansk, Poland)

Presenters: "The Direction of Accounting and Accounting Education: Raising Crucial Questions in Terms of an Integrated Framework," Hideyuki Kamiryo (Hiroshima Shudo University, Japan)

"The Search for a Better Accounting System - The Overlooked Concern," Martin Putterill (University of Auckland, New Zealand) and Roger Debreceny (University of New England-Northern Rivers, Australia)

8. **ACCOUNTING EDUCATION IN DEVELOPING COUNTRIES-Grand Salon F**

Moderator: K. G. Dutta (The Institute of Cost and Works Accountants of India, India)

Discussant: T. H. Beechy (York University, Canada)

Presenters: "Enhancing Accounting Education in Developing Countries: The Case of Iran," Ali Sagafi (Tehran University, Iran) and Adel M. Novin (Kent State University, USA)

"Needs of Accounting Education in Developing Countries: An African Case Study," R. S. Olesegun Wallace and Maurice Pendlebury (both from University of Wales College of Cardiff, UK)

10:00 AM BREAK-Exhibit Area-Arlington I and II

SATURDAY, OCTOBER 10, 1992

10:30-12:00 PM

1. RECENT DEVELOPMENTS AND ISSUES IN EDUCATION FOR GOVERNMENTAL ACCOUNTING/INTERNAL AUDITING-Grand Salon C

Moderator: Réal Labelle (Université du Quebec a Montreal, Canada)

Panelists: Jesse W. Hughes (Old Dominion University, USA)

Rowan Jones (University of Birmingham, UK)

G. Thomas Friedlob (Clemson University, USA)

2. RECENT DEVELOPMENTS AND ISSUES AFFECTING ACCOUNTING EDUCATION IN THE MIDDLE EAST & AFRICA-Grand Salon H

Moderator: Shuaib A. Shuaib (Kuwait University, Kuwait)

Reporter: Alain Burlaud (University of Paris Val de Marne, France)

Panelists: Shawki M. Farag (The American University in Cairo, Egypt)

Mfandaidza R. Hove (University of Zimbabwe, Zimbabwe)

Mohamed Ali Mirghani (King Fahd University of Petroleum and Minerals, Saudi Arabia)

B.O. Ogundele (University of Ilorin, Nigeria)

3. ACCOUNTING EDUCATION ISSUES-Grand Salon D

Moderator: Abdel M. Agami (Old Dominion University, USA)

Discussant: Phil Harper (Middle Tennessee State University, USA)

Presenters: "Is Accountancy A Profession?—Implications for Education," Tonya K. Flesher and Dale L. Flesher (both at University of Mississippi, USA)

"Vocational or Liberal? The Future of Accounting Education as an Analogy for the Higher Education Debate," Victor L. Honigberg (University of Otago, New Zealand)

4. ACCOUNTING EDUCATION RESEARCH-Grand Salon G

Moderator: Gary A. Luoma (University of South Carolina, USA)

Discussant: Rama Kashinath (The Institute of Cost and Works Accountants of India, India)

Presenters: "Incorporating Practical Significance Results in Accounting Education Research: The Use of Effect Size Information," David E. Stout (Villanova University, USA) and Thomas L. Ruble (Rider College, USA)

"Towards Understanding the Gap Between Accounting Research and Practice," Sivakumar Velayutham and Asheq Rahman both from (Massey University, New Zealand)

5. EDUCATION AND THE PROFESSION-Grand Salon J

Moderator: Howard Teall (Wilfrid Laurier University, Canada)

Discussant: Ali M. Sedaghat (Loyola College in Maryland, USA)

Presenters: "An Innovative Assessment Tool in the Accounting Curriculum: An Accounting Capstone Course Focusing on the Public Sector," Steven C. Dilley (Michigan State University, USA) and Susan C. Kattelus (Eastern Michigan University, USA)

6. INSTRUCTIONAL INNOVATIONS AND MATERIALS-Grand Salon K

Moderator: William Markell (University of Delaware, USA)

Discussant: Ian A. Eddie (The University of New England, Australia)

Presenters: "Teaching 'The Language of Business' as a Language: An Audio Approach to Elementary Accounting," Curtis L. DeBerg (California State University at Chico, USA)

"The Process of Academic Quality Improvement in the School of Accounting and Business of the National Autonomous University of Mexico," Salvador Ruiz-de-Chávez and Alfonso Orozco (both from National University of Mexico, Mexico)

7. COMPUTERS AND ACCOUNTING EDUCATION-Grand Salon E

Moderator: Kazuo Hiramatsu (Kansei Gokuin University, Japan)

Discussant: Glenn E. Owen (University of California-Santa Barbara, USA)

Presenters: "Computing In Introductory Financial Accounting Courses: A UK Example," Ruth M. King and John Whittaker (Loughborough University Business School, UK)

"Using Bitnet for International Accounting Education: A Japan-USA Study," Ichiro Shiina (Chuo-Gakuin University, Japan), M. Susan Stiner (Villanova University, USA) and Frederic M. Stiner (University of Delaware, USA)

8. ACCOUNTING EDUCATION IN DEVELOPING COUNTRIES-Grand Salon F

Moderator: David J. Fraser (University of Technology, Australia)

Discussant: Robert F. Sharp (Ohio University, USA)

Presenters: "Performance of Students in Introductory Accounting Courses: A Case Study," Can Simga Mugan and Gulnur Muradoglu Sengul (both from Bilkent University, Turkey)

"Accounting Education Development in Papua, New Guinea," Fabian Pok (University of New England, Australia)

SATURDAY, OCTOBER 10, 1992
12:15-1:30 PM
Sponsor Appreciation Luncheon-Arlington IV
Presiding: Belverd E. Needles, Jr. (DePaul University, USA), Chair, Planning Committee

1:30 PM Saturday Second Plenary Session
"CHANGE IN ACCOUNTING EDUCATION: THE PERSPECTIVES OF THREE COUNTRIES"-Arlington III

Chair: Norlin G. Rueschhoff (University of Notre Dame, USA)

"Strategies for Change in Accounting Education: The US Experiment," Doyle Z. Williams (Chairman of the Accounting Education Change Commission, USA)

"Latest Developments in Accounting Education in Indonesia," Katjep Abdoelkadir (Executive Secretary of the Coordinating Agency for Accounting Development, Indonesia) Paper was presented by Binsar Hutabaret

"Recent Developments in Accounting Education in Russia," Lorraine T. Ruffing (Chief-Accounting Section of the United Nations Transnational Corporations and Management Division)

3:15 PM BREAK-Exhibit Area-Arlington I and II

3:45 PM SATURDAY THIRD PLENARY SESSION-Arlington III
SUMMARY OF REPORTS FROM REGIONS

Chair: Andrè Zünd (University of St.Gallen, Switzerland)

Recent developments and issues affecting accounting education in Western Europe
Guiseppe Galassi, (University of Parma, Italy)

Recent developments and issues affecting accounting education in Eastern Europe
Maureen Berry (University of Illinois at Urbana-Champaign, USA)

Recent developments and issues affecting accounting education in the Caribbean and Latin America

W. John Brennan (University of Saskatchewan, Canada)

Recent developments and issues affecting accounting education in Asia and the Pacific Rim

Yukio Fujita (Waseda University, Japan)

Recent developments and issues affecting accounting education in the Middle East & Africa

Alain Burlaud (University of Paris Val de Marne, France)

Recent developments and issues affecting accounting education in the North America

W. John Brennan (University of Saskatchewan, Canada)

5:00 PM   Closing Ceremony
Sidney J. Gray President-Elect of IAAER

6:00 PM   RECEPTION -Arlington IV

7:00 PM   BANQUET-Arlington IV

8:30 PM   Entertainment-Arlington IV